James Anderson, William Alexander, Andrew Jervise, John Grant Michie

Epitaphs and Inscriptions from Burial Grounds and Old Buildings in the North-East of Scotland

James Anderson, William Alexander, Andrew Jervise, John Grant Michie

Epitaphs and Inscriptions from Burial Grounds and Old Buildings in the North-East of Scotland

ISBN/EAN: 9783337425425

Printed in Europe, USA, Canada, Australia, Japan

Cover: Foto ©Thomas Meinert / pixelio.de

More available books at **www.hansebooks.com**

FROM

BURIAL GROUNDS & OLD BUILDINGS

IN

The North-Eaſt of Scotland,

WITH

Hiſtorical, Biographical, Genealogical, and Antiquarian Notes,

ALSO,

AN APPENDIX OF ILLUSTRATIVE PAPERS.

BY

ANDREW JERVISE, F.S.A. Sc.
AUTHOR OF 'MEMORIALS OF ANGUS AND THE MEARNS,' ETC.

V. I.

EDINBURGH: EDMONSTON AND DOUGLAS.
1875.

[*All Rights Reserved.*]

'Study their monuments, their gravestones, their epitaphs, on the spots where they lie: study, if possible, the scenes of the events, their aspect, their architecture, their geography; the tradition which has survived the history; the legend which has survived the tradition; the mountain, the stream, the shapeless stone, which has survived even history and tradition and legend.'—DEAN STANLEY.

[250 *copies printed.* No. 202]

TO THE

Memory of Departed Friends,

PATRICK CHALMERS,
OF ALDBAR, ESQUIRE,

JOSEPH ROBERTSON, LL.D.,

AND

PROFESSOR COSMO INNES,

THIS VOLUME IS INSCRIBED

BY THE AUTHOR.

Sculptured Stone at Edzell.

TABLE OF CONTENTS.

PREFACE,	ix-xii	DUTHIL (Morayshire), 142-3
INTRODUCTORY REMARKS,	xiii-xxviii	DYSART (Angus), . 237
EPITAPHS AND INSCRIPTIONS,	1-376	
		ECHT (Aberdeenshire), . . . 65-6
ABERDOUR (Aberdeenshire),	55-9	EDZELL (Angus), ... 307-11
ADERLEMNO (Angus),	7-10	ELCHIES (Morayshire), . . . 297-9
AIRLIE ,,	162-3	ELLON (Aberdeenshire), . . 59-62, 347, 376
ALDBAR ,,	10-11	ELSICK (Mearns), ... 55
ALFORD (Aberdeenshire),	116-21, 339	ENZIE or ST. NINIAN (Banffshire), . 277-9
AUCHTERLESS ,,	206-9, 339	ESSIE (Angus), . . . 67-8, 371
		ETHIE ,, ... 318-19
BANCHORY-TERNAN (Mearns),	1-7, 379	
BELLIE (Morayshire),	11-16	FARNELL (Angus), . . 89-95, 350
BENVIE (Angus),	192-3, 340	FASQUE (Mearns), . . . 254-5
BERVIE (Mearns),	23-7, 341	FEARN (Angus), . . 268-70, 354
BOG WELL ,,	51	FETTERCAIRN (Mearns), . 250-6, 352
BOYNDIE (Banffshire),	199-201	FETTERESSO ,, . 75-85, 352
BRAEMAR (Aberdeenshire),	217-20	FINHAVEN (Angus), . . 334-5
BROUGHTY-FERRY (Angus),	115-16, 370, 380	FOCHABERS. See BELLIE.
		FORDOUN (Mearns), . . 62-5, 356
CARESTON (Angus),	259-60	FOYERS (Inverness-shire), . . 67
CARMYLLIE ,,	246-9, 341	
CATERLINE (Mearns),	173-4	GAMRIE (Banffshire), . 85-9, 244
CHAPEL HOUSE (Aberdeenshire),	264	GARTLY (Aberdeenshire), . . 43-5, 359
CHAPEL YARD (Angus),	159-61, 383	GLAMIS (Angus), . . . 180-6, 386
CLOVA (Aberdeenshire),	260-1	GLENMORISTON (Inverness-shire), . 66-7
COLDSTONE ,,	283-5, 342	GRANGE (Banffshire), . . . 100-4
COWIE (Mearns),	53-5, 343	
CRATHIE ,,	214-17	INSCH (Aberdeenshire), . . 20-3
CRUDEN ,,	312 18	INVERAVON (Banffshire), . 143-9, 359
CUIKSTOUN (Angus),	92-3	INVERGOWRIE (Angus), . . 193-6
CUPAR-ANGUS,	72-4, 343	INVERKEILOR ,, . . 318-26
CUSHNIE (Aberdeenshire),	187 90	INVERURIE (Aberdeenshire), . 178-80, 359
DOWNAN (Banffshire),	146	KEITH (Banffshire), . . 164-9, 360
DRUMBLADE (Aberdeenshire),	257-9	KEITH-HALL (Aberdeenshire), . 301-4
DUN (Angus),	220-6, 344, 388	KILDRUMMY ,, . . 260 7
DUNOTTAR (Mearns),	48-53, 345	KINNAIRD. See CUIKSTOUN.
DURRIS ,,	104 6, 346	KINNEFF (Mearns), . . 169-73, 119

TABLE OF CONTENTS.

KINCARDINE O'NEIL (Aberdeenshire),	238-40
KINGOLDRUM (Angus),	163-4, 385
KINKELL (Aberdeenshire),	304-7
KINMUCK ,,	304
KIRKDEN (Angus),	32-5
KIRK-MICHAEL (Banffshire),	69-71, 360
KNOCKANDO (Morayshire),	299-301
LAURENCEKIRK (Mearns),	288-94, 361
LEOCHEL (Aberdeenshire),	186-7
LETHNOT (Angus),	294-5
LHANBRYDE (Morayshire),	271-2
LIFF (Angus),	190-2
LINTRATHEN (Angus),	279-81, 364
LOCHLEE ,,	127-31, 382, 390
LOGIE-BUCHAN (Aberdeenshire),	197-9
LOGIE (Dundee), Angus,	196-7, 364
LOGIE (Montrose), ,,	209-10
LOGIE-MAR (Aberdeenshire),	281-3
LONGSIDE ,,	95-100, 364
LUNAN (Angus),	241-4, 366
MACDUFF (Banffshire),	244-6
MAINS (Angus),	201-3
MARNOCH (Banffshire),	231-5
MARYKIRK (Mearns),	132-8, 383
MARYTON (Angus),	235-8, 367
MONIFIETH ,,	106-15, 369, 380
MONQUHITTER (Aberdeenshire),	175-8, 371, 386
MORTLACH (Banffshire),	326-34
MURROES (Angus),	121-6, 381
NAVAR (Angus),	296-7, 389

NEVAY (Angus),	68-9, 371
NEWDOSK ,,	311-12
NEWHILLS (Aberdeenshire),	285-7
NEWTYLE (Angus),	138-41, 373
OATHLAW (Angus),	335-8, 374
ORDIQUHILL (Banffshire),	27-9
PERT (Angus),	210-14, 374
PETER CULTER (Aberdeenshire),	16-20
RATHVEN (Banffshire),	273-9
RESCOBIE (Angus),	155-61, 384
ST. ANDREWS (Morayshire),	270-1
ST. CYRUS (Mearns),	36-43, 376
ST. NINIAN. *See* ENZIE.	
ST. POL'NAR'S CHAPEL (Aberdeenshire),	359
SKENE ,,	226-9
SOUTHESK HOWFF (Angus),	93-4
STONEYWOOD (Aberdeenshire),	286
STRACHAN (Mearns),	29-32
STRATHDON (Aberdeenshire),	149-55
STRATHMARTIN (Angus),	204-6
TANNADICE (Angus),	45-8
TOWIE (Aberdeenshire),	229-31
URY HOWFF (Mearns),	80-4
SUPPLEMENT,	339-76
APPENDIX,	377-90
GENERAL INDEX,	391-400

ERRATA

To the more important errors in this volume.

Pg.	Col.	Line.	For	Read
6	2	14	. .	drained portion of the.
20	1	12	*Insulae*,	*Insulae*.
27	1	20	. .	Edinburgh, afterwards the celebrated banker, and grandson of Provost Coutts of Montrose.
27	1	23	brother,	uncle.
47	2	17	George IV.,	Queen Victoria.
50	1	10	. .	striving with heart and hand.
64	1	7–8	ANNE GRAHAME,	ANNA GRAHAM.
64	2	23	in infancy, .	infants.
84	2	32	Drumwhackit,	Drumwhacket.
85	1	31	. .	a poem prefixed to a.
87	1	2	1781, .	1731.
95	2	14	G, B, E, M,,	G. B. M. M.
96	2	20	79 anno,	70 annis.
99	2	13	. .	cheerful, in prosperity thankful.
112	2	34	man,	in an.
119	2	22	libel, .	label.
121	2	17	burn of Powrie,	and.
122	1	45	1857, .	1837.
134	2	27	1660, .	1680.
150	1	27	p. 45,	p. 145.
153	1	3–6	*delete*	Her husband's father, who once owned a farm in Strathdon, retired to Aberdeen, where he became a merchant.
153	1	last	p. 122,	p. 120.
160	2	7	MARY,	MARGARET.
162	1	29	M. V. G.,	M. V. M.
165	1	44	p. 134,	p. 133.
165	2	25	son,	grandson.
166	1	36	. .	eldest daughter of the Rev.
169	1	29	arrested,	detained.
172	1	25	p. 75, .	p. 352.
172	2	36	Regi, .	Regia.
176	2	34	. .	GARVOCK, senr.
178	2	last	45, .	42.
184	1	46	1777, .	1677.
190	2	37	Landaue,	Landour.
190	2	last	11th, .	7th.
195	2	23	*delete* and Co.	
202	1	28	p. 112,	p. 111.
212	1	9	uncertain,	tho' certain.
212	1	20	80, .	84.
212	1	44	divinity,	medicine.
213	1	33	. .	Mr. Lunan [*v.* p. 375].
216	2	37	. .	by desire of.
224	1	37–8	wished, etc.,	neither would decline death, nor could inflect fate.
227	1	25	p. 157,	p. 151.
228	2	6	p. 89, .	p. 245.
240	2	41	pp. 21, 121,	p. 4.
249	1	26	p. 93,	p. 94.
252	1	35	antæ, .	ante.
252	2	23	doquio,	eloquio.
255	2	44	Kenneth III.,	Kenneth II.
266	2	34	. .	et concidit.
268	1	31	*delete* line.	
270	2	13	p. 78, .	p. 53.
273	2	7	more southern chapel	south aisle.
276	2	41–3	*delete*	[*v.* p. 12, col. 1, 2d par.].
277	1	2, 10	S. MARY, .	S. GREGORY.
287	2	12	p. 79, .	p. 55.
291–2			*delete* foot and top lines,	[*v.* p. 362 *note*].
302	1	36	p. 48, .	p. 358.
324	2	26, 41	. .	[*v.* p. 351, col. 2].
348	1	30, 2, 4	I., I (? T)	T. [Thomas].
350	2	9	1831, died Dec.	1821, died Dec. 17.

☞ Clerical and typographical errors are not noticed in the above list, neither certain references to parishes and pages. The reader will kindly correct these misprints in course of perusal. The latter were caused by a change in the plan of the volume.

PREFACE.

THE Author of this volume having occupied much of his leisure during a great part of his lifetime in copying Epitaphs and Inscriptions from Burial Grounds and Old Buildings, has necessarily formed a large collection. Of these transcriptions the present volume contains upwards of two thousand, or considerably less than a fourth part of the whole.

The limited impression (250 copies) arises from the fact that this portion of the work was originally intended for private distribution only. But owing to circumstances which have happened since the Author began to print the papers which formed the nucleus of the volume, he has yielded to the wishes of personal and literary friends in offering it to the public. Had this been intended at first, not only would the number of copies have been doubled, but the arrangement of the book would have been different, and various other particulars would have received greater attention.

In addition to epitaphs and inscriptions from burial grounds, this volume not only contains inscriptions and dates from kirk bells and communion vessels, from bridges, old buildings, obelisks, and other memorials, all personally collected by the Author, but it also comprises so much that is new in genealogical, biographical, historical, and antiquarian literature, that he thinks it can scarcely fail to be locally if not generally interesting. It also contains a number of hitherto unpublished historical and family papers, extracts from kirk-session records, notices from chartularies and other authentic sources.

Although the unpublished portion of the collection has a wide range, and is pretty general in its character, it has reference mainly to the North-East of Scotland, or the counties of Fife, Forfar, Kincardine, Aberdeen, Banff, and Elgin. Besides inscriptions from most of the private and landward burial grounds in these shires, it includes collections from the towns of Dundee, Forfar, Montrose, and Kirriemuir; Aberdeen, Peterhead, Fraserburgh, Huntly, and Turriff; Banff, Cullen, Fordyce, and Portsoy; from the Cathedrals and Abbeys of St. Andrews, Dunfermline, Brechin, Arbroath, Old Machar, Elgin, Pluscardine, and Kinloss; and also from a number of churchyards in Perthshire, including those of Alyth, Bendochy, and Meigle.

But whether the remainder of this collection, or any part of it, will ever appear, or in what form, will altogether depend upon circumstances. Now that the inscriptions are collected, it would be an easy matter to give them alone; but to many, indeed to most readers, the absence of illustrative notes would render them less interesting. On the other hand, the addition of such notes as appear in this volume, however trifling and imperfect these may be considered, entails an amount of labour and research of which no idea can be formed unless by those who have been engaged on books of a similar kind, and in searching out new information regarding persons and places. Mere book-makers and plagiarists—the most contemptible of all scribblers—know nothing of 'the toil and trouble' of such works; although, unfortunately, as the Writer can testify from experience, it but too often turns out to be more for their benefit than for that of the authors of the books.

In regard to this volume, the Author has further to remark, that he has been careful to preserve as many of the *really old* inscriptions as possible, and has been at considerable trouble and expense in disinterring 'long-lost' monuments. The orthographical peculiarities of these, which constitute their value to philologists, and impart a certain charm to general readers, have been as closely adhered to as moveable type will admit of.

Some of the modern inscriptions have been abridged, but the more important and curious, particularly those which relate to 'men of mark' and to 'good and faithful servants,' are given in full.

In every instance the utmost care has been taken to secure accuracy; and the Author hopes that few 'vital errors' will be found that are not noticed either in the list of Errata (*supra*, p. vii.), or in the body of the work.

As it was impossible for the Author personally to compare all the proof-sheets with the original inscriptions, he has pleasure in stating that ministers, schoolmasters, and others have afforded ready assistance. To these (some of whose names are mentioned in the work), and to all others who have kindly aided him in what he may call his *magnum opus*, the Author begs to return grateful thanks.

He cannot deny himself the honour of stating how deeply he feels indebted to the late Right Hon. Fox, Earl of Dalhousie, who, as on former occasions, so kindly allowed the use of hitherto unpublished documents. These documents, which throw much light both upon personal and proprietary history, have been selected from the family papers at Panmure, and will be found printed in various parts of the volume.

To John Stuart, Esq., LL.D., author of *The Sculptured Stones of Scotland*, and other works of great value and interest, the Author is indebted for the revision of many of the proof-sheets of the volume. And to the courtesy of James Anderson, Esq., M.A., lately schoolmaster of Foveran, he is indebted for the excellent translations with which the book is enriched, and for much valuable and friendly assistance.

The Author has also to acknowledge the kind liberality of his friend Patrick Allan-Fraser of Hospitalfield, Esq., *H*.R.S.A., for the engraved portrait which adorns the volume. It was executed by Mr. T. O. Barlow, A.R.A., after the painting by Mr. Allan-Fraser. The Author is likewise indebted to the Trustees of the late Earl of Dalhousie for the use of the woodcut of the Sculptured Stone at Edzell, and to the Society of Antiquaries of Scotland for those at Monifieth. The *cross* which forms a portion of the ornament on the cover of the volume is from the slab at Coldstone, see *infra*, p. 283.

To facilitate ready reference, a Table of Contents has been prefixed, containing a list of Burial-places; and subjoined is an Index to the names of Persons and the more important of the Places and Subjects mentioned in the volume, and also to the first words of Poetical Epitaphs.

AND. JERVISE.

BRECHIN, *May* 1875.

INTRODUCTORY REMARKS.

IN introducing this volume, upon *Funeral and other Monuments in the North-East of Scotland*, the Author cannot help remarking that, whatever may be its reception, its preparation, imperfect as it is, has afforded him much pleasure, and enabled him to spend his leisure in such a manner as, he hopes, may be of some advantage to others, long after the ravages of Time have destroyed the monuments and their inscriptions which the work is intended to preserve.

It must have appeared to many as well as to the Author a remarkable circumstance, that, while monumental inscriptions are admitted as evidence in Courts of Law, no legal step, so far as Scotland is concerned, should ever have been taken to secure their preservation. The Author is inclined to believe that the Legislature owes a duty to the country in this respect, and that an Act of Parliament ought to be passed, not only to provide, as far as possible, against the decay of Funeral Monuments by time, but also to prohibit their destruction and removal in any and every way, whether by relatives or others. These ends could be attained with no great difficulty, and at small cost to the country compared with the outlay which is frequently incurred by individuals in cases of succession, by the employment of qualified persons to make faithful copies of all existing inscriptions, from the earliest date down at least to the introduction of the compulsory Registration Acts.

But whether viewed in this or in a less utilitarian light, the subject of Funeral Inscriptions is one of the deepest interest, and highly suggestive to all, whether as regards the past, the present, or the future of ourselves and of our country.

In all ages and nations—in barbarous as well as in the most civilised times—men have held it a duty to honour the dead by erecting such memorials over their remains as opportunity and circumstances would allow :—

> ' To honor ye sepvltor ve may be bald—
> Ve lerne of Abraham ovr father avld.'

Since the time that the Patriarch raised 'the pillar of Rachel's grave' in the wilderness of Ephrath, unembellished boulders, cairns of stones, and mounds of earth have been employed to mark the graves of pilgrims and others, who have died in lonely and uncultivated wilds, far from the site of any known burial-place.

Many of those humble but sincere tokens of gratitude still remain throughout the glens and among the mountains of Scotland. In the course of agricultural and other improvements, cinerary urns and stone cists, often containing articles of personal ornament and dress, are found in places which, from the removal of the original cairns, were never supposed to contain such 'treasures.'

As dry gravel hillocks were generally selected as places of sepulture in early times, the same spots have been frequently chosen as the sites of places of worship. This probably not only accounts for the elevated situation of many of our old churches, but also for the custom of burying *within* them,—a practice which continued to be pretty general in Scotland, in the case of heritors and ministers, down to a late date.

Since monoliths and boulders of great size and weight are so often found upon knolls, hillocks, and in dells, as guardians of 'precious dust,' it seems probable that natives as well as strangers had taken advantage of these as places of interment. Many of these stones—the removal of which from one place to another appears to be next to impossible, even with modern appliances—had probably been borne by ice or some similar agency, and deposited in their present situations, at remote periods of the world's existence.

But as it is intended in this volume to deal solely with *inscribed* slabs and monuments, the Author will not enter either upon the ancient modes of burial, or upon a history of the funeral monuments which immediately preceded the introduction of inscribed slabs. The latter are commonly called Sculptured Stones; and these, as well as the subject of ancient burial, have been so exhaustively treated by Dr. Stuart, in his work upon the *Sculptured Stones of Scotland*, as to leave nothing to be desired.

It may, however, be mentioned, that three examples of early *inscribed* monuments, of the class referred to, are to be met with in the northeast of Scotland. One lies in the churchyard of Knockando, in Morayshire; another stands at Newton of Culsalmond, in the Garioch; and the third is within the Kirk of St. Vigeans, in Angus.[1]

The first-named of these (which is the only one mentioned in this volume) exhibits the single word 'SIKNIK,' which is believed to be the name of a man. It is cut in Scandinavian runes, and is supposed to belong to the eighth or ninth century (301). No monument can be more briefly inscribed; and although in this respect it is possibly unique in Scotland, many similar instances occur in Ireland.[2]

The Newton stone, which contains six lines of an inscription, is within two miles of the church of Insch, where there is a slab to the memory of a priest named Radulph. Although the latter belongs to a more modern class of funeral monuments than the former, it is of considerable interest, and supposed to date as far back as the close of the twelfth century (20).

---

[1] See *The Sculptured Stones of Scotland*, and *Proceedings of the Society of Antiquaries of Scotland* (vols. i., v., vii., x.).

[2] *Christian Inscriptions in the Irish Language*. Chiefly collected and drawn by George Petrie. Edited by Miss Stokes, for Members only of the Royal Hist. and Archæol. Assoc. of Ireland. 4to. Dublin, 1872.

The present volume contains no other inscription that can be referred to the same or the following age.

The fragments of the monuments of the Hays and Montifixes at Cupar-Angus probably belong to the fourteenth century (72). But the most interesting inscription that the Author has met with is within the parish church of Tealing, near Dundee. It is in the vernacular of the period, and commemorates the death of Ingram of Kethenys, priest of the church of Tealing, archdeacon of Dunkeld, and a contemporary of Barbour, the more celebrated archdeacon of Aberdeen, who wrote the poem of *The Brus*. Although there is nothing regarding Tealing in this volume, the inscription is one of so much interest, that the Author may be pardoned for reprinting it here, from his own paper upon the subject, in the *Proceedings of the Society of Antiquaries of Scotland* (vol. x. p. 290). It is cut upon a freestone slab, is in fine preservation, and reads thus:—

✠ heyr : lyis : Ingram : of : Kethenys : prist
masty^r : ī : arit : eredene : of : dukeldy : made : ī : hys
xxxii : yhere : pr^{a}yis : for : hym : yat : deyt : hafa
nd : lx :   : yherys : of : eyld : in : the : yher
of : cryst : m̊ : ccc : lxxx.

The inscriptions in this volume next in order of antiquity and interest are those from the fragments of a monk's tomb at Cupar-Angus. The surname unfortunately is lost, but the remaining traces of a date show it to have been a fifteenth century work. Of the same age are the tombs of the Lyons of Glamis (181); Graham of Fintray and his wife, at Mains (201); Richard, vicar of Finhaven (338); Gilbert Greenlaw, a supposed hero of Harlaw, at Kinkell, in the Garioch (305); and those of the Leslies of Kininvie, the Constable of Balvenie Castle, and Farquharson of Lochterlandich, at Mortlach (327–30).

Probably the most interesting monuments of the sixteenth century are those relating to Abbot Schanwel (74), and to the Provost of the collegiate church of Kilmun (72), both at Cupar-Angus. The aisle of the founder of Marischal College and his father, at Dunottar (49); the fragment which indicates that the Lords of Innermeath (ancestors of the Marquis of Lorne), had their burial-place at Inverkeilor (322); the monument to the Barclays of Towie, at Gamrie (86); to Forbes of Brux, at Kildrummy (262); to the Bairds of Auchmedden, and to the father of Abbot Whyte, of the Scots College of Ratisbone, at Aberdour, Deer (57); also the interesting fragments to Wood of Bonnington, at Maryton (367), and to the Frasers, at Durris (140), all belong to the same age. The beautifully-executed inscription to Forbes of Ardmurdo, with a text in Greek capitals, which is cut upon the reverse of Greenlaw's tomb at Kinkell (305), shows how soon the work of spoliation commenced among tombstones, which, as already hinted, has been so ruinous to the interests of many families, who have had occasion to trace their descent for pecuniary or less selfish purposes.

Perhaps the most interesting monuments of the seventeenth century are those of the Lords Elphinstone, at Kildrummy (261); the Earls of Southesk, at Kinnaird (93); the Hays (75), and Barclays of Ury (80), and the Fothringhams of Powrie, at Murroes (122). Although relating to less conspicuous families, the tombs of the Gordons of Park, at Ordiquhill (28); the Irvines of Monboddo, at Fordoun (62); the Strachans of Thornton, at Marykirk (133) and at Keith (165); the Durhams of Grange, at Monifieth (109); the Inneses of Edingight, at Grange (101), of Mathie Mill, at St. Andrews, and of Coxton, at Lhanbryde (270-1); the Stratons of Kirkside, at St. Cyrus (376), are all noteworthy examples of the period; as are those of the Grahams of Largie, the Ogilvys of Barras, and that of Mr. Grainger, minister of Kinneff (172), on whom the voice of his country has conferred the honourable title of the Preserver of its Regalia. The Martyrs' Monument at Dunottar Church is another object of national interest (50). It bears the names of many who suffered for a conscientious belief in the Protestant religion; and its site is further remarkable as being the place where Sir Walter Scott met with Robert

Paterson, while engaged in retouching the inscription—a circumstance which suggested to the great novelist the idea of *Old Mortality*. The tombs of the founders of the Duffs, Earls Fife, at Mortlach (328), as well as those of young Gordon of Glastirim, and that of Bishop Nicolson, the first Vicar-Apostolic of Scotland, both at Enzie (278), must be of general interest.

But probably the most peculiar monuments of the above era are those of the Rev. Mr. Malcolm, and Roger and Euphan Rolok, at Airlie (·162). The former presents the Passion of Our Lord, carefully carved upon the copestone of the enclosure, and similar, in some respects, to the emblems upon the aumbry at Airlie Church (*infra*, p. 378); while the latter, with ornamental top, and vertically cut inscription, in raised characters, exhibits more of the Celtic type than any other noticed in this volume, although there are many and better examples of the same style in other parts of the country.

Eighteenth-century tombstones are to be met with in every variety of form. Many of these are adorned, in the style of the preceding century, with armorial bearings, ingeniously constructed monograms, merchants' marks, mortuary emblems, and representations of instruments or tools indicative of the occupations of the deceased.

Some of the last-mentioned articles are singularly interesting, and now that many have been superseded by new inventions, they are becoming of value to the antiquary, and to such as are fond of tracing the rise and progress of the useful arts.

The Author has adverted to the peculiarities of some of these in his *Memorials of Angus and the Mearns* (p. 195), as well as in several parts of this volume. In briefly referring here to a few of the most singular examples, it may be observed, that instead of the chalice, which was sculptured upon the earlier tombs of clergymen, open books became the fashion (265). That of a mill-stone picker (whose surname of 'Pickieman' had probably been assumed from his occupation) exhibits a mill-rind and a mill-stone pick (9). A cheese-press is upon the gravestone of a farmer's wife at Tannadice; and the less appropriate figures of an inkstand and two penknives are carved upon that of a schoolmaster's wife at the same place (46). A shield upon the tomb of a 'moss-grieve,' or peat-moss superintendent, is charged with the appropriate emblems of a coil of rope and a pin or short stake for laying off the moss (251). The Author has never met with any other example of the last-mentioned articles; and the two spirit-measures and a *bicker* or drinking quaich, which are well represented upon the tomb of the infant son of a roadside merchant at Cupar-Angus (344), are new to him.

In the more common cases of farmers and sailors, also of blacksmiths, weavers, and other artisans, the carvings indicative of their respective occupations are often accompanied by laudatory and uncouth rhymes, such as the following couplet from a headstone (350) at Farnell:—

'The weaver's art, it is renowned so,
That rich nor poor without it cannot go.'

Although the writers of the epitaphs which adorn the tombs of the higher classes of society are pretty generally known, it is otherwise with the epitaphs in the north-east of Scotland relating to people in the middle and humbler walks of life, if we except such as were composed by the authors of 'The Minstrel,' 'Helenore,' 'Tullochgorm,' and a few other poets.

Although anonymous epitaphs are often as fantastic in conception as they are rude in execution, and although the same lines are found in different and distant parts of the country, still they frequently possess a vigour and individuality that in some measure compensate for their want both of polish and rhythm. At Monifieth, for example, in an inscription dated as far back as 1711, we have the germ, certainly in a rude enough form, of Lover's beautiful song of the 'Angel's Whisper' (112).

A great many of our older epitaphs were probably written by parochial schoolmasters, many of whom not only possessed a considerable amount of poetical feeling, but did very much to foster and encourage healthy thought among their pupils. But besides schoolmasters, there were in Scotland, as in other countries, many other 'hobblers round the base of the Parnassus,' as the minor poets have been quaintly described, who had doubtless composed numbers of these rhymes, and possibly the most curious of the whole.

By selecting examples of these, we have given in this volume a mixture of the grave and gay. Some of the epitaphs possess unquestionable merit; and although others are utterly worthless, still, as they serve to show the taste of the times in different districts, and in various classes of society, a collection like the present would have been incomplete without them.

Those in the acrostic style (159, 183) are poor specimens; and there are only two of a punning nature, one of which refers to the surname (319) and the other to the profession (224) of the persons commemorated. In the former, it is said of Mr. Joshua Durie, that, although he could no longer en*dure* to live in this world, he en*dures* and flourishes in the next; and in the latter, we are assured that although the deceased was a learned grammarian, he neither would *decline* death nor could *inflect* fate!

One noticeable peculiarity in epitaphs is the oddly expressed oral warnings which the dead give to the living, and of which the following, from the tomb of a clergyman, is not the least peculiar:

> 'This dormitory which thou sees
> Was once the object of my eyes;
> But now my body is in dust,
> Thine also death will hither thrust' (57).

Another feature is the confidence which epitaphs exhibit in the enjoyment of future happiness by the dead, and the means by which this felicity is represented as being attained are often very singular:—

> 'He while on Earth mankind did aid
> And genarously befriend,
> For which we hope Almighty God
> Has bless'd his latter end.

> 'He by God's blessing often did
> Lame people safe restore
> To wonted health, altho' their bones
> Were bruised very sore' (373).

Some of the epitaphs contain quaint allusions to accidental deaths. One, by Skinner of Longside, refers to an ancestor of Dr. Tait, the present Archbishop of Canterbury, who 'was killed by the fall of a stack of timber' (97). Another, at Kirkden, tells us that—

> 'An old clay chimney that down fell,
> Kill'd both his servant and himsell' (34).

The death of a child by 'being drowned in a well' is referred to at Maryton (236). We have also the drowning of two brothers, while in search of their father's sheep, recorded in a Latin inscription at Lochlee (130). The death of two other brothers by drowning also forms the theme of an epitaph by Dr. Beattie (295). But probably the most curious is one by Ross of Lochlee, which has reference to a youth who was accidentally burned to death among a quantity of heather:—

> 'From what befalls us here below,
> Let none from thence conclude
> Our fate shall after time be so,—
> The young man's life was good' (128).

Of the enigmatical inscriptions given in the present work is one upon the tombstone of a blacksmith at Fearn:—

> 'Full seventy years he livd upon this earth,
> He livd to dye—the end of life is death—
> Here he was smith six lustres and three more,
> The third three wanted, it had but two before' (355).

But it is not the Author's intention, in the meantime at least, to write an essay upon the peculiarities of the inscriptions which he has collected, although many odd instances could be enlarged upon, such as the submissive husband who 'died with the concurrence of his spouse' (145); the grateful woman who erected a monument to the memory of her 'first and beloved' husband 'with concent of his successor' (371), and the considerate son,

> 'Who hindered not his father dear
> To sleep into his bed' (137).

These, and many similar points, as well as the still more interesting question of longevity, may be entered upon should the Author be spared to complete his work. But with respect to the question of longevity, he may state that, besides the casual notices of Peter Garden (209) and Lizzie Wilkin (365), who are said to have died respectively at the ages of 131 and 103, the deaths of four other centenarians are recorded in this volume. Of the lives of two of these (147, 370) little has been told. The others have been more fortunate. One, who died at the age of 110, was a sergeant-major in the rebel army at Culloden, and enjoyed a pension from George IV. (219); while the other was twice married, and had twenty-six children by his two wives, as he himself quaintly tells us, in thus speaking from his tomb:—

> 'In Wedlock's Band ue Procreat
> Lauffully us Betuix,
> Loues Pledges, whos Right number wer,
> Euen tuo tymes tenne and Six.'

Notices of nonagenarians and octogenarians occur in all parts of the volume. But the most remarkable instances are given from eight tombstones which stand within the area of the picturesque ruins of the Kirk of Cowie (53-4). It appears from these that the united ages of ten persons—five males and five females—amount to the long period of 877 years.

Among the octogenarians at Cowie are the father and paternal aunt of the late COSMO INNES, the celebrated literary antiquary, whose name must ever be dear to the lovers of Scottish history, and doubly so to those who had the pleasure of enjoying his acquaintance.

Little did the Author think, when Mr. Innes was urging the publication of this volume, for which he kindly supplied some particulars, that he so soon should have to speak of him as 'one of the past.' Although Mr. Innes, who died on 31st July 1874, had attained his 75th year, he possessed much of the buoyancy of youth, both in feeling and sentiment; and down to the very last he continued to communicate information to kindred spirits, with the geniality and exactness which are so characteristic of the true gentleman and the profound scholar.

Mr. Innes, who was born in the old mansion-house of Durris, in Kincardineshire, was Professor of History in the University of Edinburgh. He was also a Principal Clerk of Session; and on opening the Second Division of that Court on 15th October 1874, the Lord Justice-General Inglis concluded some feeling remarks on the death of Lord Benholm with this tribute to the memory of Mr. Innes:—'Nor do the calamities which have befallen us end here. We shall see no more at our table the pleasant and friendly face of Mr. Cosmo Innes, a man whose varied accomplishments added lustre to the body to which he belonged, and distinction to the office which he held. His loss will be long deplored by a much wider circle than that which frequents these halls; and having enjoyed his friendship and intimacy for more than forty years, I cannot refrain from paying this imperfect tribute to his memory.'

Apart from the portion of this volume which deals with Epitaphs and Inscriptions, the most valuable and interesting will probably be the hitherto unpublished documents so kindly lent by the late Earl of Dalhousie and others. But for these, the interesting notices concerning the life of Mr. Edward of Murroes would still have been matter for conjecture. Neither would it have come so clearly to our knowledge that, in 1701, the Earl of Panmure, and certain others of the nobility and gentry of Scotland, with a view to the improvement of the useful and ornamental arts of their country, proposed to send a son of Mr.

Edward's to the Continent, to study, sketch, and report upon the more important works in architecture, mining, planting, etc. (122-3).

Besides the interesting facts connected with Mr. Edward and his family, Churchmen will find in this volume many particulars respecting others of their old brethren, such as Mr. Dempster of Monifieth, father of the first Dempster of Dunnichen (108); and also a letter from the parson of Fettercairn, who took the wise precaution to have his vestments and 'ye silver chalice' returned to him by his cousin, the Laird of Carmyllie, in 1523, for 'feir' of an uptaking of the thirds of the benefices (352).

And now that the presentation to Scotch parish churches by heritors and others is numbered among the things that were, the quaint phraseology used in the presentation to the Kirk of Carmyllie by the laird and his curators in 1609 will be looked upon with interest (343). Nor can Lord Strathnairn's great-grandfather's own account of how he was 'supported' during his incumbency as Episcopal minister at Lochlee (382) be perused without a feeling that this worthy man had not only been strong in faith, but that, like the Israelites of old, he and his family must have been fed upon manna.

The curious letter from Erskine of Dun to his uncle, the Laird of Panmure, in which he pleads for a marriage between his neighbour, the young laird of Bonnington, and a daughter of Mr. Maule's, will please even those who have little or no turn for antiquarian lore, and may supply hints to such as take a delight in the generally thankless task of 'match-making' (389).

The letter in which Earl Marischal promises rather to break 'his necke and fortun,' than to fail in his agreement with those who became security for his 'good behaviour,' presents many points worthy of being laid to heart both by peers and commercial men in our own day (353). It shows, at the same time, how much the education of this grandson of the founder of Marischal College had been neglected, as compared with that of his friend and contemporary, the Earl of Kinghorn.

The inventories of the outfit of the latter, when he went to study at St. Andrews, and of his winter's clothing, in 1655, are most interesting; while his letter to young Arbuthnott of Findowrie, dated from the Camp at Strathblane, offering him the command of a company of horse in the Angus regiment in 1685, is highly characteristic of the dignified cavalier of that eventful period (386-8).

The account of the funeral charges of a grand-daughter of the same laird of Findowrie, who 'died of a decay' or consumption in 1704, throws much light upon the funeral customs of the period, and contains many items of expense not now to be dreamt of (383).

The first Feu-Charter of Balfour, in the parish of Kingoldrum, granted by Cardinal Beaton, 20th February 1539, to James Ogilvy of Cookstone, in Airlie, is of considerable interest, in so far as it contains a pretty full, if not a complete, list of the members of the Convent of Arbroath at that date (385). Ogilvys, possibly ancestors of Cookstone, leased Balfour from about 1478; and although tradition asserts that the castle was built by Cardinal Beaton, the Charter in question may be taken as proof of the contrary. The old houses of Claypots, Colliston, and Ethie are also said to have been built by the Cardinal as residences for female favourites; but documentary evidence shows that these were erected long after his time by the respective proprietors of the lands. Indeed, the Castle of Melgund is the only house that the Cardinal is known to have erected in Angus; and there his own initials are to be seen, together with those of Marion Ogilvy, who was the mother of a family by him, and probably his wife, by that sort of morganatic marriage which was frequent among churchmen in Roman Catholic times.

The 'testificatione' anent the wasting of Naver by 'the malitious enemie of this kirke and kingdome,' and the destruction of the minister's 'buikes' and other property by 'barbarous heighelanders,' conveys a fair enough idea of the evils attendant upon a civil war, and the hardships which the people of those days—both lay and clerical—had to undergo (389). This paper cannot fail to carry to the mind of every

d

reader the conviction, that the social condition of Scotland is far better now than it ever was in 'the good old times,' so highly lauded by writers of a certain class, and that the blessings of peace and freedom are cheaply purchased at any price, however great.

The old rentals of West Ferry of Dundee and Monifieth show that there was a considerable population, as well as shops, in these parts some two hundred and thirty years ago; and no doubt some of the local farmers, merchants, and others will be pleased to find mention therein made of namesakes, if not of ancestors (380-1).

Although not consistent with the dignity of agriculturists of the present time, the quaint manner in which the unlettered miller of Coullycan preferred his claim to the laird of Troup for a renewal of the lease of his mill must be looked upon as a curiosity in its way (87). Still, however strange it may seem, there is evidence to show that, even in recent times, similar arguments have been frequently employed for similar purposes by tillers of the soil in Scotland.

Inscriptions from funeral and other monuments have been collected and printed in most countries, and their value has been admitted not only by historians, but by all who take an interest in the past and future of a people or a country.

Scotland is by no means destitute of such collections. Many valuable inscriptions are incorporated with local histories; but the first collection, properly so called, was made by Robert Monteith, the son of an Edinburgh merchant. This unfortunate author, who was minister first at Borgue and next at Carrington, was deposed for drunkenness in the year 1685 (Scott's *Fasti*). Neither the time of Monteith's death nor the place of his burial is known. His book is entitled *Theater of Mortality*, and the first part, comprising 'Illustrious Inscriptions' from the burial-grounds of Edinburgh and its neighbourhood, appeared in 1704, and the second part, containing 'a further collection of Funeral

Inscriptions over Scotland,' was published in 1713. Both parts were reprinted at Glasgow in 1834, with eighty pages of 'Additional Inscriptions,' professedly collected from numerous burial-places in Scotland, but which appear to have been chiefly copied from local histories, magazines, and newspapers. Although the Author has, as yet, had little occasion to make use of Monteith's collection, he has tested its accuracy in many ways, and can speak of it as a trustworthy and valuable work.

Brown's *Epitaphs and Monumental Inscriptions in Greyfriars' Church-Yard, Edinburgh*, published in 1867, is also an excellent work. Besides the more modern inscriptions, it contains a number of reprints from Monteith, duly acknowledged as such by the editor. It also possesses a valuable introduction by David Laing, Esq., LL.D., of the Signet Library, Edinburgh, and some interesting extracts from the Records of the Town Council of that city.

The *Monuments and Monumental Inscriptions in Scotland*, printed for the Grampian Club (1871–3), and edited by the Rev. Charles Rogers, LL.D., is in two volumes. Besides other matter, these volumes embrace a reprint of the greater part of the Glasgow edition of Monteith, also over 360 epitaphs and inscriptions, copied from the *uncorrected* versions of the papers upon these subjects which the Author of this work contributed to the *Montrose Standard* newspaper, as noticed by him in a letter which appeared in the *Scotsman* of 12th January 1874.

These papers, as stated in the Preface, formed the nucleus of the present volume. They were corrected and supplemented after appearing in the *Montrose Standard*, but thirty-five of the notices (as detailed in the subjoined footnote)[1] are not given in this volume. These may

[1] These were notices of the parishes of—

Aberlour.	Cromdale.	Kinerny.	Rathen (Aberdeen).
Auchterhouse.	Dallas.	Leslie (Fife).	Slains.
Banchory-Devenick.	Forfar.	Leuchars.	St. Mary's (Craig).
Barry.	Fowlis-Easter.	Lundie.	St. Skae.
Botriphnie.	Glengairn.	Mary Culter.	Strichen.
Bourtie.	Glenmuick.	Meigle.	Tarland.
Cabrach.	Garvock.	Midmar.	Tibbermuir.
Cortachy and Clova.	Inchbrayock.	Migvie.	Tullich (Aberdeen).
Craig.	Kearn.	Panbride.	

possibly appear in an amplified and more interesting form at some future period.

In the course of publication, which extended from January 1868 to November 1874, these contributions frequently contained strictures upon ill-kept burial-grounds. Although these are omitted in the volume, the Author has been gratified to learn that his remarks have led to the improvement of many of those interesting and hallowed spots. He earnestly hopes that the good work will continue to be carried out wherever it is found needful, until the now too just reproach of 'out of sight out of mind'—as applied to the last resting-places of our forefathers—be wiped out, and give place to the grateful and humanizing sentiment of—

'Though lost to sight, to memory dear.'

Old Kirk-yard of Edzell.

Epitaphs & Inscriptions

FROM

BURIAL GROUNDS and OLD BUILDINGS,

WITH ILLUSTRATIVE NOTES.

Banchory-Ternan.

(S. TERNAN, BISHOP OF THE PICTS.)

THE church of *Banchorytarny*, with lands in the locality, were granted to the Abbey of Arbroath by William the Lion. The church belonged to the diocese of Aberdeen.

It is said that S. TERNAN died at Banchory, A.D. 440, and that a church was built over his remains. It is probable that Banchory was an early seat of learning, since Camerarius speaks of some of the old Scotch saints having been educated at the monastery of Banchory.

Tradition says that some of the buildings stood in the present bed of the Dee, opposite the kirk; and I am informed by Mr Stouart, inspector of poor, that "a few years ago, when a pathway was being made along the brink of the river from Banchory Lodge to the Railway Station, the men employed dug up *a small square bell*." Possibly this was the *ronecht*, or bell of Banchory-Ternan, which is said to have been presented to the Saint by Pope Gregory the Great; but, unfortunately, this interesting relic has been lost sight of.

Notices of the ownership of the bell by John Stalker (1490) "be reson of heritage pertening and mowyn to hyme be his vife," and the possession of "the Deray Croft of Banquhoriterne," are on record (Reg. Ep. 'Abd.); also legends of the bell having the power of following S. TERNAN, of its own accord, when on his religious pilgrimages!

The new church, built in 1824, has a modern bell—that upon "the watch-house" in the churchyard, which is tolled at funerals, bears:—

PETRVS. STENS. ROTTERDAMI. ME. FECIT. A⁰. 1664.
SOLI . DEO . GLORIA.

The burial-ground lies in a hollow, or *corrie*, on the north bank of the Dee. It contains a number of monuments; but all trace of the "cross church" has disappeared; also the "isle for the Burnets of Leyes." The site of their aisle is marked by an enclosure, in which there is a tablet thus inscribed:—

In memory of CHARLES-SPEARMAN BURNETT, youngest son of James H. Burnett, Esq. of Arbeadie, and Caroline his wife; born 20th July 1835, died 21st June 1836. [Mark x. 15.]

—The erector of this tablet (the ninth, and present baronet of Crathes), is directly descended from Alexander Burnett who had a grant from Robert the Bruce, 1324, of the lands of Killienach Clerach (Candieglerach), and others in the same neighbourhood. The Burnetts were also king's foresters in the North, and a small hunting-horn of ivory at Crathes, set with garnets, is said to have been given by Bruce to the first Burnett of Leys.

The celebrated Bishop Burnett (*v.* KEITH-HALL) was the son of a younger brother of Leys; and a continental amour of one of the lairds is celebrated in the ballad of the "Baron of Leys." Their residence of Crathes, built about ——, is a fine example of the Scoto-Franco style of architecture, being pretty similar to the castles of Glamis, Craigievar, and Muchals. Billings gives three plates of Crathes in his Baronial and Ecclesiastical Antiquities of Scotland.

An enclosure on the north-east of the churchyard of Banchory-Ternan contains three mural tablets of red granite. Upon the centre slab :—

In memory of THOMAS RAMSAY, second son of Sir Alex^r. Ramsay of Balmain, Bart., and of his wife Dame Elizabeth, daughter of Sir Alex^r. Bannerman, Bart. He was a Captain in H. B. M.'s Army, served in the Peninsula and at Waterloo; born 24th Feb. 1786, died 18th Decr. 1857, aged 71. And also of THOMAS RAMSAY, R.N., second son of the above Capt. T. Ramsay, and of Margaret, daughter of Sir Robert Burnett of Leys, Bart., his second wife, born 13th Jany. 1828, died 17th Jany. 1856, aged 28.

—Capt. T. Ramsay's first wife was Jane, a daughter of Pat. Cruickshank of Stracathro, Esq., by whom he had the above-named Wm., also Catherine, and two other daughters. Upon right-hand side of the above :—

CATHERINE RAMSAY, second daughter of Capt. T. Ramsay, and Jane Cruickshank, born April 16, 1822, died Augt. 21, 1843, aged 21. [Luke xii. 40.]

The third slab bears :—

WILLIAM BURNETT-RAMSAY of Banchory Lodge, late Captain in H.M.'s Rifle Brigade, and Lieut.-Colonel of the Forfar and Kincardineshire Militia Artillery, born 11th April 1821, died 6th Nov. 1865. [John xix. 25.]

—A fountain, constructed of granite, has been erected at Banchory, by subscription, to the memory of Capt. Ramsay. He was a nephew of the Very Reverend Dean Ramsay of Edinburgh, and succeeded to the estates of his grand-uncle, Gen. Burnett, a monument to whose memory, upon Scultie Hill, is thus inscribed :—

Erected to the memory of General WILLIAM BURNETT of Banchory Lodge—born 19 Feb. 1762, died 7 Feb. 1839—by his numerous Friends and Tenantry, 1842.

The burial aisle of the Douglasses of Tilwhilly, a plain building with slated roof, stands near the middle of the kirkyard. The initials and date of

J. D : M. A : 1775,

upon the door lintel, refer to JOHN DOUGLASS and his wife MARY, sister to the sixth Viscount Arbuthnott. To their only son, a marble monument (inside) bears this inscription :—

Here lies Interr'd among his Ancestors, JOHN DOUGLASS of Tilliwhilly, Advocate, who died at Edinr. March 6th 1773, in the 36th year of his Age, and in his Father's lifetime. He was only son of John Douglass and Mary Arbuthnott, was early educate in principles of true religion, which appear'd well in him all his Life. O ! Reader, here drop a Tear for a young man so soon cutt off. But let this comfort thee, that he has gain'd infinitely by dying, for Blessed are the dead that die in the LORD; and we have reason to believe that his righteous soul is now in a happy state, waiting for the resurrection of his body to eternal life.

—The above is built in the south-east corner of the vault : The next is near it :—

In memory of Mrs HANNAH DOUGLASS, widow of the late John Douglass of Tilwhilly, advocate, and daughter of the late Sir G. L. A. Colquhoun of Tillyquhonn, Bart., who departed this life 10th April 1835, aged 83 years, and lies interred here, in the same grave with her husband. This tablet is placed as a small testimony of respect and affection by her only surviving son, G. L. A. Douglass, advocate. She lived beloved, and died lamented. Blessed are the dead that died in the Lord. Rev. xiv. 13.

Upon a marble slab in the south-west corner :—

Here lies the body of JOHN DOUGLASS of Tilwhilly, who died on the 6th of July 1812, in the 40th year of his age. Here lies also the body of his only brother, GEORGE-LEWIS-AUGUSTUS DOUGLASS, Sheriff-Depute of Kincardineshire, who died on the 30th of October 1847, in the 76th year of his age. Jesus said unto her, I am the resurrection, and the life. John xi. 25.

—From a dark grey granite slab, built into the wall above the last-noticed:—

In memory of JOHN DOUGLASS of Tilquhillie, and of Falkenhorst (Thueringen Vorarlberg, Austria.) Born at Inchmarlo, March 28, 1804; died at Tilquhillie, October 11, 1870.

—Quotations from John xiv. 12; v. 28; and ix. 25 (slightly destroyed by damp), are painted upon the plaster on the north wall.

The Douglasses had a pretty early settlement on Deeside, it having been about 1479 that David Douglass, a cadet of Douglass of Dalkeith, married the heiress of Ogston of that Ilk and Tilwhilly. The Douglasses have possessed Tilwhilly from that time, with the exception of from about 1812 to 1857, when it belonged to Henry Lumsden, Esq., advocate, Aberdeen, from whom, or his heirs, it was reacquired by the Douglasses during the last-mentioned year. The castle of Tilwhilly, dated 1576, and now occupied by the tenant of the farm, is in a tolerable state of repair. Bishop Douglass of Salisbury, born at Pittenweem, in Fife, was descended of this family.

A marble slab, set in granite (on east side of the Tilwhilly aisle), is thus inscribed:—

1730, First monument erected; Second in 1776; and this by the Revᵈ. Dr Leslie of Fordoun, in 1842. Hic Jacent Reverendi Magistri JACOBUS REID, a familia de Pitfodels oriundus, Banchoriensis Ecclesiæ Pastor a Reformatione primus; ROBERTUS REID, dicti Jacobi filius, et ROBERTUS REID, Roberti dicti nepos, uterque Ecclesiæ ejusdem Pastores. Hic Jacent Magister THOMAS REID, qui obijt in Eslie, anno ætatis 76; et JOANNA BURNET, ejus conjux, quæ obiit anno ætatis 90. Necnon THOMAS REID, quondam in Pitenkirio, qui monumentum hoc erigi curavit, et obiit, 31 Januarii 1733, ætatis suæ 76, et AGNES FERGUSON, ejus conjux, quæ obiit 21 die Decembris, 1728, ætatis 70. PETRUS REID et CATHERINA REID, eorum liberi.

[Here lie the Revᵈ. Mr JAMES REID, a descendant of the family of Pitfodels, the first pastor of the church of Banchory after the Reformation; the Rev. Mr ROBERT REID, son of the said James; and the Revᵈ. ROBERT REID, grandson of the said Robert, both ministers of the same church. Here lie Mr THOMAS REID, who died in Eslie, in the 76th year of his age, and JOANNA BURNET, his wife, who died in the 90th year of her age. Also THOMAS REID, formerly in Pitenkirie, who caused this monument to be erected, and who died 31st Jan. 1733, in the 76th year of his age; and AGNES FERGUSON, his wife, who died 22st Dec. 1728, in the 70th year of her age; PETER REID, and CATHARINE REID, their children.]

—The first-named Mr Robert Reid was succeeded by Mr ALEX. CANT. Mr Alex. C. was deposed before 4th Nov. 1661, as of that date the Earl of Panmure, being sufficiently informed of his "doctrine, lyffe, and good conversatione," issued a presentation in favour of Mr George Innes, minister of Dipple. It was subsequent to this that the second Mr Robert Reid became minister of the parish. THOMAS, son of James Reid, after travelling over Europe, became Greek and Latin Secretary to James VI., and some of his Latin poems are printed in Johnston's *Delitiæ Poetarum Scotorum.* He founded the office of librarian at, and made valuable additions to the library of Marischal College, Aberdeen, among which is a Hebrew Bible, supposed of the 12th century. Another son, ALEXANDER, physician to Chas. I., published several professional works, and bequeathed books and money to King's College, Aberdeen; also money to his native parish for educational purposes. The Robert of 1620 was grand-father to Dr Thomas Reid, author of the Inquiry into the Human Mind. The Reids of Pitfodels were sprung of a burgess family of Aberdeen. Dr Leslie who erected the third and existing monument, from which the above inscription is copied, was related to the Reids through his mother. From another slab:—

GEORGIUS READ, M.D., in Classe Britannica diu, dein Londini, medendi arte functus, natalis soli desiderio tactus non inutile senium, sed quietum apud suos confecit, et inter majores ossa condi voluit, anno 1754, 87 ætatis.

[GEORGE READ, M.D., after practising the art of healing in the British Navy, and then in London for many years, feeling a desire to revisit his native soil, spent his declining years usefully but quietly among his friends, and wished his bones to rest beside those of his ancestors. He died in 1754, in his 87th year.]

From a mural tablet, within an enclosure, on left of churchyard gate:—

In memory of DUNCAN DAVIDSON, of Tillychetly and Inchmarlo, born 17th March 1773, died 8th Dec. 1849. And of his wife, FRANCES-MARY PIRIE, born 29th April 1786, died 15th Nov. 1859.

—Mr Davidson, whose ancestors came from Tarland, was an advocate in Aberdeen, and bought the prettily situated house and property of Inchmarlo from Mr Leslie of Warthill. The house of Inchmarlo was built by Mr Douglass of Tilwhilly, from whom the property passed to Mr Walter S. Davidson, a banker in London, and a son of a minister of Rayne. Inchmerlach and Arbadly (Arbeadie) were wrongously held from the Earl of Angus by Cumin of Culter in 1479 (Acta Dom.) Upon a flat stone, at eastside of Crathes aisle:—

Sub hoc marmore requiescunt Reverendus Magister ROBERTUS BURNET de Sauchen, qui pastorali officio apud hanc ecclesiam . . . sedecim annos functus est, et obiit decimo octavo die mensis Junii anno supra millesimum septingentesimo primo, et ætatis suæ quinquagesimo tert[io]; necnon JOANNA REID, sponsa eius, quæ obiit 9no die mensis Aprilis, anno 17-2, ætatis suæ -3.

[Underneath this marble rest the Rev. ROBERT BURNET of Sauchen, who was minister of this church for 16 years, and died 18th June 1701, in his 53d year; and JOANNA REID, his spouse, who died 9th April 17-2, in the -3d year of her age.]

—Sauchen, once Huntly property, was acquired by Burnets, between 1662 and 1673. On 24th February 1699, the minister of Banchory, who was some time at Fintray, was served heir to his father Thomas, in the lands of Sauchen and others (Retours, Abd.) His wife is said to have been a daughter of his predecessor at Banchory. Mr Burnet was succeeded in Sauchen, first by

a son, and then by a grandson, on whose death, in the year 1770, the property passed to the female line (v. CLUNY.)

At the top of the last-noticed slab stands a small round-headed stone, with the date of 1716, also DMS. in monogram. The initials, T.S. and M.S. are upon another part of it; but the inscription is ill to decipher, though the letters . . . . . MARGT SC . . . . and the date of 1716, are clear enough. If fully read, the inscription would probably be found to have some connection with MARTIN SCHANK, who (as shewn by an extract from the Presbytery Records of Kincardine O'Neil, kindly communicated by the Rev. Mr Mackenzie, Aboyne), became minister of Banchory on 7th Oct. 1694, and died 18th April 1747. Mr Schank married Margaret Dauney in April 1698, and at the time of his death he was a widower, with an only son, named Alexander, "above the age of sixteen years." This son bequeathed £100 to the poor of Banchory, became designed of the property of Castlerig in Fife, to which ultimately succeeded the Rev. Mr Alexander Shank of St Cyrus (v. LAURENCEKIRK.)

Mr Schank was succeeded in Banchory by Mr George Campbell, afterwards a professor in, and principal of Marischal College, Aberdeen, author of a Treatise on Miracles, &c. It was upon the removal of Mr C. to Aberdeen in 1757 that Mr Dauney came from Lumphanan to Banchory-Ternan:—

Memoriæ S. M. MARGARETÆ CHALMERS, viri Reverendi M[ri] Francisci Dauney, Banchoriensis Ternani pastoris, conjugis, quæ obiit 9no Januarii 1790, ætat 64. Necnon CATHARINÆ DAUNEY, eorum filiæ, quæ obiit 7mo Junii 1787, ætat. 34. Quatuor liberi, qui in teneris annis obierunt, juxta requiescunt. Ac etiam memoriæ S. M. præfati M[ri] FRANCISCI DAUNEY, prius Lumphanani, posterius hujus ecclesiæ per annos LVIII pastoris, qui annum ætatis LXXXII agens obiit 2do Aprilis 1800.

[Sacred to the memory of MARGARET CHALMERS, wife of the Rev. Mr F. Dauney, minister of Banchory Ternan, who died 9th Jan. 1790, in her 64th year. Also of CATHARINE DAUNEY, their daughter, who died 7th June 1787, in her 34th year. Four children, who died in infancy, rest beside them. Sacred also to the memory of the foresaid Mr FRANCIS DAUNEY, minister, first at Lumphanan, and afterwards of this church for 58 years, who died 2d April 1800, in the 82d year of his age.]

—Mr Dauney is said to have been in every respect a good example of the clergyman of the old school. Some anecdotes are still told of him on Deeside: among others, it is said, that in Mr Dauney's old age Mr Douglass of Tilwhilly charged him publicly on some occasion with inability to perform his parochial duties. This Mr Dauney determined to disprove, and one Sunday, while the laird was in church, he preached "two turns of the sand glass," and was about to commence a third, when Mr Douglass moved to leave the church, upon which Mr Dauney exclaimed, with emphasis—" Will you say noo, Tilwhilly, that I canna insist?" (*i.e.* preach.)

Sacred to the memory of the Rev. JAMES GREGORY, minister of Banchory-Ternan, who died on the 8th Sept. 1829, in the 83d year of his age, and 52d of his ministry, having been first pastor to the congregation of the Gilcomston Chapel of Ease, Aberdeen, from which charge he was translated to this parish in the year 1800. Also to the memory of ELIZABETH, his daughter, who died here 3d January 1827.

Upon a flat slab :—

1720: Hic quiescit corpus IACOBI FARQUHAR in Lochtoun de Leys, qui obiit 24 die Septembris, 1712, ætatis suæ 5-; ejusque conjugis dilectæ CHRISTIANÆ SPALDEN, quæ obiit 25 die Septembris, 1719, ætatis suæ 59.

[Here rests the body of JAMES FARQUHAR in Lochtoun of Leys, who died 24th Sep. 1712, in the 5-th year of his age. Here also rests the body of his beloved spouse, CHRISTIAN SPALDEN, who died 25th Sep. 1719, in her 59th year.]

From a flat slab :—

Here lyes WILLIAM MAIR, who departed this lyfe Janry. 20, 1710, aged 81 ; and MARGRET BURNET, his spouse, who departed Aprile 28, 1708, aged 72 years.

A flat stone, with the Reid arms nicely carved,

also mortuary emblems, and a monogram composed of a merchant's mark, and the initials A. R., bears the following :—

Here lyes ALEXANDER REID, son to Alexander Reid, Merchant in Abd., indweller in Banchory, who departed this life March 26, 1717, student at the King's College in Old Abd., in the 15 year of his age :—

. . . . and on
My last words cast an eye :—
Old and young, take Christ your rock,
And prepare to die.
Gross . . . . . and vulgar mynds take flight,
This to God's glory, my salv^{an}., & my parents' shyning light.

Haberem eum tanquam amissurus, amisi tanquam habeam.

[I would have him as if I were about to lose him—I have lost him as if I had him—*i.e.*, While I had my son, I always wished to be prepared for his loss, and now that I have lost him, I feel as if I still had him.]

ALEX. RHAEDUS de Glasel, obiit 24 Aug^{ti} anno 1726, ætatis 57. Also MARGARET REID, aged 2 years ; MARY REID, 1½ years ; and THOMAS REID, aged 1 year, all children to Alexr. Reid.

Quem amabas extulisti ; quære quem ames ; satius est amicum reparare quam flere.

[Thou hast borne to the grave him whom thou lovedst ; seek another to love ; it is better to replace a friend than to mourn his loss.]

From an adjoining head-stone :—

To the memory of GEORGE DONALD, late farmer in Bocharen, in the parish of Straen. When living, he maintained a fair character, and was a loving Husband, an Indulgent Parent to a prosperous family whom Providence had blest him with. He died Sep. the 29, 1766, aged 81 years. A. D : M. D. This stone was erected by the sons of the above deceased.

WILLIAM COLLIE, farmer in Lightwood, "after living as a dutiful and examplary parent, finished this transitory Life," 14 Nov. 1772, aged 61 years:—

Wake thoughtful in this sacred place,
Where our remains do lie ;
And meditate most seriously,
One day that thou most die.
Deep silence where Eternity begins.

Near north wall of burial-ground : —

Sacred to the memory of HOWARD L. TREW, R.N., son of Henry and Phebe Allen Trew, Grove Cottage, Banchory, 13 Feb. 1861.

Upon a table-shaped stone : —

Sacred to the memory of WILLIAM SHAW, born in Inveraven, Dec. 27, 1757, died at Bellfield, in this parish, on the 19th Dec. 1833; also of his only child ELSPET, spouse of Dr Adams, who died on 27th Dec. 1843, in her 46th year. ISABELLA ELDER, wife of William Shaw, died at Bellfield, Dec. 1849, aged 80 years. FRANCIS ADAMS, M.D., LL.D., translator of "Paulus Ægineta," "Hippocrates," and other learned works, died at Bellfield, 26th Feb. 1861, aged 64 years. ELIZA DAUNEY, his second daughter, died in Aberdeen, 2d Jan. 1862, aged 30 years. FRANCIS, his third son, Lieut. 37th Madras Grenadiers, died at Jeypore, Madras Presidency, 10th Dec. 1862, aged 28 years. WILLIAM-JAMES, his eldest son, surgeon, died at Bellfield, 25th June 1865, aged 39 years. ELIZABETH FORBES, wife of William-James Adams, died at Bellfield, 10th Jan. 1863, aged 29 years. ISABELLA-HAY ADAMS, only child of W. J. Adams and E. Forbes, died at Peterhead, on 22d March 1866, aged 3 years and 7 months. GEORGE, an infant son, and JESSIE ADAMS, granddaughter of Dr Adams, are also interred here. An infant grandson died at Kamptee, Central India, 5th Sep. 1858, aged 3 days.

—The above-named Mr Shaw was long postmaster at Banchory-Ternan. Dr Adams (whose father was gardener at Aboyne, afterwards farmer at Orkenhove), commenced practice in Lumphanan, from whence he removed to Banchory. The following inscription, composed by Professor Geddes of Aberdeen, is from a granite obelisk at Bellfield : —

In memoriam FRANCISCI ADAMS, M.D., LL.D., medicorum omnium, quotquot Scotia tulit, literarum thesauris necnon scientiarum opibus eruditissimi. Diu in hac valle reducta, ab aula et academia procul, medicinæ simul et musis, vir vere Apollinaris, fideliter inserviit. Natus Lumphanani III. Id. Mart. MDCCXCVI. Mortuus Banchoriæ IV. Kal. Mart. MDCCCLXI. Carissimi capitis desiderio amici posuere.

[In memory of FRANCIS ADAMS, M.D., LL.D., who surpassed all the physicians that Scotland has produced in the extent of his literary and scientific attainments. In this secluded valley, far from Hall and University, a true votary of Apollo, he long and faithfully served at once medicine and the muses. He was born at Lumphanan, 13th March 1796, and died at Banchory, 26th Feb. 1861. This monument was erected by his friends in token of their regret for the loss of one whom they held very dear.]

The great district of country which lies between Crathes and the Hill of Fair appears to have been early peopled, and of considerable importance in old times. There was a crannoge, or lake dwelling, in the now drained Loch of Leys, in and about which some interesting bronze relics have occasionally been discovered (v. Proceed. So. Antiq. of Scot., vol. vi.) In addition to this, there is reason to suppose that Kilduthie, about a mile from the Loch of Leys, was the seat of a religious house at a remote period. If so, the kirk or chapel had probably been inscribed to S. DUTHAC, who had several dedications in Scotland, the chief of which was at Tain.

On the west side of the parish, near that pretty spot where the Canny joins the Dee, stood the wood or forest of Trustach, which Alan the Durward bestowed upon the monks of Arbroath, 1203-14. In this locality are traces of old earthworks, which some suppose to have been the dykes of a camp, others those of an ancient township.

But the ruins of the Castle of Cluny-Crichton (near Raemoir), dated 1666, and the fragment of a coffin slab, which exhibits the top of a wheelcross, built into a dyke near the manse, together with part of the old market cross, in the last-named locality, are, along with the castles of Crathes and Tilwhilly, probably the most tangible of the existing monuments of antiquity in Banchory.

A very good account of the antiquities, &c., of Banchory is given in the Rev. Mr Anderson's Statistical Account of the parish; but the best history of ancient Banchory is in the Antiquities of Aberdeen and Banff (Spald. Club.) Guide Books contain modern histories of it; and a pamphlet—" Banchory-Ternan Sixty Years Ago" —has much that is interesting regarding the district, as well as an account of the cantrips of "The Witch of Baldarroch," which happened some thirty years ago. These, which were enquired into by lawyers, and are celebrated by more than one local poet, turned out to be nothing more than the ingenious freaks of a servant girl, though believed by many at the time to be the work of supernatural agency!

The date of 1798 is upon the bridge of Dee near the village of Banchory. In 1862 an irongirder bridge, with stone piers, was erected about four miles below the bridge of Dee, chiefly at the cost of Mr Mactier, late of Durris. The bridge of Feugh, which crosses the river of that name on the south side of the Dee, is a singularly romantic object, and has been frequently sketched and engraved.

Aberlemno.

(S. ——.)

THE kirk of *Abirkmonach* belonged to St Andrews, and was dedicated, along with a great many other churches in that diocese, by Bishop David in 1242 (Robertson's Concilia Scotiæ, vol. i.) In 1275-9 (Reg. Vet. de Aberbrothoc), the church was taxed at 20 merks.

It was dependent upon the Priory of Rostinoth, and, along with that house, became attached to the Abbey of Jedburgh. From a memorandum of 18th Jan. 1230, it appears that the church of Aberlemnach was in the gift of " Mr John" (*Miscel. Aldbar.*) This was possibly John Roman, or Romanus, " of the city of Antine, our writer," arch-deacon of York, who, in 1239, " for the good and services he did to the Roman church for a considerable time," had an annual pension of 100s., and was recommended by the Pope to the Abbot and Convent of Jedburgh, to have " some suitable or competent ecclesiastical benefice such as is given to, or conferred on secular clergy, as soon as any falls vacant."

On 24th October 1482, Mr David Stewart, pensioner of Rostinoth, held the "benefice of Abirlempno," and had Sir John Lowtholt as his chaplain. In 1567, Mr David Lindsay [of Pitairlie] was minister of Aberlemno, and of the two neighbouring churches of Forfar and Rostinoth, with a stipend of 200 merks. Mr George Lyall was reader at Aberlemno, with £20 Scots of salary. In 1574 (Wodrow Miscellany, i.), there appears to have been a different arrangement.

Possibly the most noteworthy of the succeeding ministers at Aberlemno, were the two OCHTERLONYS. The first came to the parish about 1655. He was brother of the contemporary minister of Carmyllie, and both were sons of John Ochterlony, who was provost of Brechin in 1641 (*Documents at Panmure.*) Mr Ochterlony presented a silver communion cup to the kirk of Aberlemno, thus inscribed :—

This Cup is Gifted by Mr John Ochterlonny, Minr. of Aberlemno, For the Celebration of the Lords Supper in the sd Church—1683.

—Mr O. died about 1695, and was succeeded by his nephew, also JOHN, son of the minister of Carmyllie (*q.v.*) He was served heir to an uncle and aunt in 1693, and to his father in 1699 (Retours, Forfar.) He was deprived as a nonjuror, and an intruder into parish churches ; and, after convening his adherents for some time in his own house of Flemington, he left the locality. He was afterwards consecrated Bishop of Brechin, and died at Dundee in 1742 (Keith's Lives of the Bishops.)

It was after the translation of Mr Ochterlony's immediate successor to Idvies, that Mr THOMAS MITCHELL came to Aberlemno, to whose memory, and that of some of his descendants, there are three inscribed tablets within the kirk :—

[1.]

Mr Thos. M^L. ordained 1714 ; Mr AND^w. M^L. ordained 1750 ; Mr JA^s. MITCH^L. ordained 1794.

This monument was erected by Mr Thomas Mitchel, minister of the Gospel at Aberlemno, and Marie Miller his spouse, in memorie of their two children, THOMAS and AGNES MITCHELS, who died of non age.

Below also lys interr'd yͤ Rev. Mr Tʜoˢ. Mɪᴛᴄʜᴇʟʟ, who serv'd yͤ cure in this Parish 34 years
and 9 months; For Piety, Generosity, Hospitality,
and Friendship, Extensive Charity, and Moderation,
Affability and Good Nature, Inferior to none. In
zeal for yͤ interest of Christ, and Examplifying in
his conduct what he inculcated on others, he was
Equal'd by few. He courted not human applause,
yet he obtained it. He lived in peace with all men,
and died much regretted, yͤ 9th day of Jany. 1770,
in yͤ 60th year of his age. Also here lies interred
Mr Aɴᴅʀᴇᴡ Mɪᴛᴄʜᴇʟʟ, son and successor to the
above Thomas, who lived much respected, and died
regretted by all who knew him, the 3rd day of
Jany. 1794, being the 65th year of his age, and 44th
of his ministry. Rev. Jaˢ. Mɪᴛᴄʜᴇʟʟ died 13th
May 1841, in the 72nd year of his age, and 47th of
his ministry.

[2.]

Below lie the mortal remains of Mrs Jᴇᴀɴ Cʀᴀᴡ,
sponse of the Rev. Andrew Mitchell. She died
27th Sept. 1809, the 87th year of her age. Sic
præterit species mundi.

[3.]

Sacred to the memory of Mrs Eʟɪᴢᴀʙᴇᴛʜ Sᴇᴅɢ-
ᴡɪᴄᴋ, first wife of the Revd. James Mitchell. She
departed this life on the 3d May 1821, and 54th
year of her age. Also in memory of her children,
Eʟɪᴢᴀʙᴇᴛʜ-Bᴜʀɴᴇᴛ, Aʟᴇxᴀɴᴅᴇʀ, Mᴀʀᴍᴀᴅᴜᴋᴇ,
Aɴᴅʀᴇᴡ, Jᴇᴀɴ-Cʀᴀᴡ, Gᴇᴏʀɢɪɴᴀ, Mᴀʀɢᴀʀᴇᴛ,
Eʟɪᴢᴀ-Tᴀɪʟʏᴏᴜʀ, and Fʀᴀɴᴄɪs-Nɪᴄᴏʟ Mɪᴛᴄʜᴇʟʟs,
all of whom, except Alexander and Andrew, were
dead before herself. Likewise in memory of Eʟɪᴢᴀʙᴇᴛʜ, daughter of the Rev. James Mitchell, by
Janet Webster, his second wife. Fiat voluntas Dei.

From an adjoining tablet :—

1803 : Erected by George, John, Robert, Ann,
and Jean Jarrons, in memory of their father,
Gᴇᴏʀɢᴇ Jᴀʀʀᴏɴ of Balbinnie, who died 5th Jany.
1793, aged 65 ; and of Bᴀʀʙᴀʀᴀ Wᴀʟʟᴀᴄᴇ, spouse
to George Jarron, junr., who died 15th April 1797,
aged 33 ; and Bᴀʀʙᴀʀᴀ Jᴀʀʀᴏɴ, their child, who
died in nonage ; also of Rᴏʙᴇʀᴛ and Isᴀʙᴇʟ Jᴀʀʀᴏɴ's children.

The next three inscriptions are from marble
tablets, also within, and upon the south-east side
of the church :—

[1.]

Hic conduntur reliquiæ Gᴜʟɪᴇʟᴍɪ Cʜᴀʟᴍᴇʀs de
Aldbar, qui vixit annos 65, ob. 7 Id. Jul. 1765 ;
et Cæᴄɪʟɪæ Eʟᴘʜɪɴsᴛᴏɴᴇ, conjugis adamatæ, quæ
vixit annos 58, ob. Non. Mart. 1761. Sacrum memoriæ parentum bene merentum hoc marmor filius
posuit.

[Here lie the remains of Wɪʟʟɪᴀᴍ Cʜᴀʟᴍᴇʀs of
Aldbar, who died July 9, 1765, aged 65 ; and of
Cᴇᴄɪʟɪᴀ Eʟᴘʜɪɴsᴛᴏɴᴇ, his dearly beloved wife, who
died March 7, 1761, aged 58. This monument was
raised to the memory of his excellent parents by
their son.]

—Mr Chalmers, who was a son of Chalmers of
Hazelhead in Aberdeenshire, was a successful merchant in Spain, and his wife was a daughter of
Elphinstone of Glack. The first Elphinstone of
Glack was Arthur, brother to Bishop Elphinstone,
founder of King's College, Aberdeen. Mr Chalmers bought the lands of Aldbar in 1753 (v. Mem.
of Angus and Mearns), and was succeeded by his
son Patrick, who was sheriff of Forfarshire from
1774 to 1819. To him the following refers :—

[2.]

Pᴀᴛʀɪᴄᴋ Cʜᴀʟᴍᴇʀs, Esqr. of Auldbar, advocate,
died on the 15th February 1824, aged 87.

Virtuous and learned, polished and refined,
Of pleasing manners, and enlightened mind ;
Beloved in Life, lamented in his end,
Here sleeps the Sire, the Grandsire, and the Friend.

[3.]

A Tribute of Affection to the Memory of Isᴀʙᴇʟ
Tɪɴᴅᴀʟ, who died 2d Nov. 1811, aged 67.

The church and aisle of Aberlemno, both erected
in 1722, have been much improved in appearance
by recent repairs. The belfry is upon the west
end of the kirk ; and the bell bears :—

THE BELL OF ABERLEMNO.
ROBERTUS MAXWELL ME FECIT, EDIN. 1728.

The tombstones are pretty numerous in the
churchyard. From these the following inscriptions (the earlier of which are carved in interlaced
Roman capitals), are selected :—

Heir rests ane faithfvl sister qvha livit vith hir
mariet hesbent Viliam Alerdys borges in Dundie

20 zeiris, calit IANET ADEMSON, qvha depertit in this paries the 19 day of Iuli anno 1600.

V. A : Heir rests ane faithf brother V. A. qvha departit this pnt lyfe the 17 day of Avgvst anno Christi . . . I. A.

Heir restis ane fa . . . . riet vyf IANOT VODSTER . . . . zeir and depairtit this lyf . . . . . Ivnii 1605 . . . . 66 zer of hir aig . . . .

Heir restis in the Lord ane faithfvl brother ALEXANDER WATSON svmtym in Crostvovn depairtit 28 of Febrvarii 1622 aige 51. A. W : M. D : V. W. I live to die—I die to live.

. . . AS DAIGATI qvha leivet vt his m . . . . ther dav . . . . ALIXANDR DAIGATI, IOHN DAIGATI . . . . .

Vnder this ston lyes the corps of ANDREV DALGITIE . . . . 89, and of his age 70 yier ; also EVPHAM BELL, his wife, depairted December 24, 1672, age 41 yeirs.

—The six inscriptions given above are from flat slabs. Those below are chiefly from head-stones. The first exhibits carvings of articles belonging to the weaver trade :—

JOHN NICOL, weaver, Lochead, d. 1728, a. 33 :—

Tho' this fine Art with skillfull hand,
Brings Forreign Riches to our Land ;
Adorns our Rich and Shields our Poor,
From cold our bodies doth secure,
Yet neither Art nor Skill e'er can
Exime us from the lot of man.

DAVID MILNE (1734) :—

Man's life on Earth, even From the Womb,
is Full of Troubles to his Tumb ;
He enters in with Cryes and Fears,
And paseth thro' with Cars and Tears,
He Goeth out with sighs And groans,
And in the Earth doth Loge his bons.
O that our Souls with Christ may have
A Lodging place beyond the Grave
To rest, and Hallouge sing
Eternally to Heaven's King.

From a stone, upon which a mill-rind and millstone pick are represented :—

GEORGE ANDERSON, sometime Pickieman at Balgarrock Mill, died the 9 day of March, anno 1747.

1756 : JOHN SPENCE, GRISALL COLVILL. This stone was erected by John Spence in West Milldens, in memory of his father and mother, who lived sometime in Broomhill of Balgavies :—

Here ly's an honest old race,
Who in Ballgavies land had a place
Of residence, as may be seen,
Full years three hundred and eighteen.

. . . .

This old race of Spences came there about the year 1438, where they and their offspring resided from Father to Son, till the year 1820.

—The last clause and some names were added in 1850 by Andrew Spence, Broughty Ferry.

JAMES TAYLOR (1774) :—

Here lies the man, who peace did still pursue,
And to each one did render what was due ;
With meek submission he resign'd his breath
To God, the Soverign Lord of life and death.
Here different ages do promiscuous lie :
The old man must, the young may die.

JAMES PETER (1797) :—

In hopes in peace his Lord to meet,
Here lies interr'd in dust,
One in his temper ever kind,
In all his dealings just.
Kind to the poor, the widow's friend,
He always did remain,
Till heaven's great Lord by his decree
Recall'd his life again.

———

From the peculiar symbols and other carvings upon the well-known sculptured stones which stand at, and near the kirk of Aberlemno, it is probable that the locality was an early seat of Christianity, as well as a place of considerable population in old times, long even before the district was known as a thanedom (v. Proceed. So. of Antiq. (vol. ii), and Sculptured Stone Monuments of Scotland.)

A portion of the arms of the LINDSAYS, possibly those of Balgavies, is at the kirk of Aberlemno. The foundations of their castle are on the south side of the parish. It was destroyed by order of King James, in 1593, in consequence of Sir Walter Lindsay having joined the Jesuits.

The armorial bearings of JAMES BEATON of Melgund (grandson of the Cardinal), and those of his wife, ELIZABETH MENZIES, are built into the outer and north wall of the church, dated 1604, and initialed I. B : E. M. The arms and initials M. O. (MARION OGILVY), the mother of Cardinal Beaton's children, are upon the ruins of Melgund Castle. A monogram of the initials of GEORGE, first Marquis of Huntly, and of his wife, HENRIETTA STEWART, similar to those at Gordon Castle, is built into the farm-offices at Mains of Melgund.

Melgund Castle, notices of which will be found in Memorials of Angus and Mearns, p. 278, is one of the most picturesque and interesting ruins in Forfarshire. The property of Melgund belongs to the Earl of Minto, to whom it has descended from Henry Maule, a cadet of the noble family of Panmure, and the reputed author of a History of the Picts. On the death of one of the Melgund family the following invitation to the funeral (here printed from the original at Panmure), was sent by the laird, to " his Louing Cousing Iohn Maule chamberlane off panmure":—

"Melgund 1672 May : 16
Cousing—Satturday next be ten in the forenoone is the dyet I Intend the buriale, So vith your conveniencie come or not as you find cause, either shal be taken by
Your Louing Cousing,
H. MAULE.
the buriale is on 18 Instant."

Alexander Irvine of Drum and of Kelly in Arbirlot, held considerable property in Aberlemno in the early part of the 17th century, from which he made a "mortification" of meal to the schoolmaster, and to the poor of the parish, similar to that which he made to those of Arbirlot, about the year 1629.

In 1707 Sir Alex. Murray of Melgund (an ancestor of the Earl of Minto) obtained an Act of Parliament to allow a weekly market (long since discontinued) to be held at Aberlemno "in all time coming."

Aldbar.

(S. ——)

THE church of *Aldbar*, dedicated by Bishop David of St Andrews in 1243, was given to the College of Methven, by Walter Stewart, Earl of Athol, in 1433. It is rated along with the kirk of Kinnell in the Taxation of 1275-9 (Theiner Mon. Hist. Hib. Scot., p. 114), at 4 merks 10s 8d Scots. It was served, in 1574, along with the kirk of Brechin and four others adjoining, by Mr John Hepburn, who had £202 4s 7d of stipend. Andrew Ker, then reader at Aldbar, had 20 merks and kirk lands.

The chapel is situated in the Den of Aldbar, where a sculptured stone and fragments of coffinslabs have been found. There are a few old tomb-stones, but the inscriptions are defaced.

The church, which was long a ruin, was restored as undernoted. Although private property, it is occasionally used for public service. It contains two brasses, designed by Billings. They bear respectively these inscriptions :—

[1.]
In memory of PATRICK CHALMERS, Esquire, of Aldbar, for many years a merchant in London. He was born at Aldbar A.D. 1777, and died there on the 8th day of December 1826. Also of FRANCES INGLIS, his wife, who died at Aldbar on the 10th day of February 1848, in the 70th year of her age.

[2.]
Outside the walls of this Chapel are interred the mortal remains of PATRICK CHALMERS, Esquire, of Aldbar, late Captain in H. M.'s 3d Dragoon Guards, sometime Member of Parliament for the Montrose District of Burghs, Author of the "Sculptured Monuments of Angus." He re-edified this Chapel in the year 1853. Died at Rome, on June the 23d, 1854.

—Soon after the death of Mr Chalmers, a monument, similar in design to the Ancient Sculptured Crosses of Scotland, which he did so much to preserve and illustrate in the admirable work above referred to, was erected by his late brother, John-I. Chalmers, Esq. A coffin-slab was also laid over his grave, inscribed with his name, and the dates of his birth and death.

Mr Chalmers was principal editor of the Chartularies of Arbroath and Brechin. The latter work was completed after his death, and prefaced with a genial Memoir, by his friend, Prof. Cosmo Innes of Edinburgh. The work was a free contribution by Mr Chalmers to the members of the Bannatyne Club, and contains an excellent portrait of Mr Chalmers, engraved by Bell, after a miniature by Robertson.

Mr Chalmers contributed many valuable papers to archæological publications; and at the time of his death he was a Vice-President of the Society of Antiquaries of Scotland. His remains were interred on 15th July 1854, on which occasion the following lines were written as a tribute to his memory:—

Peace to thy Soul! May'st thou in peace repose,
And no rude hand thy sacred shrine profane:
Thine was the heart that felt the poor man's woe—
Reliev'd his wants, and sooth'd his ev'ry pain.
In thee surviv'd the best of mental powers,
Combin'd with meekness, modesty, and grace;
Keen to perceive—in judgment, good and true—
Concise and fair Old Manners thou did'st trace.
How much thou wish'd poor Scotia's state to know,
And bring to light her ancient Arts and Lore,
Long hid in mists of ages past, or else
Mix'd up in fable by her Poets of yore.
Enchanted by that wish, and, doing good,
Roll'd past thy too short years of fifty-two:
Sound may'st thou sleep in that sweet lonely spot,
Where, but to-day, we bade thy corse—ADIEU!

Since the death of Mr Chalmers two magnificent folio volumes, illustrative of the Sculptured Monuments of Scotland, have been issued by the Spalding Club, under the able superintendence of Mr Chalmers' old friend, John Stuart, Esq., LL.D., Sec. A. S. Scot., &c., in which work much of the letter-press and all the engravings of Mr Chalmers' publication have been reproduced.

After Mr Chalmers re-edified the chapel of Aldbar, the remains of his ancestors were removed from Aberlemno to that romantic spot. There, too, lie the ashes of his brother and successor, JOHN-INGLIS CHALMERS, Esq.—a man of great humour and goodness of heart—who died 15th May 1868, leaving a family of sons and daughters.

Notices of the castle of Aldbar, and of the early proprietary history of the lands, are given in Memorials of Angus and Mearns. It need only be briefly remarked here that before Aldbar came into the hands of the Chalmers', it belonged first to a branch of the Cramonds of Midlothian, and next to the Lyons of Glamis, one of whom, Sir Thomas, built the oldest part of the existing castle. From the Lyons it passed to Sir James Sinclair, and afterwards to Peter Young of Easter Seaton, grandson of Sir Peter, almoner to King James VI. It was acquired by Mr Wm. Chalmers from the Youngs.

The initials and monogram of the late Mr P. Chalmers are upon some of the recent additions to Aldbar Castle. The Lyon arms and the initials, S.T.L. (Sir T. Lyon), also D.E.D., those of his second wife, Dame Euphemia Douglas daughter of the Earl of Morton, are upon the old tower.

The lintel of the mill door at Blackiemill bears the date of 1698, and the initials, R.Y: A.G. (Robert Young and Ann Graham). It was to their son that Ruddiman, the celebrated grammarian, was tutor—a fact referred to by Ruddiman in his pamphlet entitled "Animadversions" on Love's Vindication of George Buchanan.

Bellie, or Fochabers.

(S. ANDREW.)

THE patronage of the kirk of Bellie belonged to the Priory of Urquhart, in consequence of a grant of territory, by David I. about 1150-3, which included Finfans, on the west of the Spey, and

Fochoper (Fochabers) on the east, with a common for pasturage, and a fishing on the Spey, &c.

In 1574, Mr George Hay was minister of Bellie and the three parishes of Rathven, Farskan, and Dundurcus, with a stipend of £212 10s 8d. Robert Grant was reader at Bellie with £16 and the kirk lands.

In 1725, part of the east side of the parish of Bellie, including St Ninian's, and part of the west side of Rathven, including Portgordon, and Preshome, &c., were formed into a preaching station. In June 1851, these districts were erected into a *quoad sacra* parish, under the name of ENZIE where there are a parish church, manse, glebe, school, and school-house, &c.

The churchyard of Bellie is about two miles from the village of Fochabers, near to where the Spey joins the Moray Firth. In the only remaining fragment of the kirk, a much defaced tablet, with Latin inscription, bears the name of "GULIELMUS ANNAND," who appears to have died in 1770, aged 70. But the gravestone of Mr WILLIAM SANDERS, which (says Shaw) bore "that he lived 108 years, and was minister of Bellie 77 years," is not now visible. Mr Sanders was ordained about 1607. Twenty years afterwards, he was censured by the Presbytery (Scott's Fasti), "for making ane pennie brydell within Straithboggie to his dochter in law, at quhilk wer present excommunicat papists, to the greiff of all honest Christians."

It was in Mr Sanders' time, on 15th September 1632, that the Earl of Angus "wes marcit at the kirk of Bellie with lady Mary Gordon [third] dochter to the Marquess [of Huntly], be Maister Robert Douglass, minister at Glenbervie, whome the Erll of Angous brocht with him of purpoiss." On the 28th November following, the Master of Abercorn and Huntly's youngest daughter were married in the same place, "be ane Irish minister." Spalding further informs us that the "corpis" of the first Marquis of Huntly, who died at Dundee in 1636, "wes convoyit with sum freindis to the kirk of Belly," where it was kept a night, while on its way to the family tomb at Elgin.

The same authority says that Lord GRAHAM, Montrose's eldest son, lies at Bellie, but no stone marks the spot. His father had passed from Elgin on 4th March 1645, and come to the Bog of Gight, now Gordon Castle, "with the bodie of his army." While there, his son, "a proper youth about 16 yeiris old, and of singular expectatioun, takis sicknes, deis in the Bog in a few dayis, and (continues Spalding) is bureit in the kirk of Bellie, to his fatheris gryt greif."

The tombstones are numerous at Bellie. The first-quoted inscription is from a marble slab, within an enclosure, near the kirkyard-gate:—

This tablet is placed by Jean, fifth Duchess of Gordon, to the memory of her dear infant daughter, CHARLOTTE, who died the 10th of Dec. 1810; and also, to her beloved mother, Mrs SUSAN ROBERTSON, who died the 2d of June 1822, in her 91st year.

—Jean Christie, "fifth Duchess of Gordon," was a woman of humble birth and parentage, who resided at Fochabers. Her good looks and handsome person fascinated Duke Alexander long before the death of the fourth Duchess, the Lady Jane Maxwell; and probably not the least romantic part of Jean Christie's history is that almost at the very moment of her being united to a man in her own station of life, a carriage drove to the door of the cottage, where the marriage party were assembled, and Jean was abducted and carried off from her betrothed. She bore nine children to Duke Alexander, to whom, "after proclamation on three several Sabbaths," she was married "on the 30th day of July 1820, by the Rev. William Renule, minister of the parish of Bellie." According to the Bellie Register of Burials, "Jean Christie, Duchess of Gordon, Second Wife to Alexander, Fourth Duke of Gordon," was interred at Bellie upon the 2d August 1824, "aged 54 years." Her body was laid in a vault, under a handsome mausoleum of Elgin freestone, with canopy, supported by twelve pillars. Her name is not recorded; but the following, upon a marble slab, relates to her son Adam, whose remains were laid beside those of his mother:—

In this vault are deposited the remains of ADAM GORDON of Newtongarrie, son of Alexander fourth Duke of Gordon, who died at Burnside, 14th Aug. 1834, in the 37th year of his age, deeply regretted by all his friends. This marble was placed here by his spouse, Jane Grant, as a testimony of her affection.

—Mrs Gordon (like her mother-in-law, Jean Christie), was of humble parents. She belonged to Buckie or its neighbourhood, and subsequently married Mr Reid, sometime a bank agent in Fochabers, by whom she had two sons and a daughter. Newtongarrie is a property in the parish of Drumblade. Near the middle of the burial-ground at Bellie :—

Svb hoc cippo tvmvlatvr corpvs exsangve ELIZABETHÆ MILNS, Angligenæ, Andreæ Hossack ivnioris qvondam sponsæ, principis Dvcissæ Gordon qvondam ancillæ, qvæ obiit tertio Octobris, anno Dom. 1687.

[Beneath this stone is interred the body of ELIZABETH MILNS, a native of England, spouse of Andrew Hossack, junior, and formerly chief maid to the first Duchess of Gordon, who died 3d Oct. 1687.]

—The first Duchess of Gordon was Lady Elizabeth Howard, second daughter of the Duke of Norfolk. Her husband, the fourth Marquis of Huntly, was created Duke of Gordon in 1684. He died at Leith in 1716, she at Edinburgh in 1732. Although their names are unrecorded at Elgin, both were buried there.

From a flat slab :—

Heir lyes ELSPET GORDON, spous to Alexr. Gordon of Upper Dalochie, alies, Major, who departed May 12, 1690.

The next two inscriptions are from table-shaped monuments :—

Here lyes ISSOBELL KNIGHT, spous to Androu Hay, wywer in Fochabers. Shee departed the 13 of Febr. 1712 : Manney hath donn werteusly, but shee heath excideth them all.

Here lie the remains of JAMES ROSS, Esq., who, with unblemished integrity, conducted for many years the important affairs of the Great Family of Gordon ; and, whilst zealously anxious to promote their interest, raised no fortune to himself. He departed this life the 8th Sep. 1782, aged 50 years. And of KATHARINE GORDON, his wife, who discharged the duties of a daughter, a wife, and a mother, with a piety and affection offering bright example to their descendants. She was born 1st Jan. 1743, died 17th Sep. 1795. Sacred to the memory of JOHN ROSS, Esq., sometime Professor of Oriental Languages in King's College, Aberdeen, who, after passing a long life in the practice of virtues which rendered him an ornament and blessing to society, was removed to that better world, where he will meet their just reward, on 9th July 1814, in the 84th year of his age. This humble tablet has been inscribed by parental affection.

Sacred to the memory of JOHN MENZIES, Esq., who died 15th March 1831, aged 72. The best eulogium of his character is, that, for the long period of nearly 50 years, during which time he acted as cashier to the Duke of Gordon, his employer never sustained any loss by his incorrectness, or neglect of duty; and that the many thousands with whom he transacted business, were equally satisfied with the integrity of his conduct, against which no complaint was ever heard, even from those who were not his friends.

From a head-stone (enclosed) :—

Erected by Lieut.-Col. William Marshall, as a sincere but inadequate tribute to the memory of a revered parent, 1857. This stone was originally placed by William Marshall over the graves of his son Major ALEX. MARSHALL, who died at Keithmore, 31st Jan. 1807, in his 33d year ; and of JEAN GILES, who died at Newfield Cottage, Dandaleith, 13th Dec. 1824, in the 85th year of her age, whose remains lie both here interred. Here also lie the remains of WILLIAM MARSHALL, Esq. husband of Jean Giles, a man of virtue and integrity. From a humble station in life he rose to distinction by the industrious cultivation of a natural talent : eventually he became Factor on the estate of Alexander Duke of Gordon, an office which he held for many years, performing its duties with fidelity, and to the satisfaction of his Employer and the Tenantry. Although self-taught, he made considerable progress in mechanics and other branches of natural science, to which his leisure hours were frequently devoted. But he was chiefly noted for his skill and fine taste in music, the Scottish airs and melodies composed by him being widely known and appreciated. He died universally esteemed, at Newfield Cottage, Dandaleith, 29th May 1833, in his 85th year. Of a family of six children, besides the above-named Alexander, FRANCIS, a jeweller, died in London; JOHN, a Capt. in the army, died in India; and GEORGE, a Lieut. in the army, died in Spain. Jane, an only daughter, widow of John M'Innes, Esq. Dandaleith, and William, a retired Lieut.-Col. in the army, being the sole present survivors.

—William Marshall, who was originally a footman or page at Gordon Castle, was perhaps second only to the "famous Neil Gow" as a performer upon the violin, and probably superior to Neil as a composer of national airs. Marshall's music, which is still sought after in the North, consists of a number of beautiful strathspeys, named by him after people and places that he knew; and Burns was so much pleased with Marshall's music to his song, "O' a' the airts the wind can blaw," that he wrote him a complimentary letter on the subject. Marshall, who had also a taste for mechanics, employed much of his leisure in the art of clock-making, a specimen of which is preserved at Gordon Castle. A portrait of Marshall, engraved by C. Turner, from a painting by John Moir (ancestor of Moir-Byres of Tonley), with violin in hand, is to be seen in many houses in the Northern counties.

His son, Major ALEXR. MARSHALL, served in India, and at the siege of Seringapatam. Capt. JOHN, of the 26th Regt., was present in the Peninsular War, and died of cholera at Madras in 1829, and Lieut. GEORGE, of the 92d Regiment, died from fatigue in 1812. The fourth son, Lieut.-Col. WILLIAM MARSHALL (the erector of the monument at Bellie), who became a Lieutenant in the Gordon Fencibles in his eighteenth year, served in almost all the engagements during the French Revolution, including those of Aboukir and Corunna, and Marshall was so severely wounded at Waterloo, that his right arm had to be amputated. After this Lieut.-Col. Marshall was employed in Canada during the rebellion of 1837, and afterwards in various responsible military offices at home. He retired from the service in 1838, and took up his residence in the pretty cottage of Newfield, on the banks of the Spey, near Craigellachie, where he died, beloved and respected by all who knew him, on the 29th August 1870, in his 91st year. (v. *Elgin Courant* of 2d Sept. 1870.)

The next two inscriptions are from the oldest of four inscribed monuments within an enclosure :—

Here lyes the body of GEORGE GEDDES, late in Mains of Kempcairn, who dyed the twenty first day of Octr. 1746. In memory of CATHERINE MILNE, of the Mill of Towie, and relict of Thomas Geddes of Dallachy and Todholes; she survived her husband 33 years, and died the first Sept. 1821, aged 87.

In this burying ground are interred the remains of THOMAS GEDDES, of Dallachy, who died in 1789, aged — ; and of his son JOHN GEDDES, in Orbliston, who died 23d Dec. 1817, aged 64, by whose disconsolate widow this simple record is placed over his grave as a small token of her remembrance of his affection and worth.

Upon a table stone (enclosed) :—

GEO. ANDERSON, farmer, Burnside, "a man distinguished for ardent piety and pure Benevolence, whose manners were as simple as his morals were unblemished," d. 1779, a. 69; his wf. HELEN SHAND, d. 1797, a. 71 :—

Unknown to Pomp, and bred to rural Toil,
To him the Christian's Faith and Hope were given;
Unskill'd in Art, nor trained in Courtly Guile,
He liv'd to God, and died—to wake in heaven.

In same grave are deposited the remains of the Rev. JOHN ANDERSON, who was 27 years minister of the parish of Kingussie, and 11 of Bellie, previous to his retirement from the church, and who died on the 22d of April 1839, in the 80th year of his age.

—Mr Anderson knew much of the private affairs of Alexander, fourth Duke of Gordon, and long acted as Commissioner upon the Gordon estates. The circumstance of his holding that office during his incumbency having been brought before the Church Courts, and the General Assembly disapproving of his being engaged in that capacity, he demitted his charge in 1819. His mother was a near relative of Mr Shand, once in the West Indies, afterwards laird of The Burn, near Fettercairn (*q.v.*)

Upon a chest-shaped stone :—

Erected, at the expense of his fellow-servants, to JOHN BARONDON, who died at Gordon Castle, Aug. 16, 1853, aged 39 :—

It was in the bloom of manhood's prime,
  When death to me was sent ;
All you that have a longer time,
  Be careful and repent.
O, the grave, whilst it covers each fault, each defect,
Leaves untarnish'd the worth of the Just ;
His memory we'll cherish with tender respect,
Whilst his body consumes in the dust.

———

The antiquities of the parish are few—the so-called Roman Camp to the north of Gordon Castle, traces of a Druidical temple at Greencairn, and the Court Hillock, at the last-named of which places the barony courts of the district had possibly been held—being almost the only objects worthy of notice.

As to the proprietary history of the district, it appears that about 1238 King Alexander acquired the second teinds of the lands of Fochobyr, and others, from the Bishop of Moray, in exchange for lands and teinds in another part of that province. At a later date, other parts of Fochabers were exchanged for the lands of Wynn (? Whinnyhaugh), and Bynin (? Binns.)

In 1362, John Hay of Tullyboyle (Tillybody) had a charter of the whole lands from the Spey to the burn of Tynet, which are described as lying within the Forest of Awne, or Enzie. About twelve years later, the same baron (Reg. Morav.), with consent of his son, founded a chapel at the Geth (Gycht), in honour of the BLESSED VIRGIN and ALL SAINTS. This was endowed with an annuity of £20, also four acres of land at Ladardach, with a house for the chaplain, and pasture for twelve cows and a bull, sixty sheep and lambs, two horses, &c., while the jurisdiction of the foundation was given to the Bishop and Chapter of Moray. This place of worship appears to have been situated somewhere about Gordon Castle. But the old fairs or markets of S. CATHERINE, S. MUNGO, and the HOLYROOD, which were long held in the neighbourhood of Fochabers, possibly show that there were either altarages within the chapel, or that chapels in different parts of the parish were dedicated to those saints.

The Hays of Gycht and Enzie were the same as those of Tillybody, in Clackmannanshire. The male line failed about 1426-8, when Sir Alexander Seton of Gordon, afterwards Earl of Huntly, married as his second wife, Ægidia, heiress of Gycht, Enzie, and Tillybody, by whom he acquired these lands. Those of Gycht and Enzie are still in possession of descendants of the Gordons, now represented by the Duke of Richmond.

It was by the second Earl of Huntly that the House of Bog of Gight (now Gordon Castle) was founded. Since then it has been rebuilt, and from time to time altered and added to, until it has assumed the palatial appearance which it now exhibits. The Castle stands in the midst of a vast park, studded with magnificent old trees, and laid out with great taste and judgment.

Among the more interesting features within the policies are the Quarry Gardens—at one time presenting unseemly holes filled with stagnant water, and hillocks of quarry *debris*. That locality is now the most lovely and enchanting of places ; and, apart from nice walks and flowerbeds, there are some old carved stones, which fall more within the scope of our present work. Some of these, which present, in monogram, the initials of the first Marquis and Marchioness of Huntly, are said to have been brought from Huntly Castle. They are oval-shaped ; but unfortunately the centre ornaments, as well as the inscriptions, are mostly defaced. The two texts which follow (Ps. xxxiv. 9 ; Phil. ii. 10), both dated 1614, are the only parts decipherable :—

TIMETE . DOMINVM . OMNES . SANCTI . EIVS*
QVIA . NON . EST . INOPIA . TIMENTIB' . EVM.

—As there are traces of "a glory" or halo upon

the next slab, it had probably been adorned with a carving of Our Saviour—

OMNE . GENV . FLECTATVR . . . . NOMINE . IESV.

The old market cross of Fochabers is also within the policies of Gordon Castle. The town, a pleasantly situated place, is an old burgh of barony. It consists of a main street, with diverging lanes, and a spacious square, planted with rows of trees. It contains the Established Church, erected in 1789, a Free (1844), an Episcopal (1834), and a Roman Catholic Church (1828); also some excellent houses and shops, a branch bank, &c.

Milne's Institution, which was founded by Alex. Milne of New Orleans, a native of Bellie, for the free education of natives of the district, is a fine building a little to the east of the town.

The river Spey, which is of considerable width and beauty at Fohabers, is crossed by a handsome bridge, with an iron arch of great span, erected soon after 1829, the floods of August of that year having carried away the previous bridge, which was constructed of stone. The stone bridge consisted of four arches, and was opened in 1805.

GEORGE CHALMERS, who must ever be looked upon as one of the most celebrated of those men who have brought documentary and other reliable evidence to bear upon the elucidation of Scotch History and Antiquities, was a native of the town of Fochabers. He wrote several books of National value and interest, particularly "Caledonia," of which great work he lived to issue only three vols. Accounts of Chalmers' life will be found in all biographies. He was educated at King's College, Aberdeen, and after a residence of some years in America, he returned to England, when he became a clerk to the Board of Trade, and died in 1825. The following extracts from the parish register regarding the marriage of his parents, and his own baptism, may be interesting to the admirers of his works:—

Dec. 26, 1742: "GEORGE Lawfull Son to James Chalmers and Isabel Ruddoch in Fochabers, was baptized before Witnesses John Chalmers, John Geddes, Robert Chalmers, and Andw. Mitchell, all in Fochabers."

—George appears to have been the second of four sons. The first, Alexander, was born in 1740; the third, Thomas, in 1748, in the note of whose baptism his father is described as a "fewer" in Fochabers; and the fourth, Peter, was born in 1750. Their mother came from the parish of Deskford, as is shown by the following entry of her marriage:—

July 25, 1736: "James Chalmers in ffochabers and Isabell Ruddach in ye parish of Dessfoord gave up their names to be proclaimed in order to their marrige according to Law."

Peter Culter.

(S. PETER, THE APOSTLE.)

KING WILLIAM the LION bestowed the church of *Kulter*, "iuxta Abirdene," upon the Abbey and monks of S. MARY of Kelso, about 1165-99. The gift was afterwards confirmed by Mathew, Bishop of Aberdeen, within whose diocese the church was situated.

Alan of Soltre, chaplain, who had probably been an ecclesiastic of the hospital, or monastery of Soutra, in Lothian, was presented by the Abbot of Kelso, to the vicarage of the church of Culter, 1239-40. It is rated in the Old Taxation at 54s 4d.

In 1287-8, an agreement was made between the Abbot and Convent of Kelso and the brotherhood of the Knights of Jerusalem, regarding the Templars' lands of Blairs, Kincolsi (Kincousie), on the south side of the Dee, by which a chapel, erected by the Templars at their house of Culter, was recognised as a church for the inhabitants of the above lands and others belonging to them, with parochial rights (Reg. Abd.)

S. PETER'S Well, remarkable for the fineness of its water, is situated upon the Glebe Haugh, east of the church; and PETER's Heugh is the name of an adjoining part of the north bank of the Dee.

The kirk of Peter Culter, surrounded by some old trees, has a conspicuous site on the north bank of the Dee, and commands a fine view of the church and district of Mary Culter, &c. The date of 1779 is upon the church; and a slab built into the north wall, initialed M. J. K., and dated 1715, refers to the incumbency of Mr JOHN KENNEDY, who was minister from about 1704 to '23, his predecessor having been deposed (Scott's Fasti), "for lying, immorality, and negligence."

The session records shew that "the fabrick of the kirk fell to the ground vpon the 16th day of October 1673," and "the sandglasse" having been broken by the ruins, the session, on 18th January followiug, ordered another glass to "be bought."

The tombstones are numerous. The first quoted inscription is from a slab built into the outer and south wall of the church :—

Close to this wall, in front of this tablet, lie the remains of Sir ALEXR. CUMING of Culter, Bart., and his Lady, ELIZABETH DENNIS, co-heiress of Puckle Church in Glostershire. Where they now lie was formerly under their own seat in the Old Church, where they were buried.

—Philip Cumin, son of Jardine Cumin of Inverallochy, in Rathen, succeeded to Culter by marrying Marjory, heiress of Sir Adam Wauchope of Culter. Part of the property belonged in early times to Alan the Durward; and subsequently, in 1247, King Alexander bestowed Culter and adjoining lands upon Robert, son of Allan of Wauchop (Nisbet, ii., Appx. 56.)

Alexander Cumin of Culter was created a Baronet in 1672, and by him, it is said, the oldest part of the present house of Culter was erected. Sir Alex. wrote a poem on the death of Bishop Forbes (Funerals), which thus concludes :—

"Though in few acts man could abridge his playes:
In manie schens divyded are his dayes.
Since then wee see the tapers due decay,
(When 't 's dark) the candlesticke may be a prey."

The baronetcy of Culter has long been extinct; and about 1726, the estates were sold by Sir Alexander Cumin to Patrick Duff, then of Premnay. It is to the last-named that the following inscription at Culter relates :—

To the memory of PATRICK DUFF of Culter, Esq. He was born Nov. the 16, 1692. He dyed Oct. 20, 1763. He examined Christianity, believed it firmly, and loved it warmly. From Christian principles he practised social virtue; in relieving distress and promoting useful arts he delighted. The affection of his Widow raises this monument.

—In 1721, Mr Duff married his cousin Margaret, only daughter of William Duff of Braco, by Helen Taylor, "a woman of very much inferior rank to him, though come of very honest parents." Miss Duff, who was only eleven years of age at the time of her marriage, had no family to the laird of Culter; and some years after his death her second marriage is thus recorded (5th Jan. 1769), "Udny of Udny married to Mrs Duff of Culter." Besides Culter, Mr Duff acquired the "most of the low country estates of Drum," which adjoined Culter. He died at Culter House, which Baird of Auchmedden describes as "one of the most beautiful and best finished Gentleman's Seats in the North." Culter is still Duff property, being owned by R. W. Abercromby-Duff, of Fetteresso and Glassaugh, &c., Esq., M.P., who married (1871) a daughter of Sir Wm. Scott of Ancrum, Bart. P. Duff of Culter was 4th son of Craigstone, and grandson of Keithmore (v. MORTLACH.)

A table-shaped stone, on south side of church, presents a bold carving of the Irvine arms, and this inscription, the first, or oldest part being in Roman capitals :—

Here lyeth IEANE IRVINE, spovse to Maister Robert Irvine of Cvlts, in hops of a blised resvrrection, who departed this lyf the 21 of March 1678, the 32 yeir of hir aige.

Also ROBERT IRVINE, Esq. who died the 10th of April 1728, aged 89 years. Likewise MARGARET COUTTS, his second wife, who died in 1710, aged 45 years. And CHARLES IRVINE, Esq., who died the 28th of March 1779, aged 83 years. And EUPHEMIA DUGLAS, his spouse, who died 21st of Decr. 1766, aged 55 years.

—Sir Alex. Irvine of Drum had a charter from Walter Caidyow of the lands of Cragtoune of Petrycultyr, with pertinents, within the regality of St Andrews and barony of Rescobie, 23d April 1526. His grandson, Gilbert Irvine of Culairlie (fourth son of Alex. Irvine, yr. of Drum, who fell at Pinkie), was the ancestor of the Irvines of Murthil (Murtle) and Cults. A good part of the Irvine property in this locality, as above seen, was bought by Patrick Duff of Culter. From granite monuments within an enclosure :—

In memory of JOHN THURBURN of Murtle, who died 31st of January 1861, aged 80.

In memory of BARBARA-ANDERSON THURBURN, third daughter of John Thurburn of Murtle, who died 5th October 1858, aged 32.

—Mr T., who was a native of Keith (*q.v.*), bought Murtle in 1821 from the executors of Mr John Gordon, who bequeathed the Murtle Bursaries and Charities to the University and City of Aberdeen. Mr Thurburn's widow, only daughter of the Rev. Mr Findlater of Cairnie, gave £1000 towards the erection of the Thurburn Cooking Depot in Aberdeen, for the benefit of Working Men. The next two inscriptions are from flat stones :—

Here lyes the body of HELLEN SIMPSON, laufull daughter to Patrick Simpson of Coneraig, and spouse to John Milne in Brotherfield. She died March 25, 1742, aged — years, &c. :—

> So, reader, underneath ther lyes
> The virtuous, prudent, chaste, and wise;
> Of beauty great, and gentle blood,
> The darling of the neighbourhood.
> Think then of her bright generous soul,
> And first admire, and then condol.

Here lyes under the hope of a blessed resurrection, MARY GIB, spouse to William Meff, tenant in Binghill, who dept. this life the 18th of May 1710; and WILLIAM MEFF, who dep^{rt}.

Four table-shaped tombstones relate to an English family named *Smith*. The Smiths established a paper manufactory at Peter Culter, which is still carried on, and is believed to have been the first of its kind in the North of Scotland. The works are situated in the Den of Culter, one of the most lovely and romantic places in the district. Miss HESTER SMITH, who died in 1851, aged 70, (to whom one of the tombstones was erected by her niece, Jane Anne M'Leod), left the interest of £100 annually for the repair and preservation of these monuments. When not required for that purpose, the money has to be given to the poor of the parish. The most southerly of these stones bears :—

Mrs ANNE MURRAY (relict of Alex. Murray, of Elm Place, Finchley, Middlesex, Esq.), died 2d Jan. 1841. In the grave adjoining, on the north, are interred the mortal remains of her father and mother, Mr RICHARD SMITH, late paper manufacturer in this parish, and MARTHA REID, his spouse, &c.

Upon the most northerly stone :—

WILLIAM DYKAR, surgeon, R.N., died 28th June 1830, aged 74. Also HANNAH, wife of William Dykar, daughter of the late Mr Richard Smith, of Paper Mill, who died 2d May 1848.

An intermediate stone bears the following epitaph on LEWIS SMITH, proprietor of the Culter paper mills, who died in 1819, aged 42 :—

> While manly beauty in meridian bloom,
> Untimely hastning to the ghastly tomb,
> Calls from the eye the sympathatic tear;
> Pause, Friend, and shed the mournful tribute
> If social manners, with a taste refin'd, [here.
> If sterling worth, with unassuming mind,
> If filial tenderness possess a charm,
> If steady friendship can your bosom warm,
> Then, Reader, imitate, applaud, revere,
> What triumph'd in the man that's buried here.

WM. MARTIN, Grindlawburne, d. 1753, a. 88 :—

> Within this narrow house of clay,
> The bones of WILLIAM MARTIN ly;
> He was an honest man and just,
> All honest men might well him trust.
> By sweat of brow his bread he won,
> He liv'd and dy'd an honest man.
> O Lord, said he, thy strength and grace
> I ever will admire;
> For by thy sending me releif,
> Thou'st taught me to aspire.
> The heavens thou hast open set,
> And rent the vail that I
> May upward look, and thy dear Son,
> With glory cround espy.

—ISABELLA KNOWLS, spouse of Wm. Martin, d. ——, a. 96. The next three inscriptions (here abridged) are from table-stones :—

The Rev. GEORGE MARK, died 23d Dec. 1811, in the 76th year of his age, and 42d of his ministry.

The Rev. JOHN STIRLING, 27 years minister of this parish, died 5th Oct. 1839, in the 54th year of his age. His widow HELEN [FOWLER], died 4th Dec. 1862, aged 66.

—Mr Stirling, who was a native of Dunblane, left a son who studied the fine arts. In early life Mr S. painted portraits, also The Sermon, a scene in a Scotch Kirk, &c. He is presently (1872) at Tangier, engaged upon a picture of The Court of the Sultan of Morocco.

Rev. DAVID GILLATLY, minister of the Shiprow Chapel of Aberdeen, died 20th Aug. 1821, aged 58. Erected by his Relict and Congregation.

Upon the highest point of a rising ground called the Weather, or Wedder Craig, is the "Cupstone" indented in the shape of a bowl. It is commonly called the *Doupin' Stane*; and, according to an old custom, the youngest burgess of Aberdeen present at the riding of the outer marches of the city, undergoes the ceremony of being *doupit* or *dipt* in it!

There is a stone circle on the farm of Eddieston; also a single rude stone pillar (the remains of another circle), on the farm of Milltimber. Circular stone structures, supposed to be ancient, are upon the heights above Nether Anguston. Traces of the so-called Roman camp at Norman Dykes; and of the British earth work at Camphill, noticed in the Statistical Accounts, are now slight. The "Norman Well" still remains.

The Burn of Culter is bridged both upon the old and new Deeside roads. There are also stone bridges over the Leuchars (dated 1710), near Waulkmill; over the Gormack, near Milton of Drum; and over the Ord, at Nether Lasts.

An Act of Parliament was passed in 1707 in favour of Sir Alex. Cumin of Culter and his heirs, by which they were empowered to hold fairs upon the muir of Beinshill, on the second Tuesday of March and October annually, "for all kinds of vendible commodities." They were allowed to uplift the "haill profites, tolls, customs, . . . to proclaim and ryde the sd fairs," &c.

WILLIAM FORBES, A.M., author of a poem in Scottish verse, entitled "The Dominie Deposed," was sometime schoolmaster at Peter Culter. The session records (extracts from which have been obligingly communicated by Mr Smith, parish schoolmaster), bear that on 15th Nov. 1724, " Mr William Forbes entered Precentor, and is to begin to teach the school at Whitsunday next." The school was opened accordingly, and from that time nothing of any importance is recorded of Forbes until 2d Jan. 1732, when the minister "acquainted the session that (the former Preceptor, William Forbes, having entirely turned his back upon his office, one which acc^t he was not again to be received) Mr William Mories, who this day precented, was the person recommended by the heritors for the s^d office."

On 23d of same month £10 10s due to the schoolmaster "for the poor boys in the land of Culter" were "detained at the instance of William Forbes, late schoolmaster's creditors;" and upon 7th Jan. 1733, he acknowledged, by letter, the paternity of a child by Margaret Forbes, servant in Brotherfield. He was then summoned before the session; but as Forbes "compeared not," and the minister understanding that he "had gone off a recruit to Ireland," the session were "obliged to sist further procedure as to him."

"The Dominie" is generally confounded with "*Robert* Forbes, gent.," a contemporary writer, who translated into the Buchan dialect "Ajax; his Speech to the Grecian Knabbs." This poem, like that of "The Dominie Deposed," is a remarkable production; and copies of early editions, with the Latin text in the form of foot notes, are exceedingly rare. I have learned nothing of the history of ROBERT FORBES. It is clear that he was a scholar, also a native of Aberdeenshire, and much engaged in the stocking trade—then, and for long afterwards, a lucrative branch of business in that county. In one part of his "Shop Bill," Forbes says that he has "some *shanks* (stockings) to sell," also caps, gloves, and napkins. In another part of the poem (Glasgow edit., 1755) the following verse occurs :—

"I likewise tell you by this bill,
That I do live upo' Towerhill,
Hard by the house o' Roble Mill,
Just i' the neuk,
Ye canna miss't fan 'ere you will,
The sign's a buik."

~~~~~~~~~~~~~~~~~~~~~

Insch.

(S. DROSTAN, ABBOT.)

THE church of Insch (*vicaria Insulæ*), in the diocese of Aberdeen, is rated at 6 merks in Old Taxation. In 1574 it was served by the same minister as served the kirks of Clatt, Kinnethmont, and Christ's Kirk, and, like these parishes, Insch had its own "reidare," or schoolmaster. Being a part of the lordship of the Garioch, the church of Insch was probably given, as were some of the neighbouring churches, to the Abbey of Lindores, when it was founded by the Earl of Huntingdon.

The present place of worship and burial-ground are upon a slight eminence near the middle of the village of Insch. Before being *gutted*, the kirk contained some interesting carvings in wood. Among these were the arms of the Clan Chattan, which were set up in the Wardes pew by Robert Farquharson, ancestor of the Invercauld family, then proprietor of Wardes. The only remaining specimen is in the Drumrossie seat. It consists of three panels, two with scroll ornaments, and the third, or centre panel, bears a shield, charged with a fess between three boars' heads. An esquire's helmet, surmounted by a demi-soldier holding an old-fashioned musket horizontally, forms the crest. Over the crest are the words :—

VEL . PAX . VEL . BELLVM.

—The shield is flanked by the initials, G. G., and below is the date of 1678. The same arms are upon a slab at Drumrosssie House, and both refer to Gordon, the laird of the period.

The belfry of the church is of an ornamental character, with floral carvings, also the initials, M. I. L., (Mr John Logie), and the date of 1613. The bell is inscribed :—

SOLI . DEO . GLORIA.
ALBERTVS . GELY . FECIT . ADD. 1700.

—Gely was " a ffrench ffounder," who, in 1700, proposed to recast the bells of the steeple of "the colledge" of Aberdeen, a proposal which was partially agreed to.

Some years ago, during the levelling of the ground on the north side of the kirk of Insch, a coffin-slab was disinterred. It is about 6 feet long, by about 18 inches broad, and is preserved in the outer wall of the vestry. The original carving has unfortunately, by *revision* at some late date, been injured. The slab presents a dedication cross, and this inscription in Irish characters :—

✢ Orate . pro . anima . radulfi : sacerdotis.

—This is probably the grave-stone of Radulph, a chaplain of the bishop of Aberdeen, who witnessed a grant of half a carrucate of land in the parish of Rayne to the convent of Melrose, about 1172-99 (Reg. Ep. Abdns., i. 10.) If this conjecture is correct, this is among the oldest *lettered* monuments in Scotland—those at Newton of Culsamond, in Aberdeenshire, and St Vigeans, in Forfarshire, excepted.

A tombstone in the churchyard bears the name of HENRY CLERK, and the date of 1600, also a merchant's or mason's mark, resembling the figure 4, except that a horizontal line crosses the middle of the lower half of the perpendicular line. The next oldest date is possibly that upon a granite slab, placed against the south dyke, which probably relates to a son of Mr W. Burnet, who was minister of Insch from about 1661 to 1680. It bears :—

 . . . . 1669 . A . B . SONE . TO . M. W. B.

The next three inscriptions are from contiguous tombstones:—

Here lyes JAMES JOPP, feuar in Insch, who depr. this life August the 2-, 1672, and of his age 50 years. . . . .

Here lyes ANDREW JOPP, sometime merchand in Insch, who dept. this life Feby. 26, 17-2, aged 67 years; and his children, ALEXR., ANDREW, and MARY JOPPS.

In memory of JEAN JOPP, spouse of James Stants Forbes of Lochermick, who died 8th June 1822, aged 56 years.

—These inscriptions relate to ancestors of a burgess family of Aberdeen. One of them was provost of that city when Dr Samuel Johnson was presented with the freedom of the burgh—a compliment (says Boswell), "Provost Jopp did with a very good grace." Near the last-mentioned slab:—

JAS. BEATTIE in Insch, died Apr. 17, 1787.

—The above is from one of several tombstones which belong to Beatties. One of the family was a medical practitioner at Insch, and descendants still tenant the farm of Dunnideer. Near to these tombstones another, but to a different race (here abridged), bears:—

Sacred to the memory of JOSEPH BEATTIE, A.M., for 33 years parochial schoolmaster of Leslie, who died 7th Jan. 1854, aged 58 years. MARGARET MELDRUM, his wife, died 1861, aged 64 years. Their eldest son, JAMES, C.E., died 1860, aged 39 years.

Upon a round-headed stone at east end of kirk:—

Hic jacet cum familia Rev. ALEXR. MEARNS; in hoc templo fideliter ministravit annos, mirum, 60; in hoc sepulchro cum multis lachrimis depositus est anno 1789.

[Here lies with his family the Rev. ALEX. MEARNS, who was a faithful minister of this church for the wonderfully long period of 60 years, and was laid in this tomb with many tears, in the year 1789.]

—Mr Mearns, previously schoolmaster at Rothiemay, was ordained minister of Insch, 19th Nov. 1729, and died 4th Oct. 1789, in his 89th year, He was a native of the village of Drumrossie, then a hamlet of some importance, in which woollen weaving, dyeing, &c., were carried on with energy and profit. Mr Mearns married JANET SHANK, daughter of a respectable tradesman in the same place, who died in 1779. By her he had two sons and three daughters. The eldest son, Alexander, was minister first at Towie, next at Cluny. The eldest, and only married daughter, JANET, became the wife of a manufacturer and woollen dyer, whose death is thus recorded upon an adjoining head-stone of a similar shape to that of her father:—

This is the burial place of ADAM MAITLAND, late manufacturer in Insch, who died in the year 1781, aged 57.

A marble slab near east wall of burial ground bears:—

Sacred to the memory of the Rev. GEORGE DAUN, A.M., minister of Insch, who departed this life, on the 21st day of May 1821, in the 70th year of his age, and the 31st of his ministry in this parish.

—Mr Daun was previously a schoolmaster in Elginshire. His successor, a native of the Garioch, had two assistants and successors, the latter of whom, the Rev. ADAM MITCHELL, LL.D., died in 1863, aged 64. Dr M. was previously rector of the Grammar School, Old Aberdeen, which he taught with success and reputation down to the time of his appointment to the church of Insch, his native parish.

WM. BRECK, feuar, Insch, d. June 1818, a. 63; his wf., JANET MILNE, d. April same year, a. 58; their son, ALEX., student of divinity, d. 1820, a. 22:—

Nipt by the wind's untimely blast,
Scorch'd by the sun's directer ray;
The momentary glories waste,
The short-liv'd beauties die away.
Yet these new rising from the tomb,
With lustre brighter far shall shine;
Reviv'd thro' Christ with 'during bloom,
Safe from diseases and decline.

FRANCIS and PETER WISELEY, d. 17 Feb. 1843, a. 11 and 9 yrs. respectively:—

In one house they were nursed and fed,
Beneath one mother's eye;
One fever laid them on one bed,
On one bed both their spirits fled,
And in one grave they lie.

ALEX., s. of Wm. Benzie, farmer, Coldwells, d. 1834, a. 25 y.:—

Here with the aged lies a lovely boy,
His father's darling, and his mother's joy ;
Yet, Death, regardless of the parents' tears,
Snatch'd him away, while in the bloom of years.

Upon the base of a granite cross :—

In memoriam : WILLIAM GARTLY, reporter 'Scotsman' newspaper, died 6th June 1869, æt. 27 :—

"God's finger touch'd him, and he slept."

The hill of Dunnideer (? *Dun-a-tor*, or the hill fort), is about 875· feet above sea level. It is conical in form, slopes rapidly on all sides, and is one of a series of similarly shaped hills in the same district, which are best seen, as a group, from Barrabill, in Bourtie.

"Dunneleur (says Monipennie) is called the Golden Mountine, by reason of the sheepe that pasture thereupon, whose teeth are so extraordinarie yellow, as if they were coloured with gold."

There appears to have been an early vitrified work, with surrounding trenches, upon the top of Dunnideer. The vitrified walls enclose a great portion of the summit of the hill ; and within these walls, at a later period, another fort had been erected. It is the remains of this later erection which give so much character and interest to the hill ; but, as will be seen from an engraving in Cardonell's Picturesque Antiquities, the ruins were of greater extent in his time (1788) than they are now. Upon the hill top is a well, in which there was water in 1867.

The ruins are locally called *Gregory's Walls*, from a tradition that King Grig, or Gregory died at Dunnideer ; but, according to the Pictish Chronicle, he died at Dundurn or Dun-d-ern, in Stratherne. The fanciful Hardyng says that Dunnideer was one of the places where King Arthur held his round-table :—

"All of worthie Knightis moo then a legion,
At *Donydoure*, also in Murith region."

But, in the absence of authentic record, nothing can be said of the true history of Dunnideer, nor of the age of any of the masonry, the peculiarities of which have been often and fully described.

One fact only may be noted—viz., that *Gregory's Walls* are of a similar construction to the remains upon the Lady Hill at Elgin, and to those of the old castle at Duffus ; also that these places (which were inhabited by Edward I.), indicate an earlier style of building than any part of Kildrummy, and Kildrummy is said to have been the principal residence of David Earl of Huntingdon.

But, whatever doubts may exist among "the learned" as to the origin of the fort of Dunnideer, the question of the origin of the hill was long ago solved by Gordon of Rothnie, who, when reproving one of his ploughmen for "feiring" a field in such a fashion that one furrow fell upon the top of another, exclaimed in a passion—"It's needless to speak to you, man! It's been some idiot like you that rais'd the hill o' Dunnideer !"

Apart from the ruins upon the hill of Dunnideer, there are other remains in Insch, which show that the district was a place of early importance. The sculptured monument called the "Picardy Stone," and the Earl of Mar's Stone (an unadorned boulder), are both objects of interest. Some years ago part of a "brass sword" was found at Dunnideer ; and in 1867, a stone cist, containing bones and an urn, was got on Greenlaw. The urn, which was about 4¼ inches wide, bore the common zig-zag markings. Remains of stone circles are upon the farms of Wanton Wells, near Temple, and on Nether Boddam, also in other parts of the parish.

The Bass is the name of a piece of flat ground, about five acres in extent, which belongs to the Parochial Board, and is on the north side of the village. Nearer the village is the *Moatach Well*. The Moot or Moathill of the district had probably been in this locality, although no trace of it now remains.

"The Glens of Foudlen," celebrated in the ballad of the Duke of Gordon's Daughters, are in the upper part of Insch, in which there are valuable slate quarries.

But it is of the lands of Drumrossie that the earliest records exist ; and it appears that in 1257 a gift of the teinds of these, made by the abbot of Lindores, was ratified by Pope Alex. IV. to the vicar of Inchemabayn. In 1396, Thomas Earl of Mar gave a charter of the lands of Drumrossie to Andrew Barclay, lord of Gariutully. As before seen, Drumrossie was afterwards possessed by Gordons: it now belongs to Mr Leslie of Wartle, late M.P. for Aberdeenshire.

The *Village of Insch* is an old burgh of barony, in which, with other properties, Mr John Ross, minister of Foveran (called Dr John Ross of Insch), was served heir to his father in 1680, the same having been previously held by his grandfather, who was reader or teacher at the church of Birse. The superiority of Insch, held in 1724 by Mr Leslie of Balquhain, now belongs to Colonel Leith-Hay of Leith Hall. There are in Insch a Free Church, branch banks, and some good dwelling-houses and shops.

A family named Tyrie long owned the lands of Dunnideer, where there was a chapel dedicated to S. JOHN. The Tyries were Roman Catholics, and reported as such by the minister of Insch to the Presbytery of Garioch in 1704. One of the family, JAMES TYRIE, a celebrated Jesuit, who died in 1597, aged 54, wrote, under the name of George Thomson, De Antiquitate Ecclesiæ Scoticæ. John Knox wrote an answer to this work, to which Tyrie replied in a pamphlet (Paris, 1573), which is reckoned rare and valuable.

The Tyries of Dunnideer were "gryte Jacobites;" and it is told that but for the prompt conduct of one Roger, a farmer in Insch (some of whose descendants still hold responsible offices there), the life of Mr Mearns would have been in jeopardy from a Tyrie attempting to stab him with a dirk one Sunday about the '45, while engaged in Divine service. The residence of the Tyries stood near the burn of Shevock, upon the southern slope of the hill of Dunnideer. This family was possibly a branch of the Tyries of Drumkilbo and Nevay, in Strathmore (*v.* NEVAY).

———o———

Bervie, or Inverbervy.

(? S. MARY.)

THIS district is thus mentioned by Theiner in the Taxation of Scots benefices for 1275:— "De Magistro dd. De *Inuberny*, 39 sol." It is placed by Theiner within the diocese of Brechin; but is said, by others (Proceed. So. Antiq. Scot.), to lie within that of St Andrews, and to belong to the Chapel Royal of St Mary of Kirkheugh of that city. It is certain that Bervie was a seat of the Carmelite Friars down to the suppression of monasteries in Scotland (Mem. of Angus and Mearns.)

The church is said to have been dependent upon that of Kinneff until 1618, when Bervie was erected into an independent ecclesiastical district. But it had its own schoolmaster, or reader, in 1567, who had a salary of £20 a year.

A fair or market was held at Inverbervie in September (Edinburgh Prognostication for 1706), on "Latter MARY day"—a name which possibly preserves that of the titular saint of the church.

The present parish kirk, a neat and commodious building, with a square tower or steeple, was erected in 1836. It stands in the principal street of the town, to the north of the old kirkyard. The bell now in use, which was gifted to the town by the laird of Ury, while provost of the burgh, bears this inscription :—

GIVEN BY
PROVOST BARCLAY TO THE BURGH OF BERVIE, 1791.
THOS. MEARS OF LONDON FECIT.

The kirkyard is on the south-west of the town, near the railway station. The west gable is all that remains of the old kirk; and the inscriptions below are selected from some of the tombstones. The first quoted, and possibly the oldest dated, is from a much defaced slab. It also bears a shield charged with a ship in chief, the Rait arms in base, and the initials P. D : K. R.—probably for P. Davidson, and his wife K. Rait :—

. . . . DSON
BVRGES . IN . BERVI . DEPARTED . 20 . OF . DE-
CEMBER . 1634 . . . .

A much destroyed tomb, with bevelled sides, bears a shield charged, in pale, with the arms of Arbuthnott, and those of Macduff, Thane of Fife. This impalement is possibly founded upon the reputed connection of the Arbuthnotts with the Clan Macduff, by which, it is said, Hew of Arbuthnott received protection for the part he took in "boiling" Sheriff Melville and "supping his broo" on the hill of Garvock, in the time of James I. The following inscription (the concluding lines of which were printed in Monteith's *Theater of Mortality*, 1713), is upon the same stone :—

HEIR . LYIS . ANE . HONEST . MAN . ROBERT .
ARBVTHNOT . BVRGES . OF . BERVIE . VHO . DE-
PARTED   OF   IN . THE . YEAR
AND . OF . HIS . AGE   AND . MARGARET . MON-
CVIR. HIS . SPOVSE . VHO . DEPARTED . IN . THE .
1663. AND . OF . HER . AGE 65

HAVING . NOW . FOVND . BY . COMMON . SENSE .
THAT . ALL . THINGS . NOTHING . BE .
I . HEIR . REMANE . VITHIN . THIS . GRAVE .
AS . NOTHING . TO . THE . EYE .

—Margaret Moncur was probably one of the Moncurs of Knapp, in the Mearns, a branch of the family " of that Ilk," one of whom, Andrew, is a witness to a charter by Rait of (?) Hallgreen, t. Robert III. (Nisbet's Heraldry, i. 185.)

In addition to the following epitaph, a flat slab also bears that a son and daughter of the same family died respectively in 1696 and 1714 :—

☞ Hier lyes MARGARET MILL, lawful spows to Iames Dickie, swintime carpenter in Johnshaven, who departed this life the 28 of September 1713, and of hir age 47 years :

Hier lyes on bereaved of her life,
Who in her time was a most wertiovs wife ;
Her works and wertve did so her grace,
Ye might admire her cvnlie face.
Bvt willingly was to leve this world, and
Hoping to be in heaven inthroned ;
With faith continued to her death
Wntill . . . . she had any breath.

From a headstone :—

. . . . clauduntur intus fil : DAVID . nat. Jul. 28mo 175-, mort. Jan. 28mo 174- ; fil. MARIA nat. Ap. 12mo 1736, mort. Feb. 10mo 1744. Depositi hic sunt cineres HELENÆ AUSTIN, conjugis Gulielmi Clerici, Ludimagistri Ennerberviensis, quæ obiit 3^{tio} Id. Jan. anno sal. 1738 . . . . . .
[. . . . . within lie a son DAVID, born July 28, 175-, died January 28, 174- ; a daughter MARY, born April 12, 1736, died February 10, 1744. Here are deposited the ashes of HELEN AUSTIN, wife of William Clark, schoolmaster of Inverbervie, who died 11th January 1738 . . . .]

—In printing a translation of the Decreet of the Synod of Perth of 11th April, 1206, regarding a dispute between the Bishop of St Andrews and Duncan of Arbuthnott, Mr Pinkerton, in his "Enquiry into the Early History of Scotland" (vol. i. p. xiv.) says the translation was made "from the original Latin in the possession of Lord Arbuthnot about 1700 by a Mr Clerk, schoolmaster at Bervie." The next inscription is upon east side of same stone :—

Hic jacent Magister GULIELMUS CLARK, Ludimagister Berviæ, qui diem obiit 9° Decr. 1770, natus annos 7-. MARGARETA LOW, secunda G. C. uxor, nata Junii 21, 1710, nupta Aug. 17, 1745, ... Martii 16, 1762, N : 8 ; Hora tertia matutina repentino ac insolito morbo correpta spiravit moribunda, motu, linguæ usu, ac sensibus expors ; demum sub solis occasum obiit, marito ac tribus liberis relictis.

[Here lie Mr WILLIAM CLARK, schoolmaster of Bervie, who died 9th Dec. 1770, aged 7- years, and MARGARET LOW, second wife of W. C., who was born June 21, 1710, married August 17, 1745, and who died March 16, 1762. Seized at three o'clock in the morning with a sudden and unusual illness, she continued to breathe in a dying state, deprived of the power of motion, of speech, and of her senses, until about sunset, when she expired, leaving a husband and three children.]

—I have ascertained (through the kindness of Mr J. H. Stewart, the present parochial schoolmaster of Bervie), that although Mr Clark held the office of teacher there, no notice of the fact exists in the Presbytery records; and that in March 1701, the office was held by Mr James Greig. Mr Stewart has also learned from Mrs Barclay, a grand-daughter of Mr Clark, that he was the son of a Lieutenant in the Navy, and of a lady of the name of Middleton from about Laurencekirk. The Lieutenant went to sea soon after the birth of Mr Clark, and was never more heard of; and his mother being disowned by her relatives, supported herself and her son by her own industry. Two of Mr Clark's sons were watchmakers in London. One of them, David, died there, and the other, James, afterwards came to Arbroath. He had a son who entered the Navy, and two daughters who were respectively married to manufacturers of the name of Kircaldy and Butchart in Arbroath. Mrs Barclay still lives in Bervie, and her mother, Ann, a daughter of Mr Clark, by his second wife, married James Sherret, a tailor there.

From a table stone :—

W. R. : I. C.—Here ly the bodys of WILLIAM RAITT, tennant in Thre Wells, who departed this life January 4, 1743, aged 77 years; and of IANET COOK, his spovse, who departed this life 1757, aged 90 years. Also their son JOHN RAITT, sometime tenant in Hillside, who died 1776, aged 79 years; and his spouse ELIZABETH SCOTT, who died 1764, aged 88 years.

A stone near the last-quoted bears :—

. . . . . ane honest man in hop of a gloris resvrrection, GEORGE FETVS, lafvl hvsband to Margret Anderson, who departed this life Janvary 24, 1729, of his age 60.

Abridged :—

ALEXANDER ABERDEIN, late Deputy Commissary of Ordnance, Bengal, East Indies, died at Bervie, Dec. 1810, aged 53.

From a table-shaped stone (enclosed) :—

In memory of the Rev. ROBERT CROLL, who was upwards of 40 years minister of the parish of Bervie, who died on the 3d day of June 1820, in the — year of his age. And his widow, JEAN FARQUHARSON, died 12th February 1837, aged 83 years.

—Mr Croll, who had the merit of being "a self-made man," was first appointed schoolmaster, then minister of Bervie. It is said his memory was so retentive that by hearing a sermon once read or preached, he could repeat it *verbatim*. Although he was three times married, the death of his third wife only is recorded at Bervie. From a stone adjoining the last-mentioned :—

Sacred to the memory of Miss ISABELLA FARQUHARSON, youngest daughter of the late Alexander Farquharson of Balfour, who died at the Manse of Bervie, on the 19th day of April 1816, in the 27th year of her age.

Upon a head stone :—

A true Philanthropist lies here,
To whom Rich and Poor alike were dear.

JAMES SOUTER, late Post-Master in Bervie, died 12th July 1845, aged 61. His wife ANN GREIG or SOUTER, died May 17th 1861, aged 73.

From a headstone, in north-west corner of churchyard :—

1851 : Erected by James and Ann Burgon, Berwick-on-Tweed, in memory of their son ROBERT COWAN BURGON, whitefisher, aged 21 years, who was drowned, with the whole of his crew, in Berwick Bay, on the 26th of Aug. 1850. His body was picked up in Bervie Bay by a boat's crew belonging to Gourdon, and lies interred here :—

We lost him in the prime of life,
The first unto us given ;
But now we trust he's with his God,
Enjoying bless in Heaven.

On north-east side of burial ground :—

In memory of GEORGE SMALL, founder of the House of Refuge for the Destitute, Edinburgh : Born in Edinburgh, 26th May 1782 ; died at Bervie, 11th July 1861.

—Mr Small was a magistrate of Edinburgh at the time he founded the House of Refuge in that city. He also established the Lock Hospital (now amalgamated with the Infirmary), and organised and superintended the clothing stores, soup kitchens, and Cholera Hospital, and did many other kind and humane actions to the poor of

E

the Metropolis (v. Edinburgh newspapers, July 1861.) Mr Small, who was an officer in a fencible regiment until the Peace of 1802, became, in after life, a partner in the house of Muir, Wood, & Co., music-sellers, Edinburgh. He retired from business in 1848, and died in the house of his son, the Rev. Mr J. G. Small, of the Free Church, Bervie, author of "The Highlands and other Poems," &c. Upon a headstone:—

1859: Erected by James Gilchrist Gibb, in memory of his father DAVID GIBB, who was born in 1783, and died 1858, aged 76 years. A native of Perthshire, he removed to this place in 1828, and commenced Flaxspinning, which business he prosecuted up to the time of his death. An affectionate husband, a kind father, and a good member of society, he closed a usefull life by a happy death, regarding the grave as a temporary abode, and looking forward in faith to a blessed resurrection. [Though worms, &c.]

———

Bervie was erected into a royal burgh by David II., who is said to have landed near it on his return from France with his queen in 1341. Its burghal importance is still represented by the shaft of an old market cross in the square, surrounded by a few steps.

It is said that Bervie was burned in the time of Queen Mary, when, in all probability, it had consisted of only a few thatched houses. In a scarce and curious volume, entitled "A Journey through part of England and Scotland," by a Volunteer, who accompanied the Duke of Cumberland to Culloden, the following account is given of the treatment which the Royalists received at Bervie in 1746, on which occasion the Duke was the guest of the parish minister:—

"Here we put up at the Provost's House, a good honest old Fellow, whose Face shewed what he loved. His Wife told us, she had brought out Wine to present when the Duke and Army came by, but could get none of her Neighbours to back her. We were here first obliged to eat Oat-Cakes in this Journey, which was a great Hardship to several of our unexperienced Travellers."

The Viscounts of Arbuthnott had a residence or "ludgin" at Bervie; but of it, as of the house of the Carmelite Friars, the site only remains.

Interesting and varied prospects are obtained from the bridge of Bervie, including Arbuthnott and Allardyce on the north, and Craig David on the south. The present bridge, which has one handsome arch, was begun in 1797, and finished in 1799. The first bridge, which crossed the river about the same point as the present one, consisted of "2 large arches." It was built in 1695, chiefly through the enterprise of William Beattie, a bailie of the burgh, who in the same year successfully petitioned the Estates of Parliament for the vacant stipends of certain churches to assist to repay his outlay, and to enable him to finish the undertaking (Acta Parl.) Part of the middle pier of the old bridge still stands in the river. Before the time of railways this bridge was of great importance to the North, and the town of Aberdeen held a fund which was mortified for the support of the bridge of Bervie.

Hallgreen Castle, in the immediate vicinity of the town of Bervie, is the chief object of antiquity in the parish. The oldest parts, as shown by dates and armorial bearings, were erected by Raits towards the close of the 16th and in the 17th centuries.

The first Rait, according to Nisbet, took refuge in the Mearns during the 14th century, having had to leave his native district of Nairnshire for some capital crime. It is certain that Raits were settled in the Mearns, and held the lands of Owres or Uras and others at the period mentioned by Nisbet; but it was not until towards the close of the following century that they had any connection with Hallgreen.

It appears from the inventory of the title-deeds of Hallgreen (for the ready use of which I am indebted to the kindness of Messrs Morice, advocates, Aberdeen), that the lands of Hallgreen were partly held under the Crown, and partly under the family of Arbuthnott. The oldest writ concerning the property shows that on 12th June 1478, James III. confirmed a charter by Alexander Menzies, burgess of Aberdeen, dated 21st

January 1471, in favour of David Rait of Drumnagair, "of his Bleuch Lands of Inuerbervie, commonly called Hallgreen, with Twa Ninth Parts of Inuerbervie and their Roods, and Part of the Mill thereof; And an Annualrent of Twenty Shillings upliftable furth of the Stane of Benholm, To be held Feu of the said Alexander Menzies for payment of £9. 13. 4 Scots."

From the above period until the year 1724, the same family of Raits were possessed of Hallgreen; and from them all the Raits of any note in Angus and the Mearns, whether landholders, ministers, farmers, or merchants, claim to be descended. Some of the Raits of Hallgreen married into the families of Gardyne, Douglass, Symmers, and Arbuthnott. The last laird, William, died about 1724, and the lands, burdened by mortgages, were sold by order of the Court of Session. The chief bond holder was John Coutts, merchant in Edinburgh, son of Provost Coutts of Montrose, and father of the celebrated banker. The purchaser of the lands, at the judicial sale in 1724, was James, brother of John Coutts, and a burgess of Montrose, by whom they were acquired at the price of £31,500 sterling.

James Coutts was twice married, first to Jane Vanderheyden, next to Ann Crauford. By his first wife he had a son, Hercules, who, on 13th Nov. 1747, gave his father a discharge "of all legittim portion natural Bairns part of Gear, and all others which He could claim thro' his Death." Mr C.'s only son James, by his second wife, succeeded to Hallgreen, and was maternal grandfather of Mrs Scrymgeour-Fothringham of Tealing. About the year 1768, Mr Coutts sold Hallgreen to the Hon. Thomas Lyon of Pitpointy, son of the Earl of Strathmore; and in 1778 Mr R. Barclay-Allardyce of Ury purchased the estates of Hallgreen and Kingornie from Mr Lyon. Kingornie previously belonged to Mr William Johnston.

The estate of Hallgreen again changed hands in 1799, having become the property of Mr David Scott of Dunninald, by whose son, afterwards Sir David Scott, it was sold to Mr James Farquhar, M.P., in 1806. Mr Farquhar died in 1833, and was succeeded by his nephew, the present laird, who, about 1840, restored the Castle of Hallgreen. By more recent improvements Mr Farquhar has otherwise added to the value, as well as to the amenity of Hallgreen.

Ordiquhill.

(BLESSED VIRGIN MARY.)

THE office of reader, valued at 20 merks, was vacant at *Ordiquhill* in 1574. The church, sometimes called *Tulichule*, or *Tillycule* (? wood hill, or hill corner), in old writings, is said to have been originally a chapel dependent upon, and situated within, the parish of Fordyce.

The church was looked upon with suspicion as an auxiliary to the Papists by the General Assembly of 1608, when it was resolved (Book of Univ. Kirk), "that ordour be takiu with the Pilgrimages in the Chappell callit Ordiqubell, and the Chappell of Grace [in Dundureas], and ane Well in the bounds of Enzie, on the south syde of Spey." The year before this "ordour" was issued, it appears that Margaret Taylor, a woman from Castleton of Rothiemay, "was delaitit for passing in pilgrimage to Ordequhill."

Ordiquhill is said to have been formed into a separate parish about 1622-8, and the church to have been erected upon the site of a chapel which was dedicated to S. MARY. This church gave place to the present building about 1805. The bell is thus inscribed:—

IOHN MOWAT, ABD. ME FECIT, 1754,
IN USUM ECCLESIÆ DE ORDEQUHILL.
SABATA PANGO, FUNERA PLANGO.

[John Mowat, Aberdeen, made me, 1754, for the use of the church of Ordequhill. Sabbaths I proclaim, at funerals I toll.]

The kirk stands in the middle of the burial-ground, which occupies a hillock, and is surrounded by some good trees. The following is from a marble slab, within the kirk:—

To the memory of the Rev. ROBERT KNOX, A.M., for two years minister of this parish, who died 3d May 1825, aged 31 years. A token of regard from his affectionate parishioners.

—Mr Knox was tutor to the Ballindalloch family, through whose influence he got the presentation to the church.

The burial aisle of the Gordons of Park is at the east end of the kirk. Bold carvings of the family arms, with " S. I. G. OF PARK," and mottoes, appear upon the east gable of the aisle. Over the entrance are the Gordon and Sibbald arms, with the initials, S. I. G., the motto, BYDAND, D. H. S., and the date of 1665. The same initials are prettily cut in monogram upon a separate slab; and the following is round the margin of the stone:—

ERECTED . BY . SIR . JOHN . GORDON . OF . PARK,
AND . D . HELEN . SIBALD . 1665.

—The erector of the aisle was the first baronet of the family; and his wife was a daughter of Sibbald of Rankeilor, descended from the old Mearns family of that name. Sir Robert Gordon tells us that " the nixt yeir following (1617) Sir Adam Gordoun of the Parke (Carnborrow his sone) was knighted." Sir Adam appears to have been the first Gordon of Park, to which property and barony, previously known as " Corncarne," he gave the name of Park; and built the Village of Old Cornhill, which, through his influence, was erected into a burgh of barony, with weekly and yearly markets. By the establishment of these fairs, an impetus was given to agricultural industry, as well as to the growth and manufacture of lint, particulars which this well-known local rhyme appears to celebrate:—

"A' the wives o' Corncairn,
Drillin' up their harn-yarn;
They ha'e corn, they ha'e kye,
They ha'e webs o' claith forbye."

Sir William, the fourth baronet of Park, who married a daughter of William Earl of Fife, joined the Rebellion of '45, for which he was attainted. He died at Douay, about 1751, leaving two sons and a daughter. Sir William had two brothers, John and James, to the former of whom, it is said, he sold the property, or pretended to sell it, before he joined the Rebels. John left no lawful issue; and the heirs of his brother (who predeceased him), claimed the title, and succeeded to the estates. To one of them, a marble tablet, in the family aisle at Ordiquhill, is thus inscribed:—

Sir ERNEST GORDON of Park, Bart., died 6th Nov. 1800, aged 55.

—Sir Ernest's widow and a daughter lie in St Cuthbert's church-yard, Edinburgh (near the Cluny mausoleum), where two flat slabs are respectively inscribed as follows:—

Under this stone is interred the body of Dame MARY DALRYMPLE, daughter of General R. D. Horn Elphinstone of Horn and Logie Elphinston, and widow of Sir Ernest Gordon of Park, Bart. She was born on the 13th day of February 1761, and on the 3d day of July 1810, departed this mortal life in peace, and charity with all mankind, and looking with trembling hope to the mercifull judgement of a Blessed Redeemer.

In memory of Mrs MARY ELIZABETH GORDON, daughter of Sir Ernest Gordon of Park, Bart., and widow of Capt. Alexander Gordon, R.N., who died at Edinburgh, 24th June 1851, aged 65 years.

—In consequence of male-heirs of Sir William Gordon being in existence at the time Sir Ernest assumed the title, it is generally held that he, as well as his son, did so improperly; but as the legitimate male line of both brothers has failed, the title is extinct. It was a female descendant of Sir William's younger brother who married Duff of Drummuir, and brought the estate of Park to that family, in consequence of which the Duffs of Drummuir prefix *Gordon* to their paternal surname.

The following inscriptions are copied from monuments in the churchyard of Ordiquhill:—

Hunc infra [tumulum] inhumantur JOANNES MORISON, qui fatis cessit Apr. 8, anno 1686, ejusq, uxor ELSPETA MACKAY, quæ obiit Octobris 3, A° 1702.

[Beneath this mound are interred JOHN MORISON, who departed this life, 8th April 1686, and his wife ELSPET MACKAY, who died 3d Oct. 1702.]

From a plain stone :—

Here is interred the body of JOHN GOODALL, late merchant in Culphin, who died July 14th, 1760, aged 86 years. Near this place also are interred the ashes of MARGARET TAYLOR, his spouse, who died Feb. 16, 1733, aged 48 years, & of GEORGE, PATRICK, GEORGE, CHARLES, & WILLIAM GOODALL, their sons.

—The above were the parents and brothers of WALTER GOODALL, who wrote a Vindication of Mary Queen of Scots, and edited an edition of Fordun's Scotichronicon, &c. Born about 1706, Goodall became sub-librarian in the Advocate's Library at Edinburgh, first to David Hume, and next to his own countryman, Thomas Ruddiman ; but being improvident, he died in indigent circumstances. Chambers says that soon after his death (28th July 1766), his daughter presented a petition to the Faculty of Advocates, in which she stated that the furniture and other moveables in the house would scarcely defray the expenses of her father's funeral, and that " she was in such want of clothes and other necessaries, that she can scarcely appear in the streets." This sad appeal was answered by the substantial, though not extravagant, gift of ten pounds sterling.

WM. BROUN, Culphin of Park, d. 1763, a. 56 ; his wf. JEAN ROBERTSON, d. 1781, a. 71 :—

    Although by nature's firm decree,
    Parent and child must part ;
    Yet while apart, like test as this,
    Displays a Son like heart.

MARGT. LORIMER d. 1854, a. 66 :—

    Yet where, O where ! can even thy thunders fall?
    Christ's blood o'erspreads, and shields me from them all.

Abridged from a table-shaped stone :—

The Rev. ALEX. GRAY, died 26th Feb. 1823. Mrs MARY GRANT, daughter of the Rev. Mr Grant of Cullen, died 1815, aged 49.

The earliest recorded proprietor in Ordiquhill is Sir Walram of Normanville, who, by charter dated at Forfar in 1242, had a grant of the lands of Correncrare, Tulichule, and others, which are described as lying in the waste, or unimproved parts of the king's forest of Banff.

The Abernethys of Rothiemay and Salton had an interest in the district for sometime before the year 1492. According to a writer of 1724, the house of " Park was built, *anno* M.D.XXX., by a lady dowager of the Lord Saltoun of Abernethy, who was herself a daughter of Stuart Earl of Buchan."

It appears that about the year 1600 Lord Saltoun disposed of his estates of Cornearn (Park) and Rothiemay to the Lord Ochiltree, from whom they were bought by Gordons about 1606. But it would appear that the Gordons were not allowed to remain undisturbed in their possessions, for Sir John of Park as well as his kinsman of Rothiemay were forced to raise an action against the Abernethys (Acta Parl., ix. 431), for " tearing and lacerating the Decreet of lousing the late Lord Saltoun, his Interdictioun, out of the pblick Registers . . . . . and for their fraudulent concealling and keeping up of the said Decreet." In all likelihood, from the apparently " fraudulent" nature of the case, the Gordons had received a decision in their favour.

Apart from the Established Church, there is a Free Church at the present village of Cornhill, about two miles to the north-east, and within a mile of the railway station of Cornhill.

Strachan.

(? S. MARY.)

THE kirk of *Strathcichin*, which belonged to the cathedral of Brechin, is rated at 20 merks in the Old Taxation. The incumbent was the Arch-deacon of the diocese, and in virtue of his office he had a manse or residence at Brechin. It stood on the south side of the Bishop's Close in that city; and his grange or farm, called "the Arch-deacon's Barns," was near West Drums (Reg. Ep. Brechin.)

In 1574, the church of Strachan was served along with those of Nigg and Mary Culter. The contemporary reader at Strachan, John Irving, had a salary of £16 and kirk lands.

The church stood within the burial-ground until 1865-6, when a new place of worship was erected on the north side of the road. A fountain is placed in the dyke in front of the church, upon which is the date of 1866, also this inscription (v. p. 2 *supra*,) which is followed by quotations from John iv. 14-15; Rev. viii. 17 :—

IN REMEMBRANCE OF
WILLIAM BURNETT-RAMSAY
OF BANCHORY LODGE.

There is also a Free Church at the Kirktown of Strachan, in which the Rev. Mr D. S. Ferguson (son of a late minister of Maryton) officiates. He was ordained at Strachan in 1835, and seceded at the Disruption in 1843. A granite obelisk in the kirkyard bears that his successor,

The Rev. DAVID MARTIN, M.A., minister of this parish, died June 13, 1861, in the 59th year of his age, and 18th of his ministry.

The following inscription (round the margin of a flat stone) appears to be the oldest in the churchyard :—

ℌᴵᶜ. DORMIT. H. AVTHINLECT. VIR. VITÆ. INTEGER. QVONDAM. CIVIS. DEIDONEN: ET. IBIDEM NAVARCHVS. OB. AN. 1610. ET. ÆTAT. SVÆ. 48.

[Here sleeps H. AUCHENLECT, late citizen of Dundee, and shipmaster there, a man of blameless life, who died in 1610, in his 48th year.]

—The surname of *Auchenleck*, or *Affleck*—one of some note and antiquity in and about Dundee—is of territorial origin. There are various places of the name (? *Auch-na-clach*, stoney fields), in Scotland, one of which lies in the parish of Monikie.

A mural monument, to the right of the entrance to the kirkyard, bears this inscription, upon a marble slab :—

In memory of COLIN CAMPBELL, Esq. of Kilmartin and Blackhall, who died 27th April 1861, in his 33d year.

—Mr Campbell, who was an officer in the 92d Foot, and at the time of his death Major of the F. & K. Militia, left an only son, who inherits the estates. Colonel John Campbell (the Major's uncle), bought Blackhall about 1828 from the trustees of Mr Archibald Farquharson of Finzean. Mr Farquharson, who was sometime an M.P., acquired Blackhall by marrying Miss Russell, one of the co-heiresses. The house, which is beautifully situated upon the south bank of the Dee, is surrounded by extensive and thriving woods. A goat (the Russell crest), life size, is upon the top of each of the two principal pillars of the gateway, prettily cut in stone, with the motto—CHE SARA SARA (What will be, will be). Mr Russell of Blackhall was also proprietor of Strachan, which was bought, about 1822, by the late Sir James Carnegie, Bart., father of the Earl of Southesk. Sir James built the shooting lodge —a "lovely Highland home"—near bridge of Dye. In 1856, the property was sold to Sir Thomas Gladstone of Fasque, Bart.

The following epitaph is from a headstone :—

J. ABERNETHY, tenant, Gateside, d. 1703, a. 36 :—

If at this humble urn
An honest relative should come and mourn—
"Here rests my friend"—they weeping at my grave
Shall cry,—It's all the Epitaph I have.

The next inscription and lines were composed by Alex. Laing of Brechin, author of "Wayside Flowers," who wrote some verses on the death of Grant, also a brief notice of his life :—

In memory of JOSEPH GRANT, author of "Tales of the Glens," and other pieces in prose and verse, who died April 14, 1835, aged 30 years. Erected by his father and mother, Robert and Isobel Grant, Affrosk, Banchory-Ternan :—

Tho' young in years, and not unknown to fame;
Tho' worth and genius both had told his name;
Tho' hope was high, and certain honor near,
He left the world without a sigh or tear ;—

Yes! trusting in the Saviour's power to save,
No sting had death, no terror had the grave;
His parting words, in prospect of the tomb,
Were, "Dearest Mother, I am going home!"

—Grant died while the Tales of the Glens were passing through the press. It is an interesting little volume, and preserves many pieces, both in prose and verse, illustrative of the history and traditions of the Mearns. Since the stone was raised to Grant's memory, the deaths of his father and mother have been recorded upon it. The former died in 1868, aged 82, and the latter in 1855, aged 71.

Strachan was granted by William the Lion to William Giffard (ancestor of Lord Yester), who was sent on a mission to England in the year 1200. At a later date Alan the Durward is said to have had a residence upon the Castlehill, about a mile west from the Kirktown, where Fraser, Thane of Cowie, had a stronghold in 1351. The once powerful, and still common surname of Strachan, in Angus and the Mearns, is said to have been assumed from this locality. The place itself seems to have been named from its abounding in rivers and streams, the Gaelic words, *Strath-a'en*, or *Sruthan*, having some such meaning.

The LADY Bridge, which *may* indicate the name of the patron saint of the church, is between the kirk and Whitestone. The bridge of Dreip, between the Kirktown and Glen Dye, and that of the Feugh, near Banchory-Ternan, are romantic and picturesque objects. Views of the Bridges of Dye and Feugh, also of the house of Blackhall, are given by J. S. Paterson, drawing master, Montrose, in a series of interesting local views, with short notices (folio, about 1825.)

The Bridge of Dye was built at the cost of Sir Alex. Fraser of Durris, assisted by a mortification of 2000 merks, left by Mr George Meldrum [? Melville], minister of Alford. By Acts of Parliament (1681 and 1685), tolls were allowed to be levied for persons and animals, &c., for the purpose of keeping the bridge in repair.

There is also a bridge across *The Spital* Burn, a name which invariably implies that the place so called was *a hospitium*, or place of refreshment for wayfarers. In Strachan there was a Spital near the lodge of Glen Dye, for the convenience of travellers by the Cairn-o'-Mounth road, which, in old times, was one of the chief thoroughfares between the Highlands and the Lowlands (*v.* FETTERCAIRN.)

Those welcome retreats, which were one of the many holy and benevolent institutions of the Early Church, were planted in almost all the passes of the country. They appear to have been conducted upon much the same principle as the famous *hospice* of St Bernard on the Alps, and were occupied by churchmen, who were accountable for their doings to the Bishops of the Church, or the Prior of the Abbey upon which they were dependent.

But, if certain names of places in the locality and tradition are to be relied upon, something more than refreshment and shelter were required by travellers crossing *The Cairn*, since not a few places are pointed out as the haunts of robbers and murderers, stories of some of whose deeds are given in Grant's Tales of the Glens. The curious affair of Dr Rule and an apparition in a "deserted house," as related in Wodrow's *Analecta*, has formed the basis of a ballad in the Scottish Journal (i. 214), entitled "The Murder of Cairn o' Mount."

"The Stane o' Clochnaben" (? the hill of the stone), an immense granite rock which projects from the face of Clochnaben, is a striking feature in the district. It is seen from many different and distant points; and, according to local rhyme, it is one of two prominent landmarks :—

"There are two landmarks off the sea—
Clochnaben and Benachie."

It is said that the Rev. ANDREW CANT, who played a more prominent than consistent part during the times of the Covenant, was the son of the laird of Glendye. It is certain that Earl Marischal held a large part of Strachan during the Civil Wars, and that the Highlanders, on more occasions than one, plundered his lands of "horss, nolt, and scheip." Spalding also relates, 1644, that "ane feirfull vnnaturall fyre, quhilk kyndlit of itself, brynt the bigging" of the Earl's town of Gelleu, including "ane byre with nolt and oxin, none knowing quhairfra it cam;" an event which Spalding quaintly remarks, "seimit to be ane prognostick of far gryter fyre raisit on this Earllis laudis."

Dr THOMAS REID, author of the Inquiry into the Human Mind, was born at the manse of Strachan in 1710. His father was parish minister, and his mother, who had twenty-nine children by her husband, was a daughter of Mr Gregory of Kinairdy, a relative of the famous mathematicians of that name (v. MARNOCH).

Kirkden, *or* Idvies.

(? S. RUFFUS, OR S. MAELRUBHA.)

THE church of Edevyn, or Idvies, belonged to the diocese of St Andrews, and was dedicated by Bishop David in 1243. It is rated at 15 marks in the Old Taxation.

James Victie, parson of Edevyn, swore fealty to King Edward in 1296.

In an ordinance issued by the Bishop for the purpose of changing the site of the manse of Idvies in the year 1388, the new ground is described as being bounded on the east of the church by a ford upon the Vuany, at a heap of stones, near the foot of the rock, called Craignacre (Reg. Prior. S. Andree.) A well or spring in the locality still bears the name of *Siurvie*. This is probably a corruption of the name of S. RUFFUS, or S. MAELRUBHA, to whom the kirk may have been dedicated. There are other wells in the district, one is called *Tothel* (? *twathil*, the north) well, a second the *Medicie* well (a sort of chalybeate), and a third the *Spout*.

It is said that the old kirk stood upon the lands of Gask, in a field called the *Kirk-shed*, from which it was removed to its present position about the beginning of the last century. Possibly an old font, which lies in a neglected state in the burial-ground, was taken from that place. It presents a grotesque carving of a human face.

After the Reformation, the kirk of Idvies, and those of three adjoining parishes, were served by one minister, at a stipend of £133 6s 8d and kirk lands. David Guthrie, reader at Idvies, had £20 of salary.

The date of 1655 is upon the "kirk ladels," which corresponds with the time of Mr John Balvaird, who was translated to Glamis (Scott's Fasti.) I am told that the kirk bell bears the words, "BELL OF IDVIE."

The present church, which has a square tower at the west end, is in good repair. An inscribed tablet in the porch bears this account of the building:—

Hanc ædem, Rev. DAVIDE CARRUTHERS pastore, D. PATERSON et J. CARRIE presbyteris, A.D. MDCCCXXV, JOANNES BAXTER de Idvie, THOMAS GARDYNE de Middletoun, ALEXANDER LYELL de Gardyne, JACOBUS MUDIE de Pitmuies, JOANNES WATT de Kinneries, domini prædiorum in parochia jacentium, denuo struendam curarunt. ANDREA SPENCE, architecto, DON. MACKAY, JAC. MILNE, GEO. FYFE, artificibus.

[JOHN BAXTER of Idvie, THOMAS GARDYNE of Middletoun, ALEX. LYELL of Gardyne, JAS. MUDIE of Pitmuies, and JOHN WATT of Kinneries, proprietors of lands situated in this parish, caused this church to be rebuilt in 1825, the Rev. DAVID CARRUTHERS being minister, and D. PATERSON and J. CARRIE, elders. ANDREW SPENCE, architect. DON. MACKAY, JAS. MILNE, and GEO. FYFE, artificers.]

The Middletoun pew, in the south-east corner of the kirk, contains five oak panels, all charged, in pale, with the Gardyne arms, and those of the wives of various lairds. A contemporary panel presents the Gardyne and Arbuthnott coats, initialed I. G: E. A. These initials refer to John Gardyne and his wife Elizabeth, daughter of Sir J. Arbuthnott of that Ilk. This lady bore twenty-four children to her husband (v. INVERKEILOR). The other shields (which are modern) exhibit the

Gardyne arms, and those of (1), Watson of Barry; (2), Graham of Duntrune; (3), Wallace (of Arbroath); and (4), (a saltire wavy, between a heart in base and chief, and a rose, sinister and dexter, for (?) ——

The Gardynes of that ilk appear to have lost the lands from which they assumed their surname, during the latter half of the 16th century (v. Memorials of Angus and Mearns.) James Gardyne of Lawton, bought a part of the lands of the Middletoun of Gardyne about 1682, the remainder having been subsequently acquired from an ancestor of the present laird of Gardyne. The property of Middletoun, upon which there is a neat mansion-house, is possessed by Mr T. M. Bruce-Gardyne, representative, through a female, of the Gardynes of that ilk. A slab built into the farm offices at Middletoun bears the initials, D. G., the date of 1692, also the Gardyne arms and motto, MY HOIP IS ONLY IN THE LORD.

The laird of Lawton, and two namesakes, joined their fortunes with the "Royal Stuarts" under the Earl of Panmure, in the respective positions of captain, lieutenant, and adjutant. They were all at Sheriffmuir; and the laird of Lawton, and Charles Gardin of Bittisteru (Bellastrine), were among the prisoners (Patten's History), who were brought to Stirling on the 14th of Nov. 1715.

The Castle of Gardyne, (v. INVERKEILOR), is occupied by the present laird, Alex. Lyell, Esq.; and a granite monument, within an enclosure, at the east end of the kirk of Kirkden, bears this record of his father and some of the family:—

Erected by Elizabeth Gibb Lyell, in memory of her beloved husband, ALEXANDER LYELL, Esq. of Gardyne, who died Nov. 1852, aged 68 years. And of their children, viz.:—

THOMAS, who died Nov. 1821, aged 6 months,
CHARLES,   ,,   June 1825, ,, 8 weeks,
ANDREW,   ,,   Aug. 1842, ,, 11 years,
JANE,   ,,   Dec. 1842, ,, 13 years.

Also Dr ROBERT, who unfortunately lost his life on the night of the 3d July 1857, in the 32d year of his age, while quelling the Insurrection at Patna during the rebellion in India, and whose remains lie there.

—Mr Lyell, who devotes his time to agricultural pursuits, and the improvement of his property, writes that the Lyells of Gardyne are descended from

"Walter Lyell, hereditary town-clerk of Montrose, who was the son of James Lyell of Ballmaleddie and Jean Hay, daughter of William Hay of Urie. He was born in 1595, and first married a Miss Hamilton, from the South Country, by whom he had one son, Mr David Lyell of Ballhall, and Minister of Montrose, who had two sons—1. Mr James Lyell, advocate, who died unmarried ; 2. Mr Peter Lyell, married to Dowager Lady Halkerton, who also died without issue.

"Walter Lyell married for his second wife —— Findlayson, daughter of —— Findlayson of Gagie, by whom he had one son—Thomas Lyell of Dysart, —from whom I am descended.

"I may also remark that in 1798 my ancestor, Thomas Lyell of Gardyne, and merchant in Montrose, who married Marjory Renny, daughter of Patrick Renny of Usan, pulled down a large portion of the old Castle of Gardyne, and re-built a large portion of the present house.

"It appears from my old charters, 1. that, in 1602, Andrew Rollock, son of Sir Walter Rollock, conveyed the whole lands and barony of Gardyne to Sir Robert Creighton of Cluny, who held it two years ; 2. Sir Robert Creighton of Cluny conveyed to James Curle, the same subjects, in 1607 ; 3. James Curle to Jean Connolly in 1610 ; 4. Jean Connolly to Margaret Connolly in 1620 ; 5. Margaret Connolly and Sir John Scott of Newburgh, to William Ruthven in 1623 ; 6. William Ruthven, son of the former, to James Lyell, merchant in London, in 1682."

The church-yard of Kirkden contains several tombstones. The oldest, so far as I have noticed, (from a flat slab, with sand glass, skull, and cross bones), bears this inscription:—

☞ Heir lyis ROBERT DVTHIE, hvsband to Evphane Gvdlet, somtyme in Balmadie, who died in Desem. 1667, and of his age the 47 :

I rest in hope
and shal Aryse
To reigne with Christ
✝ above the Skyes.

Another slab, with the name of AGNES DALL, is dated 1668. From an adjoining stone, broken and dateless :—

..... LLIAM . STEVINSONE . hvsband . to Beatrix Stv ....
Novr. . and . of . age . the . 59 ....

The next epitaph is from a monument erected by JAMES LESLY, in memory of his wife (date defaced) :—

A N E . E P T E A F
TO . SPIK . THY . PRAISEE
THIS . SYFES . THOV . VAS
A . VYEF . VERTOVS . AN
D . VYES . OF . CHILDREN
CARFOVL . AND . TO . THY . NE
GHBOVRS . KYND . ANE
HONAST . VOMAN . AND . OF
A . LIBRAL . MYND

From a table-shaped stone :—

In hopes of a blessed resurrection, here lyis the dust of ROBERT ALEXANDER, sometime Teunent in Parconon, late husband to Isobel Scot, betwixt whom were procreate six children, vizt., William, Joan, Isobel, Robert, John, and Thomas Alexander. He died the 19 of June 1738, of age 43 years—

The penetrating art of man,
Unfold this secret never can,
How long men shall live on the Earth,'
And how, or where give up their Breath.
The person of whom this I write,
Ah ! dy'd by a mournfull fate ;
An old clay chimney that downfell
Kill'd both his servant and himself,
Which should alarm men every where
For their last hour well to prepare,
That death may never them surprise ;
For as the tree falls so it lies.

Quæ men sors hodie cras fore vestra potest.
[My fate to-day may be yours to-morrow.]

An adjoining stone, embellished with carvings of fire-tongs, a shovel, and broom, and a rose and thistle, bears this epitaph upon ISABELLA CLARK, who died in 1740, after bearing 13 children to her husband Wm. Scott, blacksmith :—

Here rests the bones of six and on
Whos ghosts are to the heavens gon ;

A parent with 5 children mō
Doth live, while death may call us so.

The next inscription is from a broken slab, richly carved. Graceful and well-proportioned figures of Justice, with a balance in hand, and of Faith, with an open book, respectively flank the first four lines :—

As death leaueth the,
So shall judgment find the.
Deall justly—fear no death.

I . H : I . R.

Here lyes JANET ROY, spouse to John Hay in Easter Idvie, who departed this life 6th of November 1716, and brought forth by her six children, tuo sous, David and John, and four daughters, Margaret, Issobel, Januet, and Agnes Hays.

JOHN, a. 16, son of David HAY and Margt. Morgan, d. 1744 :—

Here lyes a youth, an eldest son,
But ere a man away he's gone,
And left his parents both to mourn,
While here below they do sojourn.
Their hopes of him no doubt were great,
Which the more sorrow does create ;
A good advice he had to give
To those behind him he did leave.
Oh, fading, fleeting, empty show,
Is every comfort here blow ;
But cease from fears which you annoy—
He's enter'd into his Lord's joy.

DAVID HAY, a. 5, another son, d. 1746 :—

Here lyes a child, of sons the last,
Where with this family was blest ;
He like a morning flower appear'd,
By him his parents' hearts were cheer'd
But what are children but a loan—
When God calls back, are we to groan ?
He's gone to heav'n and got the start :
Long to be there, you'll no more part.

JANET GREIG, wf. of Wm. Mill (1730) :—

Let none suppose the Relicts of the Just,
Are here wrapt up to perish in the Dust ;
No, Like last fruits her time she fully stood,
Till being grown in Faith, and ripe in good—

With steadfast Hope that she another day
Should rise with Christ—with Death here down
  she lay.
The Poor her almes; the World her praise;
The Heavens her soul; and the Grave her body has.

Upon a plain headstone:—

Here lies interred the body of the Reverend Mr
IAMES MOIR, who was ordained minister of the
Gospel at Kirkden, the 30th of April 1735, and died
the 28th of January 1753.

—Mr Moir was assistant to Mr Ferguson of
Arbroath when he was appointed to Kirkden. A
plate for collecting "the offering" bears his name,
and the date of 1735. His initials also appear
upon a slab (built into the east side of the kirk-
yard gate), along with this couplet:—

M.I.M.
☞ *All ye who enter at this gate*
O now prepare for your last state.
1739.

From a flat slab:—

Erected by William, James, Elizabeth, & Mary
Cowie, &c., Elizabeth and Grizel Knox, in memory
of the Revd. WILLIAM MILLIGAN, minister of Kirkden, who died [in the] 89th year of his age, and
49th of his ministry, Nov. 15, 1823.

Adjoining the last quoted:—

Erected by Margaret Carruthers, in grateful re-
membrance of her uncle the Rev. DAVID CARRU-
THERS, late minister of this parish, who died 21st
Novr. 1840, aged 61 years.

ROBT. TAYLOR, farmer, Backboth, d. 1772, a. 65:—
Deus dedit, Deus abstulit;
Benedictum sit nomen Dei.   [Job i. 21.]

—Backboth, which is in the parish of Carmyllie
(*q.v.*), was once the site of a church. The site is
still pointed out, not far from the march between
Dunnichen and Carmyllie.

Idvies was a thanedom, and the names of two
of the thanes, Gyles and Maiise, are on record;
also those of persons who bore the surname of
Idwy.

Notices of some of the old proprietors of Idvies
will be found in Mem. of Angus and the Mearns.
It need only be here said that the property of
Idvies was bought from the heirs of Mr John
Baxter, bank agent, Dundee, by Mr J. C. Brodie,
W.S., in 1865, and that Mr Brodie, who is Crown
Agent for Scotland, and a son of Brodie of Lethen
(descended from Alexander, son of Brodie of that
ilk), has very much added to the value and appearance of Idvies. Besides new carriage drives,
and large additions to, and alterations upon, the
mansion-house, gardens, and offices, the farm-
steadings over the property are being renewed,
or otherwise made suitable to the present advanced state of agriculture.

Pitmuies belonged to a cadet of Airlie in the
time of Guynd, who (c. 1682), says it is "a good
house, well planted, and lyes pleasantly on the
water of Evenie." Pitmuies is now the property
of Mr Mudie, the worthy representative of an old
Forfarshire family (*v.* INVERKEILOR.) It is near
the Guthrie railway station, where there is a
sculptured stone, which, according to tradition,
had some connection with the defeat of the Danes
at Barry.

The village of *Friockheim* (formerly "Friock
Feus"), was begun about 183–. It is now a
populous place, situated on the east side of the
parish, and holds of Mr Bruce-Gardyne of Middleton. In the vicinity is a well-kept cemetery, with
a number of tombstones.

An Extension Church, opened in 1835 in connection with the Establishment, was erected into
a *quoad sacra* parish in 1870. The Rev. Mr Thos.
Wilson, the first minister of the church, seceded
at the Disruption, when a Free Church was
erected at the village.

The river Vinny is crossed by a number of
bridges. One of two arches, which joins the
parishes of Kirkden and Dunnichen at the village
of Letham, is dated 1820. The bridges at Pitmuies House, and Pitmuies Toll, were built respectively in —— and 1771, and that at Hatton
Mill is dated 1819.

St. Cyrus.

(S. GRIG, OR S. CYRICUS, MARTYR.)

IT is supposed (Skene's Chronicles of the Picts), that the church of St Cyrus, also called *Ecclesgrig*, was founded by Grig, or *Ciric*, who succeeded to the Pictish throne about A.D. 877.

Some writers suppose that there was a priory at St Cyrus. This opinion appears to be founded upon a charter by William the Lion, who (Reg. Prior. S. Andree), grants and confirms to the monks of St Andrews the church of *Eglesgirg*, with all its just pertinents, in free and perpetual alms gift, with the chapel of S. Rule, and with the half carucate of land in which the said chapel is situated, by all their righteous and ancient marches; and with the *Abbey land of Eylesgiry* by all its ancient and righteous marches, and with common pasture to the canons, and their own dwelling on the foresaid lands, along with my thanes (or stewards), and along with *my men* throughout the whole parish of Eglesgirg, &c. The expression "my men" in this sense means the *puri natici*—the serfs, or tillers of the soil—who were at, and for long after the date of this charter, conveyed along with property in Scotland from one landholder to another.

The site of the chapel of S. Rule is unknown; but in 1242, the church of *Eyylesgerch* was dedicated by Bishop David of St Andrews (Concilia Scotiæ.) It is rated in the Old Taxation at 60 merks. In 1574, Mr Alexander Allardes, who had "his awin pensioun, &c.," officiated there and at Aberluthnot, now Marykirk. John Burnet was reader at Ecclesgrig, and had a salary of £17 15s 6¼d.

The ancient church had a romantic site at the foot of the highest rocks, locally called "the steeples," near the sea, and thither the people repaired for worship until about 1632, when a new church was built upon "the brae heads," near the site of the present edifice. The site of the old church can be traced in the

NETHER, OR LOWER KIRK-YARD.

Interments are still made there; and the Stratons of Kirkside had their burial-place near the east end of the kirk. An old tomb (enclosed), ornamented with curious heraldic and mortuary devices, presents these traces of an inscription:—

. . . . . MARGARET. E. LEONIS . QVÆ . OBIIT . . . .
1646 . ÆTATIS . SVÆ . 68 . . . .

—This was the wife of Arthur, the first Straton of Kirkside. He acquired the lands by purchase from the Lord of the Regality of St Andrews; and in 1657, his son Mr Arthur was served heir to these, as well as to the towns and lands of Scotston and Marchrie (*ruly*. Mercury), &c. The last-mentioned were within the barony of Witston, and regality of Lindores.

The male succession of the Stratons of Kirkside failed in Joseph Straton. He was succeeded by his nephew, Joseph Muter, afterwards General Sir Joseph, who, in virtue of his uncle's will, assumed the surname of *Straton*. Upon a massive monument of Peterhead granite is the following succinct account of the General's career:—

Sacred to the memory of Sir JOSEPH STRATON of Kirkside, Companion of the Bath; Knight of the Guelphic Order of Hanover, and of the Order of St Vladimir of Russia; Lieut.-General in the British Army; youngest son of Willm. Muter, Esq. of Annfield, Fifeshire, and Mrs Janet Straton of Kirkside, Kincardineshire. This brave and accomplished officer entered the army in early life, and served with distinguished honor during the Peninsular War and at Waterloo, under Field Marshal the Duke of Wellington. At the commencement of the battle of Waterloo he commanded his own regiment the 6th Dragoons untill the fall of the gallant Ponsonby, to whose brigade it belonged, when the command of the brigade devolved upon him. Towards the close of the action Sir JOSEPH STRATON was wounded, and upon the termination of the war, in reward of his services, he had various Military Honors conferred upon him. He died Colonel of the Inniskilling Dragoons, at London, 23d Oct. 1840, in the 63d year of his age, and is interred here by his own desire.

—Sir Joseph Straton was succeeded by a nephew, to whose memory a handsome granite monument (erected by his widow), about 11 feet in height, with a medallion of Mr Straton by Steele of Edinburgh, is thus inscribed :—

In memory of GEORGE-THOMAS STRATON of Kirkside : Died 16 Feby., 1872, aged 68.

—According to tradition, Stratons possessed Lauriston from a remote period. They certainly owned lands somewhere in the Mearns in the time of Edward I. In 1411, Straton "of Lauriston" fell at Harlaw. The tower of the old fortalice still stands at Lauriston, adjoining the modern mansion-house ; and at Chapeltoun, a little to the eastward, stood an ancient place of worship, dedicated to S. LAURENCE (v. Mem. of Angus and Mearns.)

Another monument, with the Straton and Ogilvy arms impaled, and the motto, TENTO, bears :—

This monument was composed by ROBERT STRATON, Heretable tacksman of the Lands of Wardropton, descended of the antient family of Lauriston for a burying . . . .

Upon a more modern tablet, batted to the stone from which the above is copied :—

In memory of ROBERT STRATON, who erected this monument anno 1731, and died 4th March 1740 : also his spouse KATHERINE BURNET, who died 29th Dec. 1744 ; also their son ROBERT, who died 28th Oct. 1764, aged 80 years ; also his spouse GIRZAL LYON, lawful daughter of the Rev. Mr Patrick Lyon, sometime minister of the Gospel at Roscobie, who died 11th Oct. 1765, aged 74 years : had issue George, Katherine, Janet, and Helen.

—The lands of Warburton gave surname to a family in old times, one of whom, John of Wardroperisthone, granted a charter of "Wardroperisthonue in the Marnys," to Sir John of Inchmartin, knight, 1331, in exchange for certain lands in the Carse of Gowrie, (Spald. Club Mis., v. 10.)

From the door lintel of a roofless aisle :—

ANNO . DOM. 1673 . MAGISTER . DAVID . CAMPBELLVS . ECCLESIÆ . GREGORIAMÆ . PASTOR . HVNC TVMVLVM . POSVIT. VBI . SEPVLTA . IACET . CHARISSIMA . VXOR . MARGARETA . CARNEGY . ET . 4 . FILII FILIÆ . 5 . DVO . NEPOTES . CVM . TRIB' . AMICIS.

[A.D. 1673. Mr David Campbell, pastor of St Gregory's church, erected this tomb, where lie interred his dearly beloved wife MARGARET CARNEGY, 4 sons, 5 daughters, 2 grand-children, together with 3 friends.]

—Mr Campbell was previously minister at Careston. While there, on 4th April 1643, he was (Brechin Sess. Records), "contractit with Marat Carnegy in this paroch : callr for them both, Alexr. Carnegy of Cuikstoune." Carnegy of Cookstone, near Brechin, was a cadet of the Southesk family. Wodrow says that Campbell was a non-conformist ; but this (Fasti) appears to be a mistake. Dr Scott also states that Campbell attended the army to Newcastle in 1640. In 1674, he was served heir to his father, John Campbell, in the sunny half lands and town of Cowbyre, in the lordship of Cupar, and county of Perth (Retours.)

The GRAHAMS of Morphie had their chief burial place here, but no stone bears their name. The only old funeral monument, so far as I know, which belongs to the family, is a slab within the church of Kinneff (q.v.) The Morphie aisle at St Cyrus, long ruinous, was recently rebuilt by Mr Barron Graham, who is laird of Morphie, and representative of that branch of the Grahams.

Mr Graham of Morphie, who studied at the Royal Academy, London, followed the profession of a painter for several years, until his eyesight was accidentally injured. Since then he has amused himself with collecting coins and medals, &c., with the view of illustrating the progress of art from the earliest period. Besides Morphie, Mr Graham owns Stone of Morphie, a property so named from an undressed stone which stands in the farm-yard. The stone is about 11½ feet high, varying in breadth from 3 feet 4 inches at bottom to 2 feet 4 at top. It varies in thickness from about 2 feet 4 to 1 foot 9 inches. Tradition connects "the Stone o' Morphie," and a place called the Dane's Den, with the Danish conflicts of Malcolm's time. Be this as it may, when a search was made some years ago, human remains, "of large size," were found below the stone, which proves it to have been a funeral monument. Owing to erroneous information, the late Sir Jas. Simpson, in his Address to the Society of Antiquaries of Scotland, stated that the stone had been destroyed.

The Grahams of Morphie (says Nisbet) were an ancient branch of the house of Graham, in the time of Robert I., and the lands of Morphie were confirmed to them by Robert II. There were three Knights in the family of Morphie; and owing to the part which the Grahams took in the Civil Wars, and other causes, the lands were sold for behoof of creditors, after the death of the last lady of Morphie (who was a sister of Claverhouse), about 1727. The bulk of the property fell into the hands of Scott of Brotherton; but the Mains of Morphie was re-acquired by the son of the above-named lady, who served in the Wars of Queen Anne. The present laird excambed the lands of Balindarg, near Kirriemuir, for those of Stone of Morphie.

It was to his kinsmen, the lairds of Morphie and Fintray (Spalding Club Misc., vol. v.), that the second Marquis of Montrose, by letter dated 30th March 1661, requested the provost and magistrates of Aberdeen to deliver the hand of his celebrated father, which had been placed upon a pinnacle of the Tolbooth of that City by order of the Scots Parliament. According to a contemporary record, "that member of his fatheres," which had been buried in the church of St Nicholas, was disinterred, 25th February 1661, by the local authorities, and put in a coffin "coverit with ane reid crimpsone velvet cloth, and caried by Harie Grahame, sone to the Laird of Morphye" to the Town House, accompanied by the magistrates, the inhabitants "goeing before in armes . . . . . with sound of trumpet and beat of drum," and there the hand was to be kept until requested to be given over to the son of "the laite murtherit Marques."

The following is from a monument which was built into the wall of the old kirk :—

This monument was erected by Alexr. Webster, tenant in Ston of Morphie, and Bonsetter, in memory of his wife and children, viz., his wife JEAN STEVENSON : HELLEN, JEAN, JOHN, JAMES, ALEXR., MARGRET WEBSTERS.

—A group of five ill-proportioned human figures are represented upon the monument. One is in the act of setting the bones of another's arm ; a dwarf looking figure has its hand round the knee of another twice its size ; and a fifth, also of small stature, is represented holding up its arms in the attitude of wonder! The date of 1759 is upon the top of the gravestone ; and round a sandglass are the words :—

As runs the glass, man's life doth pas.
MEMENTO MORI.

Another tombstone (table-shaped), belonging to the same family, is thus inscribed :—

Here lies JAMES WEBSTER, sometime tenant in Stone of Morphie, who departed this life the 24 of December 1724, in the 53ᵈ year of his age. As also tuo of his daughters, MARY, who died in infancy, 14 June 1714, and ISOBEL . . . . . He was a person very well esteemed, and his wonderful skill and success in curing vast numbers of distressed people made him equally useful and beloved while alive, and now justly regretted.

From a table-shaped stone :—

Heir lies interred the corps of ane discreet man named DAVID WALKER, somtyme . . . . departit this lyfe the 7 of October 1693 years, and of his age 55 :—

Remember all as yov goe by
Vpon lasting eternity :
And that e'er long yov all myst
Retvrn again vnto the dvst.

The next seven inscriptions are from headstones :—

FRANCIS GRAHAM'S wife (1747) :—
Remember, man, as thou goest by,
As thou art now, so was I ;
Into that palace I will look,
Where Christ hath gone before,
To pave the way into his flock,
And keep an open door. &c.

KATREN, dr. to GEO. BARCLAY, d. 1780, a. 29 :—
  When first I drew : the breath of
    Life ; I nothing knew at all : yet
  Long before my Death I knew
  That I with Adam fell
  my body lays neer to this stone
  Waiting the morning call :
  When Christ will take me by the
    hand : he is my all and all.

ALEX. ROBERTS d. 1798 ; his wf. CATHERINE STRATON, d. 1795 :—
  If honour wait on pedigree,
    And ancient blood we boast ;
  I claim descent from Adam,
    Who of mankind was first.
  From Noah next my line I have,
    Through Cambria's hardy sons,
  To Scotia's bleak, but friendly clime,
    In earth to lay my bones.

1798.—ROBERT BURNESS and JANET RITCHIE, was married 10th April, and had the following issue [8 children recorded, 4 of whom appear to have been alive in 1798] :—
  All shall die and turn to dust ;
  We hope to rise, and be with Christ.

Anonymous :—
  The saints are Pilgrims here below,
  And tow'rds their country heaven go.

DAVID SPANKIE, writer in Montrose, son of Wm. S., tenant, Brae of Pert, was drowned, 2d Aug. 1807, while bathing, a. 21 :—
  Low here his mouldering body laid,
  Now wrapt in death's oblivious shade ;
  I trust his soul dwells with the blesst,
  In mansions of eternal rest.
  Let every one who reads his fate,
  Reflect on life's uncertain date ;
  And learn to run their worldly race,
  That they through Christ may die in peace.
  His parents hope to meet again
  Their son, beyond the reach of pain,
  And sin, and death, when saints shall rise,
  To reign immortal in the skies.

Abridged :—
  ROBERT BROWN, died 1822, aged 88. "He was an elder in said parish for 51 years."

Within an enclosure, near the south-west corner of the burial-ground, a neat monument, with marble slab, bears the following inscription from the accomplished pen of the late Mr James Burnes of Montrose :—

To the memory of GEORGE BEATTIE, writer in Montrose, who died 29th Sept., 1823, in the 38th year of his age. This monument was erected by the Friends who loved him in life and lamented him in death. In his Disposition, he was just, charitable, and benevolent ; in his Principles, firm and independent ; in his Genius, forcible and pathetic ; and in his Manners, plain and social. His virtues are deeply engraved in the hearts of those who knew him, and his literary productions will be admired while taste for original humour and vigorous expression remain.

—Beattie was the son of a crofter and salmon-fisher at Whitehills, in this parish. His father subsequently held an appointment in the Excise. Young Beattie wrote, besides other poems, that of "John o' Arnha'," a humorous and satirical production, in the style of Burns' "Tam o' Shanter." Beattie's poems, which have been often printed, possess more than ordinary merit, and his sad end has a melancholy interest : He died in the solemn and lonely spot where his remains lie buried.

— —o— —

THE UPPER KIRK-YARD.

As before stated, the parish church of St Cyrus was removed from the sea-shore to the present site, not far from the top of the cliffs, and at the Village or Kirktown, about the year 1632. This was during the incumbency of Mr Andrew Collace, who was previously minister at Garvock, and latterly at Dundee (Scott's Fasti.)

A Free Church stands near the railway station. It was built for the Rev. Dr Alexander Keith, author of the Evidence of the Truth of the Christian Religion, and other works, who seceded at the Disruption in 1843. Dr Keith, whose father was minister at Keith-hall (q.v.), succeeded Mr Trail at St Cyrus in 1816.

The corner stone of an inclosure, called *Lauriston's Aisle*—an aisle of the old parish church—bears the initials, in monogram, of I. S : E. O.

Within the same enclosure were interred the remains of ALEXANDER PORTEOUS, Esq., of Lauriston, who died there on the 7th of June 1872, in his 74th year. Mr Porteous, who made a fortune abroad, is said to have been the first to send into this country from India samples of *jute*—a kind of flax, to the successful management of which, it may be said, the manufacturers in the counties of Forfar and Fife, &c., are indebted for their fortunes. Mr Porteous, who was also the principal promoter of the Montrose and Bervie Railway, belonged to Crieff in Perthshire, and married a sister of Mr Scott of Brotherton, by whom he leaves a family.

A new kirk was erected in the burial-ground nearly twenty years ago. It contains two handsome marble tablets. One of these, built into the east wall, bears the arms of the family of Orr, and motto, TRUE TO THE END, also elaborate carvings of war trophies, and this inscription :—

To the memory of WILLIAM-ADAM ORR of Bridgeton, in this parish, Companion of the Bath, Colonel in the Royal Artillery, and Aide-de-Camp to the Queen, eldest son of the late William Orr, Esqre. of H.M. Ceylon Civil Service, and of Bridgeton, who, after an honorable and distinguished career in the service of his country, died at Weston-super-Mare, on the 11th of Sept. 1869, from the effects of illness contracted during the arduous campaignes of 1857 and 1858, in Central India.

This tablet is affectionately dedicated to a beloved brother by his sorrowing sister.

—The second slab is in the north wall (F. Leighton, inv. et sculp.) It has a handsomely carved border; and a group in relief (within a circle near the middle of the slab) represents a female kneeling by the couch of an invalid. Below the group is the following inscription, together with a verse from Ps. 88 :—

In memory of SUTHERLAND-GEORGE-GORDON ORR, Commandant of the 3rd Regt. of Cavalry, Hyderabad Contingent, who, after many years of distinguished service, fell a victim to his enduring courage, June 19th, 1858, aged 42 years. To him who, uniting every domestic with every knightly virtue, was thus prematurely summoned to the grave, this tablet is erected by his wife, as a faint token of a love for which there is no expression.

—Mr PATRICK ORR, W.S., who bought the property of Bridgeton towards the end of the last century, married Marjory, daughter of Mr Wm. Gibson of Little Fithie, in Farnell. Mr Orr was long sheriff-clerk of Forfarshire, in which office he was followed by a son, also named Patrick. An elder son, William, succeeded to Bridgeton, and was the father of the two officers above commemorated, and several other children.

Their uncle, Mr JOHN ORR, Accountant-General at Madras, died at Edinburgh about 1845. He left a considerable fortune, the interest of £1000 of which he bequeathed to the parish of St Cyrus to be distributed *annually* in the odd manner thus prescribed by his will :—

"To the Clergyman of the Established Church of Scotland, Parish of St Cyrus, County of Kincardine, for the time being, I give and bequeath for ever the annual interest accruing from the sum of One thousand pounds sterling—the interest to be divided into five equal portions, and appropriated as follows :—

"*First:* One portion to be applied to the purchase of tea, sugar, meal, candles, flannel, and any other comforts that may, by the Clergyman, be thought proper, and given by him to such Poor and Needy Parishioners as he may think fit—this distribution to be made (if possible) at the season of Christmas ;—

"*Second:* Another portion to be given as a donation to the Tallest Woman belonging to the Parish who may be Married during the year ;—

"*Third:* Another portion to be given to the Shortest Woman belonging to the Parish who may be Married during the year ;—

"*Fourth:* Another portion to be given to the Oldest Woman belonging to the Parish who may be Married during the year ; and,

"*Last:* The remaining portion to be given as a donation to the Youngest Girl belonging to the Parish who may be Married during the year. These sums to be paid to the respective parties, or, in the event of death, to the heirs of the deceased, by the Clergyman, on the Thirty-first day of December each year. The Clergyman should ascertain the height and age of every woman married in his Church during the year, and distribute the several portions according to his judgment—his decision in every case to be final."

—The mansion-house of Bridgeton, which underwent tasteful alterations during the late laird's time, is situated upon the north side of the Montrose and Bervie turnpike. Bridgeton belonged at one time to the Strachans of Thornton.

The inscriptions copied below are from tombstones in the church-yard :—

Here lyes BESSIE SMITH spovs to WILLIAM BURNET who died both in the year 1688 of ages 80 and 80 tvo years :—
Death is the end of al tribvlation,
And therefor to wyse men a swit consolation.

—The above couplet is followed by an inscription in Greek capitals, to this effect :—" To him that overcometh will be given the fellowship of angels." From an adjoining slab :—

Hier lyes DAVID BROVN, lavfvll son to Dauid Brovn and Effie Vill, indvellers in Miltovnhavien, vho departed this lyf the 6 of Febrvary 1697, and of his age 12 yiears.

From a flat stone :—

Hier lys IONN HOGE, svmtyme in Gapes Hall, who departed this lyfe the 24 of Svptember, and of age 57, in the year of God 1703 :—
Grim death arests me hier to ly,
To rest vntil the iudgement day ;
Yet me to life God will restor,
Vhom I vill praise for ever more.

—" Gapes Hall," or Gapieshaugh, was Straton property from before 1631, until about 1669, when it belonged to a Mr George Gordon. It is now part of the Ecclesgreig estate.

The next inscription is from a brass plate, fixed into an obelisk of freestone :—

Here lie the mortal remains of the Rev. JAMES TRAIL, minister of St Cyrus, at which place he died on the 1st day of May 1816, aged 59. This monument was erected by Ann Burn, his widow, and Thomas Trail, and James Dow of Montrose, his executors, to mark the spot where his ashes are deposited, and as the last tribute of regard they had it in their power to bestow towards a near and beloved relative. They would tell his worth, but that the Tomb is not the proper place for praise ; and they know that on such a subject humility and silence would have been considered a more suitable proof of their attachment by the departed spirit of their Friend.

—Mr Trail, who was a son of the Rev. Robert Trail of Panbride, published a translation from the Latin, of a curious, and now scarce, Description of the County of Angus in 1678, by the Rev. Robert Edward, minister of Murroes.

In memory of AGNES CAMPBELL, spouse of James Watson at St Cyrus, a very successful midwife there for nearly 40 years, who died 24th May 1822, aged 68. She will be longest remembered by those who knew her best.

Erected to the memory of Mr ALEXANDER ANDERSON, 33 years parochial schoolmaster, who died 15th May 1834, aged 67. Also of his spouse, MARY CAMPBELL, who died 4th January 1846, aged 74 years.

Stone cists, urns, human bones, and also implements of the stone and bronze periods, have been found in different parts of the parish, particularly in the localities of Morphie and Canterland. About twenty years ago, bones were discovered in a cave near Warburton, including, as some supposed, remains of certain extinct, or antediluvian animals.

The ruins of the Kaim of Mathers stand upon the top of an isolated rock, which juts into the sea. According to tradition, this stronghold was built by Barclay, the laird of Mathers, who joined the Mearns barons in boiling Sheriff Melville upon the hill of Garvock. This strange story, and the cause of the building of the castle are told by Balfour, in "the Kaim of Mathers, a tale in Scottish verse," which first appeared in the *Dundee Magazine* for July 1822. The following lines are copied from it :—

"The land of Mathers all was bye,
And on its steeple shore

A fearful rocke looks o'er the waves,
A-lystening to thaer roar.
So there thae buyld a lordlie Kaim
All onne the stonie rock,
Which mote defie the Sovereign's arms,
And eke the tempest's shock."

A little to the eastward of the Witston fishing station, is the entrance to a cave of considerable height and length. It is frequented by seals and other amphibious animals; and although easily reached at neap, is inaccessible at spring tides. According to tradition, the cave stretches as far inland as the Castle of Lauriston; and it is further said that a blind bag-piper and his dog having found their way into it, the wail of the pibroch and the howl of the dog were heard for some days below the kitchen hearth of the old fortalice. In course of time the sounds died away; and bleached human and animal bones having been found in or about the cave, the peasantry had no difficulty in identifying them as those of the luckless minstrel and his faithful companion!

The mansion-house of Ecclesgreig, which has a commanding position to the north of the village of St Cyrus, is surrounded by well kept grounds and thriving woods. It was greatly improved and enlarged by the late laird, whose remains were interred in a private burial place, which was consecrated by the Bishop of Brechin. It is situated within the policies; and there, shaded by yew trees, which are planted in the form of a cross, a coffin-slab of Aberdeen granite bears this inscription :—

In memory of WILLIAM FORSYTH-GRANT of Ecclesgreig : Born 10th Feby. 1804 ; died 18th Oct. 1863.
We have a building of God, an house not made with hands, eternal in the heavens. 2d Cor. v. 1.

—Mr Forsyth-Grant, who was a gentleman of large benevolence, acquired Ecclesgreig from a maternal uncle, who was a native of Strathspey. Mr Grant was succeeded by a son, late Captain in the 3d Hussars, who married a daughter of Colonel Orr of Bridgeton. The remains of Col. Orr also lie at Ecclesgreig, and the pedestal of a handsome granite cross, of the wheel pattern, about six feet in height, bears an inscription similar to that upon the monument within the parish church of St Cyrus.

The house of Ecclesgreig was called *Mount Cyrus* at one time, and at an early date the house and lands were known as *Crigie*. They bore the latter name in 1659, when they formed part of the Morphie estate, and were possessed by John, son of Sir Robert Graham of Morphie.

There are several hamlets within the parish. The Kirktown is the most considerable, and next to it in size is the village of Roadside. The established church and parish school, both of which are ornamental buildings, are situated at the Kirktown; and at Roadside are a handsome school and school-house. The last-noticed were erected by, and maintained chiefly through the liberality of, the late Mr G. T. Straton of Kirkside, who, although long an invalid, was an unostentatious and liberal benefactor to the people of St Cyrus. A little to the westward of the Straton school, a fountain of freestone bears these words :—

1870 : Erected by Mrs Straton of Kirkside,
for the benefit of the Village.

The hamlets of Milton of Mathers and Tangleha', are situated to the eastward, and close by the seashore. The former of these was erected into a burgh of barony by the name of Miltonhaven (v. Mem. of Angus and Mearns), and both are inhabited chiefly by a fishing population.

Some of the bridges in St Cyrus are objects of interest, particularly that which crosses Den Finella, on the east side of the parish. Besides being the reputed scene of the death of Lady Finella, who is said to have killed King Kenneth III., Den Finella is a singularly romantic and picturesque place, with fine waterfalls and walks. The railway viaduct crosses the lower part of the den ; and a bridge on the Montrose and Bervie turnpike is dated 1815. The old bridge is a little to the north of the last-mentioned.

Before the Lower North Water bridge was erected, the parish of St Cyrus was reached from the west, or Montrose side, by a dangerous ford and a ferry-boat. The ford was near the Mills of Kinnaber, and the boat was at *the Pon'age*, or

Pontage Pool. The pool, which has been celebrated by George Beattie in his poem of "John o' Arnha'," was a favourite haunt of the Water-kelpie, who, in allusion to the assistance he gave at the building of a mansion house at Morphie, is said to have warned passengers of impending danger at the pool, by giving vent to the following plaint, and malison against the Grahams :—

"Sair back an' sair banes,
Carryin' the Laird o' Marphie's stanes ;
The Lairds o' Marphie canna thrive
As lang's the Kelpie is alive !"

The bridge upon the turnpike road (which adjoins the viaduct of the Montrose and Bervie railway), consists of eight arches ; and the following inscriptions (the one copied from a tablet at the south-east end of the bridge, the other from a slab built into the opposite parapet), give a concise history of the building :—

[1.]

Traveller : Pass safe and free along this Bridge, built by Subscription, to which the Town of Montrose, and the two adjacent Counties, contributed a large share. The work was first projected, and a liberal sum directed to be given by THOMAS CHRISTIE, Provost of Montrose. He died before the Subscription was opened ; but the design was ably taken up and successfully followed out by his eldest son, ALEXANDER CHRISTIE, the succeeding Provost, an active and public spirited citizen, who, with the assistance of a Committee of the Subscribers, happily brought the work to a period. The foundation was laid, October 18, 1770, and the work was finished, October 18, 1775. JOHN SMEATON, JOHN ADAMS, and ANDREW BARRIE, were the architects. The same ANDREW BARRIE, mason in Montrose, and PATRICK BROWN, mason in Dryburgh, were the undertakers. The Bridge and the Approaches cost Six Thousand Five Hundred Pounds Sterling.

[2.]

This Building Erected A.D. 1775.
HIS MAJESTY gave in aid to it, out of the
Annexed Estates, £600 stg.

Viator, tuto transeas ; sis memor beneficii Regii.
[Traveller, pass over in safety ; be mindful of the King's bounty.]

Gartly, or Grantuly.

(S. ANDREW, APOSTLE.)

GRANTULY was one of the mensal churches of the Bishops of Moray.

In 1574 Mr George Nicolson had a stipend of £53 6s 8d Scots as minister of Gartly and three adjoining parishes, and John Leslye, the contemporary reader at Gartly, had a salary of 20 merks.

The present church—a long narrow building—was erected in 1621, during the time of Mr Wm. Reid, who (Scott's Fasti), "taxed the faults of his parishioners bitterli, and not in the language of Scripture, quherby the people, insteade of being edified, wer moved to laughter and derisione."

The church belfry is an ornamental work, and upon it are three slabs with these words :—

. . YIS . IS . . . RETUE
BVLT . 1621
IO . ROS . MEASON . 1621.

The bell bears an inscription in Latin, nearly similar to that at Ordiquhill (*supra* p. 27.) It is locally rendered thus :—

"John Mowat made me,
For the use of Gartly,
To call upon the Clergy,
And mourn for the Dead."

According to a writer of 1726, "the church has an aisle wherein the house of Huntley is buried." This was possibly the *Frendraught*, or *Crichton Aisle*, which entered from the nave of the church. The site is still indicated by a mound on the south side of the kirk.

Spalding states that "the ashes and brynt bones" of the unfortunate barons and their servants who perished at the burning of Frendraught in 1630, were put in "sax kistis in the haill, which, with gryte sorrow and cair, wes had to the kirk of Garntullie, and thair bureit."

The church of Gartly, which has been frequently repaired, is a sorry fabric, and the surrounding burial ground, although it contains a number of monuments, presents little of general interest. One dateless stone, fixed to the south wall of the kirk, bears this brief inscription :—

Mr GEO. GORDON, Gartly,
an honest man, regarded by all, aged 92.

From the area of the church-yard :—

Sub spe beatæ resurrectionis hoc jacent tumulo et contumulantur in uno coguati Pater, e' Filii Filiæ' Mater.

ALEXANDER SMITH, sometime in Drumbulge, dyed Novr. the 20th 1736, aged 60 years; and his spouse BESSIE CHRISTIE, dyed March 17—, aged 43 years, &c.

[In this grave lie buried together, in the hope of a happy resurrection, a Father and Mother, with their Sons and Daughters.]

From a table stone :—

WM. JESSIMAN, born in Currilaar, died there 1801, a. 84; his sp. ELSPET BURGES, d. 1759, a. 43 ;—
The smiles of fortune or her frowns
They never could me move,
My heart was fixed on God, my hope
Was in his boundless love.

The next three inscriptions are from table-shaped stones :—

Here lyes ELIZABETH CHALMERS, who died in Kirkhill, the 4th of Aprill 1768, aged 63 years, lawfull spouse to the deceased Mr JOHN CHALMERS, sometime notary public in Ersfield, in the parish of Kinnethmont. Also JANET CHALMERS, spouse of Alex. Ingram in Coxton : she died 7 Jany. 1814, aged 73 years. Also her son JOHN INGRAM, farmer, Coxton, who died 14th April 1859, aged 88 years [2 drs. recorded dead.] Also his wife JANET GREEN, who died on the 14th February 1871, in her 78th year.
Remember, man, as thou goest by,
As thou art now, so once was I.

Here lies interred the mortal remains of JAMES SANGSTER, sometime farmer in Moshead, who departed into Eternity upon the 13th April 1800 years, after he had tread the stage of Time for the space of 70 years :—
At Angel's voice and Trumpet's sound,
Shall du t arise, and bones be joined.

Under this stone is laid all that was mortal of JAMES BLACK, son to James Black in Daugh, late Lieutenant in His Majesty's 98th Regiment of Foot, who departed this life 18th of Dec. 1789, in the 25th year of his age. His merits were such that they are to be held in estimation of all who knew him while memory can record worth. As also MARY GARIOCH, espoused to James Black in Daugh, who departed this life the 9th of Jany. 1796, in the 73d year of her age.

Abridged :—

. . . . . . ALEXANDER MITCHELL, who erected this stone, died 9th Jan. 1840, aged 94 years, and is here interred. . . . .

From a headstone :—

In memory of GEORGE FORBES, late farmer in Whitelumbs, who died in 1833, aged 84; also of his spouse CHRISTIAN THOMSON, who died in 1822, aged 41.

It may be worthy of note that, within the kirk-yard of Gartly, lie the ashes of a female, who, according to local story, was lost by her husband on the day of her marriage, and whose remains were forgotten by him upon that of her funeral !

While both incidents show the convivial state of society at the time, it would be ungenerous to look upon the latter act (for the former is not unknown in Scotland even at the present day), in any other light than that of the widower's anxiety to show hospitality to those who attended the funeral of his wife, many of whom had come from distant parts of the country.

The facts of both cases are these :—A well-to-do farmer in Gartly was married at a considerable distance from his own residence ; and, when the bride left her father's for her new home in Gartly, she was placed, as was then customary, upon the pillion behind the bridegroom. When the bridegroom arrived at his house, he called to the friends, who had assembled to welcome the pair home — "Tak' doun the gudewife, sirs !" "There's nae gudewife here !" was the reply, to which the bridegroom, after a short pause, answered — "I'll wager you was her 'at gaed kloit i' the burn o' Aul' Rayne !" Messengers were despatched in search of the lost bride, who was found in a house, near the scene of the disaster, drying her garments by the side of "a blazin' ingle !"

It is told, as a sequel to this "slip," that when

the same woman died, and when the funeral procession was some distance upon the road to the kirkyard, the widower suddenly called out, " Stop, stop, sirs!—there's a mistak' here!" Strange to say the remains of his wife had been forgot to be placed into the cart (there being but few hearses in those days), in which they were to be conveyed to their last resting place!

Besides the parish kirk, at which, in 1650 (Acta Parl., vi. 608), a servant of Leith of Harthill was killed in cold blood by two of Leith's brothers, there were at one time three places of worship in Gartly. One of these stood at Kirkney (S. ——), the second at Talathrewie (S. FINNAN), and the third at Brawlinknow (S. ——.) According to tradition, an infant son of the Baron of Gartly was drowned in the Bogie, in a pool still called *Lord John's Pot*, while being carried home, after baptism, from the chapel at Brawlinknow.

Barclays, of the Towie race (v. GAMRIE), were designed lords or barons of Grantully from at least 1367; and Sir Alexander, the laird of the period, fell at the battle of Arbroath in 1445-6. About a century afterwards, the lands of Gartly appear to have passed from the Barclays to Gordon of Auchendown; and upon the death of Sir Patrick Gordon of Auchendown in 1600, the Marquis of Huntly succeeded as heir male.

The castle of Gartly, of which unfortunately very little now remains, stood upon the farm of the Mains of Gartly. According to Chalmers, Mary Queen of Scots rested at Grantuly both on her way to and from the North. It was also the scene of a ballad, called " The Barone o' Gairtly," which tells that the baron's lady, during his absence in the wars, became the wife of Gordon of Lesmore, and that, the baron having consulted " weird sisters" in a cave on the Binhill of Cairney regarding the affair, revenged the insult by burning the castle of Gartly, its faithless lady, and the rest of the inmates.

Tillieminit is perhaps the most beautiful of the many romantic glens and corries in Gartly; and there, upon a slab built into a gable of the farm steading, is a shield bearing a much defaced coat of arms, probably those of Gordon.

The parish of Gartly, which is wholly the property of the Duke of Richmond, is situated partly in the county of Aberdeen and partly in that of Banff.

A Free Church was erected on the north side of the Bogie in 1844, the parish minister having seceded at the Disruption of 1843.

There is a neat hamlet, with some shops and an inn, at the railway station of Gartly, from which the pretty district of Strathdon, and intermediate localities, may be reached daily by the mail car.

Tannadice.

(S. TERNAN, BISHOP.)

IN the year 1187, Pope Gregory VIII. granted a confirmation charter of the church of *Tanedas* to the Prior and Canons of St Andrews (Reg. Prior. S. Andree); and in 1242 (Robertson's Conciliæ), the kirk of *Tanatheys* was dedicated by Bishop Bernhame.

The church was a rectory of St Andrews, and is rated at 40 merks in one copy of the Old Taxation, at 8 merks in a second, and at £16 6s 8d Scots in a third. The old orthography of the name is as different as the rating; for, besides the examples above given, the name is spelled *Thanchais* and *Tannadyse*, &c.

In 1567, Mr James Rait was minister of Tannadice and Aberlemno, with £100 Scots of stipend. In 1574, Alex. Garden was reader, with a salary of £16 and kirklands. The patronage of the kirk belongs to St Mary's College, St Andrews.

The present kirk, which is a neat building, was erected in 1846; and, on 4th March 1866 (the day upon which the widow of the late Rev. Mr Buist died), the internal fittings were much injured by an accidental fire.

The church-yard has been considerably enlarged towards the east; and the old portion, trenched a few years ago, has been otherwise improved. But, as some of the old lying and table-shaped monuments have been set upon end (*a sin* which, unfortunately, is not confined to Tannadice), certain portions of the inscriptions are buried. The following is from a stone in the position referred to:—

☞ Hear lyes IEAN YOVNG, spovs to David Greige at the . . . . the 27 of December 1686, and of her age 19 years:—

Thir lines engraven doe record
This JEAN nov is with the Lord,
Her body in the grave doth rest in peace,
Her sovl vith saints above hath place.
Heaven keeps the sovl, here the body lies,
In earth she lived both virtvovs kind and wise.

From a headstone:—

Here rests the bodys of JAMES WILSON, sometime in Baldoukie, who died the 25 day of Aprile 1678, of age 60 years. And JEAN WOBSTER his spouse, who died the -7 of March 1718, of age 78 years. And JAMES WILSON, his son, sometime in Baldoukie.

A stone (ornamented with carvings of a cheese-press, the culter of a plough, &c.) bears:—

David Cuthbert, tenant in Mains of Murthill, raised this stone over the remains of his late spouse MARGT. MITCHELL, who died 14th May 1767, aged 68 years 6 months. She bare him seven children, vizt., Thos., David, Margaret, Elizabeth, HELEN, Jean, and JOHN, of whom HELEN died 3 years and JOHN 6 weeks of age:—

Think, ye that on these mouldring Ashes tread,
Yourselves must soon be mingled with the dead;
Prepare, prepare ye, for the silent Tomb:
The dreaded Dungeon, or the expected Dome:
Or, when the nearest, dearest joys forsake,
And all is lost which Earth could give or take;
Pleasure is fled, and Beauty quite defac'd,
The Rich lie stript of all, the Proud disgrac'd:
Or, where the Saints are husht to sleep in Peace,
While all their Labours, all their sorrows cease,
Where in firm Hope, the Friends of Jesus rest,
To rise Immortal, & be ever blest.

Upon a small headstone, embellished with carvings of pen-knives, inkstands, open books, &c.:—

This stone was erected by David Dakers, schoolmaster in Tannadice, in memory of his spouse MARORET BINNY, who died the 28th of March 1728 years, of age 68.

—The above-named were maternal ancestors of David Dakers Black, Esq. of Kergord, author of the History of Brechin, &c.

Another part of the church-yard contains a monument to the memory of the late schoolmaster, Mr HERALD, who died in 1863, aged 58. It was erected by some of his old pupils, and the inscription, which is in Latin, was composed by Mr Jas. Whamond, now schoolmaster of Dalziel, and author of an interesting volume entitled "Jamie Tacket."

It was at a meeting of the heritors and minister, presided over by Mr Wedderburn of Islabank, 24th Jany. 1824, that Mr Herald was admitted schoolmaster of Tannadice. As the minute of Mr Herald's appointment presents some peculiar features, the extracts from it, given below, may not be uninteresting, particularly since the good old Parochial system of education in Scotland has now given place to a National system. The minute provides—

"*First:* That the person elected shall have no right till Whitsunday first to any accommodation or emoluments, excepting the schoolroom and school fees; the half year's salary to be collected at the ordinary time, and in the usual way, by the schoolmaster, and to be put under the management of the Kirk Session and Heritors, to be applied for the behoof of the family of the late Mr Wm. Elmsly sometime schoolmaster;—

"*Second:* No cockfighting to be permitted in the schoolroom, under any pretence, under the penalty of two pounds to the poor of the Parish, to be prosecuted for by the Kirk Treasurer;—

"*Third:* That he shall assist the Minister of the Parish, or any other in teaching any Sabbath School, the latter may institute; and,

"*Lastly:* They, viz., the Meeting, unanimously made choice of Mr Wm. Herald, assistant Teacher to Mr John Reid, Kirriemuir, to be Parochial Schoolmaster of the Parish of Tannadice; and, on his being found properly qualified by the Presbytery of Forfar to teach the branches of literature following, viz., The reading of English in the most approved manner and Grammatically, also writing, arithmetic, Book-keeping, Practical Mathematics, Land Surveying, and Latin, as fully as to qualify the Pupils for entering into an University, the meeting find him entitled to the emoluments and fees arising from the office under the condition first-mentioned."

Four marble slabs, inserted into a freestone monument (on the south side of the burial-ground), are respectively inscribed as follows:—

[1.]

Sacred to the memory of the Rev. JOHN BUIST, who died at Tannadice, on the 9th Dec. 1845, in the 92d year of his age, and 50th of his ministry. And of MARGARET, his youngest daughter, born at Tannadice, 12th June 1812, died at Edinburgh, 1st Aug. 1846. Also in memory of MARGARET JEFFERSON, wife of the Rev. John Buist, who died at Hamilton, on the 4th March 1866, in the 86th year of her age.

And of GEORGE BUIST, LL.D., F.R.S., their eldest son, who died at Calcutta, 1st Oct. 1860, aged 55 years.

[2.]

Sacred to the memory of JESSIE-HADOW HUNTER, the beloved wife of Dr G. Buist, Bombay, who died at that Presidency, on the 5th May 1845, aged 27.

[3.]

Sacred to the memory of JAMES BUIST, merchant, Dundee, second son of the Rev. John Buist: born at Tannadice, 10th July 1810, died at Dundee, 28th March 1844.

[4.]

Sacred to the memory of JOHN BUIST, third son of the Rev. John Buist, who died at Tannadice, 7th June 1824, in the ninth year of his age. Also of CHARLES BUIST, his fourth and youngest brother, who died at Dundee, 3d Dec. 1836, in the fifteenth year of his age.

—The Rev. Mr Buist, who was a native of Abdie, in Fife, gained a premium at St Andrews in 1782 (Scott's Fasti), for the best Discourse on the Evidence of the Authenticity of the New Testament Scriptures. Mr Buist had a great sense of humour, and was ready at repartee. It is told that on one occasion, when acting as Presbytery Clerk, a late minister of Forfar remarked, on looking upon a paper that Mr Buist was writing out—" You have got a cypher too many *there*, Mr Buist." To which Mr Buist (who was the senior of his reverend brother), sharply retorted— " We have always had a cypher too many *here* since you came amongst us !"

In regard to Mr Buist's eldest son, it need only be said that he was a person of great literary attainments. He died while Editor of the *Bombay Times*, having been previously engaged upon several provincial newspapers in Scotland. He wrote, among other works, an interesting guide-book to the scenery of the Tay between Dundee and Perth, as seen from the steam-boats; an Account of the Visit of George IV. to Scotland, &c.

GEORGE SANDEMAN, d. 1822, a. 28:—
    All ye in life's gay morn who come,
    To view this youth's grass-cover'd tomb,
    Know that you to the grave are nigh,
    For youth as well as age may die.
    In early life, then, serve thy God,
    Ere thou art laid beneath the clod,
    That those who to thy grave draw near,
    To drop the sympathetic tear,
    May truly say, as of this man—
    He was an honest Christian.

CHARLES SANDEMAN (1824):—
    His was the soul that sympathy could touch,
    His was the heart that friendship's flame did warm;
    And he the pilgrim, who at death's approach,
    Lean'd for salvation on his Saviour's arm.

JOHN CUMMIN, a. 74 (1849):—
    An honest man here lies at rest,
    As e're God with his image blest;
    The friend of man—the friend of truth—
    The friend of age, and guide of youth:
    In paths of vice he never would abide,
    For even his failings lean'd to virtue's side.

———

When the Old Statistical Account of Tannadice was written by Dr Jamieson, author of the Scottish Dictionary, about 1793, there appears to have been a sculptured stone at the church; but, unfortunately, no trace of it now remains.

Tannadice was a thanedom, and farmed by the king down to 1363, when, along with that of Glamis, it was given to John of Logy, probably the father of Margaret Logy, who became the Queen of David II. (Mem. of Angus and the Mearns.) After the forfeiture of Logy, both thanedoms reverted to the crown, and were again farmed for the interest of royalty.

In 1369 (Reg. Mag. Sigill.), the same monarch granted a charter at Perth in favour of William, the son of John, who is described as " our bound and born serf of the thanedom of Tannadice." It also declares the said William to be " our free man," as well as those that shall issue from him and their posterity. The same charter provides that William and his descendants shall freely dwell in any part of Scotland they may deem expedient, and that they shall be free and at rest from all born servitude for ever. This interesting charter, which forms an additional illustration of the position of the *puri nativi* of Scotland to that before given (*v.* p. 36), had doubtless been granted for some special service to the crown, the nature of which has not been recorded.

It was in 1371-2, that King Robert II. conferred the thanedoms of Glamis and Tannadice upon Sir John Lyon, who married Princess Jane; and the Earls of Strathmore assume one of their titles of Baron from Tannadice.

A collateral branch of the Lyons, who still hold the estate of Glenogil, in Tannadice, is descended from David, the first Lyon of Cossens, second son of the fifth Lord Glamis. A door lintel at Mains of Ogil is thus initialed and dated, "16—G. L: I. N.—80."

Notices of Marcus, Murthil, and other old lands in Tannadice, are given in the Land of the Lindsays, and need not be repeated here. The modern mansion-houses are, as may be supposed, of various ages and styles of architecture, and are pleasantly situated upon the respective properties. The more considerable of these, Tannadice House, was built by Dr Charles Ogilvy; Marcus Lodge by Col. Swinburn; and Downie Park by Col. Rattray. There is a private burial-place at Downie Park, where there was, and possibly still is, a tablet thus inscribed:—

Sacred to the memory of departed worth. Lt. Col. WILLIAM RATTRAY of Downie Park, late in the Hon. East India Company's Bengal Artillery; born 30th Octr. 1752, died 20th Decemr. 1819, aged 67 years.

—Col. Rattray married a daughter of Mr Rankin of Dudhope, and his remains were removed to the burial place of that family in the *Howff* at Dundee. The estate of Downie Park, which was originally part of the Inverqubarity property, has been recently purchased by the Earl of Airlie, and that of Tannadice by Wm. Neish, Esq. of Clepington, near Dundee. Since Tannadice was acquired by Mr Neish, he has doubled the size of the house, and otherwise improved the property.

The river Noran rises in the parish of Tannadice; and, in Glenogil, it has a romantic and pleasing course, with some pretty waterfalls. It is crossed by stone bridges at Wellford, Courtford, and at Nether Careston, where it joins the South Esk. The bridge at Justenhaugh, on the Esk, about a mile above the Kirktown of Tannadice, was built in 1823.

S. ENNAN'S, popularly called *St Arnold's Seat*, is the most conspicuous hill in the parish, and is about 800 feet above sea level.

There is a Free Church at Memus, about half way between the kirks of Tannadice and Cortachy.

Dunottar.

(S. BRIDGET, VIRGIN.)

THE church of *Dunothyr* was dedicated by David, Bishop of St Andrews, in 1276. The kirk and chapel of *Dunotyr* are rated at 40 merks, in the old Taxation.

Towards the close of the fourteenth century, the church of S. NINIAN was transferred from the rock upon which the ruins of Dunottar now stand, by Sir Wm. Keith, to the banks of the Carron, near the site of the parish kirk.

A *chapel* forms part of the ruins upon the rock of Dunottar at this day; and some of the older bits—particularly the lower parts of the door lintels—are of considerable antiquity. A deep ravine, near the castle, is called S. NINIAN'S Den; and the chapel mentioned in the old Taxation roll, had probably occupied the site of the parish kirk of Dunottar.

In 1567, John Christison was minister of Dunottar and Fetteresso, for which he had "je merkis with the thyrd of his benefice extending to . . . . ." John Paton was reader at Dunottar, with a salary of £20 Scots. In 1576, John Wylie was reader, with a salary of £16 and kirk lands; and the contemporary minister was Mr Andrew Mill, "his stipend jelvjlb. xijs. ijd. with the manse and kirkland of Fetteresso," &c.

The present kirk of Dunottar, which was erected in 1782, has been recently enlarged; and the bell was made at Aberdeen in 1783.

The burial aisle, or vault, of the Earls Marischal is upon the east side of the kirk-yard. It had never been roofed, and appears to have been constructed for a recess tomb. The recess only remains. A shield upon the door lintel bears the Keith arms, also

1582: G. K.

—The above refers to George, 5th Earl Marischal, the founder of Marischal College, Aberdeen. He succeeded his grand-father the year before the date upon the aisle; and, dying at Dunottar Castle in 1623, was interred within the aisle at the church of S. BRIDGET of Dunottar.

Sir William Keith, who married the heiress of Sir Alex. Fraser of Cowie, was the first Keith of Dunottar. He was descended from Hervie, who acquired the lands of *Keith* in East Lothian from King David I., from which he assumed his surname (Chalmers' Caledonia.) The family of Keith Marischal, ennobled in 1455, was attainted in 1716, for their adherence to the Stuarts.

The Hon. Jas. Keith, brother of the tenth Earl Marischal, was perhaps the most illustrious member of his family. It need only be here remarked, however, that, having been attainted along with his brother, he entered the service of the King of Prussia, in which he rose to the rank of Field-Marshal. After a career of great bravery, he fell at the battle of Hochkirchen, where his body, stript by the Austrians, was accidentally discovered by his friend, Count Lasci, who had it hurriedly interred within the church. It was afterwards more decently buried by the local curate; and eventually removed to Berlin by order of Frederick the Great, who had a marble statue erected to the Field-Marshal's memory. This marble has recently given place to a statue of bronze, a duplicate of which the King of Prussia was pleased to present to Peterhead. Upon the pedestal of the latter :—

FIELD-MARSHAL KEITH,
Born at Inverugie, 1696,
Killed at the Battle of Hochkirchen, 14 Oct. 1758.
The Gift of King William of Prussia to the
Town of Peterhead, August 1866.
Probus vixit, fortis obiit.

—The castle of Inverugie is a roofless and picturesque ruin, about a mile north-west from Peterhead; and the baptism of the future Field-Marshal is thus recorded in the register books of the parish of St Fergus, now in the custody of the Registrar-General :—

"16 June 1696: The Earl of Marchall had a Son baptized called JAMES-FRANCIS-EDWARD, before these witnesses, John Earl of Errol, Charles Lord Hay, & Sir William Keith of Loudquharn."

—The following inscription, composed by Metastasio, copied from Douglas' Peerage (vol ii. p. 196), is upon a tablet which was erected in the church of Hockterkyre, by Sir Robert Keith-Murray of Ochtertyre, Bart., soon after the death of his cousin, the Field-Marshal :—

"JACOBO KEITH, Gulielmi Comitis Marescalli Hered. Regni Scotiæ, et Mariæ Drummond, filio, Frederici, Borussorum Regis, summo exercitu Præfecto, viro antiquis moribus et militari virtute claro, qui, dum in prælio, non procul hinc, inclinatam suorum aciem, mente, manu, voce, et exemplo restituebat, pugnans ut heroas decet, occubuit, anno 1758, mense Oct."

[To JAMES KEITH, son of Earl William, Hereditary Marischal of the Kingdom of Scotland, and Mary Drummond, Commander-in-Chief of the Army of Frederick, King of Prussia, a man distinguished for his primitive character and military qualities, who, while he was striving by voice and example, to revive the drooping courage of his troops in an action fought not far from this spot, fell fighting with heroic bravery, in the month of Oct. 1758.]

The Marischal aisle, and a mutilated stone, upon the latter of which are the supporters of the family arms, the initials E. K., the date of 1635, with the words . . . . . . DOCHTER . . . . DEPARTET . . . . . are the only traces of the Keiths in Dunottar church-yard, if we except a marble slab, built into the dyke on the left of the gate. The slab is thus inscribed:—

D. O. M. S. [et] Memoriæ ELIZABETHÆ KEITH, eximiæ virtutis et veræ generositatis, quæ obijt trigesimo Maii 1695. Georgius M'Kenzie, mæstissimus conjunx, [ponendum] curavit.

[Sacred to God the Best and Greatest, and to the memory of ELIZABETH KEITH, a lady of eminent virtue and truly honourable birth, who died on the 30th May, 1695. George M'Kenzie, her disconsolate husband, caused this monument to be erected.]

A well-sculptured skull occupies a niche on the right of the church-yard gate; and a grave-stone, which long formed a step to the church door, presents the date of 1640, and the words— ARCHIBALD BISSED ANE HONEST MAN . . . . .

Adjoining the Marischal aisle, a flat and elaborately carved stone bears:—

Heir lyes a famovs and worthy gentillman WILLIAM OGILVY of Lvmger, and CATHARIN STRAQVHAN his spovs. He being 76 yeirs of age he departed his lyfe in peace 3 Jany. 1650, & shee being 89 yeirs of age departed hir lyfe the 28 of Febr. 1651.

—Mr Ogilvy of Lumgair (? Lyn-gar, the rough linns), was the son of the laird of Balnagarrow, near Kirriemuir, and descended from the Inverquharity family. His wife was a daughter of Strachan of Bridgeton, and a niece of Thornton. Their only son, George, married a daughter of Douglas of Barras; and, from the share which Ogilvy and his lady had in saving the Regalia, when in charge of Dunottar Castle, he was created a baronet (Nisbet, ii.; *infra*, p. 170).

About thirty-five years after Ogilvy's gallant defence of Dunottar Castle, a hundred and sixty-seven men, women, and children were brought from the west of Scotland, and imprisoned in one of its dungeons, for their adherence to the Covenant (Wodrow's Hist., iv.) Nine of them died at Dunottar, and a plain head-stone, with inscription in interlaced capitals, bears this record of their death:—

HERE . LYES . IOHN . STOT . IAMES . ATCHISON . IAMES . RUSSELL . & . WILLIAM . BROUN . AND . ONE . WHOSE . NAME . WEE . HAVE . NOT . GOTTEN . AND . TWO . WOMEN . WHOSE . NAMES . ALSO . WEE . KNOW . NOT . AND . TWO . WHO . PERISHED . COMEING . DOUNE . THE . ROCK . ONE . WHOSE . NAME . WAS . IAMES . WATSON . THE . OTHER . NOT . KNOWN . WHO . ALL . DIED . PRISONERS . IN . DUNNOTTAR . CASTLE . ANNO . 1685 . FOR . THEIR . ADHERENCE . TO . THE . WORD . OF . GOD . AND . SCOTLANDS . COVENANTED . WORK . OF . REFORMATION . REV . JJ CH . 12 VERSE .

—It was in 1793, when on a visit to the Rev. Mr Walker, that the future Sir Walter Scott " saw for the first and last time, Peter Paterson, the living *Old Mortality*," who was then engaged in retouching this inscription (Lockhart's Life of Scott, i. 210.) A table-shaped stone bears the name of the said Mr Walker, also those of his parents:—

In memory of the Rev. JAMES WALKER, who was minister of this parish from A.D. 1736 to 1772, where he died aged 66; and of MARGARET SHANK, his spouse, who died A.D. 1769. Also, of their only son, the Rev. JAMES WALKER, who succeeded his father as minister of the same parish, where he continued from the time of his settlement, 23d July A.D. 1772, to his death, on the 26th Nov. 1813, in the 63d year of his age.

Heir lyes ane honest man WILLIAM LISTOVN in Stonehaven, hvsband to Agnes Richie, vha depertet ye 31 Ivlie 1644.

From an adjoining head-stone :—

Here lies THOS. HERDMAN, 1st husband to Mary White. He was principal servt. to Wm. Earl Marishall, and died ye 31 of May 1713, aged 36 years. &c.

The following inscription (from a plain head-stone, on the north side of the Marischal aisle) is prefaced by a quotation from Psal. xcv. 3 :—

Mr ALEXANDER DAWSON, parochial schoolmaster of Dunnotter, died at the schoolhouse in Stonehaven, on the morning of Wednesday the 13th day of January 1830, in the 79th year of his age. Mr Dawson was a native of the parish of Cabrach, in Aberdeenshire. He attended Marischal College for his Academical education, where he distinguished himself in the science of Mathematics. He was appointed Parochial Schoolmaster of Dunnotter in the year 1780, and continued in that office till his death. This monument to his memory is placed at his grave by a few of his Friends who had a regard for his worth as a single hearted and ingenious man.

Anonymous (1756) :—

    Reddenda ex terra terra;
    Sic super nascitur ;
    Sic itur ad astra.
    Sic transit gloria mundi.
[Earth from earth must be returned,
Such is the second birth,
Such is the path to the skies.
Thus passes away the glory of the world.]

Erected by John Ross Hutchinson, E.I.C.C.S., in memory of his grandfather the Rev. ROBERT MEMESS, Episcopal Clergyman in Stonehaven for 63 years, who died Feb. 2, 1818, aged 90 years. And his sponse ELIZABETH Ross, who died 17th June 1813, aged 78 years. &c.

—Of Mr Memess, who appears to have been a person of great individuality of character, and common sense, many anecdotes are still told in the district. When a discussion took place on one occasion regarding the difference between Popery and Presbytery, he quaintly remarked—" In one respect they are quite the same—they baith tak' siller for sin !"

Here lyes a virtuous gentlewoman HELEN GRIEGORY, sponse to James Scot, mercht. in Stonehaven, who departed this life Appril 1737, aged 78 years.

Abridged :—

WILLIAM GREGORY, late feuer in Drumlithie, died April 12, 1796, aged 95 years. CHRISTIAN SMITH, sponse to Wm. Gregory, feuer in Drumlithie, died April 20, 1788, aged 87. &c.

From a table-shaped stone :—

To the memory of ALEXANDER STRATON, late merchant in Stonehive : he died the 7th day of May 1743, aged 67 years. And of CHRISTIAN ROBERTSON, his spouse, a virtuous wife, an affectionate mother, and benevolent friend ; she died the 20th day of Oct. 1763, aged 83 years. Also of THOMAS STRATON, Esq., their son, who died in Jamaica, May 1777, aged 73 years, with a most unblemished character, esteemed by all his connections. He acquired a genteel fortune, which he left to his surviving sisters. Here lies interred PATRICK CUSHNIE, who died 23d of May 1790, aged 38. Also ELIZABETH STRATON, his spouse, who died the 24th of Nov. 1792, in the 36th year of her age. And their son, the Rev. PATRICK CUSHNIE, M.A., incumbent of St Mary's, Montrose, who died 10th June 1869, in the 90th year of his age, and 69th of his ministry.

There was a burial place at

THE BOG WELL,

vpon the brae, behind the county buildings at Stonehaven. Two inscribed slabs mark the spot : both are embellished with mortuary emblems, and the words *memento mori*. The first quoted has the letters M. T. in monogram. According to tradition the place was set apart for the burial of those who died of the plague, a statement which the first-quoted inscription appears to bear out :—

[1.]

HEIR . LEYS . ANE . HONEST . MAN . MAGNVS .
TAILLIOVR . SEYMAN . QVHA . DI . . . .
IN . STANEHYVE . . . . . . IME . OF . PEST . 1608.

[2.]

HEIR . LYES . ANE . HONEST . MANS . BEARNES .
ALEXANDER . . . . . . OKIE . SONES . LAWFWL .
TO . ALEXANDER . BROKIE . WHO . DEPARTET . THE .
12 . OF . IWNE . OF . THE . AGE . OF . TVALF . AND .
NYN . YEIRES . OLD . IN . ANO . 1648.

It was from King Grig, or Circ, that the name of the *Mearns* ("Magh-Circin, or the plain of Circin"), originated; and the "Viri na Moerne," or *Men of the Mearns*, as the inhabitants were called even at that remote period (A.D. 877-89), had their stronghold at Dunottar, then "Dunforther." This is probably the oldest known form of the name; and, in regard to its meaning, the Bishop of Brechin kindly suggests that "*Dun-forther* would be the hill of the road —*Fother* or *For* being equivalent to the Irish *Bother*, a highway."

King Donald, who succeeded Grig on the Pictish throne, is recorded to have dispersed his foes at Fotherlun (Fordoun), and to have died at Dunforther, "where he lies on the brink of the waves" (Skene's Chron. of the Picts.) It also appears that Constantine, king of the Scots, penetrated into Pictland, in A.D. 934, as far as Dunfoeder (Dunottar); and soon thereafter (c. 954), it is stated by the same authority, that Malcolm was slain by "the men of the Mearns at Fodresach," or Fetteresso. According to tradition, the body of Malcolm was buried in a gravel mound to the west of the gate of Ury. It is certain that, in 1822, a human skeleton was found there in a covering of a superior description to those generally met with (Prof. Stuart's Essays).

The ruins of Dunottar stand upon an isolated rock which, long ago, had been almost surrounded by the sea. In Slezer's print (c. 1680), some of the buildings appear to be thatched, and a flag is displayed upon the tower. The existing ruins are those of the buildings which were erected by the Keiths, to whom the rock belonged from about the end of the fourteenth century, when (c. 1390) the square tower was built. According to story, the tower existed in the time of Wallace; but record shows that in his day the rock was the site of a church only, which, in all probability, had taken the place of the older castle, and been raised over the ashes of king Donald. An admirable plan of the rock and buildings of Dunottar was made in 1872 by Mr A. Gibb, F.S.A. Scot., by whom the Sculptured Stones of Scotland, &c., were drawn and lithographed for the Spalding Club.

There are some carved stones at Dunottar, all of a late date. A triangular-shaped slab (possibly the upper lintel of a window), dated 1645, bears the initials, E. W. M., with the Keith arms, and motto, VERITAS VINCIT; also those of C. S. E. M., with the Wintoun arms, and motto, HAZARD YIT FORVARD. These initials and arms refer respectively to the seventh Earl Marischal, and his first wife, Elizabeth Seaton, the latter of whom "departed this lyffe at Dunnottar of a fewer, one Sunday, 16 of Junij 1650, aged 28."

The Castle of Dunottar belongs to Sir Patrick Keith-Murray of Ochtertyre, baronet; but the house and the greater part of the lands of Dunottar are owned by W. N. Forbes, Esq. of Auchernach (*infra*, p. 151.)

Many years ago fragments of sculptured stones were found upon the top of the isolated rock near the harbour of Stonehaven, called *Dunicare*. The rock has a fine grassy top, and upon it are traces of a rude building, which some believe to be the remains of a religious house, or of the residence of a recluse or hermit. (Sculp. Stones, i. pl. xli.)

The town of Stonehaven, anciently *Stanehythe*, is prettily situated on the west side of the Bay, where there is a good harbour. Stonehaven is a burgh of barony, and became the seat of the County Courts after the suppression of Kincardine as the county town (*v.* Mem. Angus and Mearns).

Stonehaven contains a tolbooth and the old market cross, Episcopal and U.P. Churches, also a few modern, and a good many antiquated dwelling houses. The house is still shown in which the Duke of Cumberland slept, when on his way to Culloden; and the following extract from the "Journey" of a Volunteer, previously quoted (v. p. 26), gives a graphic picture of the housing of the Duke's followers at Stonehaven :—

"We put up here to lodge at a Doctor's, named *Lawson*, who kept a Public House, his Wife was lame, and he none of the wisest of his Profession; but had great Quantities of Wormwood, Sage, and other Herbs, hanging up in the Room where we supped; the Dust of which, diffused itself amongst our Victuals, and gave it no small Relish."

The river Carron, which divides the parishes of Dunottar and Fetteresso, is crossed by several bridges. The key-stone of the principal bridge is thus inscribed:—

THEOBALD BARCLAY, 1150;
MATHERS, 1351; URY, 1647; COND. 1781.

—The first of these dates appears to refer to the time the Barclays came to Scotland, the next two to the periods at which they acquired the properties named, and the last to the building of the bridge itself.

Cowie.

(S. NATHLAN, AND S. MARY.)

THE chapel of *Collyn*, which is situated within the parish of Fetteresso, and about a mile to the east of Stonehaven, was dedicated by William, Bishop of St Andrews, in 1276, "ita quod nullum prejudicium generetur matrici ecclesie de Fethyressach" (Robertson's Concilia Scotiæ.)

The ruins of the chapel of Cowie have a romantic position upon the top of a cliff adjoining the sea. The east wall is pierced by three lancet windows of the First Pointed period; and the aumbry, although much destroyed, is still an object of interest, near the north-east corner of the church. The chapel had possibly been suppressed as a place of worship, some time before 1567 (*infra*, p. 75.)

According to Keith's Remarkable Things, the chapel of Cowie was "demolished by reason of the superstitious resorting thereto; and a certain man, called William Rait of Redclock, brought away some of the roof of the chapel, and built a house therewith, and in a little thereafter the whole house rained drops of blood." (Duncan's Descrip. of the East Coast, p. 10.)

There was an altar at Cowie dedicated to the VIRGIN; and the following rhyme, which contains the name of the principal patron of the church, is still preserved among the fishermen at Cowie :—

"Atween the kirk, and the kirk ford,
There lies Saint Nauchlan's hoard."

The area of the ruins of "the kirk of Cowie," contains some plain tomb-stones. The first two inscriptions, quoted below, refer respectively to the father and aunt of Cosmo Innes, Esq., the well-known literary antiquary, and Professor of History, in the University of Edinburgh :—

[1.]

Here rests JOHN INNES, formerly of Leuchars, and for many years sheriff-substitute of this county, who died 10th May 1827, in his 80th year.

[2.]

In memory of JEAN INNES, who died 26th June 1831, aged 82 years.

The next is from a table-shaped stone :—

To the memory of MARY SEATON, who died the 18th June 1815, aged 74 years. This stone is erected by John Innes of Cowie, in whose family she served faithfully and affectionately nearly half a century.

A flat stone, at west end of the kirk, bears :—

Here lyes the body of JOHN NEPER, late seaman in Muchall, who departed this life the 28th day of March 1766, aged 90 years.

At the opposite end of the kirk, but in less correct orthography, is this record of the death of another patriarch, and some of his descendants :—

1799 G K. A M. In memory of George Keith let Tenant In Edeslau Who died N° the 1st 1798 aged 90 years also Ann Middleton his EsPous Who died Decr the 29 1792 Aged 72 years also ther son James who died June the 3 1771 Aged 24 years also five of ther Children who died In Infency

Besides the above records of nonogenarians, four other tomb-stones (also *within* the church), present these instances of longevity, viz. :—

MARY MAIN	died	1806,	aged	97, her son,
THOS. BRIDGEFORD	,,	1825,	,,	84.
ISOBEL HOWIE	,,	1836,	,,	96.
ELSPET SMITH	,,	1868,	,,	81.
WM. SMITH	,,	1853,	,,	88, his wife,
ELSPET DONALD	,,	1868,	,,	87.

The oldest visible grave-stone at Cowie (with a shield, and mortuary emblems, &c.), bears :—

☞ HIC . IACET . VIR . PIUS . HONESTIS . GEN . . . . IOANNES . AUCHINLECK . DE . TOUNHEAD . DE . COWIE . QUI . OBIIT . ANNO . ÆTATIS . SUÆ . QUADRAGESIMO . . . . .

[Here lies a pious man of respectable parentage, JOHN AUCHINLECK of [? in] Townhead of Cowie, who died in the 40th year of his age. . . . .]

The next five inscriptions are from adjoining tomb-stones :—

[1.]

In memory of the worthy & Reverend Mr ROBERT THOMSON, Episcopal Minister at Stonehive, who died ye 7th of Nov. 1737, aged 75 years. Also ye Body of Mrs ANN LINDSAY his spouse ; she died May ye 24th 1729, aged 68.

—Mr Thomson was the first Episcopal minister at Stonehaven, and the existing church, in the old town, was built for him.

[2.]

1778.—Here lyes the body of the Rev. Mr JOHN TROUP, late Episcopal Minister at Muchalls, who departed this life at Muchalls the 17th of August 1776, aged 75 years. And REBECCA MOUAT, his spouse, died the 4th of June 1791, aged 77 years. Also three of their children, ISOBEL, REBECCA, and IRVINE.

—Mr Troup, along with his Episcopal brethren of Drumlithie and Stonehaven, suffered six months' imprisonment, for contravening the Act which prohibited Episcopal ministers from preaching to more than four persons at a time, exclusive of their own family. It is said Mr Troup carried a bagpipe to jail with him, and that on his way thither he played the Jacobite air of " O'er the water to Charlie !"

[3.]

1837 : To the memory of the Rev. GEORGE GARDEN, who for 41 years was minister of the Episcopal Congregation of Stonehaven. He died 13th Nov. 1834, aged 72.

[4.]

Beneath, in hope of a glorious resurrection, rest the remains of the Rev. JAMES SMITH, for 27 years pastor of the Episcopal Congregation of Muchals, who departed this life on the 16th day of March 1854, aged 52. This stone has been erected by the Members of the Congregation, as a testimony of gratitude for the care he bestowed on their wants, both Spiritual and Temporal. [The death of a daughter, aged 5 years, is also recorded.]

In the same grave with the ashes of Messrs Thomson and Troup lie those of Messrs Garden, Smith, and Ironside, to the last-named of whom a tomb-stone, ornamented with a Celtic cross, &c., is thus inscribed :—

[5.]

✝ GEORGIUS IRONSIDE, Eccl : Scot : Sacerdos, in Xto obdormivit iiij Non : Oct. MDCCCLXI. Det illi Dominus invenire misericordiam a Domino in illa die.

[GEORGE IRONSIDE, priest of the Scottish Episcopal Church, fell asleep in Christ, 4th Oct. 1861. May the Lord grant that he may find mercy from the Lord on that day.]

The next inscription (from a head-stone) relates to a person whose " genius" lay in constructing eight-day clocks, " which he made from beginning to end ;" and in being a superior weaver of bed-covers, and table-cloths, &c. :—

To the memory of WILLIAM KILGOUR, an original genius, who exercised the craft of a weaver at Glithnow for the long period of sixty-two years in the same house. He departed this life on the 12th day of March 1837, at the advanced age of 86 years.

By his friends :—
Here lyes the man, for ought we know,
That liv'd and died without a foe,
Now mould'ring here beneath that clod—
An honest man's th' noblest work of God.

1866 : In memory of ANNE EDWARDS, born 22d Novr. 1794, died 11th June 1866. Erected by the family of the late Arthur Duff-Abercromby of Glassaugh, and Elizabeth Innes of Cowie, as a mark of esteem and appreciation of her character during the 30 years she resided with them.

Besides the parish church, and the Chapel of Cowie, there was at least one other religious house in Fetteresso in old times, to which a burial place was attached. The site, which is called

THE CHAPEL OF ELSICK,

is situated near the mansion-house of Elsick. Traces of the church still remain within the burial-ground; and the only tomb-stone, now visible, is thus inscribed:—

Here lyes GEORG HEPBURN, indweller was at Gilibrans, who departed this lyfe the 2d day of November 1702, and was of age 67 years, who lived in the foresaid place since the year 1680.

—"Gilibrans," and a great extent of surrounding territory, which, not long ago, was owned by about a dozen different lairds, constituted the estate of Elsick, as held by the family of BANNERMAN. One of them was created a baronet in 1682; but, owing to the decline of the family fortunes, they lost all territorial interest in the district, with the exception of the old kirk-yard, until the present baronet re-acquired the estate and mansion-house of Elsick.

The more immediate ancestors of the Bannermans of Elsick were merchants in Aberdeen. According to tradition, the name originated from the family having been *bannermen*, or standard-bearers, to the kings. It is certain that, as far back as 1373 (*inf.* p. 287), Donald Bannerman was king's physician, and held property in Newhills.

Aberdour.

(S. DROSTAN, ABBOT.)

THE ruins of the old church of *Aberdovyr* are picturesquely situated within the burial-ground, which overlooks the romantic den and bay of Aberdour. *Mess John's Well* springs from a rock on the left side of the bay, and S. DROSTAN's Well is on the right.

S. DROSTAN died at Glenesk, in Angus, in the year 809. His remains were conveyed from Glenesk to Aberdour, where they were deposited in a "tumba lapidea," or stone coffin, and were long believed to work wondrous cures upon the sick and afflicted. Interesting notices of Aberdour, ecclesiastical and territorial, will be found in the Book of Deer (Spalding Club), edited by Dr John Stuart; and of S. DROSTAN, in Kalendars of Scottish Saints, by the Bishop of Brechin.

In 1318, Bishop Chein erected the church into a prebend of Old Machar.

The church of *Aberdour* is rated at 28 merks in the Old Taxation. In 1574, along with the kirks of Gamrie, Philorth (Fraserburgh), and Tyrie, it was served by Mr David Howesoun, as minister; and Alexander Ramsay was the contemporary reader, or schoolmaster at Aberdour.

The earliest parts of the old kirk of Aberdour possibly belong to the 16th century; but the piscina, or lavatory, and a hexagonal baptismal font, seem to be of an older date. The latter was brought from Chapel Den, about four miles to the westward, where, it is said, there was another place of worship.

The nave of the old church of Aberdour is used for interments. The east portion is walled off and divided into two separate aisles. A stone panel, over the entrance to the more easterly aisle, bears these words:—

This Sepulture was erected by
Chas. Leslie, Esq., M.D., Fraserburgh, 1819.

The following is abridged from a marble slab within the same aisle:—

To the memory of MARGARET ROBERTSON, wife of William Leslie of Coburty, who died 3d July 1808, aged 52. WILLIAM LESLIE, Esq. of Coburty, died Dec. 1814, aged 69. Their sons and daughter, WILLIAM LESLIE, died 11th Aug. 1819, aged 37; GRACE LESLIE, died 3d March 1821, aged 32; CHARLES LESLIE, M.D., who died at Memsie, 11th March 1839, aged 64.

—Dr Leslie, who was a native of Rosehearty, and a medical practitioner in Fraserburgh, married the heiress of Memsie.

The burial aisle of the Bairds of Auchmedden is to the west of the last-mentioned. It contains three stones, inscribed as below, each of which present carvings of the Baird arms:—

[1.]

HIC . IACET . HONORABILIS . GEORGIVS . DAIRDE . DE . AVCHMEDDEN . QVI . OBIIT . 20 . MAII . 1593 . ANNO . AVTEM . ÆTAT . SVÆ . 76 .

[Here lies the honourable GEORGE BAIRDE of Auchmedden, who died 29th May 1593, in the 76th year of his age.]

[2.]

. . . . . BAIRD . DE . AVCHMEDDEN . QVI . OBIIT . 23 . DIE . MENSIS . FEBRVARI . . . . .

[3.]

1559 : IACOBVS . BAIRD . DE . AVCHMEDDEN HOC . MONVMENT . . . . . SVORVM . ANDREÆ . GEORG . . . . . GEORGII . BAIRD . DE . EODEM . . . . . . QVORVM . CORPORA . HIC . SEPVLTA . . . . . . ET . OBIERVNT . 10 . FEB . 1543 . MAII . 29 . 1593 . ʓ . . 1620 . ET . FEB . 12 . 1642 . AC . ETIAM . ANNÆ . . . . . ER . ET . ELISABETILÆ . KETHE . MATRIS . ET . PROAVÆ . EIVSDEM .

[1559 : James Baird of Auchmedden [erected] this monument [to the memory] of his . . . . ANDREW, GEORGE . . . . GEORGE BAIRD of the same, whose bodies are here interred, and [who] died 10th Feb. 1543, 29th May 1593, ... 1620, and 12th Feb. 1642 ; and also to the memory of ANN . . . . . ER, and ELIZABETH KEITH, mother and grand-mother of the same.]

—The erector of the monument from which the third inscription is copied, was high sheriff of Banffshire, and took an active part in the public affairs of his time. He was knighted by Chas. II., and married Christian, daughter of Walter Ogilvy of Boyne. Her initials and arms are also upon the monument.

The half-obliterated name of ANN FRASER refers to a daughter of Lord Saltoun, who was the mother of Sir James Baird. Sir James' grand-mother, Elizabeth Keith, wife of the first-named GEORGE, was a daughter of Keith of Troup, brother to Earl Marischal. The name altogether obliterated (between the two Georges) had been that of GILBERT BAIRD. He was third in succession, and died 23d Feb. 1620, having had, by his kinswoman, the heiress of Ordinhuives, no fewer than thirty two sons and daughters. It was in 1597, during the absence of this laird, that James Chein from Pennan, and others attacked the house of Auchmedden. In a contemporary account of the affair, it is stated that the assailants "clam to the tops of thair houssis, kaist in staues at the chymney," and shot the lady "throw the claythis, sche being grit with barne; for feir of the quhilk schot," it is added, "she schortlie thairafter pairtit with the said barne."

In the year 1534 Andrew Baird, a son of Baird of Posso, in Peebles, and designed of Laverocklaw, in Fife, bought the lands of Auchmedden from Stewart, Earl of Buchan. The charter is attested by George Baird of Ordynhuiff and others. The Bairds held Auchmedden until 1750, when it was sold to Lord Haddo by William Baird, who joined in the rebellion of 1745.

Mr Baird married a sister of the first Earl of Fife, by whom he left a numerous family, none of whose descendants now remain, except those of his daughter Henrietta, who married Francis Fraser, Esq. of Findrack (*infra*, p. 239.) It ought to be added that Mr Baird wrote two interesting works, one, which gives an Account of his own Family, has been edited by his descendant, W. N. Fraser, Esq.; and the other, Genealogical Memoirs of the Duffs, has been privately printed by Major Gordon-Duff of Drummuir, accompanied by a photographic portrait of the author. The above notes regarding the Bairds are made up from the first of these books.

The property of Auchmedden, which has been in several hands since 1750, now belongs to Jas. Baird, Esq., one of the Gartsherrie family.

An aisle on the south side of the ruins of the church was erected by Mr Gordon of Aberdour. It contains a handsome marble tablet, with the Gordon and Rose arms, quartered; also an inscription to the following effect:—

To the memory of WILLIAM GORDON of Aberdour, who died 11 Nov. 1839, aged 67; and of his wife MARY ROSE, eldest daughter of William Rose of Ballivat, who died 18 Jan. 1828, aged 49; and of their children: JOHN, who died in October 1802, in infancy; ALICIA, who died 2 August 1810, aged 14; ANNA, who died 4 Feb. 1822, aged 16; ELISABETH, who died 28 Augt. 1826, aged 16; ALEXANDER, lieutenant of the Coldstream Guards, who died 1 April 1818, aged 20; GEORGE, who died in Surrey, 7 Dec. 1820, aged 7; and WILLIAM, who died at St Kitts, 18 June, aged 40.

—The father of the above first-named Mr Gordon was tenant of the Milltown of Aberdour, also factor for the 3d Earl of Aberdeen and for General Gordon of Fyvie. He bought the estate of Aberdour, and founded the village of New Aberdour. His son, who died as above in 1839, sold the estate shortly before his death. It is a tradition that the Lieutenant fell in a duel with a Frenchman, who appears to have been a good marksman, for it is added that he had previously shot three or four antagonists under similar circumstances. Lieut. G.'s grandfather died in 1785.

Having accidentally heard of a carved stone in the more westerly part of the nave of the church, and on the site of the old pulpit, I had diggings made when at Aberdour sometime ago, and discovered, at the depth of from one to two feet, an interesting slab of freestone, measuring four feet nine inches by two feet; but it is unfortunately broken. It is embellished in the centre with a cross, terminating in a fleur-de-lis at the top; and at the foot, within a circle or belt, there is a shield charged with three cinquifoils in chief, and a martlet displayed between two cinquifoils in base, for White. The following inscription is carved in relief round the margin of the stone:—

HEIR . LYE . . . HONE . QVHYT . SVTYM . IN ARDLAHIL . QVHA . DECEISIT . YE . XI . OF . OC. 1590.

—In a letter from Professor Baird of Lyons, to his brother of Auchmedden, dated from Lyons, 23 Jan. 1603, he remarks—" As to the Abbot, Mr John Quhyt, Quhyt of Ardlybill's son, thair is half a yeir since I hard he is in guid helth." It is stated (Edinburgh Review, No. 243, p. 180),

that John-James Whyte became Abbot of the Scots monastery at Ratisbone in 1595, and died in Germany in 1629. The above inscription appears to relate to the father of Abbot Whyte. Whytes tenanted Ardlawhill in, and long before, 1696, under Lord Pitsligo.

The following inscriptions are from stones in the churchyard:—

Heir lyes WILLIAM GORDON, sometyme in Little Byth . . . departed Feb. 9, 1724; and MARGARET DALGARNO, his spouse, who died Sept. 8, 1713.

There is a pretty complete set of tombstones to the old ministers of this parish. Upon the first noticed are the initials, M. G. C : I. O.; a shield bearing (1), a fesse-chequy, between a crescent and 2 mullets, a boar's head couped in base; (2), 2 lions rampant in chief, and 3 lozenges in base; also this brief inscription:—

Heir lyes Mr GEORG CLERK and IEAN OGSTONE his wyf. Mr GEORG CLERK entred person of Aberdovr the 20 day of Febr. 1614 years, and departed this lyf the 18 of Agvst 1644 years.

The next stone presents the initials M. W. R., and the armorial bearings, boldly carved, of a double-headed spread eagle in chief, and 3 leisters in base:—

Here lyes Master WILLIAM RAMSAY, a faithful minister of the Gospel, who was entered person of Aberdour the 2 day of Januar 1651, and departed this life the 31 day of December 1690 years.

Here lyes Mr ALEXANDER REYNOLD, a faithful servant of God in the ministry, being admitted thereto at Aberdour, September 17, 1665, and dyed August 9, 1691, and MARGARET FORBES, his spouse, who dyed Feb. 28, 1695 :—

This dormitory which thou sees,
Was once the object of my eyes;
But now my body is in dust,
Thine also death will hither thrust.

—Mr R.'s wife was a daughter of John Forbes of Pitnacalddel, by Christian, daughter of Johnston of Caskieben. The writer of the *rare verse* is not recorded!

Memoriæ Rudi admodum Dni IAC. BROUN, qui in meridionalibus hujus regionis paroœchiis de Killochoilli, natali, et Walston, aliquot annos in Evangelii laboribus versatus, huic tandem admissus parochiæ 7ᵐᵒ Cal. Sep. 1697, postquam Christo fidelitate summa et vigilantia indefessa inserviisset, fatis cessit, pridie Cal. Aug., 1732, ætatis 70, ministerii 41. Monumentum hoc extruendum curavit filius ejus unicus Ioannes, pastor Longsidensis.

[To the memory of the very reverend Mr JAMES BROUN, who, after having been employed for some years in the work of the Gospel in the south country, in the parishes of Kilbucho (his native parish), and Walston, was at length appointed to this parish, 27 Aug. 1697; and after serving Christ with the utmost faithfulness and unwearied vigilance, departed this life 31 July 1732, in the 70th year of his age, and 44th of his ministry. His only son, John, minister of Longside, caused this monument to be erected.]

Mr THOMAS ANDERSON, 31 years minister of Aberdour, died 1765, aged 65.

The Rev. ANDREW YOUNGSON, A.M., 43 years minister of Aberdour, died 15 June 1809, aged 83. AGNES ANDERSON, his wife, daughter of the Rev. Thomas Anderson of Aberdour, died 22 May 1825, aged 76. His piety, sweetness of disposition, mildness of manners, fortitude, and cheerful resignation under the greatest bodily distress, endeared him to all who knew him; and set a happy example of the power of that religion which he taught to others.

—The allusion to "bodily distress" refers to the painful fact, that Mr Y. suffered from cancer in the throat for the long period of 30 years. His son,

Major THOMAS YOUNGSON, H.E.I.C.S., died 27 Oct. 1839, aged 55. Erected by his widow.

The Rev. GEORGE GARDINER, for 46 years minister of Aberdour. He was born at Smithston in Rhynie, A.D. 1782, and died at Manse of Aberdour on the 30 January 1857.

—Many stories are preserved of Mr Gardiner's erratic habits and uncompromising disposition. He wrote the New Statistical Account of the Parish, and in speaking of the character of the people, he remarks that they are " strangers to that fanaticism which acts as a nurse to sedition, and that pharisaical hypocrisy which serves as a cloak to the most heinous sins, their maxim is, ' to fear God, honour the King, and not meddle with those that are given to change.' "

The Rev. THOMAS KIDD, A.M., ordained minister of Longside, 14 May 1829, died at Aden, where he had been tutor for several years, three days after his settlement, aged 34 years.

Here lyes the ashes of ane honest man named IAMES BRUCE, who lived sometime in Mininy, who departed this life Febry 23, 1718 years; and likewise IEAN BROWN his wife who died . . . . This stone is erected by ALEXANDER BRUCE, lawful son of the said Iames Bruce,
who departed this life May 10, 1705, also IANET SPENCE, spouse to Alex. Bruce, who departed this life May 12, 1739.

—Notwithstanding the apparent contradiction in the above inscription, it is a literal copy of the original. The middle paragraph appears to have been the last engraved part of it.

JOHN MONCUR d. 22 Ap. 1853, a. 15 y.; ROBT. d. at sea, Oct. 13, 1856, a. 22 y. :—

> Ye readers all both old and young,
> Your time on earth will not be long;
> We was like two lilies fresh and green
> Who was cut down and no more seen.
> We grew in beauty side by side,
> We filled one home with glee;
> Our graves are severed far and wide,
> By mountain, stream, and tree.

—The last verse of this epitaph, which forms such a contrast to the preceding lines, is copied from a poem by Mrs Hemans.

The parish church was removed from the old site to the village of New Aberdour in 1818. The date of 1771 is upon the belfry; and the bell was put up in 1859. A tablet outside the church bears this inscription :—

This church was erected by JOHN DINGWALL, Esq. of Brucklay, Patron and Principal Heritor of the Parish, and CHARLES FORBES, Esq., proprietor of Auchmedden. 1818.

A neat Free Church was recently erected at New Aberdour.

The Earls of Douglas were proprietors of this district before and for sometime after 1408. About the time mentioned Fraser of Philorth acquired part of the lands of the barony of Aberdour from the Earl of Douglas as superior.

Dundarg Castle of which little more than the arched gateway remains, stood upon a peninsula which juts into the sea. It is said to have been built by Cumin, Earl of Buchan, and to have been garrisoned in the 13th and 14th centuries. Tradition says that the roof was taken off the castle to replace that of the old church, which had fallen into decay.

Lord Pitsligo's cave, where that nobleman lay in hiding after the rebellion of 1715, and amused himself by scooping out a little reservoir, is between Dundarg and Rosehearty, in an almost inaccessible part of the cliffs.

Ellon.

(THE BLESSED VIRGIN.)

KING ROBERT the BRUCE gave the kirk of *Elon* to the Abbey of Kinloss, in Moray, in 1310. It was sometimes called *Kinloss-Ellon*; and possibly the church was granted to Kinloss by Cumin Earl of Buchan at the time of its foundation.

According to the Edinburgh Prognostication for 1700, MARYMASS Fair was held here in August, and RUDE Fair in May.

There was an altar within the church called the HOLY ROOD, to which, in 1380, Leask of that ilk (whose burial place was within the church), made certain grants of money and wax for saying mass, and for lights to be burned at his family tomb.

The present church was erected in 1777, within which a marble is thus inscribed:—

JOHN LEITH-ROSS of Arnage, died 15 May 1839, aged 63 ; ELIZABETH YOUNG, his spouse, coheiress of Bourtie, died 9 June, 1852, aged 70 : their third son WILLIAM ROSS, M.D., died 28 Sep. 1834, aged 22 ; GEORGE, their fourth son, and FREDERICK, their grandson, died in childhood.

—John Ross, a merchant in Aberdeen, bought the property of Arnage in 1702. The male line of Ross having failed, the succession devolved through a female on the above named John Leith Ross, who was a cadet of the family of LEITH of Freefield. The first Ross of Arnage married a daughter of Forbes of Echt, and died at Amsterdam in 1714, aged 50.

A tomb of freestone, which was built into the inner wall of the old church, is divided into three compartments. Over the centre inscription-panel (which is blank), are the Annand arms, with supporters. Below is the motto, SPER ABO. On the left, the initials, D.A.D., and on the right "Obiit 1326." The Annand and Fraser arms, with the initials, A.A : M.F., and motto, ET SALUS . . . . . are over the east panel. Upon it is the following inscription, which, though but recently restored, will, owing to the inferior sort of stone employed, require soon to be renewed :—

Monumentum marmoreum honorabilis ALEXANDRI ANNAND, baronis quondam de Ochterellon, qui obiit ix Julii, A.D. 1601 ; ejusque piæ conjugis, MARGARETÆ FRASER, filiæ quondam dō de Philorth, quæ obiit Aug., A.D. 1602.—Salus per Christum.

[The marble monument of ALEXANDER ANNAND, the late honourable baron of Ochterellon, who died 9 July 1601 ; and of his pious spouse MARGARET FRASER, daughter of the late laird of Philorth, who died Aug. 1602.]

Over the panel, on the west, are carved the Annand and Cheyne arms, with the initials A. A : M.C. ; and motto, MORS CHRISTI VITA NOSTRA. The panel bears the following renewed inscription :—

Sub hoc quoque tumulo resurrectionem expectant corpora ALEXANDRI ANNAND de Ochterellon, filii dicti Alexandri, qui obiit   , et caræ suæ conjugis, MARGARETAE CHEYNE, filiæ dō de Esselmont, quæ obiit

[In this tomb also await the resurrection, the bodies of ALEXANDER ANNAND of Ochterellon, son of the said Alexander, who died   , and of his beloved wife MARGARET CHEYNE, daughter of the laird of Esslemont, who died

—Henry Annand, who left a widow called Marjory Cullen, and who was succeeded by his son Alexander in Ouchterellon 1505-6 (of which the Earl of Crawford was superior), is the first Annaud I have found mentioned in connection with these lands. Alexander, son of the baron who died in 1601, was served heir to his father in August of that year; and the inscription last quoted, appears to refer to him and his wife Margaret Cheyne. From the Poll Book of Aberdeenshire (1696) we learn that the laird of Auchterellon was married, had three daughters, and two sons; but the surname of the laird of that period is not given. *Anan*, or *Anand*, is a territorial name, and the family were early settled in Forfarshire (Mem. of Angus, p. 288), where they subsisted down to about 1500, and were long proprietors of lands adjoining the chief residence of the Earls of Crawford. The Auchterellon branch had probably sprung from the Angus stock, and may have acquired a footing in Buchan through the Crawfords. Of the "Obiit 1326" I can offer no conjecture.

Within a railed inclosure, in front of the Annand monument :—

To the memory of KEITH TURNER of Turnerha'll, this stone is erected by his sorrowing widow. He was born January 20, 1768 ; departed this life Oct. 20, 1808, and was, by his own desire, laid into the grave of his beloved mother, ELIZABETH URQUHART of Meldrum, born July 10, 1735; died Feb. 28, 1786. Also to the memory of his widow, Mrs ANNA-MARGARET TURNER of Turnerhall, ob . . Oct. 1823, æ. 50 years.

—The author of the View of the Diocese of Aberdeen (1732), says that Turnerhall [previously Rosehill, formerly Hilton], was purchased for him (Mr Turner) by a rich merchant, who had returned home from Poland to Aberdeen, and was extremely desirous that, seeing he had no children, one of his own name should have the estate, which should be so denominated as to preserve his memory. The above *Keith* TURNER is called *John* in Burke's Landed Gentry.

Two fragments, from the Waterton aisle, which stood on the south side of the old church, are built into the church wall. One stone, with the Forbes and Ramsay arms impaled (the latter with 3 mullets or stars round the head of the eagle), is initialed and dated, I. F.W : I R., 1637, also the motto, SALVS PER CHRISTVM VIVE VT VIVAS. The other fragment bears the following words incised :—
Built by I : F. of W. . . . son to W. F. of Tolqu . . . & I. R. daut^r to Balmain, in 1637. Rebuilt by T. F. of W. and M. M. in 1755.

—Forbes of Waterton appears to have acquired the property, and to have "finished the house" of Waterton, during the early part of the 17th century. His wife was a sister to the first baronet of Balmain ; and the historian of the Forbes's says that "she bare to him Sir John Forbes of Watertonne, with diverss oyr bairns."

JAMES BOWMAN, builder and farmer, Newton of Fechil, died Aug. 14, 1806, aged 85. MARGARET TAYLOR, his spouse, died Aug. 15, 1805, aged 78. KATHERINE (their dr.) died 1796, aged 45 :—

Stay, reader, stay, remove not from this tomb,
Before thou hast considered well thy doom.
The grave that next is opened may be thine ;
With patience, then, sustain thy mortal load,
And daily strive to walk approved by God,
That when thy body's numbered with the dead,
Thy soul may rest with Christ, thy living head.

—Apart from the above lines, there are eleven others extracted from Michael Bruce's poems, beginning "The curtain of this grave." Elaborately carved masonic emblems adorn the lower part of the stone.

Mrs JANET FORREST, sometime residing in Peterhead, died 1 March 1812, aged 48.

Several tombstones bear the name of Ligertwood, two of which are respectively inscribed :—

JAMES LIGERTWOOD, born in Cairnhill, June 11, 1681, and died there January 5, 1745.

Here lys in hopse of a blessd Ressurrection, the Dust of JOHN LIGARWOOD, sometime in tartie, wh^o died Suptmb 27, 1767, aged 74 year^{rs}.

Sacred to the memory of the Rev. NATHANIEL GRIEVE, M.A., clergyman of the Church in Scotland, and Incumbent of the Episcopal Church, Ellon. He died at Aberdeen 18 Feb. 1863, in the 84th year of his age, and 60th of his ministry.

Upon monuments on the east side of the kirk door :—

Rev. ANDREW MOIR, minister of Ellon for 32

years, died Feb. 1774, aged 73. His wife JEAN, died Oct. 1789, aged 74. Their daughter JEAN MOIR [erector of the tablet], died 16 Sep. 1816, aged 70.

—Mr M., who succeeded Mr Milne (the first minister here after the abolition of Episcopacy), was father of the Rev. Mr Moir, M.D., of Peterhead, who married a Miss Byers of Tonley, in Tough. Through this marriage the present proprietor, Mr Moir, succeeded to that estate.

Rev. JAMES MILNE, minister of Ellon, died 31 May 1797, aged 79. Mrs ELIZABETH KER, his spouse, died 28 May 1807, aged 73.

The following are upon monuments on the west side of the church door :—

ELIZABETH GORDON, spouse to the Rev. Thomas Tait, minister of Ellon, died 8 Jan. 1804, aged 50. Her nephew, JAMES GORDON, son to the Rev. John Gordon, minister of Cabrach, died at Ellon, 7 July 1808, aged 13 yrs. The Rev. THOMAS TAIT, died Aug. 1810, aged 67.

The Rev. ROBERT DOUGLASS, died 21 Dec. 1831, aged 48, and in the 21st year of his ministry.

The Rev. WILLIAM BREWSTER, died 27 Aug. 1859, aged 67, and in the 16th year of his ministry in this parish.

Erected by the U.P. Congregation of Savoch of Deer, in memory of their late pastor the Rev. JOHN HUNTER, who died 3 June 1865, in the 32d year of his ministry, and the 61st of his age.

The Episcopal Church of S. MARY "on the rock" stands on the south side of the Ythan, near the bridge of Ellon. A stained-glass window of one light, in the north wall, bears, in the chief or centre compartment, a representation of Christ, with lantern in hand, illustrative of the text, " Behold, I stand at the door and knock." In the lower compartment, Christ is represented relieving a lamb from a thicket of thorns, with the words, " I am the good shepherd." The following is in the base line of the window :—

CHARLES-NAPIER GORDON, DIED 16 JUNE 1864.

—A marble tablet, on the south wall, is thus inscribed :—

In memory of CHARLES-NAPIER GORDON of Eslemont, and his sisters HARRIET, FRANCES, and GEORGINA, son and daughters of George Gordon of Hallhead, and his wife Henrietta Hope Napier.

—Gordon of Hallhead was nephew to George, Earl of Aberdeen, and his wife was a daughter of Lord Napier. The Gordons of Hallhead, in Leochel-Cushnie, who became extinct in the male line on the death of the above-named Charles-Napier Gordon, were descended from George, son of Thomas Gordon of Daach of Ruthven, who acquired Hallhead towards the close of the 14th century. Eslemont was long a part of the extensive estates of the family of Cheyne.

The Antiquities of Aberdeen and Banff (vol. iii., Spald. Club), contain valuable charters and other information regarding Ellon, from 1157, when Pope Adrian IV. confirmed to the See of Aberdeen the lands which Master Philip held in Ellon, down to a late date.

It would appear that in 1387 an inquest was made concerning the property of the church of Ellon, by which some peculiarly interesting payments were found to belong to it, such as the hereditary rights and duties of the *scologs* or scholars, who were apparently the forerunners of the readers and parochial teachers of this country. In Ellon, the " scologs' lands" were bound to furnish four clerks for the parish church, able to read and sing; while another part of the same lands had to find a dwelling-house for the scholars.

The lands of Candellon (? Candle-Ellon), were burdened with the payment of 24 wax candles yearly for the high altar of the church of Ellon ; and the lands of Ferley were held by vassals who bore the surname of FERLEY, on the tenure of maintaining a smithy at the town of Ellon.

In regard to the proprietary history of the district, it need only be stated that Ellon formed an important part of the great territory of the old Earls of Buchan. It was the seat of justice for that earldom ; and upon the moothill, or Earls' hill, these barons received formal investiture of the earldom. This mound, which was removed many years ago, stood below the bridge of Ellon, opposite to the New Inn. The Earls' hill was the last part of the Buchan property which descended with that title; and about the middle of the 17th century it belonged to the Earls of Panmure; afterwards to those of Strathmore.

The proprietors of the estate of Ellon, formerly called *Kermucks*, were Hereditary Constables of Aberdeen, the seal of one of whom, Wilyeame Kynidy, 1487, shows a key and baton, saltire-Forbes of Waterton was at one time laird of Kermucks; and, during the early part of the 18th century, the property belonged to Gordon, "son of a farmer in Bourtie, a merchant in Edinburgh, and once a bailie there, and a rich man." He built "a very great house," the picturesque ruins of the tower of which, now ivy-clad, only remain. From James, a Bordeaux merchant, and a descendant of the above-named Gordon, the third Earl of Aberdeen bought the lands of Ellon and Waterton, &c., in 1750. His Lordship died at Ellon House in 1801, aged 80; and on the death of his second son, the present proprietor succeeded, by whom the estate of Ellon has been vastly improved and beautified. A freestone slab, ornamented somewhat in the style of the old sculptured stones of Scotland, stands upon a mound near the east gate of Ellon. It is commemorative of a meeting of the different members of Mr Gordon's family under their paternal roof, and is thus inscribed:—

✠ IN MEMORIA.
THE BROTHERS AND SISTERS MEET AGAIN AT HOME,
ADVENT 1862.—DEO GRATIAS. ✠

The bridge of Ellon, which crosses the Ythan, and consists of three arches, is dated 1793. It was built at the expense of the third Earl of Aberdeen, the road trustees having previously agreed to make the Aberdeen and Peterhead turnpike to suit the locality chosen by his lordship for the bridge.

Places called the KIRKHILL of Turnerhall, and the CHAPEL of Savoch, in this parish, possibly indicate sites of early places of worship.

———o———

Fordoun.

(S. PALLADIUS, APOSTLE.)

FORDOUN is believed to have been one of the earliest seats of Christianity in the north of Scotland. After the death of S. PALLADIUS, who came to Fordoun in the 5th century, it is said that his relics were long kept there in a silver shrine.

The aisle, or S. PALLADIUS' Chapel, is all that remains of the old church. It has been for long the burial place of the families of Glenfarquhar and Monboddo. No stone preserves the names of any of the Falconers of Glenfarquhar. They were descended from William de Auceps, hawksman to William the Lion at Kincardine Castle; and are now represented by the Earl of Kintore. Sir ALEXANDER FALCONER of Glenfarquhar, who left several legacies for educational purposes, was father of the 4th Lord Halkerton, and the last of the family that was buried in the vault below. Lord Falconer, who died in 1685, whose eldest son became 5th Lord Halkerton, was of the Glenfarquhar branch; and Catherine, daughter of the 5th Peer, was the mother of Hume, the philosopher and historian.

A chest-shaped tomb (within S. PALLADIUS' chapel), embellished with bold carvings of the Irvine and Douglas arms, and the initials C.R.I: E.D., is thus inscribed:—

1668.—In spem beatæ resvrrectionis hic velvti svflitvs thalamo svaviter in Domino obdormit dux ROBERTVS IRVIN, a Monboddo, Dominvs, qui pie fatis cessit 6 Ivlii, anno salvtis hvmanæ 1652, et ætatis svæ anno 80:—

Conjvge, progenie felix, virtvtis, honesti
Cvltor, et antiqvis exorivndvs avis,
Hoc cvbat IRVINVS monvmento. Cætera norvnt
Mvsa et vitiferis Seqvana clarvs aqvis.

[1668.—In the hope of a blessed resurrection, here, as in a perfumed chamber, sweetly sleepeth in the Lord, Captain ROBERT IRVINE of Monboddo, a gentleman who piously yielded up his spirit (as above):—

Happy in his consort and in his offspring, a man of virtue and honour, descended from an ancient family, IRVINE reclines in this tomb. Moreover, the Muse had knowledge of him; also the Seine, famed for its vine growing waters.]

—Capt. Irvine, who was of the Drum family, married Elizabeth, daughter of Sir Robert Douglas of Glenbervie. From them, through a female, was descended the well-known JAMES BURNETT, Lord Monboddo, author of several metaphysical books, and who died at Edinburgh, 27 May 1799, aged 85. One of his daughters was the "Fair Burnett," celebrated by the poet Burns. Another daughter (who died about 1833, and was buried at Fordoun), became the wife of Mr Williamson, keeper of the Outer House Rolls at Edinburgh. The present laird, Capt. Burnett, is their grandson. The property came to the Irvines by marriage with the daughter and heiress of Strachan of Monboddo, a descendant of the old house of Thornton. Part of *Monbodachyn*, and other lands in Fordoun, were given to the Monastery of Arbroath, by Robert Warnebald, and his spouse Richenda.

The new church, erected in 1828-9, stands to the north of the old aisle. Upon the bell—THOMAS MEARES, LONDON FOUNDRY, 1835.

A marble slab in the lobby, above the north door of the tower, is thus inscribed:—

In memory of ALEXANDER CROMBIE of Phesdo, who lived much respected and beloved, and died deeply regretted, Nov. 21, 1832, aged 66 years. In him the Poor of this parish lost a most generous benefactor.

—Mr Crombie, who was an advocate in Aberdeen, bought Phesdo and Thornton. He was succeeded by his cousin-german, Dr Crombie, author of the Gymnasium, &c., whose eldest son is now laird of Thornton. Phesdo became, by purchase, the property of the late Sir John Gladstone, bart.

[IN CHURCHYARD] :—

Heir lyes a faithfvl brother THOMAS CROL, vho departed the 27 of April 1678, of age 81 ; and his spovs CHRISTIAN COVY, de. Ap. 28, 1668, ag. 72 :—
Theirs non in qvestion this will call,
Which I write on their dvst,
That to the poor they liberall,
And wer to all men ivst.

Upon a stone lying at south side of aisle :—
Heir lyes a faithf . . . . . . BARD spovs to
IA . . . . . . departed the 9 of De . . . . . .
Love convgal in . . . lyfe keeps amity,
Bvt death doth come and break society ;
Yet heir is love com . . . behold and see,
That vith death st . . . . . got the victory.
Together they did live, together dy,
Together ver both bvried in one day ;
Together they within this grave do ly,
Together they shall ring with Christ for ay.
Heir lyes a faithfvl brother IAMES FARQVHAR, vho departed this lyfe the 9 of December 1671, and of his age the 81.—I. F ; M. B.

WILLIAM LAY :—
Here lies WILLIAM LAY,
Sometime in Tippertie,
Who departed this life
The last Sabbath of April 1725.

ISOBEL LOUSEN, 1706 :—
Deset nor proud she covld not endure,
But still a movther to the poor.

GEORGE WATSON'S wife, 1764 :—
This dust which now obscurely lies,
Once animated was by ONE
Whose amiable qualities
Seldom, if ever, were outshone.

DAVID WALKER, d. 1772, a. 43 :—
This dust which here doth rest in sacred peace,
Once lodg'd a soul enrich'd with every grace ;
A safe companion, and a friend approv'd,
In death regretted, and in life belov'd.
Well pleased, Heaven crown'd his virtues with success,
And soon receiv'd him to the seats of bliss ;
At life's mid age he gain'd that happy shore,
Where friends unite, & death can part no more.

DAVID WATSON, by his widow, Jean Milne, who composed these lines, 1825 :—
Deeply the Widow and the children mourn
The best of husbands, & the Father kind ;
Their earthly joys & hopes were from them torn,
When he to dust his mortal frame resign'd.

DAVID GLASS, mason, aged 46, "died in consequence of a fall from the old church when taking it down on the 17th April 1828."

Upon a table-shaped stone on north side of church :—

Here are interred the remains of Dr JAMES BADENOCH of Whiteriggs, who died 26 Dec. 1797, in the 54th year of his age. Also of Mrs ANNE GRAHAME, his wife, who died 6 Augt. 1815, in the 63d year of her age. Erected by their son James Badenoch of Arthurhouse.

—Dr B., who was grandfather to the present J. Badenoch-Nicolson, yr. of Glenbervie, married a daughter of the laird of Morphie, sister to Lady Arbuthnott.

ALEX. MILNE, A.M., who, having been 46 years schoolmaster of Fordoun, died 16 Dec. 1812, aged 72.

Upon a flat stone :—

Captn. JAMES LESLIE, 15th Regt. of Foot, died at Kair, April 1, 1791, aged 55 years. Erected by his son, James Leslie, merchant, Canada.

Within a railed enclosure, on the left side of churchyard gate :—

JAMES GAMMELL, Esq. of Drumtochty, died at Drumtochty Castle, 15 Sep. 1825, aged 89, and is interred here. JANET GIRLS, spouse of the said Jas. Gammell, died 28 April 1818, aged 79, and is interred at Greenock. Their son WILLIAM GAMMELL, died in infancy. Lieut.-Gen. ANDREW GAMMELL, interred in Westminster Abbey; and Lieut.-Col. WILLIAM GAMMELL, interred at Martinique.

A granite pillar, with square base, surmounted by an urn, erected in 1850, bears the following inscription round the column :—

This monument is erected to the memory of one of Scotland's first and most illustrious martyrs, GEORGE WISHART of Pittarrow, in this parish ; and as a testimony of gratitude to the great Head of the Church, for the work of the Reformation, on behalf of which his servant suffered. He was born in 1513, and was burned at St Andrews, 1st March 1546. 'The righteous shall be in everlasting remembrance.'

—Charters show that WISHARTS were settled in this district as far back as the year 1200 ; and that they exsisted down to the early part of the 17th century. The old house of Pitarrow was demolished about 1802. Some carved stones relating to the Wisharts are still to be seen at Pitarrow. The Wisharts were succeeded in these lands by Carnegie of Kinnaird in Angus ; and Sir James (great-grandfather of the present Earl of Southesk), sold Pitarrow to a younger brother, George, one of whose descendants resold the lands to Mr Crombie, late of Phesdo.

On north wall of parish school, formerly on south wall of old church :—

Under the flat stone, 5 feet south from this wall, lies the body of JAMES LEITH of Whiteriggs, who died 20 Feb. 1788, aged 63. And on the south side of that stone, lies the body of MARGARET YOUNG, his wife, who died 6 April 1783, aged 58. The virtue of their lives made their deaths lamented, and this stone is in gratitude erected to their memories by their children. There are also interred the body of MARGARET HACKET, his mother, who died in April 1765, aged 56. And Doctor CHARLES LEITH, his brother, who died 6 of May 1731, aged 56. And also of two of his children, RAMSAY LEITH, and   LEITH, who died in infancy.

A stone, within an iron-railed enclosure, at north side of parish school, bears :—

Sacred to the memory of JAMES ARNOTT, Esq., who died at Arbikie, in Forfarshire, 3 Dec. 1799 ; and of his wife, JANET LEITH, who died at Edinburgh, 29 Aug. 1827; and of their two younger sons, CHARLES ARNOTT, Esq., formerly solicitor in London, who died at Leithfield Cottage, in this parish, 21 Sept. 1841, and whose body is here interred. And DAVID LEITH ARNOTT, Esq., a Major in the East India Company's service, who died in India, 19 Oct. 1840. And of their youngest daughter, HELEN ARNOTT, who died in Montrose, 21 Feb. 1807. JAMES LEITH ARNOTT, grandson of said James Arnott and Janet Leith, died at Edinburgh, 10 Novr. 1818, aged 2 years.

[On west front of same stone] :—

JAMES LEITH of Whiteriggs or Leithfield, and MARGARET YOUNG spouses, whose names are mentioned on a tablet erected near this stone, left six children, viz. ALEXANDER LEITH, died at sea in Jan. 1805, aged 53. JOHN LEITH, died at Surinam, in 1805, surgeon of the 16th regiment of Foot, aged 49. JAMES LEITH, died at Madras, 12 Nov. 1829, a Major-General in the service of the East India

Company, aged 65. JANET LEITH, or ARNOTT, wife of James Arnott, mentioned on the other side, died at Edinburgh, aged 73, leaving a family. MARGARET LEITH, died at Edinburgh, March 13, 1835, aged 77. ELIZABETH LEITH, died at Edinburgh 29 April 1841, aged 81. Erected by the three surviving children of the said James Arnott and Janet Leith.
—Mr Leith of Whiteriggs was father of Major-General James Leith, long Judge Advocate-General in the East Indies. "Judge Leith" bought Whiteriggs, and gave it the name of Leithfield. His nephew, James Arnott, W.S., succeeded.

JANET FRASER, relict of the Rev. Lewis Reid, minister at Strachan, died at Manse of Fordoun, 26 Jan. 1798, aged 88. The Revd. ALEXANDER LESLIE, minister at Fordoun, died Sep. 15, 1807, in the 74 year of his age, and 49th of his ministry. . . . . . . MARGARET REID, relict of the Revd. Alexander Leslie, died at Fordoun, June 20, 1829, in the 92d year of her age. Their daughter GRACE, died at Manse of Fordoun, Dec. 23, 1837, aged 62. Their daughter JANET, died at Bathlodge, 18 June 1850, aged 80; Their daughter ELIZA, relict of William Lindsay of Oatlands, died at Aberdeen, 22 July 1855, aged 83; and the Revd. JAMES, D.D., their son, died at Bathlodge, 20 March 1858, aged 94, having resigned his charge at Fordoun, in 1843, after being minister there for 55 years.

The parish of Fordoun contains many interesting historical and topographical features, such as the ruins of the royal residence of Kincardine Castle, the sculptured stone at S. PALLADIUS' chapel, &c.; as elsewhere described by the writer of these notes.

The Fordoun portion of the parish has been Arbuthnott property from at least 1608.

According to the Aberdeen Breviary, the Pictish Saint ERCHARD was a native of this parish; and it is generally agreed that JOHN of FORDUN, author of the Scotichronicon, was connected with it either by birth or residence.

Lord MONBODDO, previously referred to, and JAMES BEATTIE, professor of Natural History in Marischal College, Aberdeen, were also natives of Fordoun.

The Luther, which is bridged in various places, washes the base of the hill upon which the church stands. It flows through a pretty dell, the beauties of which are celebrated in Beattie's Minstrel, the poet having been schoolmaster here.

The burying-place of Chapelyard (S. CATHERINE), on the west side of the parish, near the site of the old town of Kincardine, contains two small head stones, bearing respectively these names and dates :—WILLIAM ROSS, 1739; and WILLIAM TAYLOR, 1786. It is marked by a few trees, and an enclosing wall.

In 1707, Sir D. Carnegy of Pitarrow had a grant (Acta Parl., xi. Appx. 144), to hold two fairs, in addition to that of Palladius, or *Paddy*, which were named respectively CAMMOCK and S. JOHN's—the first to be held on the last Tuesday of May, the other on the 3d Tuesday of June. Another fair, called LADY Market, was held at the kirk of Fordoun on 6 July.

A somewhat odd case of obstructing the designing of a manse and glebe took place at Fordoun in 1601, as fully set forth in Pitcairn's Crim. Trials, vol. ii. p. 362.

~~~~~~~~~~~~~~~~~~~~~~~~

Echt.

(S. FINCAN, VIRGIN.)

THOMAS, son of Malcolm of Lundin, granted the church of *Eych*, *Hachtis*, or *Heyth*, to the monks of Scone, about 1220.

The present parish church was built about 1804, when Mr Forbes of Echt gave a new bell in exchange for the old one, which was dated 1783. This bell was preserved at Dun Echt House until lately, when it was accidentally broken. The front of the loft of the old kirk was ornamented with carved panels, some of which, dated 1688, are preserved at Whitehill Cottage.

[IN CHURCHYARD] :—

I.E : M.L.—Here lies JOHN ELPHINSTON, late of Bellabeg, who departed this life the 10th day of

Oct. 1742, aged 70 years. Also MARY LESLIE, his spouse, who departed this life the   day of 17 , aged   years. Likewise JEAN ELPHINSTON, their daughter, who departed this life the 6th day of February 1752, aged 29 years.

—Elphinstone, who sold the small estate of Bellabeg, in Strathdon, to Forbes of Newe, is said to have gone to the Milltown of Culairlie, in Echt, to reside with a daughter who was married to the farmer. The date of his wife's death has never been cut upon the stone. The Elphinstones of Bellabeg are supposed to have been descended from the Lords Elphinstone, who held Kildrumy and other lands on the Don.

Erected to the memory of WILLIAM SMITH, A.M., who died 21 October 1830, aged 22. In 1829 he completed his studies at the Divinity Hall of the U.S. Church, where he displayed talents calculated to inspire hopes of future eminence and usefulness in the church, had it pleased the Lord to spare him :—

Ere yet his lips proclaim'd to guilty men
That Grace Divine which he had liv'd upon,
The silver cord was loosed ; Affection mourns
An only Son, an only Brother, dead,
The church below, a choisest Jewel lost,
And Friendship, all bereaved, adores, and weeps.

Revd. ALEXANDER HENDERSON, died 30 May 1813, aged 57.

Revd. WILLIAM INGRAM, died 16th May 1848, aged 79.

Cairns and tumuli lie along the base of the hill called the Barmakin of Echt. Some remarkable specimens of the so-called Druidical circles are also in the parish. These, as well as the entrenchments which surround the Barmakin, are described in the Old and New Statistical Accounts of the Parish. The summit of the Barmakin, which is from 800 to 900 feet above the level of the sea, is flat, and contains, within the upper rampart, about an acre of ground. There are a series of entrenchments, with gates, or entrances, farther down the hill. It is one of those ancient structures, known as British forts, of which class are the two Caterthuns, near Brechin, and Glenshiora, in Badenoch. Amusing stories of odd sounds having been heard at, or near the Barmakin, which were supposed to foretell the coming struggle of the hapless reign of Charles I., are told in Gordon's Scots Affairs (vol. i., pp. 56-8.)

There was anciently a chapel at *Monksecht* (S. ——), now Monecht.

Thomas, or *Thom of the Loch*, a natural son of Alex. Forbes of Brux (*Alister Cam*), is said to have acquired Echt by marrying Marjory Stewart, the heiress, and neice of the Earl of Mar, 1437-60.

The estate of Echt now belongs to Lord Lindsay, heir apparent to the Earldom of Crawford, and author of the Lives of the Lindsays, &c. Dun Echt House, an elegant castellated mansion, has been recently erected by Lord Lindsay, almost under the shadow of the Barmakin.

Glenmoriston.

(S. COLUMBA.)

S. COLUMBA's well is marked by a tall pavement slab, near the gate to the House of Glenmoriston, which, with similar stones, erected some years ago, give a strange, weird look to the locality.

The family of Glenmoriston bury within the cemetery of S. COLUMBA, where there are several handsome monuments. From some of these the following inscriptions are copied :—

This stone is erected here in memory of the much honoured JOHN GRANT, leard of Glenmoriston, who died 1736, aged 79.

A.D. 1840 : Alexander Grant, son of JOHN GRANT, fifth laird of Glenmoriston, and his spouse JANET MACKENZIE, grand-daughter of Capt. Alexander Mackenzie of Gairloch, ancestors of Capt. George Grant of the Indian Army, has erected this monument as a token of affection, esteem, and regard, with which he cherishes their memory. They died at Bre, about the year 1730.—Deut. 32, 7 ; Prov. 10, 7.

The tomb of JAMES GRANT of Burnhall, W.S., 2d son of Patrick Grant of Glenmoriston, by Henrietta, daughter of James Grant of Ruthiemurchus, died 1834, aged 66 years. His family, JAMES, died at Barbadoes, 1829, aged 20 ; SIMON-FRASER, died at Edinburgh, 1829, aged 11 ; JOHN CHARLES, E.I.C.S., Bengal, died at Singapore, 1836, aged 28, at whose desire this tomb of his father and family was erected. HELEN, spouse of Alexander Macdonald of Berbice, died at Dawlish, Devonshire, 1840, aged 34.

—John-More Grant of Culcabock (son of Grant of Freuchy), had a charter of the lands and barony of Glenmoriston from King James IV. From this John-More, the present Grants of Glenmoriston are descended. If the above inscriptions are right, the pedigree of this family, as given in Burke (Baronage, 1850), appears to want revision.

Sacred to the memory of PATRICK M'DONELL, M.D., H.E.I.S., only child of Donald McDonell of Aonach, and of Barbara Grant, his spouse. Born at Inmerick, Glenmoriston 1798, died at Mandivie, in Cutch, Bombay, 1825. Erected by his father similar to the tomb placed over his remains by his brother officers in India.

This place belongs to FINLAY M'LEOD, piper, Glenmoriston, who died 1842, aged 70. [Here follow the names of several children.]

Upon a shield built into the wall :—

Erected by PETER M'LEOD, son of Finlay M'Leod, piper to Glenmoriston. 1848.

Glenmoriston and Urquhart are united parishes in Inverness-shire. There are a number of burial places in both districts, which mostly bear the names of local saints.

Urquhart Castle, situated upon a rock overhanging Loch Ness, is one of the most imposing and picturesquely situated ruins in Scotland. It had been a place of great size and strength ; and, in addition to the ordinary means of defence known in old times, a peculiar arrangement appears about the windows, by which molten lead, or other destructive substances, could be poured upon the heads of invaders. It was besieged and taken by the forces of Edward I., 1303. In 1509, it and the barony of Urquhart came to the chief of the Clan Grant, and now belongs to the Earl of Seafield.

AT FOYERS.

Beautifully situated upon the south bank of Loch Ness, in the parish of ABERTARF, near the old mansion house and the celebrated Falls of Foyers, stands an obelisk, ornamented with the Fraser and Grant arms, and an urn upon the top. A marble slab, sunk into the pedestal, presents nicely executed carvings of two angels in alto-relievo, with upcast eyes, and the words, "Thy will be done—I am ready." The monument also bears this simple inscription :—

Sacred to the memory of JANE, spouse of Thomas FRASER of Balnain. She was the only child of Simon Fraser of Foyers, and of Elizabeth Grant, his wife. She added to superior personal graces and talents of the first order, the humblest piety, the sweetest temper, and the most devoted filial affection. Her spotless life was closed by a tranquil and christian death, on the 7th of July 1817, in the 22d year of her age. Matt. v. & 8.

—It is told that the site of this monument was a favourite retreat of the young lady whose memory it preserves, and of whose excellence and worth many interesting traits are yet remembered in the district. The first Fraser of Foyers was the fourth son of Hugh of Lovat and Kinnell, who died about 1410. Elizabeth Grant (Mrs Fraser's mother) was a daughter of Glenmoriston.

Essie.

(S. ——.)

THE churches of *Essy* and *Newyth*, both in the diocese of St. Andrews, were respectively rated at 14 and 20 merks each. In 1309, Robert the Bruce gave the advocation and donation of the kirk of Essy to the monks of Newbattle.

The parishes of "Essie and Neva" were unite in 1600.

The ruins of the old church of Essie are picturesquely situated upon a rising ground, close to the burn of Essie, which is the most considerable rivulet in the parish. It rises among the Sidlaw hills, from which it flows through the Glen of Danoon, and falls into the Dean, not far from the old kirk.

The church of the united parish, erected about 30 years ago, is conveniently situated, and nearly equi-distant from the two old churches.

Within the area of the ruins of Essie church a mutilated tombstone bears the arms of Lamy and Forbes, also these remains of an inscription :—

. . . . IOANNIS . . AMMEE, qvondam de Dvnkennie, qvi obiit 26 die mensis September . . . . . D.L : 1603 : C. F.

—Lamies were designed of Dunkenny from at least 1542. Subsequently the estate belonged to Bishop Lindsay (a cadet of Edzell), who died in 1640. Lamies reacquired it before 1682. Possibly they were of the old stock, and may have been ancestors of the present laird, Capt. L'Amy, whose father, JAMES L'AMY, was long sheriff-depute of Forfarshire, and died in 1854.

[IN CHURCHYARD] :—

THOMAS WHITE (1665) :—

We ar bvt earth, and earth is bvt fvme ;
We ar bvt novght, as novght we doe consvme.

JOHN LYON and wife (17—) :—

This man and his wife was diligent,
And in their dealings just ;
Who every way was excellent,
But now they ly in dust.
Waiting till Christ come in the skies,
With angels all around,
Commanding them straight to rise
And be with glory crown'd.

DAVID WIGHTOUN, a. 75 (1717) :—

Below this Tomb there lyeth thus,
Ean DAVID WIGHTOUN in the Bush ;
A Rabie Father was indeed ;
As you may see this tomb to read.
In English and arithmetic both
He could both write and spell ;
In Greek a great proficient—
In Hebrew did excell.

WILLIAM GIBB, Balkerrie (1737) :—

Remember man, that against Death,
There is not an antidote ;

Be rich or poor, or what you may,
You'll die & be forgot.

D. CHISHOLM's mother (1774) :—

She honoured as she bore the Christian name,
Her closet nourish'd her celestial flame ;
Her social hours with love & pleasure flow,
The love no art, no guile the pleasure knew.
Unclouded virtue shone thro' all her life—
The blameless virgin, & the faithful wife :
Long she endur'd affliction's sharpest pain
But turn'd her crosses into heavenly gain.
All this her husband, & her son who witnessed
    this express'd,—
Go live like her, & die for ever blest.

Rev. ADAM DAVIDSON, ordained minister of Essie, Dec. 1702, died Oct. 1720 :—

His soul still breathed upward, and a last,
Arrived above – the mantle's here downcast.

Rev. ALEXANDER FINLAYSON, ordained minister of Essie, Sep. 1721, died 1731.

Excepting the name, and a spring well, there is now no trace of the "Chapel of the BLESSED MARY at Balgownie, in the parish of Essie," of which there is charter evidence in 1450.

Isabella, Countess of Mar, in the time of Robert III., gave a charter of the lands of the Kirktown of Essy to Walter Ogilvy ; and his successor, Alexander Ogilvy of Auchterhouse, gave 10 merks out of the barony of Essy, for the foundation of a chaplain within the Cathedral Church of Brechin.

Nevay.

(S. ——.)

THIS church is sometimes called *Kirkinch*, or the kirk on the island, the knoll or inch upon which it stands having been at one time surrounded by a marsh, or swamp.

The date of 1651 is upon the ruins of the old church ; and the door lintel is also inscribed, 16 : D. N. 95. Upon the surrounding wall :—
BUILT BY SUBSCRIPTION, 1843.

A mutilated tombstone within the area of the church bears these traces :—

.... YRIES . IN . N .... E . FOLLOWS
—This is all that remains of an inscription which is locally said to have read when entire—" Here ly the Tyries in Nevay, honest men and brave fellows." Tyries were designed of Lunan in the 15th century. They were long proprietors of the estate of Drumkilbo, in Meigle; and one of them was slaughtered by Crichton of Ruthven, 1581. The family was knighted, and Sir Thomas of Drumkilbo was at Aberdeen with Montrose, in 1644. There were NEVOYS of that ilk, one of whom, Sir David, a lord of Session, assumed first the title of Lord Reidie, afterwards that of Lord Nevoy.

MARGARET, wf. of David BARRON, Lieut., R.N., d. 1827, a. 55 :—

> Oft shall sorrow heave my breast,
> Whilst my dear MARGARET lies at rest ;
> Oft shall reflection bring to view,
> The happy days I've spent with you.

DAVID BARRON, on two sons (1853) :—

> Here are repos'd two goodly youths,
> Which loving brothers were ;
> Endu'd with grace beyond their years,
> And virtues very rare.
> Such was their life that we may hope,
> They're gone beyond the sky,
> To sing and spend, without an end,
> A sweet Eternity.

A remarkable sculptured stone, which lay long in the burn, now stands between the burn and the old church of Essie.

A circular mound, at Castleton of Essie, appears to have been the site of a baronial residence ; and at Ingliston, traces of a large encampment are said to have existed towards the end of the last century.

Alex. Ogilvy, sheriff of Angus, had the barony of Neve, on the resignation of William Cunningham of Kilmauris (t. Rob. III.), out of the farm of which he gave 10 merks to the foundation of a chaplain in the kirk of Auchterhouse.

Kirkmichael.

(S. MICHAEL, ARCHANGEL.)

THE church of *Kirkmichel*, in Banffshire, was a mensal church of the Bishops of Moray; and the district belonged, in property, to the M'Duffs, the old Earls of Fife. S. MICHAEL'S Well adjoins the church where, at one time, " the winged guardian, under the semblance of a fly, was never absent from duty," and which the superstitious invoked to their aid on all emergencies, whether of life or of death !

The church, a plain building, erected in 1807, stands upon the haugh, on the south side of the Aven. It contains five monuments. One is of freestone, and thus inscribed :—

Here lies the body of ANN LINDSAY, spouse of John Gordon of Glenbucket, and daughter of the Right Hon. Sir Alexander Lindsay of Evelack, who departed this life on the 9th day of June 1750 aged 50 years. Also HELLEN REID, spouse of William Gordon, Esq. of Glenbucket, and daughter of the Right Hon. Sir John Reid of Barra, who died on the 5th of May 1766, aged 52 years ; and LILIAS McHARDY, spouse of John Gordon, Esqr. of Glenbucket, and daughter of William McHardy, late in Delnilat, who died May 30, 1829, aged 78 years. And of ELSPET STEWART, spouse of Charles Gordon, Esq. St Bridget, and daughter of William Stewart, Esq. Ballentrewan, who died 2d February 1856, aged 63 years.

—A slab in the churchyard, which has disappeared within the last year or two, bore the following epitaph to the lady first-named in the above inscription :—

Here l . . . . . the body of M . . . . . . LINDSEY, lady Glenbucket, d . . . . . to the Hon. Sir Alexander Lindsay . . Evelack, who in the 50th year of her . . . departed this life on the 9th of June l . . . :—

> Her stately person, Beauty, Great,
> Her charity and lowly heart ;
> Her meekness and obedience ;
> Her chastity, and her good sense,

Do all combine to eternise,
Her fame and praise above the skies.

—The Gordons of Glenbucket were descended of those of Rothiemay, whose grandfather was of the family of Lesmore (Nisbet). The Lindsays of Evelick (Perthshire), were descended of a younger brother of Sir Walter of Edzell. In 1666, a baronetcy was created in the Evelick branch of the Lindsays. The Reids, who bought Barra about 170 years ago, were created baronets in 1707.

Another tablet, within the kirk, commemorates the death of JOHN STEWART (of the Auchnahyle and Lynchork family), Captain in H.M. 39th regt., who died at Bangalore, E.I., in 1835, aged 46; also two of his brothers, ROBERT, who died at Jamaica in 1824, aged 25, and CHARLES, M.D., 86th regt., who died at Kurrachee, E.I., in 1844, aged 40, &c.

Upon a circular marble slab, built into the south wall, embellished with the Grant arms, is this inscription:—

To the memory of PATRICK GRANT, Esq. of Glenlochy, lately of Stocktoun, who died 15 April 1783, aged 74; and of BEATRIX, his wife (daughter of Donald Grant, Esq. of Inverlochy), who died 24 January 1780, aged 69. This monument is erected in testimony of filial affection and gratitude to the best of parents, by John Grant, Chief-Justice of Jamaica.

—A table-shaped stone, outside the church, is inscribed as above, except that it bears to be erected "to the best of parents by Francis Grant of Kilgraston." This branch of the Grants is descended from John of Frenchy, 4th son of Grant of Grant. The above-named John, long Chief-Justice of Jamaica, bought the estate of Kilgraston, in Perthshire. He died issueless, and was succeeded by his younger brother, the above Francis Grant, who married a daughter of Oliphant of Rossie, and died in 1819. Francis was succeeded by his eldest son John, who married a sister of Lord Gray. Lord Gray and his elder sister having both died without issue, Mr Grant's daughter (widow of the Hon. Mr Murray), is now Baroness Gray. Sir Francis Grant, P.R.A., a well-known portrait painter, is the fourth son of the above Francis Grant; and the 5th son is the brave Lieut.-Gen. Sir James Hope Grant, late Commander-in-Chief at Madras.

A beautifully executed monument of Aberdeen granite (upon which are carvings of the insignia of the Bath, a sword and shield cross ways, from which medals are suspended, and inscribed, NIVE, VICTORIA, and TO THE BRITISH ARMY, 1793-4), bears:—

Underneath lie the mortal remains of WILLIAM-ALEXANDER GORDON, Lieut.-General in H.M.S., Colonel of the 54th regt. of foot, C.B. Born at Croughly, 21 March 1769, died at Nairn, 10 Augt. 1856, aged 87.

—Two monuments relating to the same family are within the church. One to JAMES GORDON, Esq., Croughly, who died in 1812, aged 86, and his wife ANNE FORBES, who died in 1818, aged 82 (the parents of Lieut.-Gen. Gordon.) The second monument is to ROBERT GORDON, Esq., who died in 1828, aged 47, and to several of his children.

Upon the top of a table-shaped tombstone in the churchyard:—

To preserve this burying ground, and in pious regard to the memory of FINLAY FARQUHARSON of Auchriachan, who possessed this place since 1569, son to Findlay Farquharson, Esq. of Invercauld; likewise WILLIAM FARQUHARSON who died anno 1719, aged 80 years, who was the ninth man of that family who possessed Auchriachan, and JANET GRANT his spouse, who died anno 1720, aged 78. Also WILLIAM FARQUHARSON, son of Inver.... who died anno 1723, aged 30, and ELIZABETH FARQUHARSON his spouse, who died anno 1772, aged 78; also SOPHIA McGRIGOR, who died 15 May 1769 aged 59, spouse to Robert Farquharson in Auchriachan, who erected this monument, 1789.

The said ROBERT FARQUHARSON died in 179—. WILLIAM, his son died in Aprill 1811, and ALEXANDER, the last in the male line, died 11 Nov. 1835, aged 78. Janet Farquharson, Robert's eldest daughter, married James Cameron, Ballenlish, and this tablet is renewed by their son, Angus Cameron of Firhall, 1851:—

These bodies low lie here consign'd to rest,
With hopes with all to rise among the blest:

Sweet be their sleep, and blessed their wakening.
Reader! pray for those that pray for thee.
—" Achriachan, which, for about 200 years, was the inheritance of a branch of the Farquharsons, is now (1775) the property of the Duke of Gordon."

Within a railed enclosure, upon a handsome granite cross: —

In memory of Capt. JAMES GORDON, who died at Ivybank, Nairn, 9th April 1867, aged 90. He served in the Peninsula with the 92d Highlanders, and received the war medal with seven clasps. He was also present at Waterloo, and received the medal. He never made an enemy, or lost a friend.

Near the above is the following record of another race of gallant Highlanders: —

Capt. ROBERT McGREGOR, of the Clan Alpine Fencibles, and 14th Battalion of Reserve, died at Delavorar, 5 Oct. 1816, in the 80th year of his age. His sons, PETER, Lieut. 17th regt. of foot, was killed at the head of the Grenadiers of that regt., at the storming of Fort Chumera, in the East Indies, in the 26th year of his age; JOHN, Lieut. in the 88th regt., was killed at the attack on Buenos Ayres, in the 17th year of his age; JAMES, Lieut. H. P. 84th regt. died at Delavorar, in his 32d year. [The deaths of other members of this family are recorded.]

A rudely-shaped cross, formed out of a slab of gneiss, about five feet high, with a hole pierced through the shaft, between the arms of the cross, stands beside the monument to Captain James Gordon. It is said to have been used by the natives for resting their spears or lances upon when they came to Divine service; and a story is told of some of the more sacrilegious of the Highlanders having killed a priest by the side of the stone, for his being too strict in demanding attendance at church!

This, however, had very possibly been the cross of S. MICHAEL, round which, in byegone times, the people of these parts (as was customary elsewhere), had assembled for the purpose of buying and selling commodities—markets having been originally held in churchyards, and upon Sundays. As such, it is a relic of much local interest, and possibly of high antiquity.

A chapel dedicated to S. BRIDGET stood near Tomintoul in old times; and a spring in the limestone rock of Craigchalkie is known by the name of S. JESSIE.

The *Village of Tomintoul*, which was begun in 1750, occupies the top of a bleak hillock. It consists of one street, about half a mile long, built on both sides, with a market square near the middle of it. Many of the houses are ruinous. As a whole, the place has few attractions for tourists, unless about Delnaboe, where there are some fine bits of romantic scenery. But were the means of communication less difficult between the Dee, the Don, and the Spey, by the way of Tomintoul, it would improve the place, as well as the habits and tastes of the people.

A *quoad sacra* church and manse were erected at the village about 1826. The Roman Catholics being a numerous body in the district, have a chapel, school, and priest's house here. This inscription is over the front of the chapel:—

Bene fundata est Domus Dom. supra firmam petram. Deo sub tutelâ B. MARIÆ VIRGINIS et B. MICHAELIS ARCHANGELI dedicata 1837.

[The House of the Lord is well founded on a firm rock. Dedicated in 1837 to God, under the protection of the Blessed VIRGIN MARY, and the Blessed ARCHANGEL MICHAEL.]

The adjoining cemetery contains several neat tombstones. One of these, erected in 1843, presents some orthographical peculiarities:—

> Trouble sore, I shurely bore
> Physicians was in vain
> Till God above, by his great love,
> Reliev'd me of my pain.
> Adieu dear friends who laid me here
> Where I must lie till Christ appear
> And on that day I hope it 'll be
> A joyful rising into me.

———o———

Cupar-Angus.

(THE VIRGIN MARY.)

THE burial-ground of Cupar-Angus is upon the site of the Abbey, which was founded by King Malcolm in 1164. It is said to have been previously used as a Roman camp.

A monument to a monk of the monastery, who died in 1450, bears the effigy of a priest incised, the upper portion of which has been broken and lost within the last few years—possibly at the recent rebuilding of the church. When the stone was in its more entire state, these words were round the margin :—

.... monachus . de . cupro . qui . obiit . anno . dñi . millesimo . quadringentesimo . quąggesio ....

Another slab, preserved at the manse, appears to be the tombstone of ARCHIBALD MACVICAR, who was provost of the collegiate church of Kilmun, Argyllshire, 1529-48 :—

Hic . iacet . dñs . archibald' . m'vic . olim prpos . de . kilmun .

I have been told by old residenters of fragments of other two monuments : one bore :—

.... Willhelmus . de . Montefixo ....

The other :—

.... Gilbertus . de . Hay ....

—The first of these monuments had referred to some one of the family of MONTIFIX, or MUSCHET, lords of Cargill, near Cupar, of which lands they had a grant from William the Lion. They were considerable benefactors to the Abbey, and failed in the male line towards the middle of the 14th century, when one of three coheiresses became the wife of Sir John Drummond, ancestor of the Earls of Perth. By her husband she had, with other issue, ANNABELLA, Queen of Robert III., and mother of James I. of Scotland.

The other fragment belonged to the HAYS of Errol, who were by far the largest benefactors to the Abbey. It may have been part of a recess tomb, the front of which (engraved in Memorials of Angus and Mearns), still remains, as well as the mutilated effigy of a knight in armour. Possibly two of the figures in the panels are intended to illustrate the absurd story of the Hays and Luncarty. The Hays were descended of an Anglo-Norman baron who settled in the Lothians in the 11th century. He had two sons who became respectively the ancestors of the Hays of Errol, and the Hays of Tweeddale. The male line of the latter branch is still carried on ; but that of the former failed in the person of Charles, twelfth Earl of Errol (v. p. 43.) The Hays of Errol had their burial place here ; and, according to " the coppy of the Tabill quhilk ves at Cowper of al the Erles of Erroll qnhilk ver buryd in the Abbey Kirk thair," as printed in the Spalding Club Miscellany (vol. ii., pp. 347-9), the seventh Earl, who died at Slains in 1585, was laid at Cupar, beside fifteen of his ancestors. There were two GILBERTS HAY buried here, one in 1333, the other in 1436, to the last of whom the fragment above referred to had possibly related.

In south-west lobby of the church, two marble tablets are respectively inscribed as below :—

Erected by the parishioners of Coupar-Angus, to the memory of their late worthy pastor, the Rev. JOHN HALKETT, who died 21 April 1828, in the 51st year of his age, and 21st of his ministry.

Adjoining the above :—

In memoriam parentis amantissimae et percarae quae A.D. 1771, obiit 68 annos nata, filius Rob^{tus} Robertson, M.D., F.R.S., F.A.S.L., Nosocomij Reg. Grenovic Medicus ; Itemque, in memoriam ANNÆ sororis suae, hoc marmor ponendum curavit.

[To the memory of a most loving and very dear mother, who died A.D. 1771, aged 68 years ; and also to the memory of his sister ANN. Robert Robertson, M.D., F.R.S., F.A.S.L., Physician to the Royal Hospital, Greenwich, caused this tablet to be erected.]

—Dr R. wrote numerous books and essays relating to his profession. I have been unable to learn anything of his parentage ; and have to thank H. F. Prowse, Esq., senior clerk, Royal Hospital, Greenwich, for the following interesting particulars of his official career :—" Robert Robertson, M.D., was appointed Physician of the Institution

20th Dec. 1790, and was superannuated on his full salary of £500 per annum, 30th Nov. 1818, after a period of upwards of fifty years' service. During the time of his holding the office of Physician, he was also a member of the Board of Directors; and continued to be a member of the same until its dissolution in May 1829. He died 30th Sept. 1829. I may add, as a tradition amongst us, that he married when over sixty years of age, and saw two of his children attain the age of twenty-one years."

The following inscriptions are from tombstones (erect, flat, and table-shaped), in various parts of the burial-ground :—

Heir lyes ane honest woman named ANNA BLAK, spovs to Iohn Makfarland, who depairted the 16 day of Apprile 1685, and of her age 61 years.

Heir layes GEORGE MALICE, son to Androw Malice and Margaret Pinkerton in Cowper, who depr'ted 24 day of Apryl 1685, of age 10 years.

O dear child, since We Can not
Thy converss here Enjoy,
Weell heast to the Where thou shal be,
Happy without Anoy.

Heir layes ane honnest man ALEXANDER THOM, who departed in May 1684, and of his age 60; and CRISTAN CHRISTY, his spovs, died the 24 of March 1701, of hir age 62, indvellers in Bilbo. &c.

1799 : To the memory of GEORGE NICOL, Esq. of Pleasenthill, this stone is erected. He died the 3d Janr. 1798, aged 53 years.

Erected by the Relief Congregation, Coupar Angus, to the memory of JAMES STEWART, builder there, who died 3 Aug. 1861, aged 85; and who generously conveyed his whole property, heritable and moveable, for the support, in all time coming, of the preaching of the Gospel in the Relief Church, Coupar Angus.

JEAN PORTER (who d. 1800, a. 45), bore twelve children to her h. GEO. STEVENSON, farmer, Balbrogie (who d. 1836, a. 84) :—

Alexander, Jean, Robert, & Agnes,
Are here laid in the dust;
The twelth is with her in the coffin laid—
Submit to death we most.

Erected by the Kirk Session to the memory of JOHN CAMPBELL, taylor in Cuper Angus, who bequeathed £100 ster. to the Poor of the Parish, and directed the interest to be applied by the Kirk Session. A native of Badenoch, he resided the last 30 years in Cupar, & died the 23d day of May 1814, aged 50. [Acts xx. 35, cut in Greek characters.]

Upon a plain head-stone :—

Sacred to the memory of Mr THOMAS BELL, comedian, late of the Theatre Royal, Edinburgh, a respectable performer, an agreeable companion, and an honest man. While on the *Stage* of life he encountered some of the rudest shocks of adversity, and felt the chill gripe of penury in many a chequered *Scene ;* but, possessed of a happy equanimity of temper, a social disposition, and a well informed mind, the arrows of misfortune fell powerless. On the 31st of August 1815, the *Curtain* of fate dropt on the *Drama* of his existence, and he *Retired* from the *Theatre* of the world, to the sorrow and regret of all who had the pleasure of his acquaintance.

Erected by the Dundee Eccentric X Society, in testimony of their esteem and respect for Mr BELL, an honorary member.

—In noticing the death of Mr Bell, the *Dundee Magazine* (Aug. 1815) says that " he went under the appellation of 'Cousin-Bell.' He was descended from a very respectable family in Ireland; and commenced his theatrical career (we believe) in Dundee, when the celebrated 'Old Bland' was manager. Mr Bell was a very respectable performer, an agreeable companion, and an honest man."

THOMAS EDWARD (1799) :—
Each revolving year,
Each hour of Life's short span,
Damps the bige hopes,
And points Mortality to Man.

The following, said to have been at Cupar-Angus, is copied from the *Dundee Magazine* for 1799, p. 221 :—

" Erected by the *deceast* George Small, and his mother Margaret Husband, and all her children, *Except John.*"

The only remaining portion of the ancient Abbey of Cupar stands at the south-west corner of the church-yard, and consists of an arched doorway flanked by buttresses. The remains of stone coffins, mouldings, and monuments, are frequently found in the kirk-yard. About four years ago a mutilated slab was disinterred. It bore the following inscription, which has been kindly communicated by the Rev. Dr Stevenson:—

✠HIC . IACET . VENERABILIS . PATER . DOMINUS IOHANNES . SCHANWEL . QUONDAM . ABBAS . DE CUPRO . QUI . OBIIT . A . D . M . D . VI.

[Here lies a venerable father in God, JOHN SCHANWEL, late of the Abbey of Cupar, who died A.D. 1506.]

—According to the *Reg. Ep. Brechin.*, (i. 220), *Thomas* (?) Schauvel was sub-prior of Cupar in 1500, and is a witness to a deed by Abbot John Campbell regarding the lands of Redgorton, dated 6th May of same year.

Carved stones are to be seen in some old houses at Cupar; and other bits are placed round the watch-house which stands near the middle of the burial-ground. As in most cases, this building was put up during the resurrection-mania. It bears the following inscription:—

1829: Erected by Subscription of the Parish, supplemented by Messrs Jn. Storrier, Wm. Don, Wm. Hunter, Wm. Gellatly.

Towards the close of the last century, when the old waulk, or fulling mill of Cupar-Angus was taken down a door lintel was discovered which bore representations of the objects mentioned below, also these names:—

ANDREW CHAPMAN AND MARGET TOD, [The waulk-mill sheers, and the pressing brod.]

A *saying*, embodied in the three lines which follow, had, possibly, at the time been illustrative of the characteristics of the places named, but *when* is not condescended upon. The first-named parish joins Cupar on the south, and the latter is upon the north side of the Isla:—

Kettins for singin';
Cupar for ringin';
Bendochy for preachin'!

The annexed wood-cut (from *Memorials of Angus and the Mearns*, in which there is an account of the Abbey of Cupar), is part of the tomb to the Hays of Errol, referred to at p. 72, *supra*.

Fetteresso.

(S. CARAN, BISHOP CONFESSOR.)

THE church of *Fethiressach* and its chapel, the latter of which stood at Cowie (*supra*, p. 53), are rated at 20 merks in the Old Taxation. Both places of worship belonged to St Andrews; and in 1246, the kirk of *Fethirassach* was dedicated by Bishop David.

In 1425, Bishop Wardlaw converted the church of Fetteresso into a prebend, and gave it and its pertinents to the royal chapel of S. Mary *de rupe*, or Kirkheugh, of St Andrews.

The bell upon the church bears:—

FETTERESSO, 1736;

and the belfry is dated 1737. The church consisted of a nave, with an aisle upon the north side. Both are now roofless; but the walls, which are clad with ivy, are pretty entire, and occupy a rising ground in the middle of the church yard. Being situated upon the banks of the Carron, and close to the hamlet of the Kirktown, with its tile and heath-covered cottages, and surrounded by spreading trees, the locality is altogether one of much picturesque beauty. It ought to be stated that the preservation of the old kirk is due to the good taste of the late Lieut.-Col. Duff of Fetteresso, who bought the fabric to prevent its being demolished.

A skew-put stone bears .. 16 . A . F .; and the date of 1720 is upon one of the lintels of the aisle. An arched door-lintel, cut from a single block of red sandstone, and the remains of a piscina (built up), are both objects of some antiquity and interest. A fragment of a grave-stone within and over the north-west door, presents these detached letters:—

.... patr ...... anno ....

A shield in the east wall, with the arms of Mowat and Rait (?) impaled, and boldly carved, along with the initials, I. M : A—, is a 17th century work. This may have been part of a tomb to the Mowats, who were at one time in Glithno.

The following inscriptions are from monuments *within the Old Kirk*. The first is from a mutilated slab, in the area, and upon it is a shield charged with the Hay arms:—

HEIR . LYIS . FRANCI . . . . . SON
TO . THE . LAIRD . OF . WRY . 1610.
MEMENTO . MORI.

—The Hays of Errol acquired Ury about 1413, from Fraser, thane of Cowie, of which thanedom Ury formed a portion. In 1648 Ury passed, by purchase, to Colonel Barclay (*infra*, p. 82.)

A marble slab, built into the south wall of the kirk, bears this inscription:—

To the memory of the Revᵈ John Ballantyne, late pastor of the United Secession Church, Stonehaven, who died Dec. 5th 1830, in the 51st year of his age, and 24th of his ministry. He was a man greatly distinguished for his intellectual endowments and religious worth; exemplary for personal Godliness, and the diligent discharge of his official duties; zealous in teaching the young to remember their Creator, and wise and condescending in the edification of all who were placed within the sphere of his usefulness. His body lies 10 feet to the north of this monument, erected by the members of his congregation and some others, who enjoyed his friendship, and admired his character.

—Mr Ballantyne, who was a native of Kinghorn, in Fife, wrote An Examination of the Human Mind, &c. (*v.* "Recollections" of Mr Ballantyne, by the Rev. Dr Longmuir. Abdn. 1862.)

From a table-shaped stone (enclosed) within the area of the old kirk:—

Under this stone are interred the mortal remains of Margaret Kemp, wife of George Thomson, minister of this parish. She died on the 4th day of June 1836, aged 56 years. And also the remains of the said George Thomson, who died on the 15th July 1862, in the 88th year of his age, and the 62d of his ministry.

—Mr Thomson, who was a native of Grange, in Banffshire, left considerable means, the greater part of which he bequeathed to build and endow a church in the Glen of the Cowton. A church and manse have been erected in terms of Mr Thomson's will; and in August 1872, the Rev. Mr

Keith was inducted to the charge, which is known by the name of RICKARTON.

Besides that of Rickarton, there is also a kirk at COOKNEY. It occupies an elevated position about a mile north of Muchals Castle. This church was built about 1816, since which time it has been much enlarged to accommodate an increasing population; and the district was erected into a *quoad sacra* parish in 18—. A school adjoins the church, and the manse is a little to the s.-west.

The original church of Cookney stood near to Newhall. It was built about 1760, and was called the *Sod Kirk*, in consequence of the walls and seats having been constructed of turf. According to tradition, the *Sod Kirk* was the grateful offering of a seaman who was saved from a vessel which was wrecked upon the neighbouring coast.

Within an enclosure, in the north-east corner of the kirk of Fetteresso (surmounted by the Duff arms and motto, VIRTUTE ET OPERA), two slabs are respectively inscribed:—

[1.]

"Blessed are the dead which die in the Lord."

ROBERT WILLIAM DUFF, Esq. of Fetteresso, died 22d March 1834, aged 66; MARY ABERCROMBY DUFF of Glassaugh, his wife, died 6th Nov. 1833, aged 65. They were endeared to their family and friends by their benevolent dispositions, and genuine integrity of heart. This monument is erected in veneration of their memory, by their affectionate son, Robert Duff. The mortal remains of their eldest son and heir ROBERT DUFF, Esqre. of Fetteresso and Culter, repose beside those of his parents. He died aged 71, the 30th December MDCCCLXI, respected, lamented, regretted by all who knew him.

[2.]

GEORGE DUFF died the 8th July 1793, aged two years. Erected by his parents in memory of this promising child.

—Admiral Duff acquired Fetteresso about 1782. He married his relative, Helen, 4th daughter of the Earl of Fife, and dying in 1787, was succeeded by his son, the above-named R.-Wm., who was Lieut.-Col. of the Forfarshire Militia. Lieut.-Col. Duff married the only child of George Morrison, Esq. of Haddo, and by her, he succeeded to the estate of her grand-father, General Abercromby of Glassaugh. Their grand-son, M.P. for Banffshire, is now proprietor of Fetteresso, &c. (*infra*, p. 17.) Admiral Duff and the lairds of Whitehills, Culter, and Hatton of Auchterless, were sons of Patrick Duff of Craigston, who had five children by his first, and twenty-one by his second wife.

Four marble tablets, built into the south side of the north aisle, are respectively inscribed:—

[I.]

Sacred to the memory of Lieut.-Colonel WILLIAM RICKART-HEPBURN of Rickarton, who died in London in 1807. And of Mrs JANET RICKART-HEPBURN, his spouse, who died at Stonehaven, 2d Oct. 1842.

[2.]

ROBERT RICKART-HEPBURN, Esquire of Rickarton, died 17 August 1837, aged 30.

[3.]

In memory of CATHERINE JANE HEPBURN, eldest daughter of Robert Rickart-Hepburn, Esquire of Rickarton, who died 7th May 1844, in the 18th year of her age; and also of her sister JULIET, who died 22d July 1844, in the 15th year of her age. Malachi, iii. 17.]

[4.]

In memory of ROBERT WILLIAM RICKART-HEPBURN, Esquire of Rickarton, Kincardineshire, who died at Rickarton on Wednesday 28th October 1857, in the 30th year of his age. [Matt. v. 7.] This tablet is erected by his widow.

—Lieut.-Colonel W. R.-Hepburn was sometime M.P. for Kincardineshire. He was the eldest son of Catherine, daughter and heiress of David Rickart of Rickarton, and of her husband, James Hepburn, of the Congalton family. The last laird, who died in 1857, was succeeded by an uncle. The first Rickart of Rickarton was descended from the Rickarts of Arnage in Ellon, who were at one time merchants in Aberdeen. A tablet in north wall of same aisle bears:—

Sacred to the memory of ALEXANDER GORDON of Newhall, who died 16th May 1849, aged 85 years; and MARGARET LEITH, his wife, who died 3d May 1845, aged 75 years.

—Mr Gordon was the son of a farmer in Gartly.

He made money in Jamaica, and left an only daughter, who married the late Dr Thomson, a medical practitioner in Stonehaven.

The next inscriptions are from monuments *in various parts of the Church-yard*:—

. . . . ELSPET . CHALMER . SPOVS . TO . ANDROV . MIL . QVILA . DEPART . . . OF . AGE . . 3 . .

—The above is from the grave-stone of the wife of Mr A. Mill, senior. She died in 1610, and was the mother of the minister mentioned in the next inscription. His tombstone has been lately placed upon two stone rests. Upon one of the rests are the words—"The grave of Mr Andrew Milne, minister of Fetteresso, 1605-40."—The following is upon the face of the stone:—

HIC . IACENT . MARITVS . REVERENDVS . FIDELISQ'. DEI . SERVVS . MAGR . ANDREAS . MILEVS . IVNIOR . 35 . ANNIS . MYSTES . FETTERESSANVS . ET . CON-IVNX . EJ' . CHARA . FÆMINA . GENEROSA . VIZ . KATHARINA . ÆRESKINA . CVM . EOR'. LIBERIS . 18 . IS . OBIIT . 12 . OCTOBRIS . DIE . ANNO . DOI . 1640 . ÆTATIS . SVÆ . ANNO . 58 . EA . FATIS . CESSIT . KAL . MARTII . ANNO . 1631 , ÆTATIS . 44 . AC . KATHA-RINA . FARQ'RSONA . AVIA . PRÆFATI . MINISTRI ✠ SECVR' . RECVBO . MVNDI . PERT.ESVS
✠ INIQVI ✠
ET . DIDICI . ET . DOCVI . VVLNERA . CHRISTE
✠ TVA ✠
M.A.M : K.Æ : K.F : M.I.M : C.I.
MEMENTO . MORI . VITA . LABITVR .

[Here lie a revered husband, and a faithful servant of God, Mr ANDREW MILNE, junior, for 35 years minister of Fetteresso, and his beloved wife KATHERINE ERSKINE, a lady of honourable birth, with 18 of their children. He died 12th Oct. 1640, in the 58th year of his age, and she on 1st March 1631, in her 44th year. Here also lies KATHARINE FARQUHARSON, grand-mother of the foresaid minister. Weary of an unjust world I rest secure, having both learned and taught thy healing wounds, Oh Christ.]

—Mr Milne, junior, succeeded his father in the church of Fetteresso. The latter began life as a teacher in Montrose, and was preceptor to James Melvill, who describes him as "a lerned, honest, kynd man . . . . verie skilfull and diligent" (Diary,

p. 21.) Mr Milne was appointed first to the church of Dunlappy, and afterwards to Dunottar and Fetteresso (*supra*, p. 49.) In consequence of the elder Milne's services to the Church, and owing to the smallness of the living at Fetteresso, "quhilk is not able to sustane him conveniently as becometh," King James, in 1601, made a special grant to him of the third of the stipend of Cowie. Milne had much intercourse with Erskine of Dun ; and his son's wife may have been in some way related to that family.

One tomb-stone, name defaced, is dated 1600. Upon another slab, of date 1668, these words only are traceable :—

. . . . ANE WERTOVS WOMAN IEAN GORDON . . . .

From other two fragments :—

HERE LYES . . . . . ANDER FALCONER . . . TVELF IVNE 1664, OF AGE 80, AND . . . . . .

IACOBVS . . . . EST IAM OCTOGENARIVS 4 FEB . ANNO . 16-2.

From a flat stone :—

Heir lyes ane godly and vpright man, VILLIAM GREIG, somtyme in Elfhil, vho departed the 27 yeir of his age, 23 Dec. 1648 :—

And he come vho is Sharons fragrant rose,
To give his angels charge to be his train ;
This is throvgh Christ his sweit bed of repose,
While from the dvst all flesh shall ryse again.

A stone (upon which the Mowat and Harvey arms are impaled) bears :—

Heir lyes a godly and provident man IOHN MOWAT, somtime in Glithno, who departed 6 of Ivlii 1655. ISOBEL HERVY, his vertvos spovs, who departed the 1 of Avgvst 1650.

Near the above :—

✠ Heir vnder lyeth in hope of a blessed resvrec-tione, the bodie of ane honeste man, DAVID MACKIE, vho dyed the j4 May 1668, late indveller at the Milne of Covie, of age 40 yrs. ; and heir lyes his brother ROBERT MACKIE, vho dyed 24 Novr. 1661, age 50 years.

R.M : D.M : A.C.
Ovr lyfe is shorte, and tis fvlle of sorrove,
Vere here today, and straight are gone tomorrove.

Two tablets, within an enclosure at the east end of the old kirk, are inscribed as follows :—

[1.]

Burial place of the Rev. JOHN HUTCHEON, minister of this parish for 37 years, died 27th Feb. 1800, aged 67. MARY MORISON, his wife, daughter of Provost James Morison of Elsick, died 11th Aug. 1775, aged 32. DAVID HUTCHEON, advocate in Aberdeen, died 10th Dec. 1832, aged 67. ALEXANDER, their eldest son, died in the Island of St Vincent, in the year 1812, aged 46. MARY, their second daughter, died 19th April 1794, aged 63. Also two sons, JAMES and JOHN, who died in infancy. This tablet was erected by ISOBEL, their only surviving daughter, relict of the Rev. William Paul, Professor of Natural Philosophy, King's College, Old Aberdeen, in memory of her beloved parents and their deceased children, who are all buried here except the said Alexander.

[2.]

Sacred to the memory of MARY, daughter of Robert Farquhar, Esq. of Newhall, who died May 1786, aged 23 years; and of ROBERT, son of Capt. Arthur Farquhar, R.N., C.B., &c., who died 14th Sept. 1816, in the 5th year of his age; and of Dr PETER GRANT, sometime physician in Aberdeen, who died at Mansefield, 23d Feb. 1837, aged 76 years; and of AMELIA FARQUHAR, his spouse, who died at Mansefield, 1st Dec. 1838, aged 69 years.

—The first Farquhar of Newhall was Robert, a merchant and stationer in Aberdeen, who married to his second wife the eldest daughter of Provost Morison of Aberdeen, laird of Elsick. The above-mentioned Mary and Capt. Arthur were by that marriage. The latter, who became a Rear-Admiral and K.C.B., died in 1813; and another son died a general officer in the East India Company's Service.

The next two inscriptions (the last of which is abridged) are from table-shaped stones (enclosed):—

Beneath this stone are interred the remains of ALEXANDER SILVER of Balnagubs. Having acquired a moderate fortune abroad, he purchased the residence of his Ancestors, the place of his Birth, in this parish, and for many years after he lived to enjoy it, beloved, esteemed, and respected, as a husband, father, friend, and neighbour. He died 30th December, 1791, aged eighty-two. Also his daughter ANN, who died 17th August 1784, in the fourteenth year of her age.

Abridged:—

GEORGE SILVER of Netherley, died 25th Sept. 1840, aged 72; JANE SMITH, his spouse, died 2d Dec. 1830, aged 59. [3 sons & 5 daughters, aged from 4 to 19 years, recorded dead, also] GEORGE, who died at Madeira, 7th April 1843, aged 35; JOHN, Lieut. 2d Regt. Bengal Fusiliers, died at Rangoon, 4th Nov. 1853, aged 30. JAMES, died at Bath, 8th July 1870, aged 54; also three of his children.

—The estate of Netherley passed, by purchase, some years ago, from the Silvers to Horatio Ross, Esq., the celebrated deer-stalker. It now belongs to W. N. Forbes, Esq. of Dunottar.

A head-stone lies below one of the monuments above-noticed. It presents some ornamental carvings, amongst which is a shield charged with a pair of compasses and a square. It has reference to the parents of the first Silver of Netherley, and is thus inscribed:—

Here under lyeth AGNES SILVER, spouse to John Silver, wright at Maryculter, who departed the 8th of Feb. 1721, and of her age 35.

From a monument (enclosed), near west gate:—

Here lie interred the remains of Dr WILLIAM NICOL, who died at Stonehaven, 25th Nov. 1827, aged 62 years. Also of his fifth daughter, GRACE, who died 18th March 1811, aged 20 months.

—Dr Nicol, who was the son of a local farmer, and a medical practitioner in Stonehaven, married Margaret, daughter of Mr Dyce of Badentoy, in Banchory-Devenick, a merchant and burgess of Aberdeen. Dr Nicol had six daughters, all of whom married opulent merchants, and an only son, JAMES-DYCE. The latter, who entered a mercantile house in India when little over fourteen years of age, made a fortune abroad. On returning home, he added Ballogie and others to his paternal estate; and represented his native county in Parliament from 1864, until his death in 1872. He was buried in the church-yard of Birse, in which parish his residence and property of Ballogie are situated.

WM. CRUICKSHANK, tenant, Mountboys, d. 1795, a. 74 :—

"He was admitted an Elder of this parish in 1754, the duties of which he discharged with great integrity till his death. A consummation devoutly to be wished for by every good man was, by the kindness of Providence, appointed for him. On his way home from church he was instantly translated, without a groan, from earth to heaven."

DONALD CHRISTIE, d. 1813, a. 83 ; his wf. JEAN CAMERON in 1809, a. 79 :—

"They lived happy in the fear of the THREE ONE. *Dhia mor priseil;* and, as time passed on, their hope in the BRANCH grew strong." &c.

In memory of WILLIAM MONCUR, late sergeant in the 71st Regiment of Foot, who, after suffering the fatigue and calamity of war, viz., in Spain and at Waterloo, died in peace at Toadstack, in Fetteresso, the 24th Oct. 1816, aged 32 years :—

Fix'd the term to all the race on Earth,
And such is the condition of our Birth ;
No force can death resist, no flight can save,
All fall alike, the fearful and the brave ;
Live to the Lord, that thou may'st die so too,
To live and die is all ye have to do.

From a head-stone :—

In memoriam : ROBERT DUTHIE, late baker in Stonehaven, who died 8th May 1847, aged 49 years. ROBERT, eldest son of the above, died 4th January 1865, aged 39 years.

—The last-mentioned in the above inscription contributed several articles in prose and verse to local periodicals and newspapers. A volume of his poetry, prefaced by a Memoir of his life, appeared some time after his death. He left a collection of MSS. on local history, which was diposed of by his widow.

ROBERT CHRISTIE, Skaterow, d. 1856, a. 31 :—

Pain was my portion, physic was my food,
Sighs was my devotion, Drugs did me no good ;
Till Christ my Redeemer, who knows what is best,
To ease me of my pain, has taken me to his rest.

JAS. ROBERTSON, d. at Fetteresso, 1863, a. 63 :—

That JAMES had failings must be confess'd,
But he had virtues by few possess'd.

1844 : Here are interred the remains of THOMAS TAIT, who, after discharging with faithful assiduity for upwards of half a century the duties of a teacher at Gateside of Muchalls, died there 21st May 1837, aged 86. This stone is erected to his memory by some of the many persons, who gratefully remember the benefits conferred by his tuition in the days of their youth. EUPHEMIA MEARNS, his wife, died 21st Dec. 18-8, aged 81.

In memory of ALEXANDER FIELDING, late sergeant-major, Sappers and Miners, H.E.I.C.S., a native of Stonehaven, who, after serving with distinction at Delhi, and other seiges and battles, during the mutiny in India, died from sunstroke at Bareilly, 25th May 1858, aged 31 years. Erected by his widow.

It was about 1813 that the old kirk of Fetteresso was disused, and a new place of worship erected. The present church stands about a mile to the east of the old one, and within the lobby are two marble tablets inscribed as follows :—

[1.]

Sacred to the memory of JOHN LUMSDEN, Esq. of Blairmonmonth, whose remains are interred in the burying-ground of his relatives, church-yard of Fetteresso. He died 1799, aged 84.

—Blairmonmonth, now Blairmormond, or Knowsie, is at the foot of the hill of Mormond, in Buchan, Aberdeenshire.

[2.]

To the memory of Captain WILLIAM GAVIN, a native of this parish, who was born Nov. 14, 1736, and died Dec. 1, 1792. This monument is erected by desire of his affectionate wife, MARGARET GARIOCH, of the family of Mergie, who, having survived him fifteen years, was buried by his side in the church-yard of Fetteresso. As a Soldier, he had the merit of raising himself from a Private station to the rank of Captain in the 51st Regiment of Foot, in which he continued to enjoy the esteem and respect of all who knew him—a steady, brave, and experienced officer : As a Man, he was possessed of a most enlightened mind, strictly honourable and benevolent ; of a Disposition so mild, inoffensive, and amiable, that he was generally beloved while living, and regretted when he died.

—The Gariochs of Mergie were a branch of those of Kinstair, in Alford. They were followers of the Stuarts, and "Alex. Garrioch, Ensign," was among the prisoners that were brought to Stirling Castle on 14th November 1715.

THE URY BURIAL PLACE

is situated in *The Howff Park*, upon one of the most elevated spots on the estate. It is surrounded by a stone dyke and some trees, and has much the appearance of a place of worship.

The Friends, or Quakers, occasionally met in it, and some of them, although not Barclays, are interred there. The vault was added to by the first Baird of Ury, so that what was originally the outer and north wall, now separates the old part, where the Barclays lie, from that of their successors.

Capt. Barclay (*infra*, p. 83), was the last of his name who possessed Ury. He married Mary Dalgarno, by whom he had two daughters. One of them attained woman-hood, and married first Mr Samuel Ritchie, secondly Mr James Tanner. She had three sons and one daughter by her first, and one daughter by her second husband. On 12th Jan. 1859, Mrs Tanner was served "nearest and lawful heir in general" to her father; and in 1869 she resumed her family name of Barclay-Allardice. In 1870, she claimed the Peerage of Strathern, Monteith, and Airth, before the House of Lords—a claim which was previously made by her father as heir to these Earldoms, through his mother (*v.* Sir H. Nicolas' *History of the Earldoms of Strathern, &c.*, Lond. 1842.)

As above stated, the northern portion of *The Howff* is set apart for the Bairds. ALEXANDER BAIRD, Esq., of the Gartsherrie family, who bought Ury in 1854 for about £120,000, died at London in 1862. He erected the present mansion-house of Ury, and was succeeded by his brother JOHN BAIRD, Esq., who died at Naples in 1870. Both brothers were interred in *The Howff* at Ury; and the last-mentioned was succeeded by his eldest son.

A tablet over the entrance to the Barclay portion of the aisle, bears this inscription:—

Anno 1741 conditum auspicio Roberti Barclay de Ury, sumptibus autem fratris sui, Davidis Barclay, mercatoris Londonensis, ad majorum cineres tegendos, nempe Avi, Colonelli DAVIDIS BARCLAY de Ury, filii et heredis Davidis Barclay de Mathers; Patris, ROBERTI BARCLAY de Ury, Apologiæ Auctoris; nec non MATRIS, lectissimæ ob vitæ sanctimoniam et raram beneficentiam qua miseris et ægris quotidie opitulabatur. Exemplum lucidum posteris indicatum est moribus; ingenio, candore, et sanguine clari, cultores veræ religionis erant.

[Built in the year 1741, under the auspices of Robert Barclay of Ury, but at the expense of his brother, David Barclay, merchant in London, to cover the ashes of his ancestors; viz., of his Grandfather, Colonel DAVID BARCLAY of Ury, son and heir of David Barclay of Mathers; of his Father ROBERT BARCLAY of Ury, author of the Apology; and also of his MOTHER, pre-eminent for holiness of life, and for the rare beneficence displayed by her in the daily relief of suffering and sickness. In their lives a bright example was set to posterity, and they were distinguished by their intelligence, their candour, their lineage; and also for their sincere practical piety.]

—D. Barclay, the erector of the aisle (second son of the Apologist), entertained successively Queen Anne and the first three Georges, when they visited the city on Lord Mayor's day. From his second son Alexander, by his first marriage, is descended Arthur-K. Barclay of Bury Hill, Esq., Surrey, who claims (Burke's Landed Gentry) to be the male representative, and chief of the old house of Mathers and Ury.

The best account of the Barclays is given by Nisbet (Heraldry, Appx., vol. ii., pp. 236-41.) The first inscription, quoted below, is from a freestone monument within *The Howff*, at Ury:—

(1.) THEOBALD DE BERKELEY, born A.D. 1110, lived in the time of Alexander the First and David the First, Kings of Scotland. (2.) HUMPHREY, his son, cousin of Walter de Berkeley, Great Chamberlain of the Kingdom, became owner of a large domain in this county, and from the lands of Balfeith, Monboddo, Glenfarquhar, and other portions of it, granted to the monks of Aberbrothwick, donations that were confirmed by William the Lion. (3.) RICHENDA, his only child, renewed and made additions to these donations, and her grants were confirmed by K. Alexander the Second. (4.) Dying without issue, she was succeeded by JOHN DE BERKELEY, brother of Humphrey, who dispossessed the monks of all these donations, but was obliged to compromise and give them instead, a portion of his lands of Conveth, and that transaction was confirmed by K. Alexander the Second. (5.) ROBERT DE BERKELEY, son of John, had concurred in his father's compromise with the monks. (6.) HUGH DE BERKELEY, son of Robert, obtained from King Robert Bruce a charter over the lands of Westerton in Conveth. (7.) ALEXANDER DE BERKELEY, son and successor of Hugh, married Catherine, sister of William de Keith, Marischal of Scotland, A.D. 1351, and by that marriage added to the paternal estates the then extensive domain of Mathers, conveyed by charter from the Marischal confirmed by King David Bruce. (8.) DAVID DE BERKELEY, 2d of Mathers, married the daughter of John de Seton. (9.) His son, ALEXANDER DE BERKELEY, 3d of Mathers, married Helen, daughter of Grahame of Morphie. (10.) Their son, DAVID DE BERKELEY, 4th of Mathers, who built an impregnable castle called the Kaim of Mathers, and, according to tradition, there took refuge on account of his concern in the murder of Melville, the Sheriff;* married the daughter of Strachan of Thornton. (11.) His son, ALEXANDER, 5th of Mathers, married the daughter of Wishart of Pitarow; he changed the spelling of the family name to *Barclay*. (12.) His son, DAVID BARCLAY, 6th of Mathers, married Janet, daughter of Irvine of Drum. (13.) ALEXANDER BARCLAY, 7th of Mathers, son of David, married the daughter of Auchinleck of Glenbervie; and, anno 1497, sold the lands of Slains and Falside to Moncur of Kuapp. (14.) GEORGE BARCLAY, 8th of Mathers, his son, married the daughter of Sir James Auchterlony, of Auchterlony and Kelly. (15.) His son, DAVID BARCLAY, 9th of Mathers, married, first, the daughter of Rait of Hallgreen, by whom he had a son, George; and second, Catherine Home, and to John, his son by her, he gave the lands of Johnston. (16.) GEORGE BARCLAY, 10th of Mathers, elder son of David,

* *v.* above, p. 14.

married first, the daughter of Sir Thomas Erskine of Brechin, Secretary to James V. of Scotland; second, the daughter of Wood of Bonnington, to his son by her he gave the lands of Bridgeton and Jackston. (17.) THOMAS BARCLAY, 11th of Mathers, elder son of George, married the daughter of Straiton of Lauriston. (18.) DAVID BARCLAY, 12th of Mathers, son of Thomas, was born anno 1580. Polite and accomplished, he lived much at Court, incurring extravagant expenses, to the great impairment of his fortune, whereby he was obliged to sell five valuable estates; he married first, Elizabeth, daughter of Livingston of Dunnipace, by whom he had five sons and a daughter; second, Margaret Keith, grand-daughter of Earl Marischal. To his daughter he gave a handsome fortune, to his sons a liberal education; the two eldest died young. David, the third, became eminently conspicuous; Robert, the fourth, was rector of the Scots College at Paris; James, the youngest, a Captain of Horse, fell gloriously at the Battle of Phillipbaugh. (19.) Colonel DAVID BARCLAY, the first of Ury, third son of David 12th of Mathers, was born anno 1610, at Kirktonhill, the ancient seat of the family. Instructed in every accomplishment of the age, he entered as a volunteer the service of Gustavus Adolphus of Sweden, in which he so distinguished himself as to gain the favour of that Monarch; but called home by the Civil Wars which distracted Scotland, he was, anno 1640, placed in the Colonelcy of a Royal Regiment of Horse, and was repeatedly entrusted with the command of an army, and the military government of considerable portions of the kingdom, in all which positions he acquitted himself with skill and bravery, and rendered important service to his country. In 1647, he married Catherine, daughter of Sir Robert Gordon of Gordonston, who was second son of the Earl of Sutherland by Jane, daughter of the Marquis of Huntly, and was also cousin to King James the Sixth of Scotland. The estates of the Barclays of Mathers having been nearly all disposed of by his father, the Colonel acquired, by purchase from Earl Marischal, the barony of Ury, and there fixed the residence of the family. He sat in the Scots Parliament as representative successively for Sutherlandshire and the counties of Angus and Mearns. See his gravestone adjacent hereto.

Six separate tablets are inserted into niches in

the west wall of the aisle, from which the following inscriptions are copied:—

[1.]

The grave of Colonel DAVID BARCLAY of Urie, son and heir of David Barclay of Mathers, and Elizabeth, daughter of Livingston of Dunipace. He was born Anno 1610; bought the barony of Urie, 1648; having religiously abdicated the world in 1666, he joyned the Quakers, and died 12 of October 1686.

—Col. B. was the first of his family that joined the Quakers. He became farmer, but had little knowledge of agricultural affairs; and being a person of great bodily strength, it is recorded that he often had recourse to it, and effectively, not only to enforce obedience from servants, but to protect the rights of property from the incursions of his neighbours. The Livingstons of Dunipace were descended from a second son of Sir Alexander of Calendar, ancestor of the Earls of Linlithgow.

[2.]

The Grave of ROBERT BARCLAY of Urie, Author of the Apologie for the Quakers, son and heir of Colonel David Barclay of Urie, and Katherin, daughter of the first Sir Robert Gordon of Gordonston. He was born Dec^{br} 23, 1648, and died Oct^{br} 3, 1690. Also, of his wife, CHRISTIAN, daughter of Gilbert Mollison, merchant in Aberdeen. She was born, anno 1647, and died Febry 14, 1723.

—Mr Barclay was born at Gordonston, near Elgin, the seat of his grand-father. The Gordons of Gordonston are descended from Sir James, 4th son of the 2d Earl of Huntly, by his wife Annabella, daughter of James I.

[3.]

The Grave of ROBERT BARCLAY of Ury, son and heir of Robert Barclay of Ury, and of Christian, daughter of Gilbert Molleson, merchant in Aberdeen, and oldest son of Thomas Molleson, of Lauchintully. He was born March ye 25th 1672, and died March the 27th 1747.

—The estate of Lauchintully is in the parish of Kemnay, and Thomas Mollison was long town-clerk of Aberdeen. During Montrose's wars, Gilbert Mollysone and several other citizens were detained for a short time by the Covenanters

" vnder guard as prisoners in the lauch counsell hous" of Aberdeen. The following relates to Robert, surnamed *the Strong* (r. No. 7 below):—

[4.]

The grave of ROBERT BARCLAY of Ury, son and heir of Robert Barclay of Ury, and Elizabeth O'Brian, daughter of James O'Brian, Esq., of London, and son of Colonel O'Brian of the Kingdom of Ireland. He was grandson to Robert Barclay of Ury, Author of the Apology for the Quakers; was born 20th July 1699, and died 10th October 1760.

—The above Robert, who was of a turbulent and quarrelsome disposition, was fond of travelling through the country *incognito*. When on one of these excursions, it is told that he arrived at Panmure on a dark winter's morning, and going straightway to the brewhouse, the brewer, who was an Englishman, and taking Barclay for an itinerant mender of old brass, exclaimed—" You are well come tinker, for my Lord's kettle requires mending." "What sayest thou, fellow?" said Barclay in a rage; and, with a cudgel which he had in his hand, he struck the brewer over the leg and thigh, and broke both bones. When Earl William of Panmure heard of the occurrence, and guessing it to be Barclay, his Lordship traced him to the House of Fothringham, and there made him sign an obligation which secured the brewer in a small pension from the estate of Ury, which he lived long to enjoy.

[5.]

The grave of UNE CAMERON, wife of Robert Barclay of Ury, and daughter of Sir Evan Cameron of Lochiel. She was born March 1701, and died March 1762. Also of JANE BARCLAY, her daughter, who was born in 1726, and died August 1750.

—According to tradition, the Camerons of Lochiel are descended from a younger son of the royal family of Denmark, who assisted at the restoration of King Fergus of Scotland in 404! It is certain that the Camerons had possessions in Lochaber, and were a powerful clan before the time of James I. The above named Sir Evan Cameron joined the Royalists at Killiecranky, and was thrice married, his last wife being Jane, daughter of Barclay of Urie, so that his daughter UNE married her cousin german.

[6.]

The grave of ANNE BARCLAY, the eldest daughter of Robert Barclay of Ury, great-grandson of Robert Barclay of Ury, Author of the Apology for the Quakers ; and Sarah Anne Allardice of Allardice, daughter and heiress of James Allardice of Allardice. She was born 13 September 1777, and died 29th October 1782.
—Sarah Anne Allardice, who brought the estate of Allardice to the Barclays of Ury, was the grand-daughter of Lady Mary Graham, a lineal descendant of King Robert II. of Scotland, and heiress of line of the Earls of Airth and Monteith. Until the above failure of the male line, the Allardices appear to have been regularly represented, and to have held the lands from which they assumed their surname, from the time of King William the Lion.

On the east wall of the aisle four monuments bear respectively the inscriptions undernoted :—

[7.]

To the memory of ROBERT BARCLAY of Allardice, Esquire, 5th of Ury, great-grandson of the Apologist, who was born at Ury in 1731; and having acquired by marriage the estate of Allardice, thereupon assumed that additional surname. Inheriting from his father, *Robert the Strong*, symmetry of form and great muscular power, he excelled in all the athletic exercises, Succeeding to Ury on his father's death, in 1760, while it was yet in the rudest condition, he zealously devoted towards its improvement the energies of a vigorous mind, stored with a thorough knowledge of agriculture, attained by assiduous study of its theory and practice, in the best districts of England. Accordingly, he brought into high cultivation 2000 arable acres, planted 1500 acres of wood, and executed the manifold operations connected with such works, in a manner so unexampled and successful, that his practice became the conventional standard over an extensive district, and placed him in the foremost rank among Scottish agriculturists. By the grant of feu-rights on his estate of Arduthie, he laid the foundation of the New Town of Stonehaven, and lived to see it become a populous and thriving community. By unanimous election, he represented his native county in three successive Parliaments. Distinguished by his loyalty and patriotism, and honoured with the intimate friendship of the great William Pitt, and other eminent statesmen of the time, he died at Ury, the 7th of April, 1797.
—Mr B. wrote an interesting paper for "Archæologica Scotica" (vol. 1) on Agricola's engagement with the Caledonians under Galgacus, in which he gives grounds for believing that a great battle (possibly that of *Mons Grampius*), was decided at Kempstone Hill, near Arduthie.

[8.]

To the memory of UNE-CAMERON, wife of John Innes, Esquire of Cowie, who was born in 1778, and died at Cowie in September 1809. MARY, born in 1780, who died in 1799. JAMES ALLARDICE, born in 1784, who died in the Island of Ceylon in 1803. DAVID, Major in the 28th Regiment of Foot, who was born in 1786, and died at Otranto, in Italy, in 1826. RODNEY, born in 1782, who died in 1833, all children of Robert Barclay Allardice, Esquire of Ury, and Sarah-Anne Allardice of Allardice, heiress of line of the Earls of Airth and Monteith.
—The above John Innes was the eldest son of the first Innes of Cowie and Breda, by a daughter of Davidson of Newton, who was a merchant, and sometime Provost of Aberdeen. Mr I.'s father, who died in 1788, was commissary of Aberdeen, and 2d son of Innes of Edingight. His youngest son, William, bought Raemoir about 1820 ; and Cowie now belongs to the Raemoir branch of the Innes'.

The following inscription, which is cut upon a tablet of white marble, inserted into a black marble panel, presents an incorrect carving of the Barclay arms, accompanied by those of Airth and Monteith :—

[9.]

In memory of ROBERT BARCLAY ALLARDICE, Esquire of Ury and Allardice, heir of line of the Earls of Airth and Monteith, born August 25th 1779, died on the 1st of May 1854, in the 75th year of his age.

[Upon a slab, which covers the grave] :—
ROBERT BARCLAY ALLARDICE, of Ury and Allardice, born 25th August 1779, died 1st May 1854.
—Robert Barclay-Allardice, to whom the last

two inscriptions refer, was a Captain in the Army. In early life he was celebrated for pedestrian and athletic feats; latterly he acquired fame as an improving agriculturist. His Essay on Training Pedestrians, &c. (published along with Thom's account of Barclay's great feat of walking 1000 miles in 1000 hours), is now a much more rare and original piece of writing than that of his Tour to the U.S. and U. Canada, which he undertook in 1841. Captain Barclay was one of the last examples in the district of "the fine old country gentleman." He was remarkable for unostentatious kindness and warmth of heart; and, in concluding a genial notice of his career, the author of "Field and Fern" justly remarks that, "at home, his habits were very quiet and simple. He was always ready with his subscription for any good object, and every Monday 20 or 30 people would be waiting for him about the front door after breakfast for their sixpences, of which he carried a supply in his waistcoat pocket. On New Year's-day he had always his friends to dinner, and he sat obscured to the chin behind the round of beef which two men brought in on a trencher. . . . . For sometime before his death he had suffered slightly from paralysis, but a kick from a pony produced a crisis, and two days after, when they went to awake him on the May morning of '54, he was found dead in bed." Like many other human beings, he found a faithful companion in one of the kindliest of the lower animals. It predeceased him, he had it buried in the old garden, and placed a stone in the wall beside its grave with this inscription:—

To the memory of DAN, the faithful companion of R. Barclay Allardice, Esq. of Ury for sixteen years. Died 5th Feb. 1846, aged 17. A favourite Dog.

Both civilly and ecclesiastically, the district of *Kally*, or Cowie, was of early importance. The forest, which stretched almost from the Dee, to the sea at Cowie, was royal hunting ground; and the castle, which stood upon a headland near the kirk of Cowie, where the green mound, formed by the *debris* of the ruins, still remains, was an occasional residence of our kings long before there was a castle upon the noble rock of Dunottar, or, possibly, before there was a harbour at "the *Stanchythe*," or Stonehaven. Subsequently, when the thanedom of Cowie was given away by the Crown, the Frasers continued to have their principal residence at Cowie; and one of them had a royal charter by which the town of Cowie was erected into a burgh of barony.

It is also worthy of note that a great part of the road through "the Cowie Mounth," between Stonehaven and Aberdeen, lies in this parish. Although traversed now a-days by an excellent turnpike, it had, for many ages, consisted of dangerous swamps and gullys; and from the fact of these being filled up with native boulders, and a track of road thus formed, it acquired the well-known name of the *Causey Moss*, or *Causey Mouth*. It is interesting to know that in these old times, there were worthy benefactors of their race, some of whom, by gifts or mortifications of money, gave needful aid towards the support of this great thoroughfare. Among others, was Paul Crab, who, in 1384, mortified a sum of money out of his lands of Kincorth, in Nigg, to assist in its support and maintenance. The road terminated at Kincorth, where there was a ferry boat, by which passengers and goods were carried across the Dee. To the readers of Sir W. Scott's works, the *Causey Moss*, which, even yet, has a bleak and uninviting aspect, will be familiar under the name of "the muir of Drumwhackit."

The Castle of Muchals, about four miles north and east of Stonehaven, is, however, a pleasing object for the student of bygone times, it being an interesting specimen of the architecture of the 17th century. The ceiling of the large hall is ornamented (as that of Glamis) with pargetted plaster-work, containing the heads of Roman Emperors, and classical heroes of antiquity, &c.; also this admonitory legend:—

. . . CEDE ADVERSIS REBVS NEC CREDE SECVNDIS.

On the left of the building, a slab, with an inscription, in beautifully interlaced letters, puts the history of the building past all doubt:—

THIS . WORK . BEGVN . ON . THE . EAST . &.

NORTH . DE . ALR . BVRNET . OF . LEYIS . 1619 ;
ENDED . DE . SIR . THOMAS . BVRNET . OF . LEYIS .
HIS . SONNE . 1627.

— Further evidence of its history is given over a chimney in the interior, upon which is the date of 1624, Sir Thomas' monogram, and this motto :—

ALTERIVS NON SIT QVIS VTILE POTEST.

The lands of Muchals were part of the extensive barony of Cowie, which Sir Alex. Fraser obtained from The Bruce. They belonged to the Hays of Errol before the Burnets acquired them. More recently, Silver of Netherley possessed the lands and castle, which now belong to the trustees of the late Dr Milne of Madras, and are a part of the property from which certain of the schoolmasters in Aberdeenshire receive well-merited augmentations to their livings. An excellent view of Muchals Castle is given in Billings. Possibly from the umbrageous and rocky nature of the burn of Muchals, it may have been of old the haunt of badgers or wild boars, as the Gaelic words *Muich-alt* favour some such meaning.

Not far from Muchals stands a neat Episcopal church, dedicated to S. TERNAN.

PATRICK PANTER, of the Newmanswalls family, secretary to James IV., was sometime rector of the kirk of Fetteresso, as was also ALEX. GORDON, a son of Gordon of Haddo, who succeeded Bishop Elphinstone in the See of Aberdeen.

ANDREW STEVEN, or STEVENSON, who was schoolmaster at Fetteresso in 1634, wrote a life of Bishop Forbes of Edinburgh in Latin verse, published in the Spottiswoode Miscellany.

The Rev. Dr LONGMUIR of Aberdeen, a native of Fetteresso, is a voluminous writer; and among other publications, is the author of a guide book to Dunottar Castle, &c.

The NEW TOWN of STONEHAVEN was founded about 1760, by Robert, the 5th Barclay of Ury, who, shortly before, purchased the property of Arduthie, upon which the new town is built. It is a well planned, clean, salubrious place, and a favourite resort for sea bathing. The town contains some nice houses, churches, and banks, and has a population of about 3000. The present parish church, erected in 1813, stands to the north-west of the town, and in point of elegance outstrips most of our landward churches. The walks in the neighbourhood are numerous and picturesque; and there is a chalybeate spring on the south bank of the Cowie, almost under the railway viaduct. It has an elegant fountain, of Peterhead granite, above which a tablet is thus inscribed :—

ST KIERAN'S WELL.
ERECTED BY PUBLIC SUBSCRIPTION, 1860.

—There were two SS. KIERAN, the one was a bishop, the other an abbot of Ireland; the feast of the one is held on 5th March, the other on 9th September. It may be added that S. SERENUS, CARANUS, or CARAN (the patron of Fetteresso), under the name of *Corinnu*, is said to have died among the Picts.—(Liber de Arbuthnot, p. lxxxiv.)

Gamrie.

(S. JOHN, EVANGELIST.)

THE kirk of *Gamcryn* was gifted to the Abbey of Arbroath by William the Lion in 1189-98, and was subsequently confirmed to it, along with the chapel of Troup. In 1250, the whole of the church property, with the tithes of the parish, were reserved to Arbroath, the vicar only receiving the altarage and two acres of land.

The old church, which is difficult of access, was used until 1830, when a new house was erected at a more convenient spot. The old church is quite a ruin, partly roofed, and picturesquely situated upon a *kaim*, or slope, overlooking the sea, at the most precipitous and *crooked* part of the coast, in the vicinity of hills or knolls, remarkable for their pointed or peaked appearance. As *Camruie* in Gaelic means the "pointed kame or slope," possibly the church may have had its name from the physical appearance of the locality in which it is situated.

The east half appears to be the most ancient part of the ruin, the west having been added at a comparatively late date, possibly during the last century, when the walls of the east portion may have been heightened. Although, according to an inscription cut in characters of the 18th century over the lintel of the west window:—

THIS CHURCH WAS BUILT 1004,

it is more probable that the oldest existing portion had been built much about the time that the Barclay monument (noticed below) had been erected. There is an awmbry, with fluted mouldings, on the east wall. Another on the north wall, as well as an awmbry or press on the south, have plain lintels.

Three round holes, each about the size of a human skull, in the more modern part of the north wall, are said to be the places where the skulls of three Danish kings were once preserved. These unfortunate foreigners are said to have been killed in an engagement which local story avers took place at Gamrie between the Danes and Scots in the time of Malcolm I., to which circumstance also is popularly attributed the origin of the name of the parish.

A monument of some pretensions in design, and beauty in execution, built into the east wall of the church, bears this inscription :—

patricius . briay . Z . hoc . me . fiere . fecit.
hic . iacet . honorabilis . bir . patricius . barclay .
dns . de . tolly . qui . obiit   dis . mens
ano . dni . m⁰ . q¹⁰⁰   et . ioneta . ogiuy . eius .
sponca . quæ . obiit . certo . die . mens . ianuarii .
ano . dm . m⁰ . qbi⁰ . quadrage⁰ . septimo.

[Here lie an honourable man PATRICK BARCLAY, laird of Tolly, who died on the   day of anno Domini 15 ; and JANET OGILVY, his spouse, who died January 6, 1547.]

—The Barclays of Tolly or Towie early possessed lands in Gamrie, having held those of Melros towards the close of the 14th century, possibly also those of Collane and others at the same time. It was in the Castle of Cullen, in Gamrie, that William Barclay, an eminent scholar and father of the author of the *Argenis*, was born in 1541 ; and it was a descendent of these scholars who became a field-marshal in the Russian army, and figured during the wars of Napoleon. It seems doubtful (whatever may be averred to the contrary) whether the Barclays had any connection with Tolly or Towie until the time of Robert the Bruce, who gave a charter of these lands to Walter Barclay of *Kerko*, knight. It is certain that Sir Walter of Kyrko followed Bruce, and suffered in his cause, for in 1305, when King Edward made his last attempt upon Scotland, Barclay's lands were among those which the English king was petitioned to give to his follower Gilbert Peach. Barclay was subsequently accused of treason, but acquitted, along with HAMELINUS de TROUPE, the latter of whom was possibly a vassal of the old lords of the lands from which the surname was assumed.

The Barclays appear to have held Tolly until the failure of the male line, which took place during the early part of the 17th century, when Isabella, heiress of Tullie, married Charles, 2d son of the 6th Earl of Lauderdale. The date of Patrick Barclay's death has not been filled in upon the above monument. His wife had possibly (though not mentioned in peerage books) been a daughter of Ogilvy of Findlater. Some interesting notices of the Barclays of Towie will be found in Pitcairn's Criminal Trials of Scotland. Probably the Tolly race was a branch of the Berkeleys of Inverkeillor, afterwards of Mathers and Ury. (v. p. 81.)

A stone with a bold carving of the Keith arms, with a boar's head in base, the initials A. K., and motto, VICTORIÆ LIMES, is thus inscribed round the margin :—

Heir lyis the rycht honorabil ALEXANDER KEYTH of Trvp, depairtit yis lyf the xxv of Marche 1605.

—The first Keith of Troup was Sir Robert the Marischal, who married the heiress, and granted a charter of that barony to his second son John in 1413. This John was progenitor of the Keiths of Northfield, one of whom was served heir to the barony of Troup, &c., 1628. George Keith of Northfield was served heir to Sir Robert the Marischal in 1782. A mutilated stone, also within the old kirk, bears :—

Heir . . . . . ET CVMING his spovs, qvho . . . . September 1695 zeirs.

Another slab has this simple motto :—

BESSY STRACHAN, and Mrs BATHIA FORBES, ladies of Troup, 1781.

—According to Burke, Major Garden, son of the last Garden of Banchory, entered the service of Gustavus of Sweden, and returning to Scotland in 1654, bought the lands of Troup, and married Betty, a daughter of Strachan of Glenkindie. By her he had a son, Alexander, who married Bathia, a daughter of Sir Alex. Forbes of Cragievar. The same authority shows that these lastnamed were the grand-parents of FRANCIS, Lord GARDENSTON, a well-known judge in the Court of Session, and founder of the village of Laurencekirk, in the Mearns. The elegant frame of a monument only remains, which was raised in the old kirk of Gamrie to the late Lord GARDENSTONE, who died in 1793. He was succeeded by his nephew, not his brother as Burke says, for Lord G.'s 2d brother and the laird of Troup both died in 1785. Lord G.'s younger brother having married the heiress of Glenlyon, assumed the additional name and arms of *Campbell*, which continue to be used by his descendants. It was to Lord Gardenston's elder brother ALEXANDER, who died 21 Dec. 1785, that a tenant of Coullycan, in Gamrie, addressed the following letter (here printed for the first time), in which his claims to a renewal of the lease of a mill are so quaintly set forth. It was addressed " To the Oncrable Laird of Troupe," and runs thus :—

"Culy Can, June 7, 1785.

"ONERIBEL SIR,—Gif it plies your onar[1] I hop you wil lat me know how you ar to set this Mil and I will ofer as much as aney on can gif. And my forbiers[2] his bin heir so Long; and my Granmother coufred[3] your oner of the Gandis[4] when non could Dow, when you was a child; and when you fantit your grandfather, the old leard, sed whow[5] that he ould shut[6] her, and shi was nar did for fier;[7] and when you Gru[8] beter he promest to my Graufether [that] him nor yet his son, nor his sons son, would never put on[9] of his Generation out of Culy Can. And when your onars fethar cam hom, and heerd whou that your lif was scavt, he shuk hans we my[10] granmother, and said, Onest Mady,[11] I trow, he [tho'] my fethar ĥegat[12] you for kilen[13] a Sandey ; but it is you that his kepit him in live, and it shal no be forgotten to you nor yours, and my fok[14] shal niver Gar[15] your fok flit ;[16] and your oner promest the sam to her when you was a very young Gentleman, and I hop your oner his mor Gretated,[17] and likwis mor Goudnes, nor to brak ther word and your ane word, or to be on gretfoul[18] to them that seved your lif, when non but them could a savt it ;[19] and so God blis your oners Humlet Ser[t], and alwise unto death,
"JAMES MORRISON.

" Becas I was not Goud at writin lettersss right, I hafe goten a frind to do it for me.
" God blis your Onar remember me."

The churchyard of Gamrie, which is strewn with "moisty bones and broken skulls," and otherwise ill cared for, contains numerous monuments. From these the following inscriptions are selected :—

This stone is dedicated by Iames Wood in Doun, to his deceased father ROBERT WOOD, who departed in Dec. 1683 ; as also here lyis MARY REID, spous to Iames Wood in Doun, who died July 27, 1702.

Under hope of a blessed resurrection, here lyes the ashes of IOHN ROSS, sometime in the Mill of Fortrie, who departed this life Aprile 17, 1699.

Here lyes the ashes of BARBARA REID, spous to Iohn Ross, somtyme at Mill of Fortrie, who depairted this life December the 18, 1690 ; as also the ashes of IAMES ROSS, somtime in Ballgrien, lawful son to the saids Iohn Ross and Barbara Reid, who died Sept. 13, 1727 . . . . . . also here lyes ALEXANDER Ros, son to Iames Ross in Balgreen, who depairted March the 7th 1707 . . . .

Here lies interred the ashes of MARGET ROGER, spouse to Iohn Ord att Shore of Crivie, who died Jan. the 15, 1754 ; as also the ashes of MARGET WATT, spouse to Iohn Ord, sometime at Mill of Melross, who died Jan. the 7, 1707. This is erected by Alex., and John Ords, their lawful son and grandson.

1, Please your honour. 2, Ancestors. 3, Cured. 4, Jaundice. 5, How. 6, Shoot. 7, Nearly died from fright. 8, Became. 9, One. 10, Shook hands with my. 11, Honest Magdalene. 12, Frightened. 13, Killing of Alexander. 14, Folk. 15, Make. 16, Remove. 17, Gratitude. 18, Ungrateful. 19, Could have saved it.

The next three inscriptions are on the north-east side of the church, and upon table-shaped tombstones of white marble:—

Inscribed by James and Alexander Chalmers, merchants in Banff, in memory of their parents WILLIAM CHALMERS, merchant in Gardenstown, who died 3 June 1809, aged 82; and HELEN STRACHAN, his spouse, who died 9 Feb. 1811, in her 71st year. By laudable industry, joined with the strictest integrity, by a faithful discharge of the relative duties of life, and an uniform course of Christian piety, they lived respected, and died sincerely regretted.

Sacred to the memory of JAMES CHALMERS, Esq. late merchant in Banff, who died 19 Feb. 1829, aged 69. During a period of 50 years, extensively engaged in business, he uniformly maintained a character of the strictest integrity; faithfully discharged all the relative and social duties; and acquired the esteem of a numerous and highly respectable circle of acquaintances. He died universally regretted. This tablet is erected by his surviving brother Alex. Chalmers, Esq. of Clunie, as a testimony of his affectionate regard.

Sacred to the memory of ALEXANDER CHALMERS, Esq. of Clunie, who departed this life 11 Aug. 1835, aged 70. He lived exemplary for generosity, benevolence, and disinterested integrity, and died in the hope of a blessed immortality. This is erected as a humble tribute by his afflicted widow Elspet Chalmers.

—It was on the death of Alex. Chalmers of Clunie, and by mutual consent, that the large amount of £70,000 was placed at the disposal of trustees, for the "founding, erection, and endowment of an hospital and free dispensary of medicines," &c., at Banff, to be called CHALMERS' HOSPITAL. This building, which is a large and imposing structure in the Elizabethan style of architecture, has an airy position upon the rising ground, overlooking the Seatown. It has been in operation for some years, and been the means of supplying medical attendance and support to many, who could not brook the idea of receiving parochial relief, and were otherwise unable to procure the necessary comforts of life, which are so very essential in time of distress.

WM. WATT, shipmr., Gardenstone, on 3 children, (1763):—
When low in dust the mortal part doth ly,
At Christ's right hand, the soul doth dwell on high;
Then repine not parents, at your childrens' death,
The flowers which bloom in spring, cut off are first.

KENNETH FIMISTER, shipbuilder, who was put on shore hear the 13 November 1832, aged 50 years. Pleaced hear by his son John Fimister, carpenter in Burghead, in remembrance of his Father:—

My voyage is mead, my sorrow is o'er,
The troubled sea of life I'll cross no more.
My life was short, reader take notice,
Where I am now, you all most surely come.

The tradition of the landing of the Danes at Gamrie, and their defeat, have been already alluded to. In the New Statistical Account of the Parish, the affair is detailed with marvellous minuteness!

On the opposite side of the den from the old church, a conical mound, called the Castlehill, presents traces of old walls. Upon this and adjoining hills, and at a height of more than 150 feet from the present sea level, shells of various kinds are found embedded in the sand. These sandhills were a favourite retreat of the late Hugh Miller; and are still visited by students of the interesting science of geology.

The ruins of "Wallace's Castle" on the farm of Pitgair (the rough hollow), overhanging the valley and burn of Minonie, consist of two huge masses of vitrified walls, of much the same period, possibly, as the ruins of the castle of Kinedar, or King-Edward. We know that this castle was a seat of the ancient Earls of Buchan, the first recorded of whom was a contemporary of William the Lion; also that his castle of Kinedar was occupied by Edward I. in 1296; and as the Earl of Buchan was then lord of most of the district, possibly "Wallace's Castle" was erected either by him or some of his vassals.

Of the later proprietary history of certain parts of Gamrie, it is recorded that in 1226 Alex. II. confirmed the lands of Lethenoth to the monks of Kinloss, which lands had been previously granted to them by Robert Corbett. Glendowachy was a thanedom in the time of Alex. III., and valued at £20 a-year. It was given by Bruce to Hugh of Ross. In later times, the Earls of Buchan, and Moray, had an interest in Glendowachy. Doune was also a thanedom, of which John of Bothuille had a grant in 1365.

Farnell.

(? S. NINIAN, BISHOP CONFESSOR.)

THE kirk of *Ferneval* was a deanery of the Cathedral of Brechin, and is rated at 20 merks in the Old Taxation.

In 1574, Farnell and Cuikstoun (*infra*, p. 92), along with four other churches, were served by one minister, who had a stipend of £202 4s 7d Scots. Thomas Sewan, who had "the haill vicarage" and kirk lauds, was the contemporary reader or schoolmaster at Farnell.

The present church (erected in 1806), stands within the church-yard, upon a rising ground near the Pow. The bell is inscribed:—

IOHANNES . BVRGERHVYS . ME . FECIT.
ANNO . 1662.

A freestone monument, with a beautifully interlaced cross, and a representation of the Fall of our First Parents, &c., which was found upon the site of the old church, was some time ago presented to the Montrose Museum by the Earl of Southesk. It is a late type of the well-known Sculptured Stones of Scotland, and may possibly have been erected over the grave of a now unknown ecclesiastic of Farnell. This interesting stone was first engraved in Mr P. Chalmers' Sculptured Monuments of Angus, and afterwards in the Sculptured Stones of Scotland.

When the kirk-yard of Farnell was being extended and improved in 1870, the workmen came upon a line of coffins on the east side of the church, which were carefully constructed of stone slabs. The heads of two crosses were also discovered. One is pierced with four holes, and the other presents a plain cross in low relief upon one side of a circle, the same figure, in an unfinished state, being upon the reverse. Two coffin-slabs were also found: one shows traces of the figure of a sword, and the other has a smooth unornamented surface. Upon another fragment, the base of a Calvary is incised, together with two or three old English letters in relief; and a Dedication Cross is built into the kirk-yard dyke.

With the exception of the bit above noticed, the oldest lettered fragment at Farnell bears:—

.... AGNES .... DAIS CHIL ......
IAMES DA .... MARGARIT YO ......
IN CARCARI ..... AIRTED IN ....
IS .... 1638 ....

Several other fragments, less legible than the above, were discovered at the same time; as well as two flat tomb-stones. The last-mentioned are both embellished with mortuary emblems, and respectively inscribed as follows:—

[1.]

D. E: I. S. Heire lyes interd vnder this ston ISOBEL SHILGREENE, spovs to David Enererity, indweller in Fithie, who departed this life the 27 November 1675 years, and of hir age 70.

Remember man as thov goes by,
As thow art now so was I;
As I am now so mvst thow be,
Remember man that thov mvst dye.
Anno Dom. 1676—Memento mori.

—*Shilgreene* is a territorial name, probably assumed from the property of Shielagreen in Aberdeenshire. The surname of *Enererity* is of like origin, and assumed from Inverarity in Angus.

[2.]

W. T : A. A : B. C : I. A.

Heir lyes BARBRA CRICHTON, spose to Androv Andrson, indveler in Villen Yeards, vho departed this lif the year of God 1717, and of age 53. Also heir lyes WALTER TYLER, husbant to Barbra Crchton, age 49, 1698.

Memento mori—My glas is run.

—Andrew Anderson in Willanyards, 1729, was reported by the factor for the York Buildings' Co., to be "a Right honest like man, pretty well upon it, and has the Town very well plenished."

A marble tablet (enclosed) is thus inscribed :—

Sacred to the memory of Dame CHRISTIAN DOIG, relict of Sir James Carnegie, Bart. of Southesk. Died Novr. 4th 1820, aged 91 years.

—This lady was the daughter of David Doig of Cookston, near Brechin, by his wife, Magdalene, heiress of Symers of Balzeordie, in Menmuir. Symers' were designed of Balzeordie from the middle of the 15th century (Land of the Lindsays), and Doigs held property in Brechin (Reg. Ep.), from before 1532, of which city some of them were chief magistrates, 1700-41. Reswallie, in Rescobie (*infra*, p. 158), was owned by Doigs during parts of the 16th and 17th centuries.

Doig was the name of a churchman of Dunnichen in 1372. About a century afterwards, James Doig is celebrated by Dunbar, the poet, as "the wardraipper of Venus' bour," or wardrobe keeper to the Queen of James IV. But probably the most eminent person of the name, in modern times, was Dr David Doig, a native of Monifieth, and master of the Grammar School of Stirling, whom Lord Kames pronounced to be "a genius;" and said he loved him because he told him "his mind roundly and plainly" (Memoirs of Kames.)

A free-stone monument, which stood within the old kirk, bears this inscription :—

Sepulchrum Matri DAVIDIS CARNEGY de Craigo, decani Brichinen :, rectoris hujus ecclesiæ, qui primo fuit ecclesiastes Brechinen : annos 2, postea hujus ecclesiæ pastor fidelissimus annos 36, qui placide ac pie in Domino obdormivit anno Dom. 1672, ætatis suæ 77. In hac urna simul cum eo recubant prior ejus uxor HELENA LINDSAY, ac decem eorum liberi. Placuit hic inscribere anagramma a seipso compositum.

Magistro DAVIDI CARNEGY'
anagramma
Grandis Jesu, duc me Gratia.
distichon
Dum dego in terris expectans gaudia coeli,
Me ducat semper tua Gratia, Grandis Jesu.

[The burying place of Mr DAVID CARNEGY of Craigo, dean of Brechin, and rector of this church. He was at first minister at Brechin for 2 years ; and afterwards, for 36 years, the most faithful pastor of this church. He calmly and devoutly fell asleep in the Lord, A.D. 1672, in his 77th year. In this tomb, along with him, are laid his first wife HELEN LINDSAY, and ten of their children. It seemed good to inscribe here an anagram composed by himself.

To Master DAVID CARNEGY,
(Anagram)
Great Jesus ! guide me thro' Grace.
(Distich)
While I dwell on earth expecting the joys of heaven,
May thy Grace ever guide me, Great Jesus !]

—Dean Carnegy, who was descended from a laird of Cookston and Unthank, was the founder of the Carnegys of Craigo. His seal, attached to a letter of 5th March 1669, exhibits (*sans* difference and colour), a shield with an eagle displayed and a cup upon the breast, surmounted by the letters M. D. C. The charge of the cup was afterwards exchanged by the Craigo family, for that of an *open Bible*, in allusion to the Dean's profession.

The Dean's first wife was a daughter of Bishop Lindsay of Edinburgh. Two of his sons were churchmen. Robert, the youngest, was an "expectant" (*infra*, p. 210), and the eldest, James, was long minister of Barry. In a deed of 1703, David Carnegy is described as "lawful son and heir to said Mr James." The Dean left 800 merks, or about £44 2s 8d sterling, to the poor of the parish of Farnell.

Mr Carnegy's predecessor in Farnell was Mr Dugald Campbell, who went there in 1581. He was moderator of the General Assembly in 1606, and died before 8th July 1633—the date of Dean Carnegy's presentation to Farnell. Mr Campbell married Katherine Mackure, daughter of a carver and burgess of Edinburgh (Scott's Fasti). A handbell at the Manse of Farnell, which probably belonged to Campbell's time, is initialed M. D. C. It also bears a monogram, which appears to be composed of the letters, W.A.T.H.

From a monument beside Dean Carnegy's :—

Sacred to the memory of the Rev. JAMES WILSON, minister of Farnell, who died on the 18th of October 1829, in the 74th year of his age, and the 52d of his ministry, justly and universally regretted by all who knew him. Also to his two sons, JAMES and GEORGE, the former of whom died an infant, the latter in the 22d year of his age. Also to his mother, ANN BURNETT, and his sisters, MARGARET and CATHERINE, all of whom are interred here.

—Mr Wilson was translated from Maryton to Farnell in 1794. His father was minister first at Edzell, and next at Kinnaird, where he died in 1787 (*inf.*, p. 92.) The minister of Farnell married a daughter of Sir W. Nicolson of Glenbervie, Bart., and had two sons and five daughters. Mr David Smith, parochial schoolmaster at Farnell, married the eldest daughter, by whom he had Mrs Day of London, and other children. Another daughter, who married Dr Badenach of Arthurhouse, in Garvock, was mother of the present laird of Arthurhouse, J. Badenach-Nicolson, Esq. Mr Nicolson, who passed as an advocate in 1855, has published an edition of Erskine's Institutes of the Law of Scotland, which has been favourably received.

From a head-stone on south side of the kirk :—

1810 : Erected by the Reverend Andrew Fergusson, minister of Marytown, in memory of his Grand-father, the Reverend DAVID FERGUSSON, who was admitted minister of Farnell in the year 1716, and died in 1751 ; and of his father the Reverend DAVID FERGUSSON, who succeeded him in the above year, and died in 1793. Here also are interred their spouses, ANNA RUSSEL, and JANET MITCHELL, with some of their children. [Dan. xii. 3.]

—The first Mr Fergusson of Farnell gave two silver communion cups to the church, one of which is thus inscribed :—

This Communion Cupp, and another like to it, were gifted to the church of Farnwell, by the Rev. Mr David Fergusson, late minister of the Gospell there, 1751.

A monument, immediately to the south of Mr Fergusson's, is thus inscribed :—

Sacred to the memory of DAVID LYALL, Esquire of Gallery, who was born at East Carcary, in February 1733, but who left Scotland, and went to Gottenburgh in 1757, where he resided as a merchant till 1787, when he returned to his native country to enjoy the fruits of his industry, and the society of his relatives and friends. He was much respected for his integrity, benevolence, and charity, and died upon the 29th December 1815, in the 83d year of his age.

—In May 1783, Mr Lyell, merchant in Gottenburgh, gave "£250 scots to be distributed to the most indigent and needful of the poor" of Farnell. He died unmarried, and the lands of Gallery passed to James Gibson, a sister's son, who assumed the surname of *Lyall* (*infra*, p. 212.) A stone at Farnell thus records the death of Mr Gibson's parents, and a brother :—

1818 : Erected to the memory of JAMES GIBSON, who was born 22d March 1719, and died 16th Feb. 1817 ; also of MARGARET LYALL, his spouse, who was born in July 1731, and died in August 1786 ; and of DAVID GIBSON, their son, who was born 8th April 1760, and died in his seventh year.

—The father of the above-mentioned James Gibson also belonged to Farnell, but left his native country for Riga after the Rebellion of 1745, in which he took part. He became a merchant in that city, where he long resided and died. Some members of his family also settled there.

The next three inscriptions—(the first two from table-shaped stones, the third from a granite obelisk)—relate to a family who have been tenants upon the Southesk estate for considerably over two hundred years :—

[1.]

Here lies ROBERT LYELL, who dp^r. this life the 14 Oct. 1707, age 43, and 3 of his children, viz. PATRICK LYELL dp^r. this life Jun 24, 1710, of age 14 ; ROBERT L. dp^r. 28 of Nov. 1706, age ½ y^r. ; ANN L: dp^r. April the 9, 1701, of age 2 year :—

Under this monument of stone,
Here rests in peace the bones of one,
ROBERT LYELL, call'd by name,
Who fear'd God, & hated shame.
Like to the glass, man's life does pass,
  And all are born to die ;
Or as the sun, his time does run,
  Till 't grasp eternitie.

Pallida mors aequo pulsat pede
Pauperum tabernas, regumque turres.
Candide lector, vita nostra quâ fruimur brevis est.

And also in remembrance of JAMES LYALL, sometime tenant in East Carcary, and afterwards tenant of Mains of Gallery, who died there, the 27th day of Feb. 1808, in the seventy-second year of his age.

[Pale death knocks with impartial foot at the cottages of the poor, and the palaces of kings.
Candid reader, the life which we enjoy is short.]

[2.]

In hope of a blessed resurrection, here lyes ISOBEL MITCHELL, who was spouse to Charles Lyell, tennant in Carkary, who departed this life the 12 of April the year of our Lord 1727, and of age 50 years. Likewise two of her children, to wit, ROBERT, who departed July 1707, and WALTER, who died March 1717. Also here lyeth CHARLES LYELL, husband to yᵉ sᵈ Isobell Mitchell, who departed this life March the 28th 1729, aged 63 years. Also here lyeth JOHN LYELL, who succeeded his father Charles in Carkary; he departed this life September 13, 1736, aged 34 years, with one of his children called MARGARET. She died in the 3d year and 8 month of her age. Also MARGARET MUDIE his spouse, who died 20th Dec. 1761, aged 59 years. Also JAMES LYALL, tenant in Carcary, who succeeded to his father John. He departed this life the 14th day of May 1806, in the 75th year of his age. Also of ISOBEL SPENCE, his spouse, who died at Brechin the 26th day of January 1813, in the 71st year of her age.

—Margaret Mudie was a daughter of the laird of Pitmuies; and Isobel Spence belonged to a family that were notaries public and town clerks in Brechin for more than two centuries. The latter was the mother of the first-named in the next inscription :—

[3.]

In memory of ROBERT LYALL, factor on the estate of Southesk from 1817 to 1850. Born at Carcary, 27 Novem. 1778; died at Arrat, 13 January 1863. Of his wife ELIZABETH CAMPBELL, who died 25 April 1832, aged 52 years; and of his second wife, MARY BROWN, who died 11 June 1854, aged 59 years.

—Mr Lyall was succeeded in the office of factor by his second son, now at Old Montrose.

The grand-father of Sir Charles Lyell, Bart., the celebrated geologist, was descended from one of the brothers named in inscription [2.] He was bred a merchant in Montrose, became a purser in one of H.M.'s ships during the American war, and bought Kinnordy about 1780-3. He was succeeded in 1796 by his son, who was a lawyer by profession, and published a translation of Dante.

WM. son of John Cobban, shoem. in Greenden, d. 1786, a. 26 :—

O Death, fierce is thy firie dart,
No Forester like the,
Who cuts the cyder while it grows,
And spars the withered tree.

JOHN BRIMNER, bd. of Helen Smith, d. 1791, a. 75:

'Tis here the fool, the wise, the low, the high,
In mix'd disorder, and in silence ly;
No more beneath life's weighty load he goes,
But in this chamber finds a quiet repose.
O humbling thought, Pride must be thus disgrac'd,
And all distinctions here at last effac'd.

~~~~~~~~~~~~~~~~~~~~~~~~~~~~

Cuikstoun, or Kinnaird.

(? S. RUMON OR RUMALD.)

QUYGSTOUN, or CUIKSTOUN, was the "parish kirk of the Prebendary callit the Subdeaucrie of Brechin."

A place near Quygston is called *Rume's* Cross. This may possibly indicate not only the name of the saint to whom the church was dedicated, but also the site of an ancient cross. Of the cross there is now no trace; and S. RUMALD, whose feast is held on 1st July, was probably the patron of the kirk.

When the kirk or chapel at Quygston became "altogidder ruynous and decayit," Sir David Carnegie of Southesk, who died in 1598, had it rebuilt upon a site nearer to his own mansion. The district was formed into a parish at that time under the name of *Kinnaird*, and it continued to be a separate cure until the death of Mr George Wilson in 1787, (*supra*, p. 91), when the parish was divided between those of Farnell and Brechin. The only existing memorial of Mr Wilson of Kinnaird is a sun-dial in the manse garden at Farnell, which had probably been brought there by his son. It is inscribed, "1767, Mr. G. W."

The old burial-ground, which is within the deer park, and to the west of Kinnaird Castle, was enclosed, some years ago, by the Earl of Southesk. It contains a number of tomb-stones. One bears a bold carving of the Rait arms, and this inscription in raised Roman capitals :—

Heir lyes HENRIE RAIT, son to Mr David Rait, minister of this place, who departed this mortal life in the 18 year of his age, October 1669 :—

The tender grse it springs, it flovrs, it fades,
The day begins, ascens, declines, in shades ;
Frail mans like grase, his life a day, and most
Rvn ovt his race, and be disolved in dvst.

—Mr David Rait was one of three ministers who were commissioned by the General Assembly, in 1644, to supply the north-west parts of Ireland. He was settled first at Newburgh, next at Dairsie, and finally at Kinnaird, where he died sometime before 2d Feb. 1676. His father was minister of Mains, near Dundee (Scott's Fasti.)

JAMES KAR, spouse to E. Simpson (16-0) :—

MEMENTO . MORI.
HVE . DOE . NOT . THIS . FOR . NO . WTHER . END.
BWT . THAT . OWR . BWRIAL . MAY . BE . KEND.

JAS. SOUTTER, hammerman in Nether Tenements of Caldhame, d. 1760, a 54 :—

Here JAMES lyes claid with a mournfull shade,
Hath teft his Friends and Loving spouse sad,
And now is gone above the stars to sing,
Eternall prais to his imortall King.

— —o-- ·

THE SOUTHESK FAMILY BURIAL VAULT

occupies a rising ground, to the south of Kinnaird Castle, at the end of avenues of grand old trees. It is surrounded by a freestone wall, covered with ivy ; and is entered from the west by a handsome gateway. Two stone panels flank the gateway upon the north and south sides respectively. The former of these presents a carving of the Southesk arms, and the latter those of Southesk and Lauderdale impaled. Below the respective shields are these inscriptions :—

[1.]

CARNEGIORUM gentis insignia, cujus princeps, CAROLUS, Comes Southesquius, natus est Lonidni Anglorum, die 7 April anno 1661 patr . . . . . RTO, Comite Southesquio, matro ANNA, filia natu maxima atque hærede Gul., Ducis Hamiltonii, obiit in Arce sua Loucharensi, die 9 Augusti mensis, anno æræ Christianæ 1699. Hæc ianua extructa atque ornata est a MARIA MÆTELLANA eius coniuge anno sal. hum. 1704.

[The arms of the CARNEGIE family, whose chief, CHARLES, Earl of Southesk, son of ROBERT, Earl of Southesk, and ANN, eldest daughter and heiress of William, Duke of Hamilton, was born at London, in England, 7th April 1661. He died at his Castle of Leuchars, 9th Aug. 1699. This gateway was erected and ornamented by his wife, MARY MAITLAND, in the year of human salvation 1704.]

[2.]

CHARLES, Earle of Southesque, was married on Lady MARY MAITLAND, second daughter of Charles Earle of Lauderdale, brother and heir to Iohn Duke of Lauderdale, by whom he had a son JAMES, now Earle of Southesque, & two daughters, Lady ANNA and Lady MARY CARNEGY, whom he survived : Thes are the Armes of the said CHARLES Earle of Southesque & Lady MARY MAITLAND, Countes of the same, who put up thir coats, & built this gate, in the year 1704.

The burial vault, which has an arched roof, is near the middle of the enclosure, and an ornamental stone cross is placed over its entrance. The cross was erected by the present Earl of Southesk, who had the ground and dykes put into a becoming state of repair.

A neat marble monument is erected within, and upon the north wall of the enclosure, to the memory of the Earl's first wife, Lady CATHERINE NOEL. She was the second daughter of the Earl of Gainsborough, and died 9th of March 1855, leaving three daughters and a son. There is a similar monument, upon the south wall, to the memory of his Lordship's father and mother, who died in 1849 and 1848 respectively.

A free-stone slab, which lies within the enclosure, bears this inscription:—

HEIR . REST . IN . THE . LORD . A . GENTLEMAN CALLED . CHARLES . CARNEGY . WHO . DYED . THE 15 . DAY . OF . IANVAR . 1655 . YEARS . AND . OF HIS . AGE . 60 . YEAR.

—The Carnegies of Southesk first acquired a portion of the lands of Kinnaird in 1401, and the rest of the property became theirs in course of time. The valuation roll of Angus for 1682 shews that the parishes of Farnell and Kinnaird both belonged to the "Earle of Southesque" with the exception of the small estate of "Litle Foithy." The Earl's estate within the two parishes was valued at £2433 6s 8d Scots, and the latter, which was acquired by the Carnegies, during the early part of this century, is set down at £133 6s 8d Scots.

Sir David Carnegie of Kinnaird, who was raised to the peerage in 1616, took an active part in the affairs of his country. Probably he made improvements upon his Castle of Kinnaird, for, in 1656, his son wrote, on his father's behalf, to the Earl of Panmure, who at once granted the request, " for Libertie to win some stones in the quarrell of Buthergill, the lyke q'rof," adds Lord Carnegie, " he (the Earl of Southesk) has not in any part of his owne ground."

The fifth Earl of Southesk was attainted for the part which he took in the Rebellion of 1715; but the titles were restored to the present Peer in 1855. His Lordship was also created a Knight of the Thistle in March, 1869, and a British Peer in November following.

The Carnegies previously bore the surname of *Balinhard*, which was assumed from the lands of Balinhard, or Bonhard, in the parish of Arbirlot, the property of the Earl of Dalhousie. But, on examining these lands with Walter of Maule, about 1350, for those of Carnegie, in the parish of Carmyllie, and barony of Panmure, John of Balinhard and his descendants dropt their old surname of "Balinhard," and assumed that of CARNEGIE (*infra*, p. 249.)

A history of the Carnegies, edited by Mr Wm. Fraser of Edinburgh, was printed for private circulation by Lord Southesk, in two vols. 4to. This shows that the family writs are better cared for now than they were in 1646, when the Earl wrote in regard to a "bond given in to him by Argyll," that, " Be reasone of the troubles my writes are not presently beside me ; and if they were," adds his Lordship, " they are so confusedly cast togither, that I cannot fall vpon it in a sodantie."

———

During the spring of 1868, a Pict's House, or underground chamber, about ten feet long, was discovered to the west of the farm-house of Fithie. Among other evidences of human occupation, it contained the remains of an urn of red embossed Samian ware, also bones of animals, &c. These relics are now in the National Museum, and an account of "the find" is given in the Proceedings of the Society of Antiquaries of Scotland, vol. viii.

The lands of Farnell belonged at one time to the Cathedral of Brechin ; and the Castle of Farnell was a palace or residence of the Bishops of that diocese. It was visited by Edward I. in 1296 (*v*. Mem. of Angus and Mearns.) One of the skew-put stones bears the sacred monogram ihs ; and another has the crowned ſH, as symbolical of the Virgin—both here represented :—

Kinnaird Castle, which was remodelled by the present Earl of Southesk, is one of the finest buildings in the district. It stands within a park of about 1000 acres in extent, which is well stocked with deer, and studded with many fine old trees. It is described by Guynd (c. 1682), as "without competition the fiynest place, taking altogether, in the shyre."

The Pow runs through the parish of Farnell, and is crossed by two stone bridges. One bridge is near the church, the other near the junction of the Pow with the South Esk. The former is dated 1802, and the latter was originally built in 1617, to accommodate James VI., when on a visit to his friend Lord Carnegie. This appears from the Kirk-Session records of Brechin, in which, under date of 18th Oct. 1620, it is stated that a collection was ordered to be made "for help to the Pow bridge betwixt Kinnaird and Auld Montrois q^{lk} ovr Sovereigne K. James the Sext caused lay ovr for leading of his Maties provision to Kiunaird in anno 1617 yeiris."

~~~~~~~~~~

Longside.

(S. ——).

THE parish of Longside was formed out of that of Peter-Ugie, now Peterhead. The church was erected in 1620, under the name of "the ower kirk of Peter-Ugie;" and its disjunction was ratified by Act of Parliament in 1637. In 1641, it acquired the name of LONGSIDE, and was "erectit in ane severall paroch kirk be it selff, and disvnited fra the said mother kirk of Peterugie" (Acta Parl.)

Mr Alex. Martin, brother of the minister of Peterhead, appears to have been the first minister of the parish. Being there only for a few months, he was succeeded by Mr Alex. Irvine, who demitted about 1661. From that period to the present time, there have been eight incumbents.

The old church of Longside, which stands within the burial ground, a little to the south of the new kirk, is a long, narrow building, with an ornamental belfry. Upon the west side of the belfry are the Sibbald arms, and the initials, A. S. Mr Abraham Sibbald was minister of Old Deer at the time of the building of the church at Longside, but I am not aware that he, or any of his name, had an interest in the latter parish.

The Bruce arms, dated 1620, with the initials, G. B., and the words, "MR. MEASON," are also upon the belfry; and these, as at Gartly (*sup.*, p. 43), may indicate the name of the builder of the church. A third slab presents the initials, A. R., accompanied by a mason's mark.

One of the skew-puts upon the church exhibits the initials, G. B : E. M., and the date of 16 . . Upon another are the Keith and Cheyne arms, quarterly. This quartering has reference to the marriage of Keith with the heiress of Cheyne of Inverugie, by which the Keiths acquired the greater part of their territory in Buchan.

The area of the old kirk, which is now used for burial purposes, contains several tomb-stones. The oldest, formerly in the church-yard, is thus inscribed:—

Here lyes the corps of ANDROW TAYLOR in Over Kinmundy, who deperted ovt of this lyfe the 23 of Apryli 1712.

The rest of the monuments within the kirk are modern. One was erected by Keith Forbes, Esq., solicitor in Peterhead, who is said to be the last direct male descendant of Forbes of Brux. A second monument bears this inscription:—

Erected in memory of JAMES BRUCE, Esquire of Innerquhomery and Longside, second son of James Bruce, late farmer, Middleton of Innerquhomery, and Barbara Gray, his spouse: Born at Middleton 3d June 1787, died there 16th May 1862.

—Mr Bruce, who acquired a fortune as a shipowner, &c., bought the above-named estates from Mr Fergusson of Pitfour about 1820-24. His landed property was heired by a nephew, and upwards of £40,000 were willed to the clergy of the Presbytery of Deer, for distribution among the non-pauper poor within their bounds, Roman Catholics excepted!

The supposed builder of the church may have been an ancestor of "laird Bruce," for the surname is one of the oldest in the parish. Besides a tomb-stone, which Mr Bruce erected to his parents in the church-yard, there are several other monuments to the same race. One of these bears the following epitaph:—

ALEXANDER, MARGARET, and HELEN BRUCE, by their parents, Alex. Bruce and Margt. Cuming, Netherton of Inverquhomry. Erected 1771:—
Here lies, consigned a while to promis'd rest
In hope to rise again among the blest,
The precious dust of one whose course of life
Knew neither fraud, hypocrisy, nor strife.
A Husband loving, and of gentle mind,
A Father careful, provident, and kind,
A Farmer active, with no greedy view,
A Christian pious, regular, and true.
One who, in quiet, trod the private stage
Of rural labour, to a ripe old age.
Belov'd by neighbours, honour'd by his own;
Liv'd without spot, and dy'd without a groan.
Long may his humble virtues he rever'd;
Long be his name remember'd with regard;
And long may Agriculture's school produce
Such honest men as ALEXANDER BRUCE.

He died April 25, 1785, in the 81st year of his age, and 51st of conjugal felicity with his one beloved wife MARGRET CUMING, who survived him only 3 months, and was then laid down here, aged 78.

None of the monuments at Longside can be called ancient. The oldest is possibly that of the Keiths of Ludquharn, in whom a baronetcy was created in 1629 (Douglas' Baronage.) Only traces of the family arms are to be seen upon the tomb, which is built into the east dyke of the kirk-yard. Ludquharn also came to the Keiths by marriage; but the family and title have been long extinct. The property now belongs to James Russell, Esq. of Aden.

There is possibly no older date upon any grave-stone in the church-yard, than that in the following inscription:—

Here lyes ane honest werteous man called THOMAS DUNCAN, sometym of Elneruerdy, who depairted this life the 8 of September 1694, and of his age 58 years; and MARGARET ROBERTSON, who departed this life the 8 Sept. 1697.

—In the Poll Book of Aberdeenshire (1696), Margaret Robertson, "widow of Inververdy," is described as a portioner of the lands of Kinmundy and as having above 500 merks, and under 5000 merks of stocked money.

Here lyes the corps of FRANCIS DUNCAN, sometime Chamberlain to Kinmundy, who departed this life the 20 of June 1716, of age 89; also JEAN REID, his spous, who departed this life the 15 of August 1706.

—About the time above referred to, Nether Kinmundy belonged to a branch of the Gordons of Pitlurg and Straloch.

The next two inscriptions relate to ancestors of Dr Tait, Archbishop of Canterbury:—

[1.]

Sub hoc lapide cineres GULIELMI TAIT, carpentarii in Ludquharn, et AGNETIS CLERK, ejus conjugis; ille, humanæ salutis, 1725, ætatis suæ 57; illa, 1739 ætatis 79 anno, obierunt; necnon JOANSIS, GULIELMI, alterius GULIELMI, et AGNETIS TAIT, sobolis eorum qui prædecesserunt, sepulti sunt. Hic quoque conduntur exuviæ THOMÆ TAIT in Thunderton, filii S. D. Gulielmi et Agnetis natu maximi, qui in arte lapidaria, dum potuit, gnavus, in alenda familia fælix, moribus probus, animo æquus, vicinis amicus, tandem, annorum satur, fideque et spe fultus, ad patres migravit anno 1770, æt. 79. R. I. P.

[Under this stone are interred the ashes of WILLIAM TAIT, cartwright in Ludquharn, and of AGNES CLERK, his wife, who died, he in the year of human salvation, 1725, aged 57, and she in 1739, aged 70; and also of their children, JOHN, WILLIAM, a second WILLIAM, and AGNES TAIT, who predeceased them. Here also are laid the remains of THOMAS TAIT, in Thunderton, eldest son of the above William and Agnes, who, dilligent, while strength permitted, in his calling of stone-mason, happy in his family, a man of virtuous character and even temper, and a friendly neighbour, at length full of years, and sustained by faith and hope, departed to his fathers, in the year 1770, aged 79. May they rest in peace.]

[2.]

To the memory of GEORGE TAIT in Redbog, who, after having liv'd 48 years in the fear of God, and love of all good men, was, upon the 30th of May

1758, killed by the fall of a stack of timber at Peterhead, justly lamented by his friends, and sincerely regretted by all who knew him :—
> Stay, reader, and let fall a tear,
> On looking at this stone ;
> But call not anything severe,
> That Providence has done.
> Expecting death, the good man lives,
> Prepared from day to day ;
> And when God's will the summons gives,
> He's ready to obey.
> This good man lived by all belov'd,
> And dy'd by all deplor'd ;
> Dwelt here awhile, and then remov'd,
> To dwell with Christ the Lord.

—The above-named George was third brother of Thomas Tait, and his wife was Ann, daughter of Alex. Mundy, in Ennervedie. She was baptised 28th Nov. 1713, and died 14th Sep. 1772, after having had a family of three sons and four daughters. (*v.* Burke's Landed Gentry.)

Taits have been long resident in Longside. One of them lived at Savoch in 1625, and others were located, down to a pretty late date, in different parts of the parish. Probably the more important of the family were Alexander and John, the former of whom was in Mains of Ludquharn in 1729, and the latter in Mains of Kinmundy in 1741 (*Par. Reg., v. y.*) The bridge over the Ugy, near the railway station at Longside, is said to have been built by Thos. Tait, mentioned in inscription [1.] He is also locally said to have been the great-grand-father of Archbishop Tait.

In connection with the fact of Dr Tait being the first Scotchman who has filled the Archiepiscopal chair of England, and the travelling about London on underground railways, the following curious prophecy of 1601, by Richard Burbage, of the Globe Theatre, London, may be said to have been fulfilled :—

> "A Scot our King ? The limping State
> That day must need a crutch.
> What next ? In time a Scot will prate
> As Primate of our Church.
> When such shall be, why then you'll see,
> That day it will be found,
> The Saxon down through London town,
> Shall burrow under ground."

John, the son of Thomas Tait, acquired the property of Harvieston, in Clackmannanshire, about 17— ; and about 1805, his son Craufurd Tait, Esq. (the Archbishop's father), bought the adjoining estate of Castle Campbell from the Duke of Argyll. Both properties now belong to Sir Andrew Orr, a publisher in, and sometime Lord Provost of, Glasgow.

A table-shaped tomb-stone at Longside bears this epitaph :—

> And, is she gone, the once so lovely maid ?
> Gone hence, and now a dear departed shade !
> Call'd from this world in early dawn of life,
> Where but beginning to be called a wife ?
> Ye virgin tribe, whom chance may lead this way,
> Where brightest beauty moulders in the clay,
> Behold this stone, nor be asham'd to mourn
> A while o'er MARY ALEXANDER's urn—
> Then pause a little, while these lines you read,
> And learn to draw instruction from the dead :—
> She, who lies here, was once like one of you,
> Youthful and gay, and fair, as you are now :
> One week beheld her a young blooming bride,
> In marriage pomp, laid by her husband's side :
> The next we saw her in Death's livery drest,
> And brought her breathless body here to rest.
> Not all this world's gay hopes, nor present charms,
> Nor parents' tears, nor a fond husband's arms,
> Could stamp the least impression on her mind,
> Or fix to Earth, a soul for Heaven design'd ;
> Calmly she left a scene so lately try'd,
> Heav'n call'd her home, with pleasure she comply'd,
> Embrac'd her sorrowing friends, then smil'd, and dy'd.

Here lies the body of MARY ALEXANDER, spouse to John Robertson, mariner in Peterhead, who departed this life January the 3d, 1767, aged 24 years.

Also from a table-shaped stone on the south side of the church :—

S. M. of JAMES ARBUTHNOT in Rora, an affectionate husband, a tender parent, and faithful friend. Conspicuous for benevolence of heart and integrity of conduct, he gained the esteem of all. Possessed of the virtues which adorn the man and the Christian, his life was amiable, and his end was peace. He dy'd Apr. 16th 1770, aged 73 :—

Happy the man whose God, who reigns on high,
Hath taught to live, and hath prepared to die ;
His warfare o'er, and run his Christian race.
Ev'n Death becomes the messenger of peace—
Dispells his woes, then wafts his soul away,
To endless glory of eternal day.

Here also ly in hopes of a blessed immortality, MARGARET GORDON, his spouse. An affectionate wife, a tender mother, and sincere friend. She dy'd Nov. 1st, 1783, aged 84. Here are also deposited the remains of ELSPET ARBUTHNOT, their daughter, an amiable young woman, who, upon the 15th day of Nov. 1750, in the 21st year of her age, resigned her soul to God.

The next inscription is from a marble slab, fixed into an upright monument, within an enclosure, on the north-east side of the church-yard :—

Glory to God above. Sacred to the memory of the Revd JOHN SKINNER, for 64 years and upwards Episcopal clergyman in this parish, whose attainments as a Scholar, and Scriptural Research as a Divine, of which many written documents remain, acquired him a name, never to be forgotten in the Church in which he exercised his ministry, while his Pastoral Labours in the charge committed to him endeared him almost beyond example to the sorrowing flock, by whom, in testimony of their heartfelt regard, this monument is erected.
On the 16th day of June 1807, aged 86 years, he slept the sleep of death in the arms of the Right Rev. John Skinner, Bishop of the diocese of Aberdeen, his only surviving son, who, with his family, and other numerous descendants, shall never cease to feel the most devout and lively veneration for the talents, the acquirements, and character of a progenitor, who lived so justly respected, and died so sincerely lamented.

[From a flat stone, in front of the above] :—

In the same grave over which the adjoining monument is placed to the memory of her venerable husband, lie the remains of his beloved wife GRIZEL HUNTER, who died on the 21st day of Sept. 1799, in the 80th year of her age, having shewn herself, through life, the humble Christian, and, for nearly, 58 years, a partner of every conjugal virtue.
" When such friends part, 'tis the survivor dies."

—Mr Skinner was a native of Birse, Aberdeenshire, where his father was schoolmaster. His mother was first married to Donald Farquharson, laird of Balfour, in the same parish. She survived the birth of her son only about two years. His father afterwards went to Echt, where he died in 1776. In obedience to his own expressed wish that—" Where the Pitcher breaks let the shells lie; but let not a stone tell where *I* lie"— no monument marks the grave of Mr Skinner. An epitaph, however, was composed to his memory by his eldest and youngest sons, which is engrossed in the sederunt book of the Kirk-session of Echt. It is here printed from a copy, kindly made by the late Mr Malcolm, schoolmaster :—

"Dilectissimi parentis, JOANNIS SKINNER, M.A., scholæ in hac parochia per 50 annos magistri dignissimi, qui in officio ad extremum sedulus idem et probatus, in alenda prole, qua pater optabat, qua pauper potuit liberalitate, felix, animo æquus, moribus inculpatus, religionis tenax, ad vitia severus, jucundus amicis, discipulis charus, probis omnibus in pretio habitus, tandem octogenarius et secunda quam per 40 annos habuerat conjuge nuper orbatus, dysuriæ morbo intra biduum extinctus est, May 22° 1776."

[Erected to the memory of their beloved parent JOHN SKINNER, M.A., for 50 years a most deserving schoolmaster of this parish. He was diligent and approved in his office to the last, and successfully brought up his children with all the liberality that the limited means of an affectionate father permitted. He was even in temper, blameless in character, strict in the observance of his religious duties, a stern reprover of vice, pleasant to his friends, beloved of his scholars, and esteemed by all good men. He died at length of dysuria, after an illness of two days, 22nd May, 1776, in his 80th year, having been a short time before bereaved of his second wife, with whom he had lived 40 years.]

—Mr Skinner of Longside is believed to have written the contemporary epitaphs printed in this notice of Longside. An excellent account of his Life is prefixed to his Poetical Pieces (Edin. 1809), to which the reader is referred. It need only be here said that, among other works, Mr Skinner wrote an ecclesiastical history of Scotland, which is much sought after. His name, however, is more generally, and popularly associated with his poetical writings, of which Tullochgorum, the Ewie wi' the Crookit Horn, &c., are too well known to require comment; and every reader of Burns is aware of the friendly nature of the correspondence which passed between these two great masters of Scottish song. Mr S. lived in a thatched cottage at Linshart, with little more accommodation than "a but and a ben;" and there he reared a large and meritorious family, one of whom became Bishop of Aberdeen long before his father's decease. (v. p. 32.) Mr Skinner continued to reside at Linshart until 4 June 1807, when it was thought advisable to remove him to the house of his son, the Bishop, at Aberdeen; but he survived the change only for the short space of twelve days, when he died as above. Combined with his scholarly acquirements, and devotedness to his church and people, he possessed "infinite humour," which he enjoyed and exercised almost to his last moments. Being at a marriage in the parish soon after he came to the district, and remaining to enjoy the festivities beyond the time that a worthy dame thought scarcely decent for a minister, she took the liberty of advising Mr S. to leave the company by saying that—"If ye dinna gae hame, sir, folk 'll be speakin' aboot ye!" to which he curtly replied—"Maybe, gudewife; but I'll wager there'll be naebody readier than yersel'!" It is also told that a poor woman called one day at Linshart, while he was busily employed in some matter of importance; and, with the view of not being detained by her, he at once gave her some pecuniary assistance, when the woman, in the gratitude of her heart, exclaimed—"May the Lord bless you and your family, sir; an' may ye a' be in Heaven the nicht!" "I'm very much obliged to you, my good woman," quo' the old man, "for all your kind wishes; only, you needna be so particular as to *the time!*"

WILLIAM KIDD, d. 1834, a. 84 :—
Tho' 84 be long, 'tis gone and past,
And here in peace I'm resting at the last.

PETER and MARGARET SANGSTER, Kinmundy, died, aged respectively 25 and 29 years, in 1791-98 :—
Reader, suppose thy neighbour's case thine own,
And breath a fellow feeling o'er this stone.

FRANCIS GREIG, Torhendry, d. 1786, a. 72 :—
The man of honest heart, and prudent head,
Is lov'd while living, and esteem'd when dead,
And such was he whose epitaph we read.

S. M. In dutiful remembrance of an attentive husband, an exemplary parent, an agreeable neighbour, an expert farmer, in business active, in adversity cheerful, in principle conscientious, in practice irreproachable, the sensible man and sincere Christian—this small monument of family love is laid over the mortal part of ANDREW KIDD, who dy'd in Rora, March 10, 1795, aged 75 :—
Peace to his body in its bed of rest,
Till call'd to join the soul it once possest,
And soul and body be for ever blest.

His spouse ELIZABETH SELLER, died Dec. 27, 1801, aged 79.

Near Mr Skinner's monument, enclosed by a low wall, a stone with a long laudatory inscription, is prefaced by these words :—
S. M. Dy'd Febr. 3, 1790, in the 85th year of his age, and 58th of his ministry, JOHN BROWN, A.M., minister of Longside, &c. (v. p. 58.)

On the right of the churchyard gate, two inscribed monuments, the oldest in Latin, the other in English, record the death of two of the parish ministers :—

The Revd JOHN LUMSDEN, 15 years minister of the parish, died January 1732, aged 47 : His wife's name was FRANCES FULLARTON.

The Revd WILLIAM GREIG, aged 72, died on Sunday 17 Aug. 1828, "having that day preached to his people." His wife MARGARET SKINNER, died 7 Oct. 1827, aged 69.

Amelia Milne, widow of CHARLES MCDONALD, Burnside, in memory of her beloved son WILLIAM, whose life was taken away near the Kirktown of St Fergus, on the 19 Nov. 1853, in the 29th year of his age. . . . . . The secret of his death is with the Lord, who also hath the record of his humble faith, his Christian character, and his blameless life, to be all disclosed on that great day when He shall come to judge the world in righteousness, and give to every one according to his deeds.

—It was for the murder of this person that Smith, an unqualified medical practitioner at St Fergus, was tried at the Spring Assizes, Aberdeen, in 1854. It appears that Smith had effected an assurance on the life of M'Donald, and met him by appointment on the evening of 29th November, when the young man came by his death from a pistol shot. Smith, who afterwards went to New Zealand, was acquitted on the verdict of *not proven*; but the insurance money was never paid to him.

Near the north dyke of the churchyard, a granite obelisk bears :—

Erected in 1861 to indicate the grave of JAMIE FLEEMAN, in answer to his prayer—"Dinna bury me like a beast."

—This singular being was born at Ludquharn in 1713, and died at Kinmundy in 1778. His remarkable sayings and doings are narrated in an interesting pamphlet entitled The Life and Death of Jamie Fleeman, the Laird of Udny's Fool, by Rev. Dr Pratt, Episcopal minister, Cruden. It ought to be added that Dr PRATT, who was also the author of "Buchan," and other meritorious works, died on 20 March 1869, beloved and respected by all who could appreciate unobtrusive worth, and real merit.

A handsome Episcopal church, built of native granite, with nave, side aisles, and chancel, also a central tower about 90 feet high, is the most striking object in Longside. It was founded in 1853, and dedicated to S. JOHN. A stained glass window of three lights, illustrative of the principal events in the life of Our Saviour, ornaments the church; and a brass below the window is inscribed to Mr Skinner :—

In memoriam admodum Reverendi JOANNIS SKINNER, M.A., per sexaginta quatuor annos hujus gregis pastoris, qui natus iij Octob. 1721, obijt 16 Jun: 1807.

The south window of the chancel contains a painting of S. JOHN, with the following :—

M. S. JOANNIS CUMMING, qui per multos annos in hoc grege curam pastoralem fidelissime exercuit.

—Mr C., who was a grandson of Mr Skinner, died pastor of this place in 18—, and a portrait of him, by Mitchell, is preserved in the vestry.

There is a painted window of two lights in the south aisle; one picture is illustrative of the Lord's Prayer, "Thy kingdom come, thy will be done;" another of the text, "Suffer little children to come unto me." Brasses record the death of JOHN HUTCHISON, late in Monyruy, who died in New Zealand, 1863, aged 54; and his wife CATHERINE ARBUTHNOT, who died 1856, aged 43. Another window of one light, representing the good Samaritan, is in memory of ROBERT CHEVES, who was born in 1791, and died in 1856.

The Established and Free Churches are also good plain buildings; and the village of Longside, which is on the increase, contains some neat dwelling houses.

The Reverend CHARLES ARBUTHNOTT, Abbot of the Scots College of St James' in Ratisbon, who died 19 April 1820, aged 84, was a native of Longside. So highly was the Abbot respected for his worth and learning by the German Princes, that, when it was resolved, by the Diet of Ratisbon, to secularise the church lands of the Empire, an express exception was made in the Abbot's favour. The respect and esteem for him never abated; and his funeral was attended by the highest dignitaries in Germany.

Grange, or Strathisla.

(BLESSED VIRGIN MARY.)

THE church of Grange was originally a chapel belonging to the Abbots of Kinloss, to which Abbacy the lands of *Strathylaf*, with their pertinents, &c., were granted by William the Lion, 1195 6.

Grange was formerly a part of the parish of Keith, from which it was disjoined in 1618.

The old church, which stood in the burial ground, was in a ruinous state in 1793. In 1795, the present kirk was erected upon an adjoining mound.

ALEXANDER, the first DUFF of Braco, who died in 1705, was buried in the aisle of the old church, where there was a handsome monument to his memory, now buried, or otherwise lost. It was in consequence of the failure of the male succession in the person of William, son of the above Alexander Duff, that Alexander's next brother of Dipple succeeded to Braco; and it was the eldest son of William Duff of Braco and Dipple who was the first Earl of Fife.

A slab of Portsoy marble, encased in free stone, built into the churchyard dyke, is thus inscribed:—

ALEXANDER KERR, doctus, non doctor, ecclesiæ hujus ab instaurata religione pastor secundus, verum officii fideli exercitio nemini secundus, vir magni ingenii ac indefessi laboris, donis omnibus foris domique mystæ necessariis abunde refertus veritatem, pietatem, charitatem, voce, vita, exemplo docuit, coluit, promovit. Hic, ubi vires exantlavit, exuvias deposuit, anno Dom. 1693, ministerii 43, ætatis 66. Memento mori.

[ALEXANDER KERR, a learned man, although not a doctor, second pastor of this church after the Reformation, but second to none in the faithful discharge of his sacred duties; a man of great ability and unwearied activity, richly endowed with all the gifts necessary to a minister at home and abroad, taught, cultivated, and promoted, by voice, life, and example, truth, piety, and charity. Here, where he spent his strength, he laid down his remains, A.D. 1693, in the 66th year of his age, and the 43d of his ministry. Remember death.]

Upon another stone:—

Associatæ August 16, 1666: Hic cõquiescunt in Dõino, ANA GORDONA, uxor piissima D. Alr. Keri, symmystæ Grangen., natæque 4 eodè busto.

[Associated (married) Aug. 16, 1666: Here rest together in the Lord, ANNA GORDON, the most pious wife of Mr Alex. Kerr, joint minister of Grange, and four daughters, in the same tomb.]

Upon the wall of the burial aisle of the Innes' of Edingicht, the gate of which is dated 1816:—

This monument is erected by John Innes of Mwiryfold to the memory of THOMAS INNES, of Mwiryfold, his father, who lyes here interred. He died the 12 of Sept. 1754, aged 73 years.

—Thomas Innes of Muiryfold was a son of the laird of Edingicht, and long factor for the Earl of Fife, in which capacity he was succeeded by a son. Another son was a W.S. in Edinburgh, and became founder of the family of Innes of Netherdale, in Marnoch. The Innes' of Edingicht are cadets of Innes of that ilk in Morayshire, and have held the property of Edingicht from about the middle of the 16th century. On the death of Sir William, the 8th in succession from Robert of Innermarkie and Balveny, who was created a baronet in 1628, the title descended to John of Edingicht, whose 2d son is the present baronet. It is told that one of the family of Edingicht, who was an officer in the army, when on his way to Holland during the war towards the close of the last century, was reprimanded by his commander for not having a proper hat on his head, upon which Innes jocularly remarked (in allusion to the coming struggle, and the source from which, if spared, he meant to supply himself), "that there wad soon be mae hats than heads!"

Upon a tablet built into the wall of the churchyard:—

Mr ARCHD. CAMPBEL, minister of Grange 22 years, was Diligent in Office, Learned in Science, the Animated Friend, and Chearful Companion. He lived 66 years. Died the 16, was buried here his birth day, the 19 October 1774. His intimate Friend and Trustee, John Innes of Muryfold, erects this monument.

JAMES SHEPHERD, Poolside of Keith, d. 1817, a. 83:—

As a mark of respect for his virtuous life
Now reaping the fruit of his gain,
This stone is erected by ISOBEL his wife,
Till in glory she meet him again.

[ISOBEL BIRNIE, wife of J. Shepherd, d. 1832, a. 84.]

Upon a table-shaped stone:—

A morte et potestate sepulchri nulli redemptio. Vive memor lethi. Beati in Domino qui obeunt. Hic conduntur cineres PATRICII WILSON, quondam in Cantlie, et ISOBELLÆ STRACHAN, ejus conjugis, qui mortem obiere, ille Apr. 4, 1723, illa Dec. . . 1709. P.W. I.S. Hic itidem GUL. WILSON, eorum natu filius minimus, et ALEX. GAIRDEN, eorum nepos, flore ætatis exuvias deposuere.

[From death and the power of the grave there is no redemption. Live mindful of death. Blessed are they who die in the Lord. Here lie the ashes of PATRICK WILSON, sometime in Cantlie, and of ISOBELLA STRACHAN, and his wife, who died 4 April 1723, and Dec. . . 1709, respectively. Here also are laid the ashes of WILLIAM WILSON, their youngest son, and of ALEX. GAIRDEN, their grandson, who were cut off in the flower of their age.]

An adjoining monument bears :—

Sacrum memoriæ, GEORGII WILSON, nuper in Cantly, qui mortem obiit 22 die Martis, A.D. 1742, ætatis suæ 64. Hoc amoris et doloris monumentum uxor superstes et mœrens posuit.

[Sacred to the memory of GEORGE WILSON, late in Cantly, who died 22 March 1742, in the 64 year of his age. His surviving and sorrowing wife erected this monument in token of her love and grief.]

—This was the father-in-law of James Ferguson, the astronomer. His mother-in-law (whose death is not recorded upon the stone) was ELSPETH, daughter of Archibald GRANT of Edin Valley. She died 29 Jan. 1771. It was on 31 May 1739, that "James Ferguson, in the parish of Keith, and Isobel Wilson" were married at Grange. They had one daughter and three sons, all born in London, where the two eldest sons died respectively in 1772 and 1803. The youngest son died in Edinburgh in 1833. The daughter Agnes, who was born in 1745, was, says Dr E. Henderson, in his Life of Ferguson (p. 468), "remarkable for her beauty and intelligence; she suddenly disappeared about the end of July, or early in Aug. 1763, and was never more seen by her parents. Our late researches regarding her show that she was decoyed by a young nobleman and taken to Italy. He abandoned her, and she, being probably ashamed to return to her parents, whom

she had disgraced, to maintain herself, wrote articles for the magazines. She afterwards became an actress, for a brief period. She ultimately led an irregular life, and died in poverty in a miserable garret, in Old Round Court, Strand (now removed), 27 January 1792, aged 47 years." Ferguson himself was born in a secluded but picturesque spot on the Deveron, at a place called the Core of Mayen, in Rothiemay, Banffshire, upon the left side of the road from Rothiemay to the kirk of Marnoch. His parents were in poor circumstances. He was the 2d son of John Ferguson and Elspeth Lobban, and was born 25 April 1710, and died at London 16 November 1776. For other interesting particulars, see Dr Henderson's Life of Ferguson.

JOHN PRIEST died, Nov. 1803, aged 62 :—

 As pensively you pass,
 Above the silent dead,
 Improve your time—note this—
 And at your leasure read
   from

Psa. 37 3, 6; Prov. 3, 5, 6; Isa. 1, 16-18; 53, 6, 13; Matt. 7, 7, 14; John, v. 39-40; Rom. viii. 1, 14; 2d Pet. 1, 5, 11; Rev. 23, 12-17.

Revd. ANDREW YOUNG of the Associate Congregations of Keith and Grange—"after the disjunction of the two congregations in 1785, minister of Grange only"—died 21 May 1788, in the 37th year of his life, and 12th of his ministry.

Revd. JOHN PRIMROSE of the Associate Congregation, Whitehill, Grange, died 28 Feb. 1832, aged 81, and in the 43d year of his ministry.

Revd. JOHN SMITH of the Wesleyan Methodist Society, sometime missionary in Barbadoes and St Vincent, West Indies, died 17 Sep. 1855, aged 27.

A recently erected mural tablet to the memory of the father of Mr Duff, who, under the assumed name of *Andrew Halliday*, is the author of several popular plays and other works, bears :—

The Rev. WILLIAM DUFF, 23 years minister of Grange, died 23 Sep. 1844, aged 53.

The district of Grange, or Strathisla, having belonged to the Abbey of Kinloss, the whole lands were anciently held under the superiority of that house (v. Records of the Monastery of Kinloss, by John Stuart, LL.D.) The monks had a castle, or residence, upon the knoll now occupied by the church of Grange. It was surrounded by a ditch; and about 1574, a "tour, fortalice, and orchard," adorned the mound.

The neighbourhood of the church of Grange possesses much natural beauty. Near it stands the hamlet of the Kirktown, with "the noisy mansion," in which the youth of the district have been long taught by a most accomplished master.

Although, now-a-days, there is no ale-house at *the clachan of Grange*, the door-lintel of the old hostelry is at Muiryfold, and upon it is this quaint couplet:—

YE GENTLEMEN, AS YE GO BY,
COME IOIN YOVR PLACK, FOR IAMIE'S DRY.

Besides the Established Church, there are also Free and U.P., Churches in the parish. The former is at no great distance from the parish kirk, and the latter is situated at Whitehill, where there has been a congregation for about a century.

A bridge which crosses the Isla, near the church, "was built in 1699, by Alexander Christie, tenant in Cantly, for the glory of God, and the good of the people of Grange." The stone which bore this inscription is said to have fallen into the Isla; and the Kirk-session records shew that the sum of 100 merks Scots, which was left by Christie for the maintenance of the bridge, was expended before 1740. The bridge was originally built for foot passengers. It was repaired and widened in 1783, for horses and carts, &c.

The two extracts below, copied from the Kirk-session records of Grange, are interesting. The first shows the gravity with which old Kirk-sessions treated a seemingly harmless circumstance, while the latter implies a belief in another act of even a more superstitious character than the former. The first entry, dated 21st April, 1686, is as follows:—

"Isabell Reid compeared for charming, and confessed that she used to charme the eyes for the mark, by spitting, blowing, into the eye, and repeating an orison, one of which she repeated before the Session, bot denyed that she could charme for any other distemper. That in respect it is not an ordinarie sin, it is referred to the presbyterie."

The next extract (11th June 1683) goes to prove that a young woman in the parish of Grange was so sorely afflicted with scrofula, that she resolved to go to London, in the hope of being cured of the disease, by the *Royal Touch*, which was long deemed to be efficacious in that complaint:—

"Marjorie Gray being to go up to London for seeking remedie to her disease, supposed to be the King's Evil, got a Testificat declairing her to be free from church censure and public scandal."

—William of Malmesbury says that Edward the Confessor was the first prince who pretended to have the power of curing scrofula; and that the miracle was first performed upon a young married woman. He farther states that the ceremony was done by the king stroking the afflicted parts with his hand dipt in water; also, that the cure was perfected within a week, and the woman, previously childless, gave birth to twins in due time! The celebrated Dr Samuel Johnson was *touched* for the same disease, when a child, by Queen Anne, but without any good effect; and, doubtless, although unrecorded, the visit of Marjory Gray to King Charles was attended with no better success.

Additional Inscriptions at Grange.

The following is from a recently erected monument within the Edingight burial aisle:—

Near this tablet, mingling with the dust of his Ancestors, lie the remains of Sir JOHN INNES, of Balvenie and Edingight, Baronet, who died at Aberdeen, 23rd March 1829, aged 71. Also those of his spouse, Dame BARBARA FORBES, who died 12th August 1844, aged 74. Of his eldest son, Sir JOHN INNES, Bart., who died 3rd December 1838, aged 37. Of his daughter, BARBARA, who died 14th March 1865, aged 61. Also of his grandson, ALEXANDER, who died 3rd March 1845, aged 3.

—Sir James Innes, Bart., the erector of this monument, succeeded to the titles and estates of Edingight on the death of his brother in 1838. He married a daughter of Alex. Thurburn, Esq., sometime tenant of Drum, and a sister of Wm. Thurburn, Esq., solicitor and bank agent in Keith (*infra*, p. 167.)

In memory of ALEXANDER HOWIE, carrier, Rothiemay, who died on the 14th Sep. 1839, aged 26 years. This stone was erected by those Merchants in the district, who were his principal employers, in token of their respect for his uniform integrity, and his unremitting attention to business.

The next inscription (from a flat slab), is chiefly remarkable for its odd orthography :—

    Sub hoc Saxo Jacet Alex^r Long
    muir Antiquis InteJerrimisque Pro
    genitoribus editus qui post
    30 Annor^r Stadi^r SePtris 11mo
    Anno Supra mill^r Sepr 20mo
    4to fatisCesit*
    trAnsuverio* patres Sic est"   [* *sic*.
    trAnsib^{l}mus Omnes
    Vita in pati^{e}ntia mors in
    desiderio
    non est mortale qd opto

Under this stone lies ALEXR. LONGMUIR, descended from an ancient and most respectable family, who, after a career of 30 years, died 11th Sep. 1724. Our fathers have passed away, in like manner shall we also all pass away.
Life in patience, death in desire, what I wish for is not mortal.]

—The above inscription probably relates to an ancestor of the Longmuirs in Keith (*infra*, p. 166), one of whom has recently presented his fellow-townsmen with a handsome public hall. The surname may have been carried to the North from Ayrshire, where there is a place called *Langmure*. In 1477 (*Reg. Honoris de Morton*), James Langmour, presbyter, witnesses a deed regarding the Collegiate Church of Dalkeith.

The next two inscriptions (from tablets built into the kirk-yard dyke), and note, are more fully given here than below (*v.* pp. 101-2). The first slab was "removed from the church" in 1795 :—

[1.]
Associat$_e$ Agvst 16, 1666: Hic cōqviescvt in Doino, ANA GORDONA, vxor pictissia D. Ari. Kori, symystæ Graugeu : natæque 4 eodē busto.

[2.]
Sacred to the memory of the Rev. WILLIAM DUFF, 23 years minister of Grange, died 23rd Sept. 1844, aged 53 ; and of his children, JAMES DUFF, died in infancy, July 1826 ; MARY-KEITH DUFF, died Sep. 1848, aged 16 ; JOHN DUFF, A.M., died Feb. 1849, aged 21.

—Mr W. Duff, who came from Dumfriesshire, had one son who has attained the rank of a General in the American army, and another, under the name of " Andrew Halliday," has acquired fame as the author of several popular plays, &c. The latter was named after his father's friend and fellow-student, Sir Andrew Halliday, sometime Domestic Physician to the Duke of Clarence.

~~~~~~~~~~~~~~~~~~~~~~~~~~~~~~~~~~

Durris.
(S. CONGAL, ABBOT.)

THE church of *Durris*, which is rated in the old Taxation at 10 merks, was a rectory in the diocese of St Andrews.

Messrs George Fraser and Archibald Hog were ministers of Durris in 1568 and 1574 respectively. The former had probably been related to the Frasers of Durris, and the latter to the Hogs of Blairiedryne. I have seen no record of any old " reidar" at Durris.

After the Reformation the church was attached to the Presbytery of Fordoun ; but, in 1717, it was annexed to that of Aberdeen, from which city it is distant about 12 miles.

The present kirk, which is a plain building, pleasantly situated on the south banks of the Dee, was erected in 1822. The bell (*sup*., p. 27), bears this inscription :—

    IOHN MOWAT OLD ABD. FE. 1765 ;
    IN VSVM ECCLESIÆ DE DVRRIS.
    SABATA PANGO, FUNERA PLANGO.

The burial aisle of the Frasers of Durris is at the east end of the kirk. It contains a recess tomb, dated 1594. The Fraser arms, with the initials, T. F., and motto, CONSTANT, are upon a panel below the date. Sir A. Fraser, chamberlain, and brother-in-law to Bruce, had a grant of the thanedoms of Durris and Cowie from that king.

The Fraser tomb has been used by subsequent proprietors. It was re-edified in 1869 by the late laird of Durris, who put up six granite slabs, four of which are respectively inscribed as follows:—

1869: To the memory of ANTHONY MACTIER, Esq. of Durris: Died 5th Aug. 1854, aged 81.

Of MARIA MACTIER, wife of the late Anthony Mactier, Esq. of Durris: Died 30th Dec. 1852, aged 52.

Of ELIZA-ROSE MACTIER, eldest daughter of Anthony and Maria Mactier: Died 14th Oct. 1841, aged 16.

Of HENRY MACTIER, 8th son of the said Anthony and Maria Mactier: Born 1st Sept. 1836, died 15th Sept. 1836.

—Mr Mactier, who bought Durris about 1837, made money in India as a merchant. He belonged to Galloway; and his wife was a daughter of Alex. Binny, Esq., who resided in St Andrews, Fifeshire. Her uncle, Thomas Binny, Esq. of Fearn and Maulesden, in Angus, possessed a large painting, by Sir Thos. Lawrence, of Mrs Mactier and her father, &c.—possibly one of Lawrence's grandest family groups. Mr T. Binny had also a number of early pictures by Sir H. Raeburn, Sir J. Watson-Gordon, and Colvin Smith. The Binnys were come of a burgess family in Forfar.

By judicious management and improvement, Mr Mactier is said to have doubled the value of the estate of Durris. He was succeeded by a son, who sold the property in 1867 to James Young of Kelly, Esq., F.R.S., paraffin oil manufacturer.

When the Fraser Aisle was undergoing repair, two mutilated grave-stones, were found with the following remains of inscriptions:—

[1.]

Here lyes ISOBEL FR . . ER, spous . . . . aster Iohn . . . . . . minister of Duries, who departed this life the 13 of May 1716, in the -2 of her age.

—This is possibly the grave-stone of the first wife of Mr John Reid, for according to Scott's Fasti, he left a widow. The same authority states that Mr Reid, previously schoolmaster at Banchory-Ternan, was appointed minister of Durris in 1675, and that he was deposed in 1716.

[2.]

. . . . . . Magister ANDREAS
. . . . Magistri Ioannis
. . . . ris ecclesiæ Dur
. . . . . sacrosanctæ . . . .
. . . . . . heologiæ studiosus
. . . . decimo die Sept.
. . . . 26 . 17 . .

A walled enclosure, on the west side of the kirk-yard, is called the *Innes Aisle*. Although it was long used as the burial place of the Inneses, who were lessees of Durris, the tomb contains no monument. The last of this branch of the family was John Innes, Esq., sheriff-substitute of Kincardineshire, who was descended from the house of Leuchars, in Moray, and father of Professor Cosmo Innes of Edinburgh (*sup.*, p. 53.)

The next four inscriptions are from flat stones in the burial-ground:—

[1.]

1715 : I. F : C. F. Here under lyeth IOHN FRASER in Mill of Doors, who departed the 6 day of July 1711, in the 63 year of his age.

[2.]

Here lyes WILLIAM BISSET, late farmer in Darnfourd, who died ye 2d . . . . 1743, aged 70 years. Also ISOBEL PIERIE, his spouse, who died Nov. — 1742, aged 70.

Vain mortals, learn from hence to know,
Its vain to search for bliss below,
Since here ye virtuous, wise, and just
Lies mould'ring to his ancient dust.

[3.]

Here lyes the body of WILLIAM HOGG, late farmer in Mickle barns, who died 26th Feb. 1751, aged 72 years. We see impartial death cuts down, &c.

[4.]

DAVID WALKER, farmer, Mill of Montquigh, d. 1775, a. 76 :—

No lingering sickness, or long warning pains,
The pious want to purify their Stains ;
To pray forbearance from impending fate,
And urge repentance on a death-bed state,
Heaven found him fit in any hour to die,
And sudden snatch'd him kindly to the joy.

P

The district of Durris—the history and traditions of which have been given in Memorials of Angus and Mearns—was a thanedom, with a royal hunting forest, &c. The castle of Durris stood where a monument to the late Duke of Gordon is erected. It was a place of some note during the times of Alexander III. and Edward I.; and (as shewn by Spalding) the house and lands were oftener than once harried during Montrose's Wars.

A bridge crossed the Dee near the old castle in the time of Alexander III. There are at present two iron-girder bridges in the parish—one at Park, and another near Crathes, the latter of which was erected chiefly at the cost of the late laird of Durris. The Shiach or Fairy's burn—a pretty Highland stream—is crossed by a stone bridge near the parish kirk.

The Free Church of Durris and Mary Culter stands about a mile to the north-west of the parish kirk of Durris.

Statutory fairs are still held in the parish, near the Bridge of Park. Probably these represent "St Congal's fair," which (Edinburgh Prognostication for 1706) was held " at the kirk of Doors in Mernshire."

As in most parts of the country, Superstition had a firm footing in Durris in old times; and, according to story, it was fostered there by a pedagogue who played upon the credulity of his neighbours by occasionally personating his Satanic Majesty! On one occasion he appeared among the rafters of the church at an evening meeting, in the guise of a horned ox, with glaring eyes, and nearly terrified the people out of their wits. Mr Reid, minister of Banchory, being in the locality at the time, was asked to go to the kirk to *lay* Satan; and it is said that, upon seeing the parson, who was remarkable for strength of body as well as of mind, " horney" bawled out :—

" What are you doin' here, Rob Reid,
    Wi' your hard head ?"
To which Mr Reid naively replied :—
    " Whether my head be hard or saft—
      Come you doon,
    Or I'll crack your croon !"

Monifieth

(S. RULE, or REGULAS.)

GILCHRIST, EARL of ANGUS, gave the church of *Munifod* to the monks of Arbroath soon after the foundation of the Abbey. In 1220, his grand-son, Earl Malcolm, gifted the Abthane lands of Monifieth to Nicolas, the son of a priest at Kirriemuir. About twenty years later (1242) Countess Maud confirmed a donation to Arbroath, of lands, with a toft and croft, on the south side of the kirk of Monifieth, which were held by the Culdees, in her father's time (Reg. Vet. de Aberb.)

A number of Sculptured Stones, which were found at the church of Monifieth, are now preserved in the National Museum. They were first engraved by Mr P. Chalmers of Aldbar, and afterwards by the Spalding Club. Descriptions of the locality are given in both these works, also in Proceedings of the Society of Antiquaries of Scotland, vols. i. and ix. The engravings upon the opposite page (kindly lent by the Society of Antiquaries of Scotland), represent two of the latest discovered of these remarkable monuments.

The church of Monifieth and its chapel, the latter of which was at Broughty Ferry (*infra*, p. 114), are rated (Old Taxation) at 40 merks.

Some writers affirm that a chapel, dedicated to OUR LADY, stood in ancient times upon the *Lady Banks*, in the Tay, opposite to Monifieth. This would imply the existence of a population upon, or near that spot, which, although at a considerable distance from the shore now-a-days, had likely been of comparatively easy access at the period referred to. I am told that, within the last twelve years, the Tay has encroached fully twenty feet upon the Links of Monifieth.

"TRUEL Fair at the Kirk of Kinnethmont, and at Kirktown of Monifieth," appears under Oct. in the Edinburgh Prognostication for 1706.

In 1574 the churches of Monifieth, Barry, and Murroes, were served by Mr Andrew Auchenleck, as minister; and James Lovell was the contemporary reader, or schoolmaster, at Monifieth.

[Two Sculptured Stones at Monifieth.]

The present church was erected in 1812-13. It occupies much the same site as the previous building, which possessed considerable architectural beauty. The bell, which is a fine toned, prettily moulded instrument, is adorned with two medallion portraits. It has also a floral ornament round its rim, and this inscription :—

HENRICVS : IE . SVIS . TOVT . FOVR . VRAI.
IACOB . SER . M. F. MDLXV.

[Henry : I am all for truth. Jacob Ser made me, 1565.]

From a marble monument within the church :—

Here lyes the Body of GEORGE DEMPSTER of Dunnichen, Merchant in Dundee, who died 2d June 1752, in the 75th Year of his Age. And also the Body of MARGARET RAIT, his Spouse, who died — April 1740, in the — Year of her Age. And also his Father, *JOHN DEMPSTER*, Minister of this Parish, who died April 1710.

—The above inscription contains some inaccuracies. According to the Kirk-session records, George Dempster and his wife were interred within the church of Monifieth, on 2d June 1753, and 9th May 1741, respectively ; while the Presbytery books show that the minister died in 1708.

The above-named George Dempster was an extensive general merchant and corn-dealer in Dundee. He was also chamberlain or factor to the Countess of Panmure ; and at the time of his death he not only owned the barony of Dunnichen, but also the estates of Newbigging, Laws, Omachie, Burnside, Restenuet, Wester Denhead, Galry, Hillock, Ethiebeaton, and New Grange, now Letham Grange. In 1753, these properties yielded a gross annual rental of £9233 16s Scots, or £769 8s 4d sterling.

Mr Dempster was married 19th Oct. 1699. His wife was a daughter of Mr Wm. Rait, minister of Monikie, and laird of Pitforthy, near Brechin, by Margaret Yeaman, a daughter of the laird of Dryburgh. Pitforthy came to Mrs Dempster's grand-father, who was minister of Dundee, and Principal of the College of Aberdeen, through his marriage with the heiress. She was a daughter of the last Guthrie of Pitforthy, and a niece of the Rev. James Guthrie of Fenwick, author of the Christian's Great Interest.

Mr George Dempster took a very decided part in politics ; and whether owing to that circumstance, or to an outburst of the populace at a time of dearth and scarcity, is not stated ; but it appears that, during his absence from Dundee in February 1720, his premises were broken into and plundered by the inhabitants. This affair is described in the following letter, addressed by Mr Dempster to the Hon. Harrie Maule of Kellie :—

"DUNDIE, 27th Febry. 1720.

"SIR,—I am honoured w^t yours of the 16th, signifying your simpathy in my most melancholly affliction. I seed at my Returne to this wicked Place, the Ruins of a well plenished Hous, Shope, and Cellars ; and of all the hundreds that Robed me in a most Barberous maner, there is not one secured ; but, upon the Conterar, are incouraged by the Magistrats, whose slackness in punishing any of them, hath, in place of quieting the minds of the People here, inraged them more than formirly, soe that if there were not some souldeirs here to supress the Mobe, they would be up againe. I am still perswaded that, if it were layed before the Parliment, the Town would be found layable for my damages, which will amount to £1000 str., Besids the loss of my pappers, & turning me out of all Bussiness here, for they are so inraged at me in this place, by the above incorragement, that they threaten to asationat me ; wherefor pray lett me have your asistance." . . . .

The minister of Monifieth is said to have been descended from the Dempsters of Careston and Auchterless (Douglas' Baronage). A branch of that ancient family was designed of Pitforthy, near Brechin, long before that property came to the Guthries, above noticed. Some of the Dempsters of Careston and Pitforthy were merchants and burgesses of Brechin at an early date. No fewer than three persons of the surname were rulers of the burgh in 1641, Robert Dempster being then a bailie, and Charles and James towncouncillors.

The Rev. Mr Dempster of Monifieth, who was one of three sons "laufull to George Dempster, citiner of Brechin," began life as preceptor of the Maisondieu or Grammar School of his native city. He was afterwards minister of Brechin; and on his appointment to that living, he was succeeded in the preceptorship by his brother James. When the church of Monifieth became vacant in 1675, Mr Dempster was translated to it from Brechin by his friend and patron, the Earl of Panmure.

It was sometime before 10th July 1678, that Mr Dempster married Anna Maule. She was the widow of Mr Alex. Erskine, chamberlain to the Earl of Panmure, and brother to the laird of Carbuddo. She bore at least three sons to Mr Erskine, and had a numerous family by Mr Dempster, the eldest of whom was the above-named George, the first Dempster of Dunnichen (*Documents at Panmure*). Mrs Dempster died 27th June 1722, and was buried within the church of Monifieth.

In addition to the above inscription, the names and good deeds of the minister of Monifieth and his wife were recorded upon a panel, which was taken from the church in 1812–13. It was kept in an adjoining wood-yard until about 1856, since which time it has disappeared. Along with a bold carving of the Dempster and Maule arms, the panel bore this inscription :—

QVAM AMAVI DECOREM DOMVS TVÆ. O ! DOMINE.
Lord, I have loved the habitation of thy house, and the place where thine honour dwelleth.
MR. JOHN DEMPSTER, AND ANNA MAULE HIS SPOUSE, CEILED THIS CHURCH.

Mr Dempster's immediate predecessor in Monifieth was Mr JOHN BARCLAY, a son of the laird of Johnstone in the Mearns. He was previously minister at Kinnaird, near Brechin, and was admitted to Monifieth, 9th May 1649. He took the oath of allegiance to King Charles within the church of Monifieth, 5th Sept. 1662, before Sir Jas. Ogilvy of Newgrange, knight, and Andrew Gray of Hayston, sheriff-clerk of Forfarshire. Mr Barclay, who was twice married, had a large family, and died in 1675. His son, John, followed his father's profession; and a daughter, Grizel, who married "the tutor of Omachie's relation," appeared before the kirk-session in 1688.

Before the present church was built, there was a monument to the memory of Mr Barclay within "the queer" at Monifieth. A shield, with the Barclay arms, and the initials, M. I. B., &c., now built into the gable of the church, is possibly a portion of that tomb. The following couplet, which is given by Menteith from Mr Barclay's monument, although inapplicable to himself, may possibly have reference to the condition of some member of his family :—

" BARCLAIUM forsan culpas de coelibe vita;
Falleris; uxores duxerat ille novem.
' Of Barclay's single life if you complain,
You err; he had for wife the muses nine.' "

But the most stately tomb at Monifieth was that of Durham of Pitkerro, who, in 1626, after giving 300 merks to the poor of the parish, was allowed to erect a burial aisle on "the north-side of the queer" of the kirk. This monument, along with that to Mr Barclay, was wantonly destroyed when the present kirk was built; at which time, not only were the fine mouldings of the church allowed to be utilized, but the very tombstones were carried off to pave houses and shops in the adjoining village. This disgraceful outrage upon good taste and feeling was perpetrated during the incumbency of the Rev. Wm. Johnstone, author of a pamphlet upon the Decline of Piety !

One part of the Pitkerro tomb, consisting of war trophies, lies in the church-yard; and other portions are built into the east gable of the kirk. High up in the same wall, a slab bears the following inscription, prettily cut in interlaced Roman capitals :—

HIC . SITVS . SEPVLCHRVM . HOC . SIBI . POSTER-ISQVE . SVIS . EXTRVENDVM . CVRAVIT . VIR . CLARVS . PIVS . AC . PRODVS . DVRHAME . DE . PITCARR . ARGESTARIVS . QVONDAM . R . IAC . VI . SEMPI-TERNÆ . MEMORIÆ . CVIVS . MAIORES . EADEM . HÆC . NOMEN . ET . ARMA . GERENTES . HAC . IN . PAROCHINA . REGNO . RO . R. I^{mi} . SESE . DEIN . POSVERVNT . VBI . EXINDE . HVC . VSQVE . CLARV-ERVNT .

[In this tomb, which he caused to be constructed for himself and his posterity, lies DURHAME of Pitcarro, a distinguished, pious, and good man, cashier to the late King James VI. of immortal memory;

and whose ancestors, who bore the same name and arms, were settled in this parish in the reign of King Robert I., where they have occupied a distinguished position up to the present time.]

—The "cashier" was knighted at Dundee (Balfour's Annals), "at my desyre," 21st Feb. 1651. The same author states that PATRICK RUTHVEN, Earl of Forth, who died at Dundee, 2d Feb. 1651, "was interrid in Grange Durhames ile, in the paroche churche of Monefeithe." It was from the Durhams of Pitkerro (who came to Forfarshire from Kirkcudbright), that the Durhams of Luffness and Largo, were descended.

In consequence of the family affairs having become much embarrassed, Adam Durham, second son of Sir James Durham of Luffness, with consent of trustees, sold the estate of Pitkerro to James, Earl of Panmure, in 1685, for the sum of 23,000 merks. About 1705, his Lordship resold Pitkerro to George Mackenzie, Esq. It now belongs to —— Dick, Esq., whose ancestors were Dundee merchants. The oldest or more southern part of the house of Pitkerro, though much altered, was possibly built by the "cashier" of James VI., and the northern or later portion, may have been erected by the Mackenzies. The house of Pitkerro, which is well cared for by the present tenant, John Laing, Esq., merchant, is surrounded by some fine old trees.

Grange of Monifieth also belonged to the Durhams. It will be remembered that, when on his way as a prisoner to Edinburgh, in 1650, the Marquis of Montrose was lodged at the house of Grange for the night; and, but for the noise of a drunken outsider, who wanted to gain admittance, Montrose would have escaped from his guard, chiefly through the stratagem of Lady Durham, who had him attired in a suit of her own clothes. Guynd says that the laird of Grange is of "ane ancient family and chief of his name," and describes the place as "a good house, yards, and planting, with salmon fishings in the river Tay." William, the last Durham of Grange, sold the property about 1702, to R. Martin, Edinburgh (*Mem.* by James Neish, Esq., of The Laws.) (*v.* Appx.)

Good carvings of the Durham arms are built into garden walls at Monifieth; and a tombstone, appropriated to the sacrilegious purpose of paving a workshop, presents the family arms, and this inscription:—

HEIR . LYES . ANE . WORTHIE . GENTLEMAN . CALLED ALEXANDER . DVRHAM . QVHA . DECESD . THE . 17 FEBERVAR . 1563 . AGED . 65 . YEARIS.

A more modern tomb-stone lies in the same place. It bears representations of a sailor's compass, a ship's anchor, &c., also this inscription:—

Here lyes under this stone, ANDREW SPINK, shipmaster in Dundee, who departed this life upon the 31st day of March 1748, and in the 44th year of his age.

The next three inscriptions are from flat slabs, upon the south-east side of the kirk-yard. The first presents three shields, charged with mortuary emblems; also this inscription:—

1655.
HEIR . LYES . ANE . FAITHFVLL . BROTHER
DAVID . MORAM.

—The surname of Moram or Morham, which still survives in the adjoining parish of Barry, is one of the oldest in Angus. John of Morham obtained the lands of Panbride from William the Lion; and about 1214 he confirmed the King's gift of that church to the Abbey of Arbroath (Reg. Vet. de Aberb.) The surname was originally De Malherb; but, on obtaining the lands of Morham, in Lothian, they assumed *Morham* as a surname (Chalmers' Caledonia.) The De Malherbs held the property of Rossie, in Gowrie, and also gave a donation out of it to the monastery of Arbroath.

The second slab is initialed M. I. W : I. M. It bears a shield charged with three boars' heads, for Urquhart; also, these traces of an inscription:—

Monumentum . . . . IOHANNIS
URQUHART . . . . Monufuthensis
hoc . . . . quod IANETA
MORUM . . . . . . charissima erigendum
. . . . anno Christi
MDCLXIIII anno Trigesimo Secundo obiit 16 Cal. Iulij anno Salutis humanæ
. . . .

—Since I last saw the stone with the above inscription, the Rev. Mr Young has kindly had it laid upon its face, and on turning it over, he has found traces of Hexameter verse, in which are the words, "ferulam tulit." The inscription ought possibly to read—

[This monument, to the memory of JOHN URQUHART, schoolmaster of Monifieth, who died 16th June 1664, in his 32d year, was erected by his beloved wife, JANET MORUM.]

The third stone bears much elaborate carving, also a shield charged with a flesher's cleaver, knife, and axe:—

Here lyes ROBERT LORIMER husband to Christian Horn sometime flesher in Monifieth who . . . . . . Here lyes JANET FINLAW, spouse to Robert Morum in Monifueth, who died 11th February 1676, aged 44. Also here lyes CHRISTIAN HORN, sometime spouse to Robert Lorimer, who was flesher in Monefieth. She died Dec. 8, 1742, aged 66.

A marble tablet, within an enclosure on the north side of the church-yard, is thus inscribed:—

Here lies interred the Body of JAMES ERSKINE of Linlathen, who departed this life on the 26th of August 1816, at Broadstairs, Isle of Thanet, County of Kent, aged 28 years.

"Thanks be to GOD which giveth us the Victory through OUR LORD JESUS CHRIST."

Two of his Infant Children, ANN and JAMES-KATHERINE, are likewise interred here, and Two in the Greyfriars Churchyard, Edinburgh, viz. MARY and KATHERINE.

—David Erskine, advocate, father of the above-named James Erskine, was a cadet of the family of Cardross. He bought the property of Linlathen, &c., from Graham of Fintray about 1805; and married Ann, daughter of Graham of Airth. His younger son, THOMAS ERSKINE, LL.D., the friend of Thomas Carlyle, and author of several theological works, who died at Edinburgh in 1870, aged 82, was buried at Monifieth. He was succeeded in Linlathen, &c., by a sister's son, James Paterson-Erskine, Esq., a cadet of the Patersons of Castle Huntly, in Gowrie. During the early part of the 15th century, certain portions of Linlathen and Craigow (Craigie), belonged to Fither of Spalding; and in 1459, David Gardin and Janet, his spouse, had charters of the lands of Lunleithein, which were held in ward, on the resignation of Thomas, father of David Gardin (*MS. Notes of Scotch Charters at Panmure.*)

From a table-stone to the eastward of the last-mentioned monument:—

Here lieth the body of Sir EDWARD SMITH LEES, forty-five years Secretary to the Post Office of Ireland and Scotland, and who, at Broughty Ferry, on the 24th of September 1846, fell asleep in Jesus.

—This gentleman had the honour of knighthood conferred upon him when George IV. visited Ireland in 1821. His father, originally from Ayrshire, held office under the Government in Ireland, and was created a baronet in 1804.

The next inscription is from a flat stone (enclosed), with a carving of the Scott arms:—

Her lyes ane honest man called ROBERT SCOT, vho dyed the 3 of December . . the 40 year of his age, anno Domini 16 . .

—Scotts, waulkmillers at Balmossie, are said to have had a monument (now lost) at Monifieth, with these punning lines:—

"On earth I *waulked* for many years,
But here I now do sleep;
Where I shall *walk* when I awake,
To you's a mystery deep."

A dateless slab, within same enclosure, has ten initial letters down the sides, which possibly represent those of the names of as many children of the Websters. Upon the face of the stone:—

This stone was erected by Andrew Webster tenant in Downicken, and Barbara Scott his spouse, in remembrance of his deceased Grandfather and Grandmother, vizt. ANDREW WEBSTER and MARGARET SCOTT his spouse. He was tennant in Omachie and *was* both interred here.

—These were ancestors of the Websters who bought Flemington and Meathie, the last recorded of whom (upon a marble slab at Monifieth), was "JAMES WEBSTER of Meathie and Flemington himself, who died 12th Feby. 1848."

Upon a table-shaped stone:—

Here lyes ane vertuous and honest man, called

JAMES HILL, skipper in the Ferrie, and husband to Elspeth Urquhart, who departed the 29 of December 1711, of age 37. Man's life on earth. (*sup.* p. 9.)

Here lyes ane virtuous woman called MATILDA STIVEN, spous to George Kirkcaldie, in Balgillo, who died the 8 December 1732, and of age 67.

From a small head-stone adjoining the grave of Mr W. D. Bowman, engineer, Pernambuco (son of Captain Bowman of 93d regiment), who died at Broughty Ferry in 1872, aged 55 :—

Here lyes JAMES BOWMAN, smith in Cadgertown, who died December the 9th day 1733, his age 56. Round the margin of a table-shaped stone :—

Here lyes ALEXANDER ANDERSON, husband to Margaret Sturrock, some time tennant in Kingennie, who died May 24, 1722, aged 66. Here also lyes MARGARET STURROCK, his spouse, who died November 29th, 1746, aged 86. Here also lyes IEAN ANDERSON, who died May 12th, 1716, aged 22.

—The following is upon the face of the same stone. It will be seen that the concluding couplet of the epitaph embodies the same beautiful idea as in the modern song of "the Angel's Whisper" :—

Here lyes ane vertuous young woman caled ELIZABETH ANDERSONE, daughter to Alexander Andersone and Margaret Storak, who departed the 31 day of March 1711, and of her age 22 :—

O my soul, the Lord prepare thee,
When death comes here, then I must leave thee ;
When death comes here, he stays no man's leasure,
Therefor adeu all worldly pleasure.
But what more pleasure would I have
Then the Lord to bring me to the grave.
Into my grave while I lye sleeping,
The angels have my soul in keeping.

—Kingennie has long been Wedderburn property. It still belongs to that family ; and some carved stones at the old house present their arms and initials. One is dated 1637, and another with the Wedderburn and Ramsay arms impaled, is initialed A. W. : E. R.

The farm gear carved upon the stone, from which the next inscription is copied, and the blacksmiths' arms, indicative of the origin of the family, but more particularly a skull, and thigh-bones, &c., are very elaborate pieces of carving.

Here is interred JAMES WEBSTER, late tenant in Balmadoun, lawfull son to William Webster, tenant in Ethiebeaton, who died the 11th of August 1758, aged 30 years. Also his only child WILLIAM WEBSTER, who died the 1st of Nov. 1710, aged 2 years 6 months, who was procreated by Jean Low his spouse.

MARGRET GREIG, wife of Robert Tullo, tenant in Omachie, who died April 27th 1801, aged 35 years.

MATILDA DONALDSON, dr. of Isobel Duncan, Asloody, d. in "a languishing decay," 1768, a. 17 :—

In the cold bed Christ dearest saints must ly,
Till they be wakened by the angel's cry ;—
The bed is cold, the dust lys here consum'd,
But Christ in grave did ly, and he the grave perfum'd.
Their souls dislodg'd, to mansions bright do soar,
Where Christ is gone to keep an open door ;
The clog of earth must stay a while behind—
No guest for Christ till thus it be refin'd.

—Arsludie, now Ashludie, formed part of the estate of Grange of Monifieth, and was occupied in 1692 by John Durhame, " whose house was burned in the nicht, and he in it" (*Session Records,* per J. Neish, Esq.) Ashludie belonged to the Ramsays of Bamff from about the beginning of the present centnry. It was bought from that family in 186- by Alex. Gordon, Esq., millspinner, Arbroath, who has erected a mansion house upon the property.

ALEX. PATERSON, Cotton, Arsludie, hbd. to Marg. Brown, d. 1784, a. 66 :—

All men live in the same death power,
Who seised my beloved man hour ;
One word to me he could not speak,
Though floods of tears ran down his cheek.

DAVID, son to John Cairncross, mercht., Monifieth, and Agnes Henderson, d. 1744, a. 3 m. :—

Here lyes a hermles bab,
Who only came and cryed
In baptism to be washed,
And in three months old he deyed.

SILVESTER STEVEN, d. 1734, a. 20 :—

Life's everlasting gates
For ever had been shott,
Had not the death of Christ
Them pulled up.

Since the previous sheet was printed, I have received a full copy of the inscription from the tombstone of Mr Urquhart at Monifieth (partially printed on p. 110), which the Rev. Mr Young has succeeded in deciphering sooner than he anticipated, the turning over of the slab upon its face, which was suggested by the Earl of Dalhousie, having had the effect of completely clearing the stone. The inscription, was probably composed by the Mr Barclay who (*sup.*, p. 109), "had for wife the muses nine."

It will be remembered that Orbilius, referred to in the epitaph, was tutor to Horace, and so noted for his severity that his pupil calls him "flagosus." Mr Young suggests that, as the Poet had watery eyes, Orbilius " perhaps thrashed Horace so much in his youth that watery eyes became chronic with him." The Corycian crocus, which was a famous and much esteemed perfume, is alluded to by Horace in Sat. iv., line 68. The inscription is as follows:—

Monumentum Mr JOHANNIS URQUHART, Parœchiæ Monufuthensis moderatoris fidelissimi, quod JANETA MORUM, conjunx amantissima, origendum curavit. Obiit 16 Cal. Julij anno salutis humanæ MDCLXIIII, anno Trigesimo Secundo.

Siste, Viator ! proh ! jacet hac URQVHART' in urna
Ingenuus, sceptrum qui ferulamque tulit.
Non erat Orbilius pueris, ast instar amantis
Nutricis, tribuens ubera blanda labris.
Manibus inferias igitur tu fundito vota
Corycium spiret quæ tegit urna crocum.

[The monument of Mr JOHN URQUHART, a most faithful teacher of the Parish of Monifieth, which his most loving wife, JANET MORUM, caused to be erected. He died 16th June, 1664, in his 32nd year.

Stop, Traveller ! in this tomb, alas ! lies gifted URQUHART, who swayed the sceptre of scholastic rule. To children no Orbilius was he, but like a loving nurse, he fed their infant minds with tender care. As offering to his manes, then, pour out a fervent prayer that from the tomb that covers him the fragrance of the Corycian crocus forth may breathe.]

—Mr Urquhart, who appears to have taken his degree of A.M. at King's College, Aberdeen, in 1648 (*Fasti Abd.*, p. 469), was married to Janet Moram at Monifieth, on the 24th of October 1656, and by her he had two sons, William and John, and a daughter Margaret. The last recorded was born in 1662, and the baptism of the first-named, in 1657, was witnessed by Wm. Durhame elder, and Wm. Durhame, younger of Grange.

These particulars have been kindly furnished from the Parish Registers in the possession of the Registrar-General at Edinburgh, together with the minute relative to the appointment of Mr Urquhart to the office of parish teacher of Monifieth. As the minute presents some points of peculiar interest, not only to the local, but also to the general reader, it is given in full :—

"At Monifuithe Feb^r. sixt 1653 yeares.

"Which day the heretores & sessione of Monifuith being conveened for ye electing of a Schoolmaster to ye fors^d. parishe & for setling of a provisione vnto him, after publick intimo^{u}e had beene made two severall Lords days out of pulpit that non might pretend ignorance, all who were present did declare y^t in yre judgement Mr Johne Wrqubard was fittest to be yre Schoolemaster, who, after he had presented his testimonials (on qreof uas from ye Masters of ye Colledg of Old Abd. where he was educated & made master, the other from ye minister in Barrie in whose parishe he had resided since his coming frome Abd.) after y^t they wer read was elected to be Schoolm^r to sett the psalmes & to be clerk to ye Sessione ; and for ye maintainance of ye s^d Mr Johne it was agried vpone by these heretores who wer present at his electione & the sessione fors^d. That euerie ploughe within the parishe should pay two markes zeirlie vnto him, the one halfe yreof was to be given presentlie vnto him, the other halfe at the first of August nixt, & in all tymes coming at two termes in ye zeir Candlmas & Lambmas, euerie ploughe thirteenth shilling four pennies ; the number of the ploughes extending to fourtie & seven were given vp as followes, Monifuithe two ploughes, Burnsyd & Barnhill foure ploughes, Balmossie thric ploughes, the milles of Balmossie on ploughe, Forth on ploughe, Balgillo foure ploughes, the mill of Balgillo halfe aue ploughe, Lumlethum six ploughes, Effibetoune six ploughes, Grange six ploughes, Ardounie two ploughes, Laws *two*, Pidditie & Arsludie thric

Q

ploughes, Kingennie two ploughes, Legsland ane plonghe & ane halfe, Finrack two ploughes, Omachie thrie ploughes. The minister did promise to pay foure merkes zearlie during the tyme of his ministrie, & the enjoying of his stipend at the s^d kirk. Further it was agried vnto yt everie gentleman's chyld should give threttie shillings in ye qrter, euerie husbandmans chyld twentie shillings, if he be able to pay it; these who are lesse able, threttin shilling foure pennies in the qrter. Further, it was agried vnto y^t persones of good qualitie & rank & who were able, should give tuentie foure shillings Scots at yre marriage or proclama^{o}ne, qreof the Schoolm^r is to have eightcenth shilling and the beddel six shilling. These y^t are of meaner qualitie or lesse able to pay, twelfe shillings at yre proclama^{o}ne or marriage. Strangers who live without the parishe desyring the benefit of a burial place in the kirkzard of Monifuithe were oppointed to pay to the Schoolem^r twentie shilling besyde that which is due to the beddell for ye grave making. Twelfe shillings was appointed to be given at ye baptisme of everie chyld, eight shilling qreof to be given to ye Schoolemr. Further it was agried vpone yt the nixt summer there should be a schoole builded w^t. a chamber to ye Schoolm^r, as neere the mids of the parishe as could be conveniently vpon the charges of ye parishioners, the particular place for building of ye schoole to be made choise of and condescended vpone by the greater part of the voices of ye heretores & vther persones having interest theriuto, & that the scholler's parents or others who hes neerest interest in them shall bring in ye summer seasone peets, coales, or truffes to the Schoole for ye vse of ye Schoolem^r and bairnes in ye winter seasone, & yt proportionallie according to yre rank & condi^{o}ne. Further it was agried vpone that ye Schoolem^r should have libertie to remove at auie Candlemas or Lambmas heirafter, provyding he intimate the same to ye sessione fourtie dayes befor his removall. It is agried vpon & inacted by the heretores & sessione that all heretores residing w^{t}in the parishe & all husbandmen & labourers of the lands do sett yre hand to this present act obliedgeing heirby themselfes to ye fulfilling of thir premisses.

A double heirof was given to Mr Johne Wrquhard for his suretie subscribed be James Lord Couper, William Durhame elder of Grange, Alex. Wedderburn of Kingennie, *Michael Ramsay of Forth*, James Durhame of Ardounie, heretores; Mr John Barclay, Minister, Hew Maxwell, Hendrie Dog, William Mill, James Nicoll, elders, & other elders & deacons who could not subscribe gave yre consent thervnto.

---o---

The "Temple Lands," a name which almost invariably implies an ownership on the part of the Knights' Templars, are in the neighbourhood of Drumsturdy Muir.

Besides the parish church of Monifieth, and the chapel of Broughty Ferry, there were, at least, three other places of worship within the parish in old times. One of these, dedicated to S. BRIDGET, stood at Kingennie; a second, known as "Chapel Dockie," which is a probable corruption of the name of S. MURDOCH, was situated upon the lands of Ethie-Beaton; and the third, called Ecclesmonichtie, was upon the banks of the Dichty, near Panmure Bleachfield.

It has been conjectured by Bishop Forbes (Kalendars of Scottish Saints), that S. MUREN, the daughter of Hungus and Finchen, King and Queen of the Picts, was born at Ecclesmonichtie. The site is still marked by the *Lady Tree*; and, according to the Chronicle of the Picts, Finchen gave Moneclatu (Monichtie), the place where S. MUREN was born, to God, and to the church of St Andrews. The kirk of Ecclesmonichtie was probably dedicated to Our Lady.

Although there is now no hamlet—not even a cottage, at Ecclesmonichty—and the site is known chiefly to those who have a taste for archæological pursuits, "the towns and lands of Egglismonichtie," in the regality of Kirriemuir, are particularly specified in a charter granted to James Lovell of Ballumbie, by the Earl of Angus, at Cupar-Fife, 27th Oct. 1619 (*Writs at Panmure*.)

This charter also conveys to Lovell the lands of Murrois, Carmoatie, and Labothie, with the mill and mill lands of the same, in the barony of Inverarity; the lands of West Ferry, with the salmon-fishings, called "lie Westerukis et Ferry-duris," in the barony of Dundee; also the lands and mills of Balmossie; the lands of Monifieth and Justingleyis, with cunnielairs; the Liuks, and salmon-fishings in the Tay, together with Barnhill, Balclochar, Bracquhau, and Lie Camp; lands to the west of the pont or boat of Monifieth, the salmon-fishings of Polmonichtie, which are described as adjoining the said pont and a place called the Blackcraig, all situated within the regality of Kirriemuir.

But the concentric walls upon the hill of Laws, or "Lawyes of Easter Athy," are probably not only the most ancient objects in the parish, but among the most remarkable of their kind in Scotland. The hill, which is about two miles north from the parish church, is about 500 feet in height, and the summit, which is oval-shaped, measures about 500 feet from east to west by about 200 feet in breadth.

So far as seen, the walls show a series of concentric and converging chambers, constructed of rude undressed stones. Many of the stones are of great size, and traces of vitrification run through the work. Stone cists containing skeletons, and relics of stone and iron have been found in the course of excavations; also the bones of animals, and quantities of charred barley. This curious work is described in an interesting paper by Jas. Neish, Esq., F.S.A. Scot., proprietor of Laws, accompanied by plans, in Proceedings of the Society of Antiquaries of Scotland, vol. iii.

The plan of the work at Laws presents a resemblance to the *pahs* of New Zealand; and, in all probability, it had been an abode of "our ancient forefathers"—possibly a township during the Pictish period. When the late Dr Joseph Robertson visited this remarkable structure, he felicitously described it as "the Dundee of the ninth century!"

At *Cairn Greg*, to the north of Linlathen, a stone cist was lately found. It contained an urn and a spear-head of bronze; and the more interesting object of the symbol of the elephant, so peculiar to the ancient sculptured stones, was found carved upon a fragment between the covers of the cist.

The greater part of the district, including the thanedom of Monifieth, belonged to the Maormors, or Celtic Earls of Angus, in early times. At a later date, the lands of Athy were owned by Sir David of Beaton, who was Sheriff of Angus under Edward I.; and from that knight the property acquired its present name of Ethie-Beaton (*v.* Memorials of Angus and Mearns.) Monifieth was a surname about 1310, as in that year MICHAEL DE MONIFOTH was hereditary lord of the Abthein lands thereof.

Broughty, or North Ferry.
(S. ——)

THIS place, like the village upon the opposite shore of the Tay, was called *Portincraig* in old times. It is of considerable antiquity; and, prior to the foundation of the Abbey at Arbroath, Gillebryd, Earl of Angus, contemplated the erection of an Hospital at Broughty Ferry.

From earliest record, the chapel of Broughty Ferry has been dependent upon the church of Monifieth. The old church stood near the middle of the church-yard; but no trace of it exists. In consequence of the rapid increase of the population of Broughty Ferry, handsome churches have been erected in it by almost every denomination of Christians.

A Chapel of Ease, in connection with the Established Church, was built about 1826. Ten years later, the district was formed into a *quoad sacra* parish, and sanctioned as such in 1838.

The old burial-place (recently closed against interments) is of small area, and situated close to the river Tay. The oldest tomb-stone is dated 1689, and initialed I. B : I. L. A fragment in the north wall, slightly ornamented, shows these traces of lettering:—

. . . . RET & IEAN . . . .
THE 29 OF MAY THE . . . . 1729.

A small head-stone, with a blacksmith's crown and hammer, initialed T. S : I. W., bears :—

Here lyes THOMAS SMITH, husband to Isobel Weles, who dwelt in the Ferrie, who departed the — day of Ianuarie 1712, and of his age 28.

MARGARET ROSS, wf. of John Kid, shipmr. in North Ferry, d. 1785, a. 45 :—

    Now she for whom this gravestone's placed
      Was in virtue ever steady ;
    When asked a reason of her hope,
      Had ay an answer ready.
    Tho' silent and forgotten here,
      She moulders with the clod,
    The day will dawn, a voice she'll hear
      Say, Come and meet your God.

JANET WEBSTER, wf. of David Liddell, shipmr., d. 1801 :—

    Justice and truth, even from youth,
      Adorn'd her deportment ;
    Never revenging, nor exchanging
      Evil for evil treatment.
    Tender dealing, without failing,
      Was everly her aim ;
    Even to those, who were her foes,
      Beneficent and plain.
    She had to give, while she did live,
      The sample of a mind ;
    Ever rejecting, but never respecting,
      Resentment of any kind.

GEORGE CAITHNESS, shipm., N. Ferry, d. Feb., a. 71, his wf., AGNES LYELL, d. Mar., a. 69, 1801 :—

    They were a couple good without pretence,
    Bless'd with plain reason, and with sober sense ;
    Pride to them unknown, while they drew breath,
    Lovely in their lives, undivided in their death.

From a pillar, with urn on top :—

Sacred to the memory of JOHN KID, late shipmaster, Dundee, who died the 15th April 1806, aged 61 years. Cura pii diis sunt :—

    This life he steer'd by land and sea
      With honesty and skill,
    And, calmly, suffer'd blast, and storm
      Unconscious of ill.
    This voyage now finish'd, he's unrigg'd
      And laid in dry-dock Urn ;
    Preparing for the grand fleet trip,
      And Commodore's return.

Besides a new cemetery at Barnhill, an older burying-place surrounds the *quoad sacra* church at BROUGHTY FERRY. The latter contains several monuments, one of which, an obelisk of Peterhead granite, bears this inscription :—

In memory of
THOMAS DICK, LL.D.,
Author of The Christian Philosopher, &c.
Born 1774 ; Died 1857.

—Dr Dick, who was born in Bucklemaker Wynd, Dundee, was at first a preacher in the Scottish Secession Church, but afterwards became a teacher and lecturer, and ultimately adopted literature as a profession. A few years before his death, the Queen was pleased to confer a pension upon Dr Dick, in recognition of his literary labours.

———o———

Besides the elegant modern churches before referred to, and the many costly villa-residences which have been erected in and around the town of Broughty Ferry by Dundee merchants and others, Broughty Castle and the old military fort upon the hill or law of Balgillo are both objects of antiquarian interest.

The Castle, which has a commanding position upon a rock, near the mouth of the Tay, has been called "the Gibraltar of Forfarshire." It was given to the Earl of Crawford, when he was created Duke of Montrose in 1488 (Lives of the Lindsays) ; and the property of Balgillo was gifted by King Robert the Bruce, to Patrick, his chief physician (Mem. of Angus and Mearns.)

Alford.

(S. ANDREW, APOSTLE.)

ABOUT 1199-1207, the church of *Alford* was given by Gillechrist, Earl of Mar, to the Priory of Monymusk. The gift was afterwards confirmed to Monymusk by Pope Innocent and some of his successors.

The church is rated at 18 merks in the Old Taxation. In 1574 it was served by one minister, along with three neighbouring churches. John Paton was then reader at Alford.

The bell, which appears to bear an inscription similar to that at Durris *(sup.*, p. 104), was re-cast in 1761, by John Mowat, Old Aberdeen, at a cost of £9 6s sterling, less £3 12s 2d for the old instrument and the iron work.

The former church bore the date of 1603; and the following is upon the west end of the present building:—

BUILT A.D. 1804; ENLARGED A.D. 1826.

A marble tablet within the church bears:—

The late Mr JOSEPH TAYLOR of London, a native of this parish of Alford, left, in 1816, to the Poor here, £100 sterling, and desired this inscription to be put up as an example to others.

The following inscription, kindly communicated by the late Rev. Dr Gillan of Alford, is from a slab below the pulpit:—

H. I. GULIELMUS BADENOCH, A.M., Eccles. Cortachensis in Com. Angus XII an., hujus autem Ecclie VIII an. Pastor, qui vitam LVIII an^m. explevit V die Feb. M.D.C.C.XLVI. Virtutis amans & veritatis, fidem quam docuit Christianam factis probavit et charitatem. DOROTHEA etiam, filia unica, gaudium breve VIII mensium, quæ ob. XXVI Mar. M.D.C.C.XLII. Conjugi, quocum feliciter vixit VI an., et filiolæ ab ubere raptæ Barbara Forbes hoc monumentum non sine lachrymis posuit.

[Here lies WILLIAM BADENOCH, A.M., minister of the church of Cortachy in the county of Angus for 12 years, and of this church for 8 years, who closed a life of 58 years, Feb. 5, 1746. A lover of virtue and truth, he exemplified in his life the Christian faith and charity which he inculcated. Here also lies DOROTHY, his only daughter, a brief 8 months' delight, who died March 26, 1742. To her husband, with whom she lived happily for 6 years, and to her little daughter, torn from her breast, Barbara Forbes, not without tears, erected this monument.]

—There is an inscription at Cortachy to the memory of Ann Farquharson, Mr Badenoch's first wife.

Fragments of a monument, which stood within the old church, are preserved at the west end of the present building. These consist of a skeleton and three human figures, all rudely carved. The skeleton, which is upon the base of the monument, lies in a horizontal position, and a nude, winged figure is upon the top. Two clothed figures, which flank the inscription-panel, have scrolls upon their garments, which are respectively inscribed—*Verere Deum* (fear God), and *Nosce te ipsum* (know thyself.) The panel bears:—

Within this isle inter'd behind these stones,
Are pious, wise, good MARY FORBES' *bones;*
To BALFLUIG *daughter, and of blameless life,*
To Mr GORDON, *Pastor here, the wife.*
Expirarit Apr: 27, *A.D.* 1728, *Æt. suæ* 46.

—Mr Gordon, who was Professor of Divinity in King's College, Aberdeen, before he came to Alford, was translated to Alloa in 1736, where he died about 1750. He wrote notices of some of the parishes in Aberdeenshire. Being the first Presbyterian minister at Alford, and, as is said, of a haughty disposition, he was called *The Bishop.*

His wife was probably born in the Castle of Balfluig, a considerable part of which still remains, with the date of 1556 over the entrance door. The first Forbes of Balfluig was John, fourth son of Forbes of Corsindae. John Forbes, who sold the estates in 1753, is said to have gone to Rotterdam.

A head-stone (upon the south side of the kirk), bears a shield, charged with the Forbes arms, also this inscription:—

Here lyeth MARY MORESON, laful spouse to John Forbes in Mains of Balfluig, who dyed the 30 Jan.

Here lyes J: FORBES, who died in Kinstair, Jany. 11, 1751.

The next four inscriptions are from an enclosure on the south side of the church. The first is from a panel built into the church wall, and the others are from coffin-slabs, or Templar tombs of freestone, each of which has an ornamental cross upon the top:—

[1.]

JOHN FARQUHARSON, Esquire of Haughton, inclosed this burying ground for himself and family, A.D. MDCCCXXVI.

[2.]
✠ Here resteth the body of IOHN FARQUHARSON, Esquire, who departed XIV May M:D:CCC:LIV, aged LXXVI years.

[3.]
✠ Here resteth the body of MARY-ANNE, wife of Iohn Farquharson, Esq., who departed the XVIII Oct. M:D:CCC:LI, aged LXIV.

[4.]
✠ Here lyeth the body of ANDREW FARQUHARSON, Esq., of the XXXVIII Bengal Light Infantry, son of Iohn Farquharson, Esq., died VIII Nov. M:D:CCC:XLIX, aged XXXI. Haughton.

—The first Farquharson of Haughton was " John Farquharson in Breda," who bought the lands of Over and Nether Haughton, and others, with salmon fishings on the Don, from William Reid, in 1721-22. These he conveyed to his eldest son, John, in 1730, on whose death, in 1745-6, his second brother, Francis Farquharson, accountant in Edinburgh, served himself heir to the property.

In 1750, Mr Farquharson acquired the superiority of the aforesaid lands from John Forbes of Alford; and in 1753, he bought from the same gentleman the lands of Archballoch, Morescroft, Gamphrey's croft, and the lands and barony of Alford, which comprehended Balfluig and Wellhouse, &c. It is the last-named Mr Farquharson who is spoken of by the celebrated Sir William Forbes of Pitsligo as his own and his mother's best and earliest friend.

Mr Farquharson, who died 28th Feb. 1767, married Grizle Strachan. Leaving no issue, he conveyed his estates to his nephew, Alexander Ogilvie, eldest son of the Rev. Mr Ogilvie of Rhynie. Mr F.'s nephew, who assumed the surname of *Farquharson*, married Miss Mary Hay; and, dying in 1787, was succeeded by his son, Francis, who was also an accountant in Edinburgh.

It was the last-named laird who added Brainley in 1794, also Little Endovie, and Kinstair in 1800, to the Haughton estates. He died in 1808, and was succeeded by his brother John, who made out the family burial-place at Alford. The last-mentioned, who married Mary-Anne, a daughter of Sir Archibald Grant of Monymusk, Bart., and died in 1854, had a numerous family, of whom the present laird (who has courteously supplied a note of the above particulars of his family) is the fifth and youngest son. He married a daughter of Gen. Sir Alex. Leith of Freefield and Glenkindie, and has issue.

The House of Haughton, which is pleasantly situated upon the south side of the Don, was erected in 1791 by Mr Francis Farquharson. It has lately received extensive additions and improvements, and was visited a few years ago by Her Majesty the Queen.

The Farquharsons of Haughton are said to have sprung from the Cumins of Altyre (Douglas' Baronage.) The present laird bears the Cumin garbs, along with his maternal and paternal coats.

A granite tablet, built into the south wall of the church, bears this inscription :—

In memoriam JOANNIS DAVIDSON de Tillychetly, qui obiit 31° Mar. 1802, ætat. 61, ejusque conjugis ANNÆ FARQUHARSON, et liberorum HENRICI, JOANNIS, JACOBI, ALEXANDRI, OLIVARII, et JANE, qui omnes adhuc adolescen. obierunt, et cum patre hic requiescunt; filii etiam CAROLI, qui in insula Grenada medicinam exercens decessit cœlebs, A.D. 1804, ætat. 30. Posuit hoc marmor solus dict. liberorum superstes Duncanus Davidson de Tillychetly, 1845. DUNCAN DAVIDSON of Tillychetly & Inchmarlo, died 8th Decemr. 1849, in the 77th year of his age, and lies interred in the church-yard of Banchory. 1850.

[To the memory of JOHN DAVIDSON of Tillychetly, who died 31st March 1802, in the 61st year of his age; and of his wife ANN FARQUHARSON, and of his children, HENRY, JOHN, JAMES, ALEXANDER, OLIVER, and JANE, who all died young, and rest here with their father; also of his son CHARLES; who died, unmarried, in the island of Grenada, where he was practising as a physician, in 1804, in the 30th year of his age. Duncan Davidson of Tillychetly, the sole survivor of the children of the aforesaid, erected this monument.]

—The ancestors of the Davidsons of Tillychetly, Inchmarlo, and Desswood lie at Tarland, where a flat stone, with a curious inscription, marks the spot. Mr Duncan Davidson (*supra*, p. 4), was an advocate in Aberdeen. A daughter of the present laird of Inchmarlo is the lady of Sir Francis Outram, whose father distinguished himself so greatly in India that, among other honours, he was created a baronet. He married a daughter of James Anderson, Esq., corn-merchant, Brechin, by whom he had his successor in the title.

In 1696, and for sometime afterwards, the properties of Tillychetly and Carnaveron belonged to a branch of the Gariochs of Kinstair. The above-named John Davidson bought Tillychetly from Gariochs; and, according to Tradition, Carnaveron was given in dowry with an illegitimate daughter of a laird of Craigievar, who married a person named Stewart. However this may be, the Barony Court Books of Craigievar (*M.S.*, 1707-66), show that a Duncan Stewart in Norham was bailie of the Court in 1723; also that in 1729, the same person is designed "Duncan Stewart *of* Carnavern." Duncan's last appearance as bailie is upon 5th June 1732; and in 1735, James, "son of Duncan Stewart of Carnaveron" held the same office.

It is interesting to find that the same authority confirms the tradition (*infra*, p. 174), of the Stewarts having borne the name of *Alanach*, for, it appears that in 1724, when Duncan Stewart in Norham paid his own rent, he also paid 15s. Scots "for Peter *Alanach* his brother his part of a custom wedder for Whitsunday 1725."

The above-mentioned were ancestors of the Rev. Patrick Stewart of Kinneff (*q.v.*), who was sometime laird of Carnaveron. He had a family of sons and daughters; and the property now belongs to the descendants of one of the daughters. She married a medical practitioner of the name of Stewart, and went abroad.

Upon a broken table-shaped stone on west side of Haughton enclosure :—

Sacred to the memory of the Revd. ALEXANDER JOHNSTON, late minister of the Gospel at Alford, who died the 2d of March 1778. MARGARET SYME, his spouse, who died the 16th September 1802.

—Mr Johnston was ordained minister of Alford in 1746, and in 1751 he married Margaret, daughter of the Rev. Walter Syme of Tullynessle. Mrs Johnston's elder brother, Mr James Syme, minister of Alloa, married Mary, eldest sister of Dr Wm. Robertson, the historian, by whom he left an only daughter, who became the mother of Lord Brougham.

The next inscriptions are from various parts of the kirk-yard to the west of the west walk :—

Here lys below this stons,
Pious, wirtus, JEAN WISHARTS bons,
Wife to John Dain
Some time in Bridgend*   [*pron. *Brigain*.
Of Knockandoch.
All that was dicent & deseret,
Did in her parts & in her person meet;
She mead apper thro hir wnbilemeshd life,
The tender & the loving wife,
Who departed this life the 4 day of Febry. 1759, aged 42 years.

A flat stone is adorned with a nude figure standing upon a globe : it bears a sandglass in the right hand, a scythe in the left, and a libel issuing from the mouth is inscribed—*Vice hic memor mortis*. Below the figure is this inscription :—

Here lies JEAN CONNAN, who departed life April 5, 1751, aged 73 :—

Expect, but fear not Death, Death has not power,
To cut the threed, till Time point out the hour,
Death's patent's void, till Time set to his seal,
From whose joint sentence there is no appeal.
Hold Death in mind, hold Time in high esteem,
Time lost since thou cannot recall, redeem,
Waste not thy Time in vain on trivial things,
On Time the chain of thy Salvation hings.

From one of several tomb-stones, belonging to a family named Benton :—

Here lies BARBRA BRUCE, spouse to Wm. Benton, farmer at Mickle Endovie, who died Nov. 1788, aged 50 . . . . . .

The next three inscriptions are on the east side of the church-yard. The first is upon a flat slab :—

ALEXR. THOMSON, farmer in Mains of Balfluige lies here interrd. He died May 2, 1767, aged about 80 years. He was a dutiful husband, an affectionate parent, an obliging neighbour, & kind & affable even to the poorest. JEAN GAIRDNE, his relict, who lived comendably with him near 50 years, has purchased this stone to his memory, not without grief indeed ; but considers that tis most certain all must die.

Upon a plain head-stone :—

Here lys IEAN AITKEN, lawfull daughter to George Aitken in Hoodhouse of Alfoord, aged three years, dyed May 17, 1724.

—The "Hoodhouse" or Headhouse, is an old term for an inn or hostelry. The Headhouse was generally situated near the parish kirk, as were those of Alford and Clatt.

A mausoleum upon the estate of Breda, near the Don, is surrounded by a cluster of trees. It was prepared for, and within it was buried, the first Mr Farquharson of Breda. He was a son of the laird of Cluny in Braemar, who was familiarly known as "the muckle factor of Invercauld." The factor sold Cluny to Invercauld ; and his son, having made money in the West Indies as a surgeon, bought Breda from a sister of Mackenzie of Seaforth. Dr Farquharson's wife, by whom he had no issue, was a daughter of Mr Robertson, portrait painter, Edinburgh. After a lengthened litigation, the late Mr Robert Farquharson, sometime provost of Paisley, and a thread manufacturer there, succeeded to Breda (*infra*, p. 283).

Several objects of antiquarian interest have been discovered in the parish of Alford. These consist of ancient dwellings, flint-arrow heads, stone axes, and bronze weapons. A stone mould, probably for metal castings, now in the National Museum, was found upon the farm of Dorzel (*v.* Proceed. So. Antiq. of Scotd., vol. iv. ; O. and N. Stat. Accts.)

The Battle of Alford, which was fought between the Covenanters and the Marquis of Montrose, 2d July, 1645, is supposed to have taken place to the north-west of the village of Alford. The Covenanters were defeated on that occasion ; and Montrose lost George, Lord Gordon, Mowat of Balquholly, and Ogilvy of Milton of Keith. Lord Gordon was "buried in the cathedrall church of the Old Town of Aberdeen, hard by his mother." The other two officers are said to lie at Alford. The *Battle of Alford* is celebrated in a ballad of that name ; as is also the *Chase of Callicar*, which refers to a local superstition (*v.* Laing's Thistle of Scotland, and Repertory of Scottish Ballads, Abd., 1823–31.)

The Earl of Mar possessed the greater part of Alford at an early date, and granted certain lands there to William of Rossy, 1418.

Parts of Kinstair and Endovic were acquired by Lord Forbes from the widow of James of Garviach about 1467. These were possibly the first lands which the Forbes' possessed in Alford.

William Garioche of Tillychetlie, and George, portioner of Kinstair, were at the meeting of the heritors and others in 1633-4, when an obligation was entered into " for the constant provisione of ane schoole at the kirk of Alfoord." The last-named subscribed the deed with his " hand at the pen ledd be the notar," because he " could nott writ." The surname of Garioch or Gerrie is still common in the district. Sometimes it takes the odd form of *Hericgerrie*. It is evidently of territorial origin, and had been assumed from the well-known district of *The Garioch*.

On the 30th of September 1720, the laird of Ballfluig left an annual sum of £2 sterling for the benefit of the parish school-master ; and the late incumbent, the Rev. Mr M'Connach,* in order to testify his gratitude for the donation, had a portrait of Ballfluig painted for the schoolroom. This was done by the late John Philip, R.A., while Philip and his friend Stirling were painting studies, in the schoolroom of Alford, during the vacation of 1854, for their respective pictures of The Collecting of the Offering, and The Sermon (*sup.*, p. 19.)

---

* This worthy man (*infra*, p. 281), who was nearly 50 years parochial teacher of Alford, had a favourite dog, which died in 1870. It was buried within its master's garden at Crobhlar, where the following epitaph, upon a brass plate, is fixed to a fine old fir :—

To my favourite Dog, Forres.
Almost imbued with human mind,
Throughout life faithful, true, and kind ;
Beneath this verdant fir-tree's shade,
My good Dog, FORRES, now is laid.
16th May 1870.

The principal bridge in the parish crosses the Don about two miles above the Alford Railway Station. It consists of three arches, and was built in 1811. A wire bridge, dated 1869, crosses the Don near Montgerrie.

Mr George Melvill, who was minister at Alford, 1668-79, built and endowed the bridge over the Burn of Leochel. He also founded three bursaries at King's College, Aberdeen, and gave a grant towards the building of the Bridge of Dye, in Strachan (*supra*, p. 31.)

A considerable village has arisen at Alford since the opening of the branch line of railway; and important monthly markets are now held there. The Village contains a good inn, some neat houses, and shops; also handsome Episcopal, and Free Churches.

Murroes.

(S. ——)

THE church of *Muraus*, with its chapel, were given to the Abbey of Arbroath, by Gilchrist, Earl of Angus, 1211-14. The church belonged to the diocese of St Andrews, and is rated at 20 merks in the Old Taxation.

The chapel stood in the den, to the south-east of the House of Ballumbie, where the site is still shewn. In 1574, the church of Ballumbie was served by Mr Cristeson, minister at Dundee, and that of Murroes by Mr Auchinleck of Monifieth. William Oliver was the name of the contemporary reader at Murroes. He was probably descended from David Olifer, who (Reg. Aberb.), was designed of Gagie in 1457. It is also recorded in 1574, that "Ballumby neidis na reidare." The parishes were probably united about the close of the 16th century, since Henry Duncan, who was minister at Ballumbie, and having Murroes also in charge, removed to the latter (Scott's Fasti) about 1590.

It appears from a dispute which arose in Mr Edward's time regarding the teinds of Ballumbie, that 40s. were paid "for evrie pleughe" upon the two Powries, the two Gagies, Westhall, and Brichtie; and as Mr Edward could see " no reason hou Balumbie can be exempted from paying vicarage, according as the rest of the ploughes of the parioche," he closes his note of " Information" upon the subject by stating, that

"seavin chalders victuall to be the constant and perpetual stipend of the said kirk of Murroes in al tyme coming by and attoure the vicarage teinds of the said parioch *ipsa corpora* and tuentie merks yearlie furth of the tack dutie and teinds of the lands of Balumbie according to the decroitt of the platt in anno 1618."

The church and church-yard of Murroes are upon the west side of the burn of Powrie, near the old house of Murroes. The church is a plain, but neat building, erected in the time of the Rev. Mr JOHN-IRVINE CURRIE, who died 20th July 1863, in the 43d year of his ministry. The injunction, *Ora et labora* (Pray and labour), is carved over the east door of the kirk, and that of *Laus et honor Deo* (Praise and honor be to God), is over the west door.

The jougs, a well-known instrument of punishment, which old Kirk-sessions employed in the case of scolds and Sabbath-breakers, are fixed into the south wall of the kirk. A stone panel, upon the same wall, is thus inscribed:—

A.D. 1843

Christo, Luci mundi, et humanæ salutis Auctori, hæc ædes consecrata est. I. I. C.

[This church was consecrated to Christ, the Light of the world, and the Author of human salvation, in the year of Our Lord, 1843.]

The burial vault of the Fothringhams of Powrie is upon the north side of the kirk. The remains of a figure, holding a shield with the Fothringham arms, is built into the adjoining dyke. Over the entrance to the family pew is a fine carving of the Fothringham and Gibson arms, initialed, T. F : M. G., and dated 1642. These have reference to Thomas Fothringham and his wife, Margaret, a daughter of Sir Alex. Gibson, Lord Durie, and a grand-daughter of Sir Thos. Craig of Riccarton, Lord Advocate, now represented by Sir Wm. Gibson-Craig, Baronet. A slab within the church, with the names of the same laird and lady, exhibits seven shields, labelled with the names, and charged respectively with the arms of

FOTHRINGHAM.   LYNDSAY.
GIPSONE.   SCOTE.
CRAIGE.   ÆRTHE.
        HERIT.

According to tradition, the Fothringhams came to Scotland from Hungary with the Queen of Malcolm Canmore. Record shows that Hugh of Foderingeye, of the county of Perth, did homage to King Edward at Berwick-upon-Tweed, in 1296; also, that Thomas, son of Henry of Fodringhay, had a confirmation charter of the lands of Balunie, near Cupar Augus, which lie upon the confines of Perthshire, in 1378 (Rag. Rolls; Reg. Mag. Sigill.) There was a knight, Sir Hugh, in the family of Fothringham, about 1370 (Laing's Ancient Scottish Seals, i. 223.)

The lands of Wester Powrie, which belonged to Malcolm of Powrie, and were held of John Ogilvy of Easter Powrie, are said to have been given to John of Fothringham on his marriage with a daughter of Ogilvy of Auchterhouse. Lord Lindsay (Lives, i. 145), says that Thomas Fothringham of Powrie was the "familiar squire" of David Earl of Crawford, from whom he received various lands out of gratitude for "faithful service and constant attentions." His Lordship also gracefully remarks that "The Fothringhams were always closely allied in blood and friendship with the House of Crawford, and the hereditary regard has manifested itself most kindly to our behoof in the present generation."

By the marriage of the father of the late laird of Fothringham with Miss Scrymseour, he acquired the property of Tealing which adjoins that of Powrie. In consequence of this alliance, the lairds of Powrie prefix *Scrymseour* to the surname of *Fothringham*. JAMES SCRYMSEOUR-FOTHRINGHAM, Esq. of Powrie and Tealing, died in 1857. He was succeeded by his son Captain THOMAS, who married Lady Charlotte Carnegy, sister to the Earl of Southesk. He died in 1864,

at the early age of 27, and was buried in the family vault at Murroes.

The first inscription, below, is from a table-shaped stone at the west end of the kirk. A rudely carved angel at the top of the gravestone is represented blowing a trumpet. Two blank shields, also the initials, A.E., precede the inscription, and below, amidst the words— "EXPERGISCIMINI & LAVDATE, HABITATORES PVLVERIS" (Awake and sing, ye dwellers of the dust), are four nude figures (two standing the others kneeling), with uplifted arms in the attitude of prayer. Besides the above text in Latin, the same (Isa. xxvi. 19), is repeated upon the stone in Hebrew characters; and in the latter (as the Rev. Mr Nicoll kindly informs me), the reference to the chapter is given, but not that to the verse. 1 Cor. xv. 52, is also cut in Greek, but not being a correct copy of the original, the text may have been given from memory.

The following inscription (in incised and interlaced Roman capitals), occupies the chief part the tomb-stone:—

ALEXANDER . EDVARDVS . CI
VIS . DEIDONANVS . QVI . 22 . MA
II . ANN : DOM : 1655 . ÆTATIS . AN :
67 . NEPTESQVE . BINÆ . MAG
DALENA . EDVARDA . QVÆ . VI
T.E. MENSE. 4TO . ANN : DOM : 1650*
& . MARTHE . EDVARDA . QVÆ. VI
T.E. MENSE. ITIDEM. 4TO . ANN : DOM:
*1660 . OBIERE . HIC . HVMANTVR . [*sic.

—Mr Robert Edward, son of the above-named Alexander Edward, citizen of Dundee, was presented "to the paroche kirk of the Murrays, personage and vicearage thereof," by Patrick, Earl of Panmure, 8th March 1648. The Valnations of the Shire of Forfar, 1649 and '53, show that Mr Edward owned two wadsets, one of which, Crachie or Tulloes, he had from the Earl of Strathmore. He also appears to have been a man of means, for down to past 1676 he had considerable sums of money lent upon the Ballumbie and Powrie estates, &c.

Mr Edward is best known as the author of a Description of the County of Augus, in Latin, which was accompanied by a map of that shire. It was engraved by Gerard Vale and Peter Schenk of Amsterdam, at the expense of the Earl of Panmure, whose arms are upon the map, and to whom the work was dedicated. Upon the 30th of Oct. 1671, the Earl gave Mr Edward "60 rex dollars to be bestoued on the printing of the map of Angus" (*Documents at Panmure ;*) but the publication, which was a broadside, did not appear until 1678. Edward's Angus was translated by the Rev. Mr Trail of St Cyrus (*sup.*, p. 41), and published at Dundee in 1793 (43 pp. 8vo.) In 1832, another edition (12mo), appeared at the same place, but neither has the map.

Mr Edward wrote another work, entitled The Doxology Approven (Edinr. 1683, 12mo.) It contains a curious dedication to the Earl of Aberdeen, then High Chancellor of Scotland, in which the author attributes "all the Miseries and Confusions in this Land" to schism in the Church. He describes King Charles as "a glorified Martyr ;" and compares the Earl to "the wise and greatly beloved Daniel," now sitting supreme judge "in that very City and Judgment-seat, where your Father suffered so sad and unjust a Sentence."

Mr Edward married Jean Johnstone, who was "ane old, infirm, and indigent gentlewoman" in 1697. In that year she had an assignation of the stipend of Murroes from Lord Panmure, in return for having "bein at ye trouble and expense to invite and procure severall preachers from tyme to tyme to discharge the duty of a minister" at Murroes.

Besides the twin-children named in the above inscription, Mr Edward had at least four sons, who all grew up and were educated for the church. I have not ascertained the date of Mr Edward's death; but, in 1696, when his son, "Mr John Edward, governor to Sr. James Fleeming's son," had an assignation of the stipend of Murroes from Lord Panmure, it is said that "there hath been no minister serving" at Murroes "for severall years past."

Mr Charles Edward, who had been appointed "conjunct with his father," appears to have left the parish, temporarily at least, sometime before 27th August 1692; for of that date, the Bishop of St Andrews recommended that Charles' brother, "Mr Robert, who was rabled out of his own church," should supply that of Murroes. A fourth son, Mr Alexander Edward, became minister of Kemback, and was deprived as a non-juror.

The minister of Kemback appears to have had a taste for architecture. He was much patronised by the Earl of Panmure; and many of the improvements which his Lordship made about Panmure House and Brechin Castle were executed after plans by Mr Edward, who also acted as inspector of works. Indeed, so highly had Mr Edward recommended himself as a draughtsman, that the Earl of Panmure, along with eleven other noblemen and gentlemen of Scotland, agreed, on 6th Oct. 1701, to give Mr Edward £10 each to assist him to travel through England, Flanders, Holland, and part of France, "for veiwing, observing, and takeing drawghts of the most Curious and Remarkable huses, Edifices, Gardens, Orchards, Parks, plantations, Laud Improvements, Coall-works, mines, waterworks, and other Curiosities of Nature or Art that shall occurr in his traveling Throw the saids places."

This very interesting document, which is preserved in the archives at Panmure, shows an anxiety on the part of certain of our Scotch nobility and gentry, not only to improve and beautify their native country nearly two hundred years ago, but also a wish on their part to developé, by comparison with foreign practices, its mineral and other resources. It is just possible that the publication of Slezer's *Theatrum Scotiæ*, and of similar works which appeared in England and on the Continent about the close of the 17th century, had suggested to the Earl of Panmure and his colleagues the idea of sending Mr Edward abroad. I am not aware, however, that any effect was given to this laudable proposal. It is just possible that the disasters consequent upon the Rebellion had prevented its being carried out. I have seen no evidence of Mr Edward's having gone abroad, or that any of the guaranteed subscriptions were paid except that of the Earl of Panmure, for which there is a discharge by Mr Edward among the family papers.

From a table-stone, near to that of Mr Edward :—

Erected by Colonel Henry Imlach, in the service of the East India Company, to the memory of his father, the Rev. ALEXANDER IMLACH, during XLVII years minister of this parish, who died the V day of Nov. MDCCCVIII, aged LXXXI years; and of his mother SUSAN OGILVY, who died the ninth day of Sept. MDCCXCI, aged LXIII years, both interred under this monument. Also to the memory of ANN IMLACH, his sister, who died the third day of May MDCCLXXX, aged XVIII years, and interred near this place.

—Mr Imlach obtained the church of Murroes through the influence of the Airlie family, his wife having been a daughter of Ogilvy of Baikie. He was previously a teacher at Kirriemuir.

Here lys WILLIAM GIBSON, sometime in Hole of Murhouse, who died the 13 day of October 1710, and of his age 61 ; and AGNES NICOL, his spouse, to whose memory Alexander Gibson, there son, hath caused this monument to be erected—

<blockquote>
This couple liued a uirtuous life
While here they did remain ;
Their honesty and uprightnes,
No blot did ever stain.
</blockquote>

Also his son, ALEXANDER GIBSON lyes here, he dyed April 17, 1739, aged 45 years.

Upon a stone with a bold carving of a blacksmith's hammer and "royal crown," &c. :—

Heir lyes ane honest man, WILLIAM COVPER, hammerman, vho dëcit in Leigsland vpon the 18 of November 1649, and of his aig 63 yeirs. And his spovs MATILD WOBSTER, vho deceisit vpon the 5 of Avgost 1646, and of hir aige 70.

A flat slab, at the east end of the kirk, with the following simple inscription, marks the grave of a foreigner, who came to this country to study farming, and died of fever, at the age of 26 :—

PETER ORLOFF BERGSTRÖME, from Wermeland, Sweden, died at Westhall, XXIV Nov. MDCCCLVI, is here interred. I sleep, but my heart waketh.—Song v. 11.

Upon the face of a prettily carved slab :—

This stone is erected at the expense of George Arklay, farmer in West Hall, in memory of his spouse ALISON ARKLAY, who died May 28, 1773, in the 20 year of her age, and their son PETER ARKLAY, who died Dec. 1773, in the 3d year of his age . . . . .

From a monument (within an enclosure) adjoining the above :—

In memory of DAVID ARKLEY, Esq. of Clepington, who died 2nd Augt. 1822, aged 74 years ; and of MARGARET CRICHTON, his spouse, who died 19th Novr. 1836, aged 86 years. Their son, SILVESTER, died 12th Feby 1794, aged 12 years.

—Mr Arkley was sometime tenant of Ethiebeaton ; and upon succeeding to the fortune of a relation in London, he bought Clepington, near Dundee. His son, Mr Peter Arkley, bought Duninald, near Montrose It now belongs to his two grand-daughters; and Clepington was sold, some years ago, by Mr P. Arkley's second son to Mr Wm. Neish, now of Tannadice.

Sacred to the memory of PETER ARKLAY, and HELEN KERR, his spouse, who lived in this parish. HELLEN KERR died 2d June 1810, aged 86 years ; PETER ARKLAY died 23d May 1811, aged 87 years.

From a head stone (enclosed) :—

Erected to the memory of DAVID MILLER, Esqr. of Ballumbie, who died 19th July 1825, aged 71 ; and of JANE MILLER, his daughter, who died 4th Feby 1820, aged 17 years.

—Mr David Miller, who was a tenant farmer, bought the property of Ballumbie in April 1804, from the Hon. Wm. Maule of Panmure. The present mansion-house was erected by Mr Miller in 1810. From the trustees of his son, John, the property was bought in January 1847, by the trustees of the late Mr Wm. M'Gavin, merchant, Dundee. It was afterwards arranged for with them by his brother, the present proprietor, Robert M'Gavin, Esq.

Ballumbie was long the property of the Lovells, who were among the most potent and influential of the old Angus barons. They came to Forfarshire during the 13th, and had an interest in Ballumbie down to the early part of the 17th century, when it was bought by the Earl of Panmure (v. Mem. of Angus and Mearns.) The Castle of Ballumbie is described by Guynd (c.

1682), as "ane old ruinous demolished house; but a very pleasant place." The old portion, which joins the new house, and is used as a stable, has some of the characteristics which distinguish the towers of Dunottar and Edzell, the former of which was built towards the close of the 14th century, as was probably also the latter.

Anonymous:—

Its pride and its pomp are all naked and bare;
And ruin, and pale destitution are there.

From a marble slab fixed into an obelisk of freestone:—

To the memory of JAMES HORNE, for upwards of 26 years schoolmaster of this parish. He died on the 14th day of December 1840, aged 52 years. Erected as a mark of esteem and regard by a few of those who enjoyed the benefit of his valuable instruction in their youth, and his disinterested friendship in their maturer years.

Si sapis, utaris totis, Viator, diebus;
Extremumque tibi semper adesse putes.

[Traveller! if you are wise, usefully employ all your days, and think that your last is always at hand.]

Two granite crosses (enclosed), respectively bear:

[1.]
GEORGE RAMSAY-OGILVY of Westhall.
Taken 22nd Nov. 1866, aged 44. ✠ Jesu mercy.

[2.]
ANN-MARY OGILVY,
Born 22nd April 1854. Taken 2d July 1865.

—Mr Ramsay-Ogilvy was a grandson of the Rev. W. Ramsay, minister at Cortachy, by a daughter of John Ogilvy of Jamaica, a son of the laird of Westhall. Mr R.-Ogilvy, who passed as an advocate in 1844, was sheriff-substitute first at Forfar and latterly at Dundee. He succeeded to Westhall on the death of a maternal aunt, when he assumed the additional surname of Ogilvy. Mr R.-Ogilvy's only child having predeceased him (as above), he left Westhall to his cousin-german, the Rev. Mr Ramsay (now Mr Ogilvy-Ramsay), formerly minister of the parish of Kirriemuir, now minister of the beautiful parish of Closeburn.

Beatons were designed of Westhall about 1526;

and in 1577, Sir Walter Graham of Fintry and others were delated for communing with Robert Beaton of Westhall, who was concerned in the murder of Ramsay, tutor of Laws, in 1568 (Pitcairn's Crim. Trials.) Westhall was Beaton property until past 1631. In 1662, it was possessed by the coheiresses of Thomas Scott, a bailie of Dundee (Retonrs.) It belonged to the Pearsons of Balmadies (sup., p. 160), in, and long after the time of Guynd; and was acquired by —— Ogilvy, about 17—.

———o———

The most important discovery of pre-historic remains which has been made in Murroes, is that of a weem, or Pict's house. It was of the ordinary form, and about 36 feet in length. The sides were constructed of pavement slabs, similar to those found at Gagie quarries, &c. A notice and sketch of the weem are in Proceedings of the Society of Antiquaries, vol. viii.

Although Murroes was a part of the Earldom of Angus, the Earls of Crawford appear to have held a considerable interest in it during the early ages. In 1450, Alexander, Earl of Crawford, gave a charter of Wester Brichtie to David Fothringham of Powrie; and in 1463, the same Earl gave Richard Lovell of Ballumbie, and his wife Elizabeth Douglas, whom the Earl styles "his oye," a charter of the lands of Murroes. In the year 1473, Alexander, Earl of Crawford, gave an annual of twelve merks out of the last-named lands towards the support of a chaplain in the parish church of Meigle (*MS. Notes of Scotch Charters at Panmure.*)

The Fothringhams had residences both at Powrie and at Murroes. There are still the remains of two houses at Powrie, the elder of which, with arched dining hall, and chambers below, was probably erected in the 15th, and the latter building, which is still roofed, probably belongs to the 17th century. The old house at Murroes, now occupied by farm labourers, possibly belongs to the same period as the last-mentioned. Guynd says that Powrie and Murroes are "both good houses, sweet and pleasant places, excellent yards, well planted parks, and hay meadows, and dovecoats extraordinary good."

Nothing now remains of the "very good house" of Easter Powrie, mentioned by Guynd, although there were traces of "the castle" about 1794. Tradition says it was a residence of the old Earls of Angus.

The charming little chateau of Gagie, which has a secluded site on the south bank of the Burn of Murroes, is kept in good repair, and made an occasional residence by the proprietor, John Guthrie of Guthrie, Esq. A "loupin'-on-stane," or steps for assisting one to get on horseback, is in front of the house; and a cluster of four magnificent yew trees is in the garden.

In the adjoining summer-house, a door or window-lintel exhibits the Guthrie arms, with the initials, W.G., and the date of 1614. These have reference to William Guthrie (second son of Alexander Guthrie of that Ilk,) by whom the lands of Gagie were bought from Sibbald of Rankeilor in 1610. The same person had a portion of Hallton and Milton of Guthrie, 29th Dec. 1571. On 11th June 1603, he purchased Ravensbie, in Barry, from John Cant, and in the charter of these lands William is designed brother-german to Alexander Guthrie of that Ilk (*Family papers*, kindly lent by John Guthrie of Guthrie, Esq.) The first Guthrie of Gagie is said to have married Isabella, daughter of Leslie of Balquhain. A shield, on the front wall of Gagie House, bears the Leslie coat, with the initials, I. L.

Another slab, originally over the old entrance, or court gate to Gagie, bears an elaborate carving of the family arms, with the "label," or heraldic mark of a first son. The coat, which is initialed, I. G : I. H., and dated 1737, belongs to the time of John Guthrie of Guthrie, and his wife Jean, daughter of the Rev. James Hodge of Longforgan. Their son became the twelfth baron of Guthrie, and they had two daughters who were married respectively to John Scrimgeour of Tealing, and William Alison, merchant, Dundee.

The only bequest for educational purposes, which has been made to the parish, is that by Mr George Sibbald, surgeon, Argyll Square, Edinburgh, who was a native of Murroes, and died in 1863. He left £200, the interest of which is to be applied by the minister and elders "towards the education of a boy and girl," natives of the parish, and each for the space of two years. Mr Sibbald, some of whose relatives are still in Murroes, may have been a descendant of the old lairds of Gagie and Rankeilor.

It would appear that in 1724, the wants of the teacher and pupils were so ill cared for by the heritors, that the Rev. Mr Marr was compelled to petition the Commissioners of Supply to " modify a salary" for David Crombie, schoolmaster, and also a sum to build a school and school-house, " the parish being defective in both." A hundred merks Scots, or £5 10s 5d sterling, were settled as "a competent salary" for the teacher ; and a sum was also named for building purposes. It appears, however, that a long time was allowed to elapse before the necessary house accommodation was supplied for the master and his pupils.

Like most Scotch parishes, Murroes, at the date last-mentioned, and for long afterwards, was in a very poor condition socially. In 1791, Mr Iulach writes (Old Stat. Acct.), that more money had been made in Murroes by farming, during the previous thirty years, than for two hundred years before; and adds that the farmers " even use *some* of the luxuries of life"!

It may be added that a belief in some of the superstitions of the darker ages lingered in Murroes down to a late date. Not long ago, when the body of a suicide was found in the parish, it was buried in the clothes in which it was discovered, and upon the *north*, or shady side of the kirk, which was long believed to be the peculiar property of his Satanic Majesty !

When the grave of the unfortunate man was opened, his snuff-mull, and the sum of 6s 6d in silver, and a penny in copper, were found in it. These had been buried along with the body ; and as it was conveyed to the kirk-yard in the parish hearse, the feeling was carried to such a height that the hearse was never again used, but allowed to stand in a shed and rot !

Lochlee.

(S. DROSTAN, ABBOT.)

ST DROSTAN founded the first church in Glenesk. He died there about A.D. 809, and his remains were carried to, and buried at Aberdour, in Aberdeenshire (*supra*, p. 55.)

Down to 1723, when Lochlee was erected into an independent parish, it was attached to that of Lethnot (*q.v.*) These, and other points in the history of the district, are given in "the Land of the Lindsays," including notices of the families of De Glenesk, Stirling, Lindsay, and Maule. The Glen now wholly belongs to the Earl of Dalhousie, as representative of the last-named family.

The ruins of the kirk of S. DROSTAN of Glenesk stand in the old kirk-yard, at the north-east end of the Loch of Lee. The cemetery is enclosed by a wall, and surrounded by some venerable trees. To the north of the burial-ground are the ruins of the house and school of the author of "Lindy and Nory," to whose memory a granite monument was raised by public subscription, upon which is the following:—

Erected to the memory of ALEXANDER ROSS, A.M., Schoolmaster of Lochlee, author of "Lindy and Nory; or the Fortunate Shepherdess," and other Poems in the Scottish Dialect. Born, April 1699; died, May 1784.

How finely nature aye he paintit,
O' sense in rhyme he ne'er was stintit,
An' to the heart he always sent it
"Wi' might an' main,"
An' no a'e line he e'er inventit
Need ane offen' !

—Ross was a native of Kincardine O'Neil, and at one time assistant teacher at Laurencekirk. He married the daughter of a farmer in Logie Coldstone, and her grave is marked by a head-stone thus inscribed :—

This stone was erected by Mr Alexr. Ross, schoolmaster at Lochlee, in memory of JEAN CATANACH, his spouse, here interred, who died May 5th 1779, aged 77 years :—

What's mortal here? Death in his right woud have it;
The spritual part returns to God that gave it;
While both at parting did their hopes retain
That they in glory woud unite again,
To reap the harvest of their Faith and Love,
And join the song of the Redeem'd above.
Memento mori.

The above, also the next four inscriptions, are attributed to Ross. The first is from a mural and much decayed tablet, built into the north-east dyke :—

Hoc jux . . monumentum conduntur cineres JOANNIS GARDEN a Midstrath Armigeri, necnon CATHARINÆ FARQUHARSON, conjugis ejus dilectissimæ, qui matrimonio conjuncti 29no Oct., 1696, per annos 42 vitam conjugalem degerunt, tandem apud Invermark dicm obierunt supremum, hic 26to Aprilis, 1745, ætatis 73 ; hæc vero 24to Novembris, 1738, ætatis 63.

Quos Hymen th . . . . ., ... erat annis ;
Queisq' dedit multos viv . . . . ;
Peracto vitæ, summo cu . . . . , ... ,
Componit tumulo, nosce, ... , . . .
Ast probos, providos, benevolos, atq' benignos,
Veridico vivens buccinat ore Fama.

Hunc tumulum extruxit Robertus Garden, A.M. verbi Divini ad Stı Fergusij præco ex filiis ejus . . . . . . 174 .

[Beside this monument are laid the ashes of JOHN GARDEN, Esq. of Midstrath, and CATHARINE FARQUHARSON, his dearly beloved wife, who, having been united in marriage 29th October 1696, lived together in wedlock for 42 years. The former died at Invermark, 26th April 1745, aged 73 ; and the latter, 24th Nov. 1738, aged 63 :—

"When Hymen in their youth in marriage bound,
Whom with long life and mutual bliss he crown'd,
Together having finished Life's career,
And won the crown of spotless honour dear.
Know passenger ! these now by heav'nly doom
He lays united in one friendly tomb,—
Let Truth and Fame with loud acclaims approve,
Their prudence, truth, beneficence, and love."]

—The poetical portion of the above translation is from Thomson's edition of Helenore (Dundee, 1812.) The erector of the monument was minister of St Fergus, in Buchan, from 24th Sep. 1745, until his death on 7th Nov. 1772. It appears from the Poll Book that the above-named John Garden was living *in familia* with his father at Midstrath in Birse, the year of his marriage. He sold the property of Midstrath about 1722.

The Gardens came to Glenesk as factors for their relative, Garden of Troup, who leased the estates from the York Buildings' Company. They were also factors for the family of Panmure; and the last of their race, Miss Garden, died at Brechin nearly forty years ago.

The allusion to the military life of Mr Charles Garden in the next epitaph, which is upon a slab in front of the mural tablet, has reference to the part which he took in Mar's rebellion. He was at Sheriffmuir, and taken prisoner there:—

Here lie deposited the Bodies of CHARLES GARDEN of Bellastreen, Gent., who died upon 22nd Nov. 1761, aged above 90 years; and of Mrs MARGARET GARDEN, his eldest daughter, aged above 60 years :—

Entomb'd here lies what's mortal of the man,
Who fill'd with honour Life's extended span;
Of stature handsome, front erect and fair,
Of dauntless brow, yet mild and debonair.
The camp engaged his youth, and would his age,
Had cares domestic not recall'd his stage,
By claim of blood, to represent a line,
That but for him was ready to decline.
He was the Husband, Father, Neighbour, Friend,
And all their special properties sustain'd,
Of prudent conduct, and of morals sound,
And who at last with length of days was crown'd.

—In 1696, James Garden of Bellastrain, in Glentanner, is rated at £1 of poll, but (as the record bears), "he classing himself as a gentleman, his poll is £3, and the generall poll for himself, his wife, and three children *in familia*," is £4 10s. In "Ane List of Papists" which was furnished to the Presbytery of Kincardine O'Neil in 1704 (Blackhall's Narrative), it is stated that "Bathia Gardyne, spouse to Charles Gardyn of Ballastrein, is and hath been ane obstinate papist."

Here lies DANIEL CHRISTISON, who departed this life June 4th, 1751, aged 36 :—

From what befalls us here below,
Let none from thence conclude,
Our lot shall aftertime be so—
The young man's Life was good.
Yet Heavnly wisdom thought it fit,
In its all sovereign way,
The flames to kill him to permit,
And so to close his day.

—The quaint allusion in this epitaph to future punishments had possibly been suggested from the fact of Christison having been accidentally burned to death among a quantity of heather. The next two inscriptions are from a stone near the above:

Here is reposed the Dust of DAVID CHRISTISON, farmer in Auchronie, who died 20th Decer. 1761, aged 61 years, a Man of Integrity and veracity, and charitably disposed to the Indigent. He left of children, John, David, Charles, Hugh, Jean, and Magdalene, by his spouse Helen Mill.

Here lies HELEN MILN, spouse to David Christison, late Tenent in Auchrony, who died December 19th, 1775, aged 64 years :—

Stop, Passenger, incline thine head,
And talk a little with the Dead;
I had my day as well as thou,
But worms are my companions now.
Hence then, and for thy change prepare,
With bent endeavour, earnest care,
For Death pursues the as a Post,
There's not a moment to be lost.

1800 : DONALD NICOL, who died October 9th, 1799, aged 85 years; and DAVID NICOL, his son, who died August 11th, 1798, aged 52; are interred here :—

The grave, Great Teacher! to one level brings,
Heroes and Beggars, Galley-Slaves, and Kings.

—This couplet is from the Earl of Orford's epitaph on Theodore, King of Corsica, who, after long confinement for debt in the King's Bench prison, was released in 1756, and died the same year. His remains lie in St Anne's Church, Dean Street, London.

Erected by the Revd. Peter Jolly, 57 years Episcopal Clergyman, Lochlee, in memory of his son JAMES, who died 14th of March 1798, aged 10 years. And also of his spouse, JEAN DIEACK, who died May 12th 1809, aged 56 years.

LOCHLEE.

— Mr Jolly, who was the first resident Episcopal clergyman in Glenesk from the time of the Revolution, resigned his charge in 1840. He retired to Brechin, where he died in 1845, aged 82, universally respected by all denominations of Christians for his unobtrusive, kindly disposition. One of his daughters was the wife of the late Bishop Moir of Brechin.

Glenesk was long a stronghold of Episcopacy. On 16th Aug. 1745, Bishop Rait confirmed about 70 of that congregation, and on the previous day he confirmed about 25 persons in the dwelling house of the clergyman (Rev. Mr Lunan's Diary, *MS.*) The strength of Episcopacy in Glenesk and its neighbourhood attracted the attention of the Government; and in 1716, not only did the Royalists burn the meeting-house in Lochlee, but they also carried the minister a prisoner on board a frigate which was lying off Montrose. The incumbent of that period was Mr David Rose, who dwelt at Woodside of Dunlappie. He was the father of the Hon. George Rose, and great-grandfather of Lord Strathnairn. The Episcopal church and parsonage are at Tarfside, where a hand-bell is preserved, which bears this record of the generosity of the old minister:—

MR. DAVID. ROSE. GIFT. TO. GLENESK. 1728.

—Accounts of Mr Rose and his family are given in the Land of the Lindsays; also, *infra*, p. 294.

From the sides and edges of a head-stone in the old kirk-yard of Lochlee:—

Her lays DONALD MDONEL, MARGARET DUFS, JOHN MDONEL, and MARGARET TOHOU, May the 21, 1733.

Remember man as thou goes by,
Death, Judgment and Eternity.

The next two inscriptions are also from head-stones:—

Here lies MARGARET CAMPBLE, spouse to David COUTS in Drowstie, died 5th Septr. 1794, aged 24 years. Also his mother, JEAN GIBB, died 18th March 1794, aged 65 years.

—*Drowstie*, which is a corruption of the name of S. DROSTAN, was a hamlet or village in Lochlee, where there was an alehouse. The hostelry is referred to by Dr Beattie in his address to Ross on the publication of his poems of Helenore, &c.

The next inscription relates to one who had some celebrity as a local rhymester. He tenanted the farm of Glencatt, a remote place to the north of the farm of Baillies; and, like most of his contemporaries in the Glen, he had doubtless enjoyed many a " pint at Drousty:"—

1846: Erected in memory of JOHN MILNE of Glencatt, who died on the 2d Septr. 1818, aged 50 years; and his spouse, SUSAN FARQUHARSON, who died on the 2d Sept. 1843, aged 75 years. They left two daughters, Magdalene and Agnes.

———o———

THE NEW CHURCH-YARD.

A new parish church was erected at Lochlee in 1803. It stands about a mile to the east of the old kirk, between the Mark and the Brawny; and there the deaths of one nonogenarian and two octogenarians are recorded upon head-stones. Another stone (enclosed) bears the following record of the first person that was interred within the New Burial-ground:—

Erected by the Revd. DAVID INGLIS, minister of Lochlee, in memory of his mother CHRISTIAN INGLIS, who departed this life on the 15th day of July 1808, in the 73d year of her age. *Nos omnes metam properamus ad unam.*

—The erector of the above-mentioned tombstone died at Lochlee, 28th January 1837, in the 66th year of his age, as recorded upon a marble slab, fixed into the top of an adjoining chest-shaped monument. Another marble slab (in the same stone) bears that EDWARD HART, son of General Hart of Doe Castle, Kilderry, Ireland, died at the manse of Lochlee, 1st May 1836, in his 26th year. Mr Hart's brother wrote some verses to his memory, the first of which is engraved upon the tomb:—

Far from his father's home he rests,
Cut off in early bloom;
Trusting to God and his behests,
He sank into the tomb.

The next inscription which was "written under the direction" of the late Rev. Mr John Whyte of Lethnot and Navar—a brother of the two young men whose deaths are recorded—discloses a painful instance of accidental drowning which occurred during a snow storm, and while the brothers were employed collecting their father's sheep:—

DAVIDI WHYTE an. 27, ejusque minori fratri ARCHIBALDO WHYTE, an. 18, natis, qui cum torrentem rapidum transilire conarentur, qua, dejectu gravi in barathrum profundum, et præruptis utrinque rupibus clausum, præceps defertur, prior hoc jam facile superato, fratrem in gurgitem conspicatus delapsum, amore pio, necnon ejus servandi spe vana impulsus, se statim eodem præcipitavit, unâque miserrime periit, Glenmarki valle, parochia comitatus Forfarensis Lochleio, Sext. Kal. Nov. A.D. 1820. Horum mortis immaturae, nec minus pietatis, ingenii, amoris mutui insignis, cæterarumque virtutum eximiarum, flentibus amicis heu quam subito abreptorum, hoc monumentum pro suo ingenti desiderio posuit pater Jacobus Whyte.

—The translation (reprinted from Land of the Lindsays, p. 74), was made by the late Rev. Mr Whyte:—

[" In memory of DAVID WHYTE, aged 27, and of his younger brother, ARCHIBALD WHYTE, aged 18. As the two brothers were proceeding to leap across at a spot where the Mark, contracted by craggy rocks on either side into a narrow and rapid torrent, anon pours headlong over a high precipice into a deep eddying abyss, when the elder, having already crossed with facility, perceived that his brother had fallen into the impetuous stream, urged by the impulse of holy affection and by the vain hope of saving his life, rushed in heedlessly after him, and both lamentably perished together, on the 27th of October, 1820, in the glen (or valley) of Mark, parish of Lochlee, and county of Forfar. To commemorate the premature death, as well as the illustrious example of mutual affection, the talents, the piety, and other excellent endowments which adorned the hapless brothers—alas! so suddenly snatched away from their weeping relatives—this monument was erected by their bereaved and disconsolate father, James Whyte."]

A head-stone (near the kirk-yard gate) bears the following inscription:—

1811 : Erected by William Reid, shoemaker in Aberdeen, in memory of his son GEORGE, who perished among the snow about the end of Jany. 1810, within the bounds of this parish, in the 30 year of his age.

Vos igitur estote parati : quia qua hora non putatis, Filius hominis veniet.

—When Reid's grave was opened for an interment in 1873, fragments of clothes were found, also a bonnet in good preservation. The text is from Luke xii. 40.

———o———

A number of ancient funeral cairns have been found in various parts of the Glen, as noticed in the Land of the Lindsays. But the most conspicuous "cairns" are two modern erections, the one upon the Rowan hill, the other upon the Modlach. The former, which is pyramidical in its form, was lately erected by the Earl of Dalhousie, in honour of the ancient FAMILY of MAULE; and the latter, which consists of a tower, with a place for shelter, was built a good many years ago, by the St Andrews Lodge of Freemasons, Lochlee.

A neat Free Church with spire, also a commodious manse, and the new parish school and schoolhouse, are to the east of the hamlet of Tarfside, and in the pretty district of Cairncross, out of which a davoch of land was given by Morgund, son of Abbe (the lay Abbot of Brechin), to his son Michael, in the year 1230 (*Note from Dr John Stuart.*)

But the most picturesque parts of Glenesk are in the neighbourhood of Invermark, where the old roofless and ivyclad tower of the "lichtsome Lindsays," with its ingeniously constructed *yett*, or gate of wrought iron, stands upon a rising ground at the foot of Glenmark.

In the same locality, but upon a more elevated spot, is Invermark Lodge, the shooting quarters of the Earl of Dalhousie. The Lodge overlooks the Loch and water of Lee, " the auld kirk-yard," the peak of Craigmaskeldie, and a variety of other points of great natural beauty. This grand "Highland Retreat" is also interesting to "all good and loyal subjects," for there the Queen, and other members of the Royal Family, have been guests of its noble proprietor.

The North Esk river rises from the Loch of Lee, and after a course of from 30 to 40 miles, it falls into the sea near Kinnaber. Ponskeenie, a picturesque old bridge of three arches, near Dalbrack, and another of one arch, which is just being erected by the Earl of Dalhousie across the ford at Glenoffock, are the only stone bridges upon the Esk to the north of the Gannochy.

A stone bridge was built over the *Taif* or Tarf about 1750. It was carried off by the floods of 1829, when the present structure was erected. The bridge across the *Turruthd* or Turret, which separates the parish of Lochlee from that of Edzell, is also of modern date, as is that over the Brawny, near the parish church. The old bridge over the Mark, improved in 1870 by Lord Dalhousie, was contracted for at Droustic, 14th April 1755, by John Montgomery, mason in Pitcninlaich. The work was estimated to cost £34 sterling, exclusive of the materials, which were to be brought to his hand; but it was agreed that if Montgomery should show himself to be "a real Loser thereby," his loss was to be made up when the work was completed. The bridge, which was to be ready for traffic on the 29th of September following, was to be 12 feet of breadth, with "betwixt fourty and fourty-four foot of an arch." (*Original Contract*, kindly communicated by the Rev. Mr Walter Low.) A mutilated tablet upon the bridge bears:—

"This Bridge was Built on General Contributions, chiefly of the Parishioners of Lochlee . . ."

Besides the old foot-path, or *Priests' Road* from Ponskeenie to Lethnot, there is a rugged road through Glenturret to Charleston of Aboyne. Another road leads from Lochlee by Glenmark and Mount Keen to Ballater, &c. Though seldom travelled, save by tourists, it was by the last-named route that Her Majesty the Queen, and the late PRINCE CONSORT and suit came *incognito* from Balmoral to Fettercairn in 1861.

The royal party were met on Mount Keen by the Earl of Dalhousie, and lunched in a cottage occupied by one of his Lordship's foresters. From this they passed, *en route*, through the wild pass of Glenmark, and refreshed themselves at the *Tober-na-clachan-gealaich* (the white stone well), where there is a copious spring, famous for its clear and cooling water. A fine view is obtained from the spot, which is about 60 yards east of the Mark, and about 300 yards from where the Ladder Burn joins the Mark.

In commemoration of the Royal visit, and the sad loss which followed to the Queen and the Country by the death of the Prince Consort, Lord Dalhousie had a memorial erected at the well. It is composed of six roughly-hewn arches of native granite, which converge to a centre—not unlike the top of St Giles' steeple at Edinburgh—and rise to the height of about 20 feet, the whole being finished by a cross of hewn freestone. Upon the centre arch is this inscription:—

Her Majesty QUEEN VICTORIA
and his Royal Highness the PRINCE-CONSORT,
visited this Well, and drank of its refreshing waters,
on the 20th September 1861,
the year of Her Majesty's great sorrow.

—The following is round the margin of a basin of freestone, into which the spring falls:—

Rest, Traveller, on this lonely green,
And drink, and pray for SCOTLAND'S QUEEN.

Marykirk.

(THE BLESSED VIRGIN.)

THE church of *Abirluthenot*, which is rated at 20 merks in the Old Taxation, belonged to the Priory of St Andrews, and was dedicated by Bishop David in 1242.

The name of *Abirluthenot* appears to have been assumed from the burn of Luthnot, which runs past the village of Marykirk. An early, but dateless charter (Reg. Vetus de Aberbrothoc), shows that a piece of land was granted to the church of *Maringtun*, which lay to the west of the burn of "Luffenot," and extended to a bridge called "Stanbrig," on the North Esk. This charter not only proves the existence of an early bridge upon the river; but it also discloses the interesting particular, that the donor, "Willelmus Auceps," or William the Hawker, (who is the first recorded of the old family of Falconer of Halkerton), offered a turf of the land upon the altar of the church as a symbol of investiture.

In 1574, the churches of Eglisgreig and Aberluthnot were both served by one minister (*sup.*, p. 36); and Thomas Ramsay was the contemporary reader at Aberluthnot.

The name of the parish was long ago changed from Aberluthnot to that of MARY-KIRK. Before the old church was re-roofed, it contained a ceiling of carved oak, an escutcheon of the Halkerton family, and an inscribed tablet, notices of which, along with a copy of the inscription, are given by Mr Brymer, in his excellent Account of the Parish, in 1793. The inscription is as follows:—

Hic in Domino requiescunt parentes mei charissimi M. JACOBUS RAITUS, pastor vere Evangelicus, qui præfuit huic ecclesiæ 25 annos fideliter, non sine magno emolumento; tunc vitam cum morte commutavit, calend. Maii. anno 1642, ætatis suæ 59; et dilectissima ejus conjux, ISABELLA BLACKBURNE, quæ obiit 19 Januarii, anno 1637, ætatis suæ 32. Parentavit filius, W. R.

[Here rest in the Lord my dear parents, Mr JAMES RAIT, a true minister of the Gospel, who, for 25 years, presided faithfully over this church, not without great benefit, and then exchanged life for death, 1st May 1642, at the age of 59; and his beloved wife ISABELLA BLACKBURN, who died 19th Jan. 1637, aged 32. Erected by their son, W. R.]

—The erector of the above monument succeeded his father in the church of Marykirk; and although he was unsuccessful in his application for the living of Menmuir (Land of the Lindsays, p. 338), he was afterwards translated to Brechin. He was made Principal of King's College, Aberdeen, in 1661, and during the following year became one of the ministers of Dundee. He was a cadet of the House of Hallgreen, and his wife was heiress of Guthrie of Pitforthy, near Brechin, *sup.*, p. 108.) His mother was probably related to William Blackburn, a contemporary burgess of Aberdeen, who took a great interest in church matters.

The old kirk consisted of a transept, with a north and a south aisle. The north aisle, which belonged to the Barclays of Balmakewan, presents a carving of the Barclay arms, initialed I. B., and dated 1653. The south aisle, which belonged to the Strachans of Thornton, contains an awmbry, a font, and an elegant tomb. The date and initials of "A . 1615 . S," upon a slab built into the outside of the west wall, probably refer to the time that the aisle was erected.

The old ceiling of the Thornton aisle was painted with armorial bearings. Among a variety of carvings, the tomb bears the Strachan and Forbes arms, with these initials and date:—

S.I.S . . . 61 . D.E.F.

A marble tablet, flanked by pilasters, bears an inscription, which is here printed as it now appears:—

Epicedium threnodicum . . memoriam fœminæ lectissimæ, Dominæ ELIZABETHÆ FORBESÆ, Dominæ a Thornton, æternitatis candidatæ, . . . meritorum . . . pissima, puerpera, immaturo fato . . . repta est, dum annum ætatis vigesimum quintum agebat, die decimo Ianuarij . . 61 :

Cujus fragrantissæ memoriæ, licet .... de monumentis omni ære perennioribus abunde satis litatum sit, hoc tam .. magnifico mausoleo, parentandum curavit conjunx ipsius pullatus, D. Iacobus Strachanus a Thorntone, æques auratus.

Siste, viator, habes summi monument ....
Virtutis tumulum, Pieridumq' vid ..
Omnis una fuit brevis hæc quam con ....
Lux nuper patriæ .... levis umb ....
Aurea si tantas fudere crepuscula ....
Luxisset, quanto sydere ....
Quanta fuit pietas quam stemmatis ....
Enthea uiens, roscus quam sine sento sinus.
Quantus et oris honos ; Phœnix vixitq' caditq',
Qualem non poterant reddere ..... decem,
At matura polo cecidit Christoq' ; quid .....
Ignavi numerant sæcula, facta boni.
Mors ipsa non separabit.

[A funeral song to the memory of a most excellent woman, Dame ELIZABETH FORBES, lady of Thornton, who, possessed of all the merits that can adorn her sex, became a candidate for eternity 10th January 1661, in the 25th year of her age, having died prematurely in childbed. Altho' her worth is preserved by monuments more lasting than any brass, her sorrowing husband, Sir James Strachan of Thornton, knight baronet, has caused this magnificent tomb to be erected to her most fragrant memory.

Stop, traveller, you have before you a monument of the deepest grief ; you see the tomb of a virtuous and accomplished lady—one who, lately a light to her country, now flits an unsubstantial shade. If the golden dawn showed so bright a light, with what splendour would the noontide have shone? How great was her piety, how befitting her illustrious race was her inspired intellect, how thornless her rosy bosom, how great the graceful dignity of her look ! A Phœnix, she both lived and died, such as not ten ages could reproduce. But she died ripe for Heaven :—What more was needed ? The slothful reckon ages, good men deeds. Death itself shall not part us.]

—The above-named lady, who was married in 1654, when her husband was designed of Inchestuthell, was third daughter of Forbes of Waterton and his wife Jean Ramsay of Balmain (*supra*, p.,

60). Lady Strachan left a son and two daughters, who were brought up and educated by their maternal grandmother ; but, it appears, notwithstanding the high eulogium which the baronet passed upon his lady, he took so little interest in her offspring that, in 1665, their grandmother raised a summons against him for having neglected his affairs, and abandoned his children (*Watertoune Family Papers.*) Elizabeth Forbes' son possibly grew up and succeeded to the title and estates, for in 1692, John Strachan of Belly, son of Sir James Strachan of Thornton, married Isobel, daughter of Sir John Forbes.

Alexander Strachan, who succeeded his grandfather in 1606, and married a daughter of Sir William Douglas of Glenbervie, and a sister of the 10th Earl of Angus (Doug. Peer.), was created a baronet in 1625. He had several successors in the title; but, so far as I am aware, no reliable genealogy of the family exists. The once powerful branches of Carmyllie and Glenkindie are supposed to have been offshoots of the Strachans of Thornton ; and the name is believed to have been assumed from the district of Strachan, in Kincardineshire. The property of Thornton is said to have come to the Strachans by one of them marrying the daughter and heiress of Thornton of that Ilk, in the time of David II. (*v.* Mem. Angus and Mearns.)

It may be added that, in addition to Hugh Strachan, or Ramsay (*infra*, p. 165), Dr Oliver gives the names of other five of this race who became Jesuits. Among these is Alexander, eldest son of the sixth baronet of Thornton, who " succeeded to the title and its slender income," and died at Liege in 1793. He was for some time tutor in a private family, and was succeeded by his brother Robert, who was long a mercantile clerk, and died at Exeter in 1826, aged about 90 years.

There were other two brothers. One went to America, and the other is said to have taken the title on the death of Sir Robert Strachan, after which it was assumed by his nephew, who died at Cliffden, Teignmouth. It is added that Sir Alexander, the Jesuit, was offered £5000 to give up his family papers to Admiral Sir Richard Strachan, and that, poor as he was, he refused the bribe. The Thornton papers are said to be in the possession of a family in Devonshire, to whom Sir Robert left any little that he died possessed of.

The property of Thornton now belongs to Alexander Crombie, Esq. of Pittarrow; and the old family residence has been altered and added to by Mr Crombie with much taste and judgment.

The square tower of Thornton Castle is dated 1531, and the weather vane bears, "1680." The round tower, at the north-east corner, which is supposed to be the oldest remaining portion of the building, although dateless, exhibits a carving of the old family arms. The family arms, with the initials of Sir James Strachan and Dame Elizabeth Forbes, and the date of 1662, are also upon the north wing of the building, or that part which connects the two towers.

It was probably during the time of the last-mentioned Sir J. Strachan, and possibly by some family arrangement, that Thornton passed to the Forbeses, since about or soon after the year 1686, the property was acquired by James Forbes of Saach or Savoch, in Foveran parish (*Watertoune Family Papers*). In a deed of 1723, Thomas Forbes of Thornton is described as the son of the late James Forbes of Auchmacoy, in Logie-Buchan.

Mr Troup of Hartville, Bridge of Allan, who is presently preparing an Account of the Forbeses, kindly writes that James Forbes of Thornton, who died in 1713, was succeeded by his eldest son, Thomas, and that the affairs of the latter became so much embarrassed, that the estate was sold in 1763, by authority of the Court of Session.

The only memorial at Marykirk to the Forbeses of Thornton is a mutilated slab within the family burial aisle, which exhibits these traces of an inscription :—

Hic iacet . . . . . Philippus Fo . . . . . . de Thornton . . . . . . Natus 22do Dec . . . . . . obiit 2do Octob . . . . . .

The TAYLORS of Kirktonhill have an inclosed burial-place, but no monument, within the area of the old kirk of Marykirk. Robert, a younger son of Tailzour of Borrowfield, near Montrose, was the first of this family. He bought (as the present laird courteously informs us) the lands of Kirktonhill and Balmanno, from James Aikman in 1755; and married a sister of Sir James Carnegy of Pittarrow, afterwards of Southesk, by whom he had a family. Mr Taylor died about 1780, when the properties were both sold. Kirktonhill was bought by Colonel David Gairdner, and Balmanno by Mr Alex. Smith; and from them the estates were re-acquired, in 1797 and 1798 respectively, by the grand-father of the present laird, who made a fortune in Jamaica. He also changed the spelling of his name from *Tailzour* to *Taylor*.

Kirktonhill, which is within the barony of Rescobie, was anciently called the Kirktown lands of Aberluthnot. The lands were held of the Priory of St Andrews; and in 1540, Cardinal Beaton gave a charter of Kirktonhill to David Barclay of Mathers. Barclay gave the lands of Johnstone, near Laurencekirk, to his eldest son John, by a second marriage. In a letter of 5th October 1660, Barclay of Johnstone says that "the Earle of Northesk and my uncle Cadam have now ended their differences"—a statement which proves the relationship between the Barclays of Johnstone and those of Caldhame at that time. Carved slabs, embellished with the Barclay arms, are still to be seen at Caldhame (*infra*, p. 138.)

The present church of Marykirk, which stands on the north side of the burial-ground, was erected in 1806. Within, and upon the east wall, a marble monument is thus inscribed :—

The Revd. JAMES SHAND, A.M., minister of this parish from 1805 to 1837, and previously of the College Church, Aberdeen, son of James Shand, Esquire, merchant there, born 18th August 1757, died 5th Jany. 1837. MARGARET FARQUHAR, his wife, born 11th August 1767, died 11th January 1840, daughter of Alexander Farquhar, Esq., Kintore, by his wife Elizabeth Harvey, great-grand-daughter of James Harvey of Kilmundy, and his wife Margaret Baird of Auchmedden. He was an accomplished scholar, a kind husband and father, and a devoted pastor—In all the relations of life she was equally exemplary. Both were united in that faith and hope which vanquish death, and realize the rest which remaineth to the people of God. This tablet is affectionately dedicated by their surviving sons to the memory of the best of parents. Be thou faithful unto death, and I will give thee a crown of life.

—Charles-Farquhar Shand, third son of the above-named minister of Marykirk, passed as an advocate in 1834. He edited an edition of the Funeral Sermons and Orations on Bishop Patrick Forbes, for the Spottiswoode Society, in 1845. The volume contains, among other interesting matter, a copy of the Latin inscription in the Thornton aisle, as it appeared in 1828, accompanied by a poetical translation of the verses. In 1860, Mr Shand was appointed Chief Justice of the Mauritius, and in 1869, he received the honour of knighthood.

The church-yard of Marykirk was levelled and otherwise improved in 1868, in the course of which some old gravestones were discovered. One of these presents a shield, charged with the Montgomery and Melvill arms, &c. The words—"DIED IN APRYL 5, 1591," are below the shield; and the following inscription, in rudely incised capitals, is given round the border of the stone :—

Here lyes MARGRET MELVIL, who died ye 20 Apryl 1686, hir age 60 years. She uas spous to Robert Montgomry,

    Whos corps interd belou
    Lyes hyd from eyes
    Whose souls advancd with Chryst
    Above the skyes.

—Melvill is an old surname in the Mearns, but that of Montgomery is almost unknown to the district. A heart-shaped piece of ground, to the south of Hatton House, is still called *Montgom'ry's Knap*. It appears to have been surrounded by a marsh; and, according to tradition, it was the site of a castle which was tenanted by a family named Montgomery. They are said to have led a lawless and predatory life, and to have made themselves so obnoxious that their neighbours assembled and drove them from their stronghold. No writer makes allusion to this castle; but tradition further affirms that, before leaving the place, Montgomery "hid a kettle-full of gold in the Knap!"

The next inscription is partly round the margin, partly upon the face of a well-proportioned slab of red sand stone. Near the bottom of the stone are the initials, A. G., the date of 1630, also boldly executed carvings of a blacksmith's shovel, tongs, a hammer, the horns of an anvil, a horse shoe, &c. The first portion of the inscription is cut in relief, and the last three lines are incised :—

HEIR . LYES . ADAME . GLYGE . SMITH IN . THE . HILL . . . MORPHYE . SOME TYME . HOWSBAND . TO . ISOBEL . LOW WHO . DEPARTED . THE . 10 . OF . AWGWST ADAM . GLE . . . . , DIED IN APRIL 1698 . AGED . 86.
JOHN GLEIG died May 15, 1737, aged 83; ISOBEL GLEIG died March 4th, 1761, aged 78.

—"John Gleig," (great-grandson of "Adame Glyge"), was the father of Provost Gleig of Montrose. Elizabeth, daughter of Provost Gleig, married James Burnes, cousin-german to Burns, the Poet. Mr Burnes, who was a writer in, and sometime Provost of Montrose, had a large family, among whom were Sir Alexander and Charles, who both fell at Cabul; Sir James, K.H.; and Adam. The last-named succeeded to his father's business in Montrose, where he died in 1872. He was much esteemed for his upright conduct, as well as for his great humour, and generosity of disposition.

Dr Gleig, Bishop of Brechin (the father of the present venerable and accomplished Chaplain-General of the Forces), and the Rev. Mr Gleig, parish minister of Arbroath, were both descendants of "Adame." Their fathers were both blacksmiths by trade; the former followed his useful calling at Boghall in Arbuthnott, and the latter at Balrownie in Menmuir. Some members of the Montrose branch of the family were famous for the manufacture of "Jews' Harps," or *trumps*—a fact which has made the name of *Gleig* familiar to the lovers of that instrument in many parts of Scotland.

The next inscription is also one of some general interest, in so far as it marks the grave of the mother of DAVID HERD, the celebrated collector of Ancient and Modern Scottish Songs, Heroic Ballads, &c. :—

Here lyes MARGET LOW, spouse of John Herd, sometime tennent in Muirtoun of Be .... n, who died 14th Dec. 1751, aged 60 years :—

A loving and a virtueous wife she was,
That few or none could her surpass.

—It has been stated by Chambers, and other biographers, as well as in the recent reprint of Herd's Songs, that he was born in *St Cyrus*; but about 1853, while searching the parish records of Marykirk for another purpose, I came accidentally upon the following entries of the marriage of Herd's parents and his own baptism :—

Nov. 14, 1730 : The qch day were contracted in order to Marriage, JON HIRD & MARGT. LOW, both in this parioch. Caurs for the pledges, Da. Hird, in Balmakelly, for the Bridgroom, & William Low, in Denside, for the Bride. Married on Dec. 29th.

Oct. 23, 1732 : This day was baptized DAVID HIRD, lawll. son to John Hird and Margat Low, in Balmakelly, before these wittnesses, David & William Herd, both in Balmakelly.

—These extracts, which first appeared in Willis' *Current Notes* for Nov. 1854, were accompanied by a suggestion, founded on the authority of the Retours (Kincardine, No. 88), that Herd's mother might have been descended from a family of the name of Low, who were proprietors of Little and Nether Balmakelly, in 1655.

Herd's father appears to have removed from Balmakelly to, probably, the "Muirton of *Benholm*," for the final letter *n* in the destroyed word looks like part of an *m*. Be this as it may, DAVID HERD died at Edinburgh, and was buried in the Buccleuch Church-yard of that city, where a tablet (which is being fast obliterated by the weather), is built into the north wall. The tablet, which it is to be hoped will soon be re-lettered, &c., is about 16 feet west of the east dyke, and bears this suggestive inscription :—

29 feet south from this stone are interred the remains of Mr DAVID HERD, writer: a man of probity, of a kind and friendly disposition, of mild, tolerant principles, and of taste in ancient Scotish Literature. Not solicitous to shine, nor anxious to become rich, he lost few friends, and made few enemies. These qualities had their influence ; for, they averted many of the wants and evils of declining years. He died a true believer upon the 10 June 1810, aged —.

—Sir W. Scott, who characterises Herd's work as " the first classical collection of Scottish Songs and Ballads," says that he was known and generally esteemed for his shrewd, manly common sense and antiquarian science, and that from his hardy antique mould of countenance, and his venerable grizzled locks, he was known among his acquaintances by the name of *Greystail*.

The next inscription, from a tombstone near to that of Herd's mother at Marykirk, possibly relates to some of his relatives :—

This stone is erected to the memory of MARGARET HERD, late spouse to James Strachan, who died March 30, 1763, aged 50 ; and of their son, DAVID STRACHAN, who died in infancy. JAMES STRACHAN died June 6, 1782, aged 73 years.

The next two epitaphs are from headstones : —

JOHN LYAL, Potbeidlie, d. 1742, a. 53 :—
Deaths shade is made the hiding place,
When uordly troubles do increase ;
When converts young are called home,
Before those troublous days do come,
It warning giues to older sort
To fly to Christ, their chief support,
Though ye be young as well as I,
Yet faith will learn you how to dy.

ROBERT HILL, schoolmaster, d. 1784, a. 69, in the 45th year of his office :--

Thou hast the promise of eternal truth,
Those who live well, and pious paths pursue,
To man and to their maker true,
Let 'em expire in age or youth,
   Can never miss
Their way to everlasting bliss.

The following instances are given to show the long ages attained by some of the old residenters of the parish:—

MARGARET CLARK, died 1833, aged 96; her daughter ELIZABETH SHERET, died 1864, aged 90.

ALEX. PYPER died at Rosehill, 1825, aged 72; his sponse ELSPET CRUICKSHANK, died 1846, aged 84.

DAVID TOWNS, Arrat's Mill, predeceased his wife in 1729:—

> Heel order Death, that porter rude,
> To open the gates of brass ;
> For, lo, with characters of blood
> Thy husband wrote thy pass.
> At Jordan deep then be not feared,
> Tho' dismal-like and broad ;
> Thy sun will guide, thy shield will guard—
> Thy husband paved the road.
> Heel lead thee safe, and bring thee Home,
> So still let blessings fall
> Of grace while here, till glory come—
> Thy husband's bound for all.

DAVID WOOD'S wife, aged 21 (1796):—

> Stop, passenger, here and read—
> The living may get knowledge from the dead :
> Here lies the mortal part of a beloved wife
> Who only lived 5 months a married life.
> Beside her father's dust and mother's,
> At the left side of a sister and brother's—
> Our family 7 in one arrangement be :—
> Consider this, O man, that all must die.

The church at SAUCHIEBURN, now occupied by the Independents, was built by the Bereans in 1773. One of the two remaining tombstones bears the curious inscription given below. The composition of the epitaph is ascribed to Mr M'Rae, a Berean preacher ; and the person commemorated, (a son of Robert WYLLIE, aged 12 years), is said to have been accidentally scalded to death in a cauldron of boiling water :—

> Oh, that it were with me,
> As in the days of old,
> With children about me,
> In number manifold.
> But here mine only son,
> In this dark grave is laid,
> Who hindered not his father
> To sleep into his bed.

Because that the oppressor,
Upon his side had power ;
And none to comfort me,
Altho' I mourned sore.—(1789.)

A pair of silver communion cups belonging to the parish bear:—

Given to the Kirk of Aberluthnott by David Melvill and Jean Rait of Pitgarvie, 1715.

—It appears that David Melvill was *in* Pitgarvie in 1699, as in the month of March of that year his "victual house" was broken into, and "several peckfulls of meal" stolen from it, by Wm. Edmonstone, and his three sons, who lived at Bogmuir near Fettercairn, for which, and a number of other thefts, the elder Edmonstone was sentenced " to be hanged on a gibbet till he be dead." —(Black Book of Kincardineshire.)

Aberluthnot was anciently a thanedom.

It is just possible that one of the stones, about six feet long, which was found in the walls of the old church, had covered the grave of some of the lairds of Marykirk. It "was carved round the edge ; had the impression of a large broad sword, suspended at no great distance from the top, the whole length of the stone. Opposite to this sword was engraved a figure of an elliptic form, from which proceeded a lance or spear, nearly the same length."—(Old Stat. Acct.)

At Balmanno (anciently a seat of the AUCHINLECKS of that ilk), is S. JOHN'S Well, where, possibly, there had been a place of worship in old times. With some probability, a like inference might be drawn from the ancient spelling of Inglismaldie (*Ecclesmadie*), and MAIDIE'S (? Magdalene's) Well. A circular hollow in the woods of Hatton is called the *Popish Kirk*, where, it is said, there was once a chapel.

There was an Episcopal church at the village of Luthermuir ; and there, in 1782, Bishop JOHN SKINNER of Aberdeen, son of the author of Tullochgorm, was consecrated. The church was subsequently removed to Roschill, near the bridge which crosses the Luther, on the Laurencekirk road, where it long remained. It is from this place

T

that the Earl of Northesk takes his second title of Lord Rosehill.

Inglismaldie was acquired by Sir John Carnegie, afterwards Earl of Northesk, in 1635, by whom, or his successor, the castle was erected. Like many castles of the period, the beams in the ceiling of the hall were painted with scripture quotations; but these are now covered by lath and plaster. Inglismaldie was afterwards bought by Lord Halkerton, and came by heirship to the Earls of Kintore.

There was also a castle at Caldhame. From this property the Earls of Middleton took the title of baron; and it was here, while sitting in his chair, that Montrose's soldiers shot the father of the first Earl of Middleton. A carved stone, built into the farm offices, is inscribed LAVS DEO. Two other slabs bear shields: One with the initials I. B., and the date of 16–7, is charged with the Barclay arms. The other, initialed A. B: I. S., bears the same arms impaled with those of Wood. More recently Caldhame became the property of Keiths; and a stone slab, built into the wall of the bridge at Caldhame, bears a shield, with the arms partially effaced, and this inscription:—

1744: GEORGE KEITH OF CALDHAME.
RENEWED, 1783.

—This bridge, which crosses the Luther on the road between Fettercairn and Montrose, and consists of three arches, was first built by Keith, who gave £100 Scots towards its maintenance. If not required for that purpose, the interest of the money has to be expended annually among the poor of the parish, not on the poor's roll. The last Keith of Caldhame left an only daughter. She married Ogilvy of Lunan, and he sold the estate.

Just the year before the bridge of Caldhame was built, Keith's house was broken into by Randell Courteney, an Irishman, who effected an entrance by going down the kitchen chimney. (Scots Magazine.) Courteney was hanged near Fettercairn, at a place still known as Randell's Knap, 21 Sep. 1743.

According to old charters, there was a stone bridge across the North Esk, near to where the burn of Luthnot joins that river, as early as the 12th century. The present *Marykirk Bridge* consists of four arches, each of 58 feet span: its extreme length is 350 feet. The bridge was founded in 1811, and opened for traffic in 1815, at a cost of about £10,000.

The church bell of Marykirk is dated 1826. It is said that a previous bell was broken by being hit by a stone by some of the Duke of Cumberland's soldiers in 1746. It is also told that one Sunday, while the bell was cracked, a waggish schoolmaster, or precentor, handed a paper to the minister as he entered the pulpit: and, believing it to be a *bona fide* production regarding a dying parishioner, his reverence gravely announced, at the proper time, that "the prayers of the congregation were requested on behalf of *Mary Bell, in great distress!*"

~~~~~~~~~~~~~~~~~~~~~~~~~

Newtyle.

(S. ———)

THE church of *Newtyl*, in the diocese of St Andrews, dedicated by Bishop David in 1242, was given to the Abbey of Arbroath by King William the Lion.

The present church, built in 1767 (which is about to be replaced by a new edifice), stands upon a slight eminence at the west side of the village. In early times it had been surrounded by a marsh, A tablet is fixed into the outside of the south wall, upon which is the following inscription:—

Post mortem vita. Infra conditur quod reliquum est JACOBI ALISON, hujus parœchiæ quondam incolæ et decoris; nisi quod viri præstantissimi supersunt et vigent virtutes hoc marmore perenniores: rara scil prudentia intaminata fides, et pietas nescia fraudis. Pater fuit facillimus, conjux charissimus, et certus amicus, omnibus æquus, benevolus, et charus, et ut cætera complectar, eximie probus. Itaq, cum honesto, humili, forti, sanctoq animo, hominibus, maritis, socijs omnibus exemplum consecrasset integerrimum, terris animo

major, ad similes evolavit superos. Natus erat
. . . . denatus 4 Feb. 1737.
Mors certa est, incerta dies, incertior hora ;
Consulat ergo animo qui sapit usq. suo.

[Beneath is laid what remains of JAMES ALISON, sometime an inhabitant of this parish, and its ornament, save that, more lasting than this monument, the virtues of a most excellent man—viz., rare prudence, unsullied honour, and piety without guile—survive unimpaired. He was a most indulgent father, a most affectionate husband, and a sure friend—just, kind, loving to all ; and, to sum up, a man of distinguished probity. Accordingly, after he had set before husbands, companions, and men in general, a most perfect pattern of integrity, humility, fortitude, and piety, his soul, fitted for a nobler sphere than earth, soared aloft to join the society of kindred spirits in the realms above. He was born . . . . and died 4 Feb. 1737.
Death is certain, the day uncertain, the hour more uncertain. Let him then who is wise ever consult the interests of his soul.]

—Mr Alison was long factor and manager of the estates of Belmont for Lord Privy Seal Mackenzie, in which office he was succeeded by his son Patrick. The latter died proprietor of Stonee, part of Balbrogie, and Newhall, &c., near Cupar Angus, in the year 1795, on which occasion, Mr P. Alison being a trustee appointed by the celebrated Geo. Dempster of Dunnichen to act along with him in the administration of a grant by Mr James Taylor, of Middlesex, of certain funds for the education of poor children in the parish of KETTINS, (q. v.)—Mr Dempster, in offering the vacant office to Mr Murray of Lintrose, wrote that gentleman the following characteristic letter upon the subject, which is here published for the first time : —

"Skibo, by Tain, Dec. 19, 1795.
"DR. SIR,—I learn from Mr Blair of Dundee that poor Peter Alison has paid the Debt of nature. There is a little mortification for poor scholars in the Parish of Ketins, which he took the trouble to manage. I wish you would do me and the poor Children in that Parish, the favour to take charge of this Fund. If you will have that goodness, this Letter will be Authority enough for Mr Alison's Ex^{rs} to deliver up the Book, and Col. Fotheringham's Bond to you. A minute should be made in the Book of your being chosen Trustee in Mr Alison's Room, which Mr Hallyburton would sign now, and I the first Time I come to that Country. I beg to offer respectfull Compliments to Mrs Murray and Capt. Murray, and that you will consider this offer as the secret mark of respect, with which I am, Dear Sir,
" Your most obedient and most humble Servant,
"GEORGE DEMPSTER."

Several monuments are built into the west wall of the churchyard. Not long ago, the oldest of these presented familiar quotations from Horace, &c. These stones, however, have been removed, to make room for a pavement slab, which bears that " this ground was purchased from the Kirksession of Newtyle as certified and recorded." The following Latin inscription (surmouted by a shield bearing the Blair and Pattullo arms impaled), is still in good preservation :—

Hic reqviescit vir prvdens, ac gravis, generosa de Balgillo familia ortus, Magister GVLIELMVS BLAIRVS, qvi placide ac pie obiit 16 Novem. an. Dom. 1656, ætat. svæ 58. In cvjvs memoriam conjvnx ejvs amantissima Evphana Pattvllo hvnc tvmvlvm extrvxit jvxta evm, ex qvo filiam habet octennem, sepelienda.
Vivit post fvnera virtvs.
Cvjvs hic tvmvlvm cernis nvnc incola cœli est,
Corporis exvvias qvam premis abdit hvmvs.

[Here rests a grave and prudent man, descended from the honourable family of Balgillo, Master WILLIAM BLAIR, who died calmly and piously (as above). This monument has been erected to his memory by his most loving spouse Euphana Pattullo, who intends to be herself buried beside him, by whom she has a daughter eight years of age.
Virtue survives the grave.
He whose tomb you see now lives on high,
And 'neath your feet his lifeless ashes lie.]

—There were Pattullos contemporary lairds of Kinochtry, near Cupar-Angus. Patrick Blair, 4th of Balthayock, had charters of Balgillo in Angus, 1393. One of the Balgillo Blairs was knighted.
Possibly the partial mutilation of the above

tomb and the late purchase of the ground were effected by a family named Watson, once farmers at Auchtertyre, to whom there are two or three monuments within the enclosure. One of these, with armorial bearings, and the motto, HAVE FAITH, is thus inscribed :—

Sacred to the memory of GEORGE WATSON, Esq., Bannatyne House, and JEAN ROSE, his beloved wife. He, as a magistrate and man, was most justly esteemed. She was sole heiress of the ancient families of Moray, and Kinnaird of Culbin in Morayshire. As a mother and wife most exemplary. All who knew her loved her. 1813.

—It is stated in the Kilravock papers (p. 82), that " John Rose, now of Brodley, who by Jean Kynaird, a daughter of the familie of Culbin, is father to Hugh and John Rose." This fact probably bears out the statement in the inscription. HUGH, the last of the Watsons who farmed Auchtertyre and Keilor, born 1787, died 1865, was eminent as an agriculturist.

The following inscriptions are from tombstones in the surrounding burial ground :—

Heir lyis ane famos honist man GEORG MITCHEL, of age 52, indveler in Balmav, d. 1625; and his spovs C. B. ANDRO MITCHEL, and his spovs I. R. Heir lyis ISOBEL MITCHEL, spovs to A. S. :—
    Death, oft deplor, bvt in thy dealing ivst,
    Pvtis vith the sped, the sheptor in the dvst.

Upon a stone bearing a shield with the arms impaled (a cheveron, with a rose in base), and the initials I. M : M. H. :—

Heir lyis ane famovs honest man IHON MOVO, being of age 66, departed the 2 of Agvst in an. 1632, he being hvsband to Magrat Halden.

The following inscription is from the oldest of four stones erected to the memory of members of the same family. Direct descendants still survive as merchants in Dundee, &c :—

Heir lyis IAMES IOBSON, son to Iames Iobson and Barbry Scot his spovs, indveler in the Haltown of Nevtyl, vho departed in Ivly 1660, of age 9. And heir lyes BARBRAY SCOT, his mother, frvgall and vertvovs, departed March 24, anno 1684, of age 67. My glas is rvn,

Near the foregoing .—

Heir lyes ane honest man IAMES RAMSAY in Avghtertyr . . . . of age 50, with his wif IANET WHITTON, died 15 Octor '73, of age 52 ; and IAMES RAMSAY y^r son died 11 Nov '77, of age 20 ; as also IAMES, DAVID, GEORGE, and IANET RAMSAYS, laefvll children to Wiliam Ramsay and Agnas Lovnie, in the said tovne.

WM. RAMSAY, in Auchtertyre, a. 36 (1682) :—
    Vnder this stone interred doth ly
    This man of honest fame ;
    And of his wirtues while he liv'd
    His name doth fresh remaine.
    Who to his wife and parents both
    A help and comfort was ;
    But now the Lord hath crowned him
    With joy in heavenly bless.

Upon a flat stone, initialed G. M : K . B : M. B., and dated 1675, is the following epitaph in the form of an acrostic. It will be seen that GILBERT MILLE was the name of the person commemorated, that he was the father of twenty-six children by two wives, and that he attained the long age of 100 years :—

    Great is the Wonders God hath Worked
    In Heaven, and Earth, and Sia ;
    Lykuays he many mercies hath,
    BeStoued Wpon Me.
    Euen in this World, an Hundred Years,
    Remain'd I honestlie ;
    Tuo Weded Wives the tym I had ;
    Much Comfort was to Me.
    In Wedlocks Band ue Procreat
    Laufullly Ws Betuix ;
    Loues Pledges, Whos Right number wer,
    Euen tuo tymes tenn and Six,
    My Spritt to God, I do committ,
    My Body to the Graue ;
    When Christ shall com and jidg shall sitt,
    Shall them Both Receuie.

Upon a stone near the middle of churchyard :—

Heir lyes the bodies of IOHN DON, and BARBRA THOM, his spovse, indvellers in Hill of Keilor. His age 60, hir age 65. They both dyed in the month of Ivne '98.

A stone, near the south wall, bears:—

Here lys ane honest man ALLEXANDER BADAN,

NEWTYLE. 141

w⁺ 4 wiues, and 4 children, who departed this life Inly 18, 1702, of age 59. All dyed in Bvrnmovth. Also JAMES BADAN, hvsband to Agnes Horn. He dyid in Denhead, 1715, aged 36 :—

. . . .
That tyrant Death of him did us bereave,
But we beleive that God did him receive.

ANN WILKIE, wf. of David Baxter, d. 1753, a. 59:—
O that men in this world would live, said I,
As not to be ashamed to live, nor afraid to die ;
For all our friends and neighbours to us dear,
Unto our lives can't add a single year.
The righteous need not fear the sting,
For Christ will them to heaven bring.

Heir lyis ane honest man IOHN SLIDDRS, and ISODALL MARTEN his spovs, indvellars in Ballmav. She died May 1678, her age 56. He died 18 Apryl 1702, of age 75. ISODALL SLIDDRS, dovghter to Iohn Sliddrs and Ianet Small, of her age 9 yeirs :—
This honest man Is from us gone,
Whose body Lyes Within this Tomb ;
His honest Reputation ShaLL
Remain To Generations ALL ;
His Blessed Soull for Ever more,
Doth magnify The King of Glore.

Heir lyes ane honest man WILLIAM IACKSON, merchant, and hvsband to Anna Meal, indwellers in Newbigging, with seven children, sons and davghters. He departed the 16 day of March 1703, of his age 61 :—
The man here lyes who did always
While here he being hade ;
. . . . wpright both to God and man,
To what he did or said.

. . . .

A small stone cross bears :—

In memory of Wee MAGGIE, daughter of David Duncan, leader of the psalmody in this parish. Died 4 June 1864.

Upon an obelisk :—

GEORGE BROWSTER, schoolmaster of the parish of Newtyle, died 17 Feb. 1838, aged 82, and in the 52d year of his incumbency. Erected by the pupils of the deceased, who, during his day on earth, faithfully and usefully discharged the duties of his office in this parish.—1840.
Invitum sequitur honor.

A plain headstone, near the south-east corner of the kirk, presents this inscription :—

Erected at the instance of Robert Small, farmer in Boghead, in memory of his father ROBERT SMALL, who died 1771, aged 72 :—

. Here lies the dust of ROBERT SMALL,
Who, when in life, was thick, not tall ;
But what's of greater consequence,
He was endowed with good sense.
O how joyful the day in which
Death's pris'ner shall be free,
And in triumph o'er all his foes
His God in mercy see. [Revised 1838.]

———

There was a chapel (S. ———) in old times upon the Hill of Keilor, about a mile west of the village of Newtyle, not far from which stands a sculptured stone. A weem, or underground chamber, and other traces of early occupation, have been found in the same locality.

Hatton Castle, a picturesque ruin, south of the village, bears the date of 1575, which corresponds with the period of the 4th Lord Oliphant, whose ancestor, Sir Walter of Aberdalgie, had a grant of Newtyle and Kinpurnie, from Robert I., in 1318. These lands continued in the noble family of Oliphant until the early part of the 17th century, when they were sold to Hallyburton of Pitcur, from whom they passed, in the course of 50 or 60 years, to a son of the celebrated Sir George Mackenzie. An observatory, the roofless walls of which form so striking an object upon the summit of Kinpurnie hill, was built by Lord Privy Seal Mackenzie ; and the property was inherited by the Stuart-Wortley family, now represented by Lord Wharncliffe.

Bannatyne, or Ballantyne House, near the church, which is in excellent preservation, built about 1589, belonged to the family of GEORGE BANNATYNE, the collector of the ancient poetry of Scotland. It was in honour of him that the famous literary society of Edinburgh—the *Bannatyne Club*—was named.

Duthil.

(S. PETER.)

THE kirk of *Dothol*, in Elginshire, was a prebend of the cathedral of Moray, and was given to it by Gilbert, eldest son of the Earl of Strathern, 1224-42.

In 1630, the parishes of Duthil and Rothiemurchus were united.

A rude baptismal font, of granite, stands at the church of Duthil. According to the Old Stat. Account (vol. iv. p. 311), the kirk was built in 1400, which is possibly a misprint for 1600, or some later date. It stood until about 1826, when the present house was erected.

A mausoleum of granite, belonging to the Earls of Seafield, adjoins the church; and there, it is said, the GRANTS of Castle Grant have had their place of burial since the year 1585. The first of the Grants is said to have been Gregory (sheriff of Inverness in the time of Alexander II.,) who married a daughter of Bisset, lord of Lovat. From that time the surname frequently occurs in charters and other authentic documents. It was in consequence of Sir Ludovick Grant having married Margaret, daughter of the 5th Earl of Seafield, that Grant of Grant succeeded to the estates and titles of the Earldom of Seafield, &c.

The following inscription, upon a marble tablet within the church, relates to a grandson of the under-mentioned minister of Abernethy, who was previously at Duthil:—

Capt. WILLIAM GRANT, 27th Regt. Bengal N.I., Assistant Adjutant General of Affganistan, eldest son of the late Major Grant, Auchterblair, was killed in action at Gundermuck, during the disastrous retreat of the British Army from Caboul, on the 13 of January 1842, aged 38 years. Erected by his bereaved widow.

The next bears the names of the uncle and grand-father of the above Capt. W. Grant:—

Erected by James Augustus Grant, Esq. of Viewfield, in memory of his ancestors of the family of Milton, who have had from a remote period their last resting place here; and where too are deposited the remains of his father, the Revd. JOHN GRANT, minister of Abernethy, who died 21 January 1820.

—It is told that the minister, having several sons in the army during the Peninsular war, was in the habit of reading the newspapers upon Sundays to his congregation, when anything of importance occurred regarding the progress of events.

The following is upon a stone within an enclosure:—

ALEXANDER GRANT of Tullochgorm died 25 February 1828, aged 97, and MARGARET GRANT, his wife died 15 April 1850, aged 67.

ALEXANDER GRANT of Tullichgriban, Esq., died 22d Feb. 1829, aged 98 years; and his widow MARGARET GRANT, died 15 April 1849. Erected by their only child, Isabella-Elizabeth, wife of General Sir Lewis Grant.

JOHN GRANT, and ELIZABETH LUMSDEN, his spouse, both departed this life on the 9th Feb. 1806. Their son, Colonel Sir MAXWELL GRANT, K.C., died 22d Oct. 1823.

—The above refers to one of the Muckroch family, the first of whom was the 4th son of Sir John Grant of Grant, who was knighted by James VI., and died soon after the year 1625. Muckroch castle, the ruins of which still remain, is said to have been built in 1598; also, that the lands of Muckroch were excambed with the laird of Grant for those of Rothiemurchus.

MARGARET CUMING, died 20th June 1790, aged 82, wife first of Robert Grant, farmer, Aaugormack, next to Patrick Cuming, farmer, at Easter Duthil. "Name what a Consort, a Parent, and a Friend, in her station, should be—and she was that."

A rough slab, upon which a hammer, square, chisel, and a gun, are rudely carved, bears this brief inscription:—

Here lyes DONALD CUMING, son of Patrick Cuming, Duthil. 1774.

The next three inscriptions are from tombstones erected to certain of *The Men*, as they are locally called:—

DUNCAN CUMING, merchant, Bridge of Endy, Coilum, Rothiemurchus, who died 21 Feb. 1839.

aged 65, "was the last 26 years of his life effectually called to an enlightened mind to love and to believe the Holy Scripture."

JOHN M'INTOSH, late farmer, Torspartan, died 27 Nov. 1843, aged 65 :—"A man distinguished for zeal, love, sweet communion, was, for the last 35 years of his life, called to repentance. He was gifted with a spirit of love, prayer, and charitable feelings to distressed souls, persuading them to fly from the wrath to come. This is erected by his affectionate neighbours, as a token of their regards towards him."

GEORGE CAMERON, farmer, Tullochgorm, died 5 Feb. 1848, aged 79 :—"For the last 28 years of his life he was brought to sharp repentance, to be a self-denying Christian, and to have love to the brethren."

—*The Men* were those who professed to have been brought to a sense of their error by some miraculous means, after which they made it their business to go about and expound the Holy Scriptures to their neighbours. The appellation of *The Men of Ross* has been long given to laymen of that county, who acted in the way indicated. *The Men* of Duthil had great faith : not long ago, in the time of *The Men* above named, when the Spey changed its course at a particular spot, *The Men* believed that Providence had made it do so in obedience to their prayers, and had the same recorded upon a stone, which they placed at the point where the river had diverged !

The district of Duthil appears to have been the property of the Earls of Strathearn, prior to the time it fell into the hands of the Cumins, the old lords of Badenoch. It was afterwards owned by Sir John (grandson of Gregory Grant of Grant), who is said to have married the heiress of Cumin, and thus acquired the lands. Duthil is still held by a descendant of Sir John, the Earl of Seafield, who is accounted chief of the Clan Grant. He married the youngest daughter of the late Lord Blantyre, and has issue, Viscount Reidhaven, born 1851.

On the west side of the burial-ground, unmarked, as yet, by any monument, lie the remains of JAN MANNDACH, or LÒM, the celebrated Jacobite poet, who, after the defeat of his party at Culloden, found, in his flight from the battle field, an asylum in the farm house of Lochanhully, where he died, after a brief illness, caused by fatigue and disappointment.

Although there are few objects of antiquity in the district, it can boast of many curious and interesting traditions ; the more noteworthy of which have been preserved by Sir T. D. Lauder, and by local writers, particularly by "Glenmore," in his Legends of Strathspey.

~~~~~~~~~~~~~~~~~~~~~~~~~~~~~

Inveravon.
(S. PETER.)

MALCOLM, Earl of Fife, gave the church of *Invcrhoven*, and a davoch of land, to the Bishop of Moray, 1228. Inveravon was the seat of the chancellor of the diocese ; and the vicarages of Knockando, in Moray, and Urquhart, in Inverness-shire, depended upon it.—(Shaw's Moray.)

The church, erected in 1809, stands on the south bank of the Spey ; and S. PETER's Well, which was once considered an effectual cure for most diseases, is about 400 yards south-east of the church. At no distant date, votive offerings were found in the well ; and PETER Fair, now held at Dalnashaugh, stood near the consecrated fountain.

A sculptured stone, with a raven, and other carvings, lies within the site of the old church. The burial aisle of Grant of Ballandalloch, a recent building, stands apart from the church. It contains three tablets. The first, which is of Peterhead granite, bears : —

A tribute of filial affection and grateful esteem to the memory of Sir GEORGE MACPHERSON-GRANT of Ballandalloch and Invereshie, Baronet. Born 25 Feb. 1781 ; died 24 Nov. 1846.

—Sir G., who was long M.P. for Sutherlandshire, was created a baronet in 1838. He married Mary, eldest daughter of Carnegy of Craigo, in

Angus. Their third son Thomas, W.S., Edinburgh, succeeded to the valuable estate of Craigo, &c., on the death of his cousin Thomas, the last of the male line of that branch of the Carnegys. (v. p. 90.) Sir G.'s eldest son John, to whom the next inscription refers, only survived his father four years :—

This tablet is placed here by Dame Marion-Helen Campbell, in memory of her beloved husband, Sir JOHN MACPHERSON-GRANT of Ballandalloch and Invereshie, Bart. Born 3 Augt. 1804 ; died 2d Dec. 1850.

The following, from a marble slab, records the death of Sir John's wife, who was a daughter of Campbell of Ballimore, Argyllshire :—

This tablet is placed here by Sir George Macpherson-Grant of Ballandalloch and Invereshie, Baronet, in memory of his beloved mother, Dame MARION-HELEN CAMPBELL. Born 12 Oct. 1810 ; died 5 June 1853.

—The Invereshie branch of the Macphersons claim descent from Gillies, 3d son of Ewan Baan (*the fair Ewan*), who lived in the time of Alex. II. He was of the clan Chattan ; and the succession of the clan having devolved upon the sons of Muriach, a parson or priest, the family is said to have assumed the name of MACPARSON, or *son of the parson*. George Macpherson of Invereshie and Dalraddie married Grace, daughter of Colonel Wm. Grant of Ballandalloch. On the death of his descendant, General James Grant, the Ballandalloch estates came to George Macpherson, nephew, and subsequently heir of William of Invereshie, when he assumed the surname of *Macpherson-Grant*, and, as above noticed, was created a baronet. This family claim to be descended on the Grant side from John (son of Patrick of Grant), who lived during the first half of the 16th century.

Besides the burial aisle in the churchyard, a mausoleum, now surrounded by wood, erected in 1807, occupies an elevated position in the west corner of the Bowmoon park, overlooking Ballandalloch Castle and a great part of Strathspey. Here, by special request, were deposited the ashes of the above-named General JAS. GRANT.

The mausoleum is a square building of native granite, with a column rising from the centre, overtopt by a vase. A marble tablet upon the base of the column is thus inscribed :—

Memoriae sacrum JACOBI GRANT de Ballandalloch, in exercitu Britannico Ducis, undecimae peditum legionis, Praefecti, atque Castelli de Stirling Custodis, nati—die Novembris 1720, qui decessit 13 die Aprilis 1806. Hoc monumentum posuit Georgius Macpherson-Grant de Ballandalloch.

—The body of the General rests in the vault below. The outer casing consists of a coffin-shaped tomb of light grey marble, set upon a large granite slab. Upon the top of the coffin are the Grant arms and motto, surrounded by nicely sculptured banners and other trophies of war. The following inscription (of the same import as that in Latin), is upon the top of the tomb below the family arms :—

JAMES GRANT of Ballandalloch, General in His Majesty's Army, Colonel of the 11th regiment of foot, and Governor of Stirling Castle, born — Nov. 1720, died 13 April 1806.

—Gen. G., who succeeded to Ballandalloch on the death of his nephew, Col. W. Grant, about 1770 greatly distinguished himself during the American War, and was some years Governor of Florida.

The following inscriptions are selected from tombstones in the kirkyard of Inveravon :—

Heir lyes ane honest man caled WILLAM MC-WILLIE, who livid in the Cories, who departed the 10 of Ivne 1685 ; and KETREN GORDONE his spovse.

Here lyes the . . . . . JAMES STUART, late farmer in Cuttertown of Balindalloch, who departed this life the 3 of . . . 1749, aged . .

An enclosure, on the south side of the kirk, contains a number of tombstones to Grants who have tenanted farms in Inveravon. From these the next two inscriptions are copied :—

From motives of filial esteem and respect for the memories of JOHN GRANT, formerly in Glenarder, who died 12 Nov. 1797, aged 84 years ; and WILLIAM GRANT, who was some time farmer at Dalnapot, who died 16 Jan. 1815, aged 39, this stone was placed over them by Peter Grant in Craigroy, grandson of the former, and brother of the latter.

Here lies the body of CHARLES GRANT, farmer at Boat of Aven, who died Feb. 4, 1758, aged 76, and of his spouse, ANNA CUMMING, who died Aprile 20, 1736, aged 63. In memory of them, John and Alex. Grants, their sons, erected this stone.

—Those recorded in the last-quoted inscription were the direct ancestors of Jas. Grant, writer, Elgin, who was fifteen years provost of that city, and projector of the railways from Elgin to Craigellachie, and to Lossiemouth, &c.

WILLIAM GRANT, Esq., many years tacksman of Tombreckachie, terminated his earthly course with high and well merited esteem, on Saturday 3 June 1815, at the advanced age of 85 years.

Two separate and adjoining stones bear : —

JAMES GRANT, farmer, Pitgaveuie, near Elgin, died 1771 : He was a pious and honest man, a tender husband, a most dutiful parent, and a good neighbour. His remains ly interred under this stone, which was placed over them by his son, Mr JAMES GRANT, minister of Inveravon, who died 3 Feb. 1795, in the 77th year of his age, and 43d of his ministry.

Mrs MARGARET MACGREGOR, died 7 Dec. 1841, daughter of Jas. Macgregor, Esq. of Pittyvaich.* The Rev. WM. GRANT, minister of Inveravon, died 12 April 1833, in the 75th year of his age, and 41st of his ministry.

Within an enclosure : —

Sacred to the memory of THOMAS STEWART, Esq., late of Pittyvaich,* who departed this life, 5 Feb. 1815, aged 74.

In area of old kirk : —

The Rev. WM. SPENCE, minister of the Gospel at Inveravon, died 30 July 1807, in the 46th year of his age, and 12th of his ministry.

This stone was erected here by JOHN HENDRIE who died the 24th Dec. 1815 in the 63d year of his age with the concurrence of PENUAL CAMERON his spouse who died 7 May 1818 in the 57th year of her age. &c.

PETER HAY, merchant and farmer in Dalchwrich, placed this stone here on his burying place, and his remains are interred under it. He died Dec. 30,

---

* The expression " of" must, in the above, as in many similar instances, be taken advisedly. The parties so designed are often merely *tenant-farmers*.

1793, aged 73 years. He was a fair trader, an honest man, and peaceable neighbour. Death is certain, sin is the cause of it, but Christ is the cure.

Upon a granite headstone : —

Captain GRANT, tacksman of Advie and Molderie interred here May 1828, aged 90 years. He was the 7th in descent from Duncan the 9th laird of Grant, and 6th from Patrick Grant of Ballandalloch, who held the lands of Advie, first in wadset and afterwards in tack. His youngest son Capt. LEWIS GRANT of the 71st Regt., died May 1812, of wounds received at the assault of Fort Napoleon and in the Tagus, when cheering and leading the Highlanders to victory. Erected by Coll. W. Grant of Cloghill in memory of an honourable father, and a gallant brother ; also to his grandson, CHARLES GRANT CAMPBELL, Esq., Assistant Surgeon, R.N., who died at Rio de Janeiro, S. America, 6 Feb. 1851, in the prime of life, and faithful discharge of his duty.

This stone is placed here in memory of WILLIAM FALCENER, late farmer in Pitchaish, who died at Mains of Kinermony, 4 May 1793, in the 74th year of his age ; and of seven of his children, who died infants.

—An adjoining stone records the death of his wife ANNA ROSE, in 1821, aged 78, also that of a number of their descendants. Three sons were merchants in New York, and another died farmer of Kinermony, 1849, aged 81.

ALEX. MCDONALD, farmer, Parkhead of Pitchash, d. 1809, a. 84 :—

Heav'nward directed all his days,
His life one act of prayer and praise ;
With every modest grace inspired,
To make him lov'd, esteem'd, admired.
Crown'd with a cheerfulness that show'd
How pure the source from whence it flow'd.
Such was the man whose thread, when run,
Finding the appointed time was come,
To rest he sunk, without one sigh,
The saint may sleep, but cannot die.

Upon a headstone : —

Erected to the memory of JAMES MCDONALD, Esq., late of Morant Bay, Jamacca, who died at Charleston of Aberlour, 6 April 1836, aged 42 ; FRANCIS MCDONALD, Esq. of Morant Bay, died 19 June 1833, aged 38, natives of this parish.

A costly tomb, composed of blue granite, with three marble slabs inserted, bears that—

CHARLES STEWART, Esq., Deskie, who died 30 Sep. 1826, aged 74, was upright in principle, disinterested in character, and the poor man's friend.

His widow, MARY, daughter of the late Jas. Gordon, Esq., Croughly, died 27 March 1838, aged 66.

ANN-MARGARET, daughter of the above, spouse of Harry Lumsden, died 18 Nov. 1835, aged 27. CHAS.-GEO. LUMSDEN, Asst. Surg. K. R. Hussars, died at Meerut, Bengal, 1862, aged 30. [Two other sons and a daughter are recorded.]

Upon a table-shaped stone within same enclosure :—

This stone is erected here by Robert Stewart, tenant in Wester Deskie, in memory of his spouse, ELSPAT GORDON, who died Jan. 31, 1781, aged 50 years, who bore to him eleven children.

The parish being very large, burial-places were numerous. Apart from that at Inveravon, there were others at Chapelton, Haugh of Kilmnichlie, Lagmore, Bhuternich, Downan, &c. That of

DOWNAN,

which is picturesquely situated near the junction of the Livet and the Avon, is still used for interments, and contains a number of tombstones. From one of these the following inscription is copied :—

McLAG ACHBREACK D. 1818 AG 90 ✠ ALSO HIS SPOUSE GRACE GRANT D 1814 AG 81.

—From a better-cut version of the above, upon the reverse of the same stone (where the last age is given as 80), it appears that the first named was GEORGE McLACHLAN, farmer, Auchbreck.

The foundations of the old place of worship, which appears to have been a small building, may be traced near the middle of the enclosure at Downan. A stone slab bears a cross incised on both sides. It appears to be an object of some antiquity ; and, according to tradition, near it lie some of those who fell at the battle of Glenlivet, which was fought not far from it, between the armies of James VI., and those of the Popish Earls of Errol and Huntly, in 1594.

There was long a Roman Catholic seminary at Scalan ; but on the institution of the College at Blairs, in Mary Culter, the students were transferred to that place. (*v.* p. 115.)

Handsome Roman Catholic chapels stand at Tombae, and at the Braes of Glenlivet. (S. MARY.) Over the principal entrance to the first ("The Church of the Incarnation"), are the words —

CHRISTO ET PURÆ VIRGINI.

A monument, built of granite, contains three separate tablets, thus inscribed :—

✠ Sacred to the memory of WILLIAM GORDON, Esq., Minmore, who died 5 Nov. 1829, aged 74 years. R. I. P.

✠ O Death, I will be thy death. Osee, ch. 13. Expecting a blessed resurrection, the mortal remains of ANNE, the beloved wife of James Petrie, Esq., here repose,

In the *fear* of the Lord, which, &c.
In *faith*, without which, &c., please God.
In *hope*, the anchor, &c., sure and firm.
In *charity*, which never faileth.

She placidly resigned her spirit to its Creator, 7th Sepr. 1858, aged 47 years :—

"Her children rose up, &c.
"Her husband, and he praised her.
"Favour is deceitful, and beauty is vain.
"The woman that feareth the Lord, she shall be praised. Prov. ch. xxxi. Requiescat in pace.

✠ IHS. Sacred to the memory of MARY STEWART, spouse of Captⁿ. William Gordon, Minmore, who died 1 Octr. 1842, aged 63 years ; of their son, Captⁿ. JOHN GORDON, H.E.I.S., who died at Singapore, 4th July 1833, aged 27 years ; of their daughter, ELIZABETH-STEWART FORBES, who died at the Convent of Mercy, Glasgow, 10 April 1854, aged 32 ; of their 3 sons and daughter, who died in infancy. Of LEWIS GORDON, Esq., for many years Secretary to the Highland Agricultural Society of Scotland, who died at Aberdeen, 23 January 1839, aged 72. And of Sir CHARLES GORDON, who died at Edinburgh, 25th Sepr. 1845, aged 52. Requiescant in pace.

—Gordons have been long resident at Minmore, and it is from one of them that the present Gordons of Abergeldie are descended in the male line. (*v.* p. 108.) The above Sir Charles, who married a sister of Angus Fletcher of Dunans, Esq., was trained by his uncle, and ultimately succeeded him in the office of Secretary to the Highland Agricultural Society.

Interesting, and pretty complete specimens of so-called Druidical circles are at Ballandalloch, Lagmore, Belleville, and Balnellan, at the last-mentioned of which places fragments of a sculptured stone are built into the walls of the farm-steading.

The ruins of the castles of Drumin and Blairfindy are striking objects in the landscape. The first, of which three sides of the old keep remain, appears to have been a building of the 15th century, and the latter of the 17th. The former is situated so as to command the passes of the Avon and the Livet; and the latter, which is near Minmore, in Glenlivet, is locally said to have been a hunting seat of the Earls of Huntly.

The castle of Ballandalloch, near the confluence of the rivers of Avon and the Spey, has been recently enlarged and improved. It is a fine castellated chateau, situated in a tastefully laid-out lawn, surrounded by old trees. It commands a good view of the surrounding country, and contains capital examples of the works of some of the more eminent of the old painters. The family arms are carved upon a panel over the front door, below which, flanked by the words—

ERECTED 1546; RESTORED 1850—

is this text, which was upon the old building:—

YE LORD SHALL PRESERVE THY GOING OUT AND THY COMING IN.

—The date of 1602, and the initials P.G., are upon the back or oldest portion of the house.

The bridge over the Avon, near the entrance to Ballandalloch Castle, was first built by General Grant in 1792; the present bridge, and that across the Livet at Downan, were built in 1803 and 1835, respectively. Those over the burns of Pitchaish and Tommore in 1816, and 1826. The two arches of the old bridge which crossed the Livet, from one group of rocks to another, have a singularly picturesque character, and are admirably suited for a picture. These are possibly of contemporary date with the castle of Blairfindy, for the use of the lords of which, the bridge was probably erected.

But the old house of Kilmaichlie, which occupies a height on the left bank of the Avon, with its rows of old trees, is possibly the most beautifully situated of all the residences in the district. It was long a summer retreat of the Man of Feeling, by whom its beauties have been described in No. 87 of the Lounger.

Extracts from the Kirk-session Records of Inveravon.

The following extracts, selected from the Kirk-session Records of the parish of Inveravon, may interest the general, as well as the local reader, since they bear upon some curious obsolete customs and historical events. Among these the applications of the "currachers," or ferryboat men to, and the restrictions put upon them by the Kirk-session, together with the destruction of the boats of Spey, and the burning of the house of Pitchaish in the time of the Marquis of Montrose, are possibly not the least curious.

In the first extract, dated 20th March 1636, it is stated that:—

Allister McAllim, "corrachar at Awin," applied to the Kirk-session for "2 merks of ye comone good for attending ye Watter on ye Sabboth day, and for ferreing ye people to ye kirk."

Subsequently (18 Nov. 1638):—

"Johne More, the currucher, gaif in a supplicatione to ye Sessione desyring support to bay a currach, whereypon the Sessione condescendit to give him his request providing alwayes he should be readie on the Sabbath day to attend the currach and ferrie the people over the water, comeing and going from the sermone." He received "two merkis to that effect."

The term "scourger," as applied in the next extract (1 May, 1636), appears to have been equivalent to that of "rung the beggars" of a later date, and of a policeman of the present time:—

"Johne Dow admitted scourger to hold out strong Beggars and ith' vagabonds ot of ye parish, and for his fle a peck of victuall in ye weeck."

The following is dated 12 June 1636 :—

William Lesley in Dalraachie, was prohibited, under a penalty of £10 "not to resett ane stragler woman called Marie Dow." Subsequently (23 Apr. 1637), Donald Dow, potter (?) to the baron of Kinnachlon, was also prohibited from reseting the same woman (whose character is less delicately given at this date), "aither by nycht or by day."

The next two extracts, dated respectively 20th Oct. 1639, and 6th April 1640, show the sort of articles which were given as pledges for the fulfilment of contracts of marriage, also the penalty imposed upon the illiterate of those days :—

David Ross ratified a promise of marriage with Margt. Gordon, to be performed within 20 days instant, "A targe for ye woman, and a doller for ye man, layed in pand in ye k. offrs haud vntil the day appointed forsaid."

Thos. McJames contracted with Jonet Bayne—"a targe layed in pand for the man, and a sword for the woman, and yat for thair performance ; and to get the Lords prayer, the Belief, and 10 comandements wtin 20 days inst."

There are few Session records of the period that do not contain entries similar to the following, which is dated 10th July 1642:—

The "practice of Pennie brydells" was ordered to be discontinued ; and it was also "ordained that there sall be no trouble nor pley, nor pyper, nor violer at anie brydell under the paine of ane doller."

Many of the people of Inveravon and Kirkmichael, &c., were, until the introduction of reaping machines, in the habit of going to the south of Scotland and hiring themselves as reapers, at which they were considered expert hands. This practice appears to be of an older date than is generally known, for nearly 230 years ago it was looked upon as an evil to the district ; and the Kirk-session (4th Sept. 1642), made a minute touching the case as follows :—

"It was regrated yat monie servants went out of ye cuntrie the tyme of haruest, and liued vpon the cuntrie the whole winter tyme, Therefore it was ordained that whosoeuer went out of ye cuntrie wtout the minister's testimoniall should be comptd vagabounds ; and ye Resetters of these wtin the parish agayne, except they brought wt them a Testimoniall from the minister where they wrought in haruest, sall pay 10 libs."

The next entry (12 Mar. 1643), bears upon a not uncommon feature in the art of witchcraft, and the alleged way by which the charm was effected :—

"The said daye comperat Margaret Walker and gaif in a bill of complaint against Allaster McCraw his wyff, for slandering her, alleadging yat ye said Margaret Walker hade taken awaye Allaster McCraw his wyffs milk, by going betuixt her and the fyre." Mrs M. was ordered to acknowledge her guilt before the pulpit.

The next two extracts (dated respectively 29 Sept. 1644, and 16 Feb. 1645), relate to the doings of the Great Montrose, or his army, when on their march from the north to Balveny castle. It is said that a portion of the present building of the house of Pitchaish is that which was erected after the destruction of the one referred to in the second extract :—

"About this tyme James Grahame, sometyme Earle of Montrose, joyned with the Irishes and troubled the whole cuntrey, and thus hindered both convention and discipline of the kirk."

"No preaching nor collection, the minister himself having left his awin hous, the Enemy's armie of Irishes being in the cuntrey ; at the qlk tyme the boats of Spey were broken ; and the hous of Pitchaish wes burnt immediatelie after the fight of Inuerlochy."

The following (4 May, 1645), shows the unsettled state of the times consequent on the Civil Wars, and the weakness of the executive of the kirk :—

"The minister regraited the pitiefull case of ye parish where, that no delinquents could be broght to make yair repentance or paye anye penaltyes, Notwithstanding yat he hade taken caution of sundrie who hade gotten anie benefit of ye kirk fra him, and yat there could be als litle order gotten of ye cautioners as of ye delinquents themselfs, the fovr honest men [i.e. the elders] who were put ansured, they could not help the busines bot regrate it. Likewayes in respect the heads of ye cuntrey were not at home, the one-half being against the other, some with the Enemye, and some in garrisone houses."

Under 3d August 1645 is this salutary resolution :—

It was resolved that "no ayl nor aquavitæ sould be sold in tyme of divine seruice, in respect through the troubles of ye tymes the people taks occasion to abyde from the Kirk, to fall out in pleyes and scolding."

The next extract (10 Aug. 1645), has reference to a common sort of transgression :—

"A tumult being in ye kirk yeard in tyme of divine service, after tryall it wes found yat Grisall Roy and Mariorie Andersone were scolding and flyting in ye kirkzeard, and y[e]rfore being both apprehended were pūtly put in the Jouggs, and ordained to acknoledge their fault publickly the nixt Sabboth befor the congregation."

Considering the nature of the offence, the above may have been a fair punishment for the delinquents; but that shadowed forth in the next extract (16 August 1704), so far as it relates to "children not capable of church censure," must be viewed in a very different light :—

"Ane Act against Clavies.—That whereas it hath been the custome and practise of many in this parish of Inveravine, to goe about y[r] folds and cornes with kindled Torches of firr, Superstitiouslie and Idolotrouslie asscribing y[t] power to the fire of sanctifieing y[r] cornes and cattell q[ch] is only proper and peculiar to the true and living God, a practise proper rather to the heathens who are ignorant of God, than to be practisd by them y[t] live under the light of the glorious Gospell; Therefor, the Session did, and hereby dooth enact that, whosoever shall be found guiltie of the fors[d] superstitious and heathenish practises, shall be proceeded ag[st] as scandalous persons, and censured according to the demerit of y[r] crime; and if it shall be found that they be children not capable of church censure, that in y[t] case, their names be keept in record, and they declar'd incapable of any church priviledge when arrived att the years of discretion, or any testimoniall from the session, till they remove the scandall."

Strathdon, or Invernochty.

(S. ANDREW.)

THE church of *Inuyrnochy* was given to the Priory of Monymusk by Gilchrist, Earl of Mar, 1199-1207. It was afterwards (July 1256), with consent of Thomas, Earl of Mar, erected into a prebend of the cathedral of Aberdeen. In May previously, his Lordship, on presenting Sir John of Marr, rector of Invernochty, to the rectory of the kirk of Dauachyndore (Auchindoir), vacant by the death of Sir Thos. of Meldrum, requested the Bishop of Aberdeen to join the latter church to the former; but that does not appear ever to have been done.

The present church stands upon the south bank of the Don, opposite to where the water of Nochty joins the Don. An old church, built in 1757, was erased in 1851, and the present edifice erected at a cost of about £2500. It has a spire, is a spacious and neatly finished place of worship, and contains a number of monuments.

FORBES OF NEWE :—

The burial place of Forbes of Newe, the chief heritor of the parish, is at the east end, separated from the nave of the church by a low railing. It contains four monuments, one of freestone and three of white marble. The first, which bears a carving of the Forbes arms, flanked by the initials W. F. : H. F., is thus inscribed :—

Here lyes WILLIAM FORBES of New who depart..
the 10 of Ianvary 1698, the 76 yeir of age :—
  Remember man, as thou goes by,
  As thou art now, so once was I ;
  As I am now, so must thou be ;
  Remember man that thou must die.

—According to the Poll Book, the above Forbes had a wife, a daughter, and two sons living with him in 1696. He is said to have been the first Forbes of Newe; and possibly his wife was a kinswoman of his own. "William Forbes, younger of New, a gentleman," his wife, and three children are charged under the same list. The exact connection between the above-named Forbes and the present family is not established. In 1494, Duncan Forbes pursued certain persons for withholding from him the tack and mailing of Innernochty and Bellabeg, with their pertinents, at which time these estates were Mar property. Bellabeg afterwards belonged to Gordon of Huntly, subsequently to the Lords Elphinstone. (*v.* p. 65).

Forbes of Newe claims descent from Wm., of Daach, 2d son of Sir Alex. of Pitsligo. The following inscription is from a marble to the memory of the undoubted progenitors of the present family of Forbes of Newe:—

Sacred to the memory of the Rev. GEORGE FORBES, eldest son of John Forbes of Bellabeg and minister of the Gospel at Lochell, he died at New, August 30, 1799, in the 62nd year of his age, and 37th of his ministry, and was interred in the burial ground of the family within this church, where three of his children are also buried :—CHRISTIAN, born August 4, 1770, died June 12, 1782; and two other daughters, CHRISTIAN and KATHARINE, who died in early infancy. Likewise KATHERINE STEWART, only daughter of Gordon Stewart of Drummin,* and spouse of the said George Forbes, who died at New on the 3d November 1808, in the 68th year of her age. [*v.* note‘ p. 45.]

The next mentioned John Forbes, who realised a large fortune as a merchant in Bombay, bought the property of Newe, &c., in his father's lifetime. In addition to the improvement of his property, he left large donations to public charities in Aberdeen and elsewhere :—

To the memory of JOHN FORBES, Esquire of Newe (formerly of Bombay), second son of John Forbes, Esquire of Bellabeg. Born there 19th September 1743, died in Fitzroy Square, London, 20th June 1821, and buried in this church. A dutiful son, an affectionate brother, a warm and steady friend ; his amiable manners and goodness of heart endeared him to all who knew him—his active benevolence was extended to all who stood in need of assistance. But, the "widow and fatherless" in India and in Britain, were the special objects of his protection. This monument was erected by his nephew, Sir Charles Forbes, Baronet of Newe and Edinglassie. 1837. Altins ibunt qui ad summa nituntur.

—Mr F., who died unmarried, was succeeded in the estates of Newe, &c., by his nephew CHARLES, who also spent part of his life in Bombay, where he was so much esteemed that the inhabitants erected a statue of him, executed by the late Sir F. Chantrey. He was long an M.P., created a baronet in 1823, and died at London, 20th Sept. 1849, aged 76. It was he who erected a tablet to two of his grandchildren, which is thus inscribed :—

In memory of HARRIET-BOYCOTT FORBES, eldest child of John and Mary Jane Forbes, born in London the 24th May 1830, died at Edinglassie the 27th June 1835, and buried in a vault in that part of the burial ground of Newe, which lies without the church. This monument was erected by her grandfather Sir Charles Forbes, Baronet of Newe and Edinglassie, anticipating the intention of her fond parents to record the early promise of mind and heart of one of the most interesting of children. But, before this was carried into effect, it pleased the Almighty to take to himself another of the children of the same parents, JOHN FORBES, their second son and fourth child— a lovely infant. Born in Aberdeen the 1st August 1835, died at Edinglassie the 18th January 1836, and buried in same grave with his sister.

—Sir Charles was succeeded by a grandson, who died at the age of 19, in 1852, when the succession devolved upon an uncle of the last, and third son of the first baronet. It ought to be mentioned that, on the elevation of Sir Charles to a baronetcy, his tenantry in Strathdon raised a cairn, or pile of native granite, upon the hill of Lonach, in which there are two stone tablets with inscriptions. One is in Gaelic, the other (an interpretation in English), runs thus :—

Baronet's Cairn : The Tenantry of the lands of Newe, Edinglassie, Bellabeg, and Skellater, in testimony of their affection and gratitude, have erected this pile to their highly distinguished and beloved landlord, Sir CHARLES FORBES, Bart., M.P., on his elevation to the dignity of a Baronet of the United Kingdom, by His Majesty George IV., in 1823.

THE FORBESES OF AUCHERNACH have three tablets on the south wall of Strathdon church, two of marble and one of granite :—

Sacred to the memory of CHARLES FORBES, Esq. of Auchernach, who lies here with his forefathers for upwards of 200 years. Died 5th May 1794, in the 64th year of his age. Likewise to the memory of his wife JANET, daughter of Francis Fraser, Esq. of Findrack, who died 4th Decr. 1770, aged 30. Also their sons FRANCIS, who died in infancy; GEORGE, Lieut. in the 3rd Regt. Madras Cavalry, died at sea, in India, 10th April 1796, aged 26; JAMES, a Lieut. in the 72nd Highland Regt., died 9th June 1804, in the 24th year of his age. This monument is erected by his son Nathaniel, Lieut.- Gen. in the Honble. E.I.C.S., 1845.

—Mr Charles Forbes was governor or keeper of the Castle of Corgarff, which was bought by the Government after 1746, and was long used as a barracks for soldiers, at first with a view to overawe the Highlanders, and finally as a check upon smuggling, which was extensively carrried on in the district.

Sacred to the memory of Major General DAVID FORBES, C.B., H.M. 78th Regt., or Ross-shire Highlanders. Born 13th January 1772; died 29th March 1849, whose remains are deposited beneath this stone in the same grave with his father, Charles Forbes of Auchernach: also to his sons JAMES, born 13th September 1820, died 19th April 1821; and DAVID, born 10th March 1824, died 26th April 1825.

—The following refers to the father of the present laird of Auchernach and Dunottar, &c. :—

In memory of NATHANIEL FORBES of Auchernach and Dunottar, Lieutenant-General H.E.I.C.S. and Col. of the 24 Reg. Madras Native Infantry, eldest son of Charles Forbes of Auchernach, by his wife Janet, daughter of Francis Fraser of Findrack. Born at Corgarff Castle, February 2, 1766; died in London, August 16, 1851, in the 86 year of his age. Erected by his son William-Nathaniel Forbes of Auchernach and Dunottar.

—Lieut.-Gen. F. (who was heir and representative of the Forbeses of Skellater), saw much service in India in the war against Hyder Ali and Tippoo Saib, and held high commands. He bought Dunottar about 1832.

FORBES OF INVERERNAN :—

The first of these Forbes' was *Black Jock*, to whom, as bailie of Kildrummy, the Earl of Mar wrote the celebrated letter regarding the rising of 1715. *Black Jock* was the eldest son of Skellater by a second marriage; and being out in the rebellion, was taken prisoner, and died at Carlisle the night before the day on which he was to have been executed. His son, by the widow of M'Gillivray of Drumnaglass, succeeded to Invererenan, and married Jean, daughter of Alexander Alexander of Auchmull, a bailie in Aberdeen. Their eldest son, who died unmarried, made the entail of Invererenan, and was succeeded by his next brother, Alex. Forbes, to whom there is a marble tablet, on north wall of church :—

To the memory of Captain ALEXANDER FORBES of Invererenan, born the 25th of July 1744, and died at Forbes Lodge the 5th of June 1819. Erected by his friends of the Clan, and others, in honor of a man whose kindness of heart, and hospitality to young and old, was never exceeded in the Strath.

—It was this gentleman, on the threatened invasion of Scotland by the French, that commanded the Strathdon men, who had formed themselves into a Volunteer Association for the defence of their country. He married Elizabeth, a daughter of Grant of Clury, Strathspey. She was the mother of Major Alex. Forbes, also of Mary- Anne, the wife of the Rev. Dr Forbes of Blelack. A tablet bears this record of Major F.'s death :—

To the memory of Major ALEXANDER FORBES of Invererenan, whose remains are interred underneath. He died on the 20th July 1830, in the 55th year of his age, esteemed and respected by all who knew him for his highly upright and honourable principles. Erected by his affectionate widow, Margaret-Sarah Forbes.

—This lady was a daughter of Duncan Forbes- Mitchell of Thainston, 2d son of Sir Arthur Forbes of Craigievar. She had a son and daughter, the former died in London in 1827, aged 15; and the latter, who married Wm. M'Combie, Esq. of Easter Skene and Lynturk, died in 1835, aged 26. (*v.* SKENE.)

On the south-west of the church-yard :—

The burial place of GEORGE FORBES, D.D., of Blelack and Invererenan, 25 years minister of the parish of Strathdon. Possessing the respect and confidence of his Parishioners as a faithful pastor and friendly counsellor, his death was deeply lamented throughout this district. Born at Lochel, 8th April 1778; died at Aberdeen, 16th February 1834. Erected, in affectionate remembrance, by his disconsolate widow 1835. His widow, MARY-ANNE FORBES, daughter of Captain Alexander Forbes of Invernernan, died 19th April 1848, aged 68 years.

—The above were the parents of the present laird of Invernernan, who distinguished himself in the late Persian war. He is a C.B., and a General in the H.E.I.C.S. A marble cross, within the kirk, records the death of an infant son of Gen. Forbes; and an adjoining slab that of his second brother, who died at Bombay, 1849, aged 30.

ANDERSON OF CANDACRAIG :—

Within, and upon north wall of the church :—

This stone was erected in the year 1757, by Charles Anderson of Kandocraig, in memory of his Predecessors, the ANDERSONS of Kandocraig, inter'd here for seven generations past. CHARLES the Eight, died 16th March 1776, aged 65. *Mors janua vitæ.*

Sacred to the memory of ALEXANDER ANDERSON of Candacraig, who, in succession to eight generations of his ancestors interred here, died 13th of March 1817, aged 65 years. This monument of filial love and regard for an affectionate parent is erected by Captain John Anderson of the 28th Regiment, his eldest surviving son, 1st of August 1820.

Sacred to the memory of Major JOHN ANDERSON of Candacraig, who departed this life Decr. 24th 1835, aged 45 years. This tablet is erected as a tribute of sincere affection and regard by his disconsolate widow, Catherine Anderson.

—This lady was a dr. of Alex., Duke of Gordon, by Jean Christie, his second wife. (*v.* BELLIE.) The value of Duncan Anderson's lands in the Strathdon part of Migvie-Tarland, is stated in the Poll Book (1696) at £200 Scots, where his lady is charged, also two sons and three daughters, then living *in familia.* The Andersons held Candacraig until within these few years, when it was bought by Sir C. Forbes of Newe, from a sister's son of one of the Andersons, now or lately resident in Canada.

Upon a marble tablet in north-east wall :—

In memory of HUGH-ROBERT MEIKLEJOHN, oldest son of the Revd. Robt. Meiklejohn, minister of Strathdon, and Lieut. H.E.I.C. Engineers. Killed at Jhansi in Central India, 3rd April 1858, aged xxii years. Gallantly leading one attack of the Stormers he was the first to scale the wall and there fell dead, deeply lamented by all who knew him. Erected by the inhabitants of his native Strath to testify their high admiration of his bravery and moral worth, their sincere sorrow for his premature death, and their heartfelt sympathy with his bereaved family.

—A monument in the churchyard records the death of the Rev. Mr MEIKLEJOHN, and his widow, ELIZA-GRANT, daughter of Forbes of Invernernan, the first died in 1859, the latter in 1863.

The next two inscriptions are from tablets in north-west wall of the church :—

Sacred to the memory of Mrs CHRISTIAN STUART, daughter of James Gordon, Esq., Croughly, who was born 21st November 1766, died 28th February 1821, aged 54, and was interred in the burial ground of her husband's family within this churchyard, where two of her daughters both named MARY-FORBES, who died in early infancy, are likewise buried. Sacred also to the memory of her oldest son JOHN, who died in the East Indies, 13th April 1813, aged 22. [*v.* p. 70.]

Sacred to the memory of JONATHAN MICHIE, Esq., Captain in the Honourable East India Company's Bombay Marine, who died at Aberdeen on the 25th August 1811, aged 42 years, and is interred in this churchyard. Inscribed at the desire of his son, Lieutenant Jonathan Michie of the Bombay Military Establishment. 1813.

A massive mausoleum on the left of the churchyard gate bears two tablets, with the following inscriptions :—

This mausoleum was erected to perpetuate the memory of MARY FORBES, who was the wife of Major Daniel Mitchell. Her uncommon affection for her husband, parents, brothers, and sisters, and her kindness to all her friends, joined to a delightful benevolence, which never overlooked the humble nor forgot the distressed, are here recorded for example's sake. She died in London, 27th August 1820, aged 53, and her remains rest within.

—This lady, daughter of the minister of Leochel, was aunt to the present Sir Charles Forbes of Newe. Her husband was a descendant of Thomas Mitchell, a burgess and provost of Aberdeen, who bought Thainston, near Kintore, about the end of the 17th century. The second tablet bears:—

He who raised this tomb now reposes within. DANIEL MITCHELL, Major in the Hon. East India Company's Service, who departed this life on the 17th Feb. 1841, aged 64. He fell asleep in Jesus in the hope of a glorious resurrection. This tablet is erected by desire of his surviving wife Mary, daughter of the late General Hay of Rannes, in remembrance of a most beloved, respected, and deeply lamented husband.

A monument in the churchyard bears this inscription:—

Here ly the remains of ROBERT FARQUHARSON of Allerg, who died Jany. 31st 1771, in the 77th year of his age. And of ISABEL ANDERSON his spouse, who died Febry. 18th 1749, in the 70th of her age ; And of their grand-child˚ JOHN, JAMES, MARGT, & JEAN :—

Friend would'st thou triump o'er the grave ?
Would'st thou with joy thy dust redeem ?
Belive in him who came to save,
His cross the way to bless supream.

ROBT. FARQUHARSON, their son, died 16th April 1793, aged 73. JEAN GRANT, his spouse, died 3rd July 1800, aged 80. ISOBEL, their daughter, died 2nd April 1791, aged 40 years. Memento mori.

A marble tablet within, and on south wall of church, bears :—

Erected by his widow in affectionate remembrance of ROBERT FARQUHARSON, Esq. of Allargue and Breda. Born the 13th of January 1783 ; died the 14th of February 1863 ; and of their son ROBERT FARQUHARSON, younger of Allargue : Born 22nd of July 1828 ; died 9th of November 1858.

—John Farquharson of Oklerg, " his wyfe and fyve children, to wit, Andrew, Gustavus, Roderick, Georg, and Jean Fergursons," appear in the Poll Book for 1696. Breda is a small property in Alford. The last-named laird was a thread manufacturer in, and sometime provost of Paisley. (v. p. 122.)

The following inscriptions are selected from tombstones in different parts of the kirkyard :—

JOHN LUMSDEN was minister here forty four years. MARY DUFF his first, and BARBARA LUMSDEN his second wife, with their two children, MARY and HARY LUMSDENS, were all buried here before he died himself.

Mr D. McS. Heb. ix. 27 : It is appointed unto men once to die, but after this the judgment. II Thess. II. 5 : Remember ye not that when I was yet with you I told you these things. Mr D. McS., M. A. Here ly the ashes of the Revd. and worthy sert. of Jesus Christ, Mr DONALD M'SWEEN, minr. of the Gospel at Strdon, who died June the 8, 1730, aged 38 :—

A watchman faithful, honest, just,
Who ner betrayed his sacred trust,
Whose love to Christ and to his flock
Breathed in all that or he spoke.

Hug. }
Eliz. } McS. children. Memento mori.
Hel.   }

—Mr Gordon, the writer of the Old Stat. Acct. of the parish (vol. xiii., p. 184), says that, according to tradition, the inhabitants of Strathdou were " rough and uncivilized in their manners"— that hostile lairds would have rushed upon one another in the churchyard on Sundays with their durks and shabbles, and that, on one occasion, a laird cut off the head of Mr Baxter, a minister, at the manse-door, with a Lochaber axe ; also, that Mr M'SWEEN was attempted to be smothered with a wet canvas, when at family prayers one evening ; but being a man of considerable bodily strength, he was able to save himself ! Luckily the people have changed with the times, for even on the occasion of the *Lonach* annual gatherings, it is but rare that impropriety of conduct is to be seen ; while their courtesy and hospitality to strangers are worthy of imitation in many parts of the Lowlands. Near the above :—

This monument is erected by Alex. Stuart of Edinglassie to the memory of MARGARET CRANSTOWN, his wife, a person houbly. descended, politely educated, judicious, prudent, and agreeable, esteemed and regarded : she died June 22, aged 45, A.D. 1752. The said ALEX. STUART, Esq., writer to the signet, a man eminent in his profession, much esteemed, and universally regretted, died the 19th day of Septr. aged 87 years, A.D. 1787.

JOHN SIMPSON, farmer, Shanuach, d. 1780, a. 79:—
   With temper meek his bread he wan,
   He lived and died an honest man.

Erected to the memory of JOHN McHARDY, late farmer in Easter Corryhoul, who died 26 Nov. 1813, aged 60, and whose ancestors has been there for upwards of 600 years. Done by the care of his sons Joⁿ., Ja^s., Nⁿ., Chas., and Alex^r. McHardys.

Under this stone lies interred the dust of ARCHIBALD FORBES of Deskrie, who died at Mill of Keith, the 3d of Dec. 1793, in the 80th year of his age.

Hocce in sepulchro iacet DONALD DOWNYS, vir [eximia] pietate, incorrupta fide, pauperum fautor, pater non contempta prole, beatus obiit A.D. 17.. natus ....

[In this tomb lies DONALD DOWNYS, a man of genuine piety, untainted honour, a benefactor to the poor, and the father of no contemptible offspring. He died happy A.D. 17.. aged ..]

Here lies the dust of seuen generations of Dunbars, and NATHANIEL DUNBAR who liued at Mill of New. This stone is erected for HELEN YEWEN spous to Cornelcies Dunbar at Mil of Bellabeg. She died Feby. 16, 1762, aged 49. Erected by hir son Nathaniel Dunbar.

Both under this stone doth ly the bons and ashes of JAMES and JOHN ROSS, lafull sons to George Ross in Bednagaugh. JAMES died Iulie 8, 1738, aged 28; JOHN died Decr. 6, 1763, aged 24:—
   Be mindful of your Redemer while you have breath,
   For young years cannot shun death.

Here lyes the bons and dust of GEORG GRASSICH in Coull of Earnonside, who dyed Febry. 19, 1742, aged 63 years. Also ISOBEL OGG, his spouse, who dyed Octr. 28, 1747, aged 60 years.

—*Grassick* has been long a common surname in Strathdon; a marble tablet within the church records the death of PATRICK, in Foggymill, in 1823.

Interred here IOHN MICHIE in Culquhanny, who died Iuly 13, 1760, aged 81; and JANNET GRASSICH, his spous, who died Octr. 6, 1755, aged 70. This stone was put on by Hary Miche their son, &c.

—Culquhanny is now the seat of a well-known inn. Part of the old castle still remains, under which, it is said, there is a weem, or Pict's house.

The oldest antiquities in the parish are the "cirdhouses" or weems at Glenkindie, Buchaam, and Newe, plans and descriptions of which will be found in the Proceedings of the So. of Antiquaries of Scotland, vol. iv.

The *Doune of Invernochty*, upon which a castle of the old lords of the district appears to have stood, is the next most interesting object in Strathdon. The Doune is about 30 feet in height, and the top, which is oval shaped, contains about half an acre of ground. Remains of ancient buildings are to be seen upon the west and south, from which it would appear that the walls had been constructed of stones and strongly fused lime, and built in much the same style as those of the castle of Kinedar, or King Edward, which was inhabited in the 13th century.

The Doune appears to have been originally formed, as was the Bass of Iuverurie, by deposits from a number of streams, and from a variety of points, which had met at a particular spot. Thus formed by nature, and from the Doune commanding the chief passes from the north Highlands to the Lowlands, the top of it was subsequently levelled; and ditches and trenches, constructed round its base, which in early times had made it a pretty secure dwelling-place.

The ditches which surround the Doune, or mound of Invernochty, were supplied by water from the burn of Bardoch, which rises in the hill of Braigheach, and joined a large swamp or morass upon the north. The ditches contained water until about 1823, when the new turnpike road was made, and the burn of Bardoch was deepened, with the view of draining the foss and the neighbouring marshes.

Along the top of the west embankment, and other parts of the Doune, traces of a number of huts are visible, in which, possibly, the retainers of the ancient lords of the fort, and their spare animals, were housed. As was the case at Dunottar, probably the original church of Invernochty stood upon the Doune, if, indeed, it had not been the precursor of the castle; and a number of mounds, not unlike graves, may be seen towards the east side of it. But, until the top of the Doune is thoroughly excavated and trenched over, there is no means of ascertaining whether these surmises are well founded. Excavations were made some years ago on the south side of the surrounding foss, when a log of oak was found, supposed to have been part of the drawbridge of the castle. At the same time the square chamber on the left of the entrance to the fort, and some other parts of the ruins, were brought to light.

Charter evidence shows that the Earls of Mar were the old proprietors of the district; and that Adam of Strachan, who had charters of Glenkindie in 1357, was among the earliest and most important of the landowners under Mar.

In 1512, John Mackkalloun had half of the lands of Invery, Thirueis, and Edinglas; and in the year 1550, Lord Elphinston had charters of Corgarff and Skellater, &c., all within the lordship of Mar.

Culqubanny Castle, of which only part of the keep remains, is said to have been built by Forbes of Towie in the 17th century. Corgarff Castle, reputed to have been originally a hunting seat of the Earls of Mar, was burned down in 1571, during the feuds between the Forbeses and the Gordons; and some are of opinion that Corgarff was the scene of the burning of Lady Forbes, &c., celebrated in the ballad of Edom o' Gordon. (v. TOWIE). The castle, afterwards rebuilt, was bought by Government in 1746 from Forbes of Skellater, and used as a military station.

There has been a royal bounty mission station at Corgarff for nearly 150 years, where also are a school and a burial ground.

"ANDERMAS fair" was held at Strathdon in Nov., and S. JOHN's fair in Aug. annually.

The bridges in the parish are numerous. That of Pooldhulie, which is the oldest and most romantic, bears to have been erected by Alexander Forbes of Invercrnan, in 1715. The bridge of Luib was built by Sir C. Forbes in 1832; and the Nochty, near the church, is spanned by a substantial iron bridge. Two bridges have also been thrown across the Don, near Newe Castle, upon each of which is an iron plate, embellished with the Forbes arms, and this inscription:—

Erected by Sir Charles Forbes, Bart., of Newe and Edinglassie, 1858, from a bequest by his grand uncle, JOHN FORBES, Esq. of Newe.

~~~~~~~~~~~~~~~~~~~~~~~~~~~~~~

Rescobie.

(S. TRIDUANA, VIRGIN.)

THE church of *Roscolbi*, with its chapel, belonged to the Priory of St Andrews. The present church, built in 1820, stands upon the north side of the "lake of Roskolby," a fine sheet of water, which is mentioned in a note of the marches of Dunnichen in the 13th century. Upon the kirk bell:—

A. N. D. R. E. A. S   F. H. E. M   A. N. N. O   1. 6. 2. 0.

In consequence of recent improvements, the church, although a plain building, and the burial ground, once neglected and ill cared for, present a peculiarly neat appearance. A monument within, and in the south wall of the church is thus inscribed:—

To the memory of JAMES GORDON, sometime teacher in this parish, who expired in the pulpit of Forfar on the 15 day of June 1808, in the 25th year of his age, while delivering part of his probationary trials with a view to accept of the presentation made to him of this church and parish. He was the only son of Peter Gordon, lately teacher in this parish. This stone was erected by his widowed mother as an expression of her irreparable loss.

A marble slab upon the east wall bears:—

In memory of JOHN FARQUHAR, Esquire of Pitscandly, who died 30 June 1808, aged 67 years. And of ROBY-JAMES FARQUHAR, his son, who died 16 Feb. 1819, in his 22d year.

Upon a stone in the churchyard, which relates to the same family:—

To the memory of JOHN FARQUHAR of Pitscandly, who died 14 June 1844, aged 49 years. Also of SUSANNAH-FLOYD FARQUHAR, daughter of John

Farquhar of Pitscandly, and sister to the above, who died 10 Feb. 1822, aged 23 years. Also of EMILY-LAKE FARQUHAR, daughter of John Farquhar of Pitscandly, who died 21 Jan. 1839, aged 7 years.

—Colonel Farquhar of Mounie (descended from Robert Farquhar of Mounie and Tonley, once provost of Aberdeen), had three nieces who became his co-heiresses. One of them, ELIZABETH, bought, about 1731, the estate of Pitscandly. She married James, eldest son of Stormonth of Kinclune, in Angus, who assumed the surname of *Farquhar*, Being "out in the '45," he was taken prisoner and condemned to death ; but on the day before his intended execution, he was reprieved through the interest of Mrs M'Niell, a sister-in-law of his own. A flat tombstone in the churchyard, with the initials, E. F., and the date of 1764, covers the grave of the above-named ELIZABETH FARQUHAR. Mr Taylor-Farquhar, sometime incumbent of St John's Episcopal Church, Forfar, is proprietor of Pitscandly, through his wife, Mary Anne Farquhar, a daughter of the laird who died in 1844. Mrs Farquhar succeeded to her sister Sarah some years before her marriage. Pitscandly was long in the possession of the Lindsays, the last designed of which, John Lindsay, granted a disposition of the lands to George Lauder, 7 Nov. 1726, from whom the property was bought by Miss E. Farquhar. Her son, Thomas, got a crown charter of, and was infeft in Pitscandly, 23 June 1766.

A marble, inscribed as follows, which was taken out of the wall of the last church, lies below the loft stair of the present one :—

M. S. CAROLI GRAY de Carse, Armigeri, hominis probissimi, qui obiit 28vo Aprilis 1768, ætat. 86 : et JACOBI FARQUHAR de Balmoor, Armigeri, amici ejus devinctissimi, priscae virtutis viri, qui obiit 31mo Decembris, 1759, ætat. 66. Hoc marmor Elizabetha Farquhar, vidua, marito fratrique carissimis, et Gualterus Gray, prioris haeres, grato animo propatruo bene merenti, posuere 1769.

[Sacred to the memory of CHARLES GRAY of Carse, Esq., a very worthy man, who died 28 April 1768, aged 86 ; and of JAMES FARQUHAR of Balmoor, Esq., his most devoted friend, a man of primitive virtue, who died 31 Dec. 1759, aged 66. This monument was erected in 1769 by Elizabeth Farquhar, widow, in memory of her dearly beloved husband and brother, and by Walter Gray, heir of the former, in grateful remembrance of his respected grand-uncle.]

—The above Charles, son of Gray of Balbunno, in Perthshire, a cadet of the Lords Gray, bought the estate of Carse about 1741. He was succeeded by his grandnephew, Walter Lowson, the son of a farmer in Auchterhouse. On succeeding to Carse, Walter Lowson (as shown by the above inscription), assumed the surname of *Gray*. He was father of CHARLES GRAY of Carse, who died in 1850. The grand-daughter of the latter is now proprietrix of Carse. She married a son of Hunter of Burnside. He died in 1861, and was buried in a private cemetery on the hill of Carse. (*v.* p. 32.) The erector of the above monument gifted two silver communion cups to the church of Rescobie ; both are thus inscribed :—

Rescobie Kirk, 1779 ; Donum Dominae ELIZ. FARQUHAR, conjugis et viduae Caroli Gray de Carse, Armigeri. Vivit post funera virtus.

A handsome freestone monument, built into the outer and south wall of the church, has been recently renewed. The canopy, which is supported by two pillars, is ornamented with a carving of the Lindsay arms, &c. ; and the tablet presents this inscription :—

Monumentum hoc in memoriam suorum parentum Mr David Lindsay, pastor de Mary-Toune, extruendum curavit. Juxta hunc lapidem depositæ sunt reliquiæ Dom : HENRICI LINDSAY, quondam de Blairifedden, qui obiit anno Dom : . . ætat. 72 ; et uxoris ejus ALISON SCRIMSEUR, familiæ Scrimseur de Glasswal, quæ obiit anno Dom. 1651, ætat. . . ; necnon filii eorum Dom. DAVIDIS LINDSAY pastoris de Rescobie, qui obiit anno Dom. 1677, ætat. 62 ; & ejusdem duarum conjugum MARJORÆ LINDSAY, filiæ Lindsay de Kinnettles, & BEATRICIS OGILVY, filiæ . . . Ogilvy de Carsbank, quæ obiit anno Dom. 1716, ætat. suæ 89. Ibidem loci quoque sepulti sunt nonnulli ejusdem Davidis liberi, quorum nomina cœli injuria & prioris cippi vetustate perierunt.— Hoc monumentum positum fuit anno , & instauratum anno 1752.

[Mr David Lindsay, minister of Marytown, caused this monument to be erected in memory of his parents. Beside this stone are deposited the remains of Mr HENRY LINDSAY, late of Blairiefedden, who died in the year .... aged 72; and of his wife ALISON SCRIMSEUR, of the family of Scrimseur of Glasswal, who died in 1651, aged . . ; and also of their son, Mr DAVID LINDSAY, minister of Rescobie, who died 1677, aged 62; and of his two wives MANJORY LINDSAY, daughter of Lindsay of Kinnettles, and BEATRICE OGILVY, daughter of Ogilvy of Carsebank, who died in 1716, aged 89. In the same place also are buried some of the said David's children, whose names have perished through the age of the former (grave) stone, and the action of the weather. This monument was erected in the year . . . . , and restored in 1752.]

—John, the first recorded Lindsay of Blairifedden, who flourished 1535-9, had a son slaughtered by Ogilvy of Inverquharity, before the year 1588. The Kinnettles Lindsays were of the Evelick branch. (v. p. 70.) Scrimgeour of Glasswell was of the Dudhope race, and directly sprung from a burgess family of Dundee. Ogilvys were long in Carsebank, Thomas Ogilvie having been served heir to his father in it and in the lands of Kirkton of Aberlemno, in 1657. This monument, is upheld by a payment from the town of Arbroath, which was specially left for its maintenance.

A marble on the south wall of the church records the death of the following persons, whose graves are also marked by a table-shaped stone in the area of the burial ground :—

The Rev. WILLIAM ROGERS, minister of Rescobie, died 10 Sep. 1842, in the 60th year of his age, and 34th of his ministry. His wife AGNES LYON, eldest daughter of the Rev. Dr Lyon of Glamis, died 30 July 1816, in the 30th year of her age. ANN, youngest daughter of Mr John Oldham, Millthorpe, Nottinghamshire, his second wife, died 19 June 1841, in the 56th year of her age.

There are a number of gravestones in the churchyard; from some of these the following inscriptions are selected :—

Heir lyes ALEXANDER SIMPSON, qvha departed the 3 Maii 1616, he being of age 58, ane verteovs and trev man in his tym . . . . . AGNES RYND . . . . .

—Rynd or Rhynd, although now a somewhat rare surname in Angus, is of considerable antiquity in that county. Murdoch of Rhynd had a gift from David II. of a part of the royal hunting forest of Plater, near Finhaven; and about the same time a Patrick Rhynd was alderman of Forfar. Rhynds were subsequently designed of Casse, or Carse (now Carse-Gray); and it is interesting to notice that William Rynd of Carse was one of the four Angus lairds who were sureties to the Privy Council for the printing of the first Bible in Scotland. Besides Carse, the Rhynds also owned Clocksbriggs, where a stone is initialed and dated A.R : I.S. 1659; but the property passed by marriage during the last half of the 17th century to Alexander Dickson, a *pellio*, or dresser of skins in Forfar, a descendant of whom, also Alexander Dickson, made up a title to the property in 1751, as heir of his great-grandmother's brother, Thomas Rinde of Clocksbriggs, or *Cluch-brecks* (a place abounding with freckled stones.) The following inscription upon a table-shaped stone at Rescobie refers to a brother of the last-named, who succeeded to the estate in 1776 :—

DAVID DICKSON of Clocksbriggs, died 12 Sep. 1803, aged 60. MARY CUTHBERT, his wife, died 8 July 1816, aged 72. . . . . a son JAMES, an officer on board the "Generous Friends," an East India ship, which was lost in the China Seas in 1802, is supposed to have perished in the 22d year of his age. A daughter, ISOBELLA, died 1821, aged 37.

—On the death of Mr D. in 1803, he was succeeded by his eldest son, Major Dickson; but by a family arrangement with a brother-in-law, the estate was held by the latter until about 1853, when it was acquired by a son of Major Dickson's younger brother, ALEXANDER. The last-named died in the year 1865, aged 82, and it was his eldest son, DAVID DICKSON, who acquired Clocksbriggs and Rescobie, and built the present chateau or mansion-house at Clocksbriggs. He was long a merchant at Dunkirk, in France; and "in consideration of his personal exertions for improving the industry and commerce of that district, and the northern parts of the Empire at large," he was created by the Emperor Napoleon III., a Knight, and Officer of the Imperial Order of the Légion d'Honneur. But, by a sad accident, on 10th Nov. 1869, while driving near Dunkirk, Mr Dickson's horses took fright, and, leaping into an adjoining canal, both Mr Dickson and his coachman lost their lives. Miss Dickson, who was in the brougham with her father, narrowly escaped from sharing the same fate. Mr Dickson's remains were buried at Rescobie, beside those of his wife, who predeceased him by about ten years.

Another tombstone bears this record of the Rhynd family:—

Under this stone . . . . . of CATHARINE BURNS, ... hn Burns of Clocksbridges, and MARGARET REIND his spous, who departed this life Sept. 1718, of age . . years.

Upon a flat tombstone :—

☞ Heir lyis a faithfvll sister IANET DAL, spovs to David Dog of Resvale, vho lived vith hir hvsband 15 yeir, and died the 8 of Aprill 1638, being the 37 yeir of hir age.

—Doigs appear to have owned Reswallie for a considerable period. (*v.* p. 89.) It was bought in 1816 by Mr William Powrie, a Dundee merchant, whose son, the present laird, has greatly improved the property. Mr Powrie is a well-known and successful student of geology.

Upon a stone, with a shield bearing the blacksmiths' crown, pincers, and a hammer :—

☞ Heir lyis a faithfvll brother IAMES PYOT, who depairtit in Tvring the 15 of Ianvar 1643, ye 72 yeir of his age. IANOT FITCHIT his spovs bvir to him 13 bairns. Alexander, Iames, Iohn, Patrik, Wiliam, Iaine Pyots . . . Daigite.

Tvmvlo hoc conditvs est THOMAS DALL, qvondam in Balgaies, qvi obiit 12 Feb., 1675, ætatis 63, tandem AGNAS BELLIE, ejvs vxor, decessit 2ᵈᵒ Martii, 1682, ætatis 70. Cvra Ioannis Dall, in Milldens, et Margaretæ Finlo, vxoris ejvs, monvmentvm hoc extrvxtvm est vt signvm debiti amoris et reverentiæ erga parentes.

[In this grave are laid THOMAS DALL, sometime in Balgaies, who died 12 Feb. 1675, aged 63 ; and AGNAS BELLIE, his wife, who departed 2 March 1682, aged 70. This monument was erected by John Dall, in Milldens, and Margaret Finlo, his wife, as a mark of dutiful love and respect for parents.]

JOHN ESPLINE (1717) :—
  Like to the seed in earthy womb,
  Or like dead Lazarus in the tomb,
  Or like Tabitha in a sleep,
  Or Jonas like within the deep,
  Or like the moon or stars in day,
  Ly hid and languish quite away ;
  Even as the grave the dead receives,
  Man being dead he death deceives.
  The seed springs, and Lazarus stands,
  Tabitha wakes, and Jonas lands ;
  The moon appears, and stars remain,
  So man being dead shall live again.

ARCHD. PETER's children (1721) :—
  O man liue thou ane upright life,
  Whateuer to the befalls ;
  Then dubbel hapy shalt thou be
  When God by death the calls.

JOHN COULIE (1731) :—
  Unconstant earth, why do not mortals cease
  To build their hopes upon so short a lease ?
  Uncertain lease, whose term's but once begun,
  Tells never when it ends till it be done.
  We dote upon thy smiles, not knowing why,
  And while we but prepare to live, we die ;
  We spring like flowers for a day's delight,
  At noon we flourish, and we fade at night.

ALEX. HAY's father, &c., died in 17— :—
  Know mortal as these once blossoming HAYS,
  Were by Deaths sythe too early cutted down ;
  So thou must too as fading flowers decays,
  With . . . . . blessed soon.

A stone, with a much obliterated quotation from Ovid (Met. b. x., l. 33-4), bears :—

Here lyes IOHN WALACE, who lived in Finnestoun. He died in the moneth of May 1688, his age 87 years ; and his wife CATHARINE PITER died in May 1687, of age 60.

MARGT. STROAK, wf. of Thos. Wallace, d. 1759, a. 51 :—

T his stone in memory of this old race.
H ow man comes here with a peal face :
O man may see in ages all,
M an that is born he must fall ;
A s soon's our Saviour on earth he came,
S oon made interest for mortal man.
W hen he saw them in misery,
A ssumed their ransom for to pay ;
L et us ever mind this dear price :
L o our Redeemer was not nice.
A s soon as he saw man in sin stood—
C ome I'll redeem you with my blood :
E vermore be favoured into bless.

ALEX. SMITH, and wife, JANET WHITE (1772) :—
When this man liv'd upon this earth,
The Lord endu'd him with some wealth ;
And in his days, when he did live,
He studied the poor for to relieve
With money, councel, & help of hand ;
This is the truth you'l understand ;
But now these two lies in the grave,
Till the last trump do them relieve.

ANN SMITH's husband, &c. (1811) :—
My husband's here, and daughter dear,
Also a son of mine :
In dust doth lie ; but yet on high :
I hope their souls doth shine.
I've other five this date survives,
Two daughters, and three sons ;
May they with grace, pursue their race
Till once their glass is run.

—o—

CHAPELYARD.
(? S. MADOC.)

From a well near the burial-place being called S. MADOC, it is probable that the old church or chapel had been dedicated to that saint. His name is variously written ; and according to Dr Reeves (one of the most learned of Irish archæologists), the names of S. MOEDOC, MOQUE, and AIDAN, are of the same origin.

The burial-ground of Chapelyard occupies a knoll south-east of the Aldbar railway station. This was possibly the site of the chapel which was dependent upon the kirk of Rescobie in the 13th century.

The lintle of the doorway in the surrounding wall bears :—ANO MDCLXIX. The PIERSONS of Balmadies, now of The Guynd, bury here ; and, as noted below, a number of tombstones within the enclosure bear inscriptions relating to that family. Fourteen separate headstone, in one line, present the inscriptions undernoted :—

ELIZABETH PIERSONE, spovs to Iames Piersone, died 1669.

IAMES PIERSONE of Balmadies died the 7 of December 1673.

—It was possibly the above-named James Pierson who had a ratification charter in 1641 (Acta Parl., v., 621), of the lands and barony of "Auchtermeggities, vtherwayes callit Belmades, with the milne," &c., of which his parents, Alex. Pierson and Isobella Beaton, had a feu-farm charter, in 1624, from "Johne lait pretendit archibischop of St Androis." The lands were held under payment of a money rent of 20 pounds Scots, and owed suit to the archbishop's courts at Rescobie.

Dam MARGRET MVRRAY, spovs to Mr Alexander Piersone of Balmadies, vas born the 9 of Ivne 1625, died the 12 of Septer 1694, and vas hier interred the 26 of said moneth.

MEMENTO MORI : Mr ALEXANDER PIERSONE of Balmadies vas born the 3 of Febri 1626, died the 13 of March 1700, and vas heir interred the 26 of the said moneth.

Mrs MARGARET LINDSAY, daughter to Sir Alexander Lindsay of Evlick, first married to the laird of Findourie, and thereafter to James Piersone of Balmadies, to whom she bore seven sons. She died about the 56 year of her age, on the 11 or 12 of May 1714, and here interred on the 18, a virtueus and religious lady. Memento mori.

Mrs ELIZABETH ARBUTHNOT, sister German to the present laird of Findourie, died of a deceiy about the 18 year of her age, a beautiful, virtuous, and religious young lady, and was here interred some years before her mother's death. Memento mori.

—The Arbuthnotts of Findowrie were descended from Robert Arbuthnott of that ilk, who died about 1450. The last male representative of Arbuthnott of Findowrie died April 22, 1745, when the property passed to Carnegy of Balnamoon.

1746: Exuviæ mortales IACOBI PIERSONE de Balmadies, animi in Deum pij, in familiam vere paterni, in pacisceutes justi, in omues benevoli, hic unionem et præmia expectaut. Nati 3 Nov. A:D: 1666: Donati 30 Martij, 1745. Memento mori.

[1746: The mortal remains of JAMES PIERSONE of Balmadies, a man who was gifted with a disposition pious towards God, truly fatherly towards his family, just towards those with whom he had dealings, and benevolent to all, here await reunion and reward. (Born and died as above).]

JAMES PIERSONE, son of the laird of Balmadies, died of the smallpox on the 6 of August 1714, about the 18 or 19 year of his age, and was here interred on the 9 ditto. A promising young gentleman. Memento mori.

WILLIAM PIERSONE.
ALEXANDER PIERSONE.
SUSANNA SMALL.

ARCHIBALD PIERSONE, son to Mr Alexander Piersone of Balmadies.

JOHN PIERSONE, son to Mr Alexander Piersone of Balmadies.

1763: Here lies interred the mortal part of Mr IOHN PIERSONE, lawful son to James Piersone of Balmadies, who died on the 16th of February 1763, aged 64 years. A devout worshipper of his creator, and sincere lover of all mankind.

Three headstones, standing apart from those above noticed, bear respectively the inscriptions quoted below:—

JOHN PIERSONE TAYLOR.

To this grave are committed the mortal remains of ANNE FRASER, daughter to Iohn Fraser of Kirkton, who was born on the 9 of May 1723, O.S. Married to Robert Pierson, advocate, in October 1740, to whom she bore five children, Iames, Iohn, Mary, Margaret, and David, all alive, and she died on the 9 of July 1761. A lady greatly esteemed for her benevolence, and other amiable qualities. Memento mori—Mind death.

Here are interred the mortal remains of ROBERT PIERSON of Balmadies, advocate, an affectionate Husband, a loving Parent, an easy Landlord, the poor man's Friend, never intended nor delighted to harm or injure any person, who departed this life the fourth day of April 1763, aged sixty two years one month and seventeen days. Sic transit gloria mundi. Memento mori.

The following inscription is said to have been composed by the late Rev. Mr Aitken of St Vigeans, the betrothed of Miss Pierson:—

Here lies the corps of MARY PIERSON, youngest daughter of the late Robert Pierson of Balmadies, Esq. She was born the 26th of Augt. 1746, and died the 10th of Nov. 1771:—

Mildness of temper, innocence of mind,
And softest manners were in her combin'd;
Sincere and open, undisguis'd by art,
She form'd no wish but what she might impart.
Easie and social, chearful and resign'd
Harmless thro' life, the sister and the friend.
In early age, call'd to resign her breath,
Patient in sickness, undismay'd at death,
A sister's grief ('tis friendship's sacred claim),
Pays this small tribute to a sister's name.

Two headstones bear respectively:—

Mr ARCHIBALD PEARSONE of Westhall.
ELIZABETH GAIRDEN, his spovse.

—The surname of Pierson, or Pearson, is of old standing in Angus. It occurs in the records of the Abbey of Arbroath in 1506, when Abbot George granted Thomas Pierson a charter of " ly Rude" with pertinents, in the Almory of that town. A tombstone at Arbroath, with a much effaced inscription, bears the Pierson arms and the date of 1589. Archibald Pierson, designed of Chapleton, was sheriff-depute of Forfar in 1642; and the family were proprietors of Lochlands and Barngreen before 1653, in which year Thomas Pierson was served heir to his grand-father. These, doubtless, were ancestors of the Piersons of Balmadies, now represented by the laird of The Guynd.

The following is upon a monument within a railed enclosure:—

Sacred to the memory of MARGARET OUCHTERLONY, second daughter of John Ouchterlony, Esq. of The Guynd, and widow of James Pierson, Esq. She died at The Guynd, 21st March 1849, in her 78th year:—

Dear as thou wert, and justly dear,
We will not weep for thee;

One thought shall check the starting tear,
It is—that thou art free !
And thus shall Faith's consoling power
The tears of Love restrain
Oh ! who that saw thy parting hour
Could wish thee here again ?

—The Ochterlonys of The Guynd are represented through the female line by J. A. Pierson, Esq. ; and since the property of Balmadies was sold by the Piersons, it has been in the possession of several lairds. It now belongs to Sir C. M. Ochterlony, Bart., who calls the property by his own family name Sir C. is probably descended from the old stock of Ochterlony of that ilk, since Maj.-Gen. Sir D. Ochterlony, who was of that race, and created a baronet in 1816, obtained a second patent in 1823, re-creating himself a baronet with remainder to the present Sir C. and his legitimate issue. Sir David (who was born at Boston, New England, was the grandson of Alex. Ochterlony, laird of Pitforthy, near Brechin, whose eldest son, Gilbert, succeeded to that property, and was also designed of Newton Mill.

Besides the monuments to the Piersons, a few others are within the enclosure of Chapelyard. Four record deaths of a family called SCOTT, who have long tenanted the farm of Millden, one of whom ROBERT, died in 1836, aged 92 An adjoining stone shows that GEORGE SHARP, mason in Edinburgh, died whilst superintending the building of the mansion house of Balmadies, 14 Feb. 1821, aged 42. Another headstone (of the 17th or 18th century), bears this simple inscription :—

IAMES OGILVIE.   IOHN OGILVIE.

Upon another, of apparently the same period, is merely the name of

WILLIAM GRIME.

—In 1635, a charter of alienation of the lands of Balmadies, &c., was granted by a William Grime, burgess and merchant in Montrose, to James Pierson.

It is told in monkish chronicles that S. TRIDUANA, to whom the church of Rescobie was dedicated, lived an "eremitical life at Rescoby," along with two other virgins, that S. TRIDUANA was a person of great beauty, and to evade the wiles of an amorous chief, she removed to Dunfallandy in Athol. She was followed there by certain of the chief's retainers ; and on being told by them that it was the lustre of her eyes that their chief so much admired, she plucked them out, fixed them upon a stick, and sent them to her lover ! She died at Restalrig, near Edinburgh, and was buried there. In allusion to the story of S. TRIDUANA having plucked out her eyes, Sir David Lindsay, in satirizing upon images in churches, says : —

"Saint Trodwel eke there may be seen,
Who on a stick hath both her een."

"St Trodlin's fair," held of old at the kirkstyle of Rescobie, was long ago removed to the town of Forfar ; but the stone at which the baron courts were held, and market custom collected, still stands within a small triangular-shaped piece of ground (at the east door of the church of Rescobie), the property of the Earl of Strathmore, who is patron of the parish.

Some good examples of Picts' houses, or underground chambers, were found upon the farm of Weems some years ago ; but, unfortunately, these were closed up soon afterwards.

Two large boulders at the Blackgate of Pitscandly mark the site of ancient graves, in which locality, it is said, a battle was fought between the Picts and Scots, when Feredeth, the King of the Picts, was slain. One of these stones was ornamented by circular markings. At Balhaggardy and Wellton there are other stones of the old sculptured type.

All historians agree that it was in the castle of Rescobie that King Donald Bain was so long imprisoned, and had his eyes put out with red hot irons, and where he eventually died. It is supposed that the castle stood upon some of the hillocks adjoining the loch. So far as known, the only remaining traces of an ancient stronghold or fort in Rescobie, are those of Kemp Castle, upon the top of Turin Hill, of which a good description is given in the New Stat. Account Scotland.

x

Airlie.

(S. MEDDAN.)

THE kirk of *Erolyn*, in the diocese of St Andrews, was dedicated by Bishop David in 1242. The present building, which is in the *barn* style of architecture so long common to churches in Scotland, was erected in 1783.

A coffin-slab, of soft red sandstone, with a sword and hunting horn, &c., carved upon the sides, and an ornamental cross upon the top, lies in the churchyard. The shaft of the cross bears the following brief record (in Roman capitals) of persons whose history and connection with the parish are unknown to the writer :—

LYIS . HEIR . ROGER . AND . YOFAN . ROLOK . QVA . DIED . IN . RIDIE . 1640.

The oldest visible tombstone in the churchyard bears the name of ANDROV VRIGHT, and the date of 1606. The next in point of antiquity is within an enclosure. The coping stones of the walls are embellished with carvings of the five passion wounds of Our Saviour, the scourge, the pillar to which Christ was bound, the spear and the pincers, and three fleur-de-lis. The inscription is as follows :—

This bvrial bvildet by Mr Villiam Malcolm 1609.
Disce mori vt bene moriaris
Pvlvis et vmbra svmvs.
M. V. G : G. M.

Heir lyis GIRSEL MATHOV, spovs to Maister Villiam Malcolm, minister at Airlie, qwha departed this lyf the 23 day of Febrvair, and of hir age 38 zeir, 1609.

Upon a flat stone in area of kirkyard :—

Heir lyes DAVID CARDEAN, who departed the thrid of May 1662, and his aig was 74 : and ELSPAT STIL his spovs who departed the Fovrt of Ivnij 1662, and hir aig was 68.

Hvic tvmvlo lachrimas gemitvsqve impende, viator.
Discite, mortales ! pvlvis et vmbra svmvs.
Remember al as ye go by,
As ye are nov so ons vas I :
As I am nov so most ye be,
Remember man, for al most die.

[Traveller ! upon this tomb bestow a tear, a sigh,
Learn, mortals ! dust are we ; our lives like shadows fly.]

ROBERT SMITH's spouse (1748) :—

Sure death may kill, but cannot give surprise
To those whose views are fix'd beyond the skies ;
He with his spear the vital spring untied,
And sure my spouse did sicken till she died.
With winged flight her soul did speed away,
E'en to the regions of immortal day ;
Her husband, children, left to weep & moan,
The best of wives, the kindest mother gone.

JOHN ARCHER on his parents (1764) :—

This worthy pair both free of fraud,
Made Truth their constant aim ;
You might depended on their word,
For still it was the same.
They lov'd to live with all around
In unity & peace ;
And with a spotless character,
They finished their race.

PATRICK, son of Thos. DAVIE, a. 11 (1760) :—

We of this child had great content,
For to get learning of his God & Christ was his
Tho' soon cut of the stage of time, [intent,
We dar not to relleck that we so soon did part,
For it was his Letter will,
That he God's counsel should fulfill.

ROBERT, son of R. LOUNAN, a. 13 (1746) :—

While nature shrinks to be dissolved,
Relentless Death strikes hard ;
Nor blooming youth, nor parents' tears,
Procure the least regard.
The lovely child fond parents boast,
Sunk in a sea of grief ;
Hard fate—fret we 'gainst Heaven ? No,
Submission gives relief.

The chapel of S. JOHN stood near Baikie, where there was a loch and castle in old times, but the chapel site is unknown. Apart from Baikie, the parish of Airlie contains several interesting objects of antiquity, such as the underground cave at Barns, the castle and den of Airlie, S. MED-

DEN's Knowe, &c., all of which are described in the Proceedings of the Society of Antiquaries of Scotland (vol. iv.), and in Memorials of Angus and the Mearns. A coffin slab of an early type, with cross and sword, &c., incised, found near the manse, was wantonly broken by masons, and used in repairs which were being made upon the adjoining offices some years ago.

Kingoldrum.

(S. ——)

THE church of *Kingouldrum*, in the diocese of Brechin, was given, along with a toft in "the shyra" (*shire*, a division) of the same, to the Abbey of Arbroath, by King William the Lion. But, in consequence of the fragments of ancient sculptured stones, and the old *skellach*, or bell, which have been found at Kingoldrum, it is supposed to have been the site of a church of a much earlier date than the one given to Arbroath by King William.

The old bell, which had been coated with bronze, is made of sheet iron; and when discovered in 1843, a bronze chalice and glass bowl were got beside it. These latter are supposed to have been lost; but the bell was presented to the National Museum by the Rev. Mr Haldane, whose knowledge of, and favour for, local history and antiquities are well known in the district. A curious bronze cross and chain, found in a stone cist near the church, are also in the National Museum, the gift of the same gentleman.

The present church was built in 1840, upon or near the site of the previous building, which is said to have been erected before the Reformation. A coffin slab (of soft red sandstone, about 6 feet long, embellished with a cross in relief, and a sword incised), lies in the burial-ground. Luckily this slab is more valued by the minister than that which was so wantonly destroyed at Airlie. Like the latter, it had doubtless marked the grave of some person of local note—possibly that of an old laird of Balfour. A handsome mausoleum, erected in 1863, marks the burial-place of the FARQUHARSONS, sometime lairds of Baldovie and Balfour, upon which a marble slab is thus inscribed:—

✢ The sepulchre of JOHN FARQUHARSON and ELIZABETH RAMSAY of Baldovie; and of their Children. ELIZABETH, born 4th January 1768; died 18th June 1855. AGNES, born 26th March 1769; died in infancy. THOMAS, a magistrate and deputy-lieutenant of Forfarshire, born 3d October 1770; died 21st November 1860. He was the last male representative of the Farquharsons of Brochdearg, in lineal descent from the Chieftain Findla More, the Royal Standard-Bearer, who fell in defence of his country, on the field of Pinkey, 10th September 1547, and was interred in the neighbouring cemetery of Inveresk. R. I. P.

—John Farquharson, son of Alex. Farquharson, farmer, Inzion, Lintrathen, came to the estate of Baldovie by marrying Miss Ramsay, the eldest niece of Dr Ogilvy. Their son THOMAS added the adjoining lands of Balfour to the property, and was succeeded by his cousin, Capt. Mitchell, a native of Lintrathen, whose father was long factor to the Earls of Airlie. Capt. MITCHELL who erected the mausoleum, died unmarried in 1865, aged 84. Besides numerous private legacies, he left £50,000 to erect and endow an institution for the support of poor and aged priests of the Roman Catholic Church. Balfour and Baldovie, which were sold after Captain M.'s death, were bought by Sir Thomas Munro, of Lindertis, Bart.

The churchyard is kept in good order; and the following inscriptions are selected from some of the tombstones:—

Heir lyes ane honest woman called ISOBEL WRICHT, spovs to Olifer Smal in Kingovthervm, vha departed Ianvar, ano 164–, and of hir age –9.

. . . . . .

JANET BUCHAN, wf. of John Dick, farmer, Ascreavie, d. 1748, a. 62:—

 Below this stone are here reposed
  The ruins of a Tent,
 Where divine virtue deigned to dwell,
  But, ah! how soon were spent

Her mortal years; the tyrant, Death,
Resistless gives the thrust;
The virtuous wife, and virtuous Tent,
Stricks down into the dust.

JAMES DUNCAN d. 1742 :—

What havock makes impartial death
On all the human kind;
Ganst him a virtuous life's no gard,
Nor yet the purest mind.
And most all clay—yes, it is destian'd
For every sack [sex] and age,
The old and bowed, and young robust,
And infantes quit the stage.

Upon a table-shaped stone :—

Here lyes JAMES WATSON, who lived att the Mill of Kingoldrum, who departed this life the first day of Ianuary 1719, and of his age 93 :—

Reader, repent ere tyme be spent,
Think on a future state;
Do not delay another day,
In case it prove too late.

The monks of Arbroath had the sole right to hunt in the forest of Kingoldrum, from which, by special order of Alexander III., all were excluded who had not permission from the Abbots. The Castle of Balfour, of which a mere fragment remains, is said by some to have been built by Cardinal Beaton, while Abbot of Arbroath. It is more probable, however, since Balfour was held of the Abbots by Ogilvys from at least the year 1478, that the castle had been erected by one of that family.

Stone cists, flint weapons, and other traces of the early inhabitants, have been found in various parts of the parish. There are also some peculiar-looking entrenchments, and stone circles, upon the Skurroch Hill, to the west of the manse; where, in later times, the body of JOHN CATTANACH, the victim of a dreadful and preconcerted murder, was buried in a marl pit. The particulars of this murder, which occurred in the barnyard at Meikle Kenny, 11th June 1746, as well as the account of the cost of the execution of two of the persons implicated, are printed in *Montrose Standard* of 27th March 1863.

A spring, called *Neil's Well*, is in the vicinity of the church. A tablet over the manse door bears the initials of Mr James Badenoch, minister, and writer of the Old Statistical Account of the parish :—

M. I. B.   VERITAS VICTRIX.   1792.

~~~~~~~~~~~~~~~~~~~~~~~~~~~

Keith.

(S. MAELRUBHA.)

THE name of *Keith* first occurs about 1195, in King William's grant of Grange to the Abbey of Kinloss. The church of *Ket*, or *Keyth*, which was a mensal church of the Bishops of Moray, was granted to the cathedral of Elgin about 1203. In 1214-24, it is called *Keth-Malruf*, being a combination of the names of the place and of the saint, to whom the kirk was dedicated. There is a valuable and interesting history of S. MAELRUBHA and his churches, by Dr Reeves, in Proceedings of the Society of Antiquaries of Scotland, vol. iii.

The present church of Keith, which was built in 1816-19, cost nearly £6000. It is conveniently situated at some distance from the churchyard. Painted boards (certainly not in keeping with the neatness of the internal architecture of the building) are placed over the entrance door. One bears the names of those who have contributed to a fund which was begun by Miss INNES, late of Maisley, for the benefit of Poor Householders in Keith, the total sum of which amounts to about £819; another fund for the same purpose was founded by Major PETER DUNCAN, to which he alone gave £850. The bequest of £150 by JOHN THURBURN of Murtle, for the purchase of coals, is also recorded; as well as that of a like sum by ROBERT GREEN, solicitor, for the support of the Sabbath School, and the purchase of Bibles.

A pewter basin is inscribed round the margin —" This Baptising Bason belongs to the kirk of Keith, 1777." The bell now in use is modern; and the previous instrument, though tongueless, but otherwise sound, is possibly the more harmonious of the two. It is preserved in the steeple, and has this inscription upon it :—

IOHN MOWAT ME FECIT, OLD ABD. 1755 ; VT SONAT CAMPANA, SIC SONAT VITA CIVIVM PARŒOCHIÆ DE KEITH. SABBATA PANGO, FVNERA PLANGO.

[John Mowat, Old Aberdeen, made me, 1755. As sounds a bell, so sounds the life of the parishioners of Keith. Sabbaths I proclaim, at funerals I toll.]

The old kirk, which stood in the churchyard, was a long narrow building (99 by 28 feet), with an aisle, also outside stairs to the lofts. It is said that there were thirteen lairds in Keith at one time, and that each of them had a door in the old kirk, which led to their respective pews. The only part of the old building which remains (traces of the foundations excepted), is that which contains a monument to the wife and family of Strachan of Thornton. It is of freestone, embellished with the armorial bearings of Strachan and Rose, also a monogram, and this inscription :—

Sub scamno D^d. Kinnminnitie cineres lectissimæ feminæ D. KATH. ROSSÆ D. de Thorntono, cuius etiamsi fragrantissimæ memoriæ monumentis omni ære perenniorib' abunde satis litatum sit hoc tamen mausoleo parentandum duxit coniunx ipsius pullatus D. Iac. Strachanus de Thornt : huius ecclesiæ pastor. Obiit puerpera 6 Apr. anno 1689 .... quiescunt et hic GUL, ROB., et JOSHUE STRACHANUS filii eorum.

[Under the Kinminnitie family seat lie the ashes of a most exemplary woman, Dame KATH. ROSE, Lady of Thorntone, to whose most fragrant memory, although amply perpetuated by monuments more durable than any brass, her mourning husband Mr James Strachan of Thorntone, pastor of this church, deemed the erection of this mausoleum a becoming tribute of respect. She died in childbed, April 6, 1689 .... Here also rest WILLIAM, ROBERT, and JOSHUA STRACHAN, their sons.]

—It is said that the above Mr Strachan succeeded to the baronetcy of Thornton in the Mearns: there is also a place called Thornton near Keith. The striking coincidence is recorded (v. p. 134), of a lady of Thornton having died in 1661, under the same painful circumstances as the above ; and the similarity of the diction of the prefatory part of both inscriptions is worthy of note. The following notices of Mr Jas. Strachan and his son are from the late Mr Griffin's MS. notes upon a copy of Dr Oliver's Collec. for a Biography of the Jesuits :
—" James Ramsay of Thornton, alias Sir James Strachan, Episcopal minister at Keith, ejected at the Revolution," had a son Hugh Ramsay or Strachan, born in 1672, who was converted in 1693 by Dr Jamieson, then a priest at Aberdeen. He was sent to Rome ; but, in passing through Douay became a Jesuit. He returned a missionary to his native country in 1701, and died at Douay in 1745.

A monument, which also marks the site of a family burial-place within the old kirk, bears :—

Sacred to the memory of the
GORDONS and STUARTS of Birkenburn, 1843.

—The first Gordon of Birkenburn, a son of Lesmore, in Rhynie, acquired the estate about 1550. The family failed in three co-heiresses about the middle of the last century. One married Mr Stuart, minister of Drumblade ; a second, Mr Milne, minister at Inverkeithny ; and the third, known as "Lady Catherine Gordon," died in Old Keith. John Stuart, son of the minister of Drumblade, sold Birkenburn to the Earl of Seafield, and erected the stone from which the above inscription is copied. A carved panel of the old family seat is in possession of a lady at Keith, and thus inscribed :—

THIS . DESK . ERECTED.
BY . A . G. OF . BIRKENBURN . 1604
SOLI . DEO . GLORIA ; INVIDIAM . SVPERAT . IESVS.
[To God alone be the glory ; Jesus overcometh envy.]

Upon a table-shaped stone, near the north-east corner of churchyard :—

Hugh Macky, sailor aboard the Antilope man-of-war, erected this stone to the memory of JOHN MACKY, his dear father, who was born A° 1690, died A° 1732, aged 42 ; and of ———

Near the above, a modern head-stone records the death of a long-lived race, four of whom, it will be seen, died at the age of 88 :—

Geo. Smith, feuer, Newmill, in memory of his father GEORGE SMITH, who died 1812, aged 88 ;

his mother, JEAN MILN, died 1826, aged 88 . . . . his sister, JEAN, died 1851, aged 88 ; his wife, ELIZABETH GEDDES, died 1853, aged 88. The foresaid GEORGE SMITH died 1854, aged 83.

Hear lyes the corppes of thre childrin ALEXAR. IVN, and ISBEAL HENDRYS, lawfol childring to Robert Hendry, parishoner in Keith, 1682.

Rudely cut upon the face of an adjoining stone are the initials—I. L: E. T: I. L., and the date of 1688. Upon a table-shaped stone :—

This stone is erected in memory of JAMES GLASHAN, late residenter in Keith, who was born the 11 day of Dec. 1686 years, and died the 9 day of January 1771 years, in the 85th year of his age. Also of ANNE BAIRD, his wife, who was born the — day of —— 17—, and died the 14 day of Sept. 1762 years, in the — year of her age.

—It was of the above Mr Glashan that Ferguson, the astronomer, said—" I shall always have a respect for the memory of this man." Ferguson was employed as a servant upon Mr G.'s farm of Ardneadlie, now part of Bracheads, or the croft lands of Keith. While there Mr G. afforded Ferguson many facilities to pursue his favourite studies. Ferguson in his autobiography says:—" My master gave me more time than I could reasonably expect, and often took the thrashing flail out of my hands and worked himself, whilst I sat by him in the barn, busy with my compasses, ruler, and pen." (*v.* p. 102.)

An adjoining stone, in memory of Mr G.'s daughter-in-law, shows the somewhat remarkable occurrence of her having given birth to all her children upon Sundays :—

This stone is erected in memory of ELIZABETH ANDERSON, daughter of Mr James Anderson, sometime minister of the Gospel at Keith, wife of James Glashan, writer, there. She was born 28 Feb. 1751, and died 10 July 1773, in the 22 year of her age, leaving issue James, her only son, born Sunday, 1 April 1770 ; Jean, her first daughter, born Sunday, 31 March 1771 ; and Elizabeth, the youngest child, born Sunday 2 May 1773, after whose birth, the mother, upon the day above mentioned, of a consumptive illness, died.

—The eldest daughter, JEAN, became the wife of Robert Stuart of Aucharnie, in Forgue, by whom she had several children. The survivor of these, JOHN, LL.D., of Newmill, near Edinburgh, is the well-known Secretary of the Society of Antiquaries of Scotland, and of the Spalding Club, a great many of the valuable publications of which Club, including the Sculptured Stones of Scotland, (2 vols. fol.), and The Book of Deer, have been edited and prefaced by him. Mr Anderson, who was minister first at Cullen, from whence he was translated to Keith, in 1762, died in 1770 ; but no stone marks his grave. [*v.* FORGUE.]

The following inscription is from the oldest of three monuments within an enclosure :—

M. S. ADAMI LONGMORE, ad collem de Mountgreu olim coloni, e vita A. S. H. 1770 evocati ; necnon MARGARETÆ OGILVIE, anno 1781 demortuæ, conjugum fidorum, parentum charissimorum ; Adamus Longmore, ab ærario in Scotia Regio H. C. P. F. anno 1809.

[Sacred to the memory of ADAM LONGMORE, sometime farmer at Hill (or Brae) of Mountgreu, who was summoned from life in the year of human salvation, 1770 ; and also of MARGARET OGILVIE, who died in the year 1781—faithful partners, most affectionate parents. Adam Longmore, of the Royal Exchequer in Scotland, caused this tomb to be erected in 1809.]

Round the margin of a coffin slab of yellow sandstone, embellished with a floral cross in relief, is the following, which relates to a much respected Scotch Episcopal clergyman :—

✠ Resteth JOHN MURDOCH, who for many years ministered at Rathven, Keith, and Fochabers. Ob. 29 April A.D. 1850, æt. 83.

—The Rev. Dr James F.S. Gordon, of St Andrew's Episcopal Church, Glasgow, author of a Scotichronicon and Monasticon, &c., is a native of Keith, and married a daughter of Mr Murdoch to his first wife. A table-shaped stone presents the following :—

JOHN GILES, spinning-wheel maker in Keith, died 26 Oct. 1787, aged 75 :—

Beneath this stone, in hope again to rise,
The relics of ane honest man are laid ;
So, Reader, learn superior worth to prize,
That what is said of him, of thee be said.

Such peaceful neighbour, and a friend so sure,
Such tender parent, and such husband kind ;
Such modest pattern of Religion pure,
In Keith's wide precincts we too seldom find.
His hands industrious, and his heart sincere,
Of worldly wise men, he disdained the wiles ;
Go, Passenger ! make haste thy God to know,
And in thy actions imitate JOHN GILES.

In the north-west corner of the burial ground a marble tablet, within an enclosure, is thus inscribed :—

To the memory of JAMES THURBURN of Smailholm, Berwickshire, only son of the Rev. John Thurburn, minister of Kirknewton. This stone is placed here by his three sons in testimony of their affectionate remembrance of his excellent qualities, his sound understanding, his honour and integrity, which remained unshaken through much adverse fortune. He died at Drum, near Keith, 9 May 1798, aged 59. His remains are deposited in the burial ground of Milne of Kinstair, in this churchyard.

—It is told that Mr T. was brought from the south of Scotland by the Earl of Findlater for the purpose of introducing the growth and manufacture of flax into this part of the country, both of which were long and successfully carried on by him. But, towards the close of Mr T.'s life, the trade having become depressed, he, like others who were extensively engaged in the business, lived to feel a reverse of fortune, as expressed in the above inscription. One of Mr T.'s sons, John (who gave, "in memory of his father, James," £150, the interest of which is disbursed in the purchase of coals for the poor of Keith), died laird of Murtle, on Deeside ; a second son, Robert, became an opulent merchant abroad ; and a third continued farmer of Drum. Another son became a solicitor in Keith. Of the female descendants, one is the lady of Sir J. Innes of Edingight.

The erector of the stone which bears the next quoted inscription was a ploughman to his father on the farm of Arduach. Owing to a family quarrel, he left home, enlisted as a private soldier, and raised himself to the position of a major in the army :—

This stone was erected by Captain James McKondachy, in the 93d Regt., son to Iohn McKondachy, in Arduch, in memory of his mother MARGARET FORSYTH, who died the 22d day of June 1791, aged 64 years.

Within a railed enclosure :—

The Revd. JAMES M'LEAN, minister of this parish from 1795 to 1825, and afterwards at Urquhart, Morayshire, where he died 14 Nov. 1840, aged 82. His wife ELIZABETH TOD, died at Keith, 3d April 1816.

—Another slab records the death of five daughters and two sons. GEORGE, born 1801, died at Cape Coast Castle, Africa, in 1847, of which he had been sometime governor. He married in June 1838, the celebrated authoress, L. E. L. (LETITIA ELIZABETH LANDON), who died in October of the following year. Dr Hugh M'Lean of West Park, Elgin, is another son of the minister of Keith.

Upon one side of an obelisk of freestone :—

Sacred to the memory of MARY SMITH, daughter of Edward Smith, Fochabers, and widow of Alex. Mortimer of Excise, burgess of Forres. She died 4 Jan. 1802, aged 62. This tomb is erected by desire of her son, the late EDWARD MORTIMER, Esq. of Pictou, who was an eminent merchant, and long chief magistrate of that town. He was also a judge in the Court of Common Pleas ; and for 20 years represented the county of Halifax in the General Assembly of Nova Scotia. He died at Pictou, 10 Oct. 1819, aged 51. [The names of some sisters and other relatives of Mr M. are recorded upon another side of the monument.]

A monument near the west dyke of the burial-ground is inscribed :—

This monument erected to the memory of JAMES MILNE of Kinstair, who died 9 May 1771, aged 83. SOPHIA GRANT, his wife, who died 25 Aug. 1754, aged 63. JAMES MILNE, at Mill of Towie, his grandfather, died 1712, aged 83. JOHN MILNE, portioner of Urquhart, his father, died 1709, aged 50. JOHN MILNE, younger of Kinstair, his son, died 29 July 1743, aged 29. JEAN MILNE, his daughter, died 14 Feb. 1755, aged 26. Six other children died young, &c. . . . . . all buried 49 feet due east from this, under a separate gravestone, except the said John Milne, portioner of Urquhart, who died at Urquhart, and was buried there.

A flat stone, in area of old kirk, bears:—

In hopes of ane blised resurrection, heir lyeth IANET GEDDES, spows to George Macky in Newmilln, who depr. this life the 12 of March 1690.

Upon a table-shaped stone:—

Under this stone lies the body of ALEXANDER JAMIESON, a tender husband, a good father, and a faithful friend, who departed this life May 3, 1773, aged 81.

JAMES JAMIESON, late Master in Royal Navy, died 18 July 1817, aged 82 years. His remains are interred under this stone, on which his widow, Janet Jamieson, has caused this simple record to be engraved.

—This was the *Jamie Jamieson* mentioned in Lord Nelson's Despatches; and with whom Nelson sailed when Jamieson was master of H.M. frigate the Boreas. This tombstone was originally erected by Jamieson to the memory of his father. The following is upon a granite head stone:—

Erected to the memory of Major PETER DUNCAN, sometime of the 66th Regt. of Foot, who died 16 July 1854, aged 77 years, and was interred here; where also lie the remains of his sister MARGARET, who died 13 July 1836, aged 63 years.

—Duncan had the merit of having risen from the ranks; and while Captain, he was appointed one of the guards of Napoleon the First at St Helena. It is told that Napoleon having noticed a medal on Duncan's breast, began to examine it one day; but on seeing that the decoration was for the battle of Vittoria, he allowed it to drop from his fingers. Besides (as before seen) having himself founded a fund for the benefit of poor householders, natives of the parish of Keith, Capt. D. also contributed £134 to the Innes fund, for the like purpose.

The towns of New Keith and Fife-Keith are separated from each other by the river Isla, which is crossed on the highway by a substantial stone bridge. The bridge, built in 1770, was widened in 1816. The old bridge, which is a fine specimen of the strong, narrow, and high pitched arch of the period, has a stone built into the west side, dated 1609, upon which are the Murray and Lindsay arms impaled, and these names:—

THOMAS MVRRAY.   IANET LINDSAY.

On the east side:—

ERECTED 1609 : REPAIRED 1822.

New Keith, which adjoins what may be called the ruins of the village of Old Keith, was begun by Lord Findlater in 1750; and *Fife-Keith* was founded by the Earl of Fife in 1817. Both are thriving places, with a considerable population. The village of *Newmill*, which was founded about the same time as Fife-Keith, is about a mile from the latter place.

Some of the churches, houses, and shops in New Keith are neat and spacious. The Roman Catholic Chapel, dedicated to S. THOMAS, is in the Corinthian style; and colossal figures of SS. PETER and PAUL (after those of Michael Angelo), are upon each end of the pediment. The frieze is thus inscribed:—

COLUMNA ET FIRMAMENTVM VERITATIS.

—The Chapel was erected chiefly through the enterprise of the Rev Mr Walter Lovi, R. C.C., who travelled on the Continent, as well as through Great Britain, soliciting subscriptions for its erection. In the course of his wanderings he met with, and applied to Charles X. of France, who not only gave a handsome donation in money; but that unfortunate Prince also commissioned M. François Dubois to paint an altar-piece for the chapel. The subject, which represents the Incredulity of S. Thomas, is a large picture, in the artist's best manner. It was finished in 1830; and the royal gift, with the original date of it, is upon a plate in the corner:—

Carolus X., Rex Gallorum Christianissimus, dono dedit, A.D. 1829.

—After the dethronement of King Charles, Mr Lovi, fearing that the picture might be lost to his chapel, went to Paris and had an audience with Louis-Philippe, who at once delivered it over to Mr Lovi. It reached Keith in 1831, was placed in the chapel in 1832; and, on 15 Aug. of same year, Bishop Kyle opened the chapel for Divine service.

The parish of Keith, out of which Grange was formed (*v.* p. 100), contains few objects of antiquarian or historical interest. When James V. made a pilgrimage to the shrine of S. DUTHOC at Tain, in Oct. 1497, he appears to have slept a night here, when 18s were paid "at the Kirk of Keth to the gudwif of the houss," and 1s 4d " to the prest that said mes to the King thair."

Here also the Great MONTROSE, when on his way to Edinburgh in 1650, after his betrayal for 400 bolls of meal (!) by his own companion in arms, M'Leod of Assynt, was taken upon a Sunday by his guard, seated upon a pony, meanly clad, but securely tied by ropes, to hear in the churchyard the declamations of Mr Kininmouth, the parish minister, who chose for his text (1 Sam. xv. 33), "As thy sword hath made women childless, so shall thy mother be childless among women." It is told that Montrose, who soon saw that the heartless representative of Him who ever spoke feelingly to sufferers, was to make him the object of his lecture, smiled, and nobly said—"Rail on, sir, *I am bound* to listen to you!"

The bridge at Haughs was erected soon after 1770. According to tradition, the bridge at Bridgend was built soon after 1678, in which year the 4th Marquis of Huntly, afterwards Duke of Gordon, along with his young Marchioness, were arrested there while on their marriage trip from the south to Gordon Castle, owing to the largeness of the stream. To prevent the recurrence of danger and delay at this place, it is said that the bridge, of which the picturesque arch still remains, was erected soon after.

Two stones (triangular shaped) lie near the middle of the churchyard. Both are charged in chief with the Gordon arms, and a fess in the centre, with those of Innes and Melville, respectively, in base. One stone is initialed and dated, I. G : E. I. 1677 ; the other, A. G : K. M. 1693.

A carving of the Oliphant arms, quartered with those of Ogilvy, is built into the north side of the Strachan tomb. Charles, 7th Lord Oliphant, married Mary, heiress of Ogilvy of Milton, a cadet of the Findlater family, and thus came to estates in this quarter. In addition to Milton, these appear to have consisted of Auchynanie, Little Cantlie, and the Croft and Alehouse of Keith, which latter, when John Ogilvy succeeded his grandfather in 1655, was called Craigduffscroft, or "the croft of the black rock." The tower of Milton is picturesquely situated upon the craig or rock referred to, near the Linn of Keith. It is said to have been erected by Lord Oliphant, and is sometimes called by his name. It is quite ruinous, and had never been a building either of much size or elegance.

GEORGE GORDON, who was sometime a medical practitioner at Keith, his native place, perished while bathing near the Linn in 1819. He was accomplished in almost every department of the fine arts; and, in 1820, prefaced by a memoir of his brief career, appeared " Elgiva," a long historical poem of more than ordinary merit.

Kinneff.

(? S. ARNOLD.)

THE church of *Kinef* belonged to the Priory of St Andrews, and was dedicated by Bishop David in 1242. A chapel was attached to it, possibly that of S. JOHN, which stood at Barras, or that of S. MARTIN, at the Bridgend.

The present church, near which stood S. ARNOLD'S cell, is a sorry fabric, bearing the date of 1760. Round the rim of the bell :—

PIETER OSTENS HEEFT MY GEGOTEN
TE ROTTERDAM A°: 1679.

—The initials, M. I. H. are also upon the west side of the bell. These last may refer to some one of the Honymans, four of whom, as will be seen below, were ministers of the parish.

As is well known, it was within the old kirk of Kinneff that the Regalia of Scotland were concealed during the time of the Commonwealth. Those precious articles, which were carried by the minister's wife from Dunottar Castle, through the very ranks of the besiegers, and by her own well-managed plans, and those of the lady of Governor Ogilvie, were deposited in a hole purposely made for them by the minister below the pulpit. They remained there until the Restoration; when they were delivered, by the King's orders, to the Earl Marischal. But the rewards for the important service of preserving the royal insignia, were dealt out in an inverse ratio. John Keith, brother to Earl Marischal, who knew nothing of the affair, having been himself abroad during the whole transaction, but whose name had been used in a letter for the sole purpose of misleading the usurpers, "got" (as Sir W. Scott has well expressed it) the Earldom [of Kintore], pension, &c.; Ogilvie only inferior honours; and the poor clergyman nothing whatever, or, as we say, "the hare's foot to lick!"

A monument, built into the south wall of the church, on the left of the pulpit, adorned with the Ogilvie of Barras arms, contains the following renewed inscription in which "MDCLX" has been erroneously set down for MDCLXI :—

Æternæ memoriæ sacrum D. GEORGII OGILVIE de Barras, Equitis Baroneti, qui Arci Dunotriensi præfectus strenue eam per aliquod tempus adversus parricidarum Anglorum copias tutatus, eam tandem dedere est coactus. Non ante tamen quam ipsius conjugisque suæ D. ELIZABETHÆ DOUGLASSIÆ opera Imperii Scotici Iusignia, Corona, sciz: Sceptrum et Gladius, ibi reposita, clam inde avecta atque in hac Kinneffi æde sacra in tuto essent collocata. Ob egregia hæc viri in Patriam merita constantemque et illibatam in Regiam Familiam fidem Equitis Baroneti honorem per literas patentes III. Non : Mart: anno MDCLX. a Rege datas, est consecutus : auctis ejus Paternis Insignibus gentilibus quibus in hunc usque diem familia sua utitur. Regio porro diplomate Magno Scotiæ Sigillo munito ei concessum est terrarum suarum possidendarum jus a tenura quam vulgo Wardam Simplicem appellant, in Albam quæ dicitur tenuram commutaretur. In utroque hoc instrumento Regio summa ejus in principes suos fidelitas atque egregia merita maximo cum eulogio commemorabantur. DAVID OGILVIE, Eques Baronetus, supra dicti pronepos obiit Non : Decem : MDCCXCIX. annos natus LXX. Domina OGILVIE hujus conjux obiit XIV. Kal : Ian : anno MDCCC. annos nata LIII. Ambo in hac æde sepulti.

[Sacred to the memory of Sir GEORGE OGILVIE of Barras, knight baronet, who, being in command of the Castle of Dunottar, vigorously defended it for some time against the forces of the English parricides, but was at length compelled to surrender it. Not, however, until, with the assistance of his wife, Dame ELIZABETH DOUGLAS, he had secretly renoved from it the Scottish Regalia, viz., the Crown, Sceptre, and Sword, and had them deposited and placed in safety in this church of Kinneff. For these distinguished services to his country, and for his firm and untainted fidelity to the Royal Family, he obtained the rank and title of Knight Baronet, by letters patent, granted by the King, 5th March 1660; the family arms, which his descendants still use, being added to those of his forefathers. Moreover, by a Royal diploma, under the Great Seal of Scotland, he was allowed to change the tenure by which he held his lands from that of Ward to Bleuch. In both of these Royal documents, his unwavering fidelity to his Sovereign, and his eminent services were mentioned with the highest praise. DAVID OGILVIE, knight baronet, great-grandson of the above-mentioned, died 5 Dec. 1799, aged 70 years. Lady OGILVIE, his wife, died 20 Dec. 1800, aged 53 years. Both are buried in this church.]

—Governor Ogilvie's lady was a daughter of Douglas of Barras, 4th son of the 9th Earl of Angus. She was married to Ogilvie in 1634, by whom she had an only son. In consequence of the harsh treatment which she received from the usurpers, she did not long survive the surrender of Dunottar Castle; but with a nobleness of heart characteristic of her race, she enjoined her husband when on her death-bed rather to suffer death than betray his country, a request which, under much suffering, he firmly maintained. Governor Ogilvy was the son of the laird of Lumgair (v. p. 48), and bought the property of Barras from his brother-in-law, Sir John Douglas. Barras was bought by the Trustees of Donaldson's Hospital, Edinburgh; and the male line of Ogilvie of Barras failed in the person of Sir GEORGE, the 4th baronet, who died in 1837. (v. STRACATHRO.)

A mutilated tombstone, in the north wall of the church, upon which are the initials M. I. G ; C. F., thus eulogises the share which Mr GRANGER and his wife, CHRISTIAN FLETCHER, had in saving the honours of the kingdom :—

    Scotia GRANGERI cui Insignia Regia debet
    Servata hic cineres relliquieq' jacent.
    Abstulit obsesso pœno hæc captiva Dunotro,
    Condidit et sacra qva tvmvlator hvmo.
    Prœmia dant superi ; patrii servator honoris
    Sceptra rotat superos inter athleta chor . .

[Here lie the remains of GRANGER, to whom Scotland is indebted for the preservation of her Royal Insignia. These, when on the very eve of capture, he removed from Dunotter during the siege, and concealed in the sacred ground in which he is interred. He enjoys his reward above ; the heroic preserver of his country's honour now wields a sceptre amid the celestial choirs.]

—Mrs Granger survived her husband, and was afterwards married to a neighbouring laird, named Abercrombie. The Presbytery Records of Brechin show that Mr Granger was licensed before 19th September 1639, and that on 10th October thereafter he was a "preacher in Montrose," where he "is ordained with his own consent, to keep the presbyterial meetings once in three weeks at least, vnder paine of censure." On 3d Sep. 1640, he was still a "preacher in Montrose," and of that date he desired the Presbytery's "testimonial of his lyff and qualificatione for the ministerie directed to the presbyterie of the Meirns, q^{lk} was granted." It was about this time that Mr Granger became minister of Kinneff, where he died in 1663. He was succeeded by Mr James Honyman, to whom and his family a tablet on the right of the pulpit is thus inscribed:—

In memory of Mr JAMES HONYMAN, brother of Andrew, Bishop of Orkney, and Robert, Archdean of St Andrews, who was settled minister of this parish of Kinneff, 30th Sept. 1663, and died 2d May 1693, and is here interred. And of Mr ANDREW HONYMAN, his eldest son, who succeeded in the charge, and died 30th Dec. 1732 ; and, together with his wife, HELEN RAIT, of the family of Finlawston, is here interred. (His youngest brother, Mr James, was settled minister in New-port, Rhode Island, and left a family, one of his sons being lately Attorney-General there). And of Mr JAMES HONYMAN, his eldest son, and successor in this charge, who died 16th Jan. 1780, aged 77 years, & is interred here, with his wife KATHERINE ALLARDYCE, daughter of Provost Allardyce in Aberdeen. And of Mr JAMES HONYMAN, his eldest son, who succeeded him in this charge, and died 5th Aug. 1781, aged 36 years, and is here interred. This monument is erected by Mr John, a dissenting clergyman in England, Dr Robert, a physician in Virginia, and Helen, the wife of Robert Edward in Harvieston, brothers & sister of the last deceased.

—The first Mr Honyman, who died in 1693, appears to have left a young family ; and his son, Andrew, was not licensed until 16th Aug. 1700; on which day Mr James Fleming, presentee to the church of Kinneff, complained to the Presbytery "that y^r is not a manse at Kinneff, and that the kirk y^{r}of is ruinous." It was on 20th July 1699, that the above Mr Andrew Honyman offered forcible resistance to having the kirk preached vacant, to which he himself "pretended" to have a call from the parishioners ; but having expressed sorrow for his conduct before the Presbytery, they agreed, in consideration of his "young brethren and sisters, of q^m he hath the charge," to give him the stipend and crop of the parish for the year 1699. He appears to have ultimately succeeded to the church ; and it is believed that his son, who died in 1780, wrote the popular song of "Ilie, bonnie lassie, blink over the burn." The Honymans belonged to St Andrews. The Bishop of Orkney was minister first of Ferry-Port-on-Craig, from which he was translated to, and became Archdeacon of St Andrews. He succeeded Bishop Sydserf in the See of Orkney ; and in 1668, while entering the coach of Archbishop Sharpe, at the head of Blackfriar's Wynd, Edinburgh, he received a shot in his arm from a poisoned bullet, which was intended for Sharpe, from the effects of which he never quite recovered. The shot was fired by a religious fanatic named Mitchell, who had taken part in the risings in the Pentland Hills.

Near the middle of a gravestone, built into the north wall, a death's head and the words MEMENTO

MORI are rudely carved. Also "DE LARGE," and the Graham arms, with a mullet or star of *three* points upon the chevron, which, as the inscription indicates, shows that the deceased was third son of Graham of Morphie. Round the margin of the stone is this motto :—

HOC . TVMVLO . CONDITVS . EST . VIR . PIVS . ET
GEROSVS . ROBERT' . GRAHAM' . DE . LARGIE . DOMINI
A . MORFE . FI.' . TERTI' . QVI . PIE . ET . SANCTE . IN
DOIO OBDORIIT . ANNO . CHRISTI . 1597 . ANNO
ÆTATIS . SVÆ . 37.

[Below the Graham arms] :—

Inventum est hoc monumentum reparanda hac æde A.D. MDCCCXXX.

[In this tomb is laid a pious and honourable man, ROBERT GRAHAM of Largie, third son to the laird of Morphie, who piously fell asleep in the Lord in the year of Christ 1597, in the 37th year of his age. This monument was discovered when the church was repaired in 1830.]

—The Grahams of Morphie (as shewn at p. 96) are now represented by Barron Graham, Esq., laird of Morphie, and Stone o' Morphie, &c.

Upon a monument, with the Young arms, &c. (*v.* p. 75), in the east wall of the church :—

Memoriæ JOANNIS YOUNG de Stank, vicecomitis de Kincardine, qui obijt quarto die Martij, anno 1750, aetatis 52, Gulielmus Young, M.D., filius, hoc marmor posuit.

[To the memory of JOHN YOUNG of Stank, sheriff of Kincardine, who died 4th March 1750, aged 52, his son William Young, M.D., erected this monument.]

—The Duke of Cumberland, when on his way to Culloden in 1746, was the guest of Mr Young at Stonehaven. " Stank," is now named *Bellfield.* Dr Young's grave, which is within an enclosure at the east end of the church, is marked by a monument erected by his sister MARY, which bears this inscription :—

In memory of WILLIAM YOUNG, M.D., of Fawsyde, who died 9 March 1850 ; and of his wife, MARY LOGIE, who died 18 Nov. 1838. Also of their only child JANE YOUNG, who died 2 March 1834

—Fawsyde passed by inheritance to the late Rev. Mr Torry Anderson. It now belongs to Dr Wm Nicol, H.E.I.C.S., late M.P. for Dover. He was born at Fawsyde, where he has erected a neat mansion-house and offices.

In early times (1361), it was acquired by Simon of Shaklock ; and was afterwards owned by Barclay of Mathers. In the year of the Revolution Mr Robert Napier was succeeded in Fawsyde and other lands by his son William. The property of Fawsyde, near Tranent, gave both name and title to a knightly race during the time of David II.

A table-shaped tombstone on south side of church, (which adjoins another almost illegible, relating to the same family), bears :—

Andreas Lindsay, tenens de Whisleberry, filius JOANNIS & nepos alij Joannis Lindsays, dict. prædij tenen., pronepos Jacobi Lindsay, tenen. de Brigend, & abnepos Rogeri Lindsay, tenen. de Barras, ab illustri et antiqua familia Lindseorum, primo de Glenesque, et postea de Edzel designat., orti, diversarum nobilium familiarum ancestorum, tribus ult. ment. apud Caterline sepultis, hoc posuit memoriæ dict. sui Patris, qui obijt 20 De. 1724, ætatis 57 ; JOANNÆ NAPIER, ejus Matris, quæ fatis concessit 30 No. 1743, ætatis 56 ; (sepultæ apud Bervy) ; CATHARINÆ CHRISTY, ejus uxoris, quæ decessit 25 Ap. 1743, ætatis 38 ; et CATHARINÆ LINDSAY, suæ filiæ, quæ obijt in pueritia. Obijt ille ANDREAS LINDSAY 2do Julii 1761, ætatis vero 57, hic, sepultus. Ejus liberi superstites fuere, Joannis (patris successor in Whisleberry), Hugo, (scriba in Aberdeen), Joanna (uxor Gulielmi Cruickshank, civis Aberdonensis), Helena et Anna (adhuc inuptæ) ; JACOBO, filio primogenito (apud Cork, in Hibernia, in Classe Regi mortuo), mense Februarii 1759, ætatis 30. JOANNES LINDSAY, qui patri successit in Whistleberry, obijt 14 Jul. 1809, an. æt. 74, et hujus uxor, CHRISTIAN WALKER, decessit 14 Aug. 1830, an. æt. 94. Ambo hic sepulti. ALEXANDER LINDSAY, horum filius tenens de Whistleberry, obiit 6 Nov. 1831, an. æt. 68 ; cujus filia natu maxima, MARGARET, innupta decessit 7 Nov. 1831, au. æt. 22. In hoc sepulchro una contumulati.

[Andrew Lindsay, tenant of Whistleberry (son of JOHN, and grandson of another John Lindsay, both tenants of the said farm), great-grandson of JAMES

LINDSAY, tenant in Brigend, and great-great-grandson of ROGER LINDSAY, tenant of Barras, descended of the illustrious and ancient family of the Lindsays, originally of Glenesque, afterwards of Edzell, from whom were descended many noble families, and who, with the two last-mentioned, are buried at Caterline, erected this to the memory of his said father, who died 20 Dec. 1724, aged 57 ; and to his mother, JOANNA NAPIER, (buried at Bervy), who died 30 November 1743, aged 56. CATHERINE CHRISTY, his wife, died 25 April 1743, aged 38 ; and his daughter, CATHERINE LINDSAY, died in childhood. The said ANDREW LINDSAY died 2 July 1761, aged 57, and is here buried. His surviving children were John (who succeeded his father in Whisleberry), Hugh (a writer in Aberdeen), Joanna (wife of Wm. Cruickshank, citizen of Aberdeen), Helen and Ann (still unmarried). JAMES, his eldest son (died in the Royal Navy, at Cork in Ireland), in the month of Feb. 1759, aged 30. JOHN LINDSAY, who succeeded his father in Whisleberry, died 14 July 1809, aged 74 ; and his wife, CHRISTIAN WALKER, died 14 Aug. 1830, aged 94 ; both are here buried. ALEXANDER LINDSAY, their son, tenant of Whistleberry, died 6 Nov. 1831, aged 68 ; and his eldest daughter, MARGARET, died unmarried, 7 Nov. 1831, aged 22 ; they are buried together in this tomb.]

—Descendants of the same family still tenant the farm of Whistleberry, which belongs, in property, to the Trustees of Viscount Keith who became, by purchase, about 1805 and 1810 respectively, a large heritor in the parish.

JOHN DAVIDSON, weaver, Crossgates, d. 1779, a. 33 :—

Come see the home for all ordained,
The quiet rest I have obtained;
No sorrows can bedim your eye,
When in the silent grave you lie.

CHARLES STEWART, a native of Galloway, was bred a gardener. He lived upwards of 40 years in this county, died with a respectable character, at Kinneff, 25 Augt. 1766, aged 67 years, and is buried here. This inscription by order of his second wife, Margaret Clark.

ISOBELLA DUNCAN, dr. to Ann Jamie, Johnshaven, d. 1820, a. 17 yrs. :—

Ly still, sweet maid, and take your rest,
God takes them first whom he loves best.

[On back of same stone] :—
A Brother lies interred here,
Two Fathers, and a Mother dear ;
In love they lived, in peace they died ;
Their lives were craved, but God denied.

In memory of the Buriall place of WILLIAM STRACHAN, son to William Strachan and Isobel Moer, who lived a workman in this parish, unmarried, useful, and respected in the neighbourhood, and died lamented at Kinneff, 20 March 1774, aged 62.

Caterline.

(? S. CATHERINE.)

THE kirk of *Katerin*, given to the Abbey of Arbroath, was confirmed to it by Turpin, bishop of Brechin, 1178-98.

Previously disjoined from Kinneff, Caterline was afterwards united to that parish. The church was declared vacant in 1699, at the same time as that of Kinneff, so that the parishes may then have been conjoined. In the following year the laird of Caterline applied for, and received from the Presbytery, a grant of the vacant stipend of Caterline, for the purpose of " repairing the ruinous church of that parish." The old kirk stood upon the highest point of the graveyard, where a slightly ornamented slab bears this incised inscription :—

TVMVLVS . METELLANE . LIVINGSTONE . SPONSÆ . QVONDAM . ROBERTI . DOVGLASII . A . BRIGFOORD . QVÆ . OBIIT . 13 . DIE . MENSIS . IVLII . ANNO . 1647 . ÆTATIS . SVÆ . 30.

[The grave of MADELINE LIVINGSTONE, spouse of Robert Douglas of Brigford, who died 13 July 1647, aged 30.]

—Douglasses (of the Glenbervy branch), were lairds of Barras ; and Ogilvy, the gallant defender of Dunottar Castle, as before seen, bought Barras from his brother-in-law, who was a Douglas. Possibly this inscription refers to the wife of a scion of Douglas of Barras. Mary, daughter and co-heiress of Robert Douglas of Bridgeford, was married in 1740 to John, Viscount Arbuthnott.

An adjoining slab bears:—

HIC . IACET . FŒMINA . HONORABILIS . ELIZABETA . FORBES . . . .

Upon an upright stone:—

Here lies an honest gentleman, ROGER LINDSAY, once in Barras, who died in the year of God 1619, aged 61, and his spouse ELIZABETH SIMPSON. JAMES LINDSAY, his son, in Brigend, died anno 1661, aged 52; and his spouse Margaret Innes, and his eldest son James Lindsay, and John Lindsay, his brother, who caused this stone to be laid on his two wives, MARGARET MOLISON, and AGNES MILL, or MILNE.

JAS. WATT, boatmaster, Covelin, d. 1765, a. 23 :—
A hopefull youth lies here enshrined,
Whose life threed's cut by death, confinde
In Golgotha his corps does rest,
Of heavenly joys his soul's possest.

Over the entrance to an enclosure near the south-west corner of the burial ground:—

To the memory of WILLIAM GRANT of Hillton, Esquire, formerly of Tulloch. He died 15 February 1781, aged 65 years. Vixit ut vivat.

—The property of Hilton now belongs to the heirs of the late Rev. PATRICK STEWART, who was minister of Kinneff from 1782 to his death in 1830. His mother was a Grant, and he was buried within the Hilton aisle; where, with other relatives, lie his sons, ALLAN, who succeeded him in the church of Kinneff, and WILLIAM, who was long sheriff-clerk of Kincardineshire.

The first of these Stewarts is said to have been one Duncan Allanach, who came from Strathdon, and changed his name to *Stewart*. He was farmer of Norham, in Corse, and acquired the estate of Carnaveron, in Alford, about the middle of the last century. His son and heir became farmer of Mondynes, in Fordoun; and was father of the above-named minister of Kinneff. *Peter* (as the minister was familiarly called), appears to have had more than an ordinary share of the force of character, mixed with the severity and harshness of manner, which were common in his time, to almost all classes of society. Upon one occasion, when a county gentleman, who had been previously employed in the Excise, took occasion, at a meeting in Stonehaven, to denounce the Commissioners of Supply for having sanctioned the making of a road in some part of Kincardineshire, he concluded his remarks by saying, that no man of common sense would either have proposed or sanctioned the making of the road; to which, it is told, *Peter* replied—" Aye, man! I believe I had a hand in the proposin' o' the road you're speakin' o'; an' I ken I sanction'd it; an' let me just tell you this, that I winna ha'e my common sense *gang'd* by you, or ony ane o' your coat!"

An awmbry, also the fragment of a coffin-slab, with incised cross and sword, are built into the wall on the left of the gateway. The gateway is dated 1817.

There was a kirk at KINGORNY (S. ——), ruins of which were visible some 60 years ago. Some say that it was to his paternal estate of Kingorny that the father of the celebrated Dr Arbuthnott retired, when he was expelled from the church of Arbuthnott at the Revolution, others say he went to Hallgreen.

There were several castles in Kinneff in old times. Whistleberry, of which very little remains, stood upon a cliff overlooking the sea; and that of Fiddes is still roofed, and used as a storehouse by the farmer. The Knights' Templars had an interest in Kinneff, as is still shown by a farm called The Temple.

An Episcopal church, dedicated to S. PHILIP, was erected in 1848, at a short distance to the eastward of Caterline burial ground, also a school and schoolhouse. These were raised chiefly through the exertions of the late incumbent, the Rev. Mr JAMES STEVENSON. He was a native of Brechin, died in 1868, and is buried in the cemetery which adjoins the Episcopal Church.

Monquhitter.

(S. ——).

THE parish of *Monwhcctcr* was formed out of that of Turriff in 1649, and received its name from the farm whereon the church was built.—(New Stat. Acct.)

Mr Adam Hay, a cadet of the Errol family, succeeded Mr Barclay, who was possibly the first minister of the parish. Mr Hay was inducted to the church of Monquhitter in 1678; and his initials, M. A. H., and the date of 1684, are upon a triangular-shaped stone at the manse. Mr Hay presented two communion cups of pure silver to the church, which are thus inscribed:—

The gift of the R^d. Mr ADAM HAY, late minr. of the church of Montwhitter. Obiit 15 April 1727.

—Two old pewter cups, marked, "Mqr. 1779," belong to the time of Mr Johnston. In 1868, additional communion vessels were gifted to the church of Monquhitter, by Messrs George and James Hepburn, of Bogside and Swanford.

A new and spacious parish church was erected a few years ago (outside the grave-yard), and the previous place of worship, built about 1764, was erased. The bell bears:—

I . E . EROL . PATRON . OF . MONQUHITTER .
F . KILGOUR . ABERDN . 1689.

A stone upon the old belfry bore "I. E. E. PATRON;" and two stones, with carvings of the Errol arms, are built into the manse garden walls. Another slab, built over the vestry door of the new church, is thus inscribed:—

The God of heauen wil prosper ws, therfor we his servants wil arise and bwild. Neh. 2, 20. And we wil not forsake the hovse of our God. 10, 39.

The above, which was preserved within the lately erased church, had probably been originally upon the one which, as shown by the annexed inscription, was erected by William Cuming of Auchry. His tomb, which formed part of the wall of the old church, is in good preservation, and in its original site. It bears the Cumin arms, (with a buckle between the garbs) and this inscription:—

Memoriæ viri optimi, GULIELMI COMING ab Achry et Pittuly, Elgini quondam consulis, qui ptochodochium quatuor inopum mercatorum ibidem mortificavit, ac postea templum hoc impensis suis hic condidit, ac 29 Octob. A. D. 1707, ætat. an. 74, pie obiit, monumentum hoc posuit uxor ejus dilectissima, Christiana Guthry. Observa integrum, et aspice rectum; finem illius viri esse pacem. Ps. 37, v. 37. Vive memor lethi; fugit hora.

[To the memory of an excellent man, WILLIAM COMING of Achry and Pittuly, late chief magistrate of Elgin, who there founded an almshouse for four decayed merchants, and afterwards built this church here at his own expense, and died piously, 29 Oct. 1707, at the age of 74. His beloved wife Christian Guthry erected this monument. Mark the perfect man, &c. Live mindful of death; time flies.]

—This William was the first Cuming of Auchry, at least in modern times. He claimed descent from the Altyre family (*v.* p. 10); and, on selling the property of Lochtervandich in Glenriunes, he bought that of Auchry, about 1670. He was three times married (according to Douglas); and his eldest son by Christian Guthry (daughter of Sir Henry Guthry of King Edward), succeeded to Pittuly, and the patronage of the hospital at Elgin. The Poll Book does not agree with Douglas, so far as relates to the names of Cuming's sons and the number of his family. Douglas mentions only a *John* by a first marriage, and a *George* by the third; but the Poll Book (1696) shows that, besides two sons, named WILLIAM and ROBERT, there were five daughters *in familia*, also a sister of "his ladyes," at Auchry. The property of Auchry was divided and sold about 1830 by the late Archibald Cuming; and the principal part of it was bought by James Lumsden, Esq. Before Auchry was bought by Provost Cuming, it belonged to the Urquharts. It was anciently a part of the earldom of Buchan, and came to the Hays of Errol after the forfeiture of the Cumins.

Upon a table-shaped stone:—

Sub hoc cippo requiescunt cineres sobrii justique

viri, PATRICII WILSON, quondam apud Molindinum de Auchry, qui deum pictate, vitam innoccutia, amicos officiis, proximos benefactis coluit ; moriens domum lachrymis, amicos luctu, proximos dolore cumulavit ; liberisque novem una ex uxore relictis, plurimum desideratus obiit tertio die Maii 1723, ætatis suæ quarto tertii supra decimum lustri, ac monumentum hoc posuit uxor ejus, Isabella Mackie. Hodie mihi, cras tibi.

[Under this stone rest the ashes of a sober and upright man, PATRICK WILSON, sometime in Milltown of Auchry, who shewed piety towards God, innocence in his life, prudence in his family, courtesy to his friends, and kindness to his neighbours, and whose death overwhelmed his family with affliction, his friends with grief, and his neighbours with sorrow. He died deeply regretted, leaving behind him nine children by one wife, on the 3d day of May 1723, in the 64th year of his age ; and his wife, Isabella Mackie, erected this monument. It is my turn to-day, it will be thine to-morrow.]

—In 1696, the above Patrick Wilson was "a merchant in Montwhiter," and gave up "his free stock to be 500 merks," at which period he had a daughter named Elspet, also a male and female servant.

A grave-stone, got in the foundations of the last church, bears this inscription round the margin :—

Heir lyes GEORGE PANTON, son to James Panton in Midlethird, vho departed this lyfe December the 11, 1673.

—Patrick Panton and his wife Margaret Fordyce, with their two daughters, occupied Middlethird in 1696 ; and of the same date, James Panton, in Hairmoss, was clerk and collector to the Poll-tax Commissioners.

Reader, llet a ston the tell That heir lyes the corps of THOMAS TENNANT, svntym in Tepercouan . . . who departed this life in Ivne 22, anno 1692. Here lyes the body of ISOBEL, lawfull daughter to James Teunant in Middlegullie. She died the . . .

—Tepercouan, which is probably a corruption of *Tober-Cowan*, may indicate the site of a well and old place of worship, dedicated to S. COWAN, or CONGAN. Tepercouan is situated within a mile of the village of New Byth, and Middlegullie was a place near the Garmond.

The following is dateless, but about 1780 :—

To keep in memory the burying place of the family of JAMES FAITH, part of whom lies under, and on each side of this stone :—

Reader, where I am yow will soon be. Are you young, healthy, and prosperous? So was I ; but Death seized me, and I am gone to my place. If I have lived in the fear of God, and goodwill to man, think of my happyness ; but if I have done evil—BEWARE.

Upon a table-shaped tombstone :—

Erected by Francis Garden-Campbell, Esq. of Troup and Glenlyon, to the memory of ALEXANDER GARDEN, natural son of Col. Garden of Johnston ; and ROBERT GORDON, son of James Gordon in Newbyth. ALEXANDER GARDEN was drowned in the Canals of Auchry, 2 July 1806, by adventuring out of his depth ; ROBERT GORDON gallantly strove to save his life, and shared the same fate. Reader, take warning from the awful fate of these two youths ! Shun unavailing danger ; Be ever prepared for Death.

Near to the above.—

As a Wife, Ann Towie bewails the death of her loving and beloved husband, JOHN GARVOCK, cut off in the prime of life from his infant family ; as a Mother, she bewails the death of all her pleasant children, cut off in the bloom of youth, when becoming the comfort of her declining years. But amidst the ruin of her temporal prospects, she has been enabled to resign herself to the will of heaven, and to rejoice in hope of that happy rest where friends united in God shall part no more. JOHN GARVOCK died in 1771, JEAN in 1789 ; ANN and JOHN GARVOCK, junior, were buried in the same grave, April 25, 1790.

WM. MANN, dyer, Walkmill, Auchry, d. 1802, a. 92 ; MARY CHASSER, his sp. d. 1803, a. 82 :—

Death is the Land of forgetfulness : persons and properties are soon forgot ; but the righteous shall be had in everlasting remembrance.

WM. BEATON's 7 chil. (Middlebill), all d. 1849 :—
   This little band in beauty bloom'd,
   One earthly home to cheer ;
   Death snatch'd the gems to deck his crown,
   And hid the casket here.

ALEX. JOHNSTON and BARBARA OGSTON lived in conjugal union 63 years, and both died in 1767 ;

same year died, aged 58, their son WILLIAM JOHNSTON, who was distinguished by industry, integrity, and benevolence. His wife, MARY BROWN, rests in the churchyard of Longside. Their son ALEX. JOHNSTON, A.M., who was minister of this parish for 54 years, died 1 Feb. 1829, aged 84.

—Mr J. wrote valuable notices of the parish for Sir John Sinclair's Stat. Acct. of Scotland, vols. vi. p. 121; xxi. p. 138. Near the above:—

Rev. HUGH GORDON was minister of this parish from 1829 to 1843, and minister of the Free Church of Monquhitter from 1843 until his death in June 1866.

—Mr Gordon was a son of the minister of Anwoth, and a fellow-student at Edinburgh with the celebrated Edward Irving. He was tutor to the present Earl of Fife and his brother, by which means (the living being in the gift of the Fife family), he acquired the parish church of Monquhitter, which he left at the Disruption. Upon a marble slab:—

Rev. JAMES SMITH, A.M., died 20 Feb. 1853, in the 53d year of his age and 10th of his ministry. Erected by his congregation and friends in the parish.

—Mr Smith, whose father was gardener at Cairness, in Lonmay, began life as a teacher at Tyrie; and, prior to becoming minister of Monquhitter, he was rector of Banff Academy.

The *Village of Cuminestown*, founded in 1763, had its name from Joseph Cuming of Auchry. It has a considerable population; and apart from the Established Church, it contains an Episcopal Church (S. LUKE's), also a Free Church.

There is little to interest lovers of antiquity in Monquhitter, apart from the points mentioned in the Statistical Accounts. But some notice of the CONS, or CONES of Auchry (anciently *Fintray*), may be acceptable to the reader. They were a Roman Catholic family; and the first of them, according to tradition, was an operative mason, who built the Castles of Dalgety and Craigstone. It is further averred that he got the lands of Little Auchry from Hay of Dalgety, upon which he erected a fort, called *Red Castle*

(doubtless so named from the colour of the stone) to defend himself from the incursions of his neighbour, Mowat of Balquholly. But it is added that one day, while looking at Mowat fishing in the burn of Idoch, the latter, unperceived, raised his gun and shot Con while standing in the door of his own castle!

It is certain that Cons were designed of Auchry before 1539. In the year 1564 the Gordons of Shoves and Gycht, along with others, were charged with "the hurting and wounding" of "Maister William Con of Auchry in diuerse pairtis of his body, to the greit effusioune of his blude," also with "striking and dinging with brydill" three of "his cotteries," &c. William Con, who possibly died about 1580, was succeeded in that year by a son, Patrick, in the third part of the town and lands of Rothibirsbane, in Fyvie. In an action which was raised by Forbes of Ludquharn, in 1596, against certain persons for forcibly entering his house and taking away his "haill insycht plencssing and writtis," and fearing, in consequence of the superior status and influence of his opponents, that he might get but scrimp justice, Forbes informed the King that the laird of Balquhain, lieutenant-depute of the north, "is sister and brethir bairn" to Patrick Con of Auchry, "ane of the cheif committeris of the crymis." Three years afterwards the same laird of Auchry was chancellor of a jury at Edinburgh which convicted a poor Aberdeen woman for being connected with a petty theft, for which she was sentenced "to be tane to the North Loch of Edinburghe, and thair DROWNIT quhill scho be deid"!

This laird of Auchry, who served under Lord Errol at the battle of Glenlivet, appears to have been the father of the learned GEORGE CON, or CONAEUS, the Pope's agent at the Court of the Queen of Charles I. It is said that but for his unexpected death Con would have been made a Cardinal. He died 10 Jan. 1640, and was buried in the church of San Lorenzo in Damaso, at Rome, where an inscription upon his tomb sets forth his services to the Church, and his lineage. His mother's name is there given as Isabella Cheyne; but upon the under-mentioned fragment at Auchry, the initial is *M.* ALEXANDER CON, another member of this family, was a celebrated Jesuit. He wrote (1668) against the Rev. Mr Menzies of Aberdeen the famous pamphlet of "Scolding no Scholarship," &c.

The Cons appear to have been among those who suffered after the fall of King Charles I., about which time they disappear from the district. One of them went to Paris, where (from a letter which he sent to the Earl of Errol in 1690, begging "the litle anuel rent" to be remitted to him which was yearly due from his lordship's estate) he appears to have been in destitute circumstances. It is said that descendants of Con now hold high positions in Spain.

No record of the Cons is to be seen in the church-yard. Some time-worn carvings at "the Castle" are the only existing traces of them. One of these may have been a portion of the altar of their family chapel. Upon it is a rude, but spirited representation of the sacred monogram, I.H.S., with some ornamental work—apparently a dove on the left, and a cock on the right, together with the national emblem of the (?) thistle. A second stone presents the initials "P. C. 16-1." A third, built into the gable of the farm-house, initialed P. C: M. C. (Patrick Con, and M. Cheyne), is adorned with armorial bearings (party pale, an engrailed fess between two crescents in chief and a buckle in base, for Con; quarterly, first and fourth, *three* crosses patee fitched, second and third, three leaves (?), for Cheyne and Marshall of Esslemont), and this legend—

CONSTANT AND KYND.

~~~~~~~~~~~~~~~~~~~~~~~

Inverurie.

(S. APOLLINARIS, BISHOP.)

THE church of *Inveruryn*, a vicarage in the diocese of Aberdeen, was given by David, Earl of Huntingdon, Lord of the Garioch, along with other churches in the same district, to his monastery of Lindores.

The old kirk stood in the burial-ground, south-east of the town, near to where the Urie joins the Don. The walls of the church were demolished about the beginning of the present century, and the kirk-yard dykes built with the stones.

It was in 1775 that the old kirk by the riverside became disused as a place of worship. The one which was then built at a more suitable spot, was taken down, and the present edifice erected on same site, about 1841-2. The bell, re-cast in 1845, bears merely the word, INVERURIE.

There are a number of tombstones in the burial-ground. One, "from inside wall of old church," exhibits the Innes and Elphinstone arms upon a shield, with seated angels for supporters. It has also a monogram, and this inscription:—

Heir lyis VALTER INNES in Artones, vha depairtit the 27 day of Ivnii 1616 zeiris; and MERIORIE ELPHINSTOVNE, his spovs, vha depairtit the 15 day of November 1622 zeiris.

Upon a table-shaped stone:—

Hic mortalitatis posuit exuvias vir pius et probus, benignus, modestus, Revdus. Dom. GULS. WATT, qui in ecclesia de Inverurie rerum sacrarum sategit ab anno 1716, ad annum 1755. Theologus insignis, pastor fidelis et primaevorum aemulus, maritus amantissimus, paterque decem liberorum indulgentissimus, quorum octo hic quoque sepeliuntur, quod dictis recte docuit, factis exhibuit et exemplo suo confirmavit; annis tandem maturus animam placide Deo reddidit. Beati sunt mortui qui in Domino moriuntur.

[Here lie the mortal remains of a pious, virtuous, kind, and humble man, the Rev. Mr WILLIAM WATT, who was minister of the church of Inverurie from 1716 to 1755. An eminent theologian, a faithful pastor, a Christian of the primitive type, a most affectionate husband, and a most indulgent father of ten children, eight of whom are also buried here, the sound doctrine which he taught in words he exhibited in deeds, and confirmed by example; at length, at a ripe age, he calmly resigned his soul to God. Blessed are the dead, &c.]

Upon a headstone of Peterhead granite, within an enclosure:—

Sacred to the memory of the Revd. ROBERT FORBES, during 45 years one of the masters of the

Grammar School of Aberdeen, who died 13 March 1842, aged 80. MARY LANGLANDS, his wife, died 15 March, same year, aged 70. [The deaths of two young sons and a daughter recorded.] The only surviving member of the family rears this monument in affectionate remembrance of departed worth.

—The erector of the above, the Rev. ROBERT FORBES of Woodside Church, died 21 Oct. 1859, in the 48th year of his age, and 23d of his ministry. JANE HARVEY, his wife, died 25 Dec. 1855. Their names and those of some of their family are inscribed upon a flat stone.

Here lies . . . . . of ANNA SHIELS, lawful daughter to the deceast William Shiels, chirurgeon, who died May the 29, 1733, ...

In memory of JOSEPH MCGREGOR, teacher of Port Elphinstone School; born 1817, died 1861. By pupils and friends in testimony of respect.

WILLIAM LUNDIE, watchmaker, and first postmaster of Inverury, died Dec. 29, 1816, aged 73. ELIZABETH ROBERTSON, his wife, died 12 April 1856, aged 78.

In memory of JOHN STEPHEN, sometime portioner and baillie of Inverury, and officer of customs at Peterhead, where he died 1785. ANN LEITH, his spouse, died 1797.

A granite monument, highly honourable to the erectors of it, thus commemorates the sudden death, and marks the burial place of a stranger :—

To the memory of WILLIAM BUCHAN, commercial traveller, Leith, who was suddenly taken ill whilst attending divine service in St Mary's Chapel, Inverurie, on Sunday 2 Oct. 1864, and died the same evening of apoplexy, aged 33 years. This stone is erected by a number of his friends and fellow travellers, in remembrance of his personal worth, and the respect in which he was held by them.

Within a railed enclosure :—

Sacred to the memory of JAMES ANDERSON, depute-clerk of Justiciary, who died at Edinburgh, 2 Jan. 1833, aged 66. By his own unaided merit he raised himself to a situation of great trust and responsibility, which, for the long period of 45 years he filled with the greatest credit, and concluded a life spent in the public service, regretted by all who knew him. Also MARGARET ANDERSON, his sister, who died at Edinburgh, 2 June 1850, aged 80.

—Mr A.'s father was a merchant in, and chamberlain of, the burgh of Inverurie. He died in 1801, aged 8- ; and his wife, ELSPET SHAND, died in 180-, aged 71.

HELEN BRUCE, d. ——, a. 28 years :—
O, painted piece of living clay ;
Man be not proud of thy short day ;
For like a lily fresh and green,
She was cut down, and no more seen.

Erected in memory of the Rev. WILLIAM FORBES, for many years schoolmaster of Fintray, who was born in London in 1793, and died at Aberdeen, 28 Feb. 1838, aged 45.

Rev. WILLIAM DAVIDSON, admitted minister of Inverury, 6 Sep. 1769, died 17 January 1799, aged 69. His wife JEAN BRUCE, eldest daughter of Baillie Robert Bruce of Kintore, died 5 May 1821, aged 72.

Rev. ROBERT LESSEL, minister of this parish, died 29 July 1853, aged 96, and in the 53d year of his ministry. MARY MORRISON, his widow, daughter of William Morrison, farmer, Little Colp Turriff . . . . . .

—The death of two daughters are recorded, also that of WILLIAM MORRISON, who died in 1842, aged 81 ; and JANET, widow of Francis WILSON, sister of Mr Lessel, who died in 1833, aged 90. Before being minister of Inverurie, Mr Lessel was schoolmaster at Chapel of Garioch.

In the foundations of the kirk, four interesting fragments of sculptured stones were found, which are carefully preserved within the burial-place. According to old Annalists, the bones of a Pictish king, called Aodh, or Eth, of the Swift Foot, were buried " in civitate Inrurin," A.D. 881, where he died from wounds received two months previously at the battle of Strathallan. But whether any of these monuments had marked his grave, or those of other chieftains of the period, is uncertain, although by no means improbable. Contrary to the above statement, however, the Pictish Chronicle says that Aodh was *slain* at Nurim in Strathallan, instead of " wounded " by Grig or

Grigory, who was one of the most celebrated of the Pictish rulers. Grig is supposed to have dwelt for some time among the Picts in the Mearns, and to have founded the church of St Cyrus, which stood by the sea-shore. (v. p. 35.)

The carved stones, stone circles, and other objects of antiquity which have now and again been found in the locality, (described in the Sculptured Stone volumes, in the Proceedings of the Society of Antiquaries, and in the Statistical Accounts, &c.), show Inverurie to be a place of high antiquity.

The well-known mound, called *The Bass*, near the junction of the Urie and the Don, and the Coning Hillock near the manse, are apparently alluvial deposits, of which there are other, though less remarkable examples, in the district.

It is just possible, although record and tradition are alike silent upon the point, that The Bass had been at first chosen as a place of abode by some devotee, or disciple of S. APOLLINARIS; and there subsequently, in all probability, stood the fort, surrounded by the original town of Inverurie, in which King Eth is recorded to have died. The Bass is believed to have been also the site of the royal castle of Inverurie, of which Norman, son of Malcolm, was constable in 1180. This mound has been always looked upon as a place of great strength; and, according to local rhyme, it will only cease to exist when something like a second Deluge takes place:—

"When Dee and Don shall run in one,
And Tweed shall run in Tay;
The water o' Inverurie
Will bear the Bass away."

The town of Inverurie has been long a royal burgh; and a portion of the market cross, built into the garden wall of the hotel, is dated 1671. S. POLLINAR'S Fair, held in July, and that of Latter LADY Day in Sept., were named, the first from the tutelar Saint (whose chapel is said to have stood near Manar, of old Badifurrow), and the second possibly from an altarage to Our Lady which may have been within the old church.

A writer of 1724 says, that "the town of Inverurie has ane long street, lying from north-west to south-east along the water of Urie . . . . [and] no publick buildings save a church and tollbooth." Matters are very different now-a-days. A handsome town-hall, &c., were erected some years ago; and since the opening of the Great North of Scotland Railway several new streets have been made out, and a number of neat dwelling houses, shops, and bank-offices erected. Besides the Established, there are Free, Episcopal, and Methodist Churches in the town: the last named is a chaste granite structure, with belfry, &c.

It was to Aquhorties, in this parish, that, in 1799, the Roman Catholic seminary was transferred from Scalan in Glenlivet; but in thirty years afterwards it was finally removed to Blairs. (v. p. 115.) The Roman Catholic place of worship at Inverurie (the Church of the Immaculate Conception), opened 1852, is a neat building.

The Don is crossed by a strong stone bridge of three arches, built in 1791, at a cost of about £2000. Bridges cross the Urie in several parts of the parish, all of which are of later erection than that over the Don.

Glamis.

(S. FERGUS, BISHOP AND CONFESSOR.)

THE church of *Glampnes* was granted by William the Lion to the Abbey of Arbroath. It was a vicarage of St Andrews, and dedicated by Bishop David in 1242. It is said that S. FERGUS, who lived in the 6th century, died at Glamis, and was buried there.

The burial aisle of the Earls of Strathmore, which formed, in old times, the south transept of the church, is in the Second Pointed style of architecture, with stone roof, groins, and an awmbry. The bosses bear the Lyon and Ogilvy arms, &c. The floor is covered with stone flags, two of which are old tombstones. One of these, upon which a chalice and cross may be traced, possibly relates to a priest: it bears the words:—

hic . iacet . ōns . bilelm̄s . cl . . .

Upon another slab, is the name, &c., of the lady of the third Lord of Glamis, who was a daughter of the house of Dudhope :—

..... elizab . scrimgeour ..... apritis . an ...... m⁰ . cccc . nonages ...

—Round the margin of a plain, altar-shaped tomb :—

patricus . lyon . quoba . dns . de . glamis . miles . qui . obijt . xxj . d . mesis . marcij . an . dni . m⁰ . cccc . lix⁰ . . . . . hic . cu . isobella . ogilug . sposa . et . q . obijt . xii . d . ianbarij . ano . dni . m⁰ . cccc . lxxxiiij . orate . pro . aniab' . œl . . .

[Here rest Sir PATRICK LYON, lord of Glamis, who died 21 March 1459 ; and ISOBELLA OGILVY, his wife, who died 12 January 1484. Pray for their souls now in heaven.]

—The last named were the first Lord Glamis and his wife, a daughter of Ogilvy of Auchterhouse. Sir P. was created a peer before 1450, and his two eldest sons became respectively the 2d and 3d Lords Glamis. The latter (who married Elizabeth Scrimgeour) succeeded his brother about 1487, and founded a chapel at Glamis. He also obtained a charter (1491) making the town of Glamis a burgh of barony. He died in 1497. His eldest son succeeded to Glamis, and three other sons fell at Flodden. The first LYON of Glamis was Sir JOHN (son of Lyon of Forgaudenny and Forteviot), who married Princess Jane (2d daughter of Robert II. by Elizabeth Muir), by whom he acquired Glamis and other estates. Since then the family have been represented in the direct male line, and the present Earl is the 13th Lord Glamis. The Lyons, who are of French descent, came to England with William the Conqueror, and to Scotland, about the year 1100.

An enclosure, on the east side of the Strathmore vault, was erected by the late Mr Laing-Meason, of Lindertis, where one of his children is buried ; but there is no monument. A triangular-shaped stone, built into the west dyke of church-yard, dated 1672, presents nicely carved armorial bearings, &c., and the names of ALEXR. NISBET: HELLEN WOOD.

The date of 1792 is upon the present church, which refers to the time of its being built.

Another date (1603), upon the east gable, is said to be part of an old tombstone. The bell bears :—

THE REV. JAMES LYON, MINISTER.
CHURCH OF GLAMIS, 1804.

A marble tablet within the church records the death of 4 sons and 6 daughters of Dr Lyon, together with the following notices of himself and his wife :—

To the memory of the Rev. JAMES LYON, D.D., who died 3 April 1838, in the 80th year of his age, and 58th of his ministry in the parish of Glamis. Also of AGNES L'AMY, his sponse, who departed this life 14 Sep. 1840, aged 78 years.

—Dr Lyon was come of a race of clergymen, his great-grandfather having been minister at Tannadice, his grandfather at Airlie, and his own father at Longforgan. They were remotely connected with the Strathmore family ; and one of the ministers, whose standard book for texts was the Psalms, was laird of the estate of Ogle. It is told that, while remonstrating on one occasion with a son for want of economy in his habits, the youth silenced the old man by quaintly retorting —" There's nae fear o's, father, as lang as the hills o' Ogle an' the Psalms o' Dauvid last !" Dr Lyon's wife was a sister of the late James L'Amy of Dunkenny, long sheriff-depute of Forfarshire ; and both she and Dr Lyon were buried in the churchyard. Near same place, upon a plain headstone, is this inscription :—

Sacred to the memory of the Rev. Principal Playfair's daughter MARGARET, who departed this life Aug. 1810, aged 35 years.

—Principal Playfair, a native of Bendochy, was minister, first of Newtyle, next of Meigle. He married a sister of Dr Lyon, in whose house Miss P. died. The Principal was the author of several chronological and geographical works. He had a large family : one of them was Lieut.-Colonel Sir Hew-Lyon Playfair, long provost of St Andrews, to the improvement of which venerable city he contributed so much ; another was George, Inspector-General of Hospitals, Bengal, father of Lyon Playfair, C.B., &c., M.P. for the Universities of Edinburgh and St Andrews.

Upon a flat tombstone :—

Heir lyis PATRIK PHILP, qvha depairtit this lyf in May . . day, the z. of God 1637, and of his aige 62. Chryst boith in lyf and death is my greatest advantag. PATRIK PHILP, hvsband to Isobel Vright.

Possibly the true age, in the following inscription, is 81 ; and the 4 figure at the end of 81 may be meant as a substitute for the reversed figure in the date :—

Heir lyis ALEXANDER CATHROV, vha depairtit this lyf in Ivli 24, in anno 16f3, and of his aig 814.

The following, beautifully carved in raised and ornamental letters, is upon a flat stone :—

Hier lyis THOMAS TAILYOUR, and his vif AGNIS PHILP, somtym in Haystovn, with ther children. He died the 18 of Feb. 1649, his age 60. She died the 26 of Febr. 1663, and of age 57.

Heir lyis AGNES VOLVM, spovs to Williame Lyon, in Clippithils, vha depairted 1 of May 1650, her age vas 62 yoirs.

—" Clippithils" is now called Mossend of Glamis.

Heir lyis HELEN and CATHRIN LYKE, who depairted the yeir of God, 1650.

Her lyes WILIAM ADAM, in the Meltown of the Glean, who departed from this lif wpon the 28 day of Apryl 1684, and his age 57.

—" The Glean" above referred to, is the Glen of Ogilvy. According to Monipennie's Summarie of the Scots Chronicle, there was a castle there called Glen. During the Civil Wars the property of Glen appears to have belonged to a Lady Carnegie, to whom General Monck, while employed at the seige of the town of Dundee, granted a protection in favour of herself, and her tenants, &c. I am not aware to what branch of the Carnegies this lady belonged. Neither her name nor her connection with the Glen, is mentioned in Lord Southesk's History of the Carnegies. The " protextion" (preserved in the Museum of Montrose, and here printed for the first time), is as follows :—

" Whereas the Lady Carniggee of the Glenn, in the parish of Glames, desires my protextion for her person, Childeren, seruants, horses, Catle, sheepe, their wifes Childeren, & seruants, with their horses & household goods, together with her tennants Catle sheepe & household goods, These are therefore to require all officers & souldiers vnder my comand, not to trouble the s^d Lady, her Childeren, seruants, horses, Catle, sheepe, & household goods, together with her tennants their wiues, Childeren, seruants, horses, Catle, sheepe, and household goods, but permitt them to follow their Lawfull occasions without mollestation, Provided, that the benefitt of this protextion, extend not to any which are in Armes, & that the sayd Ladie Carrniggie, her childeren, seruants, & tenant act nothing prejudiciall, to the Common Wealth of England. Given vnder my hand at the Seag^e of Dundee, the 20th of Aug: 1651.

"GEORGE MONCK.

" To all officers & Souldiers whome these may concerne."

Near last-quoted inscription :—

Erected by Patrick Mollison, late millar in Glen of Ogilvie, in memory of MERGARET FLEMING, his spouse, who died anno 1758, aged 30 :—

This stone is set to celebrate
This worthy woman's praise ;
Whose equal you will hardly find
For candour now-a-days.
She sober, grave, and virtuous was,
Belov'd by all around ;
She lived in the fear of God,
Now is with glory crown'd.

The following acrostic, dated 1680, is upon a stone to the memory of JAMES BRUCE, who had been a retainer of the noble family of Glamis :—

I am nou interd beneath this ston,
Ah Death's propitious to non ;
My name was JAMES, my surname BRVCE,
Exasperat against each abuse ;
Sure sanctity my life decord,
Bent to obey my Noble Lord.
Rest, O my soul, in sacred peace,
W . . . as from sin I find releace.
C . . . . read and prais,
Each providential act thou seas.

Heir lyes IANET LANGLANDS, spous to Iohn Blair in . . . . who . . . the . . . of Ivlie '91, and her age 77. Heir lyes IOHN BLAIR, weaver in Blakhill, who departed the 9 of October '93, and his age 75.—I was alyve, bvt now am dead, &c.

Heir lyis ALEXANDER THORNTON and HELEN BALDIRNY, his spovs. They depairted 1652, he in Ianvar 22, his age vas 60 ; she in Decemb. and vas 70 yeirs.

Heir lyes IOHN BLEAR in the Thorntoun, and his spous AGNES MVRR . . He departed this lyfe vpon the 22 day of Nouember 1687, and of his age 53 ; and she departed this lyfe vpon the 12 day of Nouember 1689, and her age 52.

Heir lyes MARGARIT WILKIE, spouse to Andrew Fairneather at the Barnss of Glamiss, who died vpon the 2 of May 1688, and her age 23 years . . .
  Return to thy rest, O my Soul, &c.

—The Barns of Glamis stood within the Castle Park. The next epitaph is upon a flat stone :—

  Dear pilgrims, read this elegy,
  And spritualiz mortality ;
  Vice I doclin'd, my lyfe was just,
  In tillage I betrayed not trust.
  DAVID by name, surnamed KID ;
  Kind to the poor, now dignified
  In blissed state, triumphant by,
  Death's sting pluckt out, sin's sourse is dry.
  Eternal praise to Christ my king,
  Lord of all lords, who makes me sing,
  Delytfull songs with angels bright,
  Enjoying day that's voyd of night ;
  Read gravely, pilgrim, mind thy doome—
  God raps me up from ill to come.
  D. K. [David Kid] E. G. [Elder, Glamis].

WM. CRUICKSHANK, tailor, d. 1731, a. 61 :—
  Rare WILLIAM, who will not thy name
  And memory still love ;
  Since you the Trade did all around,
  So wond'rously improve.
  Our Tradesmen justly did to thee
  Pre-eminence allow,
  Being taught the rudiments of Art,
  Or else refin'd by you.
  That skill of yours did on them all
  An ornament reflect,
  And as you liv'd so did you die,
  In honour and respect.

JOHN BUDWORTH, d. 1718, a. 30 :—
  Here lyes JOHN BUDWORTH, English born,
  Whose life these virtues did adorn—
  He was both curteous, kynd and just,
  A friend whom on might firmly trust ;
  With other gifts both rare and fyne,
  Tho' lodged but in a crazy shrine,
  Death smot the pott, thus sadly rent
  And here to ly, the shells has sent.

Upon a head stone, embellished with " the hammer and the *royal crown*," &c. :—
  O, dear JOHN DALGETY ! who can
  Thy praises all express ?
  A most expert artificer
  In iron and in brass.
  Discreet was't thou to ev'ry one,
  Obliging, just, and kind ;
  And still [thy] tongue ingenuous spoke
  The language of thy mind.
  Such was thy life, that now we hop
  Thy soul above doth shine ;
  For thy skill, we dedicate,
  This Crown as justly thine.

January 28, 1728 : Erected by Agnes Hood in memory of her husband, JOHN DALGETY, hammerman, Glamis, who died 1727, aged 41.

A table-shaped stone (of 17th century), is similarly embellished as the above ; but as the dates, &c., have never been cut upon it, the stone had possibly been erected in the lifetime of the parties named :—
Hier lyes WILLIAM LOV, sometymes hamer man and indweller in Glamis, vho departed this life the — of — his age — years ; also heir lays CRISTIAN BVRN, his spovs, a good and vertvos, frvitfvl vif, vho died the — of — of age — years.

ANDREW STEVEN's wife (1741) :—
  Lo, here lies one who never did
  An injury to man ;
  Of whom we cannot say enough,
  Let us say what we can :—
  Her actions all were genuine,
  Her words without disguise ;
  Kind was her heart, her generous hands
  Could not the poor despise.
  She liv'd at home, and walk'd abroad,
  Still like a harmless dove,
  Till death . . . .

JAS. RHYND, a. 1 y. 5 mo., d. 1734 :—
  Here lies a sweet and loving child,
  Ah, cover'd o'er with mud ;
  Resembling well the lillie fair,
  Cropt in the very bud.

But blessed is that happy babe,
That doth thus early die ;
Not pleas'd to dwell with sinners here,
But with the saints on high.
This charming child but just did peep
Into this world, and then,
Not liking it, he fell asleep,
And hasten'd out again.

AGNES LOW, wf. of Jas. Badenach, d. 1755, a. 58 :—
Good, sober, pious, frugal, chaste,
She wade through trouble, till at last,
The ghastly tyrant struck the blow,
And laid her bones this stone below.

HELEN GWTHRIE, spouse to And. Fyfe, brewer, Glamis, d. April 3, 17—, a. 55 :—
Below this monument, a jewel
Of womankind doth ly ;
Who night and day was exercis'd
In acts of piety.
No neighbour, mother, nor a spouse,
More worthy was : Her aim
Was to speak truth, and that her word
Should always be the same.
She long'd to leave this sinful earth,
And this poor frail abode ;
Her home was heaven, where now she sings
The praises of her God.

Upon a lying stone :—
Erected to perpetuate the memory of JAMES CHALMERS, musician to the noble family of Strathmore, who dyed March 3, 1770 :—
When minstrels from each place around,
To meetings did repair ;
This man was still distinguished
By a refined air.
His powerful and his charming notes
So sweetly did constrain,
That to resist, and not to dance
Was labour all in vain.
He played with such dexterity,
By all it is confest,
That in this grave interred is
Of Violists the best.

Here lyes ane vertuous woman called LANET SMITH, spouse to Iohne Watt in Dunkennie, who depairted this life upon the 18 day of May 1777, and of hir age 73.

A box-shaped stone bears :—

JAMES HORN, Bridge End, Glamis, d. 1773, a. 57; and his wife KATHERINE SHEPHERD, d. 1793, a. 86; both "were distinguished in their time for being very liberal to the poor."

Upon a slab of white marble, inserted into the outer and west side of the Glamis family aisle :—
Sacred to the memory of ESTHER HAMILTON, wife of Patrick Proctor, factor for the Earl of Strathmore, who died 28 June 1802, aged 54 years.

An adjoining slab of granite, tastefully set in sandstone, bears :—
Erected by Esther Proctor Alexander, in memory of her father PATRICK PROCTOR, who died here in July 1819, aged 75 years, during 50 of which he was Factor on the Glamis Estate. And of her brothers, JOHN, farmer, Mains of Glamis ; ROBERT, W.S. Edinburgh ; GEORGE, Bengal Medical Staff ; THOMAS, Bombay Army ; WILLIAM-DAVID, who died here, 3d December 1860, aged 74 years, during 40 of which he also was Factor on the Glamis Estate. DAVID, H.E.I.C. Home Service ; PATRICK, Royal Navy ; and of her sister, JANE, who died at St Andrews, 18th April 1865.

—The erector of the above tombstone was wife of the late Dr Andrew Alexander, professor of Greek at St Andrews. It will be seen that her father (who came from Morayshire, and was a son of the sheriff-substitute of that county), and her brother held the factorship of the Glamis estates for the long period of 90 years. Another tablet bears the names of CHRISTOPHER PROCTOR, and his wife ANNABELLA NEWALL, who died respectively in 1850, and 1847.

Upon an adjoining granite headstone :—
Sacred to the memory of WILLIAM HENDERSON, Esq., late of Rochelhill, who died 2 Sept. 1860, aged 44. This stone has been erected as a tribute of respect by his relict Helen Chrystal Henderson.

—The property of Rochelhill (which was long a separate estate), was bought by the late Earl of Strathmore, and now forms part of the fine property of Glamis.

The oldest existing remains of " our ancient forefathers" at Glamis are, probably, the sculptured stone monument of St Orland, at Cossins, the so-called King Malcolm's gravestone at the Manse door, and the still more remarkable example of the same interesting class of antiquities which stands in the wood on the Hunters' Hill, near the Plans of Thornton. These have all been engraved and their peculiarities described in the work referred to at p. 43.

The NINE MAIDEN Well was near the old dovecot within the castle park of Glamis, where, probably, stood a chapel which was inscribed to these holy sisters, who are said to have had their residence in the Glen of Ogilvy. According to Boece, the Glen of Ogilvy was also the place where King William the Lion's life was saved by his brother-in-law Gilchrist, after he had been stript of his dignity as Earl of Angus, in consequence of having murdered his wife for conjugal infidelity! It is further said that the Glen of Ogilvy belonged to the Celtic Earls of Angus, also that the surname of OGILVY (? *Ogail-bowie*, yellow (haired) youth), was assumed from that district.

The history of the Castle of Glamis, which is one of the best examples of the Scotch baronial style of architecture in the kingdom, is so well known that it need not be dwelt upon (*v.* Glamis: its History and Antiquities). It may, however, be briefly stated that Glamis Castle was a seat of Alex. III.; that in 1304, Edward I. gave "les Chasteux de Glames et de Morthelagh" (Murthil) to Cumin, Earl of Buchan; that the thanedom of Glamis was at one time given to Sir John of Logie, and that subsequently it was granted by Robt. II. to Sir John Lyon and his lady, Princess Jane. James V. resided at Glamis for sometime during the forfeiture of the estates; but the castle of his time was mostly erased by 9th Lord Glamis, who built the older part of the present house, which may be said to have been completed by his grandson, Earl John, about 1621. Since then, however, many alterations have been made upon it, the latest by the last and present Earls of Strathmore, the latter of whom has made out flower and kitchen gardens of great extent and beauty.

The family chapel within the castle was fitted up about 1688, and was one of the last consecrated for divine service before the disestablishment of Episcopacy. It is a peculiarly quaint and interesting place, adorned with curious paintings by De Witt. Long disused, it was restored and re-opened for occasional service by the present Earl of Strathmore; and on 21st Sept. 1869, the first confirmation was held in it by the Right Rev. the Bishop of Brechin which has taken place for at least 150 years.

It was the founder of this chapel who improved Glamis Castle so much; also Castle Huntly, in the Carse of Gowrie, to which he gave the name of *Castle Lyon*. He took an active part in the Civil Wars; and, in 1677, was created Earl of STRATHMORE. A few years after the latter event he went to France for some months, during which he had a particular account of his expenditure kept, a few items of which (here printed from the originals in the archives at Glamis) may be read with interest, as showing the cost of certain articles in Paris nearly 200 years ago, as well as the economy exercised by the nobility of those days, with whom, it would appear, the "translating" of their "cloaths" from one fashion to another, was not considered so much *infra dig.* as it might be by some now-a-days:—

Aug. 2, 1683: Given to my Lord goeing to see the fireworks, on Luc-dore and a croun, whereof there was a great part given for a window to see them, ... 14 0
  ffor a flamboe to light him home to the Academic, halfe a croune, 1 10
  ffor a pond of candle, ... 0 7
Aug. 15: ffor a par of shoes to my Lord, 3 10
  ,, 18: Payed for four dyets in a Scottsman's house, where my Lord useth to din sovmtims on fish days, ... 4 0
  ,, 19: ffor two fraish eggs to my Lord's breakfast, ... 0 4
Nov. 27: Translating my Lord's cloaths as near to the fashione as he could, and a suit of Liverio to the Frenshman, 204 livers, ... 7 0

Cossins, from which place a family took their surname, and was designed "of that ilk," is about a mile north-east from the Castle of Glamis. It belonged in property to a branch of the Lyon the first of whom was 2d son of the fifth Lord Glamis. A stone panel, over the front door of the present farm-house at Cossins is dated 1627. It also bears the names of Mr JOHN LYON and Mrs JEAN YOUNG, with the armorial bearings of both families, and the following inscription :—

Protegendam presidio Dei tradas salvtem, rem, sobolem, domvm, nec aedes vis propius tvas avt damna tangent ; Devs angelos cvstvdiae prneficit.

[Commit to the protection of God thy safety, thy substance, thy family, and thy house, and neither violence nor mischief shall come near thy dwelling, for God sets angels to guard it.]

Leochel.

(S. MARNAN, BISHOP.)

THE kirk of *Loghel*, or *Lochild*, was given to the Culdees of Monymusk, by Gilchrist, Earl of Mar, 1165-70, along with the tithes and half-davach of land upon which the church stood. Colin Durward granted additional privileges out of this district to the same convent about 1240, which were confirmed ten years later by Philip of Mon-Fitchet, or Muschet, and his wife Anna, daughter and heiress of Colin Durward.

The parishes of Leochel and Cushnie were united in 1795. The ruins of both churches are within their respective church-yards. Those of Leochel consist of little more than the west gable, with the belfry.

The Forbeses of Craigievar have a burial aisle at Leochel. Although there is no inscription, it appears that (New Stat. Acct., p. 1116-18), JOHN FORBES, commissary, and son of the Bishop of Caithness, was buried here in 1668, " at night, with torches, in the Laird of Craigievar his yle and burial-place ;" where also, in 1671, Mr JOHN YOUNG, minister of Birse and Keig, was buried. Previously, in 1618, Dr JOHN FORBES, professor of divinity in King's College, Aberdeen, who died at Corse in 1648, second son of Bishop Patrick Forbes, was interred at Leochel.

A plain slab, broken in two, bears this epitaph :—

Here lyes PETER MILNER, a sober man,
Who neither used to curse nor ban ;
ELIZABETH SMITH, she was his wife,
He had no other all his life.
He died in July 1784,
Aged 77, or little more,
And she in July 1779,
Years 55, was her lifetime.
With ROBERT and JEAN, their children dear,
ELIZABETH MILNER, and JANNET FRASER,
Their grand-children.
In Rumlie they lived just neir by
And in this place their dust doth ly.

Upon a head-stone :—

In memory of JOSEPH ROBERTSON, late merchant in Aberdeen, who departed this life 18th Feb. 1817, aged 42 years; and of CHRISTIAN LESLIE, his spouse, who died 11th March 1859, aged 83 years.

—Mr and Mrs Robertson were married in London, and had a son and a daughter. The latter is the wife of Mr M'Combie of the *Aberdeen Free Press*, and the former was the late JOSEPH ROBERTSON, who was curator from 1853, of the Historical Department of H.M. Register House, Edinburgh. He died 13th December 1866, aged 56, leaving a widow and four children. Before this melancholy event, Sir Wm. Gibson-Craig, Lord Clerk-Register, having occasion to refer to Mr Robertson in his official capacity to the Committee on the Writs Registration Bill, described him " as the most learned antiquarian in Scotland, as a man in the highest reputation at the British Museum and the Record Office, well known to all the scholars of England, and highly esteemed by scholars on the Continent." Professor Cosmo Innes spoke in equally high terms of Mr Robertson in April 1864, when the University of Edinburgh conferred the honorary degree of LL.D. upon him. Dr Robertson, who was born at Aberdeen, and educated first at Udny, then at Marischal College, was an early contributor to the local press, and became editor of several newspapers, among which were the *Aberdeen*, and the *Glasgow Constitutional*, and finally, the *Edinburgh Courant*. He and Dr John Stuart were the founders, as well as " the spirits" of the Spalding Club, which, after an existence of thirty years, and the publication of a most valuable collection of works upon the History and Topography of the North-East of Scotland, was brought to a close in Dec. 1869.

Dr Robertson edited many of these works, in particular the Antiquities of the Shires of Aberdeen and Banff. This work (which is the mine from which all future writers on these districts must dig, and to which the compiler of these notes has been very largely indebted), along with Inventories of the Jewels and Personal Property of Mary Queen of Scots, and the Statuta Ecclesiæ Scoticanæ, are probably Dr Robertson's chief productions. But, as the exclusive circumstances under which these books were printed prevent their being easily got at, it is through the Prefaces of the works of others that Dr Robertson's name will be best known to the general public, since but few antiquarian or historical works were brought out in this country during the last twenty years of Dr Robertson's life, without the treasures of his mind having been more or less drawn upon by the authors. His liberality in communicating information to others was equalled only by the extent of his own erudition; while his goodness of heart, and fund of humour and anecdote, were best known to his more intimate friends, all of whom felt, when death closed his busy and useful life, that they would "never see his like again." His remains lie in the Dean Cemetery, Edinburgh, where a memorial cross, designed by Mr Drummond, R.S.A., bears this inscription:—

Erected by Members of the Spalding Club.
JOSEPH ROBERTSON, LL.D., F.S.A.,
Curator of National Historical Documents, Register House, Edinburgh. Died 1866, aged 56.

The next four inscriptions are from monuments also in the old churchyard of Leochel:—

[1.]
In memory of the Rev. JAMES KELLIE, sometime minister of Leochel and Cushnie, who died 12 Decr. 1804. This stone is placed by his brother Alexr. Kellie. "Remember them who had the rule over you," &c.

—Mr Kelly, who was a native of Morayshire, was missionary at Portsoy before he went to Leochel-Cushnie. His successor (to whom the next inscription refers), belonged to Logie-Coldstone:—

[2.]
In memory of the Reverend GEORGE ANDERSON, late minister of the united Parishes of Leochel and Cushnie, who died the 22d December 1820, in the 54th year of his age and 15th of his ministry. Also of MARGARET CATTANACH, his spouse, who died at Aberdeen, 23d April 1847, in the 79 year of her age, and of two of their children who died in infancy. This tablet, in grateful affection, is erected by the surviving members of their family.

—Mr Anderson was at one time schoolmaster at Tarland, and while there in 1799 (Scott's Fasti), he expressed his sorrow to, and was rebuked by the Presbytery of Kincardine O'Neil, for drinking and fighting in a public-house.

[3.]
Underneath this stone doth ly
The bones and dust of MARGARET JAFFRIE,
Lawfull spouse to Andrew Law,
And daughter to Alexander Jaffrie,
Gardener at Corse,
And to his spouse Elizabeth Smith,
Who died Oct. 2-, 1760, aged 35 years.

[4.]
In memory of JEAN WALLACE, and of her husband GEORGE BAIN, "who died 13th June 1838, aged 65, and was buried by her left hand."

Cushnie.

(S. BRIDGET, VIRGIN.)

THE kirk of *Cusseny*, in the diocese of Aberdeen, had possibly been bestowed upon the Cathedral of Old Machar, by the Earls of Mar, who were the ancient lords of the district.

The church, which was covered with heather until about 1792, is a roofless and picturesque ruin, upon the north bank of the burn, and within the Glen, of Cushnie. The date of 1637 is upon a skewput stone; and the bell, which is still in the belfry, belongs to the time of Mr Patrick Copland or Kopland, who became minister of Cushnie in 1672, and died there in 1710. It is initialed and dated—P. K. 1686.

There are three niches in the east wall of the church, and it is said that in these were placed the armorial bearings of the three principal heritors of the parish. One of the slabs only remains. It lies within the church, and exhibits a rude carving of the Lumsden arms, with the date of 1637, as upon the skewput of the kirk.

The church is about 14 by 63 feet within walls, and has two arched doorways on the south. The first three inscriptions are from tablets built into the outer and front wall:—

Here lyes within this wall the precious dust of the Rev. and excellent Mr WILLIAM BIDIE, minr. of the Gospel at Cushney, who depar. this life Feb. 2d, 1730, aged 38 years :—
Wel skilled in yͤ Redemption Scheme,
Immanuel was his darling theme ;
Meek, wise, & harmless, full of zeal,
His life the Truths he preached did seal.
Mors janua vitæ.   May M'Kean.

—The initials of Mr and Mrs Bidie are thus inscribed upon a stone over the door of the old manse :—

M. W. B : M. MK.   1727.

The old manse, which is occupied by the farmer of Kirkton, appears, from a date upon the skewput stone, to have been repaired in 1763.

Within behind this ston lyes THOMAS LUMSDEN of Lyn, who departed this life June the 19, 1726, and of age 82 years ; & also his spouse MARGORY FORBES, who departed this life May 1, 1716, & of age 63 years ; & WM. LUMSDEN their 4 son, who departed this life April 28, 1716, and of his age 28 years ; & 3 of their grand children ALEXR. HELIEN, and HELIEN LUMSDENS.

A. L.—I. L.—R, L.—T. L.—C. L.   1724.
Mors janua vitæ.

—"Lyn," mentioned in the above inscription, was part of the Cairndye property, in the now suppressed parish of Kincray.

Within this wall were buried the ashes of ROBERT LUMSDEN of Corrachrie, who was married to Agnes Forbes, daughter to George Forbes of Skellitur, He dyed April the 20, 1710. This stone was erected opposite to his grave by his eldist son Iames. Solum salus per Christum.

—James Lumsden of Corrachree (son of the above-named Robert) was minister of Towie (*sup.*, p. 229), and was succeeded in Corrachree by his son. The latter wrote some clever satires, the best known of which is entitled "The Humours of the Forest, a comedy," in which an old Deeside minister is burlesqued under the name of *Grumble*. It appears that *Grumble* courted the daughter of a poor clergyman while he was schoolmaster of her father's parish ; but after he got the living of "the See in the Forest," as it is called, *Grumble* gave his "poor love" the go-bye, and married the daughter of another minister, who was in affluent circumstances. Corrachree, which is prettily situated in Cromar, near Tarland, was bought by the late Lieut.-Col. Farquharson, of the Tullochcoy race (*infra*, p. 215), who changed the name to *Logiemar*. The remains of a sculptured stone, lately discovered by the Rev. Mr Michie and Dr Arthur Mitchell, stand in a field near the house of Corrachree.

The next inscription is upon the west splay of the east, and only remaining, window of the old kirk :—

Befor this ston lyes ALEXANDER LUMSDEN, laird of Cushnie, who departed this life May the 1, 1714, and of age 70 years ; & also his spous EILIZABATH LEITH, & DAVID LUMSDEN of Cushnie, who departed this life Desr. the 23, 1718, and of age each 30 years ; & also LUDOVICK LUMSDEN.

Hoc, lector, tumulo tres contumulantur in uno
Cognati, Mater, Filius, atque Pater.
Mors janua vitæ.
[Here, reader, three relations in one tomb,
The Father, Mother, Son, await their doom.
Death is the gate of life.]

—The arms of the above-named laird and lady of Cushnie, dated 1707, are carved over the front door of the old house of Cushnie, also over the door of the adjoining meal-mill. The same laird gifted two communion cups to the kirk, which are thus inscribed :—

THIS . CUPS . WAS . DEDICATED . BY . ALEXANDER . LUMSDEN . OF . CUSHNEY . FOR . THE . CHURCH . OF . CUSHNEY . USE . 1709.

—While speaking of communion cups, it may be added that other two, of silver, were given to Leochel by John Robertson, laird of Wester Fowlis, upon which are the words :—

DEDICAT . FOR . THE . CHVRCH . OF . LEOCHEL . 1659.

—Thomas Lumsden, who came from Fifeshire in the time of David II., and had charters of Madler, in Kincardine O'Neil, from the Earl of Buchan, was the first of his race in Aberdeenshire. Lumsdens afterwards acquired (1472) the lands of Balnakelly, in Cushnie, from the Earl of Rothes ; but they were not designed "de Cuschny" until about 1579-80. Since that time the property of Cushnie has continued in the family. The old mansion-house, which stands in a hollow on the north side of the burn of Cushnie, was lately re-edified, and about the same time, a new mansion-house was built upon a rising ground, a little to the north-west.

The next inscription, from the east splay of the same window, relates to another member of the Cushnie family, who died tenant of Titaboutie :—

W. L. J. G.—Here lyes befor this ston WILL. LUMSDEN in Titaboutie, who depr. this life Novm. 26, 1722, and of age 63 years, and his laufvl son JOHN LUMSDEN, A. L : J. S. 1724. Memento mori.

From a table-shaped stone within the area of the old kirk :—

In memory of the Rev. FRANCIS ADAM, who in a very exemplary manner, for nearly 50 years, discharged the duties of the pastoral office in this parish, much esteemed by all who knew him. He departed this life 15th March 1795, aged 90. On his right side lies his spouse Mrs JEAN THAIN, and on his left side, his eldest son, Mr JOHN ADAM.

The New Church of LEOCHEL-CUSHNIE is situated upon an eminence, about midway between the old churches of Leochel and Cushnie. It was erected about 1797-8, soon after the union of the parishes, and is surrounded by a burial-ground, in which there are several monuments. Two of the monuments are inscribed as below :—

In memory of the Revd. WILLIAM MALCOLM, minister of Leochel-Cushnie, who died 24th August 1838, in the 47th year of his age, and 17th year of his ministry. This monument was erected by his parishioners in token of their high esteem for his zealous and unwearied labours among them.

—Mr Malcolm was previously schoolmaster at Cushnie. His successor, Dr Taylor, to whose memory the parishioners have erected a marble tablet within the church, was a native of Banchory-Ternan. He was sometime Librarian and Murray Lecturer at King's College, Aberdeen, and had a great taste for antiquarian and philological studies. He wrote the New Statistical Account of Leochel-Cushnie, which contains an exhaustive notice of the history of the district, ancient and modern. The following is from a granite slab in the church-yard :—

In memory of JESSIE M'COMBIE, wife of the Revd. Alexander Taylor, minister of Leochel-Cushnie, who died 10th September 1852, in the 24th year of her age. And of the said Revd. ALEXANDER TAYLOR, D.D., who died 25th March 1872, in the 66th year of his age, and the 34th of his ministry.

—o—

The Castle of Craigievar (which is still inhabited), was begun by the Mortimers of Fowlis, and finished by an ancestor of the present proprietor, Sir William Forbes, Bart. It is the most interesting object of antiquity in the district. Besides its architectural features, which are admirably represented in Billings' Eccl. and Baronial Antiquities, it presents these inscriptions :—

LVX . MEA . CHRISTVS

—[Christ is my light]—is over the principal window of the great hall. The date of 1626, and the next two inscriptions, are upon different parts of the castle :—

DEVS . MEA . COLVMNA.
POST . TENEBRAS . SPERO . LVCEM.
[God is my pillar. After darkness I hope for light.]

A shield upon the staircase, charged with the

Forbes arms, initialed, and dated, I. F., 1688, is encircled by this quaint admonition:—

DOE . NOT . VAIKEN . SLEIPING . DOGS.

The ruins of the Castle of Corse, upon which are the initials, W. F., E. S., and the date of 1581, are situated, *quoad civilia*, within the parish of Coull, as is also the mansion-house of Corse. The latter was built by James O. Forbes, Esq., younger brother of Sir William Forbes of Craigievar.

The old mansion-house of the Gordons of Hallhead, and that of the Lumsdens of Cushnie, respectively dated 1668 and 1707, are still objects of some interest. The castle of the Strachans of Lynturk is now represented by a plain building, and the property belongs to Wm. M'Combie, Esq. of Easter Skene.

Bride's Well, the Bowbutts, and the Cateran's Grave, are also places of local note. The first preserves the name of S. BRIDGET, patroness of the parish, the next is said to indicate the spot where archery was practised in old times, and the third is known as the last resting place of a riever who lost his life while attempting to carry away cattle from the Glen of Cushnie.

Cushnie is one of the most elevated parts in Aberdeenshire. It has been long proverbial for the severity of its climate and the badness of its roads. The former of those characteristics, along with certain features of other two districts, have been preserved in these words:—

"Cushnie for cauld,
Culblene for heat,
Clashaureach for heather."

The following lines were, and probably still are, descriptive of the agricultural capabilities of the places named. The first two lie in Corse, the third in Coull, and the fourth in Tarland:—

"Tillyorn grows the corn,
And Wester Corse the straw;
And Tillylodge the blawarts blue,
And Caldhame naething ava."

———o———

Liff.
(S. MARY, VIRGIN.)

THE church of *Liff* was gifted to the Abbey of Scone, by Alexander I., who is said to have had a residence at Hurley Hawkin, to the west of the burial ground.

The remains of an octagonial-shaped font, of a late type, and the upper stone of a quern, lie in the church-yard. The MARY Well is about a quarter of a mile to the north of the church.

The present church at Liff, which was built in 1838, is the church of the united parishes of Liff, Invergowrie, Logie-Dundee, and Benvie. The two first-named churches are each rated, in the Old Taxation, at 8, the third at 12, and the fourth at 10 marks.

The church bell is inscribed:—

IAN . BVRGERHVIS . HEEFT . MY . GEGOTEN . '96.

Upon a hand-bell at the parish school:—

FOR THE PARISHES OF
LIFFE, INVERGOWRIE, AND LOGIE:
PAID FOR BY THE POORE 1718:
ALEX. SCOTT, MINR.

A marble tablet, in the lobby of the church, bears this inscription:—

This tablet is erected to the memory of Major ALEXANDER WATT, K.H., late of the 27th Regt. Bengal Native Infantry, who died at Edinburgh, 18th April 1851, in the 46th year of his age. By his Brother Officers as a humble token of their respect for his worth, and the many amiable qualities by which he was distinguished during a lengthened career in India.

—The deaths of Major and Mrs Watt, two sons, and a daughter, are also recorded upon a marble monument in the church-yard of Liff. Mrs Watt died at Landaue, in the Himalaya Mountains, in August 1842.

An adjoining tablet, bears an inscription, here abridged:—

KATHERINE WEBSTER, spouse to Isaac Watt, Esq. of Logie, died 2d March 1809, aged 31. ISAAC WATT, Esq. of Logie, died 11th July 1823, aged 51.

MARGARET WEBSTER, daughter of Robert Webster late of Cransley, died 18 Nov. 1832, aged 58. The following family of Isaac Watt, Esq. : KATHERINE, died 1821, aged 15 years ; ROBERT, died at Dundee, 14 Dec. 1840 ; MARGARET, wife of Alfred Begbie, Esq., Bengal Civil Service, died in India, Dec. 1842 ; JAMES, died in India, 18 July 1848, and his wife and two children were lost in the ship "Gentoo," in 1846, off the Cape of Good Hope.

—Isaac Watt, who was a thread maker, and dyer or litster, in Dundee, sold Logie to Major Fyfe of Smithfield. The property was afterwards bought by the late Jas. Watt of Denmill in Fife, by whose heirs it was sold in 1870.

An adjoining enclosure contains five tablets, from which the following inscriptions are abridged :—

ROBERT WEBSTER, late tacksman at Cransley, died 23 Dec. 1811, aged 76.

JAMES WEBSTER, Esq. of Balruddery, died 17 May 1827, aged 62. AGNES HUNTER, his relict, died at Corriedale, Strathblane, 20 January 1863, aged 77.

PATRICK, their 5th son, died 29 Aug. 1827, aged 12 years ; THOMAS, the 4th son, died at Arthur, Canada West, 2d Oct. 1857, aged 44.

AGNES, their youngest daughter, died 13 Oct. 1830, aged 20.

CHARLES, their 3d son, government agent, died near Trincomalee, 4 April 1845, aged 34.

—The above James Webster, who was a son of the tacksman of Cransley, bought the estate of Balruddery in 1806, from Mr Baillie of Dochfour. His wife was a daughter of Hunter of Seaside and Glencarse, in Gowrie, and their son Robert Webster sold Balruddery in 1849, to the late David Edward, a flax merchant in Dundee.

A monument of light sandstone, on the west side of the kirkyard, was inaugurated with masonic honours. An inserted marble slab bears :—

To the memory of JAMES JACK, surveyor of taxes Dundee, who died there 15 Dec. 1861, aged 77, whose remains are here interred. This monument is erected by his Masonic Brethren, as a respectful record of his worth ; and of his services as a Brother of the Craft, for the long period of 53 years.

A flat stone, apparently the oldest in the church-yard, is embellished in the centre with carvings in relief of a skull and cross bones, and the motto, IN MORTE VITA. Below are the Duncan and Durham arms impaled, flanked by the initials, M. I. D., A. D., G. D. It bears these words prettily cut in Roman capitals round the margin :—

. . . R . LYIS . AGNES . DVNCAN . DAVGHTER . TO
MAISTER . IOHNE . DVNC . . . . TER . AT . LIFF
VHA . DEPAIR . . . . DAY . OF . MAI . 1615
OF . HIR . AGE . 1 . ZEIR.

A table-shaped stone, ornamented with the "royal crown" of the blacksmiths, with pincers and hammer, &c., bears :—

Heir lyis ane honest man IOHN MITCHEL, portioner of Life, spovs to Isobell Gairdine. He depairted the 16 of November 1665, of aig 50.

Upon a flat stone :—

Heir layes ane godly yong man ALEXANDER LEITHEL, son to Androw Leithel, indvellar in Gowrdy, who departed May the 22, ano 1664, and of his age 26.

A tombstone, with bold carvings of a pruning knife, hedge shears, and spade, &c., bears :—

Here lys DAVID COB, lavfvl hvsband to Elizabeth Hill, sometime indvellar in Govrlie, who departed this life 1674, and of his age 45 years :—

Death's sneading knife cvtes dovne,
. . . .
Honest man entombed here lyes.

Upon a stone, on which a weaver's shuttle, &c., are carved :—

Here lies two godly persons, KEATHREN MANCUR, who departed this life on the 2 of Agust in the year 1696, and of her age 55 ; and her husband ALEXANDER ROB, on the 9 of September 1712, and of his age 69.

JAMES WIGHTON, shoemaker, Liff, d. 1725, a. 53 :—

On stones its needless for to praise our friends when dead, for when they rise it shall appear to all the earth what life they lived before their death.

Upon a flat slab :—

Here lyes AGNES GRAY, spous to John Couper in BacksiDe of Liff, who dieD in Agust 1707, and of hir age 62 :—

With husBands tuo I Children
HAD eLeven,
With two of odds I Lived
Sixty-even ;
My Body sLeeps in hoPe,
My souL I GAve,
To Him Who suffered
death, the same to Save.
CaPut in CœLis Mem . . . . Sequent . .
[The members shall follow their heavenly head.]

A plain head-stone bears :—

This stone was erected by James Waddel, sometime brewer in Liffe, in memory of his uncle WILLIAM WADDEL, who died the 24th May, anno Domini, 1765, aged 58 years :—

Here lys beneath these sordid stones,
A father to the poor ;
To orphants, and distressed ones
He keept an open door.
Fair honesty and virtus peure,
Did strive in him for place ;
Of charity a publick store
Was lost at his decess.
Now though his body here doth ly,
To moulder into dust ;
His generous soul, the noble part,
In Christ alone doth rest.

—The session records show that Waddels were brewers at Liff for nearly 200 years, where they also carried on the trade of bakers.

Upon the site of the pulpit of the old church of Liff a monument of Aberdeen granite, erected by subscription, bears :—

Tribute of respect to the memory of the Rev. GEORGE ADDISON, D.D., for thirty-four years minister of this parish, who died January 4, 1852, aged 74. [1 Thess. iv. 14.]

—Dr Addison was the son of a miller near Huntly, Aberdeenshire. He came to Angus as assistant schoolmaster at Glamis, and was afterwards tutor in the Airlie family, by whose interest he was appointed first to the church of Glenisla, next to Auchterhouse, and finally to Liff. His remains lie near the north wall of the burial ground. His wife was a daughter of the Rev. Mr Scott of Auchterhouse, some of whose sons attained high positions in the army, &c.

Lenric.
(S. ——)

THE kirk of *Baucryn* or *Baucvill* belonged to St Andrews, and was dedicated by Bishop David in 1243. The parish was joined to Liff in 1758. A bell which belonged to the church, now at Liff manse, bears these names and date :—

MICHAEL . BVRGERHVYS . M . F . 1631 :
M . HENDRIE . FITHIE.

Remains of the old church and of a baptismal font are in the burial-ground. The enclosure has been improved by the erection of a new wall, in the outer part of which two carved stones are built. One of these is dated 1633 ; the other bears the arms of Scrimgeour, the second Viscount of Dundee, impaled with those of his lady, Isobel Car, or Ker, a daughter of the first Earl of Roxburghe, also the initials, V. I. D. : L. I. C. ; and the date of 1643. The latter stone, till lately, formed the top of a sun-dial, which stood in the burial-ground. In all probability, it had been gifted to the parish by Viscount Dundee and his lady, the former of whom died of wounds received at Marston Moor in July 1644. According to Fordun, Alexander of Carron, who did good service to Alexander I. when attacked by rebels at Hurley Hawkin, was progenitor of the Scrimgeours. He was made hereditary standard bearer of Scotland by that King ; and, for his bravery and courage, had his name changed to *Skirmischur*. A descendant was created constable of Dundee by Sir William Wallace, 1298. Another of the family fell at Harlaw, 1411. They were created Viscounts of Dundee in 1641, and Earls in 1661. The title became extinct in the Scrimgeours in 1668. Twenty years later the Viscountsy was revived in the Grahams of Claverhouse. Wedderburn of Birkhill, in Fife, is representative of the Scrimgeours, through a female, and hereditary standard bearer of Scotland.

A tomb stone, partially effaced, with the S—— and Blair arms, and the initials T. S. : C. B., is thus inscribed :—

Heir lyes ane honest and godly man THOMAS
. . . . . . axter and bvrges of Dvndie, qvha departit the . . . . . . ober 1607, of his age 47 zeirs.

A stone with the Hill and Gray arms, (initialed D. H : A. G :), bears this epitaph :—

Heir lyes IOHN HILL, son to David Hill, maltman,
To Agnes Gray son also, vas the same ;
Of age tvelve years when he from them did go,
It vas on March the eleventh six hvndred fifty tvo.
1652.

Adjoining above :—

Heir lyes ane honest man caled THOMAS HILL in Balridrie, who departit the 8 of Ianevar 1643, and of his age 69. T. H : E. S : A. H.

Heir lyis ane godly and honest man IAMES SPANZIE in Balrvdrie. He departit the 5 of Februar 1620, and of his age 67, with his wyfe MARGRET THEIN, who departit the 3 of March 1612 : hir age is 52.

JANET GIKIE, spouse to Alexr. Hill, in Fowlis, died 18 Oct. 1711, aged 32, she having born 5 children ; ANN, the youngest died 1710 :—

How short man's life ! alas, while we live we die—
To know man's life; keep death still in your eye.

ALEX. HILL, died 16 Nov. 1756, aged 80.

Five of the old tombstones are initialed and dated respectively :—I. S., 1623 ; I. W. 1630, P. G. ; A. W : E. M. 1641 ; A. S. 1646, MEMENTO MORI ; P. G. 1-38.

At the head of the last of these slabs stands a peculiar example of the sculptured stones, the existence of which shows Benvie to have been an early ecclesiastical settlement. Territorially it is also a place of considerable antiquity. David I. gave the barony to Walter of Lundin, who was followed in it by Sir Philip of Vallognes of Panmure, then by the Maules, the last named of whom held the superiority of Benvie and the patronage of the kirk down to 1716.

The Scrimgeours of Dudhope (Viscounts Dundee), held the lands of Benvie as vassals of the lords of Panmure, until 1654, when Benvie passed to John Fithie, merchant in Dundee. Fithie was possibly a relative of the minister whose name is upon the old bell.

Professor PLAYFAIR of Edinburgh, also his brother WILLIAM (who wrote several works on Scotch history and antiquities), were born at the manse of Benvie. The future professor succeeded his father as minister of the united parishes, which he left about 1783-4, and became tutor to Mr Fergusson of Raith. It is told that, while Mr P. was at Raith, an elder of Liff had occasion to write him upon some business, and thus addressed his letter :—" For Mr John Playfair, formerly servant to the Lord Jesus Christ at Liff, now servant to Mr Fergusson at Raith" !

Invergowrie.

(S. PETER, APOSTLE.)

IT is said that S. BONIFACE, who came to Scotland from Rome, during the 7th century, planted his first church upon the site of the present burial place at Invergowrie, which occupies a knoll, near to where the burn of Gowrie—the " flumen *Gobriat* in Pictavia"—joins the Tay.

The church of *Invergoweryn* was given by Alexander I. to the Abbey of Scone.

Fragments of two curiously sculptured stones are built into the south-east window of the ruins of the church. The remains of a piscina, of a primitive type, are on the right of the west door ; and the rude arch or top lintel of the door partakes much of the character of that in the lower part of the tower of Rostinoth, which was also a foundation of S. BONIFACE. (*v.* p. 27.)

The area of the church of Invergowrie is used as a cemetery by the Clayhills family, and others. It contains several mural and other monuments. The tablets from which the first three inscriptions are copied are upon the north wall :—

Underneath are interred the remains of JAMES MENZIES-CLAYHILLS, late Captain in the Royal Scots, eldest son of James Clayhills, Esq. of Invergowrie, and Henrietta Henderson-Kinloch of Hallyards. He died 5 Nov. 1817, aged 31 years, ten of which were devoted to the service of his King and Country. As a tribute to the memory of Qualities the most endearing, of a Disposition the most inoffensive and mild, of Affections the most cordial and warm, and of Filial Love and Duty never surpassed—this monumental tablet is erected by Them who mourn as Parents, but resign as Christians, a prop and comfort of their declining years.

In front of this monumental stone repose the remains of JAMES CLAYHILLS, Esq. of Invergowrie, who departed this life 16 May 1825, aged 72. Plain and unassuming in his manners, in his habits quiet and retired, with a spirit of the truest charity and disinterestedness rarely excelled, he pursued the noiseless tenor of his way in the faithful discharge of the duties of a private, rather than in the bustle and parade of a public station. As a Landlord he was humane, just, and bountiful; sincere, steady, and beneficent as a Friend; kind and indulgent as a Father. This tribute to the memory of his many, but unobtrusive virtues, is offered by his Widow and surviving Children, as a small but unfeigned testimony of their duty and affection.

To the revered memory of ALEXANDER CLAYHILLS, Esq. of Invergowrie. Born 14 January 1796; died 18 June 1865.
—Three separate slabs, initialed and dated, cover the graves of the above-named. A fourth slab bears—

H. H. C., died 6 April 1829, aged 65 years.
—Clayhills was the name of a burgess family in Dundee during the 16th century, of whom, in all probability, was ANDREW, minister of Monifieth, who died in 1617; as well as ROBERT, the latter of whom, in 1633, succeeded his father in the lands and mill of Baldovie, near Dundee. In 1669, James Clayhills of Nether Liff became laird of Invergowrie, &c., by the death of a brother's son. About —— the male line of Clayhills failed, and the property came, through a female, to MENZIES of Menzieshill, who assumed the surname of *Clayhills*. The present laird (Mr Clayhills-Henderson) of Invergowrie and Hallyards, &c., an officer in the Navy, is a nephew of the late laird. A fifth slab is briefly inscribed:—

M. M., AGED 76, 1846.

Other inscribed monuments lie in the area of the church. The first quoted below had been, when entire, a fine example of its kind, with the letters boldly cut in relief:—

I . S : I . F : — HEIR . SLEIPIS . ANE . GODLY . HONORED . FA . . . . S . AGNES . FIF . HIS . SPOVS . AIGED . 76 . ZEIRIS . . . . 1574.

Possibly the next quoted (much defaced by having been walked upon), had belonged to persons named Black and Fife:—

. . . . HON . BLA . . . . ELDER . AND . KIRKMAN . . . . . . DEPARTED . 1603 . A . F.

There is another fine stone, dated 1633, with a shield on the left bearing the Lovel arms, flanked with the initials I. L.; on the right a shield with the initials A. L. only, and between the shields are the letters M. S. Another slab, in excellent preservation, bears shields with the arms of Drummond and Howison, respectively. This inscription is round the border of the stone:—

HEIR . LAYIS . ANE . GODLY . HONEST . MAN . NAMED . IAMES . DROWMAND . LAWFVL . HVSBAND . TO . IANET . HOVSON . HE . DEPAIRTIT . IN . FEBRVARI . 14 . DAY . 1665 . AND . OF . HIS . AGE . 27 . 1 . D : I . H.

Built into the west wall, and railed off from the area:—

In memory of DANIEL MACKENZIE, Esq. of Annfield, son of Kenneth Mackenzie, Esq. of Kilcoy, Ross-shire; born 1765, died 1829.
—If this inscription is authentic, it is another of many instances which show the value of such memorials, and the necessity of our existing heraldic books being thoroughly revised. Neither Mr M. nor his father are mentioned in the published pedigrees of the Mackenzies of Kilcoy. Another marble slab bears.—

In memory of Mrs ANN MYLNE of Mylnefield, daughter of Alexander Hunter of Blackness: Born 1749, died 1832.

The family burial vault of the Mylnes of Mylnefield is on the north side of the ruins of the church, where there are three marble monuments belonging to the family. One of the slabs is to the memory of—

AGNES, wife of James Mylne, Esq.: Born 27 Aug. 1765, died 15 Feb. 1843.

—This lady was a daughter of Scott of Criggie, in the Mearns. She was mother of the next mentioned, who was the last Mylne of Mylnefield:—

Sacred to the memory of THOMAS MYLNE of Mylnefield, born 28 Nov. 1785, died 22 Dec. 1836. And his wife ELIZABETH-JANE GUTHRIE, born 8 May 1799, died 14 Nov. 1839. [A daughter AGNES, died aged 16, and a son CHARLES-KINLOCH, aged 2 years.]

Sacred to the memory of JOHN MYLNE, aged 38; ANN-DOUGLAS, aged 37; THOMAS-JOHN, aged 35; and ELIZABETH-GUTHRIE, aged 27, children of Thomas Mylne, Esq. of Mylnefield, and his wife Elizabeth-Jane Guthrie. They were drowned at sea, near Sydney, New South Wales, on the occasion of the wreck of the ship "Dunbar" on 20 Augt. 1857. Sacred also to the memory of JAMES MYLNE, aged 40, their eldest brother, who died at sea, near Malta, 28 Nov. 1857. Erected in memory of their beloved Brothers and Sisters, by William, Charles, and Graham Mylne. [1. John, iv. 12.]

—The above William and Charles were in the E.I.C.S., and Graham was an officer in the 82d regiment of foot. Their mother was the eldest daughter of John Guthrie of GUTHRIE, (*q. v.*) The property of Mylnefield was sold soon after her death, to Mr Henderson, a farmer near Carnoustie, who was also laird of Grange of Barry. Mylnefield was inherited from him by Mr Low, a dockgate keeper at Dundee harbour, and Grange of Barry, by Mr Wighton, a shipowner. The Mylnes, who were designed of Mylnefield from about the close of the 17th century, were descended from a burgess family of Dundee.

A tombstone in the burial-ground bears the name of MATTHEW, and the date of 1622. Others, simply initialed and dated (A. M. 1638; W. V. 1644; G. B. 1646; I. S. 1682, &c.), lie on the south side of the ruins of the old kirk. The following inscriptions are from adjoining stones:—

. . . . nost man nemed ROBERT IACK, who deported this lyf 2 of Ianenari 1661, and of his age 6-. ROBRT IACK, son of Robrt Iack, at the Law Brig Mil, who deceset in ano 1656, and of his age 1.

Heir lyes an honest woman named MARGRAT GAIRDN, spovs to Androv Blak, maltman bvrges in Dvndie, who deceased the 24 of Ianevare 1631, and of hir age 60:—

I rest in hop intil the tym apier,
That I shal ryse and mit my Savior.

A table-shaped tombstone near the churchyard gate presents a variety of elaborate carvings, consisting of shuttles and other insignia of the weaver trade, combined with mortuary objects. The common verse, beginning, "Stop mortal man," &c., is near the centre, and the following round the margin, of the stone:—

This stone wce David, Iames, Robert, Henry, Iohn, and Thomas Cocks erected in memory of IAMES COCK, weaver in Locheye, our father, who dyed Oct. 15, 1741, aged 65; and of ISOBEL DOIG, their mother, dyed March 31, 1733, aged 48, and WILLIAM, their brother, dyed 1731.

—The above Cockes introduced linen manufactures at Lochee—a trade which is still extensively carried on at that place by their descendants, under the firm of Cox Brothers, and Co. A plain headstone, adjoining the tomb from which the above inscription is copied, bears the following to another of the same race:—

1754: This stone was erected by Robert Cock and Margaret Kid, in memory of their lawfull son ROBERT COCK, induellers in Lochee: he died Dec. 20, 1751, aged 9 years:—

O mortal man why dost thow in
This world delight to stay;
And as a drudge by her ay hurled
Even at her fortouns sway?
She's painted our with pleasures rare
All drest in gaudy hue;
She flatter can, without compare,
Yet none of them is true.

Upon a flat stone:—

Here lyes DAVID MULLO, taylor, who liued in Ninewalls, who dyed the 2 of May 17-4, and his age 62 years. As also his sponse MARGRAT WATSON, who dyed the 6 of Aprill 1743, and of her age 74 years, &c. 1849, revised by Peter Watson, Lochee.

ELIZABETH NICKOL, wf. of Jas. Whitton, d. 1756, a. 36:—

Child, wife, and mother, dutiful,
In all a pattern wonderful ;
Her grace in life makes now her glory sure,
Her corps may rott, her good name shall endure.
After death—life.

The next two inscriptions are from marble tablets, within an enclosure, at east end of the Invergowrie aisle :—

Underneath this tablet are interred the mortal remains of the Very Rev. HENEAGE HORSLEY, A. M., Dean of Brechin, Prebendary of St Asaph, and for 40 years minister of St Paul's Chapel, Dundee. He was the only son of Samuel Horsley, Bishop of St Asaph. He was born 23 Feb. 1776, died 6 Oct. 1847, universally regretted and beloved. This tablet is erected to his memory by his children, sorrowing, but not as others, who have no hope.

In the enclosure below this tablet are interred the mortal remains of ANNE BOURKE, widow of John Bourke, Esq., of the county of Limerick. She died at Dundee, 29 Dec. 1836, in the 78th year of her age, beloved and lamented.

—This lady was a daughter of Edward Ryan of Boscobel, Tipperary, Ireland. By her husband she had three sons and one daughter. Two of the sons died young. The eldest, Richard, who distinguished himself as a soldier, and as Governor of New South Wales, &c., received the honour of knighthood. In conjunction with Earl Fitzwilliam, he edited the correspondence of the celebrated Edmund Burke, to whose will he was a witness. (Burke's Landed Gentry.) His sister, FRANCES-EMMA, married the Rev. Dean Horsley ; and a plain slab within the old kirk at Invergowrie marks her grave, and bears this brief record of her death :—

F. E. HORSLEY, 18 DEC. 1821.

Upon a marble tablet, built into the east, and outer wall of the Mylnefield aisle,—

Sacred to JOHN SMITH-SKENE, Esq., Captain of the Royal Navy, and Companion of the Bath, who died 10 Dec. 1833, aged 63 years.

—Captain S. was made a C.B. in 1813, and died at Bin Rock, a villa near Dundee. He saw much service in his time, having been master of the "Egmont" at the battle of Cape St Vincent, First Lieutenant on board the "Africa" at Trafalgar, and Commander of the "Beagle" at the reduction of St Sebastian. His paternal name was SMITH; but, upon inheriting some property, he assumed that of Skene. His son, John, lately in the Coast Guard, was a Commander in the Navy, and long employed in active service in various parts of the globe.—(O'Byrne's Naval Biography.)

The estate of Invergowrie belonged at one time to the Grays. Three carved stones, possibly taken from their old residence at Invergowrie, are built over a private entrance from the Perth road to the present house. One bears the date of 1601, with the initials, P. G: A. N., also the Gray and Napier (?) arms, and the motto,

SOLI . DEO . GRATIAS.

A second slab presents the same arms and initials, and the words, GOD . GEVIS. Upon the third stone are also the Gray arms, the initials, P. G., and the legend,

TRVST . IN . GOD.

Logie, or Logie-Dundee.

(S. ——)

LIKE the kirks of Liff and Invergowrie, that of *Logyn-Dundho* was given to the Abbey of Scone by Alex. I. It was also in the diocese of St Andrews, and dedicated by Bishop David in the year 1243.

The church stood upon a rising ground ; and a burial aisle, erected by the late Major Fyfe of Logie and Smithfield (in which no interments have been as yet made), occupies the same site. According to an inscribed stone near the gate, the surrounding walls were

BUILT BY PUBLIC SUBSCRIPTION, A.D. MDCCCXXXVII.

The fragment of a coffin-slab, possibly of the 14th or 15th century, is the only relic of antiquity within the ground. It is similar to some of those fine examples which lie at the church of

St Mary, Dundee, with a floral cross upon the face of it, and an old fashioned sword upon one of the sides. The shaft of a pillar-monument, with square hole in top, *mis*called " the holywater stane," stood long in an upright posture, though now thrown aside, and treated as useless.

The oldest lettered tombstone (so far as I have seen), is dated 1786; and though numerous, few, if any, of the inscriptions are of general interest. A plain headstone, near the south-west corner, bears this tribute :—

To the memory of JOHN BENNET, cabinet-maker in Dundee, who died 26 April 1822, aged 47. This stone is erected by a select number of Journeymen Cabinet-Makers as a mark of respect and esteem for a kind master, and a sincere friend; and their high sense of the genuine integrity of conduct, and warmth of feeling which distinguished through life him who lies below.

JOHN, son of Alex. RATTRAY, d. 1839, a. 6 y. 8 m. :—
And must this body die ?
This mortal frame decay ?
And must those active limbs of mine,
Lie mouldering in the clay ?

There are some private burial-places near the west side of the enclosure: one belongs to Edward Baxter, merchant, Dundee, laird of Kincauldrum, and father of W. E. Baxter, M.P. for the Montrose District of Burghs, presently Secretary to the Admiralty. It contains a handsome freestone monument, with a marble tablet, upon which are recorded the death of Mr E. Baxter's first wife, EUPHEMIA WILSON, who died at Balgay House, 22 Aug. 1833; also that of his second wife, ELIZABETH JOBSON, who died 2 July 1842; together with two daughters who died young.

Owing to the overcrowded state of Logie burial-ground, it was closed, with certain exceptions, against further interments, by order of the Privy Council, 19 Feb. 1870. It was used chiefly for the district of Lochee, now a populous and thriving suburb of Dundee; for the better accommodation of which, a new cemetery is about to be formed upon the adjoining property of Balgay.

As the more interesting antiquarian and historical peculiarities of the united parishes of Liff, Benvie, Invergowrie, and Logie, are given in the Sculptured Stone Monuments (vol. i.), and in the Proceedings of the Society of Antiquaries (vols. ii., v., vi.), as well as in both Statistical Accounts of Scotland, &c., notices of these matters are purposely omitted here.

It may only be mentioned that the districts of Invergowrie and Logie were both famous at one time for the abundance and purity of their water springs; and that, before the Monikie supply was brought into Dundee, the water from these springs was used in that town for all important culinary purposes. The water was driven through Dundee in barrels, and the qualities of the respective springs were loudly extolled by the different vendors. Of the former, it was declared that,

"Invergowrie's crystal spring,
For Tea, surpasses everything !"

while of Invergowrie's rival, the people were assured that—

"Of a' the wells that's here about,
There's nane compar'd to Logie Spout !"

Logie-Buchan.

(? S. ANDREW.)

KING DAVID II., in 1361, gave the patronage of the kirk of *Logie in Buchan* to the Cathedral of Old Machar. In the following year the Bishop conveyed the church itself, with its teinds, to the same house, of which Logie-Buchan was a mensal church.

The Ythan runs through the parish, and the kirk stands upon a rising ground on the south side of that river. The belfry is dated 1737; and the bell inscribed :—

LOGIE BUCHAN, 1726.

The Buchans of Auchmacoy, patrons of the church, had their burial-place within it, where two marble tablets are respectively inscribed as under :—

As a mark of affection and regard for the memory of ROBERT BUCHAN, third son of Thomas Buchan, Esq. of Auchmacoy, assistant-surgeon, H.E.I.C.S., who died at Cawnpore, 4 Sep. 1825, in the 24th year of his age. His brother, JOHN, died in London, 4 Feb. 1829, aged 22 years, and is interred in the burying-ground belonging to the Church of St John, Waterloo Road, London. Also in memory of EUPHEMIA TURNER, widow of the late Thomas Buchan, Esq. of Auchmacoy, who died at Edinburgh, 22 Dec. 1832, and whose remains are interred here.

—This lady was eldest daughter of Robert Turner of Menie, in Belhelvie. The other marble records the death of her husband and eldest son :—

Sacred to the memory of THOMAS BUCHAN, Esq. of Auchmacoy, who died on the 12 Aug. 1819, and was interred in the family burying-ground within this church. Also, in remembrance of his eldest son THOMAS, who died at Marseilles, in France, 3 Dec. 1818, aged 21 years, and was interred in the Protestant burying-ground of that city.

—The present laird of Auchmacoy, who succeeded his father, married a daughter of Garden Duff of Hatton, Esq., by whom he had a son and daughter. The former, THOMAS, died at London in 1866, aged 29, after which his father erected a mausoleum near the mansion-house, where the remains of his son repose. It is said that the first of this family was a son of Cumin, Earl of Buchan; and that the laird of the period, contrary to the wish of his chief, adhering to The Bruce, was allowed to retain his lands, on the condition of taking a new name, whereupon he assumed that of *Buchan*. The property of Auchmacoy, as originally held by this family, had been of small extent, for in 1309 two-thirds of it belonged to William of Strathbogie. But in 1505, from an inquest which was held regarding the lands of Alexander Buchan of Auchmacoy (whose son Andrew had married Marjory Craufurd), the estates appear to have been considerable. Gen. THOMAS BUCHAN, who saw much service abroad, and afterwards succeeded Viscount Dundee in the command of the forces of Scotland, was a son of the laird of Auchmacoy and his wife Margaret Seton. The General, who was also connected with the rising of 1715, "dyed at Ardlogie in Fyvie, and was buried in Logy-Buchan, A.D. M.DCCXX. . . ."

The following is upon a table-shaped stone in the churchyard, besides which a marble tablet, within the kirk, records also the death of Mr Paterson :—

The Rev. WM. PATERSON, 42 years minister of this parish, died July 4, 1816, in the 65 year of his age. ANNA OGILVIE, daughter of Jas. Ogilvie, Esq. of Culquhins and Baldavie, died 17 March 1792, aged 36. Mr Paterson remarried Mrs JANE MAIR, daughter of the Rev. John Mair, minister of Rayne, and widow of the Rev. Alex. Fullerton, minister of Footdee, who died April 4, 1833, aged 75. JOHN-JAMES PATERSON, M.D., surgeon in the Bengal medical establishment of the H.E.I.C.S., died in England, March 21, 1837, aged 40. MARJORY, a daughter, died at Aberdeen 23 Aug. 1841, aged 57.

Within an enclosure :—

Rev. GEORGE CRUDEN, minister of Logie Buchan, after an incumbency of 33 years, died 11 Sep. 1850, in the 77th year of his age. His wife SOPHIA, daughter of the Rev. Wm. Fraser of Tyrie, died 18 Dec. 1839, aged 58.

—Mr C. wrote the Statistical Accounts of Logie-Buchan in 1842, and of Old Deer in 1794, where he was then schoolmaster.

The greater part of Logie-Buchan, on the forfeiture of the Cumins, was granted to the Hays of Errol by Robert the Bruce.

It is said that there were two family chapels here in old times, one at the DOVECOT (which is still a picturesque object on the right of the turnpike road from Ellon to Peterhead), the other at the OLD YARD of Auchmacoy. There was also an Hospital, on the banks of the Ythan, with a house and some land attached to it, for the support of two old people. It was upheld by the lairds of Auchmacoy; and, in 1725, the house is said to be "in good repair." It possibly stood near to the present boat-house—a ferry boat being still the means of direct communication between the north and south sides of the Ythan.

The well-known Scotch air of "Boat o' Logie," is said to have originated from this place.

Apart from Auchmacoy, the properties of Tarty, Birnis, Fechil, and Tippertie, &c., are in Logie-Buchan, the last-named of which supplies bursaries to the Aberdeen College, in the gift of Turner of Turnerhall (*v* p. 60). It was Innes of Tippertie and some other non-subscribing lairds who, in 1644, at the head of about 80 horsemen, defeated the Covenanters while they were plundering the lands of Tarty, from which (says Spalding) the Covenanters returned "in tuais; in threis, in fouris, and not in ane bodie, schamefully buk agane to Abirdene."

Boyndie.

(S. BRANDAN, ABBOT.)

THE kirks of *Inuirboudin* and *Banef*, with certain lands in the neighbourhood, were gifted by King William the Lion to the monks of Arbroath. Both churches (which are separately rated in the Old Taxatio, the latter being much the more valuable), appear to have been subsequently united, possibly about the time of the Reformation, but were again disjoined in 1634.

The ruins of the old kirk of Boyndie, with the belfry upon the west gable, stand upon a knoll near to where the burn of Boyndie falls into the sea. The belfry bears the initials of I. L. F. (James, Lord Findlater), and the date of 1740. The bell is dated 1770.

Over the door of an aisle, upon the south side of the ruins, in raised capitals:—

Lord I have loved the habitation of thy house and the place where thine honour dwelleth. This entry door to the church was put up by me JAMES OGILVIE of Culphin, who was an elder at this place forty six years bypast, at the present year of God 1723.

—This Ogilvie, who gave two silver communion cups to the parish, which are still in use, was afterwards designed of Culvie, in Marnoch.

An arched building on the north side of the ruins, once the burial vault of the Ogilvies of Boyne, has long been used for the interment of some of the less potent resident parishioners. Within it a stone is thus inscribed:—

Here lyes the body of JAMES BYRES, principal servant in the Family of Findlater for above 20 years, and tacksman of the farm of Dallochy. A man who performed the duties of his station with the strictest fidelity, prudence, and diligence, much beloved by the *Noble Family* in which he served, by whom this stone is erected. By his early death the world lost a worthy member of society, his relatives a kind and an affectionate friend, and the poor a generous benefactor. Died 6 Oct. 1784, aged 46. An honest man's the noblest work of God.

Within area of old kirk:—

To the memory of the STUARTS, formerly of Ordens, this being the burial place of that family for many ages. This stone is placed by the Rev. James Stuart, one of their descendants, late Rector of George Town Parish, South Carolina, and Chaplain to the King's Rangers in North America, 1785.

—The erector of this tomb left a considerable amount of money for educational and charitable purposes to the parish. Ordens belonged to Stuarts in 1724, for how long before or after I am not aware, but it was held of the Earls of Findlater.

An enclosure, in the south-west corner of the kirk contains four separate tablets. The oldest bears:—

This lair belongs to James Milne, sometime at Mills of Boyndie, Alexr. Milne at Mill of Alnah, and John Milne at Mill of Boyndie, his sons. This stone is erected by James Milne at Nether Mill of Boyndie, eldest son to the s^d John Milne. Anno 1739.

Upon next oldest monument:—

Erected by James Mill in Mill of Boyndie, in memory of his eldest son JAMES, who was born April 1770, and died Septr. 1788; and of his brother JOHN, late in Boghead of Ord, who was born June 1718, and died Decr. 1792. And also in memory of the said JAMES MILNE himself, who died 14th June 1807, aged 85 years. His widow, ISABEL MILNE, who died 25th June 1823, aged 81 years, is also interred here. His youngest son, ALEXR. MILNE, Lt.-Col. of the 19th Regt. of Foot, died at Demerara, 5th Novr. 1827, aged 48 years.

The above are freestone monuments; and the following inscription is upon a marble slab, encased in yellow freestone:—

Near this place are interred the remains of JOHN MILNE, Esq., surgeon in Banff, who died in consequence of a fall from his horse, May 29th 1833, in the 26th year of his age. Distinguished by active yet unostentatious benevolence, Mr Milne, both in a professional and private capacity, uniformly shewed himself a warm friend to the poor, by whom his untimely fate is deeply deplored. Nor to them only was he an object of regard. By the openness of his manners, the warmth of his friendship, and the integrity of his conduct, he had endeared himself in no ordinary degree to the community at large. To perpetuate the memory of one who, in the morning of life, and in the active discharge of duty, was so suddenly and unexpectedly lost to the world, a number of friends, to whom that memory is dear, have caused this monument to be erected. September 12, 1833.

Upon a freestone tablet:—

Sacred to the memory of JOHN MILNE, late farmer at Mill of Boyndie, who died there 25th May 1849, aged 78 years. And of his spouse JEAN MILNE, who died there 11th June 1835, in the 63rd year of her age. Here also are interred the remains of their children, ROBERT MILNE, who died 8th February 1833, aged 23 years. JOHN MILNE, who died 20th May 1833, in the 26th year of his age, (as recorded on the adjoining tablet), and ABERCROMBY MILNE, who died 9th June 1848, aged 30 years. Their son, ARCHIBALD MILNE, died in New Zealand, 1842, in the 35th year of his age. And their son, WILLIAM MILNE, Collector of Customs at Old Harbour, Jamaica, died there 7th May 1850, aged 36 years.

From two separate stones in church-yard:—

Here lyes GEORGE GILL, in Warielip, under hope of a blessed resurrection, who departed this lyf April 3, 1689. Blessed are the dead, &c.

Here lies the corps of honest JOHN WATT, late farmer in Blairmaid, who departed this life upon the 9th day of March 1758, aged 73 years.

The district of Boyne was a thanedom, in which there was a large hunting forest, of which Sir John Edmonstone had a charter in 1368. About 1485 the lands and thanedom of Boyne came by marriage to Sir Walter Ogilvy, a son of the knight of Lintrathen, in Angus. The Castle of Craig of Boyne, on the west side of the burn of Boyne, of which very little remains, is the reputed seat of the old thanes; and during the Civil Wars the laird found it a safe retreat from Montrose and his soldiers. While searching lately among the slender traces which remain of this stronghold, particularly in the kitchen midden, Mr Garland, farmer of Cowhyth, found bones of animals of the chace, &c., also needles and pins made of bone. Some of the latter are prettily formed and polished; one (in the National Museum) has the letters b, or b. o. c. m. cut upon it.

The more modern castle, once a residence of the Earls of Findlater, and inhabited until about 1745, is among the most imposing and picturesquely situated ruins in the north-east of Scotland. Vandals, however, have been allowed to make sad havock upon these ruins, for scarcely a dressed stone of any interest has been left about the place; although, from the excellent view of it given by Cordiner in his Remarkable Ruins (1791) the lintels, &c., were then wonderfully entire; also the walls painted with figures and legends.

The present church, which is nearly two miles distant from the old one, was built in 1773. A Methodist Chapel was erected in 1838, and a Free Church in 1843, at the fishing village of Whitehills. The Earl of Seafield is patron, and sole heritor of the parish.

In 1681, Sir Patrick Ogilvie of Boyne had a royal warrant to hold two yearly markets in Boyndie, one in the Muir of Whitehills on the 2d Tuesday of May, the other on the Muir of Culfin on 2d Tuesday of October, as well as for a weekly market to be held at Portsoy.

S. BRANDAN's circle, upon the farm of Bankhead, now represented by three rough boulders, one of which exhibits cup-shaped markings, and almost all other antiquities in the parish worthy of remark, are noticed in the Stat. Accounts, &c.

THOMAS RUDDIMAN, the celebrated grammarian, was the son of a farmer at Raggel, where he was born in 1674. Mrs BUCHAN or SIMPSON, the daughter of the keeper of a small inn, and the founder of a sect of religious fanatics, also belonged to this parish. When on her deathbed in 1791, she assured her few remaining apostles, among other cant and blasphemy, that she was the veritable Virgin Mary, and Mother of Jesus!

Mains.
(S. NINIAN, A DISCIPLE OF S. MARTIN.)

THE old name of Mains was *Strathdichty-Comitis*, or the Earl's-Strathdichty. Along with the kirk of Strathmartin, that of Mains was given to the Abbey of Arbroath, by Gilchrist, Earl of Angus. The parishes were united in 1794.

Both churches were in the diocese of St Andrews; and under the name of *Strathechtyn*, that of Mains was dedicated by Bishop David in 1242. *Mains of Fintry* was a later name for the parish. It is said that the name of "Fintry" was imported, and given to the district by the Grahams, from their older property of that name in Stirlingshire. The abbreviated form of *Mains* had arisen from the old name of the locality, which, in 1485 (when "Robert Grahame de Fyntree," and his eldest son had a tack of the teind sheaves from Abbot David of Arbroath), is described as "*le mangs* Stradichyne-Comitis."

The burial-ground of Mains (lately surrounded by a dyke, and put in decent order), is near the castle, and upon the north side of the Gelly burn. The burial aisle of the GRAHAMS of Fintry, which was reserved by the family when the lands were sold, formed the south transept of the kirk, of which it is the only remaining part. It was lately re-edified and adorned with a carving of the Graham arms. The gable is pierced by three lancet windows. Upon the west side of these, and within the aisle, a stoup for holy water, in a late style of the Perpendicular, projects from the wall. A carved stone (18 by 24 inches) embellished by a peculiar representation of the Annunciation (now built over the window in the south transept), was found, in 1868, while digging a grave. The pot and lily rest upon a shield charged with the Graham arms. The lily is held by a winged angel kneeling on the left—on the right stands the Virgin, with nimbus and uplifted hands, in the attitude of prayer. The ribbons remain, but the legends are effaced, and the whole work is considerably mutilated. In all probability, this formed a portion of the altar of the old kirk, which, along with the south aisle, if not the contemporary church itself, had possibly been erected by Sir David Graham and his wife Margaret Ogilvy, whose initials, &c., as shewn below, are upon certain parts of the adjoining castle. A curious lancet window of one light, hewn out of a single stone (possibly taken from the kirk), is built into the wall of the old manse.

The first Graham of Fintry was Robert, eldest son, by a second marriage, of Sir William (ancestor of the Dukes of Montrose), by a daughter of king Robert III. Robert Graham married a daughter of Lovel of Balumby, by whom he had two sons and two daughters. The daughters were married respectively to Erskine of Dun and Haliburton of Pitcur. The youngest son, along with his father, had a lease of the teinds of Balargus and Finlarg, in Tealing, 1485, from the Abbot of Arbroath. From young Graham, who is called "of Balargus," were descended the family of Claverhouse and Duntrune, now represented by Miss Stirling-Graham, the accomplished authoress of Mystifications, &c.

Of the marriage between Graham and Balumby's daughter, an interesting proof exists, in the form of a coffin-slab, which had been taken from the burial place, and now lies upon the top of the court-yard wall. It is embellished with a Calvary Cross upon steps; also, two shields,—one bears the Graham arms, the other those of Graham and Lovel impaled. These words are upon the arms of the cross:—

in . mara . chris . mara.

Robert Graham's eldest son married a daughter

of Douglas, Earl of Angus, and had a son and successor, who was knighted. Sir David (grandson of the last-mentioned), married Margaret, daughter of Ogilvy of Airlie ; and probably the older part of the Castle of Mains was built in his time, since traces of the initials D. G. and D. M. O., and the date of 1556, appear upon the arch of the court-yard, or outer entrance to the house. To his time, also, possibly belongs the stone altar-piece above referred to. Upon a slab, built into a late portion of the castle :—

PATRI.E. ET. POSTERIS. GRATIS. ET. AMICIS. 1582.

Sir David's oldest son and heir, to whose time the above inscription belongs, having taken part in the "Popish plot" of the Earls of Huntly and Errol, was beheaded at Edinburgh in 1592. His son, who became a staunch Royalist, married a daughter of Haliburton of Pitcur. The square tower of the castle, which gives so much character to the building, belongs to his period. Upon a skew-put stone are the Graham arms, and the date of 1650.

This Graham became 9th laird of Fintry, and from him the present representative of the family is descended. This branch of the Grahams has now no landed interest in Angus, the greater part of their estates having become, by purchase, the property of Erskine of Linlathen. (*v.* p. 112.)

The burial ground contains a number of tombstones. One (with a bold carving of a mascle, with a cross at each point), is inscribed :—

Hic sitv . . . nestva vir, ALEXANDER MATHOV, bvrgen : de Dvndee, qvi obiit die 23 mensis Octobris, anno 1585, ætatis svæ 53. Discite ab exemplo, mortales, discite nostro. Svm qvod eris. Omnia svbjecta mvtabilitati.

[Here lies an honest man, ALEXANDER MATHOV, burgess of Dundee, who died 23 Oct. 1585, aged 53. Learn, mortals, learn from my example. I am what thou shalt be. All things are subject to change.]

Some tombstones exhibit curious carvings : one has the beaters of a waulk mill upon it, others weavers' looms, shuttles, &c.; but the common objects are mill-rinds, and mill-stone picks, there having been, at one time, a number of meal and barley mills upon the Dichty. A gravestone, ornamented as last mentioned, initialed I.B: I.M., and dated 1655, bears this epitaph :—

Vnder this ston interd lyes he,
Who 40 two zeers livd wt ws,
At mil & kil right honestlie,
And wt his nighbr dealt he thvs ;
But death in Apryl 55,
Frō of the stage did him rēove.
O earth, earth, earth,
Hear the word of the Lord. Ior 22. 29.

Upon a flat stone, with armorial bearings :—

Heir lyes ane godly honest voman, named KATHRINE FYF, spovs to Thomas Nicoall in Balmovre, vho depairted this lyfe the 2 of Janvar, the year of God 1648, and of agge 32.

Adjoining the above, with the carvings of a mill-rind and millstone pick :—

WIL . . . ME PAWLL : IONET IOBSON. 1645.

A table-shaped stone, initialed I. D : G. Y., bears :—

Heir one beneath this ston consvming lyes, on wirtves honest . . . IOHN DVFF by nam, who, while he lived he vas beloved of al, and did deses the 11 of Nov. 1654, and of his age 60 :—

I rest in hop intil the tym apier,
That I shal rest, and mit my Sawior.

The following, embellished with the shoemakers' crown and cutting knife, preserves an old spelling of the surname of *Butchelor* :—

Hir lyes a godlay and onest man called JAMES BESLER, bvrges of Dvndie, vha departet this lif November 29, 1665, and of his age 84. JAMES BESELER, shovmakr.

Heir lyes ane godly honest man, WALTER GID, who deceast the 25 Awgwst 1664, and of his age . . .

THOS. THOMSON, hbd. to Margt. Clerk, d. 1736, a. 63 :—

He who with . . . . did me bless,
With riches, life, and breath ;
Me from these three did take away,
By sickness and by death.

HELEN DONALDSON, wife of Jas. Kinnaird, d. 1738, a. 63 :—

To honour the dead we may be bold,
Our father Abraham hath us told. Gen. 23.

WILLIAM BUICK, Gutherston (1751) :—
  Among the rest of Adam's race,
  That in this world liv'd ;
  There's one confin'd within this Tomb
  Who upright was and pious.
  He while in life was very just,
  Gave every man his due ;
  But now he is exalted high,
  In Heaven we hope he's now.

An oval-shaped slab of white marble, which fell out of a mural monument, bears :—

This stone is erected by his widow, to the memory of JAMES MARSHALL, surgeon in Peterhead, who died at the Mains of Fintry, on the 8th of August 1813, aged 28 years.

—Dr M. "late of the Winchelsea Indiaman," was the son of a retired naval officer, who subsequently sailed a vessel from Peterhead. Dr M.'s wife was a daughter of James Skelton, a shipowner at that port.

ROBERT AIRTH, d. 1763, aged 12 mo :—
  This charming child most comely was,
  And pleasant once a day ;
  But now, alas, he lowly lies
  Here in this bed of clay. &c.

CHARLES PEEBLES, schoolmaster of Mains, d. 20 July 1801, a. 66, his wd. ANN CRABB, d. 7 Dec. following, a. 64 :—
  How useful they in training youth,
  When thoughtless of the paths of truth
    They need the guiding reins ;
  The East and West, the South and North,
  Doth testify from proved worth
    Of youth spent at the Mains.

There is a burial ground, containing a number of modern tombstones, at the present parish church of Mains. The church was erected in 1800 ; and a tablet within it is thus inscribed :—

Sacred to the memory of CHARLOTTE, Lady OGILVY, sole proprietor of the estate of Bank, in the parish of Strathmartin, eldest daughter of Walter Tullideph, Esq. of the Island of Antigua, and relict of Sir John Ogilvy, Bart. of Inverquharity, late of the Scots Grays, &c., who died at the age of 72. [No year given].

—Lady Ogilvy's father was a descendant of Principal Tullideph of St Andrews. Tullideph Hall is now called Baldovan House, and Baldovan is the present name of the estate of Bank. The first Ogilvys of Inverquharity and Airlie were brothers of Sir Walter of Lintrathen ; but the seniority of the two first named brothers is, as yet, a matter of doubt. In 1625, a baronetcy was created in the Inverquharity branch.

The Castle of Mains is one of the most picturesque ruins in Angus, and has been sketched and painted by David Roberts, and other modern artists. The oldest portion is quite a ruin ; but it is to be hoped that it will be preserved from further decay. The latest building, which is attached to the south side, is inhabited. According to tradition, the old Earls of Angus had a castle here. It is further said by Bocce, that Mains was the scene of the reputed murder of a sister of William the Lion, by her husband, Earl Gilchrist. (v. p. 185.) Be this as it may, it is certain that the district belonged in property, after the days of the Earls of Angus, to Malcolm Ramsay, possibly of Auchterhouse; afterwards to Adam Irvine ; next to the Grahams.

The Gelly burn, which runs through the romantic dell between the castle and the burial-ground had, at one time, the name of *Syran;* and Synnivic, or Sinivee, is the name of a copious spring which issues from the crevice of a rock in the den—a name which may be a corruption of that of S. NINIAN, the patron saint of Mains.

Near a dovecot, built in imitation of a ruined castle, and upon the north side of the Dichty, stood the reputed birth place of the celebrated JOHN GRAHAM of Claverhouse, Viscount Dundee. He was mortally wounded at Killiecrankie, 27th July 1689, and buried in the family vault at Blair Athol, from which, it is said, his bones (?) were secretly removed, at no distant date, and reinterred within the precincts of an Episcopal Church in Aberdeenshire.

The following oddly expressed entry, dated Oct. 5, 1726, occurs in the Session records :—

"David Duncan at Mill of Mains had a daughter baptised ANN brought forth by Isobel Johnston his spouse before the congregation."

Strathmartin.

(S. MARTIN.)

THE kirk of *Strathechtin-Martin* was dedicated by David, Bishop of St Andrews, in 1249.

The church was suppressed as a place of worship when the new one was erected at Mains; and part of the materials of the former kirk were employed in building the latter.

Sir John Ogilvy (whose ancestral burial-place is within the parish church of Kirriemuir), has a burial vault upon the site of the old kirk of Strathmartin. The last interred there was Lady JANE, second wife of Sir John Ogilvy, and daughter of Thomas, Earl of Suffolk. Lady JANE, who died 28th July 1861, was remarkable for her friendly manner to, and substantial sympathy with, the poor. As the founder of the Asylum for Imbecile Children at Baldovan, and of The Home at Dundee, her name will long live in the hearts of the sorrowful and the penitent.

On the west of the graveyard (also within an enclosure), lie the remains, unmarked, of Admiral LAIRD. He was the son of a corn-merchant in Dundee, and distinguished himself during the American war. He bought the estate of Strathmartin about 1785 for £15,500, upon the improvement of which he expended nearly as much again. The rental is now over £1000 a-year. Admiral LAIRD died in 1811, and was succeeded by his grandson, Colonel Laird, of the F. and K. Militia.

At the time the kirk of Strathmartin was demolished the burial ground was about double its present size, the public road and certain cottages on the north side of it being within the old boundary. The burial place (were it properly cared for) would be one of the loveliest in the district. It is upon a rising ground on the north bank of the Dighty, surrounded by old trees, and enclosed by a stone wall. It contains a number of tombstones, from which the inscriptions quoted below are selected:—

Heir lyes ane godly honest man JAMES HVNTER, hvsband to Isobel Wat. He decest November 6, year of God 1664, of age 58. Her children PATRICK and JANET.

The first part of next inscription is carved in raised characters, round the edge of a table-shaped tomb, the rest is incised upon the face of it:—

Heir lyes ane godly honest man IOHN HAVL, sometyme at Baldiven Mill, with CATHEN RAMSEY, his loving yovng wife,
Both in on grave vntil the tym acord
That they shall heir the earch angel of the Lord:
Ovr sovl doth bend ovr bodes straicht and even,
As with it selfe it wold theme raise to Heaven;
Bvt al in vaine it vndergoes svch toyle,
The body will not leave its native soyle.
Age pvls it downe, and makes it stoope fvll low,
Till Death doth give his fatall overthrow;
Then throvgh the bodies breach the sovl doth rise,
And like a conqverovr movnt the skies,
To its eternal rest from whence it came,
As is ther bodies in tombe heir lyes.
to wit, JOHN HAVLL at Baldiven Mill, who died in pace the 22 of March 1648, and of his age 55 yeirs, with his beloved spoves CATHEN RAMSAY, who did decese the 4 of Ianvari 1666 zeirs, and of her aige 77 zeirs, both in on grave heir lyes.

Adjoining the above:—

Here lyes an godly honest man called IOHN THANE, husband to Elspit Edentovne, who dwelt in Kirktovn of Strickmartin, who departed the 1 day of Agust 1677, and of his age 51; and besides him lyes ELSPIT EDENTOUNE, his spous, who departed the 29 day of Agust 1679, and of hir age 56.

Another stone bears:—

Heir lyes DAVID THAIN, who deceased the 26 day of February 1670. Blessed are the dead, &c.

Upon a stone lately removed from its place, and laid against south dyke:—

Here lyes ane vertovs honest woman ISOBEL MATHEW, last spous to Iohn Boyack, maltman burges in Dundie, who died 22 of October 1690, and of her age 60:—
From dust I cam, and thither do returne,
Who here abids till tribes of earth shall mourn;
Till heaven and earth wrapt in a scrol shall be,
And Christ with saints coming in clouds ile se,
When soul and bodie united shall again,
Be lifted up to Christ for to remaine.

A table-shaped stone, with a weaver's loom and shuttle carved upon it, bears :—

Here lyes ane godly honest man JAMES ANDERSONE, husband to Iean Baxter, induellers in Balkelon, who departed this life Ianury 26, the year 1690, and of his age 70 :—
 Among the earth, beneath this stone,
  Doth his forefathers lie ;
 And this has been their burial plac,
  Since man's remembrie.

Carvings of a loom and shuttle accompany next :—

Heir lyes an honest man ANDREW DAVIDSON, husband to Margrat Mavar, induellers in Auchenherrie, who departed this life the 30 of May 1695, and of his age 56, and 2 of their children :—
 A godly man lyis here
 Who was good to the poor,
 He keeped ay good companie
 And ordor in his familie.
 He's gone to Heaven to his rest,
 Among the angels that are blest.

JAS., son of Thos. Low, flour mill, Dundee, d. 1752, a. 18 y. :—
 Thy name ay, thy fame ay,
  Shall never be cutt off ;
 Thy grave ay, shall have aye,
  Thy honest epitaph.

JOHN ROBERTSON, Cotterton of Strathmartin, d. 1753, a. 74 :—
 Heir lyes a godly honest man,
  All men that knew him said—
 He was an elder of the church,
  And a weaver to his trade.
 These words gave comfort unto him
  When God's word he did read—
 If that the Son did make him free,
  He should be free indeed.

ALEXR. BELL, teuant, Kirkton, d. 1759, a. 78 :—
 I lived almost eighty years,
  Within this vale of tears ;
 At last cold death on me laid hands,
  Whome every mortal fears.
 And hath my body here enclosed
  Within this grave of earth ;
 When Christ's last trumpet gives the call
  I shall come forth in mirth.
 When to his heaven he shall me bring,
  With songs of melody,
 I shall his praises ever sing,
  To all eternity.

Upon the face of a table-shaped tombstone :—

1800 : Erected by Geo. Brown, shipmaster, Dundee, in memory of his father, brothers, and sister. His father JAMES BROWN, late farmer of Balmedown, died 26 March 1785, aged 62 years. . . . . His brothers, JAMES, died 9 March 1788, aged 25 years ; JOHN died 28 March 1795, aged 32 years :—
 While here on earth JOHN did remain,
  He liv'd at peace with every man ;
 And yet a Murderer took his life—
  But all comes from his Maker's hand.
 While on this earth they lived hear,
  They serv'd the Lord with all their mind ;
 Now in the heav'ns we hope they sing,
  Where man and angels are combin'd.

On north edge of same :—

 Farewell, vain world, Iv' had enough of thee,
 Now carles what thou sayest of me ;
 Thy love I court not, nor thy frown I fear,
 My days are past, my head lies cover'd here ;
 If fault in me, be sure take care to shun,
 Look to yo'rself, for to death you soon must come.

When the burial-ground of Strathmartin was enclosed, and subsequently in the course of digging graves, the different fragments of sculptured stones were discovered which are now to be seen at the Kirktown. The largest of these, which bears the representation of two serpents, was found in the bottom of a grave in 1813, and through the good offices of the present venerable schoolmaster, it was placed in its present position. In connection with this and the sculptured stones, which stand near Strathmartin Castle, and upon the farm of Balkello, in Tealing, and not at *Ballutheron*, as is commonly said, there is an interesting legend. Though well known, it may be briefly repeated.

Long, long ago, the farmer of Pitempan had nine pretty daughters. One day their father thirsted for a drink from his favourite well, which was in a marsh at a short distance from the house. The fairest of the nine eagerly obeyed her father's wish, by running to the spring. Not returning within a reasonable time, a second went in quest of her sister. She, too, tarried so long, that another volunteered, when the same result happened to her, and to five other sisters in succession. At last the ninth sister went to the spring, and there, to her horror, beheld among the bulrushes, the dead bodies of her sisters guarded by *a dragon!* Before she was able to escape, she too fell into the grasp of the monster; but not until her cries had brought people to the spot. Amongst these was her lover, named *Martin*, who, after a long struggle with the *dragon*, which was carried on from Pitempan to Balkello, he succeeded in conquering the monster. It is told that Martin's sweetheart died from injuries or fright; and the legend adds, that in consequence of this tragedy, the spring at Pitempan was named the *Nine Maiden Well;* and the sculptured stone at Strathmartin, also *St. Martin's Stane*, at Balkello, were erected by the inhabitants to commemorate the event.

It is further asserted that the incentive cry of *Strike, Martin!* by the maiden to her lover, when he first encountered the monster, gave name to the district; while the following rhyme is popularly believed to indicate the cause of the dragon's rapaciousness, and the progress of the conflict between it and the victor :—

> It was tempit at Pitempan,
> Draiglet at Ba'dragon,
> Stricken at Strickmartin,
> An' kill'd at Martin's Stane !

People still alive in the parish recollect of nine graves, near the east end of the old kirk of Strathmartin, which were pointed out as those of the nine sisters; and it is uniformly added that the stone with two serpents carved upon it stood at the head of these mounds. I am also told that no interments have been made in these graves during the recollection of the oldest inhabitants.

So much for tradition. Probably this interesting romance was an after thought, and may have been founded upon the fact of serpents and certain nondescript animals being represented upon the stones at the Kirktown and Balkello. In addition to this, we know that the church was dedicated to S. MARTIN; and that there was a chapel in Strathdichtie, which was inscribed to the saints, known as the NINE MAIDENS. The latter place of devotion may have stood at Pitempan, since the Irish words *Pit-teamp-an* signify a small church, or temple situated in a hollow. To indulge further in etymological speculation, one might trace the origin of the name of Baldragon to the Irish *Bal-dreighan*, a town or place abounding in black thorn, or sloe bushes.

The fatal well, which is about 100 yards from the reputed site of the old farm-house of Pitempan, and on the south side of the burn, was recently covered by a flagstone. The well at Baldragon, situated in a hollow below the farm-house, remains open; and Martin's Stane, where the serpent is said to have been killed, stands upon Balkello farm, embellished with a transfixed serpent. Another stone, with "the elephant," and other carvings common to such relics of antiquity, is in a dyke near Strathmartin Castle; and a number of fragments of the same interesting class have been found from time to time in the kirkyard.

The Dichty, which runs through the united parishes, is bridged in various places. Two of the bridges were erected through the influence of Admiral Laird, and one by the Corporation of Bakers, Dundee, all before 1794.

The Rev. DAVID MAXWELL, "minister and chief heritor of Strathmartin," who died 6 June 1774, left the interest of £100 sterling for the education of four poor scholars; but, like many similar bequests, through mismanagement or otherwise, this has been long lost to the parish. Mr MAXWELL, who was one of the last descendants of the old lairds of Tealing, was translated to Strathmartin from Essie and Nevay in 1751. He left two daughters, who were long annuitants upon the estate of Strathmartin.

~~~~~~~~~~~~~~~~~~~~~~~~~~~~~

Auchterless.
(S. DONAN, ABBOT.)

THE kirk of *Ochtirles* and its pertinents were confirmed to Edward, Bishop of Aberdeen, by Pope Adrian IV., in 1157. It was a parsonage belonging to Old Machar, of which cathedral the parson was chanter.

According to Dempster, S. DONAN'S staff, which was long preserved at Auchterless, cured fever and jaundice; but was destroyed at the Reformation. S. DONAN'S fair stood at the Kirktown of Auchterless. The bell bears:—

PETER . IANSEN . ANNO . DNI . 1644.

The church, built in 1780, was repaired in 1832. In the east end of it are two wood carvings. One bears a fess between three boars' heads erased, possibly for Gordon, the other quarterly, a lion rampant, and three papingoes, for Ogilvy of Dunlugas, dated 1644, and initialed P. G: I. O.

The Duffs of Hatton have a mausoleum, or aisle, on the south-west of the church, adorned with their arms and motto, &c. Three marble monuments, built into the north wall of the church, refer to this family. The first inscription quoted below relates to the first Duff of Hatton (v. p. 76):—

To the memory of ALEXANDER DUFF, Esq. of Hatton, born 1 Jan. 1688, died 27 Dec. 1753; and of KATHERIN DUFF, his spouse, who died 23 Dec. 1758, aged 75. Also in memory of their son, JOHN DUFF, Esq. of Hatton, born 14 Jan. 1727, died 2 Aug. 1787; and of his spouse HELEN DUFF, born 21 June 1744, died 2 Oct. 1802. There are also interred of their family here, ALEXANDER DUFF, Esq. of Hatton, their eldest son; two sons named JOHN; two daughters named BATHIA; two daughters named ANN, and a daughter named KATHARINE.

On left of the above:—

To the memory of ALEXANDER DUFF, Esq. of Hatton, born 26 March 1718, died 3 Nov. 1764, who, to a native goodness of heart, sweetness of disposition, and universal benevolence, joined the social virtues of the husband, father, and friend. This marble is inscribed by the Lady Anne Duff his widow, 1765.

On right of last quoted:—

To the memory of JOHN DUFF, eldest son of Garden Duff, Esq. of Hatton, born 14 June 1807, died 27 April 1829, whose goodness of heart, and amiable disposition, endeared him to his family, and all who knew him.

—Dying unmarried, John Duff was succeeded in Hatton by the father of the gentleman named in the next inscription, which is carved upon a neat cross of white marble:—

GARDEN-WILLIAM DUFF of Hatton, died 17 Sep. 1866, aged 52.

From tombstones in churchyard of Auchterless:— .

Hear lyes ane very honest man called GEORG RAMSAY, who departed . . . . . lyfe to blessed eternity Ag. 10, 1685.

In hope of a blessed resurrection, here lyes interred the body of JOHN DOWNIE, sometime merchant in Kirktown of Auchterless, who departed this life the first day of January 1754, in the 52 year of his age. His spouse ELSPET MURDOCH, died Jan. 19, 1770, aged 77.

Here lyes ane honest man ALEX. Co . . sometyme in Kirktoun of Auchterless, who dyed Aprill 2, 1719; and ELSPET BROUN, his spouse who died . . . . . .

GEO. SANDISON, Petts, Fyvie, hd. of Barbara Reedford, d. 1782, a. 34:—

Silent grave, to thee I trust,
This precious pile of worthy dust;
Keep it safe, O sacred tomb,
Until a wife, or child, shall ask for room.

Upon a headstone:—

ADAM MAITLAND, late servant in Cushnie. He was deaf and dumb from his birth, yet the ready and intelligible manner in which he communicated by signs his ideas on a great variety of subjects clearly proved that Mind may exist when neither Speech nor Hearing are bestowed by the Author of our Being. He died 9 Jan. 1822, aged 68. Erected by Andrew Jamieson in Cushnie, in memory of a man who had faithfully served his father and him for upwards of forty years.

Near the above:—

REBECCA PATERSON, died 23 March 1819, aged 88. As a small tribute of respect for the fidelity with which she discharged her duty as a servant in his family for three generations, and during the long period of 80 years, this stone is erected to her memory by Andrew Jamieson, Cushnie.

—Hector Jamieson is described as "grassman," or cottager, on the farm of Cushnie in 1696 and

John Paterson was the name of the principal servant on the farm. There were several Maitlands in the parish at the same time, as tenant-farmers, weavers, &c. In south wall of church :—

Near this stone are deposited the remains of GEORGE BARCLAY, M.D., physician to the Aberdeen Infirmary, who died 20 Dec. 1819, aged 27. Endowed with a cheerful, mild, and affectionate disposition ; respected for his talents and acquirements, and for zeal and benevolence in his profession ; his early death was the occasion not only of sorrow to his friends, but of regret to the community in which he lived.

Built into the church wall, upon the right, and outside of east door :—

✠ Sacred to the memory of Mrs ELIZABETH ROBERTS, late of Darra, in the parish of Turriff. Died 18 April 1834, aged 68. Erected by her affectionate brother, George Paterson, of the Island of Grenada, West Indies, 1838.

GEORGE and ROBERT MIDDLETON (1816) :—
Once lovely youths.
Called from this lowly state away,
Ere they the prime of life had seen ;
Who met their end without dismay,
Because their lives had blameless been.

A table-shaped stone bears :—

JAMES CRUICKSHANK, in Toukshill, died 13 Jan. 1814, aged 71. His mother, MARGARET TOPP, died 1769, aged 64. He endowed a bursary at King's College, another at Marischal College, each of £20 a-year, and astricted to the names of Cruickshank and Tapp or Topp, or otherwise to accumulate ; and left handsome charities and legacies to his friends. Inscribed in testimony of respect to the said JAMES CRUICKSHANK in Toukshill, New Deer, by Alex. Cruickshank, in Middlchill, his nephew, 1818.

Built into outside wall of church :—

Here ly CHRISTIN HAURES, spouse to Mr Alex. Ross, minr. at Achterles, who departed this life Oct. 5th 1710, and of her age 22. Also JAMES, ISOBELL, and KATH : ROSSES, his children by ELIZ: OGILVIE, his 2d spouse. She dy'd May 17, 1720.

Upon a lying stone :—

Rev. ALEXANDER ROSE, died 7 Dec. . . . . in . . . year of his age, and 17th of his ministry.

Upon a marble within the church : —

The Rev. GEORGE DINGWALL, the faithful minister of this parish for the long period of 50 years, was born at Smallburn, Auchterless, 3d March 1786, died 15 January 1862.

—Mr D. left two bursaries of £4 10s each to the school of Auchterless, also one of £15 to the University of Aberdeen. He was the son of a farmer at Smallburn, where his ancestors had long resided.

A conspicuous monument bears an inscription, of which the following is an abridgement :—

WILLIAM CHALMERS, late in Kirktown of Auchterless, born 22 June 1726, died 14 April 1804. MARJORY THOMSON, his spouse, died Sep. 15, 1806, aged 80, &c. A son, JOHN, born 28 Aug. 1760, died 4 Feb. 1805. A daughter MARGARET, born 26 Sep. 1767, died 10 Feb. 1827. Other three sons, JAMES, A.M., born 25 April 1763, died 22 July 1846 ; ALEXANDER, born 2 May 1765, died 13 Sep. 1848 ; and GEORGE, died at Turriff, 9 April 1852, aged 96.

—The three last-named in the above inscription erected " Chalmers' Infant School" at Turriff, and endowed it with £20 annually. They also left about £300 a-year to various public charities in Aberdeen, &c. The first brother was a merchant in Auchterless, the second a farmer there, and the third a stocking merchant, &c., in Aberdeen.

An old religious house, dedicated to S. MARY, stood near the farm house of Seggat, beside the Holy Well, which was much frequented by the superstitious, and where votive offerings were frequently deposited. There was also a burial ground ; but no tombstones remain.

Stone circles, three of which (concentric) are at Kirkhill, were at one time pretty common in the parish.

In the reign of Alex. III. the barony of Seggat was valued at 15 merks ; and that of Auchterless was held on the reddendo of paying a sparrow hawk annually. Of the last property, Alex. (son and heir apparent of Irvine of Drum), and his wife, Janet Allardice, had a charter in 1499.

Before that date Auchterless belonged to Dempsters, a family that long held the property of Careston in Angus, as hereditary doomsters to the Scotch kings, also the office of justiciary to the Abbots of Arbroath.

Of this family was Thomas Dempster (*v.* TURRIFF), who records in his Ecclesiastical History of Scotland, that MALCOLM ARDES, a Carmelite friar, who flourished early in the 14th century, and wrote an account of the battle of Falkirk, &c., belonged to Auchterless. Also JAMES LAING, whom (in speaking of the Popish writers against Knox), Dr McCrie characterises as the " most impudent of all liars !" Of a different type was HENRY SCOUGAL, who resigned the chair of Philosophy at Aberdeen, and retired to Auchterless, from which, after recruited health, he became Professor of Divinity in the same University. His tombstone is in the College-Kirk at Aberdeen.

It was at Auchterless, on 12th January 1775, that PETER GARDEN died at the age of 131. The *Scots Magazine* remarks that he retained his memory and senses to the last, and lived under ten sovereigns. (?) .... It is also said that he saw HENRY JENKINS in London, who died in 1670, aged 169, who, when young, carried arrows to be used by the English at Flodden. A now rare portrait of Garden was painted by James Walis, and engraved by H. Gavin.

Logie-Montrose.

(S. MARTIN.)

BISHOP DAVID of St Andrews, in the year 1243, dedicated the church of *Logy*, under the name of " Logie Cuthil." In the Register of Ministers (1574), it is called " Logymontrois," at which time, along with the kirks of Pert, Monmure, and Fearn, it was served by one clergyman, Mr William Gray, of whom the celebrated James Melville speaks so highly in his Diary, was then incumbent.

The churches of Logie and Pert were first proposed to be united in 1645, but it was not until 1661 that the union was ratified by Act of Parliament. Down to 1775, both church fabrics were maintained and served (probably alternately) by one minister. The present church of the united parish, rebuilt in 1840, stands nearly half way between the old places of worship. The patronage of Logie belonged to the Archbishop of St. Andrews, and that of the united parish is alternately exercised by the Crown and St Mary's College, St Andrews.

The old kirk and burial-ground have a secluded and romantic site upon the west side of the North Esk, and there the principal scene of George Beattie's poem of " John o' Arnha" is laid. S. MARTIN'S Den (near which stands a Free Church, called " the Den Kirk"), preserves, along with a spring well, the name of the titular saint of the parish.

Until the old church was restored as a burial-place for the Carnegys of Craigo, little more remained of it than parts of the south, north, and east walls. It appears to have been a sixteenth century building, with three lancet windows, or lights in the east end, and an arched doorway on the south. The old awmbry, much defaced, is preserved in the north wall. The restoration of the building, which is in the Decorated style, has been done with much taste. Lights have been inserted in the south wall; and, in the west, or entrance end, round the arch of the door, in raised antique Roman capitals, is this text:—

I am the resurrection and the life; he that believeth in me, though dead, yet shall he live.

Over the doorway are two shields, one charged with the Carnegy arms, the other with those of Grant and Macpherson, quarterly: the Carnegy eagle (in allusion to the founder of the family having been a churchman), bears an open book, instead of a cup, upon the breast. Over the shields is the date of the restoration of the building, 1857, also a triangular window near the middle of the gable. Neat stone crosses are upon each of the gable points; and the interior displays a roof of open timber. Near the middle of the

D D

north wall, a marble tablet, set in light coloured freestone, is thus inscribed :—

Here lie the remains of THOMAS CARNEGY of Craigo, Esq. ; and of MARY CARNEGY, his spouse. He died 9th June 1793, aged 64, and was survived by his Widow for many years, which she devoted to the exemplary performance of all the duties of an affectionate mother. She died 20th Novr. 1815, aged 65, leaving in the minds of her children the greatest love and admiration of her many virtues, and an earnest wish to profit by her example. Their second daughter, Elizabeth, wife of the Hon. Lord Gillies, has erected this monument as a testimony of her affection and gratitude to her Parents.

—Mrs C. was the second daughter of James Gardyne of Middleton. A flat slab in north-east of the aisle covers the graves of her son and his wife, a sister of Sir Geo. M. Grant of Ballindalloch :—

DAVID CARNEGY of Craigo, born 9 March 1776, died 10th Nov. 1843. Mrs CARNEGY of Craigo, born — Sep. 1779, died 24th Sept. 1856.

On south of last mentioned :—

MARY CARNEGY, second daughter of David Carnegy of Craigo, born 4th May 1811, died 23d Feb. 1847.

A third slab, in front of the marble monument, bears this record of the last male descendant of the Carnegys of Craigo :—

THOMAS CARNEGY of Craigo, born 9th March 1804, died 12th June 1856.

—As before shown (v. p. 90), the founder of the Craigo Carnegys was David, minister at Farnell. He had a son, Robert "expectant," who preached occasionally, but the Presbytery found such fault with him in not "exerciseing when his turn is," and as he gave no satisfactory excuse, except that he had occasion to go "about weightie affaires," he appears to have lost the kirk of Farnell, to which, on 1st May 1673, Mr John Lamy was translated from Maryton. The last-named THOMAS CARNEGY left the property to his cousin Thomas Grant, W.S., Edinburgh, son of Sir George Macpherson-Grant of Ballindalloch.

The tombstones in the burial ground are few in number, and of modern date. Possibly the oldest, which is much effaced, lies at the east end of the kirk, and bears to have covered the grave of a "religious man." The three following inscriptions are from other gravestones :—

ROBERT FINDLAY, Tolmauts, hd. to Margt. Read, d. 1742, a. 60 :—
All who pass by, behould survie,
Think on this afull shrine ;
Hers moistic bons and broken skuls,
And graves all over green.
But where the souls, those deathless things
That left these bodies hear ?
Isc not give ansuer, but reffer
Till Christ our lord appeir.

JAMES CROLL, Law of Craigo, d. 1728, a. 21 :—
Faith makes vs sones and heros to the most high,
Faith leads to gloriovs immortallity ;
By faith the povr of Satan wee defie,
If on Christ's merits wee by faith relie ;
And if trv faith wnto the end endvre
Yovr evidence for Heauen is good and sur.

ALEXANDER VALENTINE, d. 1794, a 60 ; his wf. JANET CAIRD, d. 1823, a. 92 :—
My friends in Christ that are above,
Them will I go and see;
And thou my friends in Christ below,
Will soon come after me.

Mr WM. CRUDEN, sometime minister of Logie-Pert, was the author of at least two volumes, one of Hymns (Aberd. 1761), the other, Nature Spiritualised, in a variety of poems (Lond. 1766).

Pert.
(S. ———.)

THE old kirk of *Pert* is a picturesque ruin by the side of the turnpike road from Brechin to Laurencekirk. Possibly the church and parish were erected by Superintendent Erskine of Dun, to whom the greater part of the district belonged in property, and in whose time the kirk is first mentioned.

The bell, which is preserved in the belfry, is inscribed, PERT 1704. The south-west skew-put stone of the kirk has the odd figure of a hammer incised upon it; and, from the style of the building, the ruins appear to be those of the kirk of Erskine's time.

Though undistinguished, the ashes of JOHN FALCONER, who was Bishop of Brechin from 1709, repose here. He was a cadet of the noble family of Halkerton, died at Inglismaldie July 6, 1723, and is described as "a good and grave man and very modest, tall, black, and stooping."

Seven separate stones, which appear to have been pillars or supports of a table-shaped tomb, lie in the burial-ground. The carvings are dateless, but clearly the work of the 18th century. They bear respectively the words quoted below, and the emblems, &c., described:—

UNDER . THIS . STONE . DOOTH . LY . TUO . PERSONS WHO . KEEIT . ANE . HONEST . FAMILE . BUT . NOU THEY . ARE . PAST . INTO . ETERNITY.

—The figure of a thistle follows the above words. Below the following quotation from Horace the sower of the parable is represented:—

PALLIDA . MORS . ÆQUO . PULSAT. PEDE . PAUPERUM . TABERNAS . REGUMQUE . TURRES.

—The figures of death, a dart, a scythe, and a coffin, are carved after the next:—

KOMMANDING . DEATH . THAT . CROUL . DEART DOUNE . THRO . AND . VOUND . OUR . HEART.

—Alongside of Adam and Eve at the forbidden tree:—

HOMO . DAMNAVIT.

MOSES

is represented striking the rock. A harp and lily accompany the figure, and name of—

KING . DAVID.

Upon the seventh stone is the word,

ARON.

The chief priest wears a mitre, breastplate, and a long robe; and carries a censer suspended from the end of *Aaron's Rod:* The rod is represented as a round-headed, short, knotty stick.

A burial vault or aisle is on the north of the church, and a marble tablet, within the ruins, is inscribed to

MARY ALLARDICE, daughter of James Allardice, Esq. of that Ilk, in the Mearns, second wife of James Macdonald, Esq., long sheriff-substitute of that county, and only son of Thomas Macdonald, advocate, Aberdeen. She died at Inglismaldie, 4 January 1801, in the 75th year of her age. The said JAMES MACDONALD died 23 August 1809, aged 83. They lived upwards of forty-two years together in greatest happiness, and in the practice of every Christian virtue, beloved and revered by their family, and by all who knew them. This stone is erected by their only daughter MARY, only surviving child of six children, and wife of Charles Ogilvy, Esq. of Tannadice. Also, here lyes the body of MARGARET OGILVY, daughter of the above Charles Ogilvy, and Mary Macdonald, who died 25 Oct. 1805, aged 3 weeks.

—Mary Allardice (whose mother was a daughter of Milne of Balwyllo, provost of Montrose), was aunt of SARAH-ANN ALLARDICE, who married Robert Barclay of Urie (*v.* p. 83). In 1785, Mrs Barclay was served eldest nearest lawful heir portioner of Wm. the last Earl of Airth and Monteith, brother of her great-great-grandmother. Mrs Barclay, divorced in 1793, afterwards married John Nudd; and dying in 1833, aged 78, was buried at Sprewston in Norfolk. (Sir H. Nicolas' Earldom of Strathern, &c., p. 119.) Mr Ogilvy of Tannadice was the son of a physician in Forfar (*v.* pp. 11, 33).

So far as I have seen the following is the oldest dated inscription at Pert:—

1662 Heir lyes IANNET GORME, somtym spovs to Iames Strahavchn, vho depairted in the year of God the 28 of December.

An adjoining tombstone possibly belongs to the same race. It bears:—

Here lyes ROBERT WILLACK, who departed this life in the year 1705, of his age 67, Agust 10 . . . . MARGRET SMITH and ISABEL STRACHAN his spouses.

Upon a table-shaped stone, dated 1664:—

Beneath this stone coverd is the body of IHONE ROBERTSON, bvt that pairt vhich better is, avay to

Haven is gone. The paths of Death is to be trodn
by al and every one, vho in the earth doe dvel ; bvt
faith it overcomes.

ALEX. RENNY'S wife (1696) :—
Mors certa est, incerta dies, hora agnita nulli ;
Extremam quare quamlibet esse puta.

—Eccl. xii, 7, here follows cut in Hebrew characters, then this translation of the preceding :—

Frail man, uncertain is thy death,
Uncertain is thy day ;
Non knovs the hor of his last breath,
Then look for it alvay.

Here lyes JAMES HODGSTON, who departed this
lyfe in the year 1720, of his age 80, Octob. 12 day,
and of WILIAM HODGSTON, his son, and JANET
FVLERTON his spovse.

A headstone, within an enclosure, belongs to a
family named BUCHANAN, farmers, North Water
Bridge. The first recorded died in 1751, aged
70 ; the last in 1845, aged 80. Upon one side is a
circle, with four grotesquely shaped male figures :
their feet are turned towards the circle, and over
their respective heads are the words :—

I DO RING . I DID RING.
I ONCE RANG . I SHALL RING.

—Angels blowing trumpets are also represented ;
and this couplet carved upon a ribbon :—

The trumpet shall sound, the dead shall rise,
To meet Christ Jesus in the skies.

JOHN, son of Robert GREY, d. 1755, a. 20 :—

Ingenious youth, he's gone,
Oh, thou resistless fate:
Here virtues in him shone
Not feigned, but innate.
Great happiness we trust
Rewards his pietic ;
And raisd will be his Dust
Years endless bliss to be.

JOHN DURWARD on his "relations." (1804) :—

Here rests together on the lap of earth
The Sire, the Father, and the Infant Child,
To teach surviving friends in this their day
To shun the things of time, and look to Heav'n.

ALEX. KIRKLAND, st. of divinity, d. 1822, a. 19 :—

Whose turn is next? this monitory stone,
Proclaims, oh ! Reader, 'tis perhaps thine own ;

No beauty, strength—can stay the fatal doom,
No virtue, worth—prevent the op'ning tomb;
Then trust in him whose arm is strong to save
Who gives thee hope beyond the closing grave.

Within an enclosure at east end of ruins :—

Sacred to the memory of JAMES LYALL, Esq. of
Gallery, who died 20 March 1851, aged 87.

—Mr Lyall, whose paternal name was *Gibson*, inherited the estate of Gallery through an uncle
(v. p. 90). Sometime before 1576, the barony
of Galraw, in Angus, belonged to the Lords
Oliphant ; but in less than a century afterwards
Lord Halkerton was proprietor. The house,
which is pleasantly situated near the North Esk,
is said to have been erected by Fullerton, a cadet
of the Kinaber family. Near the west wall of
the burial ground at Pert :—

Erected by the United Presbyterian Congregation
of Muirton, to the memory of the Rev. JAMES
RENWICK, who was 23 years and 7 months pastor
of that congregation. Died 22 Oct. 1845, in the
60th year of his age.

"A workman that needeth not be ashamed."

—At Muirton (now Luthermuir, in the parish of
Marykirk), there has been a Seceder church from
an early period.

Near the last-mentioned tombstone another is
inscribed :—

This monument was erected by Ann Lunan, in
memory of her Brother, the Revd. Master ALEXANDER LUNAN, here interred, who was Presbyter
of the Episcopal Church of Scotland, first at Blairdaff, and last at Roschill, where he departed this
life on the 29th Sept. 1769, aged 66 years. [Job
xix. 26.]

—Mr Lunan was ordained at Aberdeen by Bishop
Gdderar, 28th October 1729, preached his first
sermon from John xii. 35, in the meeting house at
Wartle, on the Sabbath thereafter ; and, on 9th
Nov. following, he entered upon his duties in a
heath-covered place of worship at Blairdaff, in the
parish of Chapel of Garioch. On 28th October
1730, he received orders as a Presbyter ; and his
congregation appears to have been not only highly
respectable as regards the status of its members,
but also in point of numbers, for, according to Mr

Lunan's MS. Diary (now before us), he was in the habit of dispensing the Sacrament to from 270 to 300 persons annually. But though his labours were thus successful, since his successor (even after a remonstrance on his own part and on that of the Bishop), only succeeded in getting forty members of the congregation at Blairlaff to bind themselves to give him a dwelling house and a money stipend of 234 merks yearly, or about £13 sterling, it is not likely that Mr Lunan's salary had been much better.

It was in April 1744, that Mr Lunan received a call from the congregation at North Water Bridge. It was subscribed by Lord Halkerton, the lairds of Balnakewan, Gallery, and Stracathro; and Mr Lunan made his "first appearance amongst them" on the 23d of that month, having read prayers, and preached at Gallery, from Job xxii. 21. There being no church at the time of Mr Lunan's induction, the congregation of North Water Bridge assembled "in Dalidies, a house belonging to Stricathrow," where they continued to meet until the 26th of August thereafter, when their own place of worship was opened, upon which occasion Mr Lunan "spoke to the people" in brief, but suitable terms. There Mr Lunan continued to discharge the duties of his sacred office with faithfulness and acceptance down to the time of his death. Of the 263 males and 244 females whom Mr Lunan baptised in his time, he performed the last of these ceremonies in his own house at Rosehill on the 3d of August preceding his demise. Mr Lunan's father was Episcopal minister at Daviot in Aberdeenshire, and wrote a 4to volume on the Mystery of Man's Redemption (Edin. 1712), which he dedicated to Sir James Elphinstone of Logie, bart.

Next to the old kirk, the chief object of general interest in Pert, is the bridge which crosses the North Esk. It consists of three arches, and is supposed to have been originally built by Superintendent Erskine of Dun, who died in 1591. Near the south-west end, a tablet bears the Royal arms of Scotland, with the motto,

NEMO . ME . IMPVNE . LACESSIT.

—Upon the north-west are the Erskine arms, below which,

. . . . KINE , OF . DVNE.

Wodrow says that this bridge was used as a sort of prison for the Covenanters, when on their way from the west of Scotland to Dunottar Castle in 1685, and that soldiers were posted at both ends of the bridge to prevent escape. Some writers aver that there were no parapets upon the bridge at that time; but this appears to be a mistake, since, in 1669, David Erskine, then laird of Dun, applied to Parliament to be allowed to levy custom or toll for the bridge, with the view of placing "ston rails and lodges" upon it, and putting it into a generally good state of repair. For this he was permitted to exact certain payments for the space of twenty years, from "each foot persone carying burden," and for all "bestiall, loads, and others, . . . that shall happen to croce the said Northwater Bridge." (Acta Parl. vii. 654.) The necessary repairs and improvements had been made before Mr Ochterlony wrote (c. 1682), for he says that the bridge, "built by one of the Lairds of Dun, but not altogether finished, [had] raills put upon the same of very good hewen stone, amounting to a great expence, by the present Laird of Dun."

Before the Marykirk Bridge was built (v. p. 138), there was a ferry boat at Craigo.

A great fair or market was held at the North Water Bridge in old times upon Sundays as well as week days. The Brechin Presbytery Records (Oct. 12, 1643), state that "the Sabbath was profaned by ane market holden at the North Water Brig;" at which the Presbytery were so alarmed that they ordained Mr Montgomerie, then minister of Pert, "to take notice off those that frequents that market, and acquaint ther ministers therewith, that they may be punished as Sabbath breakers."

It was in this locality, in a clay-built cottage, removed not many years ago, that JAMES MILL, father of John Stuart Mill, the celebrated political economist, was born. Mr MILL, who died at London, was buried in the vault underneath the parish church of St Mary Abbots, Kensington,

Middlesex. A marble tablet, in the south aisle of the church, is thus inscribed :—

To the memory of JAMES MILL, Esquire, author of "History of British India," "Analysis of the Human Mind," and other works. Born April 6, 1773, died June 23, 1836, and buried near this place.

Crathie.

(S. NINIAN, OR S. MANIR.)

THE kirk of *Creythyn*, or *Crethy*, belonged to the Abbey of Cambuskenneth. In 1606, the kirk and kirk lands were given to the Earl of Mar, as part of the temporal lordship of that monastery.

The time of the union of the parishes of Crathie and Kindrochet (now Braemar), is not quite clear. In 1574 both churches were vacant; and the readers were respectively named John Wilson and James Ilay.

The ruins of the old kirk stand within the burial-ground of Crathie, on the north bank of the Dee. A new place of worship was erected upon a rising ground on the north side of the turnpike road. It is a plain square building, with pavilion roof; and, when resident at Balmoral, HER MAJESTY and suite attend Divine service in it. There is a neat Free Church, near Lochnagar, on the south side of the Dee.

A monument set up against the east wall of the Farquharson burial aisle, in old kirkyard, bears the date of 1702, and the initials R. H : E. .E. The Farquharson aisle (at the east end of the old kirk), contains three tablets, inscribed as undernoted :—

1699 : Within these walls lie the remains of ALEXANDER FARQUHARSON of Monaltrie ; JOHN and FRANCIS, both of Monaltrie, his sons ; ROBERT, his youngest son, and several other children, who died in their infancy. Here also are interred ANNE FARQUHARSON, the wife of Alexander ; ANNE OGILVIE, the wife of John ; and ISOBEL KEITH and HELEN BAIRD, the wives of Robert. As also, AMELIA, FRANCIS, and JAMES, the children of Robert and Helen Baird. For their memory this stone is erected with the warmest filial and fraternal affection by William Farquarson of Monaltrie. 1808.

—The first Farquharson of Monaltrie was DONALD, (son of Donald Farchar, eldest son of *Finla Mor*), forest ranger to Jas. VI., and bailie of Strathdee to the 4th Earl of Huntly. Donald exchanged his patrimony of Castleton of Braemar, for that of Monaltrie, with the Earl of Mar about 1600. His son, also Donald, having been appointed bailie of Strathdee in his father's lifetime, was surnamed *Donald Oig*, or Donald, junior. *Donald Oig* was the most famous of his race in the traditions of Deeside, not only from the part he took in the Civil Wars as chief of his clan, but as bailie to the Marquis of Huntly ; and Spalding relates, in speaking of his slaughter at Aberdeen (15 March 1645), that he was "a brave gentilman, and ane of the noblest capitans amongis all the hielanderis of Scotland." His eldest son entered the French service and died abroad ; the second succeeded to the property, and, when an old man, about the year 1700, pecuniary straits compelled him to sell Monaltrie to Alexander, younger son of Farquharson of Invercauld. It is this ALEXANDER (the first of the second race of the Farquharsons of Monaltrie), who is the first named in the above inscription. This branch, of which there were four lairds, held Monaltrie for three generations. The most famous of these was FRANCIS (2d son of Alexander), who commanded his clan at Culloden, where he was taken prisoner. He was conveyed to London, tried, and condemned to death ; but, on the evening preceding the day appointed for his execution, he received a reprieve, and ultimately a pardon, without knowing to whose kind intercession he was indebted. His hair, from the light colour of which he was known as *Baron Ban*, hung over his shoulders in long flaxen curls ; and by the grace thus added to his handsome person, it is said that a lady of influence at Court was captivated, and procured the timely respite which saved his life. He was succeeded in Monaltrie by his nephew William, who purchased Ballater and Tullich from the last of the Inverey Farquharsons. In 1827 he sold Monaltrie to Invercauld, to which family, as next of kin, William Farquharson's whole estate devolved, on the death of his widow. (v. p. 107).

Erected A.D. 1824 by James Farquharson Esq. Balnabodach. Sacred to the memory of JAMES FARQUHARSON of Tullochcoy, who died in 1760; and his spouse MAY FARQUHARSON, who died 1729. PETER FARQUHARSON of Tullochcoy, born 1733, died 1801; ISABELLA FORBES, his spouse, born 1733, died 1780. GEORGE, FRANCIS, and DONALD, their sons, the former died 1787, the two latter in their infancy. JAMES and KATHERINE, son and daughter of James Farquharson, Balnabodach and Tullochcoy. The son died in 1805, the daughter in 1807. ANN, daughter of James Farquharson of Balnabodach, and wife of Dr Robertson, who died at Indego, 31 August 1842, aged 34.

—James F. of Inverey, a younger brother of Donald, first of Monaltrie, was ancestor of the Tullochcoy branch of the clan. He took an active part in Montrose's Wars, and after the slaughter of his nephew, *Donald Oig*, at Aberdeen, he commanded the Deeside Highlanders, and was at the battle of Alford, to the success of which he materially contributed. His wife was Agnes Ferguson, daughter of the minister of Crathie, by whom he had a large family. To his son Lewis he gave the property of Auchendryne, and to JAMES that of Tullochcoy, in Aberarder. The latter married Agnes Ochterlony, daughter of the minister of Fordoun, in the Mearns, and built a new mansion house at Tullochcoy, upon a lintel of which, still extant, are carved in relief :—

I. F. : A. O. 1693.

—Their son, JAMES (who died in 1760), married a daughter of Monaltrie; and it is a tradition that Tullochcoy having joined the Farquharsons at Culloden with seven sons, he and they all fell in battle, and the succession devolved upon the above PETER, when a boy, in 1746. Peter's wife was a daughter of John Forbes of Newe; and about 1770 Peter sold Tullochcoy to Farquharson of Invercauld. Late in life he removed to Balnabodach, in Strathdon, a farm which some of his descendants still occupy. The first mentioned in the following tablet was Peter's eldest son :—

In memory of JAMES FARQUHARSON of Balnabodach, who died at Ballater, 10th October 1843, aged 85 years; and ISABELLA MCHARDY, his wife, who died at Balnabodach, 9th September 1827, aged 64 years. This tablet is erected as a mark of filial respect and affection by their three sons, Peter, John, and Alexander Farquharson, 1844. Also of their younger brother, GEORGE FARQUHARSON, who died at Balnabodach, 26th December, 1841, aged 38 years.

—Peter and John (above-named) obtained commissions in the H.E.I.C.S. The first died at Ballater in 1849, aged —, where a marble tablet is erected to his memory in the church; and the latter is Lieut.-Col. Farquharson of Corrachree, Logie-Coldstone. He is the oldest surviving grandson of the last laird of Tullochcoy, also representative of the Inverey family, the direct line, with its branches of Balmoral and Auchendryne, having become extinct.

I have to thank the Rev. Mr Michie, schoolhouse, Logie-Coldstone, for these interesting notices of the Farquharsons, by whom the facts have been kindly culled from family papers.

Upon a flat stone near N.W. corner of churchyard of Crathie :—

Here is interred the body of the Revd. Mr MURDOCH MACLENAN, late minister of the Gospel at Crathie, who, after a life of piety and benevolence, died 22 July 1783, in the 62d year of his age, and 50th of his ministry.

—According to the poet Burns, Mr M. was author of the celebrated Jacobite ballad of Shirra' Muir. Mr M., when a preacher within the bounds of the presbytery of Kincardine O'Neil, was ordained "itinerant missionary" in the united parishes of Crathie and Kindrochet, 19 Oct. 1748; and on 11 May thereafter he was inducted minister in room of Mr McInnes, who was translated to Logie-Coldstone. The heritors described Mr McLenan to the Presbytery as a "person of prudence, literatur and piety." He married Margaret Forbes, by whom, who survived him, he left no children. A granite tablet bears :—

Sacred to the memory of Rev. ARCHIBALD ANDERSON, M.A., minister of this parish, who died 8 Nov., 1866, aged 77 years, having faithfully discharged the office of the ministry in the Mission of Braemar for 9 years, and in the parish of Crathie for 26 years. [Rev. 14-13.] Erected by the resident parishoners of Crathie and Braemar.

Although Braemar and Crathie were thinly peopled at one time, there were four chapels in the latter, and seven in the former district, apart from an hospital at the Cairnwell, and the two parish churches. Manor houses were also abundant, all of which, with three exceptions, were occupied, in 1732, by Farquharsons. Invercauld has all along been the more important residence of that clan ; and at the present time, but for the absence of "old ancestral trees," it is possibly one of the finest Highland seats in the country. Balmoral, or, as the name is anciently written, "Balmoran" (? *Bal-mohr-a'en*), was also Farquharson property, until purchased from that family by the Earl of Fife. From Lord Fife's Trustees the estate was bought by the late PRINCE CONSORT, when, for the better accommodation of royalty, the old house was taken down, and the present spacious building of granite erected, in and around which the various accessories correspond in elegant simplicity and good taste.

The plateau, upon the left of the principal entrance to the grounds, is ornamented by a bronze statue of the late Prince Consort, by Theed, which was erected by the Queen. It presents this inscription :—

ALBERT, 15 OCTOBER 1867.

Near the above, a handsome granite obelisk, about 30 feet in height, bears upon the west side of the plinth :—

THIS OBELISK WAS ERECTED TO THE MEMORY OF
H. R. H. PRINCE ALBERT,
OF SAXE COBURG AND GOTHA,
CONSORT OF HER MAJESTY QUEEN VICTORIA,
BY THE SERVANTS AND TENANTS UPON THE ESTATES OF BALMORAL, ABERGELDIE, AND BIRKHALL, AS AN HUMBLE TRIBUTE OF AFFECTION FOR THEIR BELOVED MASTER, 1862.

Several memorial cairns are upon the summits of adjoining mountains, the most considerable and important of which is the "Albert Cairn" upon Craiglourachan. It has four sides, is pyramidical in form, and constructed of native granite. Upon the east side are the initials of the Queen and Royal children, and the date of "21st AUGUST 1862." Upon the north side :—

TO THE BELOVED MEMORY OF
ALBERT,
THE GREAT AND GOOD PRINCE CONSORT,
ERECTED BY HIS BROKEN HEARTED WIDOW,
VICTORIA R.
21ST AUGUST 1862.

Upon another dressed slab, a few inches below the above, is this quotation :—

He being made perfect in a short time,
Fulfilled a long time :
For his soul pleased the Lord,
Therefore hasted He to take
Him away from among the wicked.
Wisdom of Solomon, chap. iv., versus 16 and 14.

—In connection with the death of the PRINCE CONSORT, it may be added that a magnificent mausoleum was erected at Frogmore, where his remains were deposited ; and that, over the door, within a portico, is the following inscription in bronze :—

ALBERTI . PRINCIPIS . QVOD . MORTALE . ERAT
HOC . IN . SEPVLCHRO . DEPONI . VOLVIT
VIDVA . MŒRENS . VICTORIA . REGINA,
A. D. M. D. CCC. LXII.
VALE . DESIDERATISSIME ! HIC . DEMVM
CONQVIESCAM . TECVM ;
TECVM . IN . CHRISTO . CONSVRGAM.

[The mortal remains of PRINCE ALBERT were deposited in this tomb by his sorrowing widow, Queen Victoria, A.D. 1862. Farewell, most deeply regretted ! Here at last shall I rest with thee ; with thee in Christ shall I rise.]

—The "Leaves from a Journal," lately published by Her Majesty, contains, as all readers know, many interesting notices of the happy time which the Queen and the late Prince spent on Deeside ; and it is gratifying to know that Her Majesty has shown a tangible interest in these parts of the country by granting £2500 of the profits of that work, for the general education of young men belonging to, or resident in, the district. This gift, which is to form bursaries in connection with the parish school of Crathie, the school of Girnock, and the University of Aberdeen respectively, is to bear the name of *The Balmoral Bursaries;* and the patronage is vested in Her Majesty, and her successors in the Balmoral estate.

Kindrochet, or Braemar.
(S. ANDREW, APOSTLE.)

THE kirk of Braemar, anciently *Kyndrochet*, so named from its having stood near the old bridge of Cluny, was given by Duncan, Earl of Mar, to the priory and canons of S. MARY of Monymusk, about 1230, together with an acre of land, &c., in Aucatendregen, or Auchendryne.

There is a mission church at Castletown of Braemar, which is, or was, supported by Royal Bounty; also a Free Church, together with a Roman Catholic Chapel and a resident priest. The parochial burial place, which is well kept, is a short way below the village, on the south side of the Dee, surrounded by trees. An aisle, &c., belonging to the FARQUHARSONS of Invercauld, occupies the site of the old church, being the highest point in the churchyard. The burial place is behind, and three marble tablets within the aisle, are respectively inscribed as follows:—

Sacred to the memory of JOHN FARQUHARSON, of Invercauld, who died in 1750. Sacred also to the memory of JAMES FARQUHARSON, of Invercauld, his son, who died 24 June 1805, aged 83; and AMELIA, Lady Sinclair, his spouse (daughter of Lord George Murray), who died in 1779. They had eleven children, all of whom, with the exception of the youngest, Catherine, died before them. MARY, MATILDA, JANE, JOHN, and GEORGE, lie interred with their parents in the ground adjoining; CHARLOTTE, at Arnhall; FANNY at Lisbon; and AMELIA, MARGARET, and ANN, in the burying ground, North Leith.

—John Farquharson, the first named in above inscription, entertained the Earl of Mar, when engaged in organising the rising of '15. He received the command of Mar's own regiment; and, along with "Old Borlam," conducted the division of the army which invaded England. He was left in charge of the bridge of the Ribble by Forster: being defeated, he was taken prisoner, but soon afterwards set at liberty, from which time he betook himself to the more useful and peaceful occupation of improving his estate, which he gradually added to, first by the purchase of Glenmuick, next by that of Castletown of Braemar, &c. Convinced of the hopelessness of the cause of the Stuarts, he not only declined to join in the rebellion of 1745, but sent his son with a company of Braemar men, which were joined to the brave 43d, to aid the reigning Sovereign. But his daughter (facetiously styled *Colonel Anne*), wife of the chief of the Clan Chattan, joined the cause of the Stuarts with so much ardour that she went to the field in person, on which occasion she took her own husband prisoner! At a subsequent stage of the proceedings, she saved the Prince from being captured.

James Farquharson, who died in 1805, added greatly to the extent of his estates, and planted most of the timber, for which the property of Invercauld has been so long famous. His wife, Lady Amelia Sinclair, was the widow of the 8th Lord Sinclair, and daughter of Lord George Murray, Lieut.-Gen. of Prince Charles' army in 1745. Her good deeds deserve to be recorded and imitated:—When married to Mr Farquharson, she found great idleness and misery throughout Deeside; and the primitive plan was in use of spinning lint on the distaff, and winding wool on the big wheel. The little spinning wheel, though common in most parts, was then unknown in the district; and about 1755 she applied to the Board of Trustees to aid her in procuring small wheels, and a mistress to teach spinning. After much labour and opposition to her scheme, by those who were to be benefited by it, and the awarding of premiums to the more expert scholars, she ultimately succeeded so well that there were no fewer than 120 unmarried women and little girls who received premiums on 1st January 1763 ; and the quantity of linen yarn then brought to Invercauld for inspection by Lady Sinclair was supposed to be worth at least £300 sterling. Lady S. also gave a great impetus to cattle rearing, and to the cultivation of dairy produce, which are now of such such importance to the district. (Old Stat. Acct. xiv., 342.) Upon the second tablet :—

To the memory of CATHERINE, youngest daughter and heiress of James Farquharson of Invercauld, born 4 May 1774, died 27 Feb. 1845. To the memory of JAMES ROSS-FARQUHARSON, her husband, Capt. R.N., (2d son of Sir John Lockhart-Ross, of Balnagowan, baronet), who died at Edinburgh, 5 Feb. 1809, aged 38 years. This tablet was erected after his mother's death by her affectionate son, Aug. 1845.

—According to Nisbet, the clan Farquharson derive their descent from the Shaws of Rothiemurchus, who were descended from a son of Macduff, Thane of Fife. FARQUHAR, who lived in the times of Roberts II. and III., was a son of Shaw, and having settled in the Braes of Mar, his sons were called *Farquhar-sons:* The great-great-grandson of Farquhar, known as *Finlay-More*, fell at the battle of Pinkie, while carrying the royal standard. The Farquharsons of Invercauld continued to be represented in the male line until 1805, when the above-named James was succeeded by his only surviving daughter, who married, as recorded in the last-quoted inscription, the second son of Sir John Lockhart-Ross. Mrs Ross-Farquharson continued the same course of improvement which had been so successfully followed by her father. She purchased the lands of Rhineatou and Micras from Captain Macdonald (ancestor of Col. Macdonald of Rossie and St Martins), and those of Monaltrie from her cousin, William Farquharson. To her son, the third tablet bears the following inscription :—

Sacred to the memory of JAMES FARQUHARSON, Esq. of Invercauld. Born April 25, 1808 ; died Nov. 20, 1862. This tablet is erected in affectionate remembrance by his eldest son, Lieut.-Col. Farquharson, of the Scots Fusilier Guards.

—Mr F. married a daughter of Gen. Dundas of Sanson, by whom he had a large family. She died in Aug. 1869. Their eldest son (erector of the tablet above referred to), succeeded to the estates. He married Miss OSWALD of Auchencruive, Ayrshire, by whom, who died 8th August 1870, he has two sons and one daughter. The late Mr F. was much esteemed by all who knew him ; and a granite obelisk, upon a knoll on the north bank of the Dee, opposite to the Castle of Braemar, bears the following inscription, which shows how much he was respected by those who had the best opportunity of judging of his true character:—

In memory of JAMES FARQUHARSON, Esq. of Invercauld, by his Tenantry and Servants, to whom he was greatly attached. Born 25th April 1808 ; died 20th Nov. 1862. The righteous shall be in everlasting remembrance.—Psalm cxii. 6.

JAMES GRUAR, Tomintran, d. 1807, a. 72 :—

Four hundred years have now wheeled round,
  With half a century more ;
Since this has been the burying ground,
  Belonging to the GRUERS.

A flat stone upon a timber frame bears :—

DAVIDSONS SEPULCHRE.

—Quotations from Job xix. 23-7, follow the above ; but no names of deceased persons or dates are given. Upon a table-shaped stone :—

✠ Sacred to memory of the Roman Catholic Clergymen who are interred here. The Rev. —— FORSYTH, who died Nov. 8, 1708. The Rev. JOHN FARQUHARSON spent the evening of his days as Chaplain to his nephew Alexander Farquharson, Esq. of Inveray, and died at Balmoral, Aug. 22, 1782. The Rev. CHARLES FARQUHARSON, served the Catholic Mission in Braemar for many years, and died at Oirdesrg, Nov. 30, 1799, the two former were sons of Lewis Farquharson, Esq. of Auchendryne. The Revd. WILLIAM M'LEOD, died June 3, 1809, much and justly regretted :—

They died to live, that living worth regard,
And with like virtue, seek the same reward.

—Possibly Mr —— Forsyth was in some way related to Hendric Forsyth (the son of a lawyer in Edinburgh), who died in 1690, and is characterised as "a man of great merit." Of the two above-mentioned Farquharsons (whose mother was a daughter of Farquharson of Allanquoich), Dr Oliver, in his valuable Collections illustrating the Biography of the Jesuits gives some interesting particulars, of which the following is an abridgement: He tells us that, on returning from abroad, in 1729, Mr John Farquharson was placed at Scaforth, afterwards at Strathglass, in Inverness-shire, where he acquired a competent knowledge of the Gaelic, and, by degrees, formed an immense collection of Gaelic poetry. The original folio MSS., in his own handwriting, which, unfortunately, have been lost, he deposited, in 1772, in the Scotch College at Douay, among which were Ossian's poems and many other works. He was taken prisoner about 1745 whilst saying mass, and conveyed to Edinburgh in his sacerdotal vestments. After many sufferings he was liberated, went abroad, and afterwards returned to Scotland, where he lived with his nephew of Inverey, and left £200 towards the Mission. His brother, Mr Charles, who was buried in the same grave, was first settled at Glengairn ; but having been taken prisoner along with his brother, he went to Douay after his release, then to Dasant, where he was Prefect of Studies. He returned to his native district in 1782 ; and, by request of Bishop Geddes, wrote an account of the religious changes which had taken place on Deeside. Dr Oliver has preserved the name of "William Macleod," possibly the priest named in the above inscription ; and Mr Griffin (whose copy of Dr O.'s work is now before us, covered with valuable MS. notes), adds, "Born 7 April 1729 ; came to Mission 28 Feb. 1752." In 1732, the Farquharsons of Invercy and Balmoral were brothers. In 1715, Inverey was forfeited when his estate was reckoned worth £281 sterling a year. Auchendryne is that part of the Castletown of Braemar which lies on the north side of the Cluny.

In front of the Invercauld aisle, a flat stone is thus inscribed:—

✠ Erected to the memory of PETER GRANT, some time farmer in Dubrach, who died at Auchendryne the 11th of Feb. 1824, aged 110 years. His wife MARY CUMMING, died at Westside, parish of Lethnot, in Forfar Shire, on the 4th Feby. 1811, aged 65 years, and lies interred in the churchyard of Lethnot.

—*Dubrach* (as Grant was commonly called), joined the rebel army under the Mackintoshes, and became a sergeant-major. It is told that, like most of the rebels, he felt much annoyed at not being allowed to come at once into close quarters with the enemy, and that, in the heat of his ardour, he cried out to his superior officer—" O, lat's throw awa' thae fashionless things o' guns, . 'er we get doon upo' *the smatchets* wi' oor swords !" Grant was taken prisoner, and carried to Carlisle, but contrived to escape by scaling the walls, and fled to his native hills. In course of time he and his family went to Lethnot, in Angus, where they rented a small farm. While there, Grant's adventures were made known to George IV., who settled a pension upon him, which, after his death, was continued to his daughter, Annie. The late Lord Panmure (then the Hon. Wm. R. Maule), had a portrait of *Dubrach*, painted by Colvin Smith, which is now at Brechin Castle (Land of the Lindsays). The Scots Magazine says that more than 300 people attended Dubrach's funeral, that upwards of an anker of whisky was consumed by the company before lifting the body, and that three pipers were stationed at the head of the coffin, who played, " Wha widna fecht for Charlie's richt !"

Upon a loose slab in churchyard:—

ALEXR. McDONALD, soldier, ... Leys Regt. 1751.

Upon a table-shaped stone:—

In memory of CHARLES WATSON, innkeeper, Castletown Braemar, who died Aug. 2, 1828, aged 46. He bequeathed the bulk of his fortune for the Education of Youth of a certain class, in the parish of Braemar. He was son of JOHN WATSON and CATHERINE CRAIG, who formerly kept the same inn.

Here is the burial place belonging to FINLAY and LAUCHLAN M'INTOSH, May 24, 1770.

To the memory of PETER ROY, for 51 years a faithful and attached servant in the Invercauld Family, by whom this stone is erected. Died Aug. 4, 1851, aged 68.

In remote times the lordships of Braemar and Strathdee belonged to the Earls of Mar, whose male line became extinct in 1377 (v. KILDRUMMY.) Mar fell into the female line, and after a long lapse of years, and much litigation, the estates and titles were awarded to the fifth Lord Erskine. It was his lineal descendant, the 11th Earl of Mar, who proclaimed James VII. King of Great Britain, and planted his standard at Braemar, on 6th September 1715, upon the spot now occupied by the buildings of the Invercauld Arms Hotel.

There was a castle or royal residence at Kindochet, from which Robert II. dated several charters; but tradition avers that, long before his time, Malcolm III. had a hunting seat there, which stood upon a rock overhanging the water of Cluny.

The present Castle of Braemar, which has been frequently used as a garrison for soldiers, built soon after the '15, occupies an eminence upon the south bank of the Dee, below the village of Castletown. The previous Castle of Braemar, inhabited by the English under Cromwell, was burnt by the Revolutionary army.

Corriunlzie, now a favourite and charming Highland residence of the Earl of Fife, about three miles above Castletown, though mentioned in old charters, does not appear to have been occupied as a dwelling place until a comparatively late period. A magnificent view of hill and valley scenery is obtained from this locality; but these, as well as Balmoral and other interesting portions of the Dee, will be found illustrated and described in Black's "Tourist." An account of the tenure of Balmoral from 1451 is printed as an appendix to the illustrated edition of the Queen's "Leaves," from notes of the Early History of Strathdee and Braemar, M.S, in the possession of Her Majesty, by John Stuart, LL.D.

It ought to be added that the peaks and snow-covered corries of Lochnagar (3789 feet above sea level), form the extreme background to Balmoral Palace. This hill is also a fine object in the landscape when viewed from various points of Deeside, particularly as seen from near the old kirk of Tullich. Along with the mountains of Culbleen and Morven, that of Lochnagar early inspired the muse of Lord Byron, who spent some of his early days upon the banks of the Dee, where, as in every part of the country—notwithstanding the late attacks which have been made upon his character, by, apparently, one of the most unwomanly-hearted of women—Byron's name is held dear, and his memory venerated. Where, in this age of monument-raising, or to whom more worthily, could a more fitting spot be found in Scotland to erect *a cairn* to that truly great genius, than upon some part of "dark Lochnagar," where the natural grandeur of the mountain, or its outline, would remain unskaithed?

Two ancient cists, or graves, about 33 inches long, by about 20 wide, constructed of rude flagstones, and covered with a quantity of land stones, were found in 1863, near the top of an eminence called the Tom of the Boltchach, upon the farm of Lochnagar Distillery. The bones appeared to have been calcined.

The principal bridges in the united parishes are over the Cluny at Castletown, and the Dee at Invercauld and Balmoral.

~~~~~~~~~~~~~~~~~~~~~~~

Dun.

(THE BLESSED VIRGIN.)

THE church of *Dun* belonged to the cathedral of Brechin, and became attached to Sir David Lindsay of Glenesk's foundation of the Nunnery of Elcho, Perthshire.

In 1583, on the representation of John Erskine, the "vicarage of Dwn, and personage of Eglisjohne," with the teinds of both, were united into one parish. The parsonage of Eglisjohn, which was "of auld ane chappell erectit for pilgramage," consisted only of about one plough of land; and at the time of the annexation it is stated that it had been "wanting ane kirk" for "mony zeiris bygane." The site of the chapel of Eglisjohn is still pointed out near Langley Park house.

In 1834, a new place of worship was erected in

a field to the west of the old churchyard. Upon the bell :—

R. BARCLAY, MONTROSE, 1815.

It is said that Knox preached at Dun when on a visit to his friend John Erskine, the Superintendent of Angus and Mearns; and the pulpit now in use is popularly believed to be that from which Knox held forth. This appears to be a mistake, since the date of 1615 is upon a shield on the back of the pulpit. The shield bears the Erskine and Wishart arms, quarterly, also the initials I. E.; above is the injunction—PREACH THE VORD. The pulpit is ornamented with floral carvings, but of a later style than the time of Knox.

The old kirk is used as the burial aisle of the Erskines of Dun. A pavement slab within it is initialed I.E; M.G., and dated 1703. It also presents the well-known quotation from Horace, "Mors æquo pede pulsat regumque," &c., and a reference to 1 Cor. ch. 15, 17. There are several coffins here. Two are covered with crimson velvet, ornamented with coronets, and inscribed plates. One of the plates bears :—

ARCHIBALD, MARQUIS OF AILSA, K.T., F.R.S.
Died Sept. 8, 1846, aged 76.

Upon the plate of an adjoining coffin :—

MARGARET ERSKINE OF DUN,
MARCHIONESS DOWAGER OF AILSA.
Died 1848, aged 76.

—Archibald Kennedy, who succeeded his father as 12th Earl of Cassilis, was created Marquis of Ailsa. His wife was the youngest daughter of John, the last male descendant of the Erskines of Dun. JOHN ERSKINE died in 1812, and was succeeded in Dun by his eldest daughter ALICE. At her death in 1824, Dun came to Marchioness Margaret's second son, the Hon. JOHN KENNEDY-ERSKINE. He married Lady Augusta Fitzclarence (afterwards Lady Hallyburton), by whom he had W. H. Kennedy-Erskine, now laird of Dun, and two surviving daughters. One daughter became the wife of the late James Hay Erskine Wemyss, M.P. for Fifeshire, the other that of the Earl of Munster. The lineage of Kennedy of Cassilis is well known. In regard to that of Erskine of Dun, it may only be said that Robert of Erskine obtained the lands of Dun about 1360-1; and that John, grandson of Sir Robert of Erskine, and second son by a second marriage of Sir Thomas Erskine of that ilk, " is reckoned the first of the family of Dun, as separated from that of Erskyne." He had a charter of Dun from his father, dated 25 Oct. 1393, and was alive in 1419.

JOHN ERSKINE, the friend of Knox, who did so much to promote the cause of the Reformation, is the chief historical personage of his house and family. He was born about 1508, and both his father and grandfather (Sir John), having fallen at Flodden, young Erskine had a long minority. None of the biographers of the heroes of the Reformation have noticed these points regarding Erskine's early history, nor the fact of his having been in some way concerned in the murder of a young priest in the bell-tower at Montrose.

These particulars are proved by the family writs at Dun, to the use of which (as the writer of these notes was informed by a late eminent local antiquary), the Earl of Cassilis acceeded at Dr M'Crie's request, upon the express condition that whatever was found for or against the persons concerned in, or the cause of, the Reformation, should be published without abridgment. The charter chest, however, was never examined by Dr M'Crie; and it was not until the late Patrick Chalmers of Aldbar procured the use of the "Dun Papers" for the Spalding Club, that these interesting points in the history of Erskine were known. According to the custom of the age, the laws of the country demanded heavy sums as assythment, or blood-money, to be paid to the parent of the murdered priest; on the other hand, the Church inflicted a severe penance. It was while on a pilgrimage in the performance of this penance that Erskine happened to make the acquaintance of some of the leading Continental Reformers; and, feeling the restraint under which the church had placed him, he joined the Reformers, and thus became one of the chief instruments in bringing about a salutary change in the religious government of his country. He " depairtit fra this lyff [at Dun] the 22 of Merche, the yeir of God 1589."

Erskine's uncle, Sir THOMAS, designed of Brechin, secretary to James IV., and founder of the family of Pitoddrie, in Aberdeenshire, was also a person of note; as was a later descendant, DAVID, 43 years a senator of the College of Justice. He was the first Erskine of Balhall, wrote a volume of Moral and Political Advices, and died in 1755. In his time the present mansion-house of Dun was built, after plans by the elder Adams.

Besides the coffins of the Marquis and Marchioness of Ailsa in the burial vault at Dun, another, covered with black cloth, contains the remains of their grandson. Upon the top of it, a plate bears:—

ADOLPHUS KENNEDY (son of the late Lord Kennedy), who died at Montrose.

—This was the youngest child of Lord Kennedy, by his wife, Eleanor, daughter and heiress of John Allardyce of Dunottar. Lord Kennedy having died in his father's lifetime, his eldest son became, on the death of his grandfather in 1846, second Marquis of Ailsa. Owing to the effects of an accident in the hunting field, the second Marquis died at Culzean Castle, 20 March 1870, aged 54.

The garden of Dun adjoins the churchyard on the north, and there, in a retired corner, separated from the burial ground by a railing, and within a vaulted grave, lie the ashes of the before mentioned Lady Hallyburton. A coffin-slab of Aberdeen granite (polished), with cross in alto-relievo on top, bears this inscription round the sides:—

Erected to the blessed memory of Lady AUGUSTA GORDON-HALLYBURTON. Born 3 Nov. 1803; died 8 Dec. 1865. Her faith and hope were in the Lord Jesus Christ.

The old churchyard of Dun has a secluded and romantic site at the top of a den, upon a kind of peninsula, which is washed on the south and east by burns which flow from 30 to 40 feet below the level of the cemetery. The older tombstones are of a more costly class than is commonly found in rural churchyards; and, as will be seen from what follows, some of the inscriptions exhibit considerable literary talent:—

Hoc tegitvr lapide ALEXANDR . . COBVS . . . . is, fratres germani, qvi in . . terris vitam dvxervnt piam et honestam, et æterna nvnc in cœlis frvvntvr. A. . . . obiit anno Dom. 1613, Aprilis 12. . . . Memento peccati vt doleas; mortis vt insignias; ivdicis vt timeas; misericordiæ vt spores.

[This stone covers the dust of ALEXANDER and JAMES, full brothers, who led a pious and honourable life on earth, and now enjoy eternal life in heaven. A. [F. or E.] died 12 April 1613. . . . Remember sin that you may sorrow over it; death that your end may be a noble one; the judge that you may fear; mercy that you may have hope.]

Upon a table-shaped stone:—

Infra sepultæ jacent exuviæ JOANNIS ERSKINI, quondam in Dunsmill, viri pij, probi, et honesti, ex honestis et generosis orti, omnibus grati, vitæ exemplo, morum integritate, pietate in Deum insigni, in amicos observantia et constantia, in conjugem amore, in omnes humanitate, in pauperes misericordia memorabilis.

Who ever him bethought
Seriouslie and oft,
What it uare to flit
From his death bed to the pit;
Ther to suffer pain,
Never to cease again;
Wold not commit on sin,
The vhol vorld to vin.

[Beneath lie interred the remains of JOHN ERSKINE, sometime in Dunsmill, a man of piety, worth, and honour, of high and honourable extraction, of universal popularity, and distinguished for his exemplary life, his moral rectitude, his eminent piety towards God, the warmth and constancy of his friendship, his conjugal affection, his courtesy to all, and his kindness to the poor.]

—A perpendicular line is drawn upon the face of this stone from top to bottom: the above inscription is upon the left side of the line, the following upon the right:—

Conjvgis etiam charissimæ, AGNETÆ BURN, fœminæ vere probæ, infra hoc monvmentvm condvntvr cineres; tvrtvribvs similes vixervnt, et simvl mortem obiervnt, hæc ætatis 25, ille ætatis 28, hæc qvid. Maij [Cal.] ille 17 Cal. Maij an. ære Christi. 1696:

Conjvgivm Christi ac animæ mors solvere nescit,
Sed carnale potest conjvgis atq' viri.

[Beneath this monument are also laid the ashes of his beloved wife, AGNES BURN. They lived like turtles and died together, she 1st May, aged 25, and he 15th April 1696, aged 28. Death can dissolve the carnal union of husband and wife; but not the spiritual union of Christ and the soul.]

Also upon a table-shaped monument :—

Vnder this ston doe sueetly rest
A woman piovs, wertous, and chast;
Who in hir lyfe performed tuo ducties great,
A carefull Mother, and a Loving Mate.

Infra tvmvlvm hunc sepulchralem sepulto sunt reliquiæ sanctæ in Domino defunctæ KATHARINÆ FULLARTONI, Davidis Erskin in Ballachie spousæ dilectissimæ, quæ, dum in terris degeret, vitam erga Deum pia, erga maritum casta, quoad amicos et propinquos humana, pauperesq, liberalis se illustrem fecit, circiter annos 44 vitam hanc caducam degens; 28 die Januarii, anno 1697, anima in patriam cœlestem placide migravit. Cumæea, tanquam matre tenerrima, conduntur cineres puerorum et puellarum quinq, in ætate infantili morientium, beatam resurrectionem die judicij expectantium.

Disce mori, quicunq legis mea scripta, viator: :
Omnes æqua manent funera : Disce mori :
Disce mori : Frater discat cum præsule, clerus
Cum juniore senex, cum sapiente rudis.

[Beneath this sepulchral mound are interred the remains of the pious and dearly beloved wife of David Erskine in Ballachie, KATHERINE FULLARTON, who died in the Lord. During her life on earth she was distinguished for piety towards God, fidelity to her husband, kindness to her friends and neighbours, and liberality to the poor. After she had passed nearly 44 years in this transitory state of existence, her soul calmly winged its flight to its heavenly home, on 28 Jan. 1697. And with her, as a most tender mother, are laid the ashes of five boys and girls, who died in infancy, and here await a happy resurrection on the day of judgment.

Whoe'er thou art that read'st these lines,
Which, Traveller, I have pen'd ;
O, learn to die ! and know that all
Are equal in the end.
The monk may from the abbot learn,
The young clerk from the old ;
The unletter'd from the learn'd know,
Our days must soon be told.]

The next three inscriptions are from plain headstones :—

Here lyes KATREN STEVENSON, spous to Alexr Coulie, vho died ye 18 of Decembr anno 1672, of age 42. Here lyes SUSANNA COULIE, spous to John Jap, vho died ye 24 of December anno 1692, of age 35 :—

Whose corps interd below,
Lyes hid from eyes ;
Whos souls advanced,
Uith Chryst above ye skies.—(r. p. 135.)

Here lyes ane honest virgin MARGRET SIMSON, who died ye 16 of March anno 1699, of age 21 years.

Here lyis AGNAS BERTIE, spous to William Coullie, miller, who died ye 10 of March anno 1697, of age 55 years.

Upon a table-shaped stone :—

Below lieth the ashes of MARGARET GRAY, spouse to John Erskine in Cottran, uho in her day uas a pattern of Christian verteus, and having groun up to a full ear, being 70 years of age, uas on the 5th of March, cut doun by Death's fatal blou, and nou is resting from her labours, and her works follouing her, 1702.

ALEX. COULEY, and MARGT. LYALL, Leys of Dun, on six children (1720) :—

When silver bands of nature burst,
And let the building fall,
The blest goes doun to mix with dust,
Its first original.
The tyrant death he triumphs here,
His trophies spread around ;
And heaps of dust & bones appear,
Thro all the hollow ground.

JOHN PATERSON, who d. 1724, a. 81, "left the substance of the following lines to be engraven on his gravestone :"—

Within this grave I do both ly and rest,
Because the Lord perfumed ye grave at first ;
May when I rise unto me Christ grant this,
To be with him in his eternal bliss.

JEAN EDESON, his wife, died 1704, aged 59 :—

This woman here in hope doth rest,
Again to rise and be for ever blest ;
After this lif, ue purpos here to ly,
And ris and reing with her eternally.

Erected by MARGARET PATERSON, in memory of

her brother JAMES PATERSON of Redfield, who died 15 Oct. 1791, in the 69th year of his age.

A Latin inscription, scarcely legible, commemorates the good life and actions of JAMES BURN, who died in 1706. The portion relating to his wife is in better preservation, and runs thus:—

Heir lyes JANET EDISON, his spouse, who, after living with her husband for the space of 37 years, in a godly and wertuous married state, departed this life the 18 day of March 1707, of her age 60.

Here lyes ISOBEL LINDSAY, spous to Robert Strauchen in Beuillo, who departed this lif the 29 Nouember 1703, and her age 74 years:—
This woman caled in evening of her ago,
Who left her children to suplic her stage;
Some long, some short, as lif and death doeth cast,
For she is in earth, uber al must com at last.

Here lyes DAVID COB, husband to Margret Jamsou, who died yᵉ 2 of March, anno 1698, of age 75 year.

The following is upon a table-shaped stone; and, as will be seen, the inscription contains a curious allusion to the vocation of the person commemorated, as one versed in the "declension" and "inflexion" of nouns:—

S. D. G. Hoc cippo tegitur quicquid mortale fuit ALEXANDRI CROMAR, Dunnensis per octennium ludimagistri, in juventute crudienda seduli, fausti, et felicis, qui, grammaticæ doctus, mortem nec declinare voluit, nec fatum flectere potuit. Ætatis suæ anno vigesimo octavo, ærw Christianæ 1733, obiit. Metam properamus ad unam.

[By this stone is covered all that was mortal of ALEXANDER CROMAR, schoolmaster of Dun for eight years, a diligent and successful instructor of youth, who, although a learned grammarian, neither wished to decline death, nor was able to inflect fate. He died in 1733, in the 28th year of his age. We hasten to one goal.]

1757. Tegitur hoc cippo quicquid mortale fuit GEORGII WALKER. Metam properamus ad unam.

[This stone covers all that was mortal of GEORGE WALKER. We hasten to one goal.]

Upon a table-shaped stone:—

THOMAS CROOKS, sometime gardener at Ecclesjohn, afterwards farmer at Roadside of Tayock, born in the parish of Newbattle, 29 March 1716, died 3 Jan. 1798. JEAN CORMACK, his spouse, died 27 Feb. 1802. A son WILLIAM CROOKS, M.D., died on his passage from Tobago to America, in 1802, aged 38. Thos. Cross, of the Island of Tobago, planter, erected this monument 12 Dec. 1803.

James Mwrcy erected this stone in memory of his wife AGNES LYEL, who departed this life, Feb. the 8, 1732, and of age 48 years. Here lyes JAMES MURRAY, sometyme tenant in Litelmil of Boroufield, who departed this life the 20 of June 1733, and of age . . .

Believers, comfort lies in this, &c.

A tombstone (table-shaped), ornamented with carvings of the Erskine and Stuart arms, and a rudely incised figure of death, with a dart in one hand, and a Lochaber axe in the other, bears:—

Heir lyes ane faithfvll, good, and honest man, GEORG STUART, who died in the Lord the 8 day of Febrvar, anno 1687, of age 93. Heir lyes ane honest, vertovs and godly woman MARY ERSKIN, his spovs, and who died in the Lord 13 of Ianvar, anno 1690, and of her age 81:—
Wnder this ston thir mortals doth remain,
Whil Christ shal come and reas them up again;
Altho' by death they be in Prison cast,
The Prince of Lyfe will reas them up at last,
And give them lyfe, which no more will decay,
And habitation, which wasteth not away.

Two stone cists were got to the west of the manse, and one to the north, each of which contained urns with ashes and pieces of bones. Flint arrow-heads have also been found in the parish.

According to tradition, there was a chapel at Balneillie, on the west side of the parish, where human bones and graves have been found.

Dun appears to have been a place of early importance, owing, possibly, to its proximity to the King's residence at Montrose, and to natural advantages. Its earliest recorded lay proprietor was John of Hastings, who had a grant of the manor of Dun from King William. He was sheriff and forester of the Mearns; and when the monastery of Arbroath was founded, he endowed it with a salt-work at Dun, and an acre of land.

The Hastings appear to have held lands in Angus down to about the beginning of the 14th century.

At one time the lordship of Dun stretched, on the north and west of the Southesk, from the very ports of the town of Montrose to the commonty of the city of Brechin, and included a great part of the parishes of Dun, Logie-Pert, and Stracathro; also a good portion of Craig on the south side of the river. This extent of territory was broken in upon by the Superintendent, whose circumstances, owing chiefly, it is said, to the demands which were made upon him by the less opulent of the Reforming leaders, became considerably embarrassed.

But another, and very different affair, had a much more damaging effect upon the Erskines. It appears that the laird of Dun, who married the eldest sister of the first Earl of Panmure, died young, leaving two sons, whose existence naturally precluded the succession of their uncle Robert to the estates. With the view of removing these obstacles, Robert and his three sisters, who lived together at Logie, determined to poison the " two zoung boyis." For this purpose, two of the sisters crossed the Cairn o' Mount, and met with " ane notorious Witche and abuser of the people," called Janet Irwing, from whom they received a quantity of herbs, with injunctions how to use them. It appears that they " steipit thame amangis nill ane lang space ;" and, after much deliberation, as to whether the dose should be administered, they resolved in the affirmative ; and, accordingly, " about mydsomer" in 1610, the murderers " past al togidder furth of Logy," along with the eldest of their intended victims, to the house of his mother in Montrose, where she and the other son were living for a time, and there the " poysoneable drink wes ministrat," and given to their " brother soucs." The eldest son died ; but the younger recovered. By some means or other, the Erskines contrived to evade the law until towards the end of the year 1613, when the brother was tried and found guilty. He was executed at Edinburgh 1st December 1613. By his own admission, the brother appears to have been a mere tool in the hands of his three sisters, and

that they " wer the first movearis of him to that wicked deide, that therby he might atteane to the right of the leving of Dynne." Upon this confession, the sisters were apprehended, and tried in June 1614, when they were found to have been " airt and pairt" in the poisoning ; and were all sentenced to have " thair heiadis strukin frome thair bodeyis" at the Market Cross of Edinburgh. The sisters, Isabell and Annas, suffered accordingly ; but Helen, who was confined in prison until 22d March 1615, had her sentence commuted to banishment " out of this kingdome, during hir lyftyme."

The old house, or castle of Dun, where possibly these infatuated criminals as well as their victims were born, and in which it is believed Knox visited the Superintendent, stood within the present garden of Dun, near the kirkyard, where an old arched gateway, constructed of stone, and with thick walls, prettily covered with ivy, still marks the site of the old baronial residence.

In 1669, David Erskine of Dun and his successors (Acta Parl., vol. vii. 655), were empowered to hold a fair " vpon the mure of Dun the second Wednesday after Whitsonday yeerly, for buying and selling of horse, nolt, sheip, meill, malt, and all sort of grane, cloath, lining, and woollen, and all sort of merchant commodities," with power to levy and uplift the tolls and customs, &c., in all time coming.

The Bridge of Dun, which consists of three arches, crosses the South Esk near the railway station. It was erected by the grandfather of the Marchioness of Ailsa, and was completed only a few months before his death. It bears this inscription :—

This Bridge was founded on the 7th June 1785, and finished on the 27th January 1787, by Alexander Stevens.

The Rev. WM. BURNS, who originated the Revivals at Kilsyth in 1838, and became the first missionary of the English Presbyterian Church in China, was born at Dun, where his father was parish minister. During his residence in China, Mr Burns translated, and published, in the native

F F

language, an edition of Bunyan's Pilgrim's Progress, &c. A tomb in the foreign churchyard of Niau-Chwang marks his grave (v. Life by Islay Burns), with this inscription :—

To the memory of the Rev. WILLIAM C. BURNS, A.M., missionary to the Chinese, from the Presbyterian Church in England. Born in Dun, Scotland, April 1, 1812; arrived in China, November 1847; died at Port of Niau-Chwang, April 4, 1868. 2d Cor. c. v.

Dr J. P. NICHOL, author of the Architecture of the Heavens, &c., afterwards Professor of Astronomy in the University of Glasgow, began life as parochial teacher at Dun. He was born at Brechin, where his father was a merchant.

~~~~~~~~~~~~~~~~~~~~~~

Skene.

(S. BRIDGET, VIRGIN.)

NOTHING certain is known of the early history of the kirk of Skene, except that it was a chaplainry; and its patronage vested in the Principal of St Leonard's College, St Andrews. Alan Durward, justiciary of Scotland, is the earliest recorded lay proprietor of the district; and it appears that in 1247-57, he granted Peter, Bishop of Aberdeen, an annual of 22s, from his lands of *Schene*, in exchange for the second tithes of O'Neil.

The burial enclosures of the lairds of Skene and Concraig are upon the site of the old kirk; but neither contain monumental stones. Mr SMITH of Concraig was of a farmer family in Kintore. The property now belongs to the University of Aberdeen, having been bought by King's College. The present kirk, built in 1801, has the belfry upon the south side. The bell bears :—

TO . THE . KIRK OF . SKENE.
JOHN . MOWAT . ME . FE . OLD . ABD . 1735.

A marble tablet, within the church, bears :—

Near the southern wall of this church are interred the mortal remains of GEORGE SKENE of Skene, descended from a long line of that name, who was born on the IX. day of May MDCCXLIX., and died on the XXIX. day of April MDCCCXXV.

—The above-named Mr Skene was succeeded by a deaf and dumb brother, who only survived two years. The property then came to trustees for behoof of the Earl of Fife, the heir of entail, by whom the family of Skene, through a female, is now represented. Robert Skene had a charter from The Bruce of the lands and loch of Skene, dated at Scone, 1 June 1317, from which period, until 1827-8, the family held the property in the male line. It was in consequence of the marriage of the third Earl of Fife, in 1775, with Mary, eldest daughter of George Skene of Skene, that the Duff family succeeded to the estates of Skene and Careston, &c.: it is of this lady's father and his servant, Harry Walker, that so many curious anecdotes are told by Dean Ramsay and other writers. As given in heraldic books, the origin of the family of Skene is fanciful, and said to have arisen from their ancestor having saved the king's life by killing a wild boar with a dirk, or *skein*, for which deed he received the lands, it is added, from Malcolm II., also his surname. "Skene" is also the name of a place in the parish of Arbuthnott.

A flat stone in the churchyard bears this inscription —

Hic humantur sub spe beatæ resurrectionis ossa M^{ri} LUD : DUNLOP, hujus ecclesiæ Skeenensis, et alterius, sciz. Tarlanensis, annis 43 quondam pastoris fidelissimi. Multa in ejus laudes dicere inanem gloriam forsan redoleret; attamen celandum non est campanile hujus templi, inter alia laude digna, ejus sumptu magna ex parte extructum fuisse. Potiorem ejus partem tenet cœlum ubi vivit cum Xto. Obiit Feb. 6, 1691, ætatis 71.

[Here are interred, in the hope of a happy resurrection, the bones of Mr LUD. DUNLOP, for 43 years a most faithful minister of this church of Skeen, and of another, viz. that of Tarland. To say much in his praise would perhaps savour of vain glory; but, amongst other laudable actions, it is deserving of record that the bell-tower of this church was erected in great measure at his expense. His better part now dwells in heaven with Christ. He died 6 Feb. 1691, aged 71.]

A table-shaped tombstone erected over that of Mr Dunlop bears.—

In memory of the Rev. JAMES HOGG, D.D., minister of Skene, who died much respected and regretted 28 Nov. 1823, in the 72d year of his age, and 47th of his ministry, 37 of which he was minister of the parish of Skene. His sister, JEAN HOGG, died 30 June 1835, aged 82.

—Mr H. was of the old family of Blairydryne in Durris.

A granite slab, within an enclosure in north-east corner of kirkyard, bears:—

Within this enclosure are interred the remains of KATHERINE-ANN-BUCHAN FORBES, the wife of William McCombie of Easter Skene and Lynturk, and daughter of Major Alexander Forbes of Invernan, who died on the 16th day of April 1835, in the 26th year of her age. And of their son, THOMAS, who died on the 15th day of September 1841, in the 10th year of his age.

—Mrs McCombie's mother was a daughter of Duncan Forbes-Mitchell of Thainston, second son of Sir Arthur Forbes of Craigievar, (v. p. 157.) Mr McC.'s ancestors held the estate of Finnygaund in Glenshee, also those of Forter and Crandart in Glenisla, of the first-mentioned of which "John McComy-Moir" [i.e., the big or great McComie] had a charter in 1571. The Clan M'Thomas, of which this individual was the chief, appears in the roll of the clans and broken men, and John's descendants, from a dispute about marches, seem to have borne a deadly grudge to their neighbours, the Farquharsons of Brochdarg, so much so that in 1673, when members of the two families happened to meet at Forfar, a fight took place, in which Brochdarg and a brother were killed, also two McComies. After this the Farquharsons and McComies were outlawed. One McComie fled to the south, another, Donald, took refuge in the Highlands of Aberdeenshire, and became ancestor of the McCombies of Easter Skene and Lynturk, also of those of Tillyfour.—(Mem. of Angus and Mearns.) It was the father of the present laird of Easter Skene, a merchant in Aberdeen, who bought the property of Easter Skene, since which time Lynturk has fallen to Mr M'Combie by heirship. Mr McCombie built the present mansion house of Easter Skene, the lands of which property, as well as those of Lynturk, he has vastly improved by draining, reclaiming of waste land, planting, and building, &c. Like his cousin, Mr McCombie, Tillyfour, the laird of Easter Skene has acquired fame as a rearer of polled cattle, &c.

Within an enclosure on east of churchyard:—

Sacred to the memory of ELIZABETH FORBES, daughter of Geo. Forbes of Boyndlie, who died 20 Feb. 1853, aged 80.

—Miss Forbes was aunt to Mrs Shepherd of Kirkville. A daughter of the latter became the wife of Mr Ireland, sometime F. C. minister of Skene; and the following, upon a granite monument, near the above, relates to Mrs Ireland's mother:—

In memory of CATHERINE HENDERSON, relict of the late Walter F. Ireland, D.D., minister of North-Leith, who departed this life on the 22d of January 1853, aged 63. [Rev. i. 17, 18; John xiv. 19.]

Near the above, a granite monument bears:—

Erected by the parishioners of Skene to the memory of the Rev. GEORGE MACKENZIE, A.M., for 35 years the faithful and beloved minister of the parish. He died 26 Dec. 1859, aged 72.

Upon a table-shaped stone:—

To the memory of WILLIAM CHALMERS, late of the 31st Regt. of Foot, who departed this life 17 Dec. 1809, aged 76. MARGARET MILLAR, his first wife, died in Florida; ELIZABETH GIFFERT, his second wife, died 1 Feb. 1801. MARGARET CHALMERS, his daughter by Margaret Millar, spouse of Alex. Norie, Carlogie, died 26 Dec. 1796, aged 42:—

Of manners mild, to all who knew her dear;
The tender mother, best of friends, lies here;
Whose darling wit was comfort to impart,
. . . .
Candour and meekness shone in all she said,
Peace bless'd her life, and sooth'd her dying bed.
Dearest of mothers, best of friends, farewell;
May this plain stone, children's affection tell;
Through life thy virtue was their joy and pride,
In death their best example and their guide.
Our social cares and fears, alas! are o'er,
Thy love maternal cheers the heart no more.

—ALEX. NORIE died at Aberdeen, 1822, aged 67. JEAN FALCONER, third wife of Wm. Chalmers, died at Aberdeen 1830, aged 76, a woman very much beloved and respected by all who knew her; and whose trustees have caused this stone to be erected to perpetuate her memory:—

> When the trumpet sound shall call,
> And we must leave this earthly vale;
> Then the cold tomb in brightest skies
> To joy immortal they shall rise.

The following inscription, from one of three stones which relate to the same Wilsons, presents the name of one of the last descendants of the Tyries of Dunnideer, a Roman Catholic family in the Garioch (v. INSCH):—

In memory of ALEXANDER WILSON, farmer of Auchencloch, who died 1 June 1799, aged 82. Also of ELIZABETH TYRIE, his spouse, who died 10 March 1814, aged 84. Also of JOHN WILSON of Auchencloch, who died 8 April 1820, aged 66. Also his spouse, Mrs JEAN MALCOLM, who died 17 April 1836, aged 84. ✠ Died at Allathan, parish of Monquhitter, 8 Sep. 1845, in the 49th year of her age, ELIZABETH WILSON, eldest daughter of John Wilson, Esq. of Auchencloch, and spouse of Alex. Mitchell, Esq. of Allathan. R. I. P. Requiescat in pace. May she rest in peace.

Here lyes ALEXANDER GLEN, who departed this life in the year 1725, aged 64. . . . . . . ROBSON, their relick, who departed this life in the year 1735 . . . . . .

JAMES BURNET, died 2d March 1807, aged 98; MARGARET RAEBURN, his spouse, died 10th Feb. 1803, aged 88. &c.

Upon a granite obelisk:—

1865. GEORGE MELLIS, leader of the church choir of Skene, died 13 Feb., aged 32. This tribute of regard to his memory is erected by the choir, and a few friends.

MARJORY MILNE, b. 1777, d. 1856, "was upwards of 50 years an attached and valued servant in the family of Mr Thomas Burnett of Kepplestone, by whose widow this tablet is erected as a token of regard."

A plain headstone bears:—

Erected by Alex. Carny, in memory of his father, JAMES CARNY, late farmer in Kirktoun of Skene, who died 13 Jan. 1798, aged 49. His son JAMES, died 25 Nov. 1810, aged 21. His spouse, JEAN BROWNIE, departed this life June 6, 1832, aged 74.

—These were the parents and brother of the late Provost Carny of Macduff (v. p. 89.)

The next inscription, from a granite slab in east wall of burial ground, bears the name of one who made money in India as a coach builder:—

The burial place of WILLIAM GIBSON of Kinmundy, Skene.

The next two inscriptions, (the first from a marble head stone, the other abridged from a table-shaped stone,) relate to farmer families who acquired money and property:—

Sacred to the memory of JAMES DAVIDSON, Esq. of Kinmundy, who died 3 Nov. 1827, aged 72 years.

Erected by David Low of Fiddie, in memory of ELIZABETH SMITH, his spouse, who died 1833, aged 57 . . . . . the said DAVID Low died 1841, aged 77 . . . . . HELEN REITH, spouse of Robert Low of Fiddie, died 1862, aged 58. . . . . . the said ROBERT Low, for 25 years an elder of this parish, died 1869, aged 68.

Also abridged:—

JOSEPH, son of Joseph ALLAN, schoolmr. at Skene, died 1779, aged 18 years. . . . . ELIZABETH ALLAN, spouse to And. Fowler at Broadiach, died 1799, aged 34. The said JOSEPH ALLAN, schoolmaster at Skene for 62 years, died 1819, aged 87. His first wife AGNES COLLIE, died 1784. The above ANDREW FOWLER, died 1827, aged 72 . . . ELIZABETH MALCOLM, his spouse, died 1854, aged 87 : GEORGE their son, died 1864, aged 73.

Cinerary urns, stone circles, and other traces of antiquity, have been found in various parts of Skene. The hill of Keir, the summit of which presents trenches, ditches, &c., resembling those upon the Barmakin of Echt (v. p. 66), is well worthy of being visited by the antiquary.

A rude boulder upon a rising ground on Easter Skene, near the boundary between the parishes of Skene and Kinellar, bears:—

DRUM STONE. 1411. HARLAW.

—According to tradition, Sir Alex. Irvine of Drum rested upon this stone when on his way to the battle of Harlaw, and beheld for the last time the ancient tower of his ancestors, he having, like the greater part of the flower of those barons and their retainers who fought at Harlaw (as related in the well-known ballad which celebrates that sad event), there—

"Left to the world their last gude-nicht."

As shown above, the family of Skene first acquired a grant of the lands and barony of Skene from Robert the Bruce. According to Douglas (Bar., p. 555), the house of Skene was looked upon as "the first built stone house in Marr." It is described as having consisted of three storeys, built with lime quite run together, or vitrified, with walls above ten feet thick, and to have been entered by a ladder on the second storey, while the third storey was "covered with a mount of earth upon the top." Skene House remained in this state until 1680, when the arches were taken out, and the house roofed and floored. The old part still forms a portion of the present house of Skene, which has been added to, and altered, at different periods.

The Loch of Skene is a singularly beautiful object, particularly when seen from the north, with the picturesque mountains of Clochnabane, Mount Battock, &c., in the background.

~~~~~~~~~~~~

Towie.

(? S. ——.)

KILBATTOCH, Kynbethot, and Kinbattoch, are old forms of the name of this parish. Another authority calls it "Kilbartha, or Bartha's Cell or church." It was also known as Towie-Brux, from having belonged at one time to Forbes of Brux. The church was anciently a vicarage of Old Machar.

The present kirk, which has a prominent position upon the south side of the Don, is dated 1808. It is a plain building, near the site of the previous kirk, in which was found a coffin-slab, with a cross upon it, terminating in a good example of the fleur-de-lis. The church bell bears the name of Mr LUMSDEN OF CORRACHREE. His burial aisle is upon the site of the old kirk: within it is this inscription:—

Here lies Mr JAMES LUMSDEN of Corrachree, late minister of the Gospel at Towie, who died Feb. 15, 1777, aged 73. And MARY GRANT, his spouse, who died Jan. 13, 1778, aged 77. Here lies JOHN LUMSDEN . . . . . son to John Lumsden and Katharine Kearin, Aberdeen, who died April 13, 1741, aged 5 years.

[Upon a slab in outside of wall] :—

CONDITORIUM J. LUMSDEN DE CORRACHREE.

—Mr L., who was admitted minister of Towie 9 June 1740, had at least four daughters and one son. Three of the daughters were married, Mary to Bailie Dingwall of Aberdeen; Margaret, to Mr James Gordon, Belly; and Elizabeth, to Capt. John Grant of Duthil. The son Robert (born 16 March 1745), wrote some clever satires, such as the See in the Forest, and Jean of Bogmore, (v. p. 188.) Mr L. was succeeded in Towie by Mr Menrus, who was translated to Cluny (q.v.) in 1795.

Near Lumsden's aisle, a granite obelisk, within a railed enclosure, is thus inscribed:—

Sacred to the memory of Gen. Sir ALEXANDER LEITH, K.C.B., of Freefield and Glenkindie, who died 19 Feb. 1859, aged 84. Also of MARIA THORP, his first wife, who died 2 Aug. 1834. Erected by his surviving widow, Mary Mackenzie Leith.

—Sir Alex. Leith, who was a brave soldier, served in the French and Peninsular wars, and was knighted in 1815. He rose to the rank of Lieut.-Colonel; and from an expression which he used to his soldiers when they were coming to close quarters with the enemy on one occasion, he was known in the army by the soubroquet of *Cauld Steel.* By his first wife he had his successor in the estate, and another son, Col. Disney Leith, C.B., who distinguished himself at Moultan. Since then he has married the only child of Sir H. Gordon of Knockespock. Sir A.'s "surviving widow" is a Mackenzie of Glack. The Leiths of Freefield and Glenkindie, like those of Leith-hall, &c., are descended from Wm. Leith of Barns in Premnay, provost of Aberdeen, 1352-55. One of the Leiths married a daughter of Strachan of Glenkindie; and Patrick, the last of the male line of the Strachans, sold the estate in 1738 to his cousin, Alex. Leith (grandfather of Sir Alex.), who died about 1754.

MARY DUNCAN, first wf. of Ja. Strachan, d. 1771, a. 27 :—

> Here lyes interred below this clod,
> The body of a saint of God,
> Who liv'd in hope and expectation
> Of Jesus Christ for her salvation.
> She liv'd a good and pious life,
> A loving, chaste, and faithful wife;
> She died in peace with God above,
> And rests in his Eternal love,

Erected by public subscription, in memory of JOHN PROCTER, Esq., surgeon. Born 26 July 1810; died 14 April 1854.

ALEXANDER LYON, A.M., graduate of King's College, Aberdeen, afterwards of Sydney Sussex College, Cambridge, "at both of which Universities he obtained many honourable testimonials of uncommon abilities and attainments, withdrawn by untimely death on 5th day of June 1850, in the 23d year of his age." Erected by his parents, Alexander Lyon and Helen Tough.

To the memory of the Rev. ROBERT LINDSAY, LL.D., born 19 March 1799; ordained minister of this parish 20 Aug. 1840; died 31 Oct. 1851.

It is said that there were three chapels in different parts of the parish in old times. In the neighbourhood of Kinbattoch, is the site of a rath, or fort; but this, as well as the Peel of Fechley (upon which are the slender remains of an ancient fort), and the other antiquities in the parish, are noticed in the Statistical Accounts, &c.

Of Towie Castle, which adjoins the kirk, some of the vaulted cellars, and a portion of the square tower, only remain, round the latter of which a protecting wall has been recently built. It is generally believed that this was the place which, in 1571, Captain Ker, deputed by Sir Adam Gordon of Auchendown, demanded " to be randrit to him in the Queynis name ;" and the request being refused by the lady (her lord being from home), "fyre was put to the hous, wharin she, and the nomber of 27 persons, war cruelie bryut to the death." This barbarous proceeding, which was done to revenge certain insults which the Forbeses had given to the Gordons, is celebrated in the touching ballad of Edom o' Gordon. The unfortunate Lady Forbes, who, according to some accounts, was pregnant at the time of her sad death, was a daughter of Sir John Campbell of Calder; and her charred remains are said to have been buried in the now obliterated kirkyard of Nether Towie.

The Forbeses, designed of Tollies, or Towie, in 1494, are said to have sprung from Alexander of Brux, 4th son of Sir John of Forbes, who died in 1305. The estate of Towie was Forbes property down to about the middle of the 17th century.

In 1357, Thomas Earl of Mar gave a charter to Adam of Strathauen and his wife Margaret, the Earl's cousin, of part of the lands of Glenkindie, and Glenboul, called Rummor. From a sett, 1488, of the lands of Murtlich (now Morlich), which belonged to the Abbey of Cupar, it appears that Margaret Charteris was the name of the lady of Glenkindie at the latter date; and that she had " tua sonnis callit Jhonne and Alexander of Strahaquhyn." There was a knighthood in the Glenkindie family at one time; and it is probable that they were a branch of the Strachans of the Mearns (v. p. 134.) The well-known tragical ballad of Glenkindy is intended to illustrate a tradition in the courtship of Strachan and the Earl of Mar's daughter, in which "Gib his man," or page, is represented as having played " the loon," for which he forfeited his life.

The house of Glenkindie (locally situated in the parish of Strathdon), is a snug chateau, amidst ancestral trees, and partly clad with ivy. An older castle, surrounded by a foss, stood farther up the glen. But it appears that a house had been built near the site of the present one, in 1595.

Two carved stones are still there—one, below a shield with the Strachan arms, and the initials V. S., bears:—

... b̄ns . straḣbḣin . de . glenkendic
hoc . op . ferit . annō . būi . 15—

The other slab is inscribed :—

M^cLXXX. XV.
VELAM . STRAQVHEN . OF . GLENKENDE.
BEGET . T . . . .

Two door lintels, in the present house, bear the Leith cross-crosslet, the motto, TRUSTY TO THE END; also these dates and initials:—

A. L : C. D., 1741. A. L : C. S., 1787.

JAMES WILKIE, a divinity student, and native of Towie, wrote The Holy Sabbath and other poems (Abd. 1841.) The poems are of a pensive melancholy turn, to which, unfortunately, the author fell a victim.

Aberchirder, or Marnoch.

(S. MARNAN, BISHOP.)

THE kirk of *Abirkerdour*, now MARNOCH, a vicarage of the cathedral of Moray, was given by King William the Lion to the Abbey of Arbroath. Between 1203-14, Gilchrist, Earl of Mar, gave the same convent the patronage of the church of Aberchirder, the right to which he had successfully contested with the King and the Bishop of Moray.

According to tradition, S. MARNAN, who flourished about the middle of the 7th century, "dyed very old, and was buried at Aberchirdir." A ford on the Deveron, and a well near the church, still bear his name. Possibly there was an altar to Our LADY in the church in old times, as an adjoining spring is named LADY Well.

The present church, which was removed from the kirkyard about the beginning of the present century, occupies the site of a stone circle, upon a rising ground to the north-east. Like many parish churches of the period, that of Marnoch presents little worthy of notice, save two material wants—elegance in design, and beauty of situation—to the latter of which, the old site, on the banks of the Deveron, forms quite a contrast.

Little of the old kirk of Marnoch remains; and a vault, or place where bodies were deposited, prior to interment, during the resurrection mania, "built by subscription in the year 1832," is now an object of little interest. Some of the tombs, however, are of a superior class. One, in the north-east corner of the enclosure, was, according to local story, executed by a common mason at Crombie. It is of Elgin freestone, dated 1694, and presents, impaled, the arms of Meldrum of Laithers and Duff of Braco, surrounded by an elegant scroll ornament. Within an oval, the half-length life-sized effigy of a bearded ecclesiastic, with cap, frill, and gown, is carved in bold relief: a scroll is in the right hand, and a book in the left. Below (upon an oblong oval, and convex piece of polished Portsoy marble), is the following inscription :—

Hic jacet reverendus et pius defunctus D. GEORGIUS MELDRUM de Crombie, quondam de Glass, præco fidelissimus, qui officio pastorali, dum ferebant tempora, diligenter functus erat. Dives enim fuit non avarus, lucri gratia conscientiam violare noluit, pacifice et sobrie vixit, et hinc migravit anno Dom. 1692, ætatis suæ 76.

[Here lies the late reverend and pious Mr GEORGE MELDRUM of Crombie, sometime of Glass, a faithful preacher, who, while the times permitted, diligently discharged the duties of his pastoral office. Not being avaricious, he was rich, and would not do violence to his conscience for the sake of gain; he lived peaceably and soberly, and departed hence A.D. 1692, in the 76th year of his age.]

—Mr M., who previously "exercised" at Aberdeen, was admitted minister of Glass in 1644; and there, in 1650, one of his elders, in the presence of the session (alluding to some reported *fama*,) declared he had heard a parishioner say that "he sould cause that lowne the minister haue a fowll face!" Mr M.'s father was laird of Laithers, and his mother was a sister of Adam Duff of Clunybeg. Mr George Meldrum is said to have had three daughters (Doug. Bar., 138.)

Besides Crombie, in Marnoch, Mr Meldrum held large possessions in the parishes of Turriff and Inverkeithny, &c., in all which he was succeeded by John Ramsay of Melross, in Gamrie, as heir of entail. Crombie (the old house of which still stands), was previously possessed by Walter Urquhart, who, along with a number of accomplices, was charged with the murder of a brother of Lord Frendraught in 1642.

A flagstone, which forms the entrance to a vault, within the same enclosure as the last-mentioned monument, bears :—

This is now the burial place of the family of Ardmealie, being a gift from William Duff of Crombie to JAMES GORDON of Ardmealie, his nephew, who died 31 July 1791.

—The Ardmealie Gordons were a branch of those of Craig (v. AUCHENDOIR). From Gordons the property of Ardmealie was bought by Morrison of Auchentoul, father of the present laird of Bognie. It afterwards belonged to Edward Ellice, Esq., M.P., from whom it and Mayen were bought by the trustees of the undermentioned Mr Gordon of Avochie, who sold Drumlithie, in the Mearns, to Mr Miller :—

In memory of JOHN GORDON, Esq. of Avochie and Mayen, who died the 27 of Nov. 1857, aged 60 years.

—The above-named Mr Gordon succeeded his father, a W.S. in Edinburgh, in the lands of Avochie. Upon his death in 1857, Avochie and Mayen came, by entail, to the present laird, Adam Hay. Mr Hay is also a W.S., and the son of a sister of the last-named Mr Gordon's father. Mr Hay assumes the name of *Hay-Gordon* (v. KINORE).

An adjoining enclosure contains marble tablets, respectively inscribed as follow :—

Within this vault are deposited the remains of JOHN INNES of Muiryfold, Esq. Distinguished for judgment, candour, and integrity, he employed those qualities with cheerful and unremitting application in the service of his friends and his neighbours. In domestick life, an affectionate husband and generous master ; in society a most agreeable companion. Born 11 March 1729, he died lamented 3 Oct. 1780. This vault and monument were erected at the request of his disconsolate widow, Helen, daughter of Peter Gordon of Ardmealie, Esq.

—Mr Innes, who was a W.S. in Edinburgh, was descended from the Edingight family, and inherited Muiryfold from his father (v. p. 101). Leaving no issue, he was succeeded by the daughter of his younger brother, THOMAS INNES of Monellie. The latter, also a W.S., died at Edinburgh, 6th Sept. 1779, and was buried in the Greyfriars' churchyard. Mr T. Innes' daughter married James, a son of Rose of Gask, near Turriff, who was descended from John of Ballivat, 2d son of the Hugh Rose of Kilravock, who died in 1517. Mr Rose assumed the name of *Rose-Innes*. His death is thus recorded at Marnoch upon a marble slab :—

To the memory of JAMES ROSE-INNES, spouse to Elizabeth-Mary Innes of Netherdale : died 4 Aug. 1814, aged 40. [Their eldest and second sons THOMAS and WILLIAM died in infancy respectively in 1799 and 1800.]

—The following, from another tablet, shows that Mrs Rose-Innes survived her husband for about 37 years :—

To the memory of Mrs ELIZABETH-MARY ROSE-INNES of Netherdale, who died at Netherdale, 17 Jan. 1851, aged 73.

—The property and mansion-house of Netherdale are beautifully situated upon the north bank of the Deveron. Netherdale, originally called Pittendriech, and Mains of Fyvie, was acquired by Mr Innes from the Earl of Fife in excambion for Muiryfold. The present name was given the property, and the house built, by Miss Innes about 1795, when she married Mr Rose.

To the memory of GEORGINA GILZEAN, spouse of James Rose-Innes, third son of Jas. Rose-Innes, and Elizabeth-Mary, his spouse : died 10 Oct, 1836, aged 28. ELIZABETH-MARY, only daughter of Jas. Rose-Innes and Georgina Gilzean, died aged 14 years and 9 months. JAMES ROSE-INNES, spouse of Georgina Gilzean, died 10 June 1845, aged 44.

—James Rose-Innes, W.S., who died in 1845, was 3d son of the heiress of Netherdale. His wife (who predeceased him in 1836), was a daughter of Mr Gilzean of Bunachton, Inverness-shire. Their son, T. Gilzean Rose-Innes, now laird of Netherdale, married Grace, daughter of Mr Fraser, W.S., Edinburgh. Besides the family already named, the heiress of Netherdale had a daughter (who lives at Netherdale Cottage), and three sons: John, a merchant in London, who died in 1867; Capt. Patrick, of Blachrie House, Fyvie (to whose kindness I am obliged for notes regarding his family); and George, of Ardfour, a solicitor in London.

A monument, with the Chalmers and Innes coats impaled, initialed M. H. C: E. I., and dated 1709, contains this inscription:—

Sub hoc monumento reconduntur exuviæ M^{ri} HUGONIS CHALMERS, qui ecclesiæ hujus Marnochensis A.D. 36 circiter annos pastoris officio fidelissime functus est. Doctus absque vanitate, pius citra ostentationem, gravis sed non morosus, veritatem pacemque constantissime coluit, et tandem, exacto 59 annorum curriculo, ex hac ærumnosa lachrymarum valle in patriam cœlestem commigravit quinto die Junii 1707.

[Under this monument are laid the remains of Mr HUGH CHALMERS, who, for about 36 years, discharged with the greatest fidelity, the office of pastor of this church of Marnoch. Learned without vanity, pious without ostentation, grave but not morose, he constantly studied truth and peace, and at length, after a career of 59 years, departed from this sorrowful valley of tears to the heavenly land, 5th June 1707.]

Upon a flat stone in area of burial ground:—

JOHN TAYLOR, Mill of Crombie, d. 1721, a. 44; MARGT. JOHNSTON, his wf., d. 1748, a. 61 :—
Here lyes the man and wife, whose actions just,
Still blooms afresh, tho' now they're turn'd to dust;
Unlearned were both, yet from God's laws ne'er swerv'd,
Believ'd in Christ, and him they daily serv'd.
Be thankful then, since ye're like labourers sent—
The more's requir'd of them where much is lent;
In memory of their honest lives and deaths
WILLIAM, their son, this stone Bequeatha.

Near the above :—

Here lyes the body of WILLIAM THAIN, lauful son to Patrick Thain in Euchrie, who died the 22 of March 1753 . . . . .

—Though now a somewhat uncommon surname, *Thain* is one of some antiquity in the district; and it is interesting to notice that in connection with the very place named in this inscription, "Patryk Thane the ald wycar of Innerkethny," was, in 1493, one of several persons who perambulated the lands of "Yochry et Achbrady," as part of the kirk lands of Aberchirder. Yochry, Eochry, or Echry, is a sort of peninsula or headland of the Deveron, and may have its name from having abounded at one time in yew trees.

Upon a table-shaped stone:—

Sacred to the memory of JAMES SIMPSON, who departed this life January 30, 1777, aged 62 years; and ISOBEL MACKIE, his wife, who died 26 May 1787, aged 68 years. This stone is erected by their son, John Simpson, merchant in Quebec.

When we devote our youth to God, &c.

JOHN SIMPSON died Oct 30, 1858, aged 83. WILLIAM SIMPSON died 3 Nov. 1867, aged 55.

—A stone slab in a pillar of the kirkyard gate preserves this record of John Simpson's birth, and of his liberality to the heritors of the parish of Marnoch :—

John Simpson, mercht. in Quebec, was born in the parish of Marnoch, A.D. 1747, and at his sole expense erected these churchyard walls, A.D. 1793.

JAS. WATSON, gardener, Ardmeallie, d. 1780, a. 79 :—
A humourous sympathising friend,
Whose bones lies in this dark abode ;
Companion was for high or mean,
Regarding man and fearing God.

The next two inscriptions are chiefly remarkable for their orthographical peculiarities :—

Memento moeriy. AReCTed By RObeRT GRaY shoemaker in CrANNA TO THE MEMORY OF HIS son Robert and daughter Jean who departed this life Octr. 30 Nov. 12 1817. In memory of his Mother isabel layen who departed this life 1822 aged 73.

G G

Memento mori. His Fader R. G. MaSSaN IN FOggLON WhO DEParted This LIfe The 22 OF AprIL 1782 Egged 30.

Upon a headstone :—

To the memory of the late GEORGE CHRISTIE, tinsmith and engraver, Fergustown, who died 10 Feb. 1860, aged 58. Erected by his friends and acquaintances as a token of their admiration of his honest industry, moral worth, intelligence, and self-acquired mechanical genius. Here rests a prisoner now released.

Upon a marble slab.—

Sacred to the memory of the Rev. JOHN EDWARDS, who died on the 1st day of October 1848, in the 57th year of his age, and the 9th of his ministry. Post nubila coelum.

—Mr Edwards was the son of a small farmer in the parish of Grange. He was schoolmaster first of Boharm, next of his native parish. The Earl of Fife presented him to the living of Marnoch in 1837. Being vetoed by the people, application was then made by the Presbytery of Strathbogie to the superior ecclesiastical courts for advice how to act in the matter. The church courts advised the rejection of the presentee—on the other hand, the Court of Session ordered his admission to the charge " if found competent." Four members of the Presbytery voted for the former, and seven for the latter course, upon which the General Assembly deposed the majority, and also deprived the presentee of his license. After Mr Edwards was vetoed, the patron issued a new presentation in favour of the Rev. DAVID HENRY, assistant to the previous minister. Mr Henry was " the choice of the people," and inducted by a minority of the Presbytery. Being set aside, under the above circumstances, Mr Henry continued to labour at Aberchirder to a large congregation in the Free Church, and died there in 1870. He was joined (McCosh's Wheat and the Chaff), by *two* of the original protesting ministers of Strathbogie! It need scarcely be added that "the Marnoch case" caused the passing of Lord Aberdeen's Church Act, also that it hastened the Disruption of 1843, and that *the seven*, as well as Mr Edwards, were reponed to the office of the ministry.

The district of Aberchirder was a thanedom, from which, as was the fashion of the period, the thane, or king's steward, assumed his surname. The family DE ABERCHIRDER appears to have been of considerable note ; and, according to the Innes genealogy, "Dame Janettee of Aberchirder, daughter to Sir David the Thayne of these lands," married Sir Robt. Innes, by whom he acquired " a considerable estate," and bore her arms (three boars' heads erased), along with his own.

But it is of Symon, thane of Aberchirder, that the best record exists. About 1286-9, he founded a chapel on the banks of the " Duffhern," dedicated to S. MENIMIS or MONANUS, which he endowed with four silver merks out of the mill of " Carnoussexth" (Carnousie), and other privileges, to which charter his brother William de Aberkerdouer is a witness. It appears that Symon was also thane of Cunwath (Inverkeithny), six davachs of which he granted to the Earl of Buchan with the view of being reponed in the thanage of Aberchirder, of which, for some cause or other (possibly by King Edward in 1296), he appears to have been dispossessed. Symon was dead before 12 March 1328, as of that date his daughter Sibilla was recognised as his heiress in part of the lands of Westirearingusy, which she conveyed to William of Melgdrum. Of this lady no further trace is found. Sometime after the death of Symon of Aberchirder, the thanedom was given to Walter Lesly, by whose descendant, Alexander, Lord of the Isles, it was granted in 1439, under the name of " the *barony* of Aberchirder," to Sir Walter Innes, son of the before-named Sir Robert Innes and Janet Aberchirder.

Probably the chapel of S. MENIMIS stood at a place still called Chapelton, about two miles below the bridge of Marnoch. S. JOHN'S Well and S. JOHN'S Ford are near the Chapelton ; and " Sanct HUCHOMY's Well" is in another part of the parish. All these names possibly indicate sites of old places of worship.

The bridge of Marnoch bears the date of 1806. A short distance below the bridge, situated (as the name implies) upon a promontory, stands the house of Kinairdy. It is said to have belonged at one time to the Crightons of Freudraught, more anciently it formed a part of the barony of Aberchirder. Prior to 1650, Kinairdy belonged to Mr JOHN GREGORY, minister of Drumoak, ancestor of the celebrated mathematicians of that name. The property of Kinairdy, also the patronage of the kirk of Marnoch, were acquired by Lord Fife from a family named Donaldson, the first of whom was a merchant in ELGIN (*q. v.*) A stone slab upon the front of the house of Kinairdy gives this account of the erection of the oldest existing part of it :—

REBUILT & ROOF'D BY THO. DONALDSON & ELIZ. DUFF, A.D. 1725. NULLI CERTA DOMUS.

The mansion house of Auchintoul is near the middle of the parish. Built partly by, it was long the residence of Gen. ALEX. GORDON, who obtained distinction under Peter the Great of Russia, of whose history the General wrote an account in 2 vols. (Aberd. 1755). Gen. GORDON died at Auchintoul, aged 82, and was buried at Marnoch: no stone marks his grave.

Within a mile of Auchintoul stands the *Village of Aberchirder*, or New Marnoch, sometimes called "Foggieloan." It occupies a rising ground, from which a good view of the surrounding district is obtained, and consists of a square, with diverging streets. There are some good shops and dwelling houses in Aberchirder, a branch bank, also Free, Episcopal, U.P., and Baptist Churches, together with a Roman Catholic Chapel. In 1861, it had a population of about 1263 persons, the females being 221 in excess of the males!

Maryton.

(THE VIRGIN MARY.)

THE kirk of *Marinton* was a vicarage of the cathedral of Brechin. The patronage and tithes of S. MARY of Old Munros, with its lands, called in the Scotch speech *Abthen*, were given to the Abbey of Arbroath by William the Lion The same king granted the Abbey lands of Munros, in liferent, to Hugh of Roxburgh, chancellor, to be held of the Abbots of Arbroath, on the payment of three stones of wax yearly. (Reg. Vetus de Aberbrothoc.)

S. MARY's Well is in the immediate vicinity of the present church. The church was built in 1791. A hand bell at the manse bears "MARYTOUN, 1730;" and the bell upon the kirk is thus inscribed :—

MICHAEL . BVRGERHVYS . M . F . 1642.
SOLI . DEO . GLORIA.

Within, and upon the north wall of the kirk, a handsome marble monument (adorned with the Lindsay arms, and motto, FIRMUS MANEO), bears this inscription :—

Sub hoc marmore reconditus jacet Reverendus vir, DAVID LYNDESIUS, (ex prisca Lyndesiorum familia de Dowhill oriundus), ecclesiæ de Marytown per 33 annos pastor vigilantissimus, vir singulari literarum cognitione, et summa rerum peritia ornatus; pietate in Deum, fide in Regem, reverentia in Episcopos, et humanitate erga omnes insignis, obiit 16 Septembris 1706, ætatis suæ 62. Hic etiam siti sunt duo filii impuberes GULIELMUS et ALEXANDER, et KATHARINA filia, cujus eximiam formæ venustatem omnes virgine dignæ virtutes facile æquabant.

[Beneath this marble lies interred the Rev. DAVID LYNDSAY (a descendant of the old family of Lyndsay of Dowhill), for 33 years the most vigilant pastor of the church of Marytown. He was a man of profound erudition, and of the greatest aptitude for business, distinguished for piety towards God, fidelity to the King, respect for the Bishops, and kindness to all. (He died as above.) Here also are laid two of his sons who died in childhood, WILLIAM and ALEXANDER ; and his daughter KATHARINE, in whom rare personal beauty, and every maidenly virtue shone with equal lustre.]

—Mr Lyndsay was the last Episcopal minister of Maryton. According to the Brechin Presbytery Records, *MS.* (May 1, 1673), he was "younger son of Mr David Lindsay, minister of Rescobie (and) was presented to the kirk of Marieton by the Archbishop of St Andrews." The Lindsays of Dowhill claim descent from Sir William Lindsay of Rossy, in Fife, son of Sir Alex. of Glenesk, by his second wife, a niece of Robt. II. This branch is represented by David Baird Lindsay, Esq. Mr Lindsay succeeded Mr Lamy, on his translation from Maryton to Farnell. Mr Lamy (who was maternal grandfather of the celebrated Dr John Arbuthnott), was possibly a cadet of the old Lamies of Dunkenny (v. p. 68:)

The churchyard, which is kept in good order, contains a number of tombstones, from which the following inscriptions are selected :—

WM. son of Wm. Lawrance, vintner, Usan, was drowned in a draw-well, Oct. 1787, a. 3 years :—
Doth Infant's pain and death proclaim,
That Adam did Rebel?
His destiny declares the same,
Being drowned in a Well.
Let all who mourn his early death,
Hate sin the fatal cause,
And flee to Jesus Christ by faith
Who saves from Satan's jaws.

CHARLES MILNE, d. 1786, a 56 :—
O what an awful scene is here. The adorable Creator around me and the Bones of my fellow creatures under my Feet, The fatal shafts fly so promiscuously, that none can guess the next victim. Passing over the couch of decrepit age, Death has nipped Infancy in its Bud, & blasted Youth in its Bloom, therefore be ye always ready, for in such an hour as ye think not, the final summons will come.

JAMES PETRIE, d. 1789, a. 83 :—
I, when the Trumpet Sounds with joy,
Shall quit my earthly bed ;
The voice that calls me wont annoy—
Arise, come forth ye Dead.

Heir lyis ALEXANDER LITCH, svmtyn indvelar in Old Montrois, hvsband to Beatsy Ramsy, vho depairtid 11 March 1639. The Lord gives and takes, blesed be his holy name. Memento mori noli parco.

The following, in beautifully interlaced letters, is round the margin of a table-shaped stone:—

Heir lieth ALEXANDER LEATCH, somtyme in Bonitoun, who depairted this lif December 15, 1779. JANET GLEN, his spovs, died January 8, 17-2, aged 61.   [v. LETHNOT.]

JAMES ORR, husband to Ann Hampton, who lived sometime in the Bearmeans of Old Montrose, departed this life 11 Nov. 1745, aged 57.

Upon a table-shaped stone :—

JAMES FORREST, collector of toll duties leviable at the Montrose Bridge for the space of 10 years, which office he fulfilled to the satisfaction of all concerned . . . . . . , . .
—A marble slab inserted into the top of the above stone bears that Capt. JAMES DURIE of the *Libra* of Montrose, and his brother JOHN, carpenter of said vessel, were both drowned at sea, 18 Oct. 1843. Mrs MARY FORREST (wife of J. F.), died in 1848, aged 82, &c.

ALEX. GREIG, farmer (1755) :—
Primo Deus ferro mortales vertere terram instituit.
Agricola incurvo terram dimouit aratro ;
Hinc anni labor, hinc patriam paruosq' nepotes
sustinet.

[Mortals were at first divinely taught to turn up the soil with a ploughshare. The husbandman breaks up the ground with the plough ; hence the labour of the year—hence he supports his country, and his little grand-children.]

By honest industry and guiltless toil,
He liv'd on earth manuring still the soil ;
Yet not to earth were all his thoughts confin'd,
For bread of life his labours were design'd.

An adjoining stone bears :—

Here lyes DAVID DENNIES, sometime wivor in Goukhill, who departed this life the 5th day of May anno Domnino 1742, and of his age 62 years.

Upon a brass plate (v. p. 91), sunk into the top of a table-shaped stone :—

The Rev. ANDREW FERGUSSON, born March 1769 ; ordained assistant to his father, the Rev. David Fergusson, minister of Farnell, Oct. 16, 1793 ; admitted minister of this parish March 1795; demitted May 18, 1843 ; died minister of the Free Church in this parish, Oct. 24, 1843.

—An inscription upon the same stone shows that ELIZABETH BRUCE, wife of Mr A. F., died 4 Feb. 1827 ; also that their son ANDREW-FORBES FERGUSSON, M.D., born 2 Feb. 1811, died 24 April 1853, &c. Mr F.'s surviving son (ordained minister of Strachan in 1836, seceded at the Disruption, and has ever since been Free Church minister of that parish. A granite obelisk at Maryton marks the grave of "HELEN DRIVER, widow of A. F. Fergusson, M.D., Montrose, who died in 1868." Upon a headstone :—

JAMES PETRIE, who was for many years servant to the late Robert Scott, Esq. of Duninald, performed the duties of his station with unremitting diligence and fidelity, and gave, by his conduct to all around him of his own rank, an example worthy of imitation, and died in the year 1789, aged 85. This stone, as a mark of respect and approbation, was erected by the Family of Duninald.

---o---

DYSART.
(S. —)

IN an ecclesiastical sense the name *Disert*, or *Dysart*, signifies a hermitage, or the residence of a recluse or priest.—(Joyce's Irish Names of Places.) In this view the name may be applicable in the present case; for, although the very site of the old place of worship at Dysart is now unknown, the church of *Dyserth* is mentioned in an early charter of Malcolm the Maiden. Along with its teinds, and the lands of Little Dysart, the kirk belonged to the Priory of Rostinoth.

Down to about the last half of the 17th century, when Over and Nether Dysart were "annexed to the kirk of Mariton," the inhabitants of Dysart, although about eight miles distant, were bound to communicate at " the kirk of Brechin, quhilk," it is added, " was thair paroche kirk." This arrangement had probably arisen from the fact that the lands of Dysart were held under the superiority of, and belonged to, the Cathedral of Brechin. On the abolition of Papacy, the teinds of Over and Nether Dysart were given by the king to assist in educating poor deserving youths, who chose the church as a profession.

The Law of Maryton, which is a remarkable eminence, appears to have been vitrified. It commands one of the finest views in Strathmore.

There are some interesting historical points connected with the parish of Maryton, owing, in some measure, to its proximity to Montrose. The lands of Inyanie, or Ananias, belonged to, and went with, the office of heritable gatekeeper of the king's house or palace at the town of Montrose, while the estate of Foulertou went with the office of king's fowler. The Fullertons were in Maryton from the time of Bruce ; and it appears that there was a marriage between one of them and a daughter of Ogilvy of Lintrathen, prior to 1460, which is not recorded in the genealogy of the Earls of Airlie. (Reg. Ep. Brechin, p. 108.)

The estate of Bonnyton, which belonged at one time to the knightly family of Wood, more anciently to the Tullochs, is popularly said to have been held on the tenure of supplying fresh fish to the royal table, when the king came to Forfar : an old road or track, from Usan to Forfar, is still known as " the King's Cadgers' Road." The only remains of the Castle of Bonnyton are two slabs, which are built into the farm offices. One of them exhibits a carving of the arms of Scotland, the other that of the family of Wood. Both are dated 1666, being the year in which John Wood of Bonnyton was created a baronet. It was a near relation, if not the father of this laird, who, on 27 July 1643, was charged by the Presbytery of Brechin, on the complaint of Mr John Lammie, minister, of having " cum secretlie in ane morning, accompanied vith one or two at most, to his church, and baptized ane chyld qlk is suspected to be his owne." At an after date (Oct. 5), two of the persons present at the baptism declared that " Mr Johne" not only acknowledged paternity, but allowed " tuo peck of meill weiklie for the mentenance off the mother and the chyld," though " the meill was not given in his naime." The laird of Bonnyton, father of Mr John, died in January 1642. The Woods of Bonnyton, and their cadets of Craig and Balbegno, were of local note and importance in their day. One of the Craig branch was comptroller to King James V. and to Queen Mary.

Grahame, Dukes of Montrose, take their title from Old Montrose, which was their property and family residence; and where, it is believed, the celebrated Marquis was born. Old Montrose passed from the Grahams to the Earl of Middleton. It now belongs to the Earl of Southesk, kinsman of the Marquis of Montrose. A modern mansion occupies the site of the old house.

A neat Free Church with a spire, the manse, also a schoolhouse, occupy a commanding position near Old Montrose, which add greatly to the beauty of the locality.

Kincardine O'Neil.

(S. ERCHARD, BISHOP.)

IT is said that S. ERCHARD, who lived in the time of King Malcolm I., was born at Tolmads, and buried within this, the church of his native parish.

The kirk of *Kyncardin Oncle* was given to the Cathedral of Aberdeen by Duncan, Earl of Fife, about 1338, having been previously erected by him into a prebend of Old Machar. This church was accounted the best living in the diocese.

The architectural features of the north door of the kirk (long since built up), resemble those at Tullich (*v.* p. 107.)

In 1725, the kirk of Kincardine O'Neil is described as "a good edifice, higher and wider than any other upon Dee, thatch'd with heather .... yet it's shorter by a half, as appears by the remaining walls, than it has been within these hundred years." According to tradition, the roof was accidentally burned about 1730, after which it was slated. About 1830, four buttresses were raised upon the south and north sides to support the walls; but the church fabric being deemed unsafe some years ago, a new edifice was built on the east of the village. The roof was then taken off the kirk; but the belfry and bell were allowed to occupy their old places.

In Sept. 1869, it was agreed to divide the area of the old kirk into twelve separate places of sepulture for heritors of the parish and their successors. Along the north side, beginning at the west door, are the respective burial places of the lairds of (1) Westerton; (2) Midbeltie; (3) Learnie; (4) Kincardine Lodge; (5) Craigmyle; and (6) Desswood and Dalhaikie: upon the south side (also from west) are those of (7) East Beltie; (8) Campfield; (9) parochial ministers; (10) Stranduff; (11) Tornaveen; and (12) Findrack. Two marble slabs, in the south wall, in compartment (8), are respectively inscribed as follows:—

To the memory of JOHN STRACHAN of Campfield, who died in 1777, aged 81, and JANET STILL of Morear, his spouse. JOHN STRACHAN of Campfield, their son, who died in 1817, aged 94, and CATHERINE MIDDLETON of Sheils his spouse. HENRIETTA, daughter of J. Strachan, and Janet Still, and spouse to Mr James Davidson, merchant in Aberdeen, and SARAH, daughter of J. Strachan and C. Middleton, whose remains lie here interred. This stone is placed in affectionate remembrance by John Strachan of Campfield, 1819.

—The last named Strachan, factor to Gordon of Cluny, went to America, prior to which he sold Campfield to the next named laird, who was some time a tenant, also factor upon the estate of Craigievar:—

To the memory of WILLIAM SCOTT of Campfield, who died 2d Dec. 1822, aged 41 years. Two of his Infant Children are also interred here.

The Frasers of Findrack were buried within the kirk, in what was formerly the chancel. The chancel was removed many years ago. A flat stone of rough granite, initialed F. F., embellished, with a death's head, cross bones, mattocks, and sand glass, is thus inscribed round the margin:—

HERE . LYES . FRANCIS . FRAZER . OF . PITMURCHIE . VHO . D . . . RTED . THIS . LIFE . . . RIL . 29 . 1718 . IN . THE . 60TH . YEAR . OF . HIS . AGE.

—At the head of this stands a monument, with carvings of the Fraser arms and crest; also naval trophies, &c., with the words—"FORMIDABLE, 12TH APRIL 1782." This refers to Mr F. having been on board the "Formidable," and present at (among other engagements) Lord Rodney's victory over Comte de Grasse. The monument bears :—

Near this stone, with the remains of many of his ancestors, is interred the body of FRANCIS FRASER, Esquire of Findrack, a Commander in the British, and Post Captain in the Portuguese Navy, eldest son of Francis Fraser of Findrack, and Henrietta, daughter of William Baird of Auchmedden. He served his country with distinction for a long series of years, and was present at many memorable engagements. Born 22d August 1762, died 24th April 1824.

—Francis Fraser, of the family of Durris, bought Findrack from Sir Robert Forbes of Learnie, about 1660-70. He also possessed Pitmurchie. The father of the present laird sold the last of these estates to Mr Harry Lamond about 1812. Alex. Fraser had a charter from Queen Mary, in 1549, of the lands and barony of Midbeltie in Kincardine O'Neil; and Thomas Fraser and his wife Agnes Wishart had charters of the lands of Strandulf, from Andrew Burnet of Leys, 1561, and of those of Craigton from Forbes of Corsindae, in 1581. The lands of Tolnauds and Ennets, acquired from Lord Forbes in 1705, are still possessed by the laird of Findrack, whose brother, Wm. N. Fraser, Esq., is proprietor of Tornaveen in Kincardine O'Neil, which last, and other properties, were previously held by the Frasers. An obelisk at Tornaveen bears this inscription :—

Colonel ROBERT WINCHESTER, K.H., born A.D. 1783 : died A.D. 1846. During 37 years of active service with a spirit which shunned no danger, he accompanied in sieges and in many marches and battles the 92nd Regt. Gordon Highlanders. Lieut. General the Honourable Sir William Stewart, G.C.B., thus records his merits :—" Many memor-
" able services were rendered to the division of
" the Army under my command during the ardu-
" ous campaigns of the years 1813-14, in the Pen-
" insula and South of France by him, and the
" gallant Light Infantry under his orders. I should
" be truly ungrateful if I were ever to forget the
" valuable aid that I received from him on that
" 25th of July, when we so nearly lost the Rock
" and pass of Maya. But his and his noble corps
" conduct on that and on every occasion where

" valour and self-devotion were eminently called
" for during these campaigns, and in the decisive
" conflict of Waterloo, are on record, and ever will
" be so, in the military annals of those days,"—to whom this memorial is erected by his nephew, William N. Fraser, Esquire, 1865.

—In consequence of their descent from Henrietta Baird (there being no other descendants of the ancient family of Auchmedden alive), the Frasers of Findrack are the representatives of the line of the Bairds, also the male representatives of the Frasers of Durris. The Durris family, one of whom had a charter of Beltie from Jas. III. in 1469, were long patrons of the church of Kincardine O'Neil. (*v.* pp. 56, 84, 189.)

Upon a marble slab, in outer, and south wall of kirk :—

D. JOANNES FORBESIUS, presbyter, ex nobili Dominorum de Pitsligo oriundus familiâ, doctrinæ, facundiæ, prudentiæ, integritatis, amicitiæ, pietatis ac pacis laudibus illustris, quum curam pastoralem alibi et hic per 28 annos maximo cum ecclesiæ et gregis sibi commissi emolumento sustinuisset, atq Deum in terris fœlici studio prædicasset, ad superos migravit A. Æ. C. 1708, ætatis 65. Vir quo meliorem nulla nôrunt tempora.

[Mr JOHN FORBES, presbyter, descended from the noble family of the Lords of Pitsligo, distinguished for his learning, eloquence, prudence, integrity, sincere in friendship, piety, and peaceableness, having held the office of pastor here and elsewhere, for 28 years with the greatest advantage to the church and to the flock entrusted to his care, and preached God on earth with zeal, he departed to the realms above in the year 1708, in the 65th year of his age. A better man than whom no age has known.]

—According to Lumsden, "the parson of Kincardine" (who was a son of Robert Forbes of Newton), "married Agnes Dugat, daughter to the Laird of Auchinhuife, who did bear to him fyve daughters"—the eldest married Wm. Forbes of Camphill, in Lumphanan, the second her brother in-law, John Forbes, professor of divinity in Aberdeen. The oldest visible slab in the kirkyard is dated 1627. A table-shaped stone (enclosed) bears :—

Sacred to the memory of JOHN GRANT, Esq. of Kincardine O'Neil. Ob. 9 May 1799, ætat. O.S. 63. —Mr Grant (a native of Moray), made money in India, bought the property of Kincardine O'Neil, built the mansion house, and planted the wood, &c. He was grandfather of Mr Grant-Duff, of Eden, M.P. (v. KING-EDWARD.)

JEAN FRASER, sp. to Robt. Mackay, Midbeltie, d. 17—, a. 63 :—

She was married to a former husband, was a dutiful wife, and loving mother. She had an open hand to the poor, always pitied the cries of the fatherless and widows; and her own children were clothed with her industry, although now scattered abroad in the world, &c.

A table-shaped stone, within enclosure, bears an inscription to this effect :—

The Rev. WILLIAM MORRICE, 37 years minister here, died 22 January 1809, in the 82d year of his age, and 48th of his ministry. HELEN PATERSON, his spouse, died in April 1817, aged 73. MARGARET MORRICE, spouse of the Rev. William Shand, died 10 Oct. 1793, aged 28. ALEXANDER MORRICE died 14 Nov. 1795, aged 15 years. ISABEL, daughter of the said Rev. Wm. Morrice, and spouse of Wm. Roger, died at Aberdeen, 17 Nov. 1862, in her 80th year, &c.

Upon an adjoining marble slab :—

The Rev. JOHN ROGER, died 8 July 1843, in the 81st year of his age, and 50th of his ministry here. JANE MORRICE, his wife, died Dec. 20, 1846, aged 75.

A granite headstone shews that—

The Rev. MATTHEW BROWN, appointed minister of Kincardine O'Neil, 19th Oct. 1843, died 18 Nov. 1853, aged 57.

No trace remains of the hospital which Alan the Durward founded here, and endowed with considerable property, about 1233. Tradition says that the hospital stood in a field called Bladernach, between the village of Kincardine O'Neil and the present ferryboat station on the Dee. Alan's father erected a stone bridge near the latter place, in connection with the great thoroughfare from the south to the north, by Cairn-o'-Mounth. It is believed that there were contemporary stone-bridges over the Dee, near the mouth of Glenmuick, also at Durris, and at Aberdeen, in connection respectively with the passes of Glencsk, Gleubervie, and the Causay Mounth.

Although prettily situated, and once much frequented, Kincardine O'Neil is now a sort of "deserted village," owing chiefly to its distance from the Deeside line of railway. The population is mostly in the locality of Torphins, where there is a railway station and a number of houses. One of the three parochial schools is there, also a Free Church. The Parish and Episcopal Churches are at Kincardine O'Neil, also one of the three parish schools, the third being at Tornaveen. There is also a Female School at the village, a tablet upon the front of which bears :—

In grateful acknowledgement of connexion with this parish, and as a tribute to the memory of the Revd. WILLIAM MORRICE, sometime minister, this building has been erected for a Female School, in pursuance of the will of GEORGE MORRICE, his youngest, and last surviving son. The land was granted by Francis Gordon, Esq. of Kincardine Lodge.

—The above named GEORGE MORRICE died in 1850. He and his brother John accumulated wealth as timber merchants in London, where they were long contractors for the supply of oak to the Government Dockyards. Their paternal grandfather tenanted Waulkmill of Drum.

Among the prettiest natural objects in the district were the Falls, or Slug of Dess, lately spoiled to make the cascade available for utilitarian purposes. The House of Desswood, adjoining, is one of the best situated residences on Deeside. The place, now a sort of paradise, was almost a wilderness when bought by the grandfather of the present laird (v. pp. 21, 121.)

ALEX. ROSS, author of Helenore, or the Fortunate Shepherdess, and other poems, was born at Torphins in 1699 (v. LOCHLEE.)

Lunan.

(S. ——)

THE kirk of *Innerluthnene* belonged to the diocese of St Andrews, and was gifted by King William to the Abbey of Arbroath. It was dedicated by Bishop David in 1242, and is rated at 15 merks in the Old Taxation.

The present church, built in 1844, is situated within the burial-ground, and upon the left bank of the Lunan, near Lunan Bay. A slab, built into the front wall of the kirk, and initialed D. M : E. M., probably refers to David Mudie of Arbikie and his wife.

An elegant marble monument, similar in design to that at Maryton, is within the kirk, and bears this inscription :—

P. M. Reverendi viri, ALEXANDRI PEDEY, qui per XLIV. annos in ecclesia de Lunan, summa cum laude, munere pastorali functus, ob egregiam pietatem, animi modestiam, sine fuco amicitiam, sine fastu munificentiam, mirum denique candorem & urbanitatem Deo carus, cœlo maturus, bonis omnibus desideratus, septuagenarius decessit, XVII. Februarii, MDCCXIII. Amoris debiti hoc monumentum marmoreum posuit mœstissima conjux, Marjora Lindsay.

[Erected to the memory of the Rev. ALEXANDER PEDEY, for 44 years the highly esteemed minister of the church of Lunan, who died 17th Feb. 1713, in the 70th year of his age, beloved of God, ripe for heaven, and regretted by all good men on account of his eminent piety, his humble-mindedness, the sincerity of his friendships, his unostentatious liberality, and finally, his rare candour and urbanity. This marble monument of deserved affection was erected by his disconsolate widow, Marjory Lindsay.]

—Mr Pedey gave two silver Communion cups and a bread-plate to the parish, and stipulated that any Episcopal congregation, within seven miles of Lunan, was entitled, upon application, to have the use of the same. The cups and plate (the latter of which bears a date subsequent to the death of Mr Pedey), are respectively inscribed as follows :—

"*Gifted to the Church of Lunan by Mr Alexander Pedey, minister there, these two cups.* 1709."

"*Gifted to the Church of Lounan by Mr Alexander Pedey, minister there.* 1714."

—Mr Pedey was twice married, and his second wife, who survived him, left an annuity to uphold his monument.

The following inscription at Lunan, to the memory of Walter Mill, contains an error as to the length of his incumbency there. Besides the proof afforded by the Register of Arbroath (ii. 445), Mill's reply to his accuser at St Andrews —" I served the cure of Lunan, *twentie yeires* "— must be considered conclusive as to the true period of his services at Lunan (Pitscottie's Hist., 519 :—

Sacred to the memory of WALTER MILL, for upwards of forty years pastor of this church, and the last Scottish Martyr for adherence to the Protestant Faith. He entered on his ministrations in the days when Popish error prevailed in Scotland ; but by Divine grace was brought to the knowledge of the truth ; and, having faithfully preached the Gospel for many years, in the midst of persecution, suffered martyrdom, at St Andrews, on the 28th day of April, A.D. 1538, in the 83d year of his age. This memorial was erected A.D. 1848, during the ministry of the Revd. Robert Barclay, by the Heritors and Parishioners of Lunan, in grateful acknowledgment of the blessings resulting from the Reformation. "The righteous shall be in everlasting remembrance."

—The monument with the above inscription took the place of one (said to have been of timber), which was erected by the Rev. Mr Gowans. The inscription (from Bowick's Life of John Erskine of Dun), is given in Supplement (q.v.)

From a monument, also within the kirk :—

In memory of WILLIAM TAYLOR-IMRIE, Esqr. of Lunan, who died 11th March 1849, in the 70th year of his age.

—Mr Taylor-Imrie was a grand-nephew of Mr William Imrie, laird of Lunan, who died in 1790, and left the property to his niece's husband, Alex. Taylor at Cushnie, in liferent, and to their second son (the above-named William) in feu. Mr Imrie bought Lunan in 1759, from Mr David Wise, a merchant in Dundee. In 1767 he acquired the superiority of the lands from the Earl of Panmure, to whom the feu-duty belonged as owner of the Abbacy lands of Arbroath, which he bought along with other portions of the forfeited estates of his uncle.

Mr Taylor-Imrie, who died unmarried, left Lunan to his nephew, eldest son of his sister Elizabeth, who married Captain James Blair of the old Forfar Militia. He was formerly a midshipman in the Royal Navy, but held a commission in the 70th Foot, and died at Tynemouth, when in England with his regiment. His son, Brigadier James Blair, was so much esteemed by his brother officers, that shortly after his death they erected an obelisk to his memory at Lunan. It stands upon rising ground to the north of Lunan House, and bears this inscription :—

To the memory of Lieutenant-Colonel JAMES BLAIR, of the Bengal Army. Born on the 7th November 1792, he died at sea on board the ship *Madagascar*, during a voyage to the Cape of Good Hope, undertaken for the recovery of his health, on the 12th of August 1847. High in the estimation of the Supreme Government of India, he had, for the last twelve years of his life, Commanded the Cavalry Division of His Highness the Nizam's Army, and this Monument was erected by his Brother Officers, European and Native, to commemorate their admiration of his character as an Officer, and their affectionate recollection of him as a Friend.

—Lieut.-Col. Blair, who predeceased his uncle, married Charlotte, a daughter of Gen. Vanrenan, and their son, now Major of the F. and K. Militia Artillery, succeeded to Lunan on the death of his grand-uncle in 1849. Major Blair-Imrie has done much to improve and beautify Lunan, which is one of the most desirable residences in Angus.

The Gaelic words, *Lun-an*, which have some such meaning as the "water meadows," are quite descriptive of the locality of the kirk.

The oldest stone in the burial-ground at Lunan is possibly that which bears the name of ANDREW JAMIESON, the date of 1697, and some commonplace verses. The inscriptions given below are from monuments in the same place :—

JOHN TORN, "mason St Virgins," d. 1749, a. 37 :—

This man was working at Red Castl and taking down a wall, was brussed by the fall of it, that he liuet but ane hour thereafter, and died :

As we each night lay down our head,
Each morning open our eyes ;

. . . . .

ROBERT SOUTTER'S wife d. (c. 1815) :—

"To know Death, and not to fear it, is the summit of human happiness."

In memory of ROBERT HUDDLESTON, schoolmaster, Lunan, who died 27th Feb. 1821, aged 53 years. Also of WILLIAM, his son, who died in infancy.

—Besides editing editions of Hollinshed's Scots Chronicle, Toland's History of the Druids, &c., Mr H. also contributed papers on Scotch antiquities to contemporary periodicals (Land of the Lindsays, p. 86.)

Near this spot are interred the remains of the Revd. JOHN GOWANS, the faithful minister of this parish for nearly 31 years, who died 14th Novr. 1820, greatly lamented, in the 70th year of his age. This stone is erected to his memory by his afflicted widow, ISABELLA WEBSTER, who also departed this life 2nd March 1823, in the 77th year of her age, and is here laid by the side of her husband.

—Mr Gowans, who began life as schoolmaster of St Vigeans, was sometime minister of Glenisla. He was the penultimate successor in Lunan of Mr HENRY OGILVY, who died there, 23d May 1781, in the 85th year of his age. Mr Ogilvy married Peggy, daughter of Mr Wise of Lunan, and his daughter, Isobell, was mother of Professor Hercules Scott of Aberdeen. The Wises of Lunan are now represented by Dr T. A. Wise, author of a Review of History of Medicine among Asiatics, a Commentary on the Hindoo System of Medicine, and of several papers on Scotch antiquities, &c.

Although there is no monument to Mr Ogilvie at Lunan, the name of few old ministers is better known. This is owing chiefly to the many stories and quaint anecdotes which are preserved regarding him. The more remarkable of these have been often printed.

The next inscription relates to one of Mr Ogilvy's successors at Lunan, whose ancestors, long farmers at the Upper North Water Bridge, are said to have sprung from the Barclays of Mathers:—

Sacred to the memery of the Reverend ROBERT BARCLAY, minister of the parish of Lunan, who died on the 11th day of July 1849, in the 62d year of his age, and 29th of his ministry.

A baptismal font and sand glass, which are respectively fixed to the pulpit and precentor's desk at Lunan, also a hand-bell, present each the following inscription:—

Given to the Church of Lunan by Alexander Gavin, merchant there, and Elizabeth Jamieson, his spouse, 1733.

—The donor of these articles had a shop first at Peatloch and next at Denhead of Lunan. He was also sexton and kirk officer, both of which offices were hereditary in the Gavius from at least 1679 (*Session Records*.)

Alexander Gavin had a large family by his wife Elizabeth Jamieson. The second son, David, born at Peatloch in 1720, is said to have joined an aunt in Holland, who married a Dutch seaman, whose life she had saved from shipwreck in Lunan Bay.

Having acquired a fortune as a merchant at Middleburgh, Mr Gavin bought the property of Easter Braikie, in Forfarshire, in 1752, and that of Langton, in Berwickshire, in 1757. He married, in 1770, Lady Elizabeth Maitland, daughter of the Earl of Lauderdale, and had four daughters, two of whom died unmarried.

The second daughter, who became the wife of Mr Baird of Newbyth, succeeded to Easter Braikie, and the eldest, who inherited Langton, married the Earl, afterwards the Marquis, of Breadalbane. The last-named was the mother of the second Marquis of Breadalbane, of Lady Pringle of Stitchel, and of the Duchess of Buckingham.

It will thus be seen that, through the marriage of his great-grand-daughter with the Duke of Buckingham, who is a lineal descendant of King Henry II., that the blood of the humble kirk beadle of Lunan may, like that of poor Paterson, the celebrated prototype of "Old Mortality," be said to flow in the veins of Royalty.

———

The barony of Lunan appears to have been in the hands of the Crown about the year 1377, when it was given by Robert II. to Richard of Montealt, who soon afterwards resigned it in favour of Alexander Stuart, the king's son (Mem. Angus & Mearns). It is supposed that it was vassals of those ancient lords that first assumed *Lunan* as a surname.

The property of Lunan appears to have belonged to a female branch of the Stuarts in 1476, for on the 3d Sept. of that year Egidia Stewart, who is designed "of Lounane," granted a confirmation charter "to her sone Walter Tyrie of the lands of Lunane in Forfar, and lands of Forteviot in Perth, and of her lands of Pitfour in Aberdeen," all of which were held in warde (MS. Notes of Scotch Charters at Panmure.)

This grant clearly refers to some portion, if not to the entire barony of Lunan. Taken as a whole, Lunan was a lordship of considerable extent and value, for besides Easter Lunan, with its mill, it comprehended, among other lands, those of Arbikie, Courthill, Cothill, Drumbertnot, Falsecastle, Hawkhill, Hillhead, and Newton.

It is interesting to notice that, long after the old race of Tyries ceased to hold Lunan (for a considerable part of the barony was held by Ogilvy of Inverquharity before 1589), the lands again became, in part at least, before 1610, the property of their namesakes, if not descendants, of Drumkilbo (Retours.)

A portion of Lunan was acquired by Sir John Carnegie, afterwards Earl of Northesk, in 1643 (Douglas' Peer.) In course of time the whole barony, the lands of Arbikie excepted, appears to have come to that family, and to have been held by them until 1723, when the fourth Earl was forced to dispone the "Lands and Barony's of Lunnan, Redcastle, Ethie, and Northtarrie, with the pertinents," to Messrs John Forbes of Newhall, John Ogilvie of Balbegno, and Alex. Bayne of Riress, advocates, as trustees for behoof of creditors, "excepting the South and North Mains of Ethie, with the house, yeards, parks, and office-houses thereof."

These estates were all exposed to sale within the house of John Steill, vintner, in Edinburgh, on 13th Feb., 1728, at twenty years' purchase, when "the lands and barony of Lunan" were bought by Wm. Lyon, advocate, for John Carnegy of Boysack. John Fullerton of that Ilk became security for the money, which appears to have been furnished by Lord Dun, who was previously a creditor on the estate. The whole transaction was probably accomplished by Boysack and Fullerton for the purpose of keeping Lunan in the Northesk family, to whom it still belongs.

It appears from the conditions of sale that Lunan was held blench of the Crown—one half "for payment of ane penny money, and the other half likewise blench for payment of ane penny silver money at the term of Whitsunday, if asked, allenarly." The lands and barony of Redcastle (*infra*, p. 326) were also held of the Crown, but those of Ethie and Northtarrie were held of the lordship of Arbroath, and formed a portion of the forfeited estates of the Earl of Panmure.

The lands of Easter Lunan, or Inverlunan, now Lunan—that portion which belongs to Major Blair-Imrie—appear to have been the part which was given by King William the Lion, along with the kirk and its teinds, to the monastery of Arbroath. It was this portion which Abbot Walter leased, 14th Dec., 1428, to William of Guthrie, and in which he was long followed by namesakes, probably kinsmen (Nig. de Aberb.).

It appears from notes of writs, kindly communicated by Major Blair-Imrie, that, in 1544, Lord Innermeath of Redcastle had a feu-charter of Lunan from Cardinal Beaton as Commendator of Arbroath, and that his successor had a confirmation charter of the same lands from Esme, Duke of Lennox, also as Commendator of Arbroath, in 1582.

But it is evident that Guthries re-acquired Lunan; for, on 4th Nov. 1653, John Guthrie of Over Dysart was served heir to his uncle John "in the toune and lands of Inverlounan," &c. (Retours, 326.) The writs of Lunan shew that, in 1667, the last-named John Guthrie sold the estate to Francis (afterwards Sir Francis) Ogilvy, son of the laird of New Grange, and that, on a judicial sale of the property of Sir Francis, 30th July 1702, Lunan was bought by his son-in-law, George Ogilvy, who held an heritable bond over it. George Ogilvy was the 4th son of the baronet of Inverquharity, and left a son, John Ogilvy of Balbegno (above-mentioned), who, on 30th Oct. 1723, sold Lunan to Alexander Wyse (*infra*, pp. 361, 366.) Mr Wyse is described in the title-deeds as the only son of David Wyse, "tennant in Mains of Lauriestoun;" and Ogilvy sold Lunan to him on this condition, viz., "Reserving only freedom to me to erect a monument upon my father's grave in the said church [of Lunan] if at any time hereafter I shall think proper so to do." If a monument was ever erected to George Ogilvy, no trace of it now remains.

~~~~~~~~~~~~~~~~~~~~

Macduff.

(S. ——)

IT was this portion of the parish of Gamrie that bore the name of *Doune*, and of which, as a thanedom, John of Bothuille had charters in 1365 (*supra*, p. 89.)

The name of *Doune* may have been given to the district either from the green or grassy nature of the hill which bounds the town of Macduff on the south-west, or from the word *Dun*, "a fort;" for there are still traces of old earth-works, as well as of a castle, upon the hill.

In 1413 the lands and barony of Doune were given by Sir Alexander Keith to Patrick, son and heir of Alexander Ogilvy, sheriff of Angus. At a later period (1467), Sir James Stewart, afterwards Earl of Buchan (who assumed the surname of Douglas), and his wife Margaret, daughter of Ogilvy of Deskford, had charters of the lands and baronies of Strathalva and Doune, also of Banff Castle, and fishings upon the Deveron, &c. (Coll. Abd. & Banff.)

When Maria, Countess of Buchan, was served heiress to her grand-mother, in 1615, in certain lands in Banffshire, among these are enumerated the barony of " Glendawachye *alias* Doune." (Retours.) It was through the marriage of this lady with James Erskine, son of the 7th Earl of Mar, that the title of Earl of Buchan came to the Cardross branch of the Erskines.

George, Lord Banff, held part of the lands of Doune in 1664. It was possibly through the interest of the Ogilvys that the village was erected into a burgh of barony, for, when Lord Strathmore succeeded his father, " burgo baronice de Doune" is specially mentioned in his retour of service, 29th October 1695.

The district became Fife property in 17—. Doune was then a poor fishing hamlet; but, being situated upon a finely sheltered shore, the second Earl of Fife saw the advantages that would flow from erecting a harbour there, and by giving facilities for house-building, &c. His Lordship spared neither trouble nor expense to attain his object; and it was he who changed the name of the place to MACDUFF. Long before he died, he had the satisfaction of seeing it occupied by over 1000 inhabitants, and the harbour become a place of considerable trade. It is now one of the most thriving sea-ports on the east coast of Scotland.

It was also through the second Lord Fife's influence that Macduff was created a Royal burgh. In commemoration of that event, he had a cross erected upon a rising ground, which bears his family arms, also this inscription :—

MACDUFF'S CROSS.

Rebuilt at Macduff by the Earl of Fife 1783, when the place was constituted a Royal Burgh by George IIId. May it flourish, increase in number and in opulence, while its Inhabitants gain the blessings of life by Industry, Diligence, and Temperance.

—The ancient " Cross Macduff," or rather its base, is still to be seen among the Ochil Hills, near Newburgh-on-Tay. A valuable and interesting account of Cross Macduff is given in the Sculpd. Stones of Scotd., vol. ii., pp. lxvi-lxxiii.

Although by the Reform Act the burgh of Macduff is united with that of Banff, it has an independent municipal government, and contains about 4000 inhabitants.

When the Earl of Fife built the harbour, he also erected a Chapel of Ease at Macduff; and, in 1866, the town, and some adjoining parts of the parish of Gamrie, were made into a *quoad sacra* parish.

The church, which was almost entirely rebuilt a few years ago, occupies a prominent position upon the hill behind the town, and a little to the eastward stands a commodious Free Church.

The burial ground adjoins the parish church. The tombstones are numerous, and as many of them are painted black—a not uncommon fashion in the district—they have a strange appearance, particularly when seen from a distance.

The following inscription (from a table-shaped stone), relates to the first person who was buried in the cemetery at Macduff :—

[1.]

Here lie interred the remains of MARGARET TURNBUL, who departed this life on the 27th day of October 1808, in the 85th year of her age. She was a servant in the Family of Fife for 65 years; and, as a testimony of her faithful services during that long period, this stone is erected by James, the present Earl of Fife.

The rest of the inscriptions (the third of which is abridged), are copied from monuments in various parts of the burial-ground :—

[2.]

ALEXANDER CARNY, late rope-manufacturer in Macduff, died 27th March 1829, aged 73, who, by the upright discharge of his public duties as Provost of Macduff, and Justice of the Peace, as well as by his private conduct, deserved and possessed the esteem of numerous friends and acquaintances.— Erected by his widow Catherine Lyal, and his nephew Alexander Carny.

[3.]

Erected by public subscription to the memory of ALEXANDER CARNY, who was for many years Provost of Macduff and a magistrate of the county of Banff. Born 7th May 1785; died 24th Nov. 1856. He was a just judge, a kind husband, a dutiful parent, and an honest man.

—Mr Carny's wife (who was a daughter of Mr Alex. Tocher, mentioned in the next inscription), died in 1870, aged 70. Mrs Simpson of Cobairdy and Mrs Grant of Beldornie are two of Mr Carny's surviving daughters (*supra*, p. 228.)

[4.]

Erected by the Family in memory of their mother JANE TOCHER, wife of James Smith, sometime schoolmaster in Macduff, who died 28th February 1838, aged —5 years. [2 drs. died young. Also a son ALEXANDER, who died at Toronto, Canada, 18th Sep. 1855, aged 32.] Also ALEXANDER TOCHER, who was 67 years schoolmaster in Macduff, and died 10th February 1844, aged 89 years. And of his wife, ANN HASLOPP, who died 3d January 1850, aged 83 years. [The above] JAMES SMITH, late tutor, Knox College, Toronto, Canada, and died there 3d January 1867, aged 66 years.

[5.]

As a tribute of respect to the memory of JAMES WILSON, Esq., late of the Island of Jamaica, who died at Macduff, on the 5th day of October 1829, aged 84 years. This tablet is erected by his nephew, the Rev. Thomas Wilson, minister of Gamrie.

[6.]

Sacred to the memory of MARGARET WILSON, spouse to William Wilson, shipowner, Macduff, who died the 19th of January 1837, aged 87 years. The said WILLIAM WILSON died the 7th of June 1838, in the 90th year of his age, during which period, his upright character gained him the respect of his relatives, and a numerous circle of friends and acquaintances.

[7.]

Erected by George R. Huie, Trilawney, Jamaica, and Ann S. Huie in Macduff, in memory of their affectionate mother, MARGARET RIDDOCH, relict of John Huie, merchant, Jamaica, who died 12th July 1831, in the 91st year of her age. The abovenamed ANN S. HUIE, died 9th March 1863, in the 86th year of her age.

[8.]

MARGARET WILSON, d. 182-, a. 22:—

Youth fades—life is a vapour—
The sun is but a spark of fire—
A transient meteor in the sky;
The Soul, immortal as its Sire,
Shall never die.

Carmyllie.

(THE BLESSED VIRGIN.)

THE district of *Kermyle*, or Carmyllie, was not erected into a separate parish until 1609, although David Strachan, the principal heritor, had founded a chapel there, by deed dated 5th March 1500, which was ratified 20th January 1512-13 (*infra*, p. 341.)

The older portion of the church of Carmyllie is probably the same as was built by Strachan. Before the recent additions and alterations were made, some interesting examples of masons'-marks were to be seen upon the old part of the building. The ashler work was a fine specimen of masonry, resembling, in some points, the style of the more ornate church of Fowlis-Easter.

The initials, M. J. S., and the date of 1757, which were upon a lintel on the south side of the kirk, had reference to alterations which were made upon it during the time of the Rev. JAMES SMALL, who was minister from 1720 to 1771. His son, Dr Robert Small, who became one of the ministers of Dundee, wrote a brief, but excellent account of that town, also a work on Kepler's Astronomical Discoveries.

There was neither a "school nor school-house at Carmyllie" in 1729; and the kirk, kirk-yard dykes, and bell, were all in a ruinous state. According to tradition, the bell was rent at the rejoicings which were held in 1715, when the Chevalier de St George came to Panmure House. The bell now in use is thus inscribed:—

MADE AT EDINR. 1748,
FOR THE KIRK SESSION OF CARMYLLIE.
WILLIAM ORMINSTON.

The following initials and date are upon the Guynd pew, in the kirk of Carmyllie:—

I. O : 1657 : K. M.

—These refer to John Ochterlony of Guynd and his wife Katherine Maule – probably the parents of John Ochterlony who was served heir to his father in Guynd, &c., April 12, 1676, and who wrote a valuable Account of the Shire of Forfar, c. 1682, printed in the Spottiswoode Miscellany.

The surname of Ochterlony is said to have been assumed from the lands of Lownie, near Forfar, which were exchanged, 1226-39, for those of Kenny, in Kingoldrum. Ochterlonys possessed Kelly, in Arbirlot, before 1442, and about 1614, Sir William Ochterlony sold Kelly to Sir Alex. Irvine of Drum. It was about the latter date that the Ochterlonys acquired Guynd, which was previously the property of the Strachans of Carmyllie. "Gwythen" (? *Geith-an*, an exposed marshy place), is an old spelling of "Guynd."

The following lines, from *The Temple* in the Den of Guynd, have reference to the last direct male descendant of the Ochterlonys of that Ilk. He built the present mansion house, and planted most of the trees at Guynd ; but notwithstanding what is stated in the first couplet, he was buried in the old kirk-yard of Montrose :—

Lines written by the late John Ouchterlony, Esquire, who died at The Guynd, 20th Novembr, 1843:—

In this lone spot, by mortal seldom trod,
The dust is laid, the spirit fled to God,
Of him who reared these woods, these cultured plains
With verdure cloth'd, or stored with golden grains ;
O'er these paternal scenes, by time defaced
Bade yonder mansion rise in simple taste ;
And deeming naught his own which heav'n bestow'd,
Diffused its blessings as a debt he ow'd.
O empty record ! what avails thee now ?
Thy anxious days, thy labour-warm'd brow ;
See where man's little works himself survive,
How short his life, who bade these forests live.
While they shall rear their ample bows on high
Through distant ages, and while o'er them sigh
Eve's murmuring breezes, to the thoughtful say—
Like his, so pass thy fleeting span away.

Erected in 1853.

—Mr Ochterlony was succeeded by his nephew, Mr J. A. Pierson, who greatly improved the property. He died 9th Aug. 1873, aged 73, and was buried at Chapel-yard in Rescobie (*q.v.*) Mr Pierson married a daughter of the laird of Glenmoriston, but leaves no issue.

From a marble tablet within the church :—

In memory of the Revd. PATRICK BRYCE, 45 years minister of this parish, a sincere Christian, a faithful pastor, devout, charitable, and upright. He recommended that religion which he taught, by a peculiar mildness and simplicity of manner. Conscientious in the discharge of every relative duty, beloved, honoured, and universally respected, he died in the humble hope of a far nobler inheritance beyond the grave 21st June 1816, in his 84th year. Also MARY AITKEN, his wife, who closed a well-spent life in the same hopes of a blessed immortality, 19th Sep. 1801, aged 72. A tribute of filial love and respect from their only child and affectionate daughter.

—Mr Bryce's only child married the Rev. Mr Webster of Inverarity, the son of a merchant and magistrate of Forfar. Six of her sons were bred lawyers, and one a physician. The last-mentioned wrote Statistics of Grave-yards in Scotland ; one of his brothers, who died of fever at Cairo, in 1826, wrote Travels in Egypt, and another is sheriff-clerk of Forfarshire.

Heritors and ministers were buried within the church down to a pretty late period. Among the latter was Mr Scott, who appears to have had but little sympathy for the wives and families of the exiled nobles. "The Presbyterian ministers (writes the Countess of Panmure in 1716), are bad neighbours, particularly Scott of Carmyllie, who gives all the information he can against me, and he is but too well heard." Scott died in 1720, and was succeeded by Mr Small, traditionary notices of whose kindness of heart and hand still survive in the parish.

The kirk-yard was lately extended upon the north side, and the inscriptions given below are from tombstones in the older portions of it :—

☞ Heir lyes JAMES RIND, yovnger, vho departed this lyfe the 10 of Ianr. 1664, of age 31.

✠ Heir lyes ane honest man JAMES RIND, hvshand to Helen Philp, vho departed this lyfe 8 of Ianvari 1660, of age 80.

A stone, embellished with the carvings of a pair of scissors and a tailor's goose, and initialed I. C : I. P., bears :—

. . . . sober man caled IOHN CHRISTIE who departit the 2 day of Ivle . . . . . spovs . . . EL PETER, who departit ye 24 day of — — 1624, of age 30.

On 28th Feb. 1661, David Caird in Monchur, in Carmyllie, appealed against a decision of the Presbytery of Arbroath, which he looked upon, as quaintly stated in his protest, " as contrair to the law of God and man, and practice of this kingdome [because] they intendit to excommunicate him out of the Societie of God's people over into the hands of the Devill." Kathrine Mill (mentioned below), was possibly the wife of this " worthy ":—

. . . . . KATHRINE MILL spous to David Kaierd who dicessed . . . March anno 1668, hir age being 50 yeirs :

Earth, take thy earth :
My frinds I take my leave,
My sovle to God,
My body to the grave.

Hier rests the corpes of DAVID KAIERD, who decissed the 5 of December, and of age 50 yeirs, anno 1632. Here lyes ELLEON KEARD, spovs to David Ramsay, who lived sometime in Peterly, who died the 22 of May 172-, and of her age 33 years.

—David Ramsay, Pitairly, is described (1729) as "an old man and poor, and can pay but a very little part, if any [of his arrears of rent] ; however," it is added, " his children are coming up." (York Buildings' Co's Mem. Book, MS.)

JANET CHRISTIE . . . . John Gibson, in Greystone, d. 1720, a. 41 :—

The memory of the just is blest, but the name of the wicked shall rot.
He who was sober, just, and good,
And fam'd for peity,
No panigerick now doth need,
His prais to amplefy.

His memorie on earth is blest,
His soull with glorie crown'd ;
His bodie here shal rest in peace
Till the last trumpet sound.

—John Gibson, in Greystone of Carnegie, who also farmed part of the Kirkton of Panbride, is said to be (1729) " a very honest man . . . only 'tis thought he tiples, and thereby negligent of his own affairs." James Christie, a pendicler on Greystone, at the same date, had the character of being " a very good countrey like man."

WM. ALLAN, and JEAN TURNBULL, in Bents of Guynd (now New Mains), on 3 children, 1769 :—

Now cruel death hath us all three
Right soon his captives made ;
And by his mightie arm you see,
Down in the grave hath's laid.

JAS. BALBIRNIE and wife, Mossholes, on chdn., 1769 :
When death's darts did approach so near,
We parted with our children dear ;
And for them we had this respect—
This monument we did erect.

—In 1729, David Balbirnie, in Mossholes, was so " very poor" as to be unable to pay much of his arrears of rent, " the reason whereof is not the man's own fault, but owing to his wife and children's tenderness."

ISOBEL LIECH, wf. of Wm. Scott, Drumnygar, d. 1767, a. 64 :—

Lean not on earth, 'twill pierce thee to the heart,
A broken reed at best ; oft a spear
On its sharp point ; peace bleeds, and hope expires.

DAVID KYDD, farmer, Newton, d. 1782, a. 63 ; his wife, BARBARA MORGAN, d. 1804, a. 88 :—

Let marble monuments record
Their fame, who distant lands explore,
This humble stone points out the place
Where sleeps a virtuous, ancient race.
Their sire possess'd ye neighbouring plain,
Before Columbus cross'd the main ;
And tho' ye world may deem it strange,
His son, contented, seeks no change,
Convinc'd, wherever man may roam,
He travels only to the Tomb.

JOHN WALLS, Greystone, d. 1826, a. 61 :—
Here, gentle reader, o'er this dust
We crave a tear, for here doth rest
A Father, Husband, and a Friend,
In him those three did finely blend.
Worn by disease, and rack'd with pain,
Physicians' aid was all in vain,
Till God, in his great love, saw meet
To free him from his sorrows great.
How wonderful, how vast his love,
Who left the shining realms above ;
How much for lost mankind he bore,
Their peace and safety to restore.

Sepulchral traces, of a very old type, have been found near Moncur and Monquhirr ; also at the Fairy Knowe, where a rude boulder of about two tons weight bore the representation of a human foot upon the lower side. The origin of these marks are popularly attributed to the fairies. (*v.* Jour. Kilkenny Archæolg. So., new series, vol. v., p. 451.)

The lands of Carnegie, which John of Balindard acquired from Sir Walter Maule of Panmure, about 1350, in exchange for those of Balindard, or Bonhard, in Arbirlot, lie to the west of the kirk of Carmyllie (*v.* p. 93.) On acquiring the lands of Carnegie, Balindard, as was the custom of the period, assumed his surname from his new possession, and from him sprung the Carnegies, Earls of Southesk and Northesk, &c. Carnegie was a barony, which comprised the possessions of Carnegie, Mossholes, Drum, and Greystone, also the adjoining slate quarries. In 1729, "the biggings" on Carnegie proper, which appear to have been in a sadly dilapidated state, as were the buildings upon most of the properties in Scotland at the same period, were valued at £134 3s 4d. The lands of Carnegie now belong to the Earl of Dalhousie.

The Kirk-session records of Carmyllie show that in 1707 the poor "had a considerable loss by the Doits and Lettered Turnors" which were gathered at church collections ; also that, in 1709, the Earl of Panmure gifted to the poor "the custome of the mercatt of Carmyllie," held on 25th April, and that £2 18s 2d Scots were collected on that day. *Doits* and *Turners* were copper coins : the value of the first was a penny Scots, the latter two pennies, or one bodle.

On 28 April 1743, "John Corser in Backboth, and Margt. Weir in Muirheads [were] summoned to compear before the Session for consulting such as pretend to foretell future events."

It is worthy of note that JAMES STRACHAN, Bishop of Toronto, who was a native of Aberdeen, taught a side school at Cononsyth, in this parish, about 1793-4. Also that the Rev. PATRICK BELL, LL.D., the inventor of the reaping machine, became minister of Carmyllie at the Disruption, and died there 22 April 1869, aged 69. His father was a farmer in the parish of Auchterhouse.

A freestone slab (built into the manse offices at Carmyllie) presents a much defaced carving of the Ochterlony arms, with the date of 1670, and the initials M. A. O : H. M. Those refer to Mr Alexander Ochterlony, "lawfull sone to umq^{ll} John Ouchterlony, late provest" of Brechin (who succeeded Mr Patrick Strachan in 1666), and to his wife Helen Mudie, of the Bryanton family. The stone also bears this injunction :—

QUÆRAMUS SUPERNA.
[Let us seek the things above.]

A slab, over the front of the manse, having reference to the time of the Rev. WM. ROBERTSON, who died 27 Nov. 1836, aged 50, is inscribed :—

W. R., 1820.
DOMUM EXPECTAMUS CUJUS CONDITOR EST DEUS.
[We expect a house, whose builder is God.]

Upon a door lintel at the manse garden : —

Μελέτη τὸ Πᾶν.
[Practice is everything.]

The CHAPEL SHADE at Backboath is said to be the site of an old place of worship ; and the remains of a stone circle, called THE TEMPLESTANES, were visible down to a late date.

A Free Church and manse were erected at Carmyllie in 1850, and a school and schoolhouse in 1860.

Fettercairn.

(S. MARK, EVANGELIST.)

THE kirk of *Fethyrkern*, a rectory in the diocese of St Andrews, is rated at 25 merks in the old Taxation. In 1567, Patrick Bouncle was minister of Fettercairn, and of the three adjoining parishes of Fordoun, Newdosk, and Conveth (Laurencekirk), at a salary of 24 lb., " with the support of the Priour of St Androis." John Thom was reader, or schoolmaster, with 24 merks a year. David Strachan, afterwards Bishop of Brechin, was sometime minister at Fettercairn; also William Chalmers, who presented a congratulatory address to Queen Anne from his brethren of the Episcopal Church.

The present place of worship, which stands upon a rising ground in the kirkyard, and close to the village, was built in 1803. A handsome spire, or belfry, was added, in 1838, to the west end of the church. In old times, the bell was suspended from a tree, which stood upon the *Bell Hillock*. The old bell having become useless, a new one was got, which bears:—

FETTERCAIRN KIRK,
J. DICKSON & CO., MONTROSE, 1821.

At the time of the removal of the Bell Hillock, the earth and human bones of which it was composed having been thrown into the burial vault of the WOODS of Balbegno, which was within the old kirk, it is now difficult to say whether the Woods had any funeral monuments at Fettercairn.

It is well known that they were a branch of the Bonnington family, (v. p. 237); and the first Wood I have seen designed of Balbegno, appears in the year 1539, when "Johne Wood of Bawbegno, witht my hand at the pen led be me maister Johne Bell notar publict," gave King's College, Aberdeen, a charter of certain annual rents in Belhelvie and Ellon. In 1622, John Wood of Balbegno graduated at King's College; as did his relative and namesake, a brother of the laird of Balbegno, in 1666 (Fasti Abdns.) From 1539 (how long before I am not aware), the lands were held by Woods until about 1687, when they were sold to Andrew, second brother of the Earl of Middleton (Doug. Peerage), whose son, Robert, married a sister of John Ogilvy, advocate, son of Ogilvy of Lunan. Having no issue, Robert Middleton left his estate to his brother-in-law; and Mr Ogilvy's daughter (Mrs Brisbane), sold Balbegno about 1778, to the Hon. Walter Ogilvy (New Stat. Acct.) It is now the property of Sir T. Gladstone, bart., whose father bought it from the Hon. Donald Ogilvy of Clova. As thanes of Fettercairn, the Woods of Balbegno bore, in addition to their paternal coat of an oak tree, two keys fastened to a branch (Nisbet.)

The castle of Balbegno, which is in good preservation, contains an interesting hall with groined freestone roof. Some of the bosses present grotesque ornaments, others floral, and one bears the Irvine arms. The ceiling has two shields, charged respectively with the Scotch lion, and the Wood (?) arms. The vaulted compartments, of which there are sixteen, are occupied by mural paintings of the coats and mantlings, &c., of as many Scotch peers. Upon the bartizan are three medallion heads, one male, with hat, &c., and two females. A male head with beard and helmet is over the garden door. These are all boldly carved in freestone, and in the same style as the famous " Stirling Heads." Several shields, with arms, possibly those of the founder of the castle and his lady, are upon different parts of the house. The date of 1569 is upon a carved panel on the south side, near the top of the house. Upon the southeast, near the bartizan, below a shield with the Wood and Irvine arms, are these names, probably those of the erectors:—

I. WOD : E. IRVEIN.

Unfortunately the paintings in the hall are suffering from damp, and some of the shields in the outer walls are plastered over; but in these points, it is to be hoped, there will soon be an improvement. It ought to be added that, about the end of the last century, the Ogilvys made an addition to the east side of the castle, by which the original entrance and front were spoiled; and it is said that a tenant removed the stones from Balbegno, now at Caldhame, which bear the Wood and Barclay arms (v, p. 138.)

Three burial enclosures within the churchyard of Fettercairn belong respectively to the lairds of Fasque, Balmain, and Arnhall. None of these enclosures contain tombstones. The RAMSAYS, lately of Fasque, and still proprietors of Balmain, Easly, &c., are descended from Sir John Ramsay, afterwards Lord Bothwell, who in 1510, had charters of Balmain and Fasky, &c. The male line of the Ramsays, as well as the original baronetcy, became extinct (1830) in the person of the 7th baronet, who heired the title only in 1806. The estate of Fasque, &c., passed by bequest of the 6th baronet, to his sister's son, Alex. Burnett (second son of the baronet of Leys), who was in the same year (1806), created a baronet in his own right. He assumed the surname and arms of *Ramsay*, and was grandfather of the present baronet of Balmain.

The following inscriptions are from tombstones in different parts of the churchyard. The first is round the margin of a flat slab :—

☞ HEIR . LAYS . . . . . . ITHFVL . BROTHER . ALEXANDER . . . . . ROS . MERCHANT . AND . BVRGES , OF . DVNDIE . VASE . QVHA . DEPAIRT . . . . E LYF . 2 . MAI . ANNO . 1615 . OF . HIS . AGE . 88.

The above is cut in relief, the following is incised, upon the same stone :—

This monument was repaired by David Watt in memory of his daughter MARY WATT, who departed this life 3d November 1779, aged 17 years.

Near the last quoted :—

Hear rests in the Lord WILLIAM AVSTIN, hvsband to Isobel Gentleman, who depe . . . . e the 30 of Ivne anno 1685, and of age 68.

Anonymous :—

My glas is rvn, and thine rvnneth ;
Remember dath, for Ivgment cometh.

Upon a flat stone :—

☞ Here rests in the Lord IOHN WALLENTINE, lete Mosgrive in Arnhale, who departed this lyf 23d Febryr 1679, and his age 65 years. And his spous AGNES LOWE, who departed this lyf the 12th June 1682, and hire age 68 years :—

My parents here in hope doth rest,
Again to rise, and be for ever blest ;
. . . . live in hope here to lye,
And rise and reing with them eternaly.

—The stone from which the above is copied is elaborately ornamented with mortuary and other carvings, the more interesting and (so far as I have seen) unique of which are (upon a shield) a well carved human hand, holding a coil of rope, on the left of which is a short pole, or stake. These objects possibly refer to the occupation of "mosgrive"—the rope for measuring the moss, and the pole for marking the boundaries. The surname of *Valentine*, which is still common, is of considerable antiquity in the district. I am inclined to think that it had been assumed from one of the Thorntons of that ilk, whose Christian name was *Valentine*. (v. Mem. of Angus and the Mearns.) Robert (one of the last recorded of the Valentines), was farmer of Bogmuir, where he died in 1868, aged 82. Upon an adjoining stone :—

Under this stone are reposited the bodys of DAVID MORES, aged 80, departed this life May 5, 1696, with his wife ISOBEL MITCHELL, who died March 7 1694, aged 74; as also their daughter ELIZABETH MORES :—

Under this stone the man and wife do ly,
What was one flesh, we but one dust now spy ;
Their daughter also lodgeth in this grave,
So for three bodys, we one ashes have.
The great Eternal Three and One with ease,
Will from one dust all the three bodys rise,
Which winged to the celestial joys above
Shall never cease to sing their praise and love.

—Mr Cameron, parochial schoolmaster of Fettercairn (to whom I am obliged for some particulars in this notice, also for his having kindly unearthed some of the old stones), informs me that in 1674, Alex. Morrice, a student of Marischal College, Aberdeen, was appointed schoolmaster of Fettercairn, and that the stone, with the above inscription, has lain upon its face since 1843, when a schoolmaster was buried under it. David Mores, or Morrice, had likely been related to the school-master of 1674.

Under this stone is interred the corpse of ALEXANDER CROLL, who sometime lived in Kirkhill of Fettercairn, and departed this life Dec. 25th day 1747, aged 45 years. As also the corpse of MARGARET SMITH, his spouse, who died the 21st of April 1756 years, aged 50 years :—

 The tyrant, Death, spares neither age nor sex,
 The gayist mark he haughtily affects ;
 Parents from children, Husbands from their wives,
 He often tears, when most they wish their lives ;
 Learn then to fix on nothing here below,
 But on thy God, he'll Heaven on the bestow.

—In consequence of the locality of their residence, the above Alex. Croll, and his son, were called *Kirky Croll*. Both were wrights, or carpenters, and it is said that they made the gallows tree upon which Randell Courtency was hanged, (*v.* p. 138,) after which they received the soubriquet of *Pin the Widdie !* The following, upon an adjoining stone, in memory of an ALEXANDER CROLL, is dated 1751 :—

 He as a rock amongst vast Billows stood ;
 Scorning loud winds and raging of the flood ;
 And fix'd remaining all the force defies, [skies,
 Muster'd from threat'ning seas, & thundering
 To keep ameau his end still to observe,
 And from the Laws of Nature neer to swerve.

Upon a flat stone :—

Hic conduntur reliquiæ ELIZÆ PEAT, quæ 2do. die Augti. A.C. 1779, æ. s. 19 ; & ALEXRI. PEAT, qui 25to. die Janri. A.C. 1781, æ. s. 81, mortuus est. Ad memoriam JACOBI PEAT, qui A.C. 1750, æ. s. 20, mortuus est, ALEXRI. PEAT, antæ in Bogmill, nepotis qui etiam sub hoc tumulo requiescit, hoc monumentum extructum est. Mors omnibus appropinquat.

[Here lie the remains of ELIZA PEAT, who died 2 Aug, 1779, in her 19th year ; and of ALEX. PEAT, who died 25 Jan. 1781, in his 81st year. This monument was erected in memory of JAMES PEAT, who died in 1750, in his 20th year, grandson of Alex. Peat, late in Bogmill, who also rests in this tomb. Death draweth near to all.]

Here resteth in the Lord WILLIAM CHRISTY, who departed this lyf ninth . . . . . 1677 . . . . . his spouse, MARGARET DAVIDSON, who departed this lyf . . . . . and 79 her age.

MARGARET LOW (1761) :—

 Death's equal hand reacheth a fatal blow
 To all, even Kings unto his Sceptre bow ;
 Be wise, frail man, live dying so thou'lt give,
 To death his wounds, and after dying live.

JOHN SIM (1748) :—

 Mount up, mount up, my soul,
  On contemplation's wings ;
 Leave earth's unearthly minds,
  Do thou mind heavenly things.

A stone, initialed M. A. S : E. A., and dated 1753, bears :—

M.S. Sub hoc tumulo conduntur reliquiæ ALEXANDRI SCOTT, A.M., humaniorum & aliarum artium & scientiarum, mathesion, imprimis, professoris clarissimi & eruditissimi. Natus est apud Molam Balmanice Inferiorem decimo quarto die Decembris, anno 1708. Mortuus est apud Bankhead de Birse decimo octavo Februarii, anno 1751, annum ætatis agens 43 :—

 Par mens dôquio, mens spem super æthera librans,
 Mens pia sideris [et] purior orbe nitens.

[In this tomb are laid the remains of ALEXANDER SCOTT, A.M., a most distinguished and learned professor of the more liberal and other arts and sciences, especially mathematics. He was born at Nethermill of Balmain, 14 Dec. 1708, and died at Bankhead of Birse, 18 Feb. 1751, in the 43d year of his age :—

 The mind which learning can inspire—
  The mind that soars beyond the sky—
 The mind that's pure—in lustre far
  Excels yon starry orb on high.]

Erected 1792 by James Gibb in Mill of Arnhall and Robert Gibb in Drumhendry, in memory of their parents JOHN GIBB and HELLEN LAW, in Chapelton of Arnhall. JOHN GIBB, died 19 March 1755, aged 55. HELLEN LAW died 17 June 1769, aged 62, and GEORGE, son of James Gibb, died June 1789, at the age of 14.

—In 1750, John Gibb, and his wife Helen Law, tenants of Chapelton, kept the brewhouse or inn near Sandyford, where there was a ferryboat, at which time the " rent and mess meall" of Chapelton of Arnhall were collected in name of Sir

James Carnegie of Pittarrow. The chapel was dedicated to S. MARTIN, and an adjoining pool in the North Esk is still called *Lin-Martin*. Two carved stones, dated respectively 1668 and 1704, bear the arms (the eagle being erroneously carved with two heads), and the initials of two of the Earls of Southesk. Possibly the next inscription relates to Helen Law's parents:—

Here lys MARGARET DICKIE sometime spouse to James Law in Chapelton of Arnhall, who dyed May the 28, 1737, aged 76 years; and those her children, ROBERT, JANET, ISOBEL LAWS, who dyed in their nonage.

Upon the reverse of same stone (surrounding a representation of Our First Parents at the forbidden tree), is this couplet:—

Adam & Eve by eating the forbidden tree,
Brought all mankind to sin & misery.

Upon an obelisk, within an enclosure:—

Erected by the Parish of Fettercairn, in memory of the Revd. ROBERT FOOTE, their late pastor, as a mark of their esteem for an honest man, and an able and zealous minister of the Gospel. He died on July 1, 1800, in the 67th year of his age, and the 41st of his ministry.

—The above is upon the west side of the obelisk. On the north side:—

Here is interred JANE SMITH, widow of the Rev. Robert Foote, who died in 1842, aged 83 years.

—This lady (daughter of a minister at Garvock), had a large family by her husband: the deaths of four of them are recorded upon the east panel of the obelisk, and upon the west is that of her son ARCHIBALD, merchant in Montrose, who died in 1867, aged 71. Two other sons, James, and Alex. Leith-Ross, followed the profession of their father. The first was sometime minister at Logie-Pert, afterwards at Aberdeen, and the latter is at Brechin. Both seceded at the Disruption; and having written works on theological subjects, they both had the honorary degree of D.D. conferred upon them. Their grandfather, the Rev. CHARLES FLT (a St Andrews M.A.), married BARBARA STEWART, and died minister of Kinnoul in 1758, aged 56. Their father, who was previously minister at Eskdalemuir, though inducted to Fettercairn (Sept. 16, 1773), very much against the wishes of the people, soon became a favourite in the parish. The induction day was very tempestuous, and stories of the ravages occasioned by *Foote's Wind* have been handed down to the present time! Mr Foote's opponent at Fettercairn was Mr BARCLAY, founder of the Bereans, who holds a prominent place among "Scots Worthies." He died at Edinburgh, and was buried in the Old Calton graveyard of that city, where a stone marks his grave, thus inscribed:—

In memory of JOHN BARCLAY, M.A., pastor of the Berean Church, Edinburgh, who died 29th July 1798, in the 65th year of his age, and 39th of his ministry.

Upon a headstone at Fettercairn:—

DAVIDI WHYTE, filio Alexandri Whyte, olim in Aucharno Clovæ, coloni, Monterosarum quondam chirurgo, qui, 14 Januarii anno 1839, annos 39 natus, obiit, hoc monumentum positum est. Etiam; ANNÆ WHYTE, sorori ejus paternæ, quæ 8 Aprilis 1842, annos 25 nata, hac ex vita discessit. [1 Cor. 15.55.]

[This monument was erected to the memory of DAVID WHYTE (son of Alex. Whyte, farmer, late in Aucharn, Clova), formerly surgeon in Montrose, who died January 14, 1839, aged 39. And also to the memory of ANN WHYTE, his paternal half sister, who departed this life April 8, 1842, aged 25.]

—Dr Whyte had a brother, sometime minister of Fettercairn. The latter, who died in 1858, wrote a book on Prayer, another on the Lord's Supper; also the excellent notice of Fettercairn in the New Statistical Account of Scotland.

JAMES SMITH, flaxdresser, d. 1816, a. 86:—

While in life he acted as 'a Father to the Poor;' and, with the consent of his spouse, devoted nearly all his property for their benefits, by appointing it to become at the Survivor's death a permanent fund for their aid. Erected by his widow ISOBEL TAYLOR, who died at Montrose, 18 May 1824, aged 71.

A tombstone (table-shaped) bears:—

Here rests in the Lord, JOHN KINLOCH, and his spouse JEIN KINLOCH, he died in the year 1690, aged 60, and also ELIZABETH BLACKLAWS, his second spouse, who died in the same year, aged 66. This stone was repaired by William, David, and James Kinlochs, sons of John Kinloch, late tenant in Mickle Strath, in 1803.

[Upon a brass plate, sunk into same stone] :—

Sacred to memory of JAMES KINLOCH of Wester Balmanno, formerly for 17 years of the Island of Jamaica, died 19th June 1831, aged 78 years.

Upon an adjoining headstone :—

Sacred to the memory of GEORGE KINLOCH, Esq., Deputy Judge Advocate and Master in Chancery, in the Island of Jamaica, who died at Stonehaven 22 April 1802, aged 60, and of Mrs SUSANNAH WIGGLESWORTH, his spouse, who died at Edinburgh, 7 May 1841, aged 81. Their surviving children, Alexander, George Ritchie, Lydia, and Maria Kinloch, have erected this stone as a mark of their filial affection.

—The above-named George Ritchie Kinloch, late Principal Keeper of the General Register of Deeds and Probative Writs, Edinburgh, published a volume of Ancient Scottish Ballads (1827.)

GEORGE SHERIFFS, for a long period factor on the Fasque and Balmain estates, died 27 April 1845, aged 83. MARY MONY, or SHERIFFS, his wife, died 17 Oct. 1847, aged 67 ; and their son, EDWARD· BANNERMAN SHERIFFS, M.D., F.R.C.S., died 14 Jan. 1846, aged 39.

—Dr Sheriffs was a person of acknowledged talent. He began practice at Fettercairn, which he left for Brechin. While at Brechin, he published (1832) Remarks on Cholera Morbus, also began a work upon the Osteology of the Human Ear, illustrated by casts. Being unsuccessful at Brechin, he removed first to Edinburgh (where he issued the last-named work), next to London, and latterly to Aberdeen, at the two last-mentioned of which places he lectured upon anatomy and physiology, &c. Dr Sheriffs (who was named after Dean Ramsay), kept a carriage in London, also a piper, dressed in ' the garb of Ould Gaul.'

A head stone, near the north-east corner of the kirkyard, erected by Sir T. Gladstone, bears :—

Sacred to the memory of SANDY JUNOR, a kindhearted, simple-minded, upright man, and a faithful friend. Poor himself, his heart and hand were ever open to the wants of others. Born at Fortrose, he died near Fettercairn, 27 Nov. 1863, aged 60, deeply regretted by all classes.

—*Sandy Junor's Well*, which travellers crossing the Cairn-o'-Mounth hail with gratitude, was the handiwork of this humble man, whose object in constructing the fountain is thus told upon an adjoining slab :—

This fountain was erected in memory of Captain J. N. GLADSTONE, R.N., who died in 1863, by his grateful friend SANDY JUNOR.

———o———

S. ANDREW'S EPISCOPAL CHURCH,

which stands a little to the eastward of the house of Fasque, was built by Sir John Gladstone, and consecrated and opened, 28th August 1847, by Samuel, Bishop of Oxford, now of Winchester· The original building has been greatly improved, by the erection of a new chancel, which was consecrated by Alexander, Bishop of Brechin, 15 April 1869. It is in the early English style of architecture, with deep splayed lancet windows. The east window, which contains representations of S. ANDREW and the FOUR EVANGELISTS, &c., is a fine specimen of art. As shown by the following inscription (copied from a brass plate upon the north wall), the additions were made by the present Baronet, in memory of his third brother, the late Capt. GLADSTONE, who was sometime M.P. for Walsall :—

𝔈𝔫 𝔤𝔩𝔬𝔯𝔦𝔞𝔪 𝔥𝔬𝔫𝔬𝔯𝔢𝔪𝔮𝔲𝔢 𝔇𝔢𝔦 𝔢𝔱 𝔦𝔫 𝔪𝔢𝔪𝔬𝔯𝔦𝔞𝔪 𝔡𝔦𝔩𝔢𝔠𝔱𝔦𝔰𝔰𝔦𝔪𝔞𝔪 𝔍𝔬𝔥𝔞𝔫𝔫𝔦𝔰-𝔑𝔢𝔦𝔩𝔰𝔬𝔫 𝔊𝔩𝔞𝔡𝔰𝔱𝔬𝔫𝔢, 𝔦𝔫 𝔊𝔩𝔞𝔰𝔰𝔢 𝔕𝔢𝔤𝔞𝔩𝔦 𝔑𝔞𝔳𝔞𝔯𝔠𝔥𝔦, 𝔮𝔲𝔦 𝔬𝔟𝔦𝔦𝔱 𝔄.𝔇. 1863, 𝔥𝔲𝔫𝔠 𝔠𝔞𝔫𝔠𝔢𝔩𝔩𝔲𝔪 𝔢𝔠𝔠𝔩𝔰𝔦𝔵 𝔖𝔱𝔦. 𝔄𝔫𝔡𝔯𝔢𝔵 𝔞𝔟𝔰𝔱𝔯𝔟𝔦 𝔠𝔲𝔯𝔞𝔟𝔦𝔱 𝔣𝔯𝔞𝔱𝔢𝔯 𝔪𝔬𝔢𝔯𝔢𝔫𝔰, 𝔗. 𝔊., 𝔄.𝔇. 1867.

[To the glory and honour of God, and in the deeply cherished memory of JOHN-NEILSON GLADSTONE, Captain in the Royal Navy, who died A.D. 1863, his sorrowing brother, T. G., caused this chancel of St. Andrew's Church to be erected.]

—A monument of white marble, in the north wall of the nave of the church, presents a group of two figures, in high relief, nearly life size, and in the attitude of prayer. These represent the founder of the church and his lady. Along the base of the monument is this inscription:—

Sacred to the memory of Sir JOHN GLADSTONE of Fasque and Balfour, Baronet: born 11 Dec. 1764; died 7 Dec. 1851. And of his wife, ANN ROBERTSON, born 4 Aug. 1772; died 23 Sept. 1835.

—Sir John, who was a grandson of John Gladstone of Toftcombs, Lanarkshire, was a native of Leith. He was an eminent merchant at Liverpool, and created a baronet in 1846. By the above-named lady (who was his second wife), daughter of Provost Robertson of Dingwall, he had two daughters and four sons—Sir Thomas, his successor; Robertson, of Courthey, Lancaster; the late Capt. John, of Bowden Park; and the Right Hon. W. E. Gladstone, Prime Minister of England. Sir John bought the estates of Fasque and Balfour from the late Sir Alex. Ramsay, bart., in 1829. He subsequently acquired from other proprietors the lands of Phesdo and Balbegno; and his successor, Sir Thomas, in 1856, added the fine Highland estate of Glendye to his paternal inheritance. Two memorial windows (also on the north side of the church, inscribed as below), refer respectively to a sister, and two children of the present baronet:—

In memory of ANN MCKENZIE GLADSTONE, born 1802, died 1829. Lord, I believe, thou hast the words of eternal life.

—The next window contains a representation of Christ blessing little children.—

In memory of EVELYN-MARCELLA GLADSTONE, born 1847, died 1852. FRANCES-MARGARET GLADSTONE, born 1850, died 1853.

A window (over the entrance to the church) is commemorative of ROBERT GLADSTONE (a brother of Sir John), who died at Fasque in 1835. A flat stone, in the area of the church, over the family vault, bears this record of the death of a daughter of the Premier:—

In the vault beneath sleep the mortal remains of CATHERINE-JESSY GLADSTONE, second daughter of W. E. and Catherine Gladstone. Born July 27, 1845, died April 9, 1850. "And in their mouth was found no guile: for they are without fault before the throne of God." Rev. 14, 5.

A memorial window on the south side of the church is embellished with two subjects. The upper one is S. JOHN the Evangelist leading the BLESSED VIRGIN home from the Crucifixion, the lower represents S. JOHN leaning upon his Master's breast. Along the base is the following:—

✠ In memory of Sir JOHN HEPBURN-STUART-FORBES, Bart. Born Sept. 25, 1804, died May 28, 1866.

—Sir John, who was the eldest son of Sir William Forbes of Pitsligo, baronet (v. p. 244), died in London, and was interred in the family tomb in the Greyfriars' Churchyard, Edinburgh. Sir John married Lady Harriet, 3d daughter of the Marquis of Lothian, by whom he left an only child and heiress. She married her cousin, Lord Clinton, by whom, having died in 1869, she left a family. The property of Fettercairn was bought in 1777 by Sir John Belshes-Wishart, bart., afterwards the Hon. Baron Sir John Stuart, maternal grandfather of the late baronet. The late proprietor, who, shortly before his death, succeeded to the property of Invermay—"the birks" of which are celebrated in Scottish song—was well-known throughout Scotland for the interest he took in promoting the advancement of agriculture, as well as the improvement of the social condition of the labouring classes. In testimony of the esteem in which he was held in the neighbourhood of his own residence, it is sufficient to mention that a handsome memorial fountain, designed by Mr Bryce of Edinburgh, has been erected at the village of Fettercairn. A panel of Peterhead granite bears this simple inscription:—

Erected to the memory of Sir JOHN H.-S.-FORBES, baronet, of Pitsligo and Fettercairn, by his neighbours and other friends, 1869.

The ramparts or walls of the vitrified fort or site of Greencairn Castle, about a mile to the west of Fettercairn village, are still traceable. Some suppose that this was the residence of a Maormor or Earl, and that it was the scene of the murder of Kenneth III. by Lady Finella.

The proprietary history of Balbegno and Fasque,

&c., has been already noticed. These were probably parts of the old thanedom of Fettercairn, for *Fettercairn* appears to have been at one time the general name of the district; but as portions of the lands were gifted by the Crown to vassals and others, distinctive names were given to each; and these, as a rule, were descriptive of the physical aspects of the different places.

By far the earliest lay proprietors in the district were the MIDDLETONS, of the existence of whom there is authentic evidence from at least the year 1221. They long had their residence at Fettercairn House, and there a stone panel (inscribed 1666, E. I. M : C. G. M.), relates to the time of the celebrated John, Earl of Middleton, and his first Countess, Grizel Durham, a daughter of the laird of Pitkerro, and mother of the second Earl of Middleton. This slab, and the market cross at Fettercairn, the latter of which is dated 1670, and ornamented with the Middleton arms and those of Scotland, are, so far as I know, the only visible traces of the Earl now at Fettercairn.

It is told in Law's Memorials that one of the lairds of Balbegno was a companion in arms with Middleton long ere he had acquired much fame; and that before entering the field of battle on one occasion they agreed, in the event of either of them being killed, that the other should return and give the survivor some account of the other world! It is added that Balbegno fell; and one day, while Middleton was a prisoner in the Tower of London, and just as he had finished reading a portion of Scripture, Balbegno's ghost appeared, and taking him by the hand, said—" Oh, Middleton, do you not mind the promise I made to you when at such a place, such a night on the Border?" But, without giving him any account of " the other world," it is added that Balbegno prophesied Middleton's future greatness, and vanished from his view, exclaiming :—

"Plumashes above, and gramashes below,
It's no wonder to see how the world doth go."

About the time of the Reformation, a portion of Fettercairn belonged to a family named OGSTOUN, one of whom was a **Commissioner to the first General Assembly (1560),** " for the Kirks of the Mernes." He was also present at the Assembly in July 1567; and in that which was held at Aberdeen in March 1592, " Walter Ogstone of Fettercarne subscrived the Band anent the Religion" (Booke of the Univ. Kirk.) The Ogstons of Fettercairn were possibly cadets of an Aberdeenshire family, who were anciently designed " of that Ilk."

The old market cross of Fettercairn was possibly erected by the Earl of Middleton at the time he obtained an Act of Parliament to hold a weekly market there. He received this privilege in 1670 — the date upon the cross — but long before that, S. MARK's fair (named doubtless in honour of the saint to whom the kirk was dedicated), was a market of considerable importance. S. CATHERINE's fair (originally held at the old town of Kincardine), had probably been transferred to Fettercairn when the county courts, &c., were removed to Stonehaven (Mem. of Angus and Mearns.)

The North Esk, which separates the parish of Fettercairn from that of Edzell (*q. v.*) on the west, is crossed by the Gannochy Bridge. The Craigmoston burn, which separates Fettercairn from Fordoun on the east, is bridged in several places: The upper, or Craigmoston bridge, is in connection with the ancient thoroughfare of Cairno'-Mounth, which Sir James Balfour calls " the sext of the cheiffe mountain passages" to the Dee, " It passes (he contiuues) from Fittircairne in The Mernis to Kincardlyne of Neill one Dee, in Mar, and conteins aucht miles in mounthe."

The *Village of Fettercairn*, where stand the Established and Free Churches, is a clean, salubrious place, with a number of neat houses. Accompanied by the late Prince Consort, Princess Alice and Prince Louis of Hesse, the Queen (*v.* Her Majesty's " Leaves") spent the night of 20 Sept. 1861, in the inn of this village, in honour of which event, a triumphal arch (planned by Mr Milne, St. Andrews), was erected by public subscription. It is briefly inscribed:—

VISIT OF VICTORIA AND ALBERT,
SEPT. 1861.

Drumblade.

(S. HILARY.)

THE church of *Drumblat* belonged to the See of Old Machar. *Tillery's* Well (a corruption of S. HILARY), is in the neighbourhood of the kirk. There were two saints of this name, a Bishop and Archbishop, whose feasts were held respectively on 14 January and 5 May.

The present church was built in 1773, and improved in 1829. In the Old Stat. Account it is said that the former church was erected in 1110: this is clearly a misprint for 1641, the same stone from which the writer quoted being still in existence, and built into the belfry. A hand bell lately removed to Lessendrum House is inscribed, GEORGE BISSET, 1604.

Prior to the rebuilding of the church in 1773, there was an aisle on the south side, which belonged to the Bissets of Lessendrum. This has given place to a railed enclosure, with a low stone wall, in which a free stone slab is inserted and thus inscribed:—

This is the burial place of the Family of Lessendrum.
Done by ANNE BISSET, 1775.

—Another free stone slab (the oldest now visible) bears this inscription:—

Hic iacet honorabilis vir, GEORGIVS BISSET de Lessendrvm, qvi obiit 25 Ianvarii 1623, et ætatis svæ anno 73°.
Ætatem ornavit primam mihi vivida virtvs,
Et prisca at lapsv sors rediviva domvs
Famam terra sol . . . . . . perennem
Indigetvm ; reqviem posthvma vita dedit.

[Here lies an honourable man, GEORGE BISSET of Lessendrum, who died 25 January 1623, aged 73. Active virtue adorned my youth, and the restoration of the decayed fortunes of my ancient house won for me an enduring reputation among my countrymen on earth ; in the life beyond the grave I enjoy repose.]

—A flat stone covers the grave of the gentleman, to whose memory a marble slab is erected, within the church. Upon the marble :—

Sacred to the memory of MAURICE-GEORGE BISSET, Esq. of Lessendrum, who died at Lessendrum, on the 16 of Dec. 1821, in the 64th year of his age. This tablet is jointly inscribed by Harriot, his affectionate and mournful widow, and his brother, and immediate successor, William, Lord Bishop of Raphoe, in honor of his name, and in grateful recollection of the many virtues that adorned his endearing character.

—Opposite to the last mentioned another marble tablet (with a bishop's cap, &c., resting upon a cushion), is thus inscribed :—

Sacred to the memory of WILLIAM BISSET, D.D., late Lord Bishop of Raphoe, and proprietor of Lessendrum, who died on the 4th Sept. A.D. 1834, aged 75 years.

—On the death of Bishop Bisset, Lessendrum descended to his nephew William Bisset (son of Alex. Bisset), who married Lady Alicia Howard, daughter of the Earl of Wicklow. WILLIAM BISSET died Jan. 8, 1858, upon which, on failure of male heirs, the estate devolved upon Jane-Harriet, daughter of Maurice-George Bisset, who died in 1821. She married her cousin, Archdeacon Maurice-Geo. Fenwick, who assumed the name of *Bisset* ; and their son Mordaunt Fenwick-Bisset, succeeded to Lessendrum on the death of his mother JANE-HARRIET FENWICK-BISSET, in 1866. Her grave at Drumblade is covered by a coffin-slab of polished Peterhead granite, with a cross in high relief upon the top.

It is not quite clear at what time the Bissets acquired Lessendrum. Charter evidence shows that they held it about the middle of the 14th century ; and it is probable that Walter Bisset, who swore fealty to King Edward in 1296 for lands in Aberdeenshire, had been in possession of Lessendrum. The Bissets first settled in Scotland under William the Lion. One of them founded an hospital in the Merse, and another founded the monastery of Beauly, in Ross-shire. The clan was numerous and powerful until about 1242, when the Border Bissets, out of revenge, treacherously assassinated the young Earl of Athol at Haddington. For this, the chief actors were outlawed and disgraced ; still the family continued to have considerable influence; and the older branches having died out, that of Lessendrum has been looked upon for a long period of years as the chief of their race. Upon the fragment of a slab in the burial-ground:—

Hic iacent cineres mulieris ornatissimæ . . . .

Another small headstone bears the name of a grand-daughter of Sir Robert Gordon of Straloch (v. CAIRNIE), the celebrated geographer :—

ELIZABETHÆ GORDON quæ nupserat GEORGIO CHALMER, p. de Drumblade, qui obiere, hæc 6 Ianr⁰ 1692, ille . . . . Linquenda tellus et dom' et placens uxor.

[Here lie the ashes of a highly accomplished woman, ELIZABETH GORDON, spouse of GEORGE CHALMER, pastor of Drumblade, who died she 6 Jan. 1692, and he . . . . Earth, home, and pleasing wife must be left.]

—According to the interesting notice of the parish of Drumblade, in the New Stat. Account, which was written by Mr Geo. Ramsay Davidson (now of Lady Glenorchy's Free Church, Edinburgh), two silver communion cups were gifted to the parish by Mr Chalmer, and two by Mr Abel. Upon the reverse of Mr Chalmer's stone:—

This stone belongs to the "GORDONS," and the family of ALEXANDER BARCLAY, late feuar in Huntly, who was born in 1752, and died in 1835, aged 83 years.

Upon the tombstone of Mr Abel, who wrote the Old Stat. Account of the parish :—

Sub hoc saxo Magistri GEORGII ABEL, pastoris Evangelii apud Drumblade, reliquiæ inhumantur. 14° Septemberis 1794, ætatis 56°, officii 28° anno diem obiit.

[Under this stone are interred the remains of Mr GEORGE ABEL, minister of the Gospel, Drumblade, who died 14 September 1794, in the 56th year of his age, and 28th of his ministry.]

The Rev. WILLIAM RAINY died at Monelly, 2 Nov. 1842, aged 77. His wife, MARY TAYLOR, died 16 Feb. 1861, aged 53.

An enclosure on south-east of the church contains several monuments. Two of white marble, set in granite, bear respectively the names of ELIZABETH (wife of Capt. Chas. Gordon, R.N.), who died in 1843, aged 31 ; and of Major-General JOHN GORDON, R.A., born 1789, who died in 1861 (v. p. 51.) Upon a table-shaped stone :—

Here lie the remains of the Rev. ROBERT GORDON, minister of Drumblade, who died 27 Nov. 1820, aged 70 ; also the remains of JEAN FARQUHARSON, his widow, who died 23 June 1829, aged 79.

—A mural tablet bears the name of Mr G.'s daughter, ELIZA, first wife of Captain Henry of Corse, who died in 1802, aged 21 (v. FORGUE.) Another tablet shows that a second daughter, MARGARET, died in 1867, aged 82; also that her husband, ANDREW McPHERSON, predeceased her in 1836, aged 67. Mr M. was local factor on the Huntly estates, in which office he was succeeded by his son, to whose memory there is a marble monument, within an adjoining enclosure : —

Erected to the memory of the late GEORGE McPHERSON, Esq., Gibston, factor on the Huntly estates for 27 years, who died at Gibston, 8 Sep. 1864, in the 56th year of his age, by the Tenantry of the Duke of Richmond, and other Friends of the deceased, as a mark of their respect for his memory.

The writer of the Old Stat. Account (vol. iv. p. 55) says that there were "large stones with inscriptions upon them, now all broken down and carried away," upon a small hill called Robin's Height. These were possibly sculptured stones. Near to this is the Sliach, where there had been a camp or place of *strinth*, for it was to it that Bruce was carried when taken ill at Inverurie in 1308. According to Barbour :—

"Tharfor in littar tha him lay
And till the *Sterach* held thar way,
And thocht thar in that strinth to ly
Quhill passit war his malady."

There had possibly been a chapel (? Christ Jesus) at Sliach in early times, since, in "Aberdeen's New Prognosticator" for 1720, a market held on second Tuesday of June is set down as "JESUS Fair at the Park of Slioch in Drumblate Parish."

There are tumuli at Meethillock at the foot of Robin's Height, and spear heads of various sizes have been found in the same locality.

The Bissets are by far the earliest recorded possessors of land in Drumblade. Early in the 15th century, the Angus families of Fenton, Lindsay, and Ogilvy appear to have held considerable property in it; also Alex. Seton, lord of Gordon, Barclay of Gartly, and others.

Careston.

(S. —)

THE parish of *Caraldstone*, or *Careston* (one of the smallest in Scotland), was formed from those of Brechin and Fearn, by Act of Parliament, in 1641, upon petition of Sir Alex. Carnegy of Balnamoon, a brother of the first Earls of Southesk and Northesk. It was in 1720 that Careston came, by purchase, to Major Skene, cadet of the family of that ilk, now represented by the Earl of Fife, through a female (*v.* p. 226 *supra ;* Laud of the Lindsays.)

A hand-bell, initialed A. F., C. F., and dated 1756, was given to the parish "by Alex. Fairweather in Balglassic." Two communion cups are inscribed CARESTON, and dated 1779.

In consequence of a whim of Mr George Skene, the gravestones were turned out of the churchyard, when the present dykes were built. After Skene's death, a few monuments were recovered and replaced in the kirkyard. One of these, dated 1755, bears to have been erected by JAMES CLARK and AGNES BEAN. As if in anticipation of Mr Skene's sacrilegious proceedings, it presents these lines :—

> This stone doth hold these corps of mine,
> While I ly buried here;
> None shal molest nor wrong this stone,
> Except my friends that's near.
> My flesh and bones lyes in Earth's womb,
> Wntill Judgment do appear;
> And then I shall be raised again,
> To meet my Saviour dear.

Upon a plain headstone, at west dyke :—

In memory of Mr JOHN GILLIES, who was ordained minister of Carraldston, Sept. 1716, and departed this life the 1st March 1753, aged 72 years. Six of his children are likewise buried here, of which five died in infancy, and one, viz. THOMAS, in March 1736, aged 13 years. His spouse, Mary Watson, survives him, as also five of his children, viz. John, minister in Glasgow; Robert, merchant in Brechin; and Mary, Isobel, and Janet Gillies. [Ps. 37; Phil. i. 31; Col. 3, 4.]

—The Rev. Mr Gillies came to Angus as schoolmaster at Fearn, and was the first minister at Careston after the abolition of Episcopacy. His son John wrote the Life of Whitfield and other works; and Robert was the father of Dr John Gillies, historian of Greece, and of Lord Adam Gillies, &c. (*v.* BRECHIN.) From a headstone adjoining the above:—

Hic iacet ALEXANDER BURNET, V.D. minister de Careston, olim de Footdee in vicinio Aberdoniæ, æt. 62, qui maximam vitæ partem Londini in disciplinis literariis, in præsenti ævo parum fructuosis, parce ac duriter egerat, etsi literis haud mediocriter imbutus ; tandem amicitia Patroni, Georgii Skene de Skene, ministerio hujus parœchiæ donatus, et quod supererat vitæ in muniis debitis exsequendis feliciter ducere sperans, intra biennium, heu ! mortuus est, dum vixit hilaris, comis, facetus, et nomini inimicus, Janⁱⁱ. 25, anno æræ Christ, M.D.CCC.

[Here lies in his 62d year ALEXANDER BURNET, minister of Careston, formerly of Footdee, in the vicinity of Aberdeen, who spent the greatest part of his life in London engaged in the pursuits of literature, so unprofitable in the present age, by which, although possessed of no ordinary literary attainments, he earned only a scanty and precarious livelihood ; having at length been presented to the ministerial charge of this parish through the friendship of the Patron, George Skene of Skene, and hoping to pass the remainder of his life happily in the discharge of the duties of his office, he died, alas ! within two years, 25 January 1800. In life he was distinguished for cheerfulness, courtesy, humour, and goodwill towards all.]

Near the last quoted inscription, within an enclosure :—

In memory of DAVID LYELL, who was ordained minister of Careston, A.D. 1800, and died there on the 15th July 1834, in the 86th year of his age. His spouse, the Hon. CATHARINE ARBUTHNOTT, died 16 Dec. 1853, aged 65. Their son STUART-THOMAS LYELL, surgeon, H.E.I.C.S., died at Ballary, in India, 17 July 1853, aged 45.

—Mr Lyell's father was laird of Fernyflatt and Hallhill, or Easter Kinneff, also of Largie, in the Mearns. He was a cadet of Lyell of Dysart, the first of whom was town-clerk of Montrose. The Hon. Mrs Lyell was a daughter of the seventh Viscount Arbuthnott. A son, Mr Hew Lyell, is minister of Auchterhouse. Against east wall :—

This stone was erected by George Mitchell in memory of his father, GEORGE . . . . ELSPET FAIRWEATHER, who died 1736, aged 80 . . . . . . AGNES GALL, who died 1731, aged 33 ;- -

    As our shorter day of light,
    Our day of life posts on ;
    Both show a long course to the night,
    But both are quickly run.
    Both have their night, And when that spreads
    Its black wing o'er the day,
    There's no more work, All take their beds,
    Of feathers or of clay.
    Chuse then before it be too late,
    For choice will end ;
    Remember on thy choice thy fate,
    Thy good or ill depends.

A slab, set up against the front wall of the kirk, records five deaths which occurred in the family of JOHN RITCHIE, from 8th to 25th March 1767 :—

MARY, aged 9 years ; DAVID, aged 7 months ; MARGARET, near 5 years ; JEAN, aged 7 years ; ELIZABETH, aged 2 years, 7 months. They lie interred within 12 foot of the fore wall of the kirk by west the door, and a foot without the straught of the geavel. [Matt. xix. 14 ; Psal. lv. 14.]

But the oldest visible tombstone is a much-effaced fragment, of the 17th century, upon which is the name of IOHNE WOOD ; also the rhyme of "Remember man, as you go by," &c., in Roman capitals. Wood is one of the oldest family names in Careston.

The castle of Careston, which has been frequently added to and altered, is still inhabited. The oldest part of the building, which was erected by the 13th Earl of Crawford, presents some interesting architectural features. Among these is a bold carving of the royal arms of Scotland, over the chimney of the great hall, flanked by banners, &c. Below, in interlaced capitals :—

THIS . HONORIS . SINGE
AND . FIGVRIT . TROPHE . BOR
SVLD . PVSE . ASPYRING . SPRE
ITIS . AND . MARTIAL . MYND"
TO . THRVST . YAIR . FORTVNE
FWRTH . & . IN . HIR . SCORNE
BELEIVE . IN . FAITHE
OVR . FAIT . GOD . HES . ASSINGD

The proprietary history of Careston can be traced from a remote date. It is said that the lands went along with the office of "hereditary dempster" of Scotland ; also that, from this circumstance, the surname of DEMPSTER was assumed, and originated with the old lairds of Careston (v. p. 209.) But other places in Scotland have the same name, amongst others are Careston in Banffshire, of old the property of the lords of Deskford, now that of their representative, the Earl of Seafield; also Careston in Fife, long owned by a branch of the noble family of Seton, now represented by George Seton, Esq. of St Bennet's, advocate, author of the Law of Scottish Heraldry, &c.

Kildrummy.

(S. BRIDGET, VIRGIN.)

KILDRUMMY parish, as now constituted, consists of the old ecclesiastical districts of *Kindrumyn* and *Cloueth*. The first church is rated at 7 merks in the Taxation of 1275, and the latter at 4 merks.

CLOUETH, or CLOVA,

was a foundation of considerable antiquity and importance, having been a sort of sub-monastery

KILDRUMMY.

to that of Mortlach. By charter dated at Forfar in 1063, King Malcolm granted and confirmed to the church of S. MARY of Mortlach, "my lands of Murthue, the church of Cloveth, with its lands, and the church of Dalmeth (now Glass), with its lands."

In 1157, Pope Adrian IV. confirmed *the monastery* of Cloueth to Edward, bishop of Aberdeen, and his successors. More than a century afterwards (1266), the Dean and Chapter of Aberdeen confirmed the grant made by Bishop Richard of the churches of Dummeth and Cloueth, for the lights of the great altar, and the ornaments of the cathedral of Aberdeen. At a much later date (1511), the Bishop's lands at Clova are stated to consist of two ploughs, and to have been let to four tenants. In 1549, the lands of Clowetht, and the mill of the same, were leased for 19 years by the Bishop, to Master Robert Lumisdane, probably an ancestor of the future lairds of the property.

It was in 1520, that the kirk of Cawbraucht or Cloueth was constituted *one* of the common churches of the chapter of Aberdeen, a fact which possibly shows that Clova and Cabrach were then one district.

The monastery, or church of Clova, stood upon a rising ground, which slopes rapidly towards a burn on the south, where there is a copious spring called *Similuak*—possibly a corruption of the name S. MOLOCH, to whom the kirk was dedicated. The site is planted, and inclosed by a rude stone dyke; and although the foundations of the kirk can be traced, which show it to have been about 31 feet long and about 15 feet broad, only one dressed lintel remains. There are no tombstones; and the site is about four miles to the eastward of the kirk of Kildrummy, at no great distance from the mansion house of Clova.

The date of the permanent union of the kirks of Kildrummy and Clova has not been ascertained. It is true that as far back as 1363, owing to the smallness of the revenues of the parishes of Kildrummy and Clova, which are said to have been wasted by frequent wars, the Bishop ordained one vicar to serve both cures, and to have a stipend of 100s., with the kirk lands; but this agreement was not lasting. In the previous year, Thomas, Earl of Mar, gave over the right of the patronage of the kirk of Kildrummy to the dean and chapter of Aberdeen, possibly with the view of having the two churches united.

It is said that the church of

KILDRUMMY

was once "called *the Chappel of the Lochs*, being situated upon an eminence surrounded on all sides with a marsh." Now, however, the marsh has almost disappeared, and a great part of the space it occupied is under cultivation.

The old kirk, which stood on the north side of the burial-ground, was removed outside the kirk-yard about 1805. The only remains of the old church are parts of the north and east walls, and the Elphinstone burial place. Upon the latter portion, which formed the south aisle of the kirk, a slab presents this inscription:—

YIS . YLLE . VAS . DVILT . BE . A . E . IN
160- . ZEIRS . LORD . BLIS . VS.

—A tombstone built into the west wall of the aisle presents a bold carving of the Elphinstone arms in the upper half; in the lower are three figures, with their hands in devotional attitudes. These are possibly intended to represent the persons named in the next inscription, which is cut (with the initials, V. E : P. E : D. E.), round the margin of the tomb:—

. . . . VILLIAM . PATRIK . AND . DAVID ELPHINSTOVNES . . . . . ALEXANDER . LORD . ELPHINSTOVN . . . . TIT . YIS . LYF.

—The above appear to have been sons of the 4th Lord Elphinstone; but their names are not given in Douglas' genealogy of the family. A slab in the floor of the aisle bears:—

✠ HEIR . LYIS . ANE . . . . . MAN . MASTER LO . . . ELPHYNSTOVN . ALEXANDER . LORD . ELPHYNSTOVN . QVHA . DEPARTIT . FRA . YIS . LYF YE . LAST . OF . MAII . 1616 . BEING . OF . YE AGE . OF . XXX . ZEIRIS.

—The following (also from a slab in the floor of aisle), refers to James of Barnes, second son of the 4th, and father of the 6th Lords Elphinstone :—

. . . . R . OF . THIS . COVE
. . . . . MEMBRIT . EVER . ON . DEATH
. . . . ATH . MOST . GLORISLY . MAY . RINGE
. OD . . . AND . WITH . HIS . SAVLS . REDIMER
. . . . . HINS . . . NE . OF . BARNS.

—The surname of Elphinstone (supposed to have been assumed from the property of Elphinstone, near Edinburgh), first appears in charters about 1250. Alex., who was ennobled in 1509, was the first of his race that held lands on Douside. These consisted of the barony of Invernochty, the king's lands of Kildrummy, with the keepership of the castle, all acquired in 1507-8. He fell at Flodden; and it was his great-grandson who built the burial aisle. It was also in the time of the latter, about 1626, that Kildrummy was lost to the Elphinstones, owing to the Earl of Mar having been restored to his old family estates, of which Kildrummy formed a part. Until recently, the Elphinstone tomb at Kildrummy was ill-cared for; but the present Peer, with a feeling which cannot be over-rated, made a pilgrimage to the spot, and gave orders for its repair, which latter fact is thus recorded upon a panel over the entrance:—

RESTORED BY WILLIAM, 15TH LORD ELPHINSTONE, 1862.

Besides the tombstones above-mentioned, there are other three within the aisle. Upon one with the Elphinstone arms much effaced, the words, SOLI . DEO . GLORIA, are only traceable. The second stone appears to have commemorated the death of a daughter of Gordon of Lesmore. There is nothing to show that the Elphinstones and Gordons of Lesmore were related; but according to the Forbes genealogy, "Duncan Forbes in Findlest married a daughter of James Gordon of Leshmoir." Possibly the slab had been removed from the Forbes burial ground. These words only remain upon it:—

. . . . ORDVNE . DE . LESMOIR . ET . SPONSA . MA . . .
—The next, which is the most perfect inscription within the aisle, relates to a grieve, or farm overseer. The initials, T. E., and the Elphinstone arms are cut before the words, "he being":—

LORD . HAIVE . MERCIE . VPON . HIS . . . .
BEFOR . YIS . LYIS . THOMES . ESPLIN . QVHA .
ENTERIT . IN . SERVICE . VITH . ALEXANDER . LORD .
ELPHINSTOVNE . INTO . YE . ZEIR . OF . GOD . 1580 .
ZEIRIS , ... HE . BEING . OF . YE . AIG . OF FOVR-
TEINE . ZEIRS . AND . REMENIT . IN . HIS . LORD-
SCHIPS . SERVICE , GRIEF . IN , KEILDREME . TO . YE .
ZEIR . OF . GOD . 1636 . ZEIRS.

A slab within a recess-tomb, in the north wall of the old kirk, is embellished with two effigies, in bas relief, representing a knight in armour and a lady, habited in the costume of the period. Upon the outer edge of the stone are these traces of an inscription:—

hīc . iacet . alexr . de . forbes . qvondam . dns . de . bvrchis . et . marjora . . . .

—According to Lumsden's Genealogie of the Houss of Forbes, Alister Cam had two sons, "John Forbes with the sleick hair, called the Whit Laird, and Duncan Forbes of Drumalachie." The first died without male issue. The latter succeeded to the estate of Brux, in which he was followed by his second son, John, "alias the gleyed Laird." John was succeeded by his son ALEXANDER (misnamed *Gilbert* in Douglas' Peerage), recorded in the above quoted inscription, whose wife was MARJORY, 3d daughter of the sixth Lord Forbes, by a second marriage.

The last of the direct lineal descendants of the Forbeses of Brux was JONATHAN, who was out in the '45, and who contrived, by appearing in a variety of menial capacities, after his escape from Culloden, to evade the Royalists. He died about 1802, and was buried, within a walled enclosure, in the *Howff Park* at Brux, which was constructed by his own hands. The site overlooks the Don, and commands an extensive view of the lands of Brux, &c. It is told that when his mother was dying, she remonstrated with her son against being buried in the spot he had selected by assuring him that she would not "lie in that cauld out-o'-the-warld place!" To which Brux is said to have replied, "We'll try ye there first, mither, an' gin' ye winna lie, we'll then shift ye to the auld kirkyard!" He entailed the lands of Brux, &c., upon the second sons of the Lords Forbes. Old

Brux is said to have belonged to the Society of Friends.

It is said that the properties of Brux and Drumallochie came to the Forbeses by one of them marrying the daughter and heiress of Cameron, the previous laird. The Brux tomb at Kildrummy kirk is still known as *The Cameron Aisle*. It is certain that, about 1365, Thomas, Earl of Mar, gave the lands of "Burchis and Wester Drummalochy" to John Camerou, who is described as his shield-bearer, also that Cameron married Ellen Monte Alto, or Mowat, a daughter of Fowlis in Cushnie. Alexander Forbes was designed "de Burchis" before 1409, in which year he had charters of Glencarwe, Glenconro, and Le Ord, from the Earl of Mar.

The top stone and right lintel of a monument (originally within the old kirk), is thus inscribed in raised antique capitals :—

DEFOR . YIS . LYIS . IHON . REID . OF . YE . NEV. MIL . QVHA . DESEIST . M . Z . YE . . . . ZEIR . OF . GOD.

—The face of the stone exhibits two shields: one (flanked by the initials, I. R.), is blank, the other (flanked by the initials, I. R : S. H.), has the Reid arms below the first-mentioned shield, and the carving (in relief) of the upper part of a cherub. Round the margin of this slab, and upon part of its face, is this inscription :—

HEIR . LYIS . ANE . HONORABIL . MAN . ALEX-ANDER . REID . IN . THE . CVLTS ✠ AND . IHONE . REID . OF . THE . NEV . MIL . QVHA . DECEST . THE . ZEIR . OF . GOD . 1563 . AND . IAMES . REID . OF . . . NEV . MIL.

—The estate of Newmill now forms part of the Clova property, and Cults or Culsh is in the same locality. Although the Reids of Newmill were of old standing in the parish, it would appear, if the following *unengraved* epitaph is to be relied upon, that the sayings and doings of at least one of them were unworthy of imitation :—

Here lies the Great Newmill,
Wha liket aye the ither gill;
Aye ready wi' his aith an' curse,
But never cared to draw his purse!'

Reid, which is one of the oldest surnames in the parish, occurs upon many of the tombstones. The following relates to one whose father is said to have been out with the Earl of Mar :—

PETER REID, farmer in Nether Kildrummy, who for 40 years, faithfully discharged the duties of an elder in this parish, and died 11 April 1803, in the 83d year of his age.

—It is told that this worthy was in the custom of remarking in the church, in a half audible and sarcastic tone, when well-dressed females failed to contribute to the offering—" Aye, aye ! a bonny lass, an' a braw plaid ; but nae a bawbee !" Speaking in a half audible tone in Scotch churches about the period referred to was not uncommon. Many ludicrous instances are preserved : One of these may be mentioned. The farmer of Jellybrands, in the Mearns, was an elder of the Sod-Kirk (*v.* p. 80.) Money was then of so great value that a halfpenny was often put into, and a farthing taken out of, "the ladle," by donors. On one occasion, a neighbour of *Jeally* (as the farmer was commonly styled), put in the larger coin into the ladle, and the elder, not giving him time to take out the lesser, his "friend" repeatedly called out, in a low tone, "Jeally ! come back wi' my fardin' !" upon which Jeally curtly and sacrilegiously replied, in the hearing of most of the people in church—" Go to h— !"

The New Mill inscriptions are from an enclosure at the west end of the area of the old kirk. The Lumsdens of Auchindoir and Clova, &c., bury at the east end, and to that family the next five inscriptions relate :—

Before this ston lyes ROBERT LUMSDEN of Cushnay, and JOHN LUMSDEN of Auchnder, his second son, and AGNES GORDON, his spous ; and also CHARLES and MARJORIE LUMSDENS, laufvll son and daughter to John Lumsden and Agnes Gordon. JOHN LUMSDEN dyed Janure 8, 1716, and of age 71 years, 1724 : H. L : K. G. :

Hoc, lector, tumulo tres contumulantur in uno,
Cognati, Mater, Filius, et octù [? atque] Pater.
Mors janua vitæ. [*v.* p. 187.]

D.O.M. H. L : K. G. Befor this ston lyes KATHRIN GORDON, daughter to the laird of Buckie, and spouse to Hary Lumsden of Cushnie, and 5 of her children ; and she depr. this life August the 22,

1733, aged 31 years. Also the said HARRY LUMSDEN of Cushnie died the 8 day of June 1754, in the 69th year of his age.

Befor this stone lyes JAMES LUMSDEN, eldest lawfull son to William Lumsden in Titaboutie, who depr. this life in Nov. 1730, aged 40 years.

—The Titaboutie Lumsdens (v. p. 188), were the progenitors of those of Auchindoir and Clova, &c.

In this ground are deposited the remains of JOHN LUMSDEN of Cushnie, who died 12 June 1795, aged 68; and Mrs ANNE FORBES, his spouse, daughter of John Forbes of New, who died 11 Nov. 1811, aged 76. In testimony of warm affection for their memory, this tablet is erected by their son, John Lumsden, now of Cushnie, 1814.

—It was from the above-named John (who died in 1795), that his cousin Harry, of Kingston, in Jamaica, bought (1782), the estates of Auchindoir and Clova. Harry's name appears in the next inscription, copied from a table-shaped stone:—

The grave of WILLIAM LUMSDEN of Harlaw, who died at Mid Clova, Feb. 1758. RACHEL LUMSDEN, his spouse, daughter of Chas. Lumsden, second son of John Lumsden of Auchindoir: She died at East Clova, Feb. 11, 1788, aged 77. KATHARINE, his daughter, spouse of John Leith, died at West Hills, Feb. 2, 1792; also HARRY LUMSDEN of Auchindoir, who died in April 1796. MARGARET RANNIE, widow of Dr. Jas. Young, R.N., died at Mid Clova, 6 June 1841, aged 76 years. Also HARRY LEITH-LUMSDEN of Auchindoir, youngest son of John Leith and Kathrine Lumsden, who died at Aberdeen, on the 27 March 1844, in the 68th year of his age, and was interred here, 4 April following. (The Lord gave, &c.) Also JANET YOUNG, or DUNCAN, wife of Harry Leith-Lumsden of Auchindoir, who died at Edinburgh, 7 Jan. 1861, aged 73 years, and was interred here on the 16th of same month.

—Harry Leith-Lumsden, who was sometime a carpenter in Aberdeen, and died in 1844, was a sister's son of the first laird, and succeeded to the estates on the death of his cousin, Sir H. Niven-Lumsden (v. below). H. L.-L.'s wife, by whom he left no family, was previously married to Thomas Duncan, an Aberdeen advocate, by whom she had several children: One daughter is the wife of Prof. Piazzi Smith; another (as recorded upon an adjoining tombstone), married T. H. Bastard, younger of Charlton Marshall, Dorsetshire; and a third married Dr Kilgour, Aberdeen. H. Leith-Lumsden, being the last descendant of the original entailer of Auchindoir and Clova, the estates passed, by virtue of the entail, to HENRY, son of Lumsden of Belhelvie and Pitcaple. It is said that this arose from the fact that Mr Lumsden of Belhelvie, advocate in Aberdeen, who made the entail, after having exhausted the line of succession proposed by the entailer, asked of him "who next?" when the laird is said to have answered, "The devil if you like!" "Weel, weel," quo' Belhelvie, "instead o' puttin' in *Auld* Harry, what wad ye think o' puttin' in my son *Young* Harry?" The suggestion being assented to and acted upon, "Young Harry" of Belhelvie, in default of other heirs, succeeded to the estates of Auchindoir and Clova. He died in 1856, aged 72, as the seventh Lumsden tombstone at Kildrummy shows; and his grandson is now the proprietor of the estates.

Sir Harry Niven-Lumsden (above referred to), was buried within a mausoleum, near Lumsden Village, at a place called Chapel House, so named from an Episcopal Church having stood near it. The mausoleum is enclosed by a wall. A slab of white marble, inserted into a massive granite tomb, is thus inscribed:—

Sacred to the memory of Sir HARRY NIVEN-LUMSDEN of Auchindoir, Baronet, who died 15 Dec. 1821, aged 36 years 8 months. Also of his affectionate spouse, HARRIET-CHRISTIAN, eldest daughter of General Hay of Rannes, who died 26 Aug. 1820. Also their three children interred here, viz. MARY-CHRISTIAN NIVEN, who died in Aberdeen, 22 March 1817, aged 3 years 6 months; RACHEL-ANN NIVEN who died at Clova, 3d May 1817, aged 4 months; JOHN-HARRY NIVEN-LUMSDEN who died at Clova, 2d May 1820, aged ten months.

—Sir Harry Niven-Lumsden was the only surviving son of John Niven, sometime of Peebles, near Arbroath (q.v.), and of his wife Rachel Lumsden, sister to Harry Lumsden, who bought Clova and Auchindoir. He was knighted, 5 July 1816, upon presenting a congratulatory address from the county of Aberdeen, when Princess Charlotte and Prince Leopold, were married. In 1821, shortly before Sir H.'s death, through the influence of the Duke of Gordon, he was created a baronet. Leaving no issue, the title became extinct. Sir Harry was succeeded (as above) by his cousin Harry Leith, another sister's son of the original entailer.

Besides the monuments previously noticed at Kildrummy, possibly the oldest inscribed is one initialed M.C., and dated 1679. A table-shaped stone, on east side of burial ground, with a book carved upon the top, covers the grave of Mr JOHN ALEXANDER, who was minister at Kildrummy before and during Mar's rebellion. He offered up the prayer at the raising of the Rebel Standard in 1715, for which he was deposed. The initials J. A. may yet be traced upon the stone. A tablet, built into the west wall of the Elphinstone aisle, bears :—

Before this tomb the Rnd. WILLIAM MILN, minr. of the Gospell at Kildrumie, and HELEN KERR his wife lyes. DAVID MILN, their son, who dyed May 10, 1730, aged 8 years and 7 months.

—Mr M., who was settled at Kildrummy in 1720, and died in 1762, had in 1760 seven children alive, " all above the age of 21 years complete." A table-shaped stone (in front of the above) gives a detailed account of Mr M.'s family. It was erected by his youngest son, DAVID, who was translated from the church of Dallas to that of Edinkillie in 1793. A table-shaped stone bears this epitaph to Mr M.'s successor :—

Here lies the Rev. JAMES McWILLIAM, late minister of the Gospel here, who died April 6, 1771, aged 71 years, 11 months, and 6 days :—

Rev^d. and grave, he Preached heaven's King,
Because he knew it was a weighty thing ;
And at his hearers, as he aim'd the dart,
You'd well perceive it from his heart.
Now called Home, a Faithful serv^t., lov'd
Of his Great Master, and by him approv'd,
Poses^d. of joys eternal, and above,
He Sings, he Shines, he Reigns, where all is love.
No pain is y^r., no tears flow from his eyes,
His Master purchas'd, he Enjoys the prize.

Done by the care of John, James, and W^m. Homs, his nephews.

To Mr. McWilliam succeeded Mr ROBERT LUMSDEN, who died in Jan. 1795. To him there is no monument : upon that of his successor :—

To the memory of the Rev. JOHN HARPER, who discharged with fidelity the office of a minister for the space of 25 years, first in the parish of Leslie, afterwards in Kildrummy, and died 23d April 1807, in the 63d year of his age. Also of his sisters, CHRISTIAN HARPER, who died 1796, aged 47 ; and also of MARGARET HARPER, another sister, who died in Nov. 1837, aged 86.

Mr BENJAMIN MERCER, previously at Forbes, followed Mr Harper. He died in 1815, and was buried at Towie. Three years before Mr M.'s death, Mr ALEX. REID was appointed assistant and successor; and to the latter, who died in 1849, in his 67th year, succeeded his son-in-law, the Rev. John Christie, D.D., Inspector of Schools under Dr Milne's Bequest. Dr Christie's father was 52 years schoolmaster at Kildrummy, in which office he was succeeded by his youngest son—four elder sons having been educated for the church.

A flat stone, embellished with carvings of a death's head and cross-bones, bears this inscription, recently revised :—

1724. R. D. Mors janua vitæ. D. D.

Here lyes MICHAEL DUMBAR, who died Decr. the 9, 1722, and of age 100 years, and ARTHUR, his son. JRM. D : A. D. D : AS. D.

—According to tradition, Michael Dunbar was a sort of brigand, who lived by murder and plunder ; but inquiry shows that this was not the fact. Being a man of great bodily strength and daring, he was made Captain of the parish of Kildrummy, or the leader of those who, as was essential in these times, combined to protect their lives and property against the incursions of the Cateran, or Highland robbers, in the course of which, Michael had doubtless led a rough enough life. Michael, who was a Roman Catholic, and a keen supporter of the Stuarts, dwelt in the Den of Kildrummy ; and it is told that, when upon his death-bed, Mr Miln, the parish minister, paid him a visit; and, while exhorting Michael upon the rough life he had led, and that he had much need to repent of his sins, Michael replied—" Repent o' my sins! What the deevil cou'd I dee whan thae Heelan' thieves cam' doun to take awa' our nowt?" "Ah, but Michael," said the parson, "that 'll a' stand against them at the day o' Judgment." "Weel, weel," quo' Michael, "ilka chiel' 'll get's ain then!" And, grasping a dirk which lay beside him in the bed, he exclaimed, to the terror of the minister, who, it is said, made a quick retreat— "That's the hand, an' that's the dirk that loot oot fifteen sauls o' them a' in ae nicht!" Upon an adjoining slab:—

Hear lyes ALEXANDER DUNBAR, who lived in Miltoun of Neu Mill, who dayed 1729, aged 43; and his spons HELEN GIBON, lawful daughter to John Gibon, sometime farmer in Newbeggin, and her age is 74. She dayed 1761. Don by the care of James, John, and George Dunbars.

Upon a flat stone :—

George Cattenach in Bridgend of Mossat, and Helen Gordon, his spouse, has placed this stone here in memory of their deceased children, vizt., ANN, aged 22 years; MARY, aged 18 years; JEAN, aged 13 months. And also GEORGE GIBB, their grandchild, aged 13 months. The above-named GEORGE CATTENACH died 28 May 1821, aged 88 years; and also HELEN GORDON died 25 Dec. 1814, aged 74.

—Helen Gordon's father, who was a son of Dalpersie, or Terpersie, in Tullynessle, was out in the '45. He was long a fugitive; but was at last captured by the Royalists while hiding in an aperture in his own house. Being identified, or, in other words, betrayed by, it is said, his neighbour, the minister of Kinnethmont, he was taken to Carlisle, where he was executed along with other ten rebels, 15 Nov. 1746. Helen Gordon was the grandmother of the Rev. Harry Stuart, minister of Oathlaw, who has done so much to improve the condition of agricultural labourers, &c.

In memory of DAVID HUNTER, sometime farmer at Barns, Deskry, thereafter brewer in Aberdeen, who died 1 Jan. 1816, aged 59 years. This stone is erected by Mrs Helen Hunter, wife of Mr Charles Macdonald, banker in Huntly, Mary, his daughter, and John Hunter, Writer to the Signet, his son, 1828.

It will be seen that the united ages of the three persons next recorded amount to the uncommon period of 255 years:—

Here lies JEROM RITCHIE, sometime farmer in Hardhuncher, who died 15 March 1798, aged 99; and also his spouse MARY JEALS, who died 2 Aug. 1796, aged 84 yrs. And also JOHN RITCHIE, who died 20 May 1817, aged 72. Done by the care of their son, Alexander Ritchie, Esq., in the Island of Jamaica.

To the memory of WILLIAM SHERIFF, farmer in Upper Whidlment, parish of Auchindore, who died in the year 1762, and was buried in this place. And of his wife BARBARA CLARK, who died in the year 1773, and was also buried in this place. And of their son ALEXANDER SHERIFF, Esquire, who died in the year 1801, in the Island of Jamaica. To fulfil whose intention this stone was erected by the Rev. Dr James Sherriffs, Aberdeen.

—The last-named in the above inscription was minister of St Nicholas from 1778 to 1814; and having been made residuary legatee to his kinsman "of Jamaica," Dr Sherriffs was, in consequence, proprietor of 163 Negro slaves at the time he was Moderator of the General Assembly of the Kirk of Scotland. The Dr's brother Andrew, a bookseller in Aberdeen, was author of a volume of meritorious Scottish Poems.

ALEXANDRO LEITH, V.D.P., Alex. f. viro docto, benevolo, probo, qui in Schola Grammat. Abredon., ubi annos amplius XXI juventutem literis humanioribus felicissime instituerat, labori ut semper intentus, XV Jan. A.C. MDCCXCIX, æt. LIII, subito, cheu! conticuit concidit, hæredes merito H.M.P.

[To the memory of ALEXANDER LEITH, preacher of the Gospel (son of Alexander), a learned, benevolent, and worthy man, who, while engaged in work with his habitual energy in the Grammar School of Aberdeen, where for upwards of 21 years he had been a most successful instructor of youth, suddenly, alas! dropped down, 15 Jan. 1799, in his 53d year. His heirs erected this well-deserved monument.]

The ruins of the Castle of Kildrummy are the chief objects of interest in the parish, engravings of which will be found in Pennant, Cordiner, Grose, and Billings, &c. According to Gordon's Genealogy of the Earls of Sutherland, Gilbert, Bishop of Caithness (1222-45), "built the castle and fortresse of Kildrume in Marr, with seaven tours within the precinct of the said castle." This assertion is not supported by any authority; and it is generally supposed that Kildrummy is of an earlier date, also that it was the residence of David Earl of Huntingdon, lord of the Garioch, brother of William the Lion. Earl David's second daughter was grandmother of Robert the Bruce, by which marriage, it is believed, Kildrummy came to the Bruces; and it was through this relationship that Bruce claimed the Crown. Bruce himself married a daughter of Donald Earl of Mar to his first wife; and Gartney, Earl of Mar, married a sister of the Bruce. It was probably in this way that the old Earls of Mar became possessed of Kildrummy Castle, which was long their chief seat, as well as the capital of Mar and the Garioch.

Like the architectural features of this grand ruin, its historical associations have been often described. Without dwelling upon these, it may be briefly remarked that Edward I. rested at Kildrummy and received homages in 1296; and that it was an asylum for Bruce's Queen and other ladies after the battle of Methven, soon after which it was captured (by betrayal some say), and the brave defender, Sir Nigel Bruce, taken to Berwick, where he was beheaded. It was besieged by the Earl of Athol in 1335; and in 1361, owing to some quarrel between the Earl of Mar and the king, the castle was captured by David II. In the early part of the following century, it was stormed by the son of the Wolf of Badenoch, who not only took the place, but obtained the hand of the widowed Countess—by " violence or persuasion"—together with a charter of all her possessions in favour of himself and his own heirs, to the exclusion of those of the Countess. After this, in 1412, it was stormed and taken by Sir Robert Erskine, who considered himself the legal heir to the Earldom of Mar. The castle was also besieged in the time of Lord Elphinstone by young Strachan of Lynturk, who, besides hereschip, was charged with committing slaughter at the siege.

As already seen, Kildrummy Castle belonged to, and was occupied by the Lords Elphinstone from about 1507-8 until 1626, when it was restored to the Erskines as nearest lawful heirs to Countess Isobel. It was from Kildrummy that John, Earl of Mar, dated some of his manifestoes regarding the rising of the '15, the year after which saw him deprived of his titles and his estates. But, if not restored, the castle must have been in a sadly dilapidated condition in 1715; for, about twenty years previously, it is stated that, "by the insurrection of the heighlanders," the castle, then "surrounded with great walls wherin their was much building, [was] totallie burnt and destroyed;" and, in estimating the extent of the damage, it is added that "the repairation of it cannot be under nyne hundred pound sterling."

Besides the castle, where it is said there was once a burial place, Kildrummy contains a number of interesting points for the antiquarian. Of the castle cemetery, possibly the coffin slab, with ornamental cross, which lies on the north side of the ruins, is the only remaining trace. It is a good example of its kind; but a short slab in the parish churchyard, upon which a wheel cross, and a pair of scissors are represented, is probably the more interesting of the two. Numerous specimens of flint arrow heads and stone axes have been found in the parish, also stone coffins, &c. The Picts' houses in the muirs of Kildrummy have been described at length by the late Professor Stuart of Aberdeen, and are still worthy of being visited.

Although no trace now remains, there was a burgh of barony at Kildrummy, which contained persons designed "burgesses," so early as 1403, and which had probably arisen, as did most of our towns, under the care of the lords of the castle, and been situated almost under its shadow. Two consecrated wells indicate the sites of old religious houses—that of S. MACARIUS, on the east of the parish, is in Macker's Haugh; and another on the west is at Chapel RONALD (? *S. Ronan*) in Glenkindie. The Templeton, near the church, was held under the Knights' Templars.

Fearn.

(S. NINIAN, BISHOP.)

THE church of Fearne, in the diocese of Dunkeld, was a prebend of that cathedral. A piece of ground near the kirk is called *Dunkeld Riggs*. When improving the public road which passes the church, some years ago, human remains and an urn were discovered in a coffin, which was hewn out of the solid rock (Proceedings of the So. Antiq. of Scotland, vol. iii. p. 80.)

The bell, which was lately cracked, and replaced by one uninscribed, bears:—

IC . BEN . GHEGOTEN . INT . IAER . M. D. VI.

The church and burial-ground are situated in the middle of a romantic dell. Within an enclosure, on the west side of the graveyard, a monument bears:—

Sacred to the memory of THOMAS BINNY, Esq., who died March 5, 1843.

—Mr Binny, who died at his residence of Maulesden, near Brechin, bought the barony of Fearn about 1836, which, by marriage with his daughter Elizabeth, came to the late Hon. WILLIAM MAULE, third son of the late Lord Panmure.

The oldest tombstone inscriptions at Fearn are not quite legible. One, upon which a human figure is represented climbing a ladder, guarded by angels blowing trumpets, bears:—

By power of Christ, and trumpet sound,
Our bodies shall be raised from ground.

Upon a table-shaped stone:—

Here lyes JANNET LYON, who dyed in the year of God, 1687. JEAN, and MARGARET CRAIG, children to George Craig, and Beatrix Black:—

Blest is the man, who, since he naked came
Into the world, and must return the same.
Doth by the shelter of his quick fire,
Make food and raiment crub his vast desyre.
For worlds, empires, and courts, and crowns, and kyngs,
Are rich in cares, when rest hath better things.

But peace of conscience makes the soul rejoyce,
More than the world, and al her fading toyes.
For vhoe belive earth shal not stil enfold
Us in her arms, that wer too base a hold,
For any in whose soul the sprit of grace
Hath made his mansion, or a duelling place ;
For he who was dead is alive, and shall,
To us be Alpha, and Omega still.

Remember man as thow goes by,
Behold yowth here intombd doth ly,
Could youth or years a purchase make,
Or strength from death a release take,
Then they as thow had lived to say,
So youth as age may soon decay.

Trust not to yowth, though thou be strong,
Thy years therby for to prolong ;
But know, O man, thy frailtie,
For therof they examples be,
Who in their prime al pulled away,
So youth as age may soon decay.

JOHN REID, blacksmith, d. 1702, a. 70 :—

Full seventy years he liv'd upon this earth,
He liv'd to dye ; the end of life is death :
Here he was smith six lustres and three more,
The third three wanted, it had two before.

ISABELLA BLACK, d. 1723, a. 15 years :—

O death, o grave, why so severe ?
Even youth may se thy look austere ;
This young maid did by living die,
By death she lives eternilly.

ANN THOMSON, wife of John Black, tenant, Vain, died 1810, a. 51 :—

The loving wife, the steady friend,
Beneath is lowly laid ;
Some ponderings at Affection's call,
May not be ill repaid.
Does self control thy purpose rein ?
Benevolence warm thy heart ?
Or hope divine such transports raise,
As heavenly joys impart ?
Such graces should thy mind adorn,
Such hope inspire thy breast ;
Like her's thy life shall yield content,
Thy death like her's be bleast.

—The above lines are upon the back of the stone. Upon the front is the verse, "A few short years of evil past," &c. Blacks have farmed in various parts of Fearn for many generations; one of them, DAVID, servant to the Rev. Mr Wemyss, became tenant of a portion of the farm of Dubb in 1731. Upon a head-stone :—

1826.—Erected by James Deuchar of Demarara, in memory of his father, GEORGE DEUCHAR of Deuchar, who died 20th January 1802, aged 55 years; and of his mother, ELIZABETH PETER, who died 27th February 1823, aged 65 years.

—Tradition says that the Deuchars received the lands from which they assumed their surname, and the designation "of that ilk," for services performed at the battle of Barry in 1010! Record shows that Deuchars held the lands of Deuchar as vassals of Lindsay of Glenesk, lord of Ferne, in 1379. Deuchars continued in possession of Deuchar until about the year 1815, when their male representative sold the property, and went to New Zealand.

JAMES WATSON, 40 yrs. tenant of Balquhadlie, d. at Ledmore, in 1835, a. 81; MARY WEBSTER, his wf., d. 1818, a. 49 :—

When mortals to the eve of life draw near,
And death's dark shades upon their eyelids close,
The wise through faith in Christ are void of fear;
How calmly sink the righteous to repose.
While here envelop'd in the grave's dark night,
The body mixes with its kindred clay,
The soul unfetter'd soars to realms of light,
To live in sunshine of eternal day.

—Mr John Watson, lately farmer at Ledmore, in Menmuir, the only survivor of a family of twelve, six of whom died in the flower of their days, erected this monument, and wrote the above lines. Mr W. is author of several pieces of poetry: among these is Whistlin' Tam, published in the 5th series of "Whistle Binkie."

GEO. RICKARD, d. 1840, a. 90; his nephew, JAMES RICKARD, farmer, Windsor, d. 1842, a. 48, " whose generous heart ever rejoiced to relieve the wants of the needy" :—

Death daily walks his active round,
On time's uncertain stage ;
He brakes up every fallow ground,
Spares neither sex nor age.

A rude boulder, with a hole in it, very much resembling a field-gate post, was taken out of a grave some years ago, near the spot where it now stands. It is said to mark the grave of JOHN MACINTOSH, sometime farmer of Leadendrie, who did good service to the district in the fight which occurred at Sauchs, in Lethnot, between the men of Fearn and a gang of Cateran, when the latter were defeated, and deprived of their plunder. An account of this affray, as well as of the historical and antiquarian peculiarities of Fearn, will be found in the Land of the Lindsays.

The ancient lords of Fearn were the Montealts, or Mowats, who had a grant of the barony from William the Lion. The Lindsays followed the Montealts, and to the Lindsays succeeded Carnegie of Southesk, the last-named of whom held the barony until the attainder in 1716.

The castle of Vayne (now in ruins), overlooked the river Noran. It was built or improved by the Earls of Southesk. Three door or window lintels, preserved in the farm offices, bear respectively the following legends and dates :—

DISCE . MEO . EXEMPLO . FORMOSIS . POSSE . CARERE.
[Learn by my example to be able to want the beautiful.]
. . . . . PLACITIS . ABSTINVISSE . BONIS .
ANNO . DOM . 1678.
[. . . . . to have abstained with a good will.]
NON . SI . MALE . NVNC . ET . SIC . ERAT .
ANNO . DOM . 1678.
[If it is ill with me now it was not so formerly.]

—The first of the above inscriptions is carved upon a stone on which are an earl's coronet, and the monogram, E. R. S.,—i.e., Robert Earl of Southesk, whose lady, as one of the historical characters of the time of Charles II., occupies a conspicuous place in the Memoirs of Count Grammont. A beautiful monogram of the same Peer is built into the manse at Fearn, also some other carved stones relating to the Carnegies.

In the manse of Fearn were born JAMES, and Dr H. W. TYTLER. Both have acquired places in the literary annals of their country: the first, known by the soubriquet of *Balloon*, was a ready and effective writer in prose and verse, and the latter translated the poems of Callimachus from the Greek, &c.

The principal bridges in Fearn are those which cross the Noran at Courthill and at Wellford. A bridge appears to have been erected at the first of these places about 1620, and at the latter about 1807. The Cruick, which rises in Fearn parish, and joins the North Esk near the kirk of Stracathro, is crossed by a number of stone bridges. All are of comparatively modern erection.

St Andrews.

(S. ANDREW, APOSTLE.)

ANCIENTLY called *Kil-ma-Lemnoc*, ST ANDREWS was a mensal church of the cathedral of Elgin, as was also that of OGSTON, on the opposite side of Loch Spynie. Both kirks were served by one vicar. There was a chapel at Inch, on the north side of the parish; and the kirk of Kilma-Lemnoc stood originally at Forrester's Seat (Shaw's Moray.)

In 1567, Alexander Leslie was "exhorter" at St Andrews kirk, with 40 merks a year. Subsequently, in 1574, " Elgin and St Androis kirk" were served by one minister. There was also one reader for both places. The minister had, along with the kirk lands, £115 11s 1½d Scots, the reader £40 Scots. The parishes of St Andrews and Lhanbryde were united in 1782, about which time the two old kirks were demolished, and a centrical one erected about midway between the original sites.

The burial-place, which is surrounded by a stone wall, occupies a rising ground upon the west bank of the Lossie. The old font is broken in three pieces. Two enclosures, one at the east end of the kirk, the other near the south-west corner of the cemetery, built up on all sides, belonged to Inneses. The first, called the Leuchars Aisle, contains two slabs: one bears the Innes arms, and this inscription :—

HEIR . LYES . ANE . HONORABLE . MAN . ALEXANDER . INNES . MATHI , MILNE , WHO . DEPARTIT NOVEMBER . THE . FIRST . 1636.

—This is probably the tombstone of Alex. Innes, who witnesses a grant to his brother-german, John Innes of Leuchars, of the lands of Corskie, Mathie Mill, and three parts of Garmocht, in 1587 (Ane Account of the Familie of Innes, Spalding Club edit., p. 148.) It is from the Leuchars branch that Professor Cosmo Innes is descended (*supra*, p. 78), by whom the interesting family history, just quoted, was edited.

The second stone in the Leuchars aisle also presents the family arms, with A.I : I.K. in monogram, and this inscription :—

ALEXR. INNES, IEAN KINNAIRD—1638.

—These were Alexander Innes, son of George Innes of Calcots, and his wife Jean Kynaird, a daughter of Cowbin. They were married about 1655, when Innes received from his wife's mother a " present portion of 4000 merks, with that part of the stell fishing callit the Eath stell."

Upon a marble slab, set in freestone, within the area of the old kirk :—

In this church lie interred Mr JOHN PATERSON, once minr. of Dipple, and 47 years minr. of this parish, who died April 20, 1778, in the 81st year of his age, and 51st of his ministry. And HELEN GRANT his spouse, died Jan. 5, 1769, aged 76 years. Love to God and charity to men, were their prevailing dispositions. He was fervent in the work of the Gospel, and she was a pious, but humble Christian. This mont. is erected to their memory by their son Mr Robert Paterson, minr. of New Spynie.

Upon two flat slabs in burial ground:—

Here . lyes . IESPAR . WINCHESTER, . who . died . in . Spynie. 27 . of . October . 1688 . also . IAMES . SIM , who . died . at . Pitgavnie . May . 1658 . WILLIAM . WINCHESTER . his . son . Worship . Him . that . made . the . Heaven . the . Earth . & . the . Sea . & . the . fountain . of . water . MARGARET . SIM . his . spouse . I.W ; M.S.

Heir lyes AGNES GEDDES, spous to Iohn Grant in Kirkhill, who departed the 20 day of May 1-81. I.G : A.G.

From a table shaped stone :—

Here lies interr'd the body of ANDREW GILL, late schoolmaster at St Andrew's, who departed this life, Sep. 5, 1791, aged 66 years. He was an affectionate husband, a tender parent, supported the noble character of an honest man, lived much respected, and died much lamented by his family and friends.

Lhanbryde.

(S. BRIDGET, VIRGIN.)

IN Bishop Bricius' great charter of the foundation of the canonries at Spynie (1208-15), mention is made of the assignation of the Chantors' church of *Lamnabride*, with a davoch of land. In 1225, when Bishop Andrew granted the manor of Lamanbride, with its pertinents, and the davoch of Petnassare, to Robert Hood, and Matilda his spouse, the manse and kirk davoch were reserved. The next mention of Lhanbryde is in 1280, when Malcolm of Moravia, knight, granted a charter of his whole lands of Lamabride to his son William. In 1529 (Douglas Peer.), James Stewart, Earl of Moray, had charters of Cookstoun, Longbride, &c., from his father James IV.

In 1574, the churches of Langbride and Urquhart were served by one minister, and each locality had its own reader. The burial place, which occupies a rising ground, is near the middle of the village of Lhanbryde, one of the loveliest hamlets in the north.

The Inneses of Coxton buried within the choir of the old kirk, and a recess tomb, which contains the recumbent and well-proportioned effigy of a knight in armour, is still preserved at Lhanbryde. On the left is a freestone slab (adorned with the Innes arms, also a skull and cross bones), upon which is this inscription :—

HIC . REQVIESCIT . IN . DNO . ALEX . INNES . COKSTOVNS . EX . ILLVSTRI . FAMILIA . INNERMARKIE . ORIVNDVS . QVI . FATIS . CONCESSIT . G . OCTOB . -612 . SVE . VERO . ÆTATIS . 80.

[Here rests in the Lord, ALEX. INNES of Cokston, descended from the illustrious Invermarkie family, who died 5 Oct. -612 in the 80th year of his age.]

—This old man was the father of John Innes of Haltoun, whose son James, against the "advyis" of his father and grandfather, "unduitfully coupled him selff in marriage with Mariory Innes, dochter to Alexr. Innes of Cotts," an act which so much offended his "guidsir and father" that they mutually bound themselves to "seclud the said James during all the dayes of the said Mariorey's lyftyme, and the airs quhatsumever gotten, or to be gotten betwix them, for ever fra all benefit of inheritance that may appertein to them ather be birth richt, tailzie, succession, or ony other provysion quhatsumever." John Innes of Coxton appears to have died between August 1634, and July 1635. He was probably succeeded by Alexander, who married a daughter of Gight. A slab (with the Innes and Gordon arms), is thus inscribed :—

HIC . REQVIESCIT . MARIA . GORDON . FILIA . . . . EQVITIS . DE . GIGHT . QVE . FATIS . CONCESIT . 20 . AVGVSTI . AÑO . . . 1647 . . . . IN . PIAM . . . . . . MEMORIAM . HOC . MONVMENTVM . CONSTRVEDVM . ALEXANDR . INNES . DE . COXTON . MARITVS . CVRAVIT.

[Here rests MARY GORDON, daughter of Sir . . . . of Gight, who died 20 Aug. 1647, to whose pious memory her husband, Alex. Innes of Coxton, caused this monument to be erected.]

—It was in the time of the above-named Alexander of Coxton (c. 1635) that his brother, Innes of Leuchars, and other members of "the clan," were ordered to restore the property of the "umquhil Mr John Innes of Coxtoun," to his executors, also the charter kists of Coxton and Balvenie, as well as to pay 1000 merks for the "wrong and insolence committed in the taking of the place of Coxtoun."

There were Inneses of that Ilk (a property in the adjoining parish of Urquhart), from the time of William the Lion, and from Walter of Innes, who died in the time of Alexander II., have descended the various branches of Invermarkie, Balvenie, Leuchars, &c. It was through the marriage of Sir James Innes of Innes, in 1666, with Margaret, third daughter of Harry, Lord Ker, that their great-grandson, Sir James Innes-Northcliffe, bart., became, by decision of the House of Lords in 1812, fifth Duke of Roxburghe.

A flat stone, with carvings of the blacksmith's crown and hammer, bears :—

Heir lyes the . . . . . honest man called DAVID RUSSEL in Longbry, who died in yeir 1665.

The following inscription contains the somewhat odd, but not unique notice, of a man erecting a monument to his own memory :—

This is the burial place of PATRICK PAUL, who lived in Darklin, and died 16 . . Jan. 17th, and his spouse GRIZEL MAVER, and their children James Paul who placed this stone in memory of his father and of himself, who dyed Nouer. ii. 1756, and ELIZABETH MILN, his spouse, who dyed the 29 of Septr. aged 66, the year 1771.

Here lys the body of ELIZABETH WALTON, first beloved spouse to William Tulloch, merchant in Elgin, who dyed Nov. 23, 1763, justlly lamented by all hir acquaintances :—

In God I liv'd, in him I died,
I live with him, tho' dead I ly.

In area of old kirk :—

This stone is placed here by Mrs Ann Macfarlane to the memory of, and over the remains of her husband, the Rev. THOMAS MACFARLANE, late minister of Lhanbryde, who died November 1781 ; and of their son, the Rev. THOMAS MACFARLANE, late minister of Edinkillie, who died on the 7th August 1827.

Within an enclosure :—

Sacred to the memory of ELIZABETH TOD, relict of the late Rev. James McLean, minister of Urquhart, who died in Elgin, on the 25th day of Jan. 1851, aged 75 years.

—This was the second wife of Mr M'Lean; his first wife, whose name was also Elizabeth Tod, died at Keith (v. p. 167.)

Near the south-west corner of burial-ground :—

Sacred to the memory of JOHN SADLER, who died on the 24th of Dec. 1858, in his 65th year. He was for many years the faithful servant of James, fifth Earl of Fife, by whom this stone was placed. St John xi. 25, 26 verses.

The most remarkable object of antiquity in the district of St Andrews-Lhanbryde is the Tower of Coxton. Although a niche over the doorway presents the family arms and the date of 1644, &c., possibly the tower was erected by the laird, Alexander, who died in -612. It is certainly older than 1644. As a building, Coxton partakes much of the characteristics of the Border towers, and consists of four storeys, with a high-pitched roof, and turrets at the angles. It is entirely fire-proof, no timber having been used in its construction, with the exception of the two doors. One door is upon the ground floor, and the other, which is reached by a ladder, is upon the second flat. Both are guarded by massive iron yetts.

"Not a crack (says Billings, who gives two views of this interesting tower) is visible ; and we predict that until the stone disintegrates, the Castle will stand. Within the rooms is a singular provision for communication, perfectly independent of the staircase. In the centre of each floor is a square stone, fitted into a groove. These stones, when lifted up, show an opening from the summit to the base of the tower, and by the aid of a rope and pulley, the requirements of its inmates might be attended to, and all the inconveniences of carriage up the narrow staircase avoided."

It need scarcely be added that, although "lifts" are of comparatively late introduction into large mansion-houses and hotels in this country, the contrivance at Coxton shows that the value of them was long ago discovered and appreciated by our ancestors.

———o———

Rathven.

(S. PETER, APOSTLE.)

THE churches of *Rotht-uen* and *Freschane*, both in the diocese of Aberdeen, were annexed by Bishop William in 1483.

The kirk of Freschane, Forscan, Farskin, or Faskin, was dedicated to the VIRGIN MARY. It stood in a field about a mile to the west of the town of Cullen, where *the site* is still pointed out. The three churches of Rathven, Dundurcas (now part of Rothes), and Bellie, were served by one minister in 1574. It is stated at the same period that " Forsken neidis na reidare."

A freestone slab, built into a wall at Farskane, initialed E. H., and dated 1677, presents a carving of the arms of Hamilton of Raglen—a family, so far as I know, that never had any connection with the locality, unless it may have been that a laird of Farskane married a Hamilton. Gordons were designed of Farskane in 1649, how long before, or afterwards, I am not aware; but one of them, who joined Mar's rebellion, is said to have found a safe retreat for some time in a cave, which still bears his name, among the cliffs by the seashore.

In early times, a family was named FARSKIN, and designed of that Ilk. Farskin, or Faskin, is still a surname in Banffshire. The property, once owned by Hay of Rannes, now belongs to the Earl of Seafield.

The present church of Rathven, built in 1794, is a plain house, near the old burial-ground, about a mile from the populous village of Buckie. About the year 1660 there was "a good church, with a square steeple, and an aisle for the Hays of Ranis." The nave of the old church is used as the burial-place of heritors and others. The aisle for the Hays of Rannes, or the south aisle of the kirk, which is still in good repair, bears this account of its erection upon a slab on the right of the entrance :—

IN . DEI . HONOREM . ECCLESIÆ . VSVM . ET
IA . HAYI . DE . RANNES . KA . DVNBAR . EI'
CONIVGIS . EORV . POSTERORV . GRATIAM . FIT
HÆC . AVSTRALIOR . ÆDIOLA . AN . DNI . 1612.

[To the honour of God, for the use of the church, and in grateful remembrance of JAMES HAY of Rannes, KATHERINE DUNBAR, his spouse, and their descendants, this more southern chapel was erected in 1612.]

A marble monument (with the family arms quartered, and a crescent, over all, indicating the descent of the Hays from a second son, also the motto, SPARE NOUGHT), contains this notice of the Hays:—

To the memory of the HAYS of Rannes and Lenplum. 1421, Sir WILLIAM HAY of Locharat was ancestor of the noble family of Tweeddale : 1474, he married a second wife ALICIA, daughter of Sir William Hay of Errol, by whom he had Sir EDMUND HAY of Lenplum and Morum, who married MARGARET KERR, and had DUGALD HAY of Lenplum, who married HELEN COCKBURN, daughter of Cockburn of Newhall. Their children were, 1520 (I.), EDMUND HAY of Lenplum; (II.), GEORGE HAY of Rannes; (III.), WILLIAM HAY of Edderston ; (IV.), ANDREW HAY of Ranfield. 1562, The above GEORGE HAY was Superintendent of Glasgow and Aberdeen, Secretary to the Privy Council in the year 1567, and Rector of Rathven. He added the lands of Faskin and Findachy to his patrimonial inheritance. He also acquired the lands of Edderston, which he bestowed on his brother WILLIAM, and the lands of Ranfield, which he gave to his brother ANDREW. 1567, The above GEORGE HAY married MARRIOT, daughter of HENDERSON of Fordel, of whom there were (I.), GEORGE, who died unmarried in the year 1586. 1603 (II.), JAMES HAY of Rannes and Lenplum, who married Katherine, daughter of Dunbar of Grange. Their children were (I.), GEORGE HAY of Rannes ; (II.), JAMES HAY of Muldavit; (III.), JOHN HAY of Langsbed; (IV.), ANDREW ; (V.), WILLIAM ; (VI.), KATHARINE; (VII.), ANNE. The above JAMES HAY of Rannes succeeded to the estate of Lenplum in consequence of the failure of heirsmale of William Hay of Lenplum, as is instructed by a deed recorded in the Books of Session, 28th of May 1599 ; but afterward sold this property to Sir William Hay, a younger son of the family of Tweeddale. 1630, In the estate of Rannes he was succeeded by his eldest son GEORGE, who married

AGNES, daughter of Guthrie of Guthrie, Bishop of Murray, and had, 1645, JAMES HAY of Rannes, who married MARGARET, daughter of Gordon of Park. Their children were (I.), JAMES HAY of Rannes; (II.), ANDREW HAY of Mountblairy, of whom the Hays of Cocklaw and Faichfield are descended. 1684, The above JAMES HAY of Rannes married MARGARET, daughter of Gordon of Glengerrack. Their children were (I.), CHARLES HAY of Rannes, born 1688, and died in London in 1751; (II.), JAMES HAY, who married HELEN LAUDER, dowager Lady Banff, of whom were JAMES, CHARLES, and WILLIAM HAYS. 1710, The above CHARLES HAY of Rannes married HELEN, only child of Dr Andrew Fraser, Inverness. Their children were (I.), ANDREW HAY of Rannes; (II.), ALEXANDER HAY, died 1771, aged 47; (III.), MARY, married to Leith of Leithhall; (IV.), KATHERINE, married to Gordon of Sheilagreen; (V.), CLEMENTINA, married to Duff of Whitehill; (VI.), MARGARET, married to Russell of Montcoffer; (VII.), JANE, unmarried.

1789, The above ANDREW HAY died unmarried, the 29th of August 1789, aged 76, and his remains are deposited in this aisle. Mr HAY was distinguished for those qualities which add grace and dignity to human nature. Possessed of true piety, he was an affectionate kinsman, a steady friend, a pleasant companion, and an honest man. The urbanity of his manners, and the kindness of his disposition, were universally felt and acknowledged. He made use of his fortune with that happy prudence which enabled him, while alive, to share enjoyment with his friends, and to leave to his successor an ample and independent inheritance. Rev. xiv. 13.

—Sir William Hay, sheriff of Peeblesshire, 1420, founded the collegiate church of Yester, for a provost, six prebendaries, and two singing boys. His first wife was a daughter and coheiress of Giffard of Yester, and their grandson, ennobled as Lord Hay of Yester, was ancestor of the present Marquis of Tweeddale. Douglas, in his Peerage, says that Sir William died soon after 1420; and that by his 2d wife Alicia, daughter of Sir *Thomas* Hay of Errol, he had a son, EDMUND, *who married a daughter of Maxwell of Tealing*, in Angus; also a daughter who became the wife of Macdowel of Makerston—discrepancies between the above inscription and Douglas which some one acquainted with the matter may be able to rectify. Possibly the male line of the Hays of Rannes failed in Charles, who died in 1736; at least he left a daughter, MARY, who became the wife of John Leith of Leith Hall, in Kinnethmont. Rannes has long been a portion of the Seafield estate; but the patronage of the church of Rathven belongs to Leith-Hay.

The area, or nave of the kirk is partly enclosed, and contains a number of monuments. In the western part is the following:—

JAMES GORDON of Glastecrum, dyed Febry. the 20th, 1783, aged 64.

—The Gordons, who were designed of Glastecrum, or Clystirim, before 1662, were descended from a second son of the Huntly family. One of them (who was the laird of the period), became R. C. Bishop of the district; another has a tomb at St Ninian's, or The Enzie (*v*. p. 278.) Within an adjoining, but separate enclosure at Rathven:—

This stone was erected by Katherine Duncan to the memory of ALEXANDER INNES, Capt. of the Enzie Volunteers, her husband, who died at Loanhead the 15 Sept. 1799, and is interred here, aged 45.

—His widow died in 1851, aged 85. Within the more easterly part of the nave are the next two inscriptions:—

Here lyes WILLIAM GORDON of Farskan, who departed this life the XVI. day of June MDCXCII. Memento mori.

The burial grounds of the Families of FARSKIN and FINDOCHTY were enclosed by William Gordon-Duff of Eden, and William Dunbar of Nether Buckie, descendants of these families, A.D. 1799.

—Gordon (*v*. p 273), who was designed of Farskan in 1649, married Helen, daughter of Duff of Braco, and niece to the first Earl of Fife. The remains of the castle of Findochty (which property belonged at one time to the Hays of Rannes) now form part of the buildings at the farm of Mains of Findochty. A well off Findochty, called *Samel Figgot* (?) is covered by the sea at high tides, at low water it is a fresh water spring.

An enclosure, on S.E. of the Rannes aisle, contains tablets, from which the next three inscriptions are copied. The first is upon a freestone slab :—

Memoriæ charissimæ suæ conjugis ELIZABETHÆ GORDON, quæ decessit die decimo quinto Januarij calendas, 1725, ætatis suæ 31, monumentum hoc extrui curavit maritus superstes Alexander Gordon de Cairnfield, Signeto Regio Scriba.

[To the memory of his dearly beloved wife, ELIZABETH GORDON, who died Dec. 18, 1725, in the 31st year of her age. Her surviving husband, Alexander Gordon of Cairnfield, W.S., caused this monument to be erected.]

—The above lady was heiress of Cairnfield. Her husband (by whom she had three daughters), was of the Gordons of Dykeside, in Morayshire. He married a second time, and had (says Burke) two sons, John his successor, and James, late of Roseburn (v. BANFF), to the last of whom the next quoted inscription appears to refer :—

Sacred to the memory of JAMES GORDON, second son of ALEXANDER GORDON of Cairnfield, who died at Banff on the 1 January 1813, aged 77; and JANET MERCER, his spouse, who died at Nairn, on the 24 May 1842, aged 84. This tablet is placed by Adam-Garden Gordon, their youngest son, and Francis Gordon of Kincardine, 1844.

—There is no monument to John Gordon before referred to; but one (white marble) to his son Adam (of Arradoul and Cairnfield) is thus inscribed :—

"Byland"—To the memory of ADAM GORDON of Cairnfield, who died 17th March 1847, aged 74. ELIZABETH CRUICKSHANK, his wife, eldest daughter of the late Patrick Cruickshank of Stracathro, Forfarshire, died 29th January 1847, aged 67, and their two sons and two daughters, who predeceased them. Erected as a tribute of respect and affection by their surviving sons—John Gordon of Cairnfield; Patrick, Major, H.E.I.S.; George, merchant, U.S., America; James C. Duff, and William, Lieutenant, H.E.I.C.S.

—Patrick Cruickshank, who went from Rossshire to the West Indies as a mechanic, made a fortune abroad, and bought the estate of Stracathro on his return to Scotland. He was twice married, and Mrs Gordon was the only child by the first marriage (v. STRACATHRO.)

The next two inscriptions are from the same enclosure—the first is from a marble slab :—

Sacred to the memory of the late family of STEUART of Tanochy, all of whom, but two, lie interred here. PATRICK STEUART of Tanochy, died 31 Dec. 1779, aged 50; ELIZABETH, his wife, died 4 April 1804, aged 60. Their three sons, GEORGE STEUART of Tanochy, W.S., died Oct. 1814, aged 45; ALEXANDER, Major 75th regt., killed in Callabria, April 1813, aged 40; ANDREW died in the Island of Jamaica, ——. Their two daughters, HARRIET-MARY, died 19 July 1864, in the 93d year of her age; ELIZABETH-MARGARET, died 24 July 1858, aged 82. [Titus ii. 10; Rev. xiv. 13.]

—This family is now represented by Steuart of Auchlunkart, who is proprietor of Tanochy. A flat freestone slab bears :—

Here lies JAMES GORDON, son of the late George Gordon, Esq. of Buckie, who departed this life at Cullen, 27 May 1860, in the 58th year of his age. Mrs HELEN ORD, his spouse, and daughter of Mr Wm. Ord of the family of Findochty, late merchant at Deskford, died at Cullen, 1 Dec. 1803, aged 78. This stone is placed over their remains by Mrs Anne Rannie, eldest daughter of the late Col. Browne, &c.

The oldest visible stone at Rathven bears the name of ISOBEL MACKIE, and the date of 1698. The following inscriptions are from tombstones in different parts of the burial ground :—

This ston belongs to Iames Forbes, dueller in Nyr. Buckie . . . . IANET REID somtime his spous who departed . . April . . . .

Heir lyes the body of KATHRIN SIM . . . . somtime spous to Iohn Lobban, who doesest the 2 dayes of September 1713. I. H. S. Here also lyes CHRISTEN SCOT, who doesest the 11 of Iune 1708.

Here lies the body of JEAN GARDEN, spowse to Iohn Smith, skipper in Rottenslogh, who died March 31, 1779, aged 68 years; here lies also three of their children. As a small testimoney of regaird to their memory this stone is erected here by the affectionate husband whos desire is that his body may be interred near theirs, and now

 Tho' ÆEleos blasts & Neptunes waves,
 Hase driven him to and fro,
 Yet now at last, by Heavens decree,
 He harbours here below.
 And at an anchor he does ride
 With many of our fleet,
 Till the last trumpet raise him up.
 Our Saviour Christ to meet.

Here lies the body of JOHN REID, sometime skipper in shore of Buckie, who died the 26th Oct. 1786, aged 65 years; and MARGRAT WOOD, his spowse, who died 2d Oct. 1785, aged 62 years.

The four preceding inscriptions are from flat stones—the next two from headstones:—

Erected by the Rev. David Carment, minister of Rosskeen, in memory of his father JAMES CARMENT, late schoolmaster at Enzie Chapel, who departed this life on the 28th of July 1812, and is interred here.

WM. SMITH, hd. to Ann Flett, d. 1844, a. 50:—
 Thy life, dear man, through every scene,
 Has active, useful, lovely been.
 Whoe'er design'd more liberal things?
 Who higher stretch'd devotion's wings?
 Could friendship, trade, at home, abroad,
 Be sacred more to Christ than God;
 How far from fear, to heaven how nigh—
 Thus WILLIAM liv'd, and learn'd to die.

The antiquarian peculiarities of Rathven are but few. The circle which stood at Corriedoun was long ago destroyed; and the King's Cairn, the reputed grave of King Indulphus, who tradition says was slaughtered there by the Danes—but according to the Pictish Chronicle, he died at St Andrews—is still pointed out. Cairns and tumuli are to be seen upon the Muir of Bauds, the traditionary scene of the conflict. Some of the cairns have been opened, and found to contain stone coffins, of the common construction and size, with urns of the ordinary type.

Three isolated rocks upon the sea beach below Farskin are called the *Three Kings of Cullen*. These are popularly said to have been named from a Dane, a Scot, and a Norwegian, who fell in battle. More probably, owing to the similarity of the name of Cullen to that of Cologne in Prussia, these rocks had been named after the *Three Kings*, or Wise Men of the East, to whom the Cathedral of Cologne was dedicated. The rocks are near the town of Cullen.

About 1224-6, John Byseth (one of a race of potent barons of William the Lion's time, and who were anciently lords of Lovat), gifted to God, and to the Church of S. PETER of *Rathfan*, for the maintenance of seven leprous persons, and other pious uses, the patronage of the kirk of Kiltalargy (Kiltaralty), in Inverness-shire.

The bedehouse, now in ruins, stood at the village of Rathven. It was a thatched house of one storey. The walls appear to have been built of a mixture of rough boulders and sandstones, differing in no respect from the surrounding cottages except that the door and window lintels were dressed. The pensioners, now lodged in different parts of the district, are maintained from the rent of some acres of land in the neighbourhood, and by gifts of meal, which are doled out by Lord Seafield, the patron and administrator of the bequest. In the rental of the parsonage of Rathven (1563), appears the item of "the kirk of Kintallartic sett for 24lbs.," as well as those of the kirk of Dundureas, and the lands of Mulben.

The parish of Rathven (locally called *Raffan*) was probably named from a rath or fort, which may have stood upon one of the promontories which overhang the burn of Rathven, near the kirk. The parish, which extends about ten miles from east to west, contains the fishing villages of Portnockie, Findochty, Portessie, Peterhyth, Buckie, Gollachy, and Portgordon, &c., also the inland village of the Kirktown of Rathven. The largest of these villages is Buckie, which promises to become the most important town in Banffshire.

Apart from the parish church, there are *quoad sacra* churches at Portnockie, or Seafield, at Buckie, and at the Enzie (of old *Awne*). There are also Free Churches at those places, besides an Episcopal and a U. P. church at Buckie, and a Methodist chapel at Rottenslogh, now Portessie.

There are three Roman Catholic chapels in the district. One at Preshome (S. MARY), a second at Tynet, or Auchenhalrig (S. NINIAN), and the third at Buckie (SS. PETER and PAUL). The first, built in 1788, was the scene of the labours of Bishop KYLE, who died there in 1869, in the 80th year of his age, and 41st of his Episcopate, respected by all who knew him for his generosity of heart, and his uncommon scholarship and antiquarian knowledge. S. MARY'S Chapel contains a magnificent altar piece, representing S. GREGORY, painted by the Carracci—considered one of the most valuable pictures in Scotland.

The chapel at Buckie, consecrated in 1857, is a large cathedral-looking structure, with nave and side aisles, flanked in front by two well-proportioned towers. The interior is neatly fitted up, and some of the windows present figures in stained glass and diaphany. Two marble tablets are built into the south wall: the one nearest the altar is thus inscribed :—

✠ Pray for the Soul of Sir WILLIAM GORDON, Baronet, of Gordonstone and Letterfourie. Born 20th December 1804; deceased 5th Decr. 1861, whose remains are interred in this church. May he rest in peace.

The second tablet bears :—

✠ Pray for the Souls of Sir JAMES GORDON, Baronet of Gordonstown and Letterfourie, born in the year 1779; deceased on the 24th December 1843. And of his spouse, MARY GLENDONWIN of Glendonwin, born in the year 1783; deceased on the 18th May 1845; whose remains are interred within this church. May they rest in peace. Amen.

—The first Gordon of Letterfourie was James, Admiral of the Fleet in 1513, and fourth son of the second Earl of Huntly, by his wife, a daughter of James I. A baronetcy was created in the family in 1625. The present proprietor, Sir Robert Glendonwin-Gordon of Letterfourie, a direct descendant of the admiral, is Premier Baronet of Scotland. There is little worthy of note regarding the House of Letterfourie. Near the village of Buckie, upon the side of a romantic burn, stands a dovecot, in the south side of which are two freestone slabs, with traces of inscriptions. Although much defaced, enough remains of the one over the door to show that it is a quotation from Prov. iii. 10. The initial, G., is upon each side of the door.

It was near Buckie that the celebrated Dr ALEX. GEDDES was born, who appears to have been the Colenso of his time, both as regards his notions of the Pentateuch, and his treatment by the Bishops. He died at London, and was buried in Paddington Church-yard, where a monument with the following inscription (kindly communicated by the Rev. Mr Bucklings), marks his grave :—

"Rev. ALEXANDER GEDDES, LL.D., translator of the historical books of the Old Testament, died February 26, 1802, aged 63—

'Christian is my name, and Catholic my surname. I grant that you are a Christian as well as I, and embrace you as my fellow disciple in Jesus. And, if you were not a disciple of Jesus, still I would embrace you as my fellow man.'—Extracted from his works. Requiescat in pace. This stone is erected by his friend, Lord Petre, in 1804."

—Besides being remarkable for his scholarship and his works on biblical criticism, Dr Geddes was also a writer of Scottish verse; and when elected a corresponding member of the Society of Antiquaries of Scotland, he conveyed his thanks to the Society in a long poem (Archael. Scotica, i. p. 445), in which he strongly advocates the preservation of the Scotch language :—

"'Tis yours, my gen'rous, gentle brithers!
T' assert the honor of your mithers,
An' shaw they gaif as pure and gude
A language, as they gaif a blude."

St. Ninian's, or The Enzie.

(S. NINIAN, BISHOP CONFESSOR.)

THIS burial-ground, which is sometimes called St. NINIAN'S, at other times CHAPELFORD, is octagonal in form, and occupies a slight eminence in a field upon the farm of Braes of Enzie, about half-way between the parish kirks of Rathven and Bellie.

It is enclosed by a substantial wall, shaded by a few trees; but no ruins remain of the chapel, which a writer of 1726 says was "rebuilt about thirty years ago by . . . . . . Dutchess of Gordon."

Although the site of the grave-yard partakes little of the picturesque or the romantic, a fine view is obtained from it of the hills of Sutherland and Caithness. To the lovers of worth and genius the enclosure is peculiarly interesting, for within it lie the ashes of some of the most scholarly and holy men of their time. The first epitaph is from the oldest visible grave-stone :—

Here lyes ADAM GORDON, youngest son of Thomas Gordon of Glestirim, and Anna Gordon, eldest daughter of the Laird of Bucky. He dyed the 44th year of his age, the 30 of March 1695 :—

Here one doth ly of honorable birthe,
Sanoring of Heauen, while he liud on earth
Who by deuotion made his frequent flights,
And sheus desire to be with heauenly lights.
To God his king & contry
& True & dutifull in all relations,
Too, fors children, seruants, neighbours, & his
Found him exemplar by an holy life,   [wife,
He's mised by those & by the endigent ;
Then let him haue what to the Lord he lent.
    Requiescat in pace. ✝

The stone from which the above inscription is copied lies near the site of the altar of the old chapel. The next three inscriptions are from table-shaped monuments in the same locality. The first is embellished with carvings of a sand glass, skull, cross bones, and bells, &c. :—

D.O.M. Reue^{nus} D. THOMAS NICOLSON, Epis. Peristach. Vic. Ap. in Scotia, hic iacet. Wir fuit primeva pietate, insignis candore et simplicitate christiana, admirandus integritate, et morum innocentia eximius, ingenio acutus, doctrina et eruditione clarus, prudentia et sapientia singularis, zelo et charitate fidelibus charissimus, beneficentia, comitate, et liberalitate, etiam iis qui foris sunt, wenerabilis. Abi, wiator, et bene precare. Wixit annos circiter 76, obiit quarto Idus Octobris anno reparatæ salutis 1718.

[Here lies the Very Rev^d. THOMAS NICOLSON, Bishop of Peristachium, Vicar Apostolic in Scotland. He was a man of primitive piety, distinguished for candour and Christian simplicity, justly admired and esteemed for his integrity and the spotless purity of his character, acute of intellect, eminent for learning and erudition, gifted with rare prudence and wisdom, deeply endeared to the faithful by his zeal and charity, respected even by those who are without for his beneficence, courtesy, and liberality. Go hence, traveller, and bless him. He lived about 76 years, and died 12th Oct. 1718.]

—Mr Nicolson, who was the first Vicar Apostolic of Scotland, was originally a Protestant. About 1682, he embraced the Catholic Faith, and after a residence abroad, returned a missionary to his native country. At the time of the Revolution, he was cast into prison, and subsequently banished. He went to France, and while there, in 1695, he was raised to the Episcopate by the title of Bishop of Peristachium. On his way to Scotland, which he did not reach until July 1697, he again suffered imprisonment for a time; but once in Scotland, he spent an active and unmolested career, and died at his residence of Preshome. Bishop Nicolson was a younger son of Thomas Nicolson of Kemnay, by his wife, a daughter of Abercromby of Birkenbog, at which mansion the Bishop was born about 1645. His epitaph is said to have been written by his coadjutor, Bishop Gordon.

Besides Bishop NICOLSON, who was born in Banffshire, the number of Roman Catholic Prelates, natives of the Enzie and its vicinity, is worthy of being noticed. Of these Bishop GORDON was born at, and was laird of Glastyrum; Bishop SMITH was born at Fochabers; Bishop GRANT at Wester Boggs; Bishop JOHN GEDDES at Corriedoun; Bishop PATERSON at Path-head; Bishop SCOTT at Chapelford; Bishop MURDOCH at Wellheads; and Bishop SMITH at Cuttlebrae. Bishop GRAY of Glasgow was born at Buckie; and the late Bishop GILLIS of Edinburgh, though a native of Montreal, in Canada, was connected with the locality, in so far as his parents had emigrated from near Fochabers. Adjoining Bishop Nicolson's tomb :—

✠ Sub hoc lapide sepultus est R. D. GEORGIUS MATHISON, natus die 12 Januarii, 1756, qui e Seminario Scotorum Vallisoletano in Scotiam rediit presbyter anno 1778, ac, cum per 50 fere annos Missionem S. Niniani apud Bellay fideliter administrasset, ad meliorem vitam transiit die 14 Januarii 1828.

[Beneath this stone is interred the Rev. GEORGE MATHISON, born 12 Jan. 1756, who returned a priest from the Scotch College of Valladolid to Scotland in 1778, and after he had faithfully conducted the Mission of S. Ninian at Bellay for nearly 50 years, departed to a better life, 14 Jan. 1828.]

—Mr M. was a native of Bellie. He was educated first at Scalan, in Glenlivet, afterwards at Valladolid, in Spain, and continued missionary of S. NINIAN, or Auchinhalrig, down to the time of his death. Upon a table-shaped stone :—

To the memory of the Rev. WILLIAM REID, who, having received Holy Orders at Douay, served in the Mission of Scotland 45 years, and departed this life at Kempcairn, on the 25th of April 1825, in the 71st year of his age. This stone was erected by his niece Sophia-Helena-Maria Reid.

—Mr Reid, who was a native of Fochabers, was a favourite with all sects of Christians. He was one of those right-minded men who could give or take in repartee. Being at a dinner party on one occasion, soon after the death of a favourite pony, the loss of which he was lamenting, an Anti-Burgher, or Seceder, who was present, profanely inquired of Mr Reid if he gave his horse *extreme unction* before it died ; to which Mr Reid goodnaturedly answered, " Deed no, sir ; the beastie deeit *a Burgher !*" (Gordon's Scotichron.) A flat stone within an enclosure bears :—

Here lie the remains of JOHN STUART, Esq. of Bogs : born the 29th of June 1702, died the 7th of July 1780. May his soul rest in peace.

Upon a head stone adjoining the above :—

To the memory of JOHN STUART late of Bogs, and of JEAN LINDSAY, his spouse ; and of their daughters, HENRIETTA, BARBARA, JEAN, KATHARINE, MARY,

and CHARLOTTE, all of whose remains are interred here. Erected at the desire of Barbara, the last surviving daughter of the family, who departed this life on the 20 of August 1823, in the 86th year of her age, and whose benevolence, charity to the poor, and amiable manners, gained her the general and just respect and esteem of all ranks of society where she was known.

Though not solely devoted to the burial of members of the Roman Catholic Church, the graveyard of S. NINIAN may be said to have been hitherto pretty generally used by them ; and it is much to be wondered that, in this large and populous district—where there are Established and Free Churches—so many Protestants should prefer carrying their dead to Rathven, &c., when, with but little trouble and expense, S. NINIAN'S could be enlarged and made available for interment by all denominations in the district.

There is a copious spring at a short distance from S. NINIAN'S ; but whether it was "ane Well in the bounds of the Enzie, on the south syde of Spey," which was considered one of the " causes of the growth of Papistrie" in that locality, and as such ordered, by Act of Assembly in 1608, to be destroyed, is less certain, than that the water is of the best and purest kind (*v.* BELLIE.)

~~~~~~~~~~~~~~~~~~~~~~~~

Lintrathen.

(S. MEDDAN.)

THE church of *Lautrethyne*, or *Luntrethen*, valued at 20 merks in the Old Taxation, was a vicarage in the diocese of St Andrews.

During a vacancy in 1386, the rents of the vicarage were uplifted by order of the Bishop, and applied to assist in the repair of the cathedral church of St Andrews, which, in 1378, had been much destroyed by fire (Reg. Prior. S. And.)

The patronage and teinds of the chapel of *Glentrathen* were given to the Priory of Inchmahome, in Lake Monteith.

The present church, built in 1803, was repaired and enlarged some years ago. It is said to stand upon, or near the site of a chapel which was erected by Alan the Durward. It had, more probably, succeeded a later building, since the Durwards ceased to have connection with the parish towards the beginning of the 15th century, when (says Douglas), Sir Walter Ogilvy acquired Lintrathen by marrying Isabel, the heiress of Durward.

In old times the bell of S. MEDDAN of Lintrathen was an object of considerable importance. It was hereditary in certain noble personages; and charter evidence shows that " its resignation included a house or toft, near the church of Lintrathen, as a pertinent; and the right of the Countess of Moray, wife of Sir John Ogilvy, was completed by shutting her ladyship into the said house by herself, and the delivery of the feudal symbols of earth and stone" (Spalding Club Miscell., iv.)

Of the fate of the bell of S. MEDDAN, I have heard nothing reliable: More than twenty years ago an old man told me that some years previously, when an aged woman died at Burnside of Airlie, and her effects were disposed of, " an auld rusty thing like a flaggon, that fouk ca'd *Maidic's Bell*," was sold along with a lot of rubbish! Whether this article had been the old bell or not, the description of it corresponds with that of the *skellachs*, or bells of the Middle Ages. The present church bell is inscribed:—

MICHAEL . BURGERHVYS . ME . FECIT . 1632.

The church and burial-ground of Lintrathen are prettily situated upon the north bank of the Melgam, near a romantic linn, or water fall. The churchyard is kept is good order, and the inscriptions quoted below are selected from some of the tombstones. Possibly the oldest is that which bears the date of 1695, and the words "JOHN DICKSON, Little Kenny." Upon another near the same spot:—

Here lys interred ALEXR OGILVY wt. his tuo wiues MG: LAWSON and IANNET DAVIE, wt. nine of his children JO: HE: JS: JHO: AND: WM: ALEX . & . . . . OGILVIES.

Hear layes ELISABETH SMART, spouse to Iohn Eduart in Nether Sheithens. She departed this life the 27 day of December 1713 years, her age was 36 years.

Heir lyes ane honest woman called ISABEL MACHER, spows to Iohn Dens, who departed this lif wpon the 21 of Ianewar, and of her age 38, 1713.

Heir lyes ane honest man called JAMES OGILVY. He lived in Little Kilrie, husband . . . . departed this life the 16 of August 26 years, 1719 . . . . .

The above inscriptions are from flat stones — the next two are from headstones:—

JOHN CRAICK, farmer, Breas of Old Allan, d. 1740, MARGT. DAVIDSON, his spouse, d. — :—

All Time relations here below,
Tho' knit with strongst bands,
Death soon disolves; when time is spent,
No bond his power withstands.
He snatched of the virtuous wife,
The husband fond doth mourn;
But death his days it soon did cut —
Here his beseide her urn.

ANDREW HAY's daughter (1759) :—

A deep and rapid stream divides —
Death is the name it bears;
But o'er it Christ has laid a bridge,
For heavenly passengers.

Upon a table-shaped stone: —

JAMES FENTON, farmer, Purgavie, d. 1742, a. 55; CHIRSTON JOHNSTON, his spouse, d. 1746, a. 52 :—

Below this tomb are laid the bones
Of a good virtuous pair;
Both scholars, pious and discreet,
Accomplishments most rare.
Whose knowledge serv'd not to puff up,
But for a nobler end;
That lowlyness might them prepare,
A glorious life to spend.

According to tradition, the Durwards possessed the greater part of Lintrathen in old times, and Alan, the most celebrated of his race, is said to have had a residence upon the south-west side of the hill of Formal, overlooking the loch. As before stated, Sir Walter Ogilvy is said to have acquired the property by marrying the heiress of Durward ; but it also appears that the same knight had charters of Purgavie and other parts of the district from Archibald Earl of Douglas, which were confirmed in 1406 by the Duke of Albany.

Not far from the reputed site of Durward's Castle, and about the year 1831, a quantity of Roman coins were found in a hillock, some of which are preserved in the locality. Monoliths, possibly remains of so-called Druidical circles, are in various parts of the parish ; and these, as well as the supposed abodes of the early inhabitants, which are pointed out upon certain of the hill sides, &c., particularly about the Torrocks, were noticed at length in the *Montrose Standard*, 13th March, 1868.

The chief object of natural beauty and interest in the parish is the Loch of Lintrathen ; but, owing to an agreement between the Earl of Airlie (chief heritor of the parish) and the inhabitants of Dundee, the space which the loch now occupies is to be very much extended, and the natural aspect of the locality altered, for the purpose of constructing a reservoir to supply water for that large and increasing community.

The only mansion house in the parish is that of Balintore—an elegant building—recently erected by David Lyon, Esq.

Mr THOMSON, grandson of Ross, author of *Helenore*, of which poem Mr Thomson published an edition at Dundee, in 1812, with a biographical notice of the author, was long minister at Lintrathen, and died in 1813.

Logie, or Logie-Mar.

(S. WOLOK, BISHOP.)

DUNCAN, EARL of MAR, 1239-44, gave the church of *Logymar*, or *Logyrothuan in Mar*, to Old Machar, and provided that his body should be buried within that cathedral. The church of Logie was previously granted by Gilchrist, Earl of Mar, to the Culdees of Monymusk.

Until 1473, the chaplainry of Glenbucket, in Strathdon, was attached to the kirk of Logie ; but at that period (Reg. Ep. Aberd., i. 307), in consequence of the dangers and difficulties which were encountered in travelling through an uninhabited country, and desert mountains, in which five or six people perished in one day whilst going to hold Easter at Logie, the Bishop of Aberdeen had the chapel of Glenbucket erected into a separate parish kirk, with baptismal font, &c.

The parishes of Logie and Coldstone were united in 1618. A new church was erected about half way between the old sites ; and the present kirk was built in 1780. The *Pooldow well*, a little to the south of the kirk, is a strong mineral, once famous for the cure of scorbutic and other disorders.

The burial ground of Logie lies in the Vale of Cromar, near Loch Kinord. It is kept in good order, protected by a stone wall, and contains a number of gravestones. Within a walled enclosure, called the *Blelack Howff* lie (unmarked by any monument), the Gordons, who were lairds of Blelack from an early part of the 16th century.

The last laird was out in the '45, and many anecdotes are told of his hairbreadth escapes from the Royalists, which appear to have been chiefly effected by the personal strength and daring of his henchman, M'Connach, whom he rewarded by a long and cheap lease of an adjoining farm. The last direct survivor of M'Connach is the reverend, the ex-schoolmaster of Alford, one of the finest living examples of "the old school," whether as to kindness of heart, individuality of character, or honesty of purpose.

In speaking of the rebel laird of Blelack, it may be added that *the fairies* abode in the Seely Howe, a hollow in the Carne Hillock, upon that property ; and, before leaving for the wars of the '45, the laird, determined to dislodge them from his lands, employed for that purpose a reputed magician, named John Farquharson, tacksman in Parks. The fairies, however, refused to obey his spell until he should assign them some other place of abode, which he did by sending them to the Hill of Fare, near Bauchory! But, disliking their new quarters very much, the superstitious aver that the fairies pronounced this imprecation upon Gordon :—

> "Dool, dool to Blelack,
> And dool to Blelack's heir,
> For drivin' us frae the Seely Howe,
> To the cauld Hill o' Fare !"

—The malediction of the fairies against Farquharson was still more eldritch :—

> "While corn and girs grows to the air,
> John Farquharson and his seed shall thrive nae mair !"

It is added that Farquharson, whose circumstances went to the bad from the day he dislodged the fairies, left his native country and was never again heard of. Matters also went ill with the Gordons. The rebel laird died without lawful issue, when the estate passed to Charles Rose, a sister's son, who prefixed *Gordon* to his own surname. Having light hair (that of the Gordons being dark), he was known as "the Red Laird." He left a half-witted son KEITH GORDON, who died almost a pauper, in 1869, aged 73, at Fairnrae in Towie.

Keith was the last legitimate descendant of the old Gordons of Blelack, for although the property was bought in 1794 from "the Red Laird" by *a* Gordon, the latter had no connection, so far as known, with the original stock. It is true that he was a native of the district, having belonged to Balneyan, which he left in early life for Dundee, where he carried on the trade of a vintner, or innkeeper, so successfully that he bought the estate of Blelack with the profits of his business.

"Gordon's Inn" was long a well-known hostelry in Dundee. It stood opposite to the Town House, and was only removed when Reform Street was made out in 1834. Before buying Blelack, the "vintner" showed his goodness of heart by erecting a monument (table shaped) at Logie, to the memory of an uncle, upon which is this inscription :—

DONALD GORDON from Ballneyan, died 11 January 1776, aged 98, in gratitude to whose memory, his nephew, William Gordon, vintner, Dundee, caused this stone to be erected :—

Altho' this tomb no boasted tittles keep
Yet silent here the private virtues sleep ;
Truth, candour, justice, altogether ran
And form'd a plain, upright, honest man.
No courts he saw, nor mixt in publick rage,
Stranger to all the vices of the age ;
No lie, nor slander did his tongue defile—
A plain old Britton free from pride and guile.
Near five-score years he numbered ere he died,
And every year he number'd he enjoy'd.
This modest stone, which few proud Marbles can,
May truly say, Here lies an honest man ;
Ye great whose heads are laid as low,
Rise higher if you can.

—The first appearance of the "vintner" laird of Blelack in the Parish Church is thus noticed (May 3, 1794), in the books of the kirk treasurer :— "Mr Gordon, the new proprietor of the lands of Blelack, being in the church, gave a guinea to the poor, which made that day's collection to be £1 3s 7d."

Blelack was sold soon after this laird's death to John Forbes of Newe, who bequeathed it to his relative, the Rev. Dr Forbes of Strathdon, for behoof of his son, now General Forbes of Invercrnan (*v.* p. 151), by whom it was sold in 1862 to Sir Alex. Anderson (*v.* p. 119), from whose trustees it was bought in 1869, by Mr Coltman, a neighbouring proprietor.

It may be added that the mansion house of Blelack was accidentally destroyed by fire in the autumn of 1868. Also, that the Dundee vintner had a sister, who married James Clark, farmer, Carue, by whom she had at least one son and three daughters. The son, who was a preacher, became schoolmaster of Daviot, in Aberdeenshire, where he died in 1849, aged 49. He was father of the present vicar of Taunton, in Somersetshire, and other children. The following is from another stone at Logie:—

Here lies JOHN M'LAGGAN, who died in Newgrodie, and MARGARET LEY, his spouse ; also WILLIAM M'LAGGAN, their lawful son, who departed this life March 20, 1794, aged 28.

Unmark'd by trophies of the great and vain,
Here sleeps in silent tombs an honest train ;

No folly wasted their paternal store,
No guilt, no sordid avrice, made it more;
With honest fame, and sober plenty crown'd
They liv'd and spread their cheering influence
    round.

Coldstone.

(S. ——.)

THE name of this district appears in a variety of forms, among which are those of *Collesen*, *Colcon*, *Corlilstan*, *Culquholdstane*, &c. The first of these spellings appears in the Old Taxation of 1275, in which the kirk is rated at 12 merks, and the last is in the Register of Ministers, &c., for 1574, when the kirks of Coldstone, Coull, Kincardine O'Neil, and Banchory-Ternan, were all under the superintendence of one minister.

In 1402, when Isabella, Countess of Mar and the Garioch gave the patronage and advocation of the kirk of Coldstone to the monastery of Lindores, it is described as "Colilstane in Cra Mar;" and, when it was added to the canonry of Old Machar in 1424, it is called "Coldstane."

Coldstone and Coull may be said to form respectively the west and east corners of Cromar, and as water is much more abundant in the former district than in the latter, "Collesen" is probably the closest to the true etymology of the name, since the Gaelic compound, *Cul-esvan*, means a corner or district which abounds in streams.

The church-yard of Coldstone is situated upon the south side of a hill, from which there is a good view of Cromar and the surrounding country. A granite stone, about 24 by 12 inches in size roughly dressed on one side, presents a beautifully incised cross within an oval. It is an object of considerable antiquity, and had probably marked the grave of an old ecclesiastic.

The site of the kirk, which can still be traced, is about 58 feet in length by about 30 in width, and has a chancel or burial aisle, on the east, of about 26 by 30 feet in size. At the east end of the chancel or aisle lies a stone, in the centre of which are the Forbes arms, with initials, R. F., and M. C. This inscription is round the margin :—

Heir lyes Mr ROBERT FORBES, minister of Coldstane, who departed ovt of this lyfe xii of Ianvarie 16-3.

—It was in the time of Mr Forbes that the parishes of Logie and Coldstone were united. According to Lumsden of Tillickerne, he was a member of the Balluig family. After the death of two successors (Scott's Fasti), the living was held in succession by the ministers whose deaths are recorded in the next five inscriptions :—

In memory of the Rev. JOHN SHEPHERD, minister of Logie-Coldstone, who, after he spent his life in love to God and mankind, dyed March 1, 1748, aged 74.

—Mr Shepherd, who was translated from Midmar to Logie-Coldstone, had at least two sons and two daughters. One of the daughters married Forbes of Bellabeg, and became the mother of the Rev. Geo. Forbes of Leochel, and of John Forbes, afterwards of Newe (*sup.*, p. 150). The second daughter, who married Gordon of Crathienaird, was the mother of the late Rev. Mr Gordon of Aboyne. The sons were both clergymen. One was settled first at Tarland and next at Newbattle, while the other went to Bourtie. A son of the last-mentioned became minister of Daviot, and by his wife, a daughter of Dr Garioch of Gariochsford, he had a pretty large family. One son, Captain John, was sometime Chairman of the Board of Directors of the E I.C., and another, Thomas, laird of Kirkville, in Skene, was also an officer in the Co.'s Marine Service.

Here lye the remains of the Revd. Mr JOHN McINNES, late minister of the Gospel at Logie-Coldstone, who died the 10th Octr. 1777, in the 62d year of his ministry, and the 88th of his age.

HELEN FORBES, spouse of the Revd. Mr John McInnes, minister of Logie Coldstone, who died on the 26 of Decr. 1774, aged 71 years.

—Mr M'Innes, who was previously at Crathie, supported the Royalists, and having prayed one Sunday during the rebellion, "that the Rebels might be scattered like mist upon the mountains," it is told that the lady of Blelack, who was present, rose up in her pew, and with uplifted arm and clenched fist, exclaimed, with an oath —" Will ye say that au' my Chaarlie amo' them?" As Mr McInnes was not translated to Logie-Coldstone until 1748, this circumstance (if ever it had happened) must have occurred before that time.

Beneath this stone are interred the remains of the Rev. ROBERT FARQUHARSON of Allargue, minister of Logie-Coldstone, who died 5 Jan. 1826, in the 78th year of his age and 56th of his ministry. And also those of his spouse, ELIZABETH, daughter of the Rev. James Innes, minister of Marnoch, who died the 31 Aug. 1836, aged 76.

—A son of the above-named succeeded to the property of Breda, in Alford (*supra*, p. 120).

In memory of the Rev. ANDREW TAWSE, for 7 years minister at Grey Friars' Church of Aberdeen, who, in the 8th year of his ministry in this parish, and 47th of his age, while conducting the solemn service of God's House, on Sunday 15 Dec. 1833, was called from the faithful discharge of his pastoral duties, and expired in presence of his sorrowing people.

—Mr Tawse, who was sometime tutor in the Whitehouse family, had a taste for painting and music, and it was through the influence of the Farquharsons that he got the kirk of Logie-Coldstone. He was a native of Aberdeen, where his father was a well-to-do flaxdresser.

In memory of the Rev. JOHN MCHARDY, for 32 years minister of this parish. Born 13th Jan. 1785; died 17th Jan. 1866.

A table-shaped stone bears:—

To the memory of Mr GEORGE FORBES, Master in the Royal Navy, who served many years in that rank, and gained high praise for his courage and conduct in many engagements, particularly in the memorable battle at Trafalgar, when Lord Nelson fell. On retiring from the Service, he became tacksman of Kinord, where he died on the 11th of June 1821, aged 62. And his wife MARGARET FORBES, who died on the 7th Oct. 1847, aged 74.

In the church-yard of Coldstone, unmarked by any monument, lie the remains of ALEXANDER LAING, author of the Donean Tourist. He was born in Coull, and died at Boltingstone—a roadside tavern between Tarland and Strathdon—on 20th April 1838, aged about sixty. He was the illegitimate son of an Aberdeen advocate, and a staunch Roman Catholic (Inf. Rev. Mr Michie.)

Although pretty well educated, and a person of good natural abilities, Laing was of an erratic temperament, and never succeeded in the world. At the time of his death, he was employed as a book canvasser, in allusion to which he was known as *Stachie* (*i.e.* Stationer) *Laing*, and being blind of an eye he sometimes went under the sobriquet of *Gleyt Laing*. In addition to the work above mentioned, Laing published the Caledonian Itinerary, The Thistle of Scotland, a collection of Ballads, A Repertory of Ballads, the Eccentric Magazine, &c. His books, which are now rare, and much sought after in the North, are all curious. A few pages of " the copy " of the Donean Tourist (now before us) exhibit an incredible amount of patience and labour. Instead of being *written*, as in ordinary cases, it is composed of single letters and words, cut out of a variety of publications, and pasted upon sheets of foolscap! From this " eccentric " copy the printer appears to have set the book in type.

———o———

Some traces of early occupancy still remain in Logie-Coldstone, such as artificial cairns; a paved road on the farm of Cairnmore of Blelack; an old sculptured stone formerly at Mill of Newton, but now removed to the grounds at Tillypronie House; a peculiar hollow near the church, called the Picts' Howe; and the only remaining boulder of a stone circle, stands at Logie (*supra*, p. 188.)

The whole district belonged at one time to the Earls of Mar. In 1364, Ego, the son of Fergus, had a charter from Mar of the lands of Huchtircrue (Watercarn) in Cromar, and from that place, 1305-7, a family, as vassals of the over lord, assumed the surname of OUCHTIRARNE.

The House of Groddie, at the foot of Morven, though now a plain building, presented at one time some of the characteristics of a mansion-house. It then belonged to Gordons; and the mantle or chimney-piece, besides being adorned with the Gordon and Forbes arms, bore the initials of A. G.: M. F., and an inscription, of which these traces only remain :—

.... GORDOVNE ..... BES ; GRACE ...
.... PEACE ; VE ..... YST . IESVS ✠

The lands of Old and New Groddie, along with those of Whitehouse, belong to the Marquis of Huntly; and the mansion of Whitehouse, although now represented only by a thatched cottage, was long the property and residence of a branch of the Farquharsons. When Miss Elizabeth Farquharson of Jamaica, who was known as *Black Bess*, bequeathed the interest of £400 for the support of a school at Glengairn, and to aid the most necessitous poor of the united parishes of Tulloch, Glenmuick, and Glengairn, in all time coming, she included in her bequest the poor upon Old and New Groddie, in consequence of these lands having been part of the Whitehouse estates. As Miss F.'s legacy was not realized for many years, the capital sum increased to about £600.

This lady was sister to Harry Farquharson of Whitehouse, who fell at Culloden, and great-grandaunt to Andrew Farquharson, Esq., now representative of the Whitehouse branch.

But, although the Farquharsons have ceased to hold their ancient paternal estate in Cromar, it ought to be stated that, as is not unfrequently the case, the name of their old inheritance of Whitehouse has been transferred to another property. This was done by the father of the present laird, who, on acquiring the lands of Abercattie, in the parish of Tough, changed the name to that of Whitehouse. He was an advocate in Aberdeen, and his father was long an eminent medical practitioner and consulting physician in Dundee.

During the Wars of the Covenant, the district of Cromar was sadly plundered and ravaged by Argyle's soldiers (Spald. Cl. Misc., vol. iii.); but it is uncertain whether the couplet—

"Culbleen was burnt, an' Cromar herriet,
An' dowie's the day John Tam was marriet,"

has reference to that period. More probably, from the *style* of the rhyme, it refers to some calamity which had befallen the country during one of the later rebellions, in both of which the people of Cromar were concerned.

A market or fair was long held at the Kirk of Logie, and a well-known rhyme preserves both its name and celebration-day :—

"WALLOCK fair in Logie-Mar,
The thirtieth day o' Januar."

The hill of Morven, which is celebrated by Lord Byron in one of his earliest songs, bounds Logie-Coldstone on the west. According to "weather prophets," and an old rhyme, when the summit of the mountain is enveloped in mist, a rainfall over the district may be expected :—

"When Morven has a tap,
Cromar 'ill get a drap."

The next rhyme (not now true, doubtless!) contains the lost names of some places about the Burnside of Logie-Coldstone :—

"Frae Faandhu to Tamgleddie,
Frae Paddock-pool to Allalogie,
There never dwalt an honest bodie !"

~~~~~~~~~~~~~~~~~~~~~~~~~~~~

Newhills.

(? THE BLESSED VIRGIN.)

IT was "in 1663 (Old Stat. Acct.), that the lands of Capelhills were mortified for the maintenance of a minister, and a church was built upon them, by George Davidson of Pettens, burgess of Aberdeen; in consequence of which the south-west corner of the extensive parish of St Machar was erected into a separate parish in 1666. These lands of Capelhills (probably derived from *Capella*, a chapel), now assumed the name of Newhills, and from them the whole parish was denominated."

Besides erecting and endowing the church and parish of Newhills, Davidson, who is said to have acquired a fortune as a pedlar, built the first stone bridge over the Buxburn, repaired that of Insch, and "bigit" the kirk-yard "dyk" at Footdee.

The oldest ecclesiastical site in Newhills is probably that which lies nearly two miles to the north of the parish church, and upon the south side of the Aberdeen and Inverurie turnpike. It was dedicated to the VIRGIN, and is called the

CHAPEL OF STONEYWOOD.

The Holy Well, which is still a copious spring, near the south-west corner of the kirk-yard, is "reckuod medicinall," and said "to be good for the stomach, and for cleausing and curing any ulcerous tumours on any part of the body, when bathed with it."

"The ruines of ane old popish chappell" were to be seen here in 1725. These were probably the same of which traces still remain. The burial-place, which was enclosed by a substantial stone wall, 1834, is chiefly used by Roman Catholics. It contains a few tombstones, but none of old date. A tablet in the west wall bears this inscription, which is partially defaced:—

Within this tomb lies the body of DONALD M'QUEEN, late farmer in Bogfairlie, who departed this life the 31st July 1813, in the 66th year of his age; also of his wife MARGARET FORBES, who died the 10th Oct. 1813, in the 65th year of her age . . . . . From a sense of filial duty, not more the dictate of nature than the tribute of willing gratitude, this tomb is erected by their surviving son, Donald M'Queen.

The kirk of S. MARY at Stoneywood was probably disused when the district was made into a separate parish in 1663. The ivy-clad ruins of the first erected place of worship at Newhills stand within the burial-ground. About 1830, a new church was built a little to the eastward.

The first incumbent of Newhills is supposed to have been Mr George Melvill (Scott's Fasti); but the following inscription from a stone built into the splay of one of the windows of the old kirk is, so far as I know, the oldest monumental trace of any of the ministers of Newhills:—

To the memory of the Reverend Mr JAMES HOWE, for 52 years the worthy minister of the Gospel of this parish of Neubills, who died 3rd October, A.D. 1768, aged 80th years. Also of his brother the Reverend Mr ALEXR. HOWE, the worthy minister of the Gospel of the parish of Methlock and of Tarues for 36 years, who died September 3rd A.D. 1765, aged 60 years. And also of their aunt, Mrs ANN HOWE, who died December 8th, A.D. 1748, aged 89 years, all interred in this church. Also Mrs BETTEY HOWE, their sister, who died July 15th, 1769, aged 78.

—Mr Robert Burnett (Mr Howe's immediate predecessor), was admitted to Newhills in 1704, and in June 1715, when about 60 years of age, he destroyed himself within the church with the bell rope. It is locally said that the kirk bible was found lying open beside the body of Mr Burnett, and that the 13th, 14th, and 15th verses of Job, ch. vii., were marked by his own hand— "Thou scarest me with dreams, and terrifiest me through visions; So that my soul chooseth strangling, and death rather than my life."

From a marble tablet in E. wall of kirk-yard:—

Vir Reverendus JOANNES BROWN, SS. T. D., primum apud Rhynie fere XX. annos, deinde apud Newhills fere XXXII. V. D. M., probus, benevolus, hilaris, facetus, amicisque semper carissimus, obiit A. D. MDCCCIII., ætat. LXXIX. Uxor ejus BARBARA GORDON, pia, placida, benigna, obiit A. D. MDCCXCVIII. ætat LXV. Vir Reverendus GEORGIUS ALLAN, apud Newhills XL. amplius annos V. D. M., obiit Kalendis Juliis, A. D. MDCCCXXIII., ætat. LXVI. ANNA BROWN, Joannis Brown, supramemorati, filia, eademque Georgii Allan, item memorati, uxor, obiit XXIV. Decembr., A. D. MDCCCXXXV. annos LXXII. nata.

[The Rev. JOHN BROWN, D.D., minister of the Word of God, first at Rhynie for nearly 20 years, and afterwards at Newhills for nearly 32 years, a man virtuous, benevolent, cheerful, pleasant, and ever deeply endeared to his friends, died 1803, aged 79. His wife, BARBARA GORDON, pious, gentle, and kind, died 1798, aged 65. The Rev. GEORGE ALLAN, minister of the Word of God at Newhills for upwards of 14 years, died 1st July 1823, aged 66. ANN BROWN, daughter of the above-mentioned John Brown, and wife of George Allan, likewise mentioned, died 24th Dec. 1835, aged 72.]

—Mrs Brown, who was a daughter of the laird of Craig, in Auchindoir, had three sons and five daughters. One of the latter, as shown above, married Mr Allan (a son of a schoolmaster at Skene, *v.* p. 228), who was her father's assistant, afterwards his successor. Elizabeth became the wife of Mr Brown, minister of Glenmuick (*v.* p. 108.) Upon another slab:—

BARBARA ALLAN, eldest daughter of James Nicol, advocate in Aberdeen, died 21 March 1838, aged 5 years. His wife, BARBARA ALLAN, died 30 Dec. 1852, aged 52 years. The said JAMES NICOL died 18 March 1855, aged 55 years, and was buried at Old Aberdeen, owing to a snow storm preventing access to Newhills.

A granite monument (thus inscribed) marks the grave of Mr G. A.'s successor, who was previously schoolmaster at Chapel of Garioch:—

Erected in memory of the Rev. JAMES ALLAN, for 33 years the worthy minister of the parish of Newhills, who died in 1857, aged 83 years. JANE RONALD, his wife, who died in 1859, aged 64 years. Their children, JESSIE ALLAN, died 1849, aged 20; WILLIAM-K.-E. ALLAN, surgeon, who died in 1843, aged 23 years; FIFE ALLAN, Ensign, 30th Regt. Madras N. I., died at sea in 1858, aged 22 years.

JOHN PHILIP, d. 1845, aged 78; his wife, CHRISTIAN WALKER, d. 1856, aged 85; a dr. d. 1841, aged 36; and a son, JOHN, in 1856, aged 32:—

Here in this bleak and elevated spot,
Parents and sister, ye are not forgot:
This lettered headstone at your grave appears—
A faint memorial which affection rears,
But doom'd to perish in a few short years.
They do not reck released from this world's strife,
Whose names are written in the Book of Life;
They shall be satisfied who live to wake
In Jesus' likeness, when Death's sleep shall break.

The proprietary history of some parts of the district of Newhills is interesting. It is said that the lands of Slatie were granted to Edward, Bishop of Aberdeen, by King Malcolm, about 1150–65. Charter evidence shows that Robert the Bruce gave the custody of the royal forest of Stocket to the burgh of Aberdeen; and that, subsequently (1493), Wood of Overblairtone having received a royal grant of the same forest, together with that of the Castlehill of Aberdeen, his claim was challenged by the Provost and community, who, in the following year, had judgment given in their favour.

In 1373, Donald Banerman, king's physician, had certain portions of Clyntreys, Achrinys, Waterton, and Welton from the king, also the lands of Slatie from Bishop Kyninmond. Donald had a son, or near relative, Alexander, provost of Aberdeen in 1382, of whom were the knightly family of Elsick (*v.* p. 79), also probably the Banermans who, until a comparatively late period, were extensive merchants in, and otherwise connected with, Aberdeen.

On the south-east of the parish is the interesting old house of Kingswells, long ruinous, but lately restored with much taste, by the present proprietor, Mr F. Edmond, advocate. It belonged at one time to Alexander Jaffray, provost of Aberdeen, whose Diary of the transactions of the times of Charles and Cromwell is not only valuable on account of the history it gives of the leading political events of the period; but Jaffray having been one of the first to join the Quakers in this country, his book embraces very much that is interesting, and not elsewhere to be found, regarding the rise and progress of that sect in the North of Scotland.

Owing to the extensive trade which has been carried on for some years in the manufacturing of paper, and the quarrying and dressing of granite in Newhills, the villages of Auchmull, Buxburn, Bankhead, and Stoneywood, have become places of considerable importance. Near Stoneywood are the handsome school buildings, erected by the Messrs Pirie, for the education of the children whose parents are employed about their paper works at Waterton, &c.

Besides the Parish, there are Free Churches both at Auchmull and Kingswells. That at Kingswells is a neat building, erected chiefly at the expense of Mr Edmond.

---o---

Laurencekirk.

(S. LAURENCE, PRIMATE OF ENGLAND.)

THIS parish has been long known by the name of the patron saint of the church, who, the late laborious Dr Joseph Robertson discovered, contrary to popular belief, to be not S. Laurence of the Roman Calendar, but the ancient Primate of England, who bore the same name.

It appears that S. LAURENCE visited Pictland about A.D. 605-19, and that in honour of this visit the church of Conveth was dedicated to him. It also appears that, long afterwards, in 1073-93, our own "good Queen Margaret" made a pilgrimage to the church of S. LAURENCE of this place; and in her anxiety to do honour to the Prelate's memory, she went disguised as a canon; but having thus violated the traditions of her country, she was repulsed from entering the church (Concilia Scotiæ.)

CONVETH, however, was the name of the district, during and for long subsequent to the middle ages. The old church of *Cuneveth*, of which no trace remains, is said to have stood about a mile to the east of the present village. It was a rectory belonging to St Andrews, and was dedicated by Bishop David in 1244. In the old taxation of the Scotch Churches, which was made about 1275, the kirk of *Cuneveth* is rated at 30 marks. It does not appear that there were any chapels attached to the church at that period.

Among the more eminent of the early ministers of Conveth, was Mr William Lamb, nephew of Patrick, Abbot of Cambuskenneth, who, in 1540, having been previously admitted "to heir and understande the practik," was appointed an Ordinary Lord of the Court of Session.

After the Reformation, and in 1567-74, the kirks of Conveth, Fordoun, Fettercairn, and Newdosk, were all served by one minister, Mr Patrick Bouncle, who had a stipend of £160 Scots, and kirk lands. Patrick Ramsay was then reader or schoolmaster at Conveth, with £30, and a share of the kirk lands.

In 1571, it was ordained by the General Assembly, that Mr Bouncle, as one of "the auld chaptoure" of St Andrews, and as one of the "ministeris professouris of the trew religioun," should continue, during his life, to be one of the chapter, and to have a voice in the "electioun of the Archbishop," &c. In the Assembly of 1582, Mr Bouncle reported, "anent the constitutione of Presbyteries," that in the Mearns, "They had erected there a Presbytrie of Ministers, but not as yet of any Gentlemen or Elders." (Booke of the Univ. Kirke.)

It is said that the present parish kirk, erected in 1804, took the place of one which was built in 1626; and that, when the old house was being taken down, a stone was found (New Stat. Acct.) upon which " the figure of a man lying on a gridiron was carved, representing, it was supposed, the martyrdom of St Laurence." This stone, which is unfortunately lost, had probably been a Pictish monument.

The church is a plain building, surrounded by the burial-ground. A handsome marble tablet (the only one within the church) is thus inscribed :—

In memory of WILLIAM DUIRS, M.A., M.D., Deputy Inspector-General of Hospitals and Fleets, a native of this parish, who fell a victim to yellow fever, contracted in the execution of his duty at the Royal Naval Hospital, Jamaica, 8 June 1867, aged 47 years. This tablet is erected by sixty-two of his brother medical officers as a testimony of their high appreciation of his sterling worth, kindness of heart, and professional abilities.

— Dr Duirs, who began life as a teacher, but afterwards studied medicine, was the son of a builder and contractor at Laurencekirk. A few years before his death Dr Duirs married a daughter of Dr Fettes, who has been long the principal physician of the district, and sometime chief magistrate of Laurencekirk. By his wife, who did not long survive him, Dr Duirs left several children.

The churchyard of Laurencekirk contains a number of tombstones; and, so far as I have seen, the first quoted inscription bears the oldest date. It is carved in prettily interlaced capitals, upon a stone with sloped ends and sides. It lies near the outer and south wall of the church: upon one end are the initials W. L. and a shield charged with two crescents in chief, and a mullet in base, upon the other end is a death's head. The south bevel or slope of the stone bears:—

READERS CON . . . . T ICE HEIR LYE
WHO LYES HEIR NOV WAS ONC AS YE WILIAM
AS HE IS NOV SO YE MVST DE LAWSONE SON TO
REMEMBER AL THAT YE MVST DIE DAVID LAWSONE
IN POVDVRNE DEPARTED THE 13 YEAR OF HIS AGE 1656.

[Upon the north bevel of the same stone]:—

HER LYES ONE WHILE HE LIVED DID SEEME
TO VERTVES PATH ADDICTED. THE HOVRIS RVN.
SHORT TYME WEIL SPENT HEIR WILL CONDEMNE
THE LONG LYF OF THE WICKED. MEMENTO MORI

Upon another stone, similarly formed as the above, with inscription incised:—

Heer lyes DAVID LAWSON in . . . . who departed this lyfe the . . . . O ctober 1670, of age 52 years. In death . . . .

The slab, from which the next inscription is taken, has been batted to the east end of the kirk. It bears rude carvings of a sand glass, skull, and crossed mattocks, the initials M. P. B., the date of 1695, also these words incised:—

HER . LYES . MASTER . PATRICK . DELLIE . SCHOOLLE.
MASTER . WHO . DEPARTED . THIS . LYFE . FEBRUARY .
THE . 10 . 1695 . OF . AGE . 20 . YEIRS . 5 . MONETHS .
AND . 16 . DAYES.

—The above, as given in Chalmers' admirable Life of Ruddiman (p. 16), is slightly incorrect, the day of the month being misprinted " 20th," instead of 10. It was, while tutor at Aldbar, to the great-grandson of Sir Peter Young of Seton, that Ruddiman, afterwards the grammarian, heard of the death of Mr Bellie, and, applying for the situation of schoolmaster at Laurencekirk, he succeeded in procuring it. Ruddiman was then 21 years of age, and he continued at Laurencekirk until accident brought him into personal contact with Dr Pitcairn, the celebrated Latin poet in 1699, through whose influence he went to Edinburgh, where he became librarian to the Faculty of Advocates, and after a long and useful life he

died in 1757. Although not Ruddiman's immediate successor at Laurencekirk, the poet Ross was schoolmaster there before going to Lochlee.

The following is upon a table-shaped stone, near the middle of the burial ground:—

Viro admodum Reverendo JONATHAN WATSON, in Ecclesia Scotiæ Episcopo, pietatis aliarumque virtutum vere evangelicarum æmulo; in bonis literis, inque theologia exercitato; animo firmo; filio, patri, conjugi amantissimo. Sui omnibus officii sacri muneribus per 17 annos apud Laurencekirk fideliter functus, multum defletus obiit 28 die Janu., 1808, annum 46 agens. Vidua et mater mœrentes H. M. P.

[To the memory of the Very Rev. JONATHAN WATSON, Bishop of the Church in Scotland, distinguished for his piety, and other truly evangelical virtues, conversant with good literature and theology, firm of purpose, and a most affectionate son, father, and husband. Having faithfully discharged all the duties of his sacred office at Laurencekirk for 17 years, he died much regretted, 28 Jan. 1808, in his 46th year. His sorrowing widow and mother erected this monument.]

—Mr Watson, who was the first resident Episcopal clergyman at Laurencekirk after the troubles, was brought from Banff by Lord Gardenstone in 1791. In the following year he was consecrated Bishop of Dunkeld; and continued to labour at Laurencekirk, where he "lived universally esteemed, and died universally regretted." His widow was a daughter of Edgar of Keithock, near Brechin (*q. v.*). Their daughter, Miss Watson of Pitt Street, Edinburgh, who is possessed of a number of Jacobite relics, furnished some interesting particulars for Chambers's History of the Rebellion.

Bishop Watson was succeeded in the charge at Laurencekirk by Mr Milne, who was first stationed at Muchals, after which he became assistant to Bishop Strachan at Dundee:—

M. S. Reverendi GULIELMI MILNE, A.M., presbyteri Ecclesiæ Episcopalis in Scotia, qui apud Laurencekirk munere pastorali octo circiter annos fideliter functus est; pietate in Deum, verecundia et morum comitate, insignis erat; obiit innuptus anno Dom. 1817, sacri muneris 20, et ætatis suæ 42. Fratres sui reverendi Diocesis Brechinensis.

[Sacred to the memory of the Rev. WILLIAM MILNE, A.M., presbyter of the Episcopal Church in Scotland, who for about eight years discharged the duties of pastor at Laurencekirk. He was distinguished for his piety, modesty, and courtesy of manners, and died unmarried in 1817, in the 42d year of his age, and 20th of his ministry. His reverend brethren in the Diocese of Brechin erected this monument.]

An adjoining headstone bears this inscription to Mr Milne's successor:—

Sacred to the memory of the Rev. ROBERT SPARK, sometime Episcopal clergyman at Laurencekirk, who died 3 May 1837, in the 81st year of his age, and 57th of his ministry. And of his wife, Mrs JEAN BEATTIE, who died 30 March 1838, aged 76. Also of their family, JOHN and CHRISTINA, who died in infancy; and JOHN, surgeon H.E.I.C.S., who died at Bombay, 5 May 1829, aged 36.

—Before coming to Laurencekirk, Mr Spark officiated first at Redmyre, where he succeeded Mr (afterwards Bishop) Strachan, and next at Drumlithic. The Redmyre mission was abolished in Mr Spark's time, and the congregation divided between the churches of Laurencekirk and Drumlithic.

Like the Episcopal church of Drumlithic, that of Laurencekirk was burnt by the Duke of Cumberland in 1745; after that, the Episcopalians met for a time at Mill of Halkerton, from whence they removed to Redmyre. Subsequently, owing to the centrical situation of Laurencekirk, it was fixed upon as the seat of the Convention of the Bishops and Clergy of the Episcopal Church in Scotland, when they met (11th November 1789), and resolved to apply to Government for a repeal of the obnoxious penal laws under which they were then suffering—an application which was attended with the success it so well deserved.

It is told that when Lord Gardenstone heard of Laurencekirk being selected as the place of the meeting of Convention, he was so much gratified that he intimated his intention to the parish minister of being at the expense of entertaining the Bishops and Clergy, and begged of Mr Forbes to show them attention, and act as landlord in his absence. But, as "his reverence" declined to recognise ministers proscribed by law, his Lordship—himself "a lawgiver," and an Established churchman, and who has not been inaptly designated "the friend of human kind"—felt so indignant at Mr F.'s conduct, that he not only entertained the *unlawful* clergy himself, but set about the erection of the present church, &c., at Laurencekirk.*

The Episcopal church was founded on the 15th of September 1791, and built after plans by Captain Rudyerd, commanding engineer of Scotland. It contains an altar piece, which was presented by a Mr Mitchell of Bath in the time of his fellow-student, the Rev. Mr Milne. The subject is said by some to be the Presentation of the Virgin in the Temple, by others S. Laurence. Whatever the picture may represent, there is no doubt as to its being a fine work of art, possibly by Nicholas Poussin, to whose broad and telling style it bears a striking resemblance.

The church is a plain, but neat structure, with baptismal font of freestone, gifted by Mr Goalen, a late incumbent. The east end of the church is crescent shaped, and a plain belfry and clock are upon the west end. Over the door (which is reached by a few steps), a slab contains this account of the erection of the edifice:—

Ædis hujus Divino in Scoticana sub Episcopis Ecclesia cultui, per illustrem FRANCISCUM, Dominum de GARDENSTON, devotissime dicatæ, ejusque et aliorum complurium munificentia elegantissimo tandem extructæ, die Martii XXIV., anno MDCCXCIII.

[This edifice, most devoutly dedicated for Divine worship in connection with the Scottish Episcopal Church, by the illustrious FRANCIS, Lord GARDENSTON; and by his munificent liberality and that of several others, at length completed in a style of the greatest elegance, 24 March 1793.]

* Since this notice appeared on 9th June 1871, it has been resolved to erect, upon the site of the old Episcopal church of Laurencekirk a new edifice in the Early English Gothic style of architecture, after plans by Mr Ross, Inverness. The foundation stone—solemnly blessed and dedicated to God and Saint Laurence, the Archbishop and Confessor—by the Lord Bishop of the diocese—was laid by the Hon. the Lord Forbes, 4th July 1871, in presence of the Rev. Dr Flemying, the incumbent, and a large assemblage of spectators.—(v. Montrose Standard, July 7, 1871.)

According to the Aberdeen Magazine for Aug. 1791, in which there is an account of the laying of the foundation stone of the church of S. LAURENCE, it was at first intended that the inscription over the doorway should present a fuller account of the history of the building. This idea having been abandoned; and as the bit proposed to be added may be said to perfect the account of the rearing of the edifice, it is here quoted:—

"Johanne Phair et Johanne Gibson, architectonibus. Ad ichnographiam Henrici Rudyerd, artificum militarium in Scotia præfecti. Lapidem primum solenniter posuit Collegii Architectonici symmystes, Johannes Ewen, Aberdonensis, die Septembris decimo quinto, anno salutis humanæ MD.CC.XCI.
Qui tantæ in terris pietatis signa dedere,
His debit in coelis præmia digna Deus."

[John Phair and John Gibson, architects. After a plan by Henry Rudyerd, chief of the military artificers in Scotland. John Ewen of Aberdeen, a member of the College of Architects (Freemasons), solemnly laid the first stone, 15th September 1791. To those who have given proofs of such piety on earth, will God give due rewards in heaven.]

—In addition to being the chief subscriber towards erecting the Episcopal Church, Lord Gardenstone also burdened the estate of Johnston with a perpetual annuity of £40 sterling, and as many bolls of oatmeal, also three acres, &c., of the best land in the village, for the maintenance of the clergyman. When James Farquhar, Esq. of Hallgreen, M.P., bought the lands from Lord Gardenstone's heirs, he was bound by them to try to set aside these payments; but, luckily for the church, the supreme courts decreed in its favour. As previously shown (v. p. 87), Lord Gardenstone, who died 22d July 1793, was the second son of the laird of Troup, and his remains lie within the family burial place at the old kirk of Gamrie.

The estate of Johnston is now the property of Alex. Gibbon, Esq., to whom it was left by his maternal uncle, the above-mentioned Mr Farquhar (v. NIGG). Upon a headstone in churchyard of Laurencekirk:—

The Rev. David Forbes minister of St Laurencekirk, erects this stone to the memory of his father, ALEX. FORBES, who payed to nature its last debt, Augt. 7, 1768, aged about 80 years:—

Shall venal flattery prostitute the Muse,
To senseless titles spurious honours pay,
And yet to rural worth such lays refuse,
Which Truth may burnish with her brightest ray?
Forbid it Equity! The task be mine
To yield his memory all the praise I can;
The whole's compris'd in this conclusive line—
God's noblest work (here lyes) an Honest man.

—Alex. Forbes was a blacksmith to trade, and the above lines were composed by his relative, Dr Beattie. A brass plate, inserted into the top of a table-shaped stone (beside the above), is thus inscribed:—

The Rev^d. DAVID FORBES, who was 34 years minister of the parish of Laurencekirk, died March 24th, 1795, aged 70 years. This stone is placed over his remains by his widow, KATHARINE MORISON, who died 22d Oct. 1820, aged 70 years. She was buried in the grave of her husband.

The patronage of the church being in the gift of St Mary's College, St Andrews, it was given after Mr Forbes' death to the Rev. George Cook, second son of Professor Cook. He remained at Laurencekirk until 1829, when he became Professor of Moral Philosophy at St Andrews; and was succeeded at Laurencekirk by his nephew, Mr John Cook. He was also translated to St Andrews, and gave place to the present incumbent, Mr M'Gowan.

Dr George Cook married Diana, a daughter of the Rev. Mr Shank, sometime minister at St Cyrus, whose monument (within an enclosure near the N.E. corner of the kirkyard of Laurencekirk) bears this inscription:—

Sacred to the memory of ALEXANDER SHANK of Castlerig, sometime minister of the Gospel at St Cyrus, who died at Laurencekirk on the 5th Jany. 1814, aged 75 years:—Also, DIANA, his wife, daughter of the late Robert Scott of Dunninald, parish of Craig, who died here on the 24th Feby. 1825, aged 84 years:—And, JANE, their youngest daughter, who died at her house in Laurencekirk, on the 23d of Nov. 1840:—Also, in memory of HENRY SHANK of Castlerig and Gleniston, Esq., last surviving son of the above Alexander and Diana Shank, who died January 4th 1860, aged 81.

—Mr Shank, who was a son of the minister of

Drumoak (*q.v.*), was appointed to St Cyrus in 1732. About 1784, he resigned that church on succeeding to the estate of Castlerig in Fife, which came to him by the death of his cousin, Alex. Schank. By his wife, Diana Scott, Mr Shank of St Cyrus had several children, the last-named of whom in the above inscription became a Director of the E.I.C., and left a family of sons and daughters (*v.* Burke's Baronage.)

It ought to be added that the present representatives of the minister of Drumoak trace his descent from one Murdoch Shank, who, it is said, found the body of King Alexander III. among the cliffs at Kinghorn. For this service, it is also stated that Murdoch received a gift of the lands of Castlerig, near Kinghorn, which " Estate (writes Mr Shank of the Villa), has descended from Father to Son in the family of Shanks of Castlerig up to the present day, a period of nearly 600 years."

So far as I have seen, there is no trace in printed records of the name of Castlerig until a late date, nor of a family of Shank, or Schanks, as landowners from 1360—when, according to Nisbet's Heraldry (1st edit., ii. 229), Robert Shank held lands at Kinghorn, which bounded those of a chapel and hospital upon the north and west—until 1695, when the name of Henry Shanks appears among the heritors of that parish (Sibbald's Hist. of Fife, 452.)

But, apart from these printed particulars, the Rev. Dr Cook of Haddington kindly informs me that a Martin Shank witnesses several baptisms at Kinghorn in 1575; also that Henry Shanks, bailie, and Agnes Balfour, his wife, had a son named Martin born 28th June 1670, who became minister of Banchory-Ternan—a point which disproves a tradition that Mr Shanks of Banchory (*q.v.*) belonged to the Garioch, in which district the Poll Book and other authorities show the surname of Shank to have been pretty common during the 17th century.

I am also indebted to Dr Cook for a reference to the charter in favour of Alex. Shanks, dated 12th February 1735 (Reg. Mag. Sigil., Lib. xcv., No. 46), which proceeds on the resignation of Alex. Shanks, of the lands and barony of Kinghorn to the Crown. It also appears that, by entail of 1769, Alex. Shanks of Castlerig, having no legitimate male issue, left his estates to the son of his cousin-german, by whose descendants Castlerig and Gleniston are now possessed.

ALEXANDER BEATTIE, d. 1788, a. 26:—

Ah! early lost! ah! life I thou empty name,
A noontide shadow, and a midnight dream;
Death might have satisfy'd his craving rage,
And mow'd down all the vices of the age.
But Heav'n who saw, offended with our crimes,
Begrug'd thy virtues to the abandon'd times;
By his cold hand transplanted thee on high,
To live and flourish thro' eternity.

—The above lines are locally attributed to Dr Beattie, author of the Minstrel, who, as is well known, was born at Laurencekirk in 1735. Upon a headstone:—

Sacred to the memory of JAMES THOMSON, late teacher in Laurencekirk, who received the degree of Master of Arts from the Mar. Coll. of Aberdeen in the year 1800. He died the 17th May 1812, in the 34th year of his age.

Upon a headstone:—

Erected by Charles Stiven, boxmaker, Laurencekirk, to the memory of MARGARET BURNETT, his spouse, who died the 20th Oct. 1813. The said CHARLES STIVEN died the 6th Aug. 1821, aged 68 years, and is here interred.

—The last-named was the first of the Laurencekirk snuff-box makers. He was born in the parish of Glenbervie; and his father, "a gryte Jacobite," named his son after the young Pretender. The first of the Laurencekirk snuff-boxes was made about 1783, for Lord Gardenstone's factor, in imitation of a box which Stiven mended for him. Stiven improved upon the original; and, on its being shown to Lord Gardenstone, his Lordship advised Stiven to settle in Laurencekirk, where he afterwards carried on, with success and reputation, the business of a fishing-rod and snuff-box maker. Some years ago his son was appointed box-maker to Queen Victoria.

ELSPET MORES (1720) :—
Wain tears give ore, for I am far aboue
The highest reach of any human loue ;
My soul's in Glory. Death's wuseemly shade,
A pleasant groue is to my body made.
Where heauenly rest I'le take until the day
That (come my Father's Blessed) Christ shall say,
Then shal our joys begune, perfected be
With lasting peace blest in the Lord that die.

Although, as already shown, Conveth, now Laurencekirk, was a place of note in the 7th century, the existing remains of antiquity in the parish are few and uninteresting. Records show that John (brother of Humphry of Berkeley), having dispossessed the monks of Arbroath of the lands of Balfleth, Monboddo, and Gloufarquhar, &c., was bound, in the time of Alex. II., to allow them a part of the lands of Conveth, of which Berkeley was then proprietor.

At Halkerton, the remains of an old seat of the lords of that title are still visible ; and it seems probable that it was there that " William the Hawker" resided. He is the reputed ancestor of the noble family of Falconer, and was possibly contemporary with William the Lion.

Tanton Fair (S. ANTHONY), probably shows that there had been either a chapel in the district, or an altar in the church of Conveth, dedicated to that saint. *Katie's Market*, which was established in Lord Gardenstone's time, and named after an old woman in the village, is still held there ; as is also *Lowran Fair* (S. LAURANCE). The last named is one of the oldest of the local markets, and has its name from the titular saint of the kirk.

It was soon after 1764 that Lord Gardenstone bought the property of Johnston—then a poorly cultivated and almost barren district—and began those improvements upon it, which, great as were his talents as a lawyer and writer, &c., have done more to hand down his name to posterity than any other of his many good deeds. The village had advanced so much from 1764 to 1779, that he obtained a royal charter, by which it was erected into a burgh of barony, on which occasion he addressed a Letter of Advice to the inhabitants, for their commercial and social guidance, which has been much admired for its sound common sense. His Lordship also had portraits drawn, in crayons, about 1790, of the original feuars and others (21 in number), including Brich, the artist. These curious productions are preserved in the Gardenstone Arms Hotel, at Laurencekirk.

It is superfluous to say that, since Lord Gardenstone's time, Laurencekirk, like other places, has been very much altered and improved in its appearance. And while but little waste land is to be seen around it, the village (apart from the Parish and Episcopal Churches) contains a neat Free Church, branch banks, and many good shops and houses, together with a public hall.

Very few of the old or original houses are now in existence, and but few of them present (as was fashionable at one time) either the date of erection or the initials of the proprietor. One exception, however, is worth noting, the inscription being quaint, and significant as to the state of the proprietors at the time they built the house, and at a brief period thereafter :—

1814 WE THOUGHT OF BETTER TIMES ;
1816 BUT WORSE CAME.

There is a library and reading-room at the north end of the Gardenstone Arms Hotel, which was erected and furnished with books by Lord Gardenstone. Although neither the number nor the selection of the books met the approval of Dr Johnson, who visited the place in 1773, there was possibly then not another library of the kind between Edinburgh and Aberdeen ; and his Lordship had at least the merit of establishing in these parts a place of intellectual resort to which the inhabitants could repair, at a time when good books were comparatively difficult of attainment.

It was at Laurencekirk, in 1782, while a student at Aberdeen, that Colman the younger, the future dramatist (whose love for Scotland and the Scotch was much like that of Dr Johnson), " deposited (as he humorously says) upon a profane altar his virgin offering to the muse. This maiden effort (he continues), a ballad, was a contemptible piece of doggerel," and was written in the album of the Boars' Head Inn. On returning soon after, Colman was pleased to find the following couplet written below his effusion :—

"I like thy wit ;—but, could I see thy face,
I'd claw it well, for Scotia's vile disgrace."

Which Colman curtly answered by writing :—

"Is, then, a Scotchman such a clawing elf?—
I thought he scratch'd no creature but himself!"

Lethnot.

(THE VIRGIN MARY.)

LETHNOT and NAVAR (the early history, &c., of both of which parishes will be found in the Land of the Lindsays), were united in the year 1723.

A curious font, of possibly the 15th century, lies in Lethnot kirkyard. The present church of Lethnot was built in 1827 ; and two slabs in the belfry (respectively initialed and dated — 1672 N., and J. R. 1742), relate to the incumbency of Mr ROBERT NORIE and Mr JOHN ROW. To the memory of the last-named a tablet within the church is thus inscribed :—

1747.—Here lies what was mortal of the late Reverend Mr JOHN ROW, minister of the Gospel in the united parishes of Navar and Lethnot, who discharged the sacred office with unwearied diligence in the first of these parishes alone for 5 years, and afterwards in both together for 22 years, and whose labours, through the blessing of God, produced such effects as convinced all who observed them that he had neither run unsent, nor spent his strength in vain. He died upon the 24 day of Decr 1745, while the Nation was distracted with Civil Wars, but had the pleasure to see his People adhering to their religion and liberties, while many others had joined those who wanted to overturn both ; and soon after Affairs had taken such a turn as he had foretold, both in public and private, the disturbers of our peace being dispersed by ye glorious Duke of Cumberland. His spouse, ELIZABETH YOUNG, who had lived 43 years married with him, died upon the 8 day of Septr 1746, and was interred beside him.

—Mrs Row bequeathed a sum of £10 towards the support, or repair, of the bridge of Lethnot, which was erected about the time of the union of the parishes, and when her husband was transferred from Navar to Lethnot. The next inscription is also within the church:—

Here lies ye Body of GEORGE DAVIDSON, Son to Mr Will. Davidson, Minr of the Gospel in Navar & Lethnot, & Janet Farrier, his Spouse, who died 16th Aug. 1760, in the 16th year of his age, having finished his first Session at College. His good Dispositions, Sweetness of temper, uncommon application, progress in Latin and Greek, and other amiable Qualities, afforded pleasing Prospects, made his short life endearing to his Parents, and his early Death much regretted by all who knew him. But blessed are ye Dead which die in the Lord. His Brother ALEXANDER DAVIDSON, was born 2d Nov. 1746, and coming from Riga, a Sailor, died 23 July 1763, and Burried in Woulosound Burial place in the 17th year of his age, much lamented.

—Mr Davidson, who was ordained minister of this parish in 1746, died in 1775-6. He was buried within the church of Lethnot, as was also the Rev. DAVID ROSE, long Episcopal clergyman of the district, and his second wife (v. Land of the Lindsays). The last named were the parents of the Hon. Geo. Rose, and the great-grand parents of Lord Strathnairn. While turning over some papers of the late Rev. Mr Symers, a scrap was found by the Rev. Mr Cruickshank, containing the following copy of an inscription for a monument which was intended to be raised to the memory of Mr and Mrs Rose by a daughter :—

"DAVID ROSE, Episcopal clergyman, served the cures of Lethnot and Lochlee. Died in the year 1758, aged 63, and lies buried in the Kirk of Lethnot. His spouse, MARGARET ROSE, died in the year 1785, aged 80, and was buried beside her husband. The above Rev. DAVID ROSE was twice married, and by his first wife had four children, all of whom died at an early age. By the second he had five children, of whom two only survive—the Honourable GEORGE ROSE, and a daughter, MARGARET, by whom this marble is erected."

—The daughter, who proposed to erect the monument, died unmarried in Montrose about 1820, and was buried in St Peter's cemetery there.

The next inscription, from a chest-shaped tomb, covers the grave of the founder of the Gannochy Bridge, &c. (v. Land of the Lindsays) :—

This stone was erected by James Black, tenant in Wood, in the parish of Edzell, in memory of his spouse JANNET WALLIS, who died the 6 of June 1745, aged 65 years; and sd James Black was of age 68 years :—

Ah Sin ! hence momentary life, hence breath,
Sighs for ye silent grave and pants for death :
What means ye warning of ye passing bell ?—
A soul just gone to Paradise or Hell.
To darkness tends ye broad, but slippry way,
O frightful gloom, deny'd each cheering ray ;
While such as walk in paths divinely bright
Shall shine within ye Courts of endless light.

JAMES BLACK,

Born at Mill of Lethnot, dy'd Oct. 24, 1750, at Wood of Dalbog. Chiefly built the Bridge of Gannochie, and doted for the support of it 50 merks Scots : Besides 1000 merks for other Bridges and pious uses : viz. 500 merks for a Schoolmr. at Tillibardin : and 300 merks toward building a Bridge at Balrownie, with 200 merks to the poor of Fettercairn.

No Bridge on Earth can be a Pass for Heav'n,
To generous deeds Let yet due Praise be given.

Memento—1746—mori.

Upon another chest-shaped stone :—

To this grave is committed all that the grave can claim of two Brothers, DAVID and JOHN LEITCH, who on the 7th of Oct, 1757, both unfortunately perished in the West Water, the one in his 23d, the other in his 21st year. Their disconsolate father John Leitch, tenant, Bonnington, erects this monument to the memory of these amiable youths, whose early virtues promised uncommon comfort to his declining years, and singular emolument to Society.

O Thou ! whose reverential footsteps tread
These lone dominions of the silent Dead ;
On this sad stone a pious look bestow,
Nor uninstructed read this tale of woe ;
And while the sigh of sorrow heaves thy breast,
Let each rebellious murmur be suppress'd ;
Heaven's hidden ways to trace, for Thee, how vain !
Heaven's just decrees, how impious, to arraign !

Pure from the stains of a polluted age,
In early bloom of life, they left this stage ;
Not doom'd in ling'ring woe to waste their breath,
One moment snatch'd Them from the power of Death !
They liv'd united, and united dy'd ;
Happy the Friends, whom Death cannot divide !

—This epitaph, composed by Dr Beattie, author of "The Minstrel," appears (slightly altered) in the first edition of his poems (Lond. 1760.) The sad accident to which it alludes arose from the two brothers being upon one horse, while attempting to cross the river during a flood.

Here lyes AGNES GIBB, spous to James Laing, Drumcairn, in the parish of Lethnot, who departed this life the — day of Iannary 1737, aged 48, who left behind her thes children lanfully procreat betuixt her and her said husband, Iohn, Iames, David, and William Laings, and tuo daughters, Ann and Margaret Laings :—

Remember all who pass by, &c.

A slab of Peterhead granite (encased in a handsome freestone monument), presents this inscription :—

In memory of the Rev. ALEXANDER SYMERS, late minister of the united parishes of Lethnot and Navar, who, after an incumbency of 33 years, died on the 9th day of May 1842, aged 76 years. And of CLEMENTINA CARNEGY, his spouse, and daughter of the late James Carnegy of Balmachie, Panbride, who died on the 14th February 1851, in the 84th year of her age. And of their children, DAVID-LYELL, who died on the 6th May 1821, aged 19 years ; ALEXANDER, Commander of the ship *Haidee*, who perished in the Indian Ocean with all on board, in the year 1838, in the 34th year of his age ; JOHN-PETER, who died on the 2d June 1821, aged 17 years ; CLEMENTINA-LYELL, who died on the 24th August 1824, aged 18 years ; MARGARET, who died in June 1820, aged 11 years ; PATRICIA-ALISON-CARNEGY, who died in January 1817, aged 2 years.

—Mr Symers was previously schoolmaster at Barry. The monument was erected by two of his sons—George, surgeon, R.N., and Stewart-Lyell, merchant, Trancnt, the latter of whom changed the spelling of his name to *Seymour*.

Navar.

(S. ——.)

THE kirk of *Netheuer*, a parsonage of the cathedral of Brechin, had possibly been granted to that church by one of the ancient lords of Brechin, who took one of their titles from this district. From Navar, at the present time, the title of Baron is assumed by the Earl of Dalhousie, a descendant and representative of the old lords De Brechin.

The burial-ground, which is surrounded by a dry stone dyke and a few trees, is situated upon the sunny side of a hill near Blairno. Although the kirk was "down" before June 1729, its size can yet be traced. Near the middle of the enclosure, a belfry, to which a stone slab is fixed, bears this record of the subscribers to the building :—

Ann Wylie in Westside omitted.
This bell-house was built in the year 1773, at the expense of the following persons and their interest—
Mr Alex. Gold Tenant in Argeith
James Cobb in Ledbreakie
Frances Stewart in Nathrow
James Molison in Craigendowy
Ja. Lighton in Drumcairn
John Molison in Oldtown
Alexr Jolly in Witton
Will Speid in Blarno
Thos. Gordon in Lightney
Da. Wyllie in Tillyarblet
Jon & Andr Cobbs in Tillicbirnie
George Cobb in Achfearey
John Cobb in Room.

Owing to a miscalculation on the part of the builder, the receptacle in the "bell-house" was made too small for the instrument; and it continued to be suspended from a tree in the church-yard until stealthily removed. The bell was long concealed; and on being brought to light (a new bell having meantime been got for the kirk of Lethnot), the Navar bell was sent by the late Lord Panmure to the parish kirk of Arbirlot, where it long remained. It is now in the Arbroath Museum, and thus inscribed :—

SOLI . DEO . GLORIA
M . IO . FIFVS . PASTOR . NAVARENSIS . DON . DEDIT.
C . OVDEROGGE . FECIT . ROTTERDAM . 1655.

—Mr Fife, who was admitted to Navar in 1650, and died in 1658, left 1000 merks in charge of the ministers of the Presbytery of Brechin "for helping to entertaine and maintaine ane pious young man ane student at the new college of St Androwes yearlie" (*v.* Land of the Lindsays.)

There are a few tombstones in the burial ground. From one of these the following is copied :—

Here lyes the relicts of a very honest woman MARGARET FYFE, sometime spouse to James Molison in Craigendowie, who chearfully left this life in hope of a better, the 25 of November year of God 1712, and 70th year of her age.

A pearl precious here doth ly,
As signifies her name;
Still shining to posterity,
By her deserved fame.
Death battered down those walls of clay,
To let her soul goe free;
And soar aloft to praise for ay,
The Triune Deitie.
Sleep then, frail dust, within thy closest urn,
Till the morning of the resurrection dawn,
When thou shalt wake, the heaven & earth shall
And be rejoined to thy immortal pawn.   [burn,
Memento mori.
My glass is run, & thine runneth.

Although unmarked by any memorial, it may interest some to know that the ashes of JOCK GUDEFELLOW lie at Navar. Jock, who was a well-known and much-feared vagrant, died, while upon a begging tour, at Tillyarblet, in Nov. 1810, where (Session records) "he was taken care of and got every thing he desired while in life, and after his decease was decently dressed by David Wyllie and his mother, at their own expences." A note of "the expences of his fourdrel" is also preserved, the total cost of which, it appears, amounted to £2 9s 11d, of which sum 13s were expended on "spirits used betwixt his death and burial." Gudefellow is thus spoken of by the late James Bowick of Montrose, in his meritorious volume of Characters and Sketches (1824) :—

"There's he who slid from Perth to Aberdeen
Upon his hands and buttocks, as they say;
JOCK GUDEFELLOW was the creature's name, I ween,
Who ofttimes scared the children from their play;
But now the fearful wight hath passed into the clay."

Jock is said to have been a *gourmand;* and it is told that, upon entering a farm house one day, and finding a female the only inmate, he demanded a dish of "fried collops!" It seemed at first impossible to comply with Jock's demand ; but on recollecting that the remains of a pair of old buckskin breeches were in the garret, the wylie damsel frankly acceded to his request. These she soon procured, and, like Paddy Haggerty of Irish song, having cut them into suitable bits, and fried them with onions and butter, set "the dainty dish" before Jock, who, upon clearing the platter, gruffly remarked—" Aye, lass, your collops are tough (tough), but tastie !"

Withal, Jock had humour : upon asking "ane o' the gudeman's sarks" (shirts) from a farmer's wife one day, who told him she had no old shirt to give away, Jock replied by answering, " Ye ken, gudewife, an *auld* sark's nae compliment to ony body—gi'e me a gude ane !" Upon handing Jock a shirt, aware of his traducing propensities, the gudewife (who was more famed for worth than personal beauty) remarked, "although that's ane o' the gudeman's best sarks, ye'll just gae to the next toon an' misca' me." " Me misca' you, gudewife !" quo' Jock ; " I cou'dna do that if I didna ca' ye bonnie ; an' if I ca'd ye that, ye ken yoursel', I wad be speakin' against my conscience !"

JONATHAN DUNCAN, sometime Governor of the Presidency of Bombay, was born upon the farm of Blairno in 1756, a part of which his father occupied. His parents were buried at Edzell (*q.v.*).

The principal stone bridges in the united parishes are those of Lethnot, or Pikehardie, and Stonyford, both over the Dye, or West Water. The first bears the date of 1723, and the latter this inscription :—

Built in 1787 by . . . . stones carried . . . . mason work cost £75 ster., contributed by the Public. Centre valued at 15 guineas, given by Earl Dalhousie. Persons most active in forwarding the undertaking : — John Spence, Esq., Commissary, Brechin ; John Taylor, minister of ye Gospel, Lethnot ; Thomas Molison, tenant, Craigendowie; Charles Will, Tilliebardines ; John Will, Mill of Glascory ; John Smart, Auchouric ; John Wyllie, Ballindairg. Foundationstone laid by John Smart, Hunthill : Keystone driven by George Molison, shoemaker, Craigendowie.

An excellent account of the history of the West Water Bridge, and of the other bridges in the united parishes, was read before the Presbytery of Brechin, by the Rev. Mr Cruickshank, minister of Lethnot and Navar (*v. Montrose Standard* of 7th October 1870.)

Elchies, or Macalen.

(S. MACALEN, BISHOP AND CONFESSOR.)

ELECHYN and BOTTHARY (Botaric) were classed as one of the eight canonries of the Cathedral of Moray, which were erected by Bishop Bricius, who died in 1222 (Reg. Morav.) In the old taxation of 1275 (Theiner), the prebendary churches of Duthary (Botaric) and of *Elchyn* are jointly rated at 5 merks 6s. Scots.

The churches of Pettaric (Botaric) Elchies, and Glass, were served by one minister, Mr Alex. Leslie, in 1574. He had £66 13s 4d of stipend ; and William Hay, reader at Elchies, had £16, with the kirklands.

I am kindly informed by the present minister (Mr Pirie) that there is no proof, either in the records of the church or the Teind Court, of the parish of Elchies having been legally annexed to Knockando ; but from about the beginning of the 18th century, until about 1760, when the kirk of Elchies appears to have become ruinous, the minister of Knockando officiated at both places.

At the present time the people of Elchies have weekly service, either by the parish minister or an assistant.

The church-yard of Elchies, or MACALEN, is situated upon the north bank of the Spey, and is still used for interments. It is near the house of Easter Elchies, surrounded by a substantial stone dyke, and shaded by some good old trees. Parts of the north and west walls of the kirk, covered with ivy, stand near the middle of the enclosure; and the Easter Elchies burial aisle is in the south-east corner. The aisle is still roofed; but the door, and the entrance to the vault being both open, and the place otherwise ill-cared for, it will soon go to ruin unless speedily repaired. In the east wall is a handsome monument of Elgin stone, with a tablet (flanked by two Corinthian pillars), thus inscribed:—

Sub hoc marmore in Christi adventum conduntur cineres JOANNIS GRANT de Elchies, viri æternum lugendi, qui, dum inter vivos, nunquam adeo sibi suisq. quam aliis officia præstare solicitus fuit; amicum certissimum amicis, egenis levamen promptum, singulis hospitem liberalissimum ubiq se præstitit; de patria vero, propter operam ei in bello posteriore civili non minus fideliter quam feliciter navatam, optime meritus, et postquam tam in sacris quam negotiis secularibus omnium cujuscunq. generis virtutum constanti exercitio verae nobilitatis characteristicon adeptus esset, a virtutis Auctore vocatus, fatis cessit Martii IV^{to}, anno salutis humanæ MDCCXV, ætatis LVI^{to}, hoc unicum, ædificium in debitæ filialis observantiæ justiq. doloris tesseram, Patricio, filio unico, extruendum relinquens.

[Under this marble, until the advent of Christ, lie the ashes of JOHN GRANT of Elchies, an ever-to-be lamented man, who, while among the living, was never so anxious to promote the interests of himself and his family, as those of others; to his friends he ever showed himself a very sure friend, to the needy a ready benefactor, to all a very liberal host; by the not less loyal than successful services which he rendered to his native land during the late Civil War, he earned a just title to the deepest gratitude of his countrymen; and, after he had by the constant practice of every kind of excellence in sacred as well as in secular affairs, acquired the distinctive mark of true nobility, being summoned by the Author of virtue, he departed this life 4th March 1715, in his 56th year, leaving this unique structure to be erected by his only son, Patrick, in token of due filial respect and just regret.]

—The erector of the mausoleum, and in all probability the composer of the Latin inscription, was admitted an advocate in 1712. Having attained considerable eminence as a barrister, he was raised to the bench in 1732, and assumed the title of Lord Elchies. He was subsequently a Lord of Justiciary, and died at Inch House, near Edinburgh, in 1754. His collected Decisions of the Court of Session were published in 1813, and his Annotations on Lord Stair's Institutes in 1824. His Session papers and notes of his decisions are preserved in the Advocate's Library, all of which "exhibit a wonderful degree of application and industry" (Senators of College of Justice.) Lord Elchies' son, John Grant, sheriff-depute of Moray and Nairn, afterwards a Baron of Exchequer, sold Easter Elchies to the Earl of Findlater, to whose descendant, the Earl of Seafield, the property now belongs. "Esterelloquhy" belonged in property to John Grant of Grant in 1565, and was then teld of the Cathedral of Moray for an annual payment of £11 5s 4d. (Reg. de Morav.) This laird appears to have given Easter Elchies to his third son Duncan, who became the founder of this branch of the Grants. Lord Elchies' father was a captain in the royal army, and fought at the skirmish in Cromdale, under Sir Thomas Livingstone, in 1690.

The burial ground contains a few tombstones, one of which (uninscribed) appears to have been used originally as a millstone, since it presents the socket for the rind, &c. The following are a few of the inscriptions:—

Here lyes ane honest woman called MARIORIE CHALMERS, spous to William M'Conachie in Hillhall, who departed this lyfe the — day of Decr. 1687.

Here lyes ane honest woman called ISABEL WARDEN, spous to John Sharp in Hillhall, who departed the 29 day of December 1704.

Here lyes the body of ALEXANDER CUMMING, lawful son of Robert Cumming indweller in Colargreen, who dep⁴ this life the 3 day of October 1707 years.

Under this stone is laid til the coming of Christ, the dust of an honest man caled IOHN PROCTOR, sometime indweller in Clayfurs at Easter Elchies. He died the .... and ELSPET GRANT, his first spouse, who died the 29 of July 1709, and .....

Upon a stone bearing representations of a rake, hedge shears, and a pruning knife, are the initials, G.M: C.C. Adjoining:—

JEAN GRAY, wf. of John Skakell, mercht. Elgin, died in "the flower of her age," 1737, a. 22 :—
In one coffin, below this stone,
Lys both the mother and the son.

Knockando.

(S. ——)

THE church of *Knockandoch*, which is within the diocese of Moray, is said to have been a vicarage dependent upon the kirk of Inveravon before the Reformation (Shaw's Moray.) The fact is not mentioned in any record that I have seen, until 1574-6. Alexander Sandeson was then reader, and, along with the kirk lands, he had 20 merks of stipend. In 1574, Alexander Gordon was minister of Knockando, and of the two neighbouring parishes of Kirkmichael and Inveravon, with £160 Scots of stipend.

It is just possible, since the kirk of Knockando was dependent upon that of Inveravon, that the former district, like the latter (v. p. 143), had belonged in property to the old Earls of Fife; but of this there is no record.

The kirk of Knockando, which is a long narrow building with outside stairs to the galleries, has a commanding position upon a rising ground, from which there is a fine view of mountain scenery. A slab over the kirk door bears the following text and date: the date refers to the building of the present place of worship :—

ROM . X . 14 . 15 . MDCCLVII.

The church has lately been much improved by the enlargement of the windows, &c.; and an inscribed slab of white marble, set in black, is in the Wester Elchies loft :—

Sacred to the memory of MARGARET, wife of James-William Grant, Esq. of Elchies, who died in London, Jan. 28, 1855, born April 10, 1791. Her mortal remains were laid in Kensal Green Cemetery, in the sure and certain hope of the resurrection to eternal life. Isa. 26. 3.

A Templar's tomb (formed of composite) within an enclosure in the church-yard, covers the ashes of the husband of the above-named lady. It bears the words " CRAIG-O'-CROACHAN " (the slogan, or war cry of the Grants), also this inscription :—

The vault of Elchies. In remembrance of JAS.- WILLIAM GRANT of Elchies, in this county, who died the 17th day of Dec. 1865, aged 77 years. His mortal remains are laid in this vault. Jesu mercy.

—Mr Grant, who long held a high position in the Civil Service in India, was a gentleman of superior learning and refined tastes, and cultivated the interesting science of astronomy with no ordinary success. It was Mr Grant who bought the " Trophy Telescope of the First Exhibition" (v. Good Words for 1863, p. 126). He had it fitted up at Elchies, where it was an object of attraction until Mr G.'s death, when it was bought by the late Mr Aytoun of Glenfarg. Mr Grant's father made a fortune abroad, and acquired by purchase, about 1783-4, the estate of Wester Elchies, to which were afterwards added those of Knockando and Ballintomb.

Grants appear to have occupied Wester Elchies from at least 1565: In the rental of the bishopric of Moray of that date (Reg. Morav.), it is stated that Wester Elchies, with the mill and fishings of the same, the "ferrie cobbill," also Kincardic with fishings on the Spey, were held by James Grant, for the annual payment of £16 9d Scots. This old branch of the Grants (who were cadets of Grant of Grant), held Wester Elchies, &c., for several generations.

Apart from the slab bearing the Runic inscription, and the curious old incised stones in the churchyard (referred to below), possibly the oldest inscribed stone at Knockando is a fragment which bears a shield with the Dunbar and Grant arms impaled, the initials I. D., and these words:—

  . . . . ODEV . OF . MARY . D . . . . .
  LAVFVL . DAVGHTER . TO . . . .

—In consequence of so many of the ministers of Knockando having died in early life, a tradition has long existed in the parish to the effect that when a manse was being built long ago, the minister refused to give the workmen *a founding pint*, upon which they are said to have pronounced a malison against future incumbents; and, in token of their sincerity, it is added that they built a gravestone into some part of the manse. Whether the fragment above-noticed (which was found in the old offices of the manse a few years ago), had been the fatal stone, or that any malediction was ever pronounced, is more difficult to say than that no parish in the district has had so many changes of ministers, through death, as that of Knockando. The Separate Register of the Presbytery of Aberlour shows that from April 1788, until December 1866, there have been no fewer than seven ministers at Knockando, all of whom died there with the exception of Dr Asher, who was translated to Inveravon after being seven years at Knockando. The next three inscriptions are from the tombstones of some of these ministers:—

In memory of the Rev. JOHN WINK, minister of Knockando, who, after 11 years of faithful service, died 11th March 1851, aged 54.

In memory of the Rev. FRANCIS W. GRANT, who, after 3 years of an earnest ministry, died 25th Jan. 1855, in the 32d year of his age. By his sister, Margaret, teacher, Kirknewton.

Erected by the Parishioners of Knockando in affectionate remembrance of the Rev. JOHN CLARKE, minister of Knockando, who, after an acceptable ministry of 11 years, died 18th Dec. 1866, aged 47.

—In addition to the above, other three parish ministers are buried at Knockando, who have no tombstones—viz., Messrs FRANCIS GRANT, who died in 1805; LAUCHLAN M'PHERSON, who died in 1826; and GEORGE GORDON, who died in 1839.

. . . . LEAN, an honest and laborious man that died 17th June 1746, and of MARGARET WALLACE, his wife, a woman of unaffected simplicity and chearfulness in manners, with unspotted integrity, and by her industry reared a young family. She died 16th May 1769. This monument is erected by Alex. M'Lean, their dutiful son, gardner at London.

WM. WATSON, Excise Officer, d. 1834, a. 34; his dr. HANNAH d. 1840, a. 9 yrs.

To Death's despotic sceptre all must bend,
He spares not parent, child, nor weeping friend;
Not manhood's bloom, nor youth's fair tender
Can move his pity, or resist his pow'r. [how'r,
Meagre consumption here a FATHER laid,
And BURNING FEVER slew his LOVELY MAID.
'Twas sin that gave tyrannic pow'r to Death,
And, at his summons, these resigned their breath,
Until their Saviour calls them from the grave,
Destroys grim Death, and shews his pow'r to save.

Erected by Isabella McQuine in Memory of hir Son JAMES ROBERTSON upar Tamdo, who died the 5th My 1810 aged 21 years :—

Remember friends as you pas bay
 what you ar now so once was I.

In memory of the Rev. ANDREW SPROTT, who was born at Stranraer, in July 1806, ordained at West Kilbride in 1837, inducted at Archiestown in April 1845, and died 4 May 1864. A laborious & faithful minister greatly beloved.

In affectionate and hallowed remembrance of the Rev. JOHN MUNRO, for 50 years the pastor of the Congregational Church of this parish. He was an eminently devout, able, and faithful minister of Christ, greatly beloved and respected in all the relations both of private and public life. He finished his long, laborious and useful course, March 26, 1853, in the 79th year of his age. "Well done," &c.

Upon a headstone :—

Erected by Hellen, Jessie, and Isabella Tulloch, in memory of their beloved parents MARGARET GILLAN, who died on the 19th Feb. 1840, aged 55 years; and her husband ALEXANDER TULLOCH, farmer, Crofthead, who died on the 17th Oct. 1840, aged 55 years.

—Alex. Tulloch was killed by his son-in-law, Peter Cameron, Balintomb. Cameron, who was tried for the murder at Inverness, 14th April, 1841, pleaded that he had no intention to kill Tulloch, but only intended to maim or disable him, so as to prevent him from marrying a woman to whom he was attached. Cameron was found guilty of culpable homicide, and transported for life. It is added that, under the circumstances, much sympathy was felt for Cameron.

Neither Elchies nor Knockando contain much of antiquarian interest, if we except the remains of a stone circle at Ballinteem, near the Bishop's and Priest's Crofts, and the Sculptured Stones in the kirkyard of Knockando. These latter are said to have been carried from an old burial place called Pulvernan, on the Spey, near Knockando House. One of them bears the name of "SIKNIK" in Scandinavian Runes, being the same name that appears upon another Runic monument in Sweden (v. Sculpd. Stones of Scot., ii., p. 61.)

A place called Lady Croft is in Elchies, but whether it refers to an old ecclesiastical dedication is uncertain.

The *Village of Archiestown*, so named from its founder Sir Archibald Grant of Monymusk, was begun about 1760. In 1783, a number of the houses were destroyed by fire, among others that of the session-clerk and schoolmaster, when, unfortunately, the parochial registers perished. Lately a miserable village, Archiestown has now assumed, in consequence of improved roads, and its proximity to the railway stations of Carron and Craigellachie, &c., a clean tidy appearance. It consists of a square, a main street, and bye-lanes; and contains Free and U.P. churches.

The Spey is crossed by an iron girder bridge at Carron railway station, and by the fine picturesque bridge of Craigellachie (v. p. 26.) There are also ferry-boats at Charleston of Aberlour, and at Black's Boat, near Inveravon.

Keith-hall, or Monkeigie.

(S. SERF, OR SERVANUS, BISHOP.)

ABOUT the year 1175, William the Lion granted a charter at Edinburgh, by which he confirmed the gift made by his brother, Earl David of Huntingdon, to the church of S. MARY, and to the Bishop of Aberdeen, of the tithes of *Munkegyn*, and those of some adjoining kirks.

"Sancte Serwe altar in the parochie kyrk of Monkego" is mentioned in a deed of 1481; and the present parish church (built in 1771), stands upon a portion of "Sant Sares' bank," where, it is said, St Sares' fair was held previous to its removal to the parish of Culsamond. Another fair called S. MARGARET'S was long held on the farm of Mains of Keith-hall; but whether it was named in honour of Margaret, who was the heiress of the last of the De Garioclis, or of any other lady of local distinction (a practice which, as at present was not uncommon in old times), or in honour of S. MARGARET of the Roman Calendar, is not clear. If after the last-named, there had probably been an altar at Monkeigie dedicated to S. MARGARET. An eminence to the eastward of the old kirkyard is called *The Monk's Hill*; and *The Spital*, or site of the ancient *hospice*, is upon the extreme east of the parish.

The name of KEITH-HALL was given to the parish, as well as to the principal mansion house (previously *Caskieben*), after 1662, about which year the property was bought by Sir John Keith, who was created Earl of Kintore.

The parishes of Monkeigie, *alias* Keith-hall, and Kinkell, were united in 1754, when about one-third of Kinkell, which included Thainston, was added to Kintore, and the rest to Keith-hall.

The old kirk of Monkeigie stood near the middle of a basin-shaped hollow, and upon a mound or eminence, which having been surrounded by a moss, or marsh, in early times (the bed of which is still visible), the site of the kirk must have had quite the appearance of an island. Taking these facts into consideration, the site had probably suggested the name of the locality, since the Gaelic words *Mon-keig-ie* have some such meaning, as an island, or mound, in "a cogue," or basin-shaped situation.

Only the foundations of the old kirk are traceable in the burial-yard. Within an enclosure in the north-west corner lie some of the Kintore family, and within it are two small stones—one bears their arms, the initials E.I.K., and the date of 1698; the other is dated 1710. Both refer to the time of the first Earl, who died in 1714. A plain granite headstone is thus inscribed:—

In memory of ANTHONY-ADRIAN, eighth Earl of Kintore, who was born 20th April 1794, and died at Keith-hall, 11th July 1844, in the 51st year of his age. ✠ And also of his son WILLIAM-ADRIAN, Lord Inverury, who was born 2d Sept. 1822, and died Dec. 17th, 1843, aged 21 years.

—The above-named Earl had no family by his first wife, a daughter of R. Renny, Esq. of Borrowfield, near Montrose. By his second wife, a daughter of F. Hawkins, Esq., he had two sons and two daughters. The eldest son (Lord Inverury) was accidentally killed in England while fox hunting. The second son is the present Earl of Kintore, who married his own cousin, a daughter of Capt. Hawkins, by whom he has issue. The next inscription is from a granite slab inserted into the wall of the family burial place:—

Erected by Kintore to the memory of his beloved Aunt the Lady MARY KEITH, daughter of William, 7th Earl of Kintore, who died at Bath, July 5, 1864, aged 69 years.

—The first Earl of Kintore was John, fourth son of the sixth Earl Marischal (*v.* p. 48). He was raised to the dignity of a Peer, &c., in 1677, in consequence of the share which it was *said* he had in the preservation of the Regalia of Scotland. It was through the marriage of David, fifth Lord Halkerton, with the eldest daughter of the second Earl of Kintore, when she was only 13 years and 5 months old, that the Kintore family succeeded to the estates of Glenfarquhar, Inglismaldie, and Dunlappie (*v.* p. 62).

Upon a marble slab built into a monument on the south wall of the churchyard:—

Near this wall are interred the mortal remains of the Rev. Dr GEORGE-SKENE KEITH, minister of the parish of Keith-hall for 44 years, and of Tulliallan in Perthshire for 8 months. Born at Auquhorsk, Nov. 6, 1752, he died at Tulliallan House, March 7, 1823. Distinguished and beloved as the clergyman of a parish, remarkable in a wider sphere for his learning and science, of great mental and bodily activity, he preserved in age the same vivacity and cheerfulness, the same love of knowledge, warmth of feeling, and untiring Christian benevolence, which characterised his youth and manhood. Some gentlemen of this county, who had intended to present him with a memorial of their high respect for his character, but were prevented by his death, have erected this monument to his memory.

—Besides sermons and kindred publications, Dr Keith wrote treatises on political economy, the View of the Agriculture of Aberdeenshire, &c. His son JOHN, who died in 1867, succeeded to the church of Keith-hall, so that the father and son were in uninterrupted possession of the same charge for about ninety years. Another son, the Rev. Dr Alex. Keith of St Cyrus, born 13 Nov. 1792, and who seceded at the Disruption, is the author of Evidences of the Truth of the Christian Religion, and other works. Auquhorsk is a farm in the parish of Kinellar, from which Keiths, a reputed branch of the Marischal family, were long designed.

A flat slab, in front of Dr Keith's enclosure, is inscribed round the margin:—

Here lyes JOHN KEITH, servant to the Earle of Kintor, who departed ye 27 of Sep. . . . . . .

Upon a headstone:—

In memory of JOHN H. J. BUCKLITSCH, who died 1 Jan. 1831, aged 76 years. He was brought from Saxe Weimar by the late R. H. Anthony, Earl of Kintore, in whose family he acted as jager for 45 years.

Upon a table-shaped stone:—

DAVID CRAB, died 27 Nov. 1834, aged 75. "He was 40 years in the service of the Earls of Kintore, the last of whom he served raised this tablet.

Here lies departed worth
God's noblest work—
An honest man."

JEAN STEWART, wf. of D. Crab, d. 1858, a. 92.

In memory of Mr ARCHIBALD M'LEAN, road contractor, a native of the parish of Killin, who died Aberdeen, 31st Dec. 1825, aged 78. Erected by his widow, ELIZABETH SANGSTER. She died 1846, aged 77.

To the memory of Provost WILLIAM MOLLISON, of the burgh of Inverury, who was born 8 Sep. 1746, and died 7 Dec. 1824, aged 78. A tribute of respect for an upright and honest man. H. M. P. 1826.

In memory of GEORGE REID, sometime one of the baillies of Inverury, who departed this life 22d June 1806, aged 81. This stone is erected by his son, Lieut. ANTHONY REID, 81st Regt.: He died 1813, aged 29.

In memory of JOHN BODDIE, late residenter in Aquhithie, who died 6 Sep. 1828, aged 84. ELIZABETH CHRISTIE, his spouse, died 29th April 1829 aged 70.

Abridged :—

The Rev. JAS. COCK, minister of the Gospel at Keith-hall, died 17 Feb. 1776, in the 78th year of his age, and 38th of his ministry. BARBARA REID, his spouse, died 27th April 1800, in the 80th year of her age. [Deaths of 3 sons and 5 daughters recorded.]

The district of Monkeigie belonged to the Earl of Huntingdon, and subsequently to the De Gariochs, one of whom, Andrew de Garioch, was sheriff of Aberdeenshire, in 1264. The Gariochs ended in a daughter Margaret, who married Stiven Johnston, a reputed brother of the laird of Annandale (Doug. Baronage.) By this marriage the lands of Caskieben and others came to the Johnstons, in whom a baronetcy was created in 1626, which title is now held by Sir W. Johnston of that ilk and Hilton.

Dr ARTHUR JOHNSTON, the celebrated scholar and Latin poet (uncle to the first baronet), was born at Caskieben in 1587, and died at Oxford in 1641. His elegant verses, *De loco suo natali* (Del. Poet. Scot., i. 601), are highly descriptive of the locality of his birth-place. No stone in the burial ground bears the name of any of the Johnstons, although it is said that " Monkeigie was a chapel, built at first by the Johnstons of Caskiben for their own family"—an assertion, however, which is contrary to the recorded facts.

The house or castle of Caskieben stood upon a rising ground, where a moat is still visible, at a little distance from the present mansion of Keith-hall. Keith-hall is a large building in the Elizabethan style. It has been frequently added to and altered, and the front is embellished with several family shields. The oldest shield is initialed E.I.K : C.M.K., and dated 1665. This legend adjoins :—

   MAY . TRVTH . AND . GRACE,
   REST . HERE . IN . PEACE.

The old mansion house of Kendal (previously *Ardiharrall*), surrounded by a few venerable trees, still conveys an idea of its former importance, though it has been long occupied as a farm house. It was here (Collec. Abd. and Banff), in 1643, that the future Bishop BURNET was born, whose History of his Own Times, and the prominent part he took in contemporary events, have made so famous. The Bishop's father, who died a Senator of the College of Justice, under the title of Lord Crimond, was proprietor of Kendal and Crimond, and fourth son of the baronet of Leys. His mother was a sister of Sir Archd. Johnston, the celebrated Lord Warristoun, who was executed at Edinburgh in 1663.

The property of Kinmuck lies to the south-east of the parish church ; and according to tradition a battle was fought there between the Scots and Danes. It is further averred that in consequence of a wild boar having been captured upon the lands, the name of Kinmuck was conferred upon the district ! But, since the Gaelic words *Kinmuich* mean a " boar's head," and as the outline of certain parts of the lands suggest a resemblance to that object, it is more probable the name had originated from that circumstance.

It ought to be mentioned that the property of Kinmuck was acquired by Sir Alexander Irvine of Drum, who, in 1629, mortified the rents of the lands for the support of bursars at the University of Aberdeen, the patronage being vested in his successors in Drum.

THE HAMLET OF KINMUCK

is nearly half-way between the kirks of Keith-hall and Fintray. It has been long a chief seat of the Friends or Quakers, of whose history, in connection with the locality, interesting notices will be found in the Diary of Provost Jaffray of Aberdeen, and in Barclay's Apology for the Quakers.

The meeting-house, which has been recently enlarged, is a neat place of worship. Upon the opposite side of the road is a small but well-kept cemetery, with a few tombstones. From these the following inscriptions, which relate to a farmer family at Lethanty, are copied :—

JAMES GLENNY died 7 month 31st, 1804, aged 27 years. ELIZABETH GLENNY died 8 month 4th, 1854, aged 76 years. ELIZABETH GLENNY died 12 month 9th, 1823, aged 19 years.

JOHN GLENNY died 5 month 30th, 1844, aged 44 years; and ELIZA GLENNY died 12 month 26th, 1845, aged 10 years.

KATHARINE GLENNY died 10 month 16th, 1863, aged 65.

~~~~~~~~~~~~~~~~~

Kinkell.

(S. MICHAEL, ARCHANGEL.)

BISHOP HENRY of LYCHTON, in 1420, erected the church of *Kinkel* ("alias dictumplebaniam"), belonging, with its chapels, to the Knights of Jerusalem, into a prebend of the cathedral of Old Machar (Reg. Ep. Abd., ii. 253.)

The church, of which little more than the north wall remains, appears to have been an elegant structure. According to a writer of 1732 (Coll. Abd. and Banff, 571), it "had, formerly, a turret in the middle (for a steeple), and a great window in the east end. . . . Its chancel was separated from the rest of the church by a timber wall ; and in the south side of the chancel, it had three pillars. . . . In the north side (opposite to the pillars), is a place in the wall, wherein of old the host was preserved, with these inscriptions over it in green stone :—' HIC . EST . SERVATVM . CORPVS DE . VIRGINE . NATVM.' Underneath is written ; —' OBIIT M. A. G.' (that is, Mr Alexander Galloway), ' 1528.' His name is also written a little beneath the crucifix. . . . A little farther westward, on the same side, is a little crucifix set in the wall, made also of a sort of green stone, having some other figures on it. Here is also a very large Font. But this church is now so lamentably polluted and profaned," adds the writer, "that one is ashamed to write of it."

The " little Kirktoun," at which the kirk was situated in 1724, has long ago disappeared ; and the east end of the kirk is filled with rubbish and loose stones, among which are bits of the old mulions of the east window, &c. The language employed by the scribe of 1732, as to the place being " lamentably polluted and profaned," is applicable to the present state of the ruins, as well as to the burial-ground.

Although the peculiarities of this interesting old church have been often described, and the more curious of its ornaments engraved (v. Archæol. Scotica, vol. iii., p. 10), the following brief notes upon its present state may not be out of place here. Of the "great window" of 1732, the north side or lintel is all that remains ; and some of the plaster still adheres to the north and east walls of the church. The north wall is the most entire part of the building ; but the " three pillars" of 1732 are gone. With the exception of some of the carvings upon the upper lintel, the awmbry appears to be in pretty much the same state as it was in 1732.

The awmbry is flanked by two graceful scrolls, embellished with the above-mentioned legend, which appears to mean, " Here is preserved the Body born of the Virgin." It is carved in the contracted form represented below, and in ornamental Roman capitals :—

A̅   HIC . EST . S̅V̅A̅T̅V̅   G̅
A̅   CORP' . DE . V̅G̅I̅E̅ . NATVM   G̅

Below, and in the centre of the sill of the awmbry, a shield bears the Scotch lion, over which is the word

MEORARE.

Upon the right are the initials A.G. ; on the left—

A͞NO . D͞NI . 1528.

In the same wall, a little to the westward of the awmbry, within a plain stone frame, is a fine carving of Our Saviour upon the Cross, with the legend INRI upon the arms of the calvary. A winged angel, in the act of raising the host (?) kneels upon the left side of the cross, below which a ribbon, between four human heads, bears : p͞r͞s . sa͞to͞m (? preces sanctorum.) Upon the right of the cross stands a draped figure with nimbus—below (at the foot of the cross), is the fragment of a smaller figure, apparently seated. The calvary, or cross, is raised upon three steps, in front of which is a chalice, also the remains of some other object. Below are the initials A.G. ; and incised upon the frame—

A : G . ANO . 1525.

The initials so often repeated refer, as before shown, to ALEXANDER GALLOWAY, who was parson of Kinkell, and of whom, as the above inscriptions imply, the church itself had been intended to be a memorial. The earliest date, 1525, possibly refers to the year the work was begun, that of 1528 to the time it was finished.

Besides building the kirk of Kinkell, Mr Galloway, as early as 1505, bought two acres of land for a manse and glebe to the chaplains at Colliehill, in Bourtie, which he presented to that church (v. p. 132). He also gifted costly ornaments to the cathedral of Old Machar, and some property at Fittie. For the last-mentioned donation he requested prayers to be said upon the 7th of March annually for the souls of his father and mother, WILLIAM GALLOWAY and MARJORY MORTIMER.

Mr Galloway's liberality to the church, as well as his devout piety and learning, are recorded in the obituary of the Franciscan Convent of Aberdeen, and in the Register of the Cathedral, &c. He held, at the time of his death, which happened in 1552, the joint offices of a professor in King's College, Aberdeen, and rector of Kinkell. According to Dempster, he wrote a work (now lost) upon the natural history of the Hebrides, in which he gives an account of *claik geese*, and the trees upon which they grow !

A pavement slab, originally carved upon one side only, now embellished on both sides, stands in a socket (lately renewed) within the area of the old kirk. The incised effigy of a warrior in mail armour, with the hands in a devotional posture, covers the west face of the stone ; and the following remains of an inscription are round the margin :—

Hic . iacet . nobilis . armiger . Gilbertus . de . Erie . . . . anno . . om . m . cccc . xi.

—A shield is upon each side of the helmet of the effigy. One shield is blank, the other is charged with a chevron, between two water budgets in chief, and a hunting horn in base. The same arms are upon the breast of the figure ; and as these (with the bugle possibly for a difference) are the armorials of the GREENLAW family, the tomb probably relates to a person of that name, and one who may have been a relative of the contemporary bishop of Aberdeen, who was of the Greenlaws of that Ilk, in Berwickshire. It is also probable that the person commemorated was one of those noble preservers of the liberties and independence of Scotland who fell at Harlaw, since the date upon the stone corresponds with the year in which that battle was fought. This tomb has been long and erroneously described as that of Scrimgeour of Dudhope, whose fate is celebrated, along with many others, in the well-known ballad of the Battle of Harlaw.

Upon the reverse, and round the margin of Greenlaw's tombstone :—

Hic iacet honore illustris et sancta morum pietate ornat' Joanes Forbes b' Arbmurd' ej' cognois haeres 4 qui anno ætatis suæ : 66 : 8 iulii A.D. 1592 obiit.

[Here lies, bright with honor, and adorned with saintly piety of character, JOHN FORBES of Ardmurdo, fourth successor of his name (?), who died 8th July 1592, in the 66th year of his age.].

The Forbes arms (with a hawk's head between the three boars' heads) are boldly incised upon the upper part of the slab: below is the text (Phil. i. 21) in Greek capitals.

"John Forbes of Ardmurdo (says Lumsden), married   Graham, daughter of the Laird of Morphie, who did bear to him Mr Alex. Forbes, bishop of Abd. and John Forbes of Ardmurdo." The last-named is possibly the laird mentioned in the above inscription. Lumsden tells us that his wife was a daughter of John Forbes of Towie, to which property she had probably succeeded, after "ye houss of Towie failled," which appears to have been sometime before 1598. William Forbes of Towie had a confirmation charter of the lands of Ardmurthach from John Narne of Cromdale, 1500-1. From a flat slab, south of the ruins of the kirk :—

Heir lys under the hope of a ioyful resurection A ... R King, sometyme in Kinkel, who deperted this lyf the 2 of Febrie 1658, and Margrat Sime, his spous, who deperted the 28 of Iuly.

At south gable of church :—

Hic jacent Mr Ioannes Gellie, quondam pastor eccliae de Kinkell, qui obiit Aug. 4, 1683; & Maria Jaffray eius uxor, quæ obiit Feb. 4, 1705.

[Here lie Mr John Gellie, sometime minister of the church of Kinkell, who died 4 Aug. 1683; and Mary Jaffray, his wife, who died 4 Feb. 1705.]

A slab (in the east gable of the ruins) bears :—

Jacet hic sepulta Dña Maria Gordon, Mri Geo. Skene, pastoris, uxor, quæ obiit Aug. 1, 1712, ætatis 32.

[Here lies interred Dame Mary Gordon, wife of Mr George Skene, minister, who died 1st Aug. 1712, aged 32.]

Upon a flat stone on south side of gate :—

Here lies the body of John Walker, sometime farmer in Ardmurdo, who died April 17, 1750, aged 63 years; and his two wives, viz., Margaret Smith and Anna Walker; as also his 2 children, Margaret and Barbara Walkers. Done by ye care of Janet Caie, his relict. Mors janua vitæ.

Here lies John Emslie, sometime gairdiner at Theinston, who departed this life March 23, 1785, aged 75 . . . . . .

1832: Erected by Jas. Moir, mail guard in Aberdeen, in memory of his father, who departed this life the 2d Feby. 1829, aged 72 years :—
Stop, stranger, stop, don't walk along;
Stop one moment and read my stone;
And as you read the end of me,
Be sure for Death prepared to be;
Death did to me short warning give—
Be mindful, therefore, how to live.

Three table shaped stones belong to the next mentioned family. The oldest (embellished with mortuary emblems) bears :—

Here lies Thomas Tait, elder, sometime farmer in Mill of Thainstone, who died Feby. 8th, 1759, aged 80 years; and also his spouse Anna Moir :—
Now slain by Death who spareth none,
And lies full low under this stone,
Rotting in dark and silent dust,
Prepare for death, for die thou must,
Life is uncertain—Death is sure,
Sin is the wound—Christ is the cure.

Sacred to the memory of John Tait, Esq., late cooper, Savannah-la-Mar, Jamaica, who died at Aberdeen, the 30th July 1818, in the 60th year of his age. Also of his father Thomas Tait, in Mill of Thainston, who died 1782, aged 60; and of his mother, Margaret Cruckshank, who died in July, 1818, aged 96.

—The third monument shows that William Tait at Mill of Thainston, afterwards at Crichie, died in 1823, aged 70, and that his widow, Elspet Smith, died in 1843, aged 83. The same family still tenant the farm of Crichie, and also carry on the business of paper making.

Here lies the body of William Smith, sometime farmer in Ardmurdo, who died June 17, 1772, aged 89 years. And also his spouse Margt. Smith; their sons, John, late in Toftbills, who died in 1804, aged 84; and of James, late in Ordifold, who died in 1809, aged 83 :—

Now slain by death, &c.

—An adjoining gravestone shows that one of the above family, William, in Toftbills, died in 1823, aged 68, and that his spouse, NICOLAS MACKAY, died in 1853, aged 91.

Some years ago the burial ground at Kinkell was extended towards the south. The next inscription is from a monument in that locality :—

In memory of PETER-JAMES, infant son of Captn. P. W. Lanore Hawker, and grandson of Lt.-Col. Peter Hawker of Longparish House, Hants, who, like a spring flower, was cut down on the 18th March 1852, at the early age of 1 year and 8 months.

Being, as before shown, an ancient *plebanian* church, Kinkell had a number of dependent kirks. These were Monkeigie, Kintore, Drumblade, Dyce, Kinellar, and Kemnay. All were served by vicars under the parson of Kinkell, who, as one of the chapter of the cathedral, had his residence at Aberdeen.

Apart from Mr Galloway, some of the rectors of Kinkell were men of note in their day. On 4th July 1296, Peter de Champayne, parson of the kirk of Kinkell, did homage to Edward I. at Forfar; but, although probable, it is not quite so certain whether Champayne was parson of Kinkell in the Garioch, or of Kinkell in Strathearn, as that the same king, on 15th August 1298, gave a letter of presentation to the then vacant kirk of Kinkell in Aberdeenshire, to John Bousche of London (Prynne, 791.) Among the later parsons were James Ogilvie, a son of Ogilvie of Boyne, who became Abbot of Dryburgh; and Alexander Anderson, the last Roman Catholic principal of King's College, was previously designed vicar of Kinkell.

Kinkell has long been, and still is, the seat of an important market, named after the titular saint, whose "well" is in the neighbourhood of the church-yard. When Geo. Forbes was served heir to his father, Dr John Forbes of Corse (1649), among the lands and property enumerated, were the kirklands of the Kirktoun of Kinkell, also the liberty of "ane frie fair called Michael-fair," which was held upon the kirklands of the same yearly.

A ferry-boat has long plied upon the Don, opposite to the old kirk.

Balbithau, a turreted old mansion to the eastward of the kirk, is surrounded by venerable trees. The estate belonged to a family named Chalmers, from at least the middle of the 16th, to about the close of the 17th century, one of whom, John, "gudeman of Balbithan," slew Alexander Keith of Ochorsk (Auquhorsk) at Aberdeen, in 1584. The testament and inventory of the effects of David Chalmers, laird of Balbithan, (possibly John's father), who died in 1580 (Ant. Abd. and Banff, iii. 425), presents some curious items which ought to interest both lairds and tenants of modern times.

The Chalmers' were succeeded in Balbithan by James Balfour, an Edinburgh merchant. It now belongs to the Earl of Kintore, by whom the property was bought from Mr Abernethie-Gordon, whose remains lie within an aisle at Kinkell. Mr A.-Gordon, who left an only daughter, was a person of great corpulency; and while being carried to the grave, the weight of his body broke the spokes, and the coffin fell to the ground, luckily, without sustaining injury. Upon a tablet within the Balbithan aisle :—

Sacred to the memory of BENJAMIN ABERNETHIE-GORDON, Esquire, the last Heir of Entail of Balbithan. Born 22d May 1782, died at Strand Villa, Ryde, Isle of Wight, 4th February 1864.

Edzell.

(? S. LAURENCE.)

THE kirk of *Adel* was a rectory in the diocese of St Andrews, and the district appears to have been a place of early ecclesiastical importance. Besides having its "Abbe," or Abbot, it was the site of one of those sculptured stones, with interlaced and other carvings, which are believed to belong to Pictish and Celtic times. This interesting object, of which all trace had been lost, was brought to light in 1870, when the old dykes of the kirk-yard were being renewed.

Whether Edzell had been a seat of learning in old times, like some other places where the name or title of "Abbe" existed, and where sculptured stones have been found, is difficult to say; nor is there any way in accounting for the name of S. LAURENCE being associated with the locality, unless, when at Laurencekirk (*v.* p. 288), that Primate may have visited Edzell. It is certain, however, that the old bell, or *skellach*, which was in existence within the recollection of old inhabitants, was called "The Bell of St Laurence," and a spring, near the kirk-yard, bore the name of "St Laurence's Well." Dr Stuart seems to think (Book of Deer, p. iv.) that the kirk of Edzell, like that of Newdosk, was dedicated to S. DROSTAN.

Down to the year 1818, when the present place of worship was erected at the village of Slateford, the church stood within the burial-ground, which occupies a slight eminence, on the north bank of the West Water, about a mile north-west from the present church. The bell, which so long occupied the belfry at the old kirk (now in the session-house) appears to have been an article of local manufacture—at least it bears this inscription:—

THE . PARISH . OF . EDZELL.
MR . IAMES . THOMSON . MINR.
MADE . AT . SCLAT . FORD . BY . IOHN . EASTON . 1726.

The bell upon the kirk at Edzell bears:—

D. BARCLAY, MONTROSE, 1819.

From the slender traces of a window lintel still remaining, the old kirk appears to have been in the Early English style of architecture. It was composed of a nave and south aisle; and the aisle, separated from the nave by a graceful arch, was the family seat or pew of the lairds of Edzell. An awmbry (about 13 by 30 inches), with circular moulding, is built into the south wall; and there is a recess below the east window, possibly for an effigy.

A broken octagonal-shaped font, about 20 inches in diameter, of rude workmanship, is preserved within the aisle; also fragments of a tombstone, bearing the Lindsay arms, much defaced,

the initials A. L · W . . ; also these words and letters:—

```
. . . . . VMINE . TVO . LVMEN . V . . . . .
IN . VITA . ET . IN . . . . . . . . . . . . . .
CHRISTVS . . . . . . . . . . . . . . . . . . .
HÆC . IOANES . L . . . . . . . . . . . . . .
ER . GERMANVS . O . . . . . . . . . . . . .
ORIS . ERGO . POSVI . . . . . . . . . . . . .
. . RS . IANVA . V . . .
```

The family burial vault (below the aisle), is reached by a few steps. It has a groined freestone roof, and the keystone is ornamented by four skulls carved in relief. There is a square niche in the west wall of the vault, which had possibly been intended for an inscribed tablet; but the fragments above referred to, bear the only visible record of the Lindsays at the church of Edzell.

The first LINDSAY of Edzell was Sir ALEXANDER, a lineal descendant of Walter of Lindsay, an Anglo-Norman, who came to Scotland about 1116. Sir Alexander acquired the lordships of Edzell, Lethnot, and Glenesk, by marrying Katherine, a daughter and co-heiress of Sir John of Stirling. Sir Alexander's eldest son succeeded to his mother's patrimony; and in 1397, on the death of his uncle, Sir James Lindsay of Crawford, he became chief of his family, and heir to the Lindsay estates in Clydesdale, &c. He married Elizabeth, daughter of Robert II., and was created Earl of Crawford, 21st April 1398.

The fifth Earl was created Duke of Montrose, a title which none of his successors appear to have assumed; and when it was claimed by the late Earl of Crawford, the House of Lords gave an adverse decision, owing to some real or supposed restriction in the patent. His lordship, who died at Dunecht House, 15th Dec. 1869, aged 86, was Premier Peer of Scotland. He was succeeded by his eldest son, Lord Lindsay, author of the "Lives of the Lindsays," and other interesting and valuable works. The present Lord Lindsay, though young, is a student of the science of astronomy, and was one of those who went to Spain to witness the great solar eclipse in 1870.

It was shortly before the breaking out of the Rebellion of 1715 that the last Lindsay of Edzell parted with his paternal estates. He sold them to the Earl of Panmure, by whom they were soon afterwards forfeited. After being in the hands of the York Buildings' Company, the property was bought back about 1764, by William, the last Earl of Panmure, from whom, by entail, it came to the Earl of Dalhousie.

A flat stone, in the kirk yard, with initials and monogram, &c., is thus inscribed :—

Hier lyes THOMAS DON, who died in the year 1672, and AGNES STEVARD his spouse, who died in the year 1686, and ELIZABETH ther daughter who died in the year of God 1661.

Round the margin of a flat stone (the face of which is embellished with carvings of articles used by waulkmillers), is the following :—

Heir rests in the Lord ALEXANDER WALKER indualler in Uackmiln of Corstouns, uho departed this life the 12 of . . . 670, and his age 90 ; and his spovs ISOBEL BURN, uho departed this life 17 of Februar 1679, and hir age 68 year. Here rests in the Lord ALEXANDER WALKER, indualler in Caepo, uho departed this life the 10 day of Februar . . . . his age 69 ; and his spous IANNET BALFOUER, uho departet this life the 14 of Febraro 1692, hir age 57 years.

Upon a headstone :—

This monument was erected by John Bishop, tenant in Slateford, in memory of his spouse JANET DUNCAN, who departed this life August 6th, 1747, aged 53 :—

> Reader, cease thy pace and stay,
> Harken unto what we say ;
> As you are such once were we ;
> As we are such shall you be.
> Then provide whilst time you have,
> To come Godly unto your grave.

The following traces of an inscription are upon a flat stone, which is said to have covered the grave of Major Wood (v. Land of the Lindsays, p. 14), on the south side of the Lindsay aisle :—

. . . . BENEATH . THIS . STON
. . . . MAN . IAMES . DONALDSON
. . . MORTAL . MAN . . . SOVN . LO . LAID
. . . . THAT . TO . GOD
VHOS . EVER . . . . . ND . IVST
HEIL . PARDON . THOSE . THAT . ON . HIM . TRVST
MANKYND . HATH . NO . REPOS . BVT . ON

Another slab, near the one last mentioned, bears the names of ANDREW IAMIE and ELSPET ANDERSON, with the date of 1675. Upon a small headstone :—

Here lyes JAMES DURAY, son to John Duray of that Ilk, who departed this life February 13, 1743, agd 36 : —

> Remember, man, as you pass by,
> That grave stone under which I ly,
> Read, and remember what I tell,
> That in the cold grave thou must dwell,
> The worms to be your companie,
> Till the last trumpet set you free.

—The above relates to a family who are said to have been heritable doomsters or dempsters to the old lairds of Edzell. Along with that office, it is added, they had a grant of the lands of Durayhill, from which they assumed the designation " of that Ilk."

Round the edges of an elaborately ornamented stone, with monogram, &c. :—

☞ Hier lyes IAMES BELLY, who departed this life the 20 of Avgvst 1711 : His spovse ISOBAL STEVRD.

Remember man, as ye go by, &c.

Upon a plain headstone :—

Erected to the memory of DAVID LOW, late tenant in Meikle Tullo, who died 25th May 1852, aged 78 years. Also of his spouse JEAN JOLLY, who died 15th March 1861, aged 83 years. [&c.]

—The above-named David Low was the last liferenter and occupant of his name in Meikle Tullo —a possession which his ancestors held from a pretty early period, as appears by the under-quoted copy of a lease, still in possession of the family. It is in the handwriting of the penultimate Lindsay, laird of Edzell, and is a good example of the simple narration of fact and contract which existed at the period :—

"J david Lyndesay of Edzell Binds and oblidges me my airs exrs and successors q'homever, that

John Low and James Low in mickl Tullo, shall peacablie possess and Bruick ther possessiou ther for the space of five years nixt to com, they alwayes paying ther yearlie duties mys as formerlie, usd & woutd: in witt. wherof, J have subscrived this, my obligatione, at Edzell, the sixt day of Junn j^m vi^c nyntie six years.
"D. LYNDESAY.
"Notta that within ther taks jlk on of them ar to pay a wedder sheep."

—John and James Low, who were both in Meikle Tullo in 1729, were, like almost every tenant in the district, found to be in arrears of rent to the York Buildings' Co.; but they were so far ahead of many of their neighbours, that it is stated, they "may pay all," if allowed crop of 1715. Probably the Rev. GEORGE LOW, of Birsay and Harray, was of this race. He was one of the most accomplished naturalists of his day, and was born at Edzell, where his father was kirk officer (*v.* Land of the Lindsays.)

Upon the only remaining panel of a chest-shaped monument:—

> But yet the weight of flesh and blood,
> Doth see her flight restraine,
> That oft I prease, but doth small good,
> I rise and fall again.

A headstone bears:—

This monument was erected by David Bruce, in memory of his father JAMES BRUCE, 1749. Here lies IAMES BRUCE, sometime tenent in Westsyde of Edzell, who departed this life Julie 28, 1738, aged 72 years; and IAMES BRUCE, his son, who died in infancy. [&c.]

Intomb'd we with our fathers lie, &c.

From a plain headstone:—

This stone was erected by Iohn Fitchet, tennant in Blackymill, in memory of his wife MARGARET VALENTINE, who died the 19th of June 1775, in the 60th year of her age. She had by her first husband William Tindal, tennant also in Blackymill, three children, Anne, David, and Isabel Tindals, who survived their mother; and by the said Iohn Fitchet, six, of whom Martha, Margaret, and Cecilia survived their mother, and IOHN, IAMES, and another CECELIA died before her.

Upon a table-shaped stone:—

This monument is erected to the memory of JAMES DUNCAN, late of Wardhouse, who died on 13th January 1792, aged 75; and of JEAN MICHIE, his spouse, who departed this life on 13th July 1795, aged 63 years. As also of their children, MARGARET, ELIZABETH, JEAN, BETTY, SOPHIA, and JAMES, the latter of whom is interred in the vault of the Church of St Martin's, London.

—These were the parents, sisters, and brother of Jonathan Duncan, sometime Governor of the Presidency of Bombay. He was born at Blairno, in Navar, where his father was farmer (*v.* p.297.) Wardhouse is a small property near Montrose, which Governor Duncan bought as a residence for his parents. Upon a freestone monument:—

Sacred to the memory of GEORGE COOPER, merchant in Slateford, who died 29th Nov. 1831, aged 82 years, 4 months. Also of JANE LINDSAY, his spouse, who died 19th April 1841, aged 90 years.

—Mr Cooper acquired a large fortune as a merchant in the village of Slateford, and left a number of legacies for educational and other purposes, to Edzell and some adjoining parishes.

To the memory of the Revd ANDREW HUTTON, who died on the 5th May 1842, after having faithfully discharged the duties of parochial minister of Edzell for 53 years, and by his piety and benevolence endeared himself to all. "He being dead, yet speaketh."

Upon a monument in the area of the old kirk:—

Sacred to the memory of THOMAS WYLLIE, tenant, Mains of Edzell, who died 21st May 1795, aged 67; and ISOBEL BLACK, his spouse, who died 17th May 1790, aged 61 years.

—The monument from which the above inscription is quoted, also bears that WM. WYLLIE (son of the above) died in 1829, aged 58, and his wife, ANN MITCHELL in 1836, aged 61. The monument was erected by JAMES WYLLIE, son of the last-named, who died in 1858, aged 65. Mr Wyllie was life-renter, and the last of his race that tenanted Mains of Edzell.

The chief objects of interest in the parish are the ruins of the Castle of Edzell, the history of which and its old proprietors have been admirably told in the Lives of the Lindsays. And, as the antiquarian peculiarities of the parishes of Edzell and Newdosk, are detailed in the Land of the Lindsays, notices of those points are purposely omitted in this place.

It need only be here said that the ruins of Edzell Castle are the most extensive and imposing in Angus; and that, along with the unique stone carvings which adorn the garden walls, few places in Scotland are more worthy of being visited by "lovers of the past."

The ruins are about a mile west from the village of Edzell; and the Gannochy Bridge, with its romantic scenery, is about a like distance to the north. This bridge, which crosses the North Esk, was first built at the cost of James Black (v. p. 295), farmer of Wood of Edzell, in 1732; and in 1795 it was widened at the expense of the adjoining proprietors. About two miles further north, upon the Glenesk road, a bridge crosses the burn at Auchmull, near to the site of an old castle. A tablet upon the south side of the bridge preserves this account of its building:—

1820: Built by the Honourable WILLIAM MAULE of Panmure, M.P., and JOHN SHAND of The Burn, Esq. Mr SHAND having contributed to the Bridge and road one Hundred Guineas, as a mark of his Friendship for his Neighbours in the Waterside and Glenesk. Q.D.B.; J.A. Ædif.

—The Hon. Mr Maule, created Lord Panmure in 1831, was father of the present Earl of Dalhousie. Mr Shand, who belonged to about Fochabers, made money in Demarara, and bought the Burn and Aruhall, in which he was succeeded by his brother William, from whose creditors Colonel M'Inroy, the present laird, purchased these estates. They belonged at one time to Lord Adam Gordon, afterwards to Mr Brodie, whose daughter became Duchess of Gordon (v. p. 252.)

A substantial bridge of three arches crosses the West Water on the road to Brechin. A tablet in the north wall bears this inscription:—

This Bridge was built by Publick Contrabution, the Countie paid a 100 pound, and the remander was raised by subscription. The undertakers was John Molison of Ballichie, Provest of Brichine; David Allardice, of Memus, Baillie in Brichine; John Spence of Bodwarts, Commisar in Brichine; George Erskine in Westside; Thomas Wyllie in Mains; David Christison in Carneskorn, tennants in Edzel; and George Fairwather, tennant in Smidiehill. Anno Dominic 1771.

—Before this bridge was built, there was one of wood for foot passengers, which was often swept away by the stream; also a boat at a place adjoining, called Trailsound. "Bodwarts," mentioned in the above inscription, is now called *Cairnbank*, a small estate near Brechin. The other places have still the same names.

With the exception of the Newdosk or Balfour portion of Edzell, which belongs to Sir Thomas Gladstone, the rest of the parish is owned by Lord Dalhousie. The *Village of Edzell* (of old Slateford, and a Burgh of Barony), has lately much increased in size and importance. The soil being dry, and the air salubrious, it has become a favourite resort for summer visitors. The Established and Free Churches are at the village. It contains a reading room, a bank office, and good inns, and the streets and houses are lighted by gas.

Newdosk.

(S. DROSTAN, ABBOT.)

THE kirk of *Newdos*, like that of Edzell, was a rectory belonging to St Andrews, and a place of early ecclesiastical importance. The district, which was a thanedom, is locally situated in the Mearns. Along with the kirk, the parish was annexed, in whole or inpart, to that of Edzell, some time before the year 1662.

A spring to the east of the kirkyard is known by the name of S. DROSTAN; and a baptismal font, of a very early type, broken in two, lies within the burial-ground, where the foundations of the church—about 7 paces wide, by 20 long—are still visible.

A dressed, but unornamented slab of soft redsandstone, about 5 feet high, stands near the east end of the site of the kirk, and three venerable ash trees are upon the south of the cemetery.

Interments are still made at Newdosk, where there are a few tombstones. A headstone, profusely ornamented, bears this inscription :—

Here lyes the corps of MARGARET DURY, sometime spous to William Adam, tennant in Achmol. She departed this life sometime in March 1735 years. Also here lyes the corps of MARGARET DUNCON, second wife to William Adam. She was born the first of January, and departed this life the 34th year of her age, year of God 1740.

The following, from the oldest of two adjoining headstones, relates to an ancestor of Alex. Gold, tenant of Hillock of Edzell, who died in 1871, aged 89 :—

Here lyes ISOBEL GOLD, spous to Robert Carnegie in Pitnemon, who departed this life September 30, 1741, being the 31st year of her age, liweing behend her a son that she and her husband bade betuixt them, Alexander Carnegie, his age 2 years.

~~~~~~~~~~~~~~~~~~~~~~~~~~~~~~~

Cruden.

(S. OLAUS, KING AND MARTYR.)

BOETHIUS and other chroniclers aver that a battle having been fought at Cruden between the Danes and Scots in Malcolm III.'s time, in which the latter were victorious, Malcolm " biggit ane kirk," which he "dedicat in honour of Olavus, patron of Norroway and Denmark, to be ane memoriall, that sindry noblis of Danis wer sumtime buryit in the said kirk . . . . . The kirk that was biggit to this effect, as oftimes occurris in thay partis, was ouireassin be violent blast of sandis. . . . Sindry of thair bonis war sene be us, schort time afore the making of this buke, mair like giandis than common stature of men : throw quhilk, apperis, that men, in auld times,

hes bone of mair stature and quantite than ony men ar presently in our days."

The old kirk referred to stood upon a knoll in the Links of Cruden, to the east of the present church. The site is still pointed out, also some "grave-shaped" mounds; but no trace of the building remains. A slab of blue lime-stone, or "Iona marble," lies at the new kirk. It presents hollows or grooves for brasses and supports for lamps. Such tombs were commonly placed near the high altars of churches. Story says that a Prince or King of Denmark, who was slain in battle at Cruden, was buried below this stone in the ancient kirk of S. Olaus, and after the destruction of that edifice the slab was removed to its present site. In speaking of the patron of Cruden, Arthur King, who gives 30 March as his celebration day, calls him " S. Ole, king of Norwege, and martyr under Henric ye crowkit." According to " An Almanack and New Prognostication" for 1706, " S. OLES Fair at Cruden, in Buchan," was held on the first Tuesday of April.

The Chronicler also tells us that on the destruction of the old house, "ane kirk was biggit efter, with mair magnificence, in ane othir place, mair ganand." The Earls of Errol had a burial aisle at that church, in which Dr JAMES DRUMMOND, Bishop of Brechin, was buried. Being deprived at the Revolution, he retired to Slains Castle, where he lived with the Earl of Errol, and died in 1695.

Contemporary with Bishop Drummond was the Rev. JOHN BARCLAY, parson of Cruden, who translated Dr Arthur Johnston's Epigrams upon the cities and principal burghs of Scotland, and who also wrote a curious Description of the Roman Catholic Church (1689). Barclay had possibly been buried within the church of Cruden; but of this there is no monumental evidence.

The kirk of Invereroudon, or Crudan, with its pertinents, were confirmed to the See of Aberdeen by Pope Adrian, in 1157, of which cathedral Cruden was a prebend in 1256.

The present kirk, erected in 1777, was much enlarged and improved about 1834. In the passage, near the south door, a slab, initialed

P. C ; M. C. (with shield in centre bearing mortuary emblems) is thus inscribed :—

Heir lyes waiting for a blessed resvrrection, PATRICK CRVIKSHANK, lawier in Abdn. who departed 22 Ivly 1656. He that believeth in me thovgh he wer dead yet shal he leive 11 of John 2 v. I shall be satisfied when I awak with thy likness 17 Psal. 15 v.

—Possibly the "lawier in Abdn," was related to Gawine Cruickshank in Ardiffrie, notary public, who received seisin of the town and lands of Easter Auchleuchries from John Gordon and his wife Marie Ogilvie, 1637; and who, in 1652, had a wadset of the same property from Gordon and his wife, redeemable upon the payment of 5500 merks (Diary of Gen. P. Gordon.)

A granite monument (enclosed) near west dyke bears :—

In memory of the Lady FLORENCE-ALICE HAY, infant daughter of the Earl and Countess of Erroll : born May 28th, 1858, died May 15th, 1859. (Jer. 31. 3 ; Mal. 3. 17.)

—The Earl of Errol, who married Eliza-Amelia, daughter of the Hon. General Sir Charles Gore, succeeded his father as 18th Earl in 1846. As before observed (v. pp. 42, 172), the Hays were first settled in Buchan by Robert the Bruce, and their old residence of Slains Castle was destroyed by James VI., in consequence of the Earl's adherence to Popery. Soon after the latter event, a castle was erected within the parish of Cruden, upon the promontory of Bowness, a singularly romantic site, overhanging the sea. It was this castle, added to and improved, which Dr Samuel Johnson visited when on his tour to the Hebrides, and of which, and the neighbouring scenery of the Bullers of Buchan, as well as of his kind reception by Lord Erroll, he speaks so highly. A slab, facing the old piazza at Slains Castle, bears this inscription :—

GILBERTI'S Errollie Comes, Domin' HAY, Scotiæ Constabularius, huius operis fundamentum quindē die Martii, anno Dom. 1664, fecit et —— die mensis —— anni sequentis perfecit.

[GILBERT, Earl of Erroll, Lord HAY, Constable of Scotland, laid the foundation of this edifice, 15th March 1664, and completed it the following year, on the —— day of the month of ——]

—Upon a second tablet, over the entrance to the stables :—

Built 1664 by GILBERT XI. Earl of Erroll, Great Constable of Scotland, and rebuilt 1836 and 1837, in the reign of William the IV., by WILLM.-GEORGE, XVII. Earl of Erroll, Great Constable, and Knight Marischal of Scotland.

—The 17th Earl married Lady Eliz. Fitzclarence (a sister of the Earl of Munster), by whom he had the present Peer, and three daughters. Two of the daughters became respectively the Countesses of Gainsborough and Fife.

Within a vault in the south-east corner of the kirk-yard of Cruden, shaded by an old spreading elm, lie the remains of a young English lady of quality, who, according to one story, died by unfair means, and to another of a broken heart. Not far from the same place, upon a neatly carved slab of about 2½ by 1½ feet in size, is the following :—

Heir under lies waiting for a blessed resurrection, ALEX^R. ANDERSON, who dept. this lyf the 7 of Oct. 1681, I am the resurrection & the lyf, &c.

Adjoining the west wall :—

Here lyes JOHN RON, who died in Wards of Cruden, upon the 19 Sept. 1702, and of his age the 72 years.

Upon a flat slab, within an enclosure on the south side of burial-ground :—

Under this stone lies the remains of CHARLES GORDON of Auchleuchries, who departed this life the 9th of June 1777, aged 73 years.

—The above-named was a descendant of Alex. Gordon in Sandend, who bought the lands of Auchleuchries from Patrick, grandson of General Gordon, in 1726. So far as known "Gordon in Sandend" was in no way related to the previous Gordons of Auchlenchries.

The most celebrated of the old set of Gordons (who held Auchleuchries from about 1489) was General PATRICK GORDON, who obtained high rank in the army, and favour at the Court of Peter the Great. The Czar, who frequently visited the General during his last illness, was by his bedside when he died; and, as beautifully remarked by Dr Joseph Robertson, the learned editor of the General's Diary, "the eyes of him who had left Scotland a poor unbefriended wanderer, were closed by the hands of an Emperor."

In a vault, before the high altar of the first-erected Roman Catholic chapel at Moscow, and which was chiefly reared by General Gordon's munificence, his body was laid with great pomp and honour, in presence of the Czar, and other dignitaries of the Empire. This inscription (Diary, p. 193), marks the General's tomb :—

"Sacræ Tzareæ Majestatis Militiæ Generalis, PATRICIUS-LEOPOLDUS GORDON. Natus anno Domini 1635, die 31 Martii. Denatus anno Domini 1699, die 29 Novembris. Requiescat in pace."

[PATRICK-LEOPOLD GORDON, General in the Army of His Sacred Majesty the Czar. Born 31st March 1635. Died 29th Nov. 1699. May he rest in peace.]

It was General Patrick Gordon's son-in-law, Alexander Gordon (the son of a merchant in Aberdeen), who saw much active service in Russia, and rose to the rank of Major-General, that wrote a History of Peter the Great, and died at Auchintoul, in Marnoch (*v*. p. 235).

CHRISTIAN FORBES, sp. to John Ramage, d. 1728, a. 39 :—

When mortal man resigns his transcient breath,
The body only I give ore to death ;
The part dissolv'd, and brokenframe I mourn,
What came from earth, I see to earth return.

ROBT. JOHNSTON, Midmiln, d. 1745, a. 42 ; ANNA SUTHERLAND, his wf. d. 1758, a. 54 :—

Come shed a tear, whoever passeth by,
For his unwisht for death ; Whose memory,
For justice, mercy, honesty, and peace,
Shal last till time, and death itself shal cease.

The next inscription, from a table-shaped stone, relates to (*v*. Peterhead) the parents of the Right Rev. Bishop Kilgour :—

Here are deposited in hopes of a happy resurrection, the remains of ROBERT KILGOUR, sometime litster at Walk Mill of Cruden, where, having lived upwards of LI years, he died the XXIIId day of Sept. in the year of Our Lord, MDCCLVIII, and in the LXXIId year of his age. And the remains of ISOBEL BARRON, his spouse, who died the XXIId day of Dec. in the year of God MDCCLXII, and of her age the LXXVIIth. &c.

The next epitaph, which is upon a flat slab in the kirkyard, with the face downwards, was composed (as Mr Ranken of St Drostan's Episcopal Church, Deer, kindly informs me, upon the authority of the late Dean Cumming, the author's grandson), by the Rev. Mr Skinner of Longside, author of Tullochgorm, &c. :—

S. M. of the Rev. Mr ALEXANDER KEITH, whose probity of heart, sanctity of manners, easiness of conversation, and unwearied attention to all the duties of his office as a minister of the Church of Scotland, under the many trying events of 8 and 40 years, rendered his life valuable, his death lamentable, and his memory precious. Ob. Oct. 27, 1763, æt. 68 :—

Ultime Scotorum in Crudenanis, KETHE, Sacerdos,
Fratribus et plebi diu memorande, vale.
Posuit unici nati pietas.

[Priest KEITH, farewell ! Last of the Scots,
Who taught in Cruden's vale ;
Long will thy people—brethren all—
Thy much-felt loss bewail.

The piety of his only son has placed this memorial.]

—Aware that the name of " Al. Keith " was associated with a work entitled a " View of the Diocese of Aberdeen," edited for the Spalding Club by my much lamented friend Dr Joseph Robertson, I felt anxious to know (particularly from being so largely indebted to that work in the compilation of notes upon the church-yards within the Diocese of Aberdeen), whether the Parson of Cruden and the author of that valuable production could be identified.

After much unsuccessful correspondence, and personal inquiry in Buchan—and when I had almost lost hopes of attaining my object—the Rev. Mr Ranken of St Drostan's, kindly transmitted the following valuable particulars regarding the old Priest of Cruden. It will be seen from these that Mr Ranken has succeeded in identifying Mr Keith as the author of the work in question:—

"I am happy (writes Mr Ranken), in being able to furnish you with some particulars concerning Mr Keith—probably all that can, at this distance of time, be got at.

"On referring to one of the Spalding Club volumes ('Collections on the Shires of Aberdeen and Banff,' vol. I.), I find the following in the Preface, p. xi. 'The VIEW OF THE DIOCESE OF ABERDEEN,' which takes the last place in the volume, is printed from a manuscript in the Library of the Faculty of Advocates at Edinburgh. This is the only copy of the work now known to exist, although another was extant about the middle of the last century, among the MSS. in the library of the Earl of Errol at Slaines Castle, although traces of other transcripts have been found, much more recently, in different quarters of the Diocese.

"Of the writer nothing is known beyond what may be conjectured, as to his name, from a note on one of the boards of the volume :—'*Al. Keith finl. haec MSS. Novr. 25. 1732 ;*' and beyond what may be gathered, as to his calling, from the work itself. A perusal of its pages will leave no room for doubt that its author was a zealous presbyter of the Episcopal Church of Scotland; and the persecutions which afflicted that communion, in his day, and during many following years, as they may help to explain more than an occasional acerbity of expression, or peculiarity of phrase, into which he has been betrayed, so, perhaps, they may sufficiently account for the complete oblivion which has fallen upon the learned and industrious compiler."

After giving a copy of the inscription, which Mr Ranken made about 1844, he continues, "I well remember standing at the side of the tombstone, along with my good old friend, Dean Cumming, copying the inscription; and on my remarking on the expression '*Ultime Scotorum,*' he said, 'Ah! you little know the condition the church and the clergy were in in those dreadful days. Utter extinction, to all human appearance, was coming upon them: the clergy never expected to have successors.'

"I regret that I never made my friend and classfellow, the late Dr Joseph Robertson, aware of the identity of the Parson of Cruden with the Alex. Keith, the author of the 'View of the Diocese of Aberdeen.' He would, I have no doubt, deemed the information valuable. Slaines Castle, the noble proprietors of which clung to the disestablished and proscribed church, for many years, was one of the likeliest places to possess a copy of the manuscript, although even *their* Jacobitism was at last tired out, and they took the oaths to the Hanoverians, and got a 'qualified' English clergyman to Cruden, where, in course of time, Mr Keith would be quite forgotten.

"As to Mr Keith's parentage, he was the son of the Rev. George Keith, minister of Deer during the latter years of the Episcopal Establishment, which the Prince of Orange put his heel upon. Mr George Keith was in possession when the crash came; and through the local power of the Marischal, the head of his clan, and the Patron of the Parish, as well as from the esteem in which he was held by the Parishioners at large, he kept possession until his death in 1711. Then came 'the rabble of Deer,' commemorated by Meston the poet, in which the Presbyterian authorities were deforced in attempting to induct Mr Keith's successor; and their being obliged to perform the ceremony in the neighbouring kirk of Longside.

"The following is the extract of Alex. Keith's Birth and Baptism, which shews that he was a boy of 16 at his father's death :—

"'May 21, 1695, Friday.—Mr Geo. Keith minr. of Old Deer had a sone baptised by Mr David Sibbald minr. at New Deer, and named ALEXANDER, & brought forth by Sophia Ross his wife upon the 22 of the sd. moneth. Godfathers Alexr. Gordon of Pitlurg, Alexr. Gordon in Mill of Aden, Alexr. Keith in Miltoun of Durney, & Mr Alexr. Ross sometym Parson of Rathen, & Mr Alexr. Robertson the minister of Longsyd. Witnesses Pitfour, Captn. Binney, & Gaval.'

"Mr Alex. Ross, the 'exanctorated' Parson of Rathen (adds Mr Ranken), was Mr George Keith's father-in-law, and seems to have lived after his ejection at the manse of Deer. There is a tradition that Mr Geo. Keith was Parson of Keithhall, near Inverurie, before he was translated to Deer."

It need only be added that the above extract relating to the birth and baptism of Mr Keith is a noticeable instance of the curious custom which prevailed in Scotland during Episcopal, and even in later times, of having godfathers and godmothers present at baptisms, who bore the same Christian name as was conferred upon the child.

Here lys interred the corps of Mr GILBERT STERLING, minister of the Gospel, and schoolmaster at Cruden, who departed this life upon the 17th of April 1744 years, aged 43 years ; as also the corps of ANN FORBES, his spouse :—
Here lys intomb'd under this mould'ring dust,
A man whose soul was truely virtuous :
A woman, too, whose baseness did despise,
And they both rest, in hopes again to rise
To happiness ; thou, reader, drop a tear,
And virtue's paths to follow, learn bear.

The above, and the next two inscriptions are taken from table-shaped stones :—

S. M. If goodness of heart and charity of hand, united to the tender husband, the indulgent father, and the social neighbour, can claim a respectfull remembrance, Then, friend, behold this monument of faimly love, and drop a tear of veneration to the memory of GEORGE FORREST, surgeon, ob. Jun. 24, 1761, æt. 42.

Probably the last and next quoted epitaphs were composed by the Rev. Mr Skinner :—

REBECCA HAY, daughter of the Rev. Mr Hay, minister of the Gospel at Cruden, died on the 15th day of Nov. 1771, aged 18 years. IEAN HAY died June the 3d 1772, aged 24 years :—

Here in one grave two lovelie virgins ly,
Two sisters dear, destined in youth to dy ;
Their persons beauty, grace their souls adorn'd,
No wonder then their death is deeply mourn'd.
In glory they shall rise and bless their doom,
Then shall they have an everlasting bloom—
Learn hence, fair virgins, in your early days,
Your great Redeemer by your lives to praise.

Within an enclosure, in which it is said a family named ALEXANDER lie buried, who were tenants in Nether Mill, and factors to the Lords Erroll, are two slabs thus inscribed :—

P.G ; M.M ; B.C. In hope of a blessed resurrection here lyes the corps of PETER GORDON, who lived in Neither Milln of Cruden, and dyed Nov. 17-7, aged 58 years. Also the corps of MARY MACKIE, his spons, who died August 4, 1767.

T.S ; I.S. Here lyes in hope of a blessed resurrection, the corps of GEORGE, THO., and MARY STUARTS, children to Thos. Stuart and Iean Stell, his spouse, anno 1750.

There are several tombstones to a blacksmith family of the surname of *Smith*. From one of these bearing the blacksmith's crown, &c. :—

Here lyes in hope of a blessed resurrection, the corps of THOMAS SMITH, sometime smith in Keplaw, who departed this lyfe the 22d of Feb. 1767, in the 59th year of his age. [Psal. 39. 4.]

Upon one side of a headstone, now lying flat and broken in two pieces :—

Beneath this Stone is deposited, in Sure and Certain hope of a Joyfull Resurrection, the remains of a Sinner, redeemed by an inestimable price, and Created by divine grace, an Heir of Eternal Glory.

Upon the reverse of same stone :—

To the memory of PETER LION, sometime at flour mill of Slains, who died 4th Dec. 1813, aged 91 years : Also HELEN WITHERSPON, his spouse, who died 5th Janry. 1805, aged 81 years.

Upon a table stone :—

To the memory of PETER SMITH of Aldie, physician, who died the XXIId Nov. MDCCCXIII, in the LXXIId year of his age ; CATHERINE, his daughter, who died in infancy, and JOHN, his son, who died VIIth March MDCCXCIV, in the XVIth, year of his age: Also MARGARET MOIR, his spouse, who died on the Xth day of August MDCCCXXVI, in the LXXVIth year of her age.

From a headstone placed against the west wall of the kirkyard :—

Sacrum memoriæ Reverendi JOANNIS DUNCAN, Verbi Divini ministri in parœchia Dunrossness, in Insulis Zetlandicis ; qui naufragio periit XXII Februarii, anno Domini MDCCCXIII, et ætatis suæ XXXVI.

[Sacred to the memory of the Rev. JOHN DUNCAN, minister of the Word of God in the parish of Dunrossness, in the Shetland Islands, who perished by shipwreck, 22 Feb. 1813, in the 36th year of his age.]

—Mr Duncan was one of sixteen passengers, along with a crew of seven men, who were lost in the schooner *Doris*, which left Leith for Lerwick on the afternoon of Saturday, 20th Feb., and perished among the rocks opposite Slains Castle, during a dreadful gale of wind, on the evening of the 22d, when (Scott's Fasti), " this respected and highly useful individual closed a life ' embittered by all the evils of unmerited poverty and domestic affliction.'" "Many of the passengers (Scots Maga.) were highly respectable characters, and their loss will be severely felt in the islands to which they belong. It is added that Mr Craigie (the master), was " long known to possess all that constitute an upright character."

ALEX. OLDMAN, Kirkhill, d. 1803, a. 63 ; ELIZABETH GRANT, his sp., d. 1820, a. 86 :—
After the cares of former life,
And many labours past ;
Here is the harbour of old age—
Its safe-guard now at last.

From a table-shaped stone :—

To the memory of JAMES JOHNSTON, son to Andrew Johnston in Sand End of Cruden, who departed this life on the 24th day of Febry. 17—, aged 25 years :—
Man like a flower doth rise & fall,
Return to dust when God doth call.
Also of ANDREW JOHNSTON, his father, late farmer in Sand End, who departed this life the 20th day of Dec. 1804, aged 64 years. Also of his son ALEXANDER JOHNSTON, who was Surgen on board of his Majesty's ship L'Aimable, who departed this life off a Martinico the 27th day of August 1795, aged 24 years. Also KATHEREN DWGWJD, spouse to the foresaid Andrew Johnston, who died the 6th of Aprile 1829, aged 90 years.

John, the son of Uthred, gave his lands of Slanys and Cruden to Fergus, Earl of Buchan, before the year 1214, in exchange for those of Fedreth in New Deer, and Ardindrach in Cruden. Two villas at Ardindrach, with pertinents, were given by Bruce to Sir John of Bonville in 1321.

Traces of ancient burial cairns, rude sepulchral stones, and old personal ornaments, &c., have been found in many parts of the parish ; but the more tangible of these remains—the Standing Stones, or circle which stood near the church—having been demolished in 1831, the district is now-a-days more famous for its romantic coast scenery than for its antiquities. Of its scenery, the Bullers, the promontory of Dunboy, and the Bow of Pitwartlachie, are the more remarkable. The first is well represented by two plates, in Cordiner's Antiquities and Scenery of the North of Scotland (1780), and has been frequently engraved and photographed.

Tradition avers that the parish of Cruden had its name from the reputed defeat, or *crushing* of the Danes in the battle before referred to—a point which is thus advocated in a popular rhyme :—

"*Crush-Dane*, the field and parish then were styl'd
Though time and clever tongues the name hath spoll'd."

The true origin of the name is difficult to find. Possibly the last syllable of the word may have reference to the stream which flows through the parish, and the first to the round-shaped knolls or hillocks which are so common in the district, particularly in the valley of the Cruden, where the old kirk stood.

A neat Episcopal Church (S. JAMES THE LESS), with a spire about 90 feet high, has a commanding position upon the rising ground south-west of the parish church. It was built in 1843, and there the late Rev. Dr PRATT, author of " Buchan " and other useful topographical works, continued to labour until his death in 1869 (*v.* p. 100.) Dr Pratt's Buchan contains a a good account of the history and antiquities of the parish of Cruden.

The principal bridge across the river Cruden is called the *Bishop's Bridge*, It consists of one arch, and three separate tablets are built into the south side of the bridge. One of these presents a carving of the Errol arms, and the initials E. I. E.; the second, flanked by two pastoral staffs, bears the arms of (? the See of Brechin), and Drummond impaled, dated 1697, and initialed, B. I. B. Upon the third slab are the words :—

REBUILT BY JAMES E. OF ERROL, 1763.

Besides building the bridge across the Cruden, or causing it to be built (for it will be seen that it bears a date subsequent to the death of Bishop

Drummond), that prelate also presented the church with two silver communion cups, which bear the following inscription:—

Dedicated to the Service of Jesus and his church at Cruden, by Dr IA. DRUMMOND, late Bishop of Brechin, who died at Slains, 13th Ap. 1695.

There are other four communion cups of silver belonging to Cruden. Upon one:—

Dedicated to the service of Iesus and of his church at Cruden, by SAMUEL HUTCHEON, who dyed at Craighead the 16 Aprile 1611.

Upon each of the remaining three:—

Dedicated to the Service of Jesus, and of his church at Cruden, by ROBERT CUMMING of Birness, 1712.

—I am indebted for these cup inscriptions, and other kind services, to the late Mr ROBERT DAWSON, M.A., schoolmaster of Cruden. Being an accomplished conchologist, Mr Dawson was occasionally employed on the Dredging Committee of the British Association for the Advancement of Science, in the course of which, and by his own unaided exertions, he made important additions to the Mollusca of the North-East Coast of Scotland, and contributed papers to the Reports of the Association. Mr Dawson, who also excelled in geology and botany, was a native of Ordiquhill, and died in the prime of life, after a short illness, 29th Dec. 1871.

The only villages in Cruden are those of Bullers, Ward, Whinnyfold, Northhaven, and Hatton. At the last-named of these places is a Free Church. With the exception of Hatton, these villages are occupied by a fishing population. In 1603-4, some of those "portis," in common with others in the locality, were visited by "the pest." But, according to local rhyme, the Well of the royal patron of the parish, which is near the Bay of Cruden, is proof against all such calamities:—

"ST. OLAVE's Well's low by the sea,
Where pest nor plague shall never be."

———o———

Inverkeilor.

(S. MACCONOC, or CONON.)

INVERKEILOR, as now constituted, is composed of the two parishes of *Inuirkileder* and *Athyn*. Both were in the diocese of St Andrews; the first is rated at £70 and the second at 50 merks in the Old Taxation.

These were separate and independent ecclesiastical districts for several years subsequent to the Reformation, for in 1574 Inverkeilor had its own minister and reader, and Ethie was served, along with three other churches, by a different clergyman, and a different reader from those at Inverkeilor.

Chapels were attached to both churches; and these, along with the kirks, were granted to the Abbey of Arbroath at the time of its foundation. Those of Inverkeilor were given by Walter of Berkeley, lord of Redcastle, and those of Ethie by Wm. the Lion. But, according to the Stat. Accounts, "Conghoillis" (? now Cowholes) was the old name of the parish. This idea appears to have been founded upon a misreading of the name of "Achinglas" in King William's charter, which is probably a corruption of the Gaelic words, *Athin-eglish, i.e.*, the church of Athyn, or Ethie. The ruins of the kirk of

ETHIE, OR S. MURDOCH,

stand in a lonely and romantic spot near the cliffs, east of the Redhead. Like the kirk of S. Skae, and similarly situated places of worship, that of S. Murdoch possibly owed its origin to some recluse who had taken up his abode there with the view of affording succour to shipwrecked sailors, and pilgrims along the coast. Whether the founder of the church was S. MURDOCH, (Dempster's Eccl. Hist., ii. 476), a hermit and bard who dwelt in a cell at Kilmurdach, in Argyll, the walls of which he ornamented with pictures of his lections; or of S. MURDOCH, bishop of Killala, in Ireland, who, about A.D. 440 (Butler's Lives, 12th Aug.), had a church near to where the river Moy falls into the sea, or whether it was founded by a disciple of either of those holy men, is not certain. But it is to be noticed that another of the comparatively rare dedications in Scotland to S. MURDOCH was at a similarly named place—*Ethie*-Beaton in Monifieth—where the site still retains the name in the odd form (*v.* p. 114) of "*Chapel Dockie.*"

Only a portion of the west wall of the kirk of S. Murdoch of Ethie remains: It is from about 16 to 18 feet in height, by about 30 feet in width. The wall is about 3½ feet thick, pierced in six different parts by holes of about 8 inches square. The corner stones and a string course are good specimens of ashler work; but the rest of the building is of rubble.

The area of the kirk of S. MURDOCH measures about 57 by 22 feet. The cemetery, a pretty green sward, upon the south and east, presents no grave-mounds, although interments have been made there within the last hundred years. In the adjoining burn, which runs through a small den upon the south, and falls over the cliffs into the sea, there had doubtless, though now unknown, been a consecrated well; and the banks of the burn are covered by those interesting terraces, resembling sheep walks, regarding the origin of which geologists hold various notions. The ford or crossing, by the cliff road, in old times, to and from the Redhead, had been by this burn; and, as the Gaelic words *Ath-yn* (? Athaen), imply a place of this nature, the name may have originated from that fact. The parish church of

INVERKEILOR,

which was erected about a hundred and fifty years ago, has been altered and added to at different times. It is situated upon the point of a rising ground (? *Kil-ard*, a church upon a height), and overlooks the valley of the Lunan.

An octogonal font of freestone, embellished on each of the eight sides by sacred emblems and monograms, stands before the pulpit. "SUFFER LITTLE CHILDREN TO COME UNTO ME" is carved round the lip of the font: upon the base :—

Presented to the church of Inverkeilor by AGNES RAIT, Anniston, on the occasion of her Marriage, 1802.

—Miss Rait was married to H. A. F.-Lindsay-Carnegy, of Spynie and Boysack, Esquire. Mr Lindsay-Carnegy not only represents the oldest landowners in the parish; but is also the representative of the Lords Spynie, the first of whom, Alexander (youngest son of the tenth Earl of Crawford), was accidentally killed by his kinsman, young Lindsay of Edzell, upon the High Street of Edinburgh, in 1607 (*v.* Lives; also Land of the Lindsays.) The present house of Kinblethmont, which occupies a rising ground, and commands a fine view, is modern, and surrounded by tasteful planting.

A slab, built into the left splay of one of the S. E. windows of the church, presents a shield, charged with (? by mistake) a double-headed eagle. The initials, M.D.R., in monogram, flank the base; I.R. and the date—"1628, 2 FEB.," are over the shield; and below it is a death's head. Possibly this slab has reference to some of the RAMSAYS, contemporary lairds of Cairnton. "Euphan Mudie" (mentioned in an inscription below), was a daughter of David Mudie (son of John Mudie of Brianton), and his wife Janet Ramsay of Cairnton.

A second slab, with a shield bearing the Durie arms, and " 3 SEP. 1631, M.I.D ;" is built into the splay of another window. The words "MEMENTO MORI" are over the shield. The following epitaph, which seems to be a sort of play upon words, is below the shield :—

QVOD . DVRVM . EST.
FRACTVM . NEC . PLVS.
DVRARE . VIDETVR.
DVREVS . AT . DVRAT.
CLARAQVE . FAMA . VIGET.

[That which is Durable is broken, nor appears any longer to enDure; but DURIE still enDures, and flourishes with bright renown.]

—Joshua Durie, possibly while minister at Logie-Montrose, was present at the General Assembly of the Church of Scotland, at Edinburgh, in 1602. He was (Scott's Fasti) admitted to the second charge at St Andrews in 1607, from whence he was translated to Inverkeilor in 1613. Dr David Laing of the Signet Library, Edinburgh, kindly informs me that Joshua was a son of Mr John Durie, minister of Edinburgh, who died in the house of his son-in-law, the celebrated James Melvil, at Montrose, 25th Feb. 1600; and that, in 1590, John Durie, his wife, and Joshua, their son, had a grant from the king of an annual pension of £75 Scots, which was confirmed by Act of Parliament in 1592: also that a letter from the Archbishop and Bishop to the King, for the continuation of this pension, is dated 16th May 1606; likewise, that after the death of John Durie's widow, this grant was again ratified in favour of Mr Joshua Durie, then minister at St Andrews, Eupheme M'Kane, his spouse, and John Durie, their son, 23d Oct. 1612. The date of 3d Sept. 1631, upon the monument at Inverkeilor, probably refers to the time of Joshua Durie's death ; and the initials M.I.D : D.E.M., in monogram, which flank the shield, refer respectively to Mr and Mrs Durie.

Built into the right hand splay of the S.E. window is a monument, with the carving of a cherub on the top, and the text, Heb. ix. 27, in Greek characters. This inscription follows : —

Infra sepulta cum sex liberis iacet ELIZABETHA BETTIE, prior conjunx M^{ri}. Ioannis Raithi. Mortem obiit in Dno. Kal. Novemb. A.D. 1661. Filius IOANNES A.D. 1675, ætatis suæ xxii. apud Iudos in insula Mevi huic mundo valedixit. Ex liberis Euphamiæ Mudie de Braintone conjugis M^{ri}. Ioannis Raithi, ROBERTUS et IANETA jacent infra sepulti.

[Beneath lies buried, with six of her children, ELIZABETH BETTIE, first wife of Mr John Rait, who died in the Lord, 1 Dec. 1661. Her son, JOHN, bade farewell to this world in the island of Mevis, [? Nevis] in the [West] Indies, A.D. 1675, in the 22d year of his age. Of the children of Euphan Mudie of Brainton, wife of Mr John Rait, ROBERT and JANET lie interred here.]

—Two compartments (below the Latin inscription), present figures, incised, in the style of Holbein's Dances of Death. Of these the Rev. Mr Hay has kindly communicated the following description :—" In the compartment on the right are two figures, a male and female, evidently, by the dress of the male figure, intended to represent John Rait and his wife. Death, in the usual form of a skeleton armed with a dart, is forcing his way between the two, and pushing them asunder. This compartment or panel, bears these inscriptions—below 'Congugium carnale' (the carnal marriage),—above, ' In morte dividimur' (in death we are divided.)

" The other compartment has the same two figures, representing the same persons ; but in addition to the gown and bands which distinguish the minister as in the above panel, he and his wife are both now represented with wings indicating that they have attained the spiritual state, and are trampling Death, the same figure that was thrusting them asunder before, under foot. This panel has the inscription below, ' Conjugium æternum' (the spiritual and eternal marriage) ; and above, ' Omnia vincit mors Christi' (the death of Christ vanquishes all.)

" Between the two panels, crosswise, is inscribed, 'Quis mihi dabit pennas columbæ?' (Who will give me the wings of a dove?)" Across the width of the stone, under both panels, is inscribed the same motto which appears upon a tombstone at Dun (v. p. 222):—

Coniugium Christi ac animæ mors solvere nescit;
Sed carnale potest coniugis atque viri.

Another slab (with the text, Eccl. xii., cut in Hebrew characters, together with mortuary emblems, M:I.R:I.R., &c), bears the following remains of an inscription in Roman capitals : —

Reverendi viri Magistr . . . .
IS RAITHI antistitis e . . . .
diserti perspicu . . . .
lithum conduntur . . . .
Montrosarum trio . . . .
vero . . . spem lustris . . . .
stora . functus . . . .
Cal . Dec . A.D. . . . .
is LXII. a labo . . . . quiev . . . .

[1 Cor. iii. 6, cut in Greek letters.]

RETÆ sacræ RETE sacrum . . . . . .
frvctifer . . . . . asti . . . .
 re docendo
acivit . . . .
 re . . . .

[Under this stone were laid the remains of the Rev. JOHN RAIT, a clear and eloquent preacher of the Gospel in this church, who was previously three years in Montrose. He rested from his labours 1st Dec. A.D. —— in the 62d year of his age, &c.]

—The Brechin Presbytery Records show that Mr John Rait had "a communication" as 2d minister of Montrose, 10th Dec. 1646. His first wife had possibly been from Montrose, or its neighbourhood, where the name of Beattie has long been common. His second wife, as above seen, was a daughter of David Mudie, by his wife, Janet Ramsay of Cairnton.

Mr John Rait, whom Mr Ochterlony calls "a gentleman of the House of Hallgreen in the Mearns," was laird of Bryantou about 1682, and was succeeded in the kirk of Inverkeilor by his son JAMES. As a Non-juror, the latter was deprived of his living by the Privy Council, when the vacant stipend fell to the Earl of Panmure, patron of the parish, and lord of the abbacy of Aberbrothock. It appears that his Lordship resigned his right to the half-year's stipend of 1695, as well as to the stipends of seven succeeding years, "in favours of Mr Dauid Rate of Breyington, one of the heretors," by whom the stipends were to be uplifted and applied "touards such pious and charitable uorks and uses as he shall condescend on uithin or about ye sd parochin and church of Inuerkillor." This arrangement had probably been made with the view of aiding the deprived minister, to whom, during that period, no successor was appointed (*Assignations of Vacant Stipends at Panmure.*)

A panel in front of the east loft of the kirk exhibits the Carnegie and Hallyburton of Pitcur arms impaled. The panel is dated 1635, and initialed, S. I. C.: D. M. H.—the initials being those of Sir JOHN CARNEGIE, and his first wife, Dame MAGDALEN HALLYBURTON. The Northesk burial-vault is at the east end of the kirk.

Over the entrance, surrounded by carvings of angels with trumpets, &c., are the words:—

DIES . MORTIS . ÆTERNÆ . VITÆ . NATALIS . EST
FIDELIBVS.

[The day of death is the birth-day of eternal life unto the faithful.]

—Possibly the burial-vault was erected by the first Earl of Northesk after the death of his first wife, which had taken place sometime before 1652, as Lamont states in his Diary (p. 49), that on the 29th April of that year, and on the same day as his widowed daughter, Lady Scotstarvet, the younger, was married to Preston of Erdree, in Fife, "the Earle of Etthie, in Angus, her father (being about 73 years of age), was maried upon one of his owne tennants, surnamed Malle."

This Earl, who was a younger brother of the Earl of Southesk (*v.* p. 93), got Ethie and other lands from his father about 1595-6, and acquired Inglismaldie, &c., about 1635 (Doug. Peer.) In 1639, he was created a peer by the title of Lord Lour. He was created Earl of Ethie in 1647, which title, in 1662, was changed to that of Earl of Northesk and Lord Rosehill. To his descendant, the sixth Earl, and his lady, a marble tablet within the church is thus inscribed:—

Sacred to the memory of GEORGE, VIth Earl of Northesk, Admiral of the White Squadron of His Majesty's Fleet: born 2d Aug. 1716, o.s., and died 22d January 1792. And ANN LESLIE, Countess of Northesk: born 22d Feb. 1730, o.s., and died 11th Nov. 1779.

—Lady Northesk (a daughter of the Earl of Leven and Melville) had three sons and three daughters. The eldest son, who became a Vice-Admiral, saw much service under Earl St Vincent and Lord Nelson, and was third in command at the battle of Trafalgar. His lordship, who died in 1831, married a sister of Earl St Vincent, by whom he had four sons and as many daughters. The eldest son, a midshipman, was lost in the *Blenheim* when in his 16th year. The second son, born in 1794, is the eighth and present Earl of Northesk. His son, Lord Rosehill, is Aide-de-Champ to the Commander-in-chief of the Forces in Scotland.

A slab, built into the front wall of the kirk of Inverkeilor, presents a carving of the arms of the Stewarts of Lorne. It is initialed I.S., and bears the motto :—

QVHIDDER . VIL . ZE.

—Sir Robert Stewart of Innermeath, father of the first Lord Lorne, acquired the lands and barony of Redcastle about the middle of the fourteenth century. The square tower or keep of Redcastle was probably built by one of the Stewarts, in whose hands the property continued until about the close of the sixteenth century. (*v.* Mem. of Angus and Mearns, p. *13.) The Stewarts, while in the locality, had doubtless been buried at Inverkeilor; and the above-mentioned slab had possibly ornamented their aisle. The Stewarts of Redcastle and Lorne are now represented by the Duke of Argyll, whose eldest son, the husband of Princess Louise, has the title of Marquis of Lorne. From a marble tablet, within the kirk :—

Sacred to the memory of JOHN MUDIE of Arbikie, Esq., who died June 1728, aged — years. And of his wife, MAGDALEN CARNEGY, daughter of James Carnegy of Craigo, who died 27th Decr. 1771, aged 89 years ; and of their Family, & Descendants. Of their family, which consisted of six sons and eight daughters, three daughters only came to maturity, viz. 1st ELIZABETH, married to Robert Smith of Forret, Esq., who left an only son, WILLIAM SMITH of Forret, Esq., married to his cousin-german, 29th April 1784, the after mentioned Magdalen Hay: He died 2d Feby. 1785, leaving no issue. 2d AGNES, married to James Hay of Cocklaw, Esq., who left two sons & a daughter. Their eldest son, CHARLES HAY, Esq., advocate, afterwards Lord Newton, one of the Senators of the College of Justice, a man of distinguished talents & inflexible integrity, died Octr. 1811, aged 64 years. Their youngest son, JAMES HAY, Esq., died at Edinr. 6th June 1787, & was interred there. 3d ANNE, married to Robert Stephen of Letham, Esq., left an only daughter ANNE, who died Novr. 1806. Magdalen Hay, only daughter of James Hay, Esq., & Agnes Mudie, and relict of William Smith of Forret, Esq., the last survivor of the family, has erected this monument as a tribute of respect to the memory of her relations who lie buried here. And it is her desire also to be interred in the spot which contains the ashes of her husband & of her grandmother, and mother, MAGDALEN CARNEGY, and AGNES MUDIE, parents, with whom she was long united in the closest bonds of love and affection, whose virtues she reveres, and whose example she most earnestly wishes to follow. 1818.

—James Mudie, son of James Mudie, merchant in Montrose, was served heir to his father of Arbikie, April 26, 1664 (Retours, Forfarshire.) According to Burke, John Mudie of Brianton, living in 1600, son of John Mudie of Gilchorn, living in 1570, was ancestor of the Arbikie and Pitmuies family. Forret and Cocklaw are properties in the shires of Fife and Aberdeen respectively : Letham is in the parish of St Vigeans.

Lord NEWTON, who assumed his judicial title from his property of Newton, in Stracathro, passed as advocate, 1768, and was raised to the bench in 1806, being accounted one of the foremost lawyers of his time. His Lordship possessed a great fund of humour and anecdote ; and it was he and Mr Smellie, the printer, that " drilled" the poet Burns, on his introduction to "The *Crochallan* Fencibles" (a bacchanalian club), in Jan. 1787, a circumstance which gave rise to one of Burns' happiest poetical fragments. Lord Newton, who became excessively corpulent, died at Powrie House, near Dundee ; and never having been married, he left the estate of Faichfield, in Longside, &c., and his large fortune, to his only sister, Mrs Hay-Mudie who survived until 1823 (*v.* Memoir of Lord Newton, and Portraits of him, in Kay's Edinburgh Portraits). The Hays of Cocklaw and Faichfield were descended from a second son of Hay of Rannes (*v.* p. 274).

The family of GARDYNE were of old designed of that Ilk, a property in the adjoining parish of Kirkden, where their castle, ornamented with the family arms, dated 1568, is still in good preservation, and inhabited by the present laird, Alexander Lyall, Esq. (*v.* Mem. of Angus and the Mearns.) The Gardynes, who have long possessed the lands of Middleton, &c., bury at Inverkeilor. Their tomb consists of an enclosure of about 42 by 18 feet in extent; and, before the old walls were removed, the door lintel (now lost), bore the following lines :—

Were death denied, poor man would live in vain;
Were death denied, to live would not be life;
Were death denied, e'en fools would wish to die.

—The Gardyne burial place contains a number of tablets, from which the following inscriptions are copied. The first of these shows the remarkable fact of a lady having given birth to no fewer than *twenty-four* children :—

[1.]

DAVID GARDYNE of Lawton marrd. JANET LINDSAY of Edzell, 1603. Their only issue, JOHN, marrd. ELIZH., daughr. of Sir John Arbuthnott of that ilk, 1643, who had issue 4 sons and 20 daughters. ROBERT, their heir, marrd. GRIZEL, daughr. of Alexr. Watson of Barry, 1676, their issue, DAVID, WILLIAM, ELIZAH., who marrd. 1st Scott of Hedderwick, 2d Barclay of Johnston; GRIZEL, who marrd. 1st Wedderburn of that ilk, and 2d David Graham of Duntrune. DAVID, heir to Robert of Lawton, marrd. ANN GRAHAM of Fintray, 1706. Their issue, ELIZAH., who marrd. James Guthrie of Craigie, 1733.

[2.]

AMELIA, who married Alexar. Hunter of Balskelly, 1741; DAVID fought under Prince Charles at Culloden, and died at Newport, in Flanders, 1749; JAMES, who married MARY WALLACE, 1741; CLEMENTINA, who marrd. Alex. Graham of Duntrune, 1751; ROBERT, who died in minor age. JAMES GARDYNE had by his wife Mary, daughr. of Thomas Wallace of Arbroath, issue, viz. :—

	Married.	Decd.
DAVID, to Mary Taylor of Kirktonhill,	1784.	1802.

[3.]

ANN, to James Bruce, ...	1777.	1827.
CHARLES, ...		1813.
MARY, to Ths. Carnegy of Craigo,	1775.	1815.
ELIZABETH, ...		1831.
CLEMENTINA, to Charles Greenhill,	1787.	1835.
AMELIA, ...		1763.
THOMAS, ...		1841.

MAGDALENE, to Peter Ranken of Forfar,	1793.	
AGNES,		
GRIZEL, ...		1823.
AMELIA, 1st to Anderson of Baldovie,	1782.	
2nd to John Kirkaldy,	1797.	1830.
JAMES, ...		1794.
ALEXANDER, ...		1792.

[4.]

Sacred to the memory of CHARLES GREENHILL, Esquire of Fearn, who died 3d of May 1829, in his 88 year; and of CLEMENTINA GARDYNE, his wife, who died 12th January 1835, in her 82 year.

—Mr Greenhill, who was more than forty years factor to the Southesk family, acquired considerable wealth and position in Angus. Besides the children recorded in the next inscription, he had a son DAVID, who succeeded to the estate of Finhaven, &c., on the death of his cousin James Carnegy-Gardyne (*v.* OATHLAW.)

[5.]

Sacred to the memory of ALEXANDER & JAMES GREENHILL, sons of Charles Greenhill, Esquire of Fearn, and Clementina Gardyne. ALEXANDER died 22d May 1832, aged 44 years; JAMES died 25th June 1817, aged 26 years.

[6.]

In memory of MAGDALINE, widow of Peter Rauken, sheriff-substitute of Forfarshire, who departed this life at Rosely, near Arbroath, 10th July 1853, on her 96th birth-day; also of MARY, only daughter of Major Macan, H.E.I.C.S., who departed this life at Rosely, on same day, aged 6 years. The old go to death.—Death comes to the young.

Upon a slab with the Gardyne arms and motto, " Cruciata cruce junguntur" :—

[7.]

WILLIAM BRUCE-GARDYNE, Esquire, of Middleton, Major 37th Regiment, born 1777, died 15th June 1846. Also their children, ANNE, born 1826, died 15th May 1831; JAMES MACPHERSON, born 1828, died 23 April 1828; AGNES-MARY, born 1835, died 25 March 1847.

—Major Bruce succeeded to Middleton, &c., on the death of his uncle THOMAS GARDYNE, who died unmarried (as above) in 1841, aged —. In accordance with his uncle's settlement, Major Bruce assumed the name of *Gardyne*, and was succeeded by his son, the present laird of Middleton. To a son of the last-mentioned the following inscription refers :—

THOMAS, born 1859, died 20th February 1864.

The family of RAIT of Anniston bury within an enclosure near to that of Gardyne. The Rait enclosure contains a freestone monument, which encases a graceful group in marble, representing the spirit of consolation, in the form of a female figure, ministering to the support of a person in sickness. Below is the following :—

In memory of the Right Hon. the Lady CLEMENTINA RAIT, who died 16th October, A.D. 1848, aged 29 years, the beloved wife of James Rait, Esq. of Anniston, second daughter of David, seventh Earl of Airlie.

Upon the upper part of the monument :—

In memory of JOHN RAIT, Esqr. of Anniston, born 1748, died at Anniston, 1823; and of his wife, ELIZABETH GUTHRIE, daughter of James Guthrie, Esqr. of Craigie, who died 1814. And of their children, viz. WILLIAM, died at Anniston, 1806; GEORGINA-HENRIETTA, died 1812; JOHN, died 1815; AGNES, married George Arbuthnott, Esqr. of Mavisbank, third son of Sir William Arbuthnott, Bart., and died in London, 1842; AMELIA, married Patk. Geo. Skene of Pitlour, died at Pitlour, 1830; WILLIAM, died in India, 1837; ALEXANDER died 1830, whilst home on sick leave from the 1st Madras Cavalry; MURRAY died at Anniston, 1819. James, who erected this monument, is the only survivor.

—The Raits of Anniston claim descent (Burke's Landed Gentry) from the Raits of Hallgreen, an account of whom is given in Nisbet's Heraldry. Some of the Hallgreen family became small proprietors, others churchmen, merchants, and farmers in Angus, &c.; and it is said that the first Rait of Anniston—who also owned Balmadies at one time—acquired a fortune as a merchant in Dundee.

The present mansion-house of Anniston, which has been greatly improved by Mr Rait, was previously called Little Inchoch, and the farm, now Myreside, was anciently Anniston.

The next two inscriptions are from table-shaped stones, elaborately ornamented :—

ALEXANDER DEAS (1746) :—

Methinks I hear the doolfull passing Bell,
Setting an oneset to its lowder knell;
Methinks I hear my dearest friends lament
With sighs, and tears, and wofull drieryment.
Methinks I see my children standing by,
Vewing the death bed whereupon I ly;
Methinks I hear a voice in secret say—
Thy glass is run, and thou must die to-day.

Here lies ane Godlie and ane honest man JOHN MILL, who departed this life the 10 of Iuly 1646, and of his age 56 years. Likewayes here lies honest and verteus ELSPET AIR, his wife, who departed this life the 20 of February 1668, and of her age 66 years.

From a headstone :—

Here lyes the dust of WILLIAM RUXTON, sometime tenant in Mireside, who had three wives that brought forth 14 children, the first one; the 2d five; and the 3d eight, of which number 4 lyes here, viz. WILLIAM and JAMES of the 2d; ANDREW & JOHN of the 3d; he died the 9 of April 1841, aged 84. As also MARGARET, daughter of David Ruxton and Margaret Brown, his spouse :—

Age and decay of Nature wore him of this stage;
He laid down into a good old age,
To rest and sleep, till the last trumpet sound,
And then to rise and with his soul be joynd—
To live with Christ his praises for to sing,
That overcame the grave, and took away Death's sting.

—Upon the reverse of the above monument are three shields: the middle shield, dated 1742, contains the names of WILLIAM RUXTON and his three wives, viz., KATRIN LAIRD, JANNET HENDERSON, and MARGET WILLIAMSON; the shield on the left has the names of the families of the two first wives (Elizabeth, Alex., John, Wm., and Anna); that on the right those of the third wife (David, Margt., Alex., Elspeth, Andrew, John, Thos., and Wm.) DAVID, of the third family, was the first of four generations of RUX-

TONS who have tenanted Mains and Mill of Farnell. The Ruxtons, farmers at Balinhard in Arbirlot, and those in Foveran and Belhelvie, Aberdeenshire, all sprung from David Ruxton, tenant of Myreside. Within the church, upon the left of the pulpit:—

By Alexr. Carnegie, minister of Inverkielor, to the memory of his father JOHN CARNEGIE, late minister thereof, from 20th Feby. 1755, to 28th Feby. 1805, when he died, aged 81. And of his mother CATHERINE WALKER, who died 25th Nov. 1790, aged 57; and of four of his brothers, who died in nonage, all interred in the area before the pulpit.

—The erector of this tablet, and his wife ELIZABETH SKIRVING, are buried within an enclosure on the north side of the kirk-yard. He died in 1836, aged 73, she in 1835, aged 66. Mr C. was proprietor of Baldovie, near Montrose, which belonged to the Melvilles (v. p. 129.) He sold that property to the Southesk family, and bought Redhall, &c., in the Mearns, now held by his son John Carnegie, Esq. An adjoining obelisk was erected by the congregation to Mr Carnegie's successor, Mr GEO. ARKLAY, who died in 1866.

JAS. PETER, hd. of Elizab. Rait, d. 1745, a. — :--
No beavty, strength, can stay the fatal doom;
No virtve, worth, prevent th' op'ning tomb.

GEO. PAUL, schoolmr., Inverkeilor, d. 1850, a. 47:
Grave; the guardian of his dust,
Grave; the treasury of the skies;
Every atom of thy trust
Rests in hope again to rise.

The most remarkable natural object in the parish is the Redhead, the *Rubrum promontorium* of Boethius—"a point of land which runneth far into the sea"—near to which the Danes are said to have landed when they invaded Scotland in king Malcolm's time.

Referring to the same locality, Monipennie writes that "a falcon engenders yearly upon a high rock, past memorie of man." Mr Ochterlony (c. 1682) corroborates this statement, and adds that there is "abundance of sea-foul and kittiewaicks .... nothing inferior in tast to the solan geese of the Basse." Ochterlony also tells that "sea-calves, who gender as other beasts doe, bring forth their young ones in the dry caves" betwixt Arbroath and Ethie, and that "the old ones are of a huge bignes, nigh to ane ordinare ox, but longer, have no leggs, but in place thereof four finnes, in shape much like to a man's hand, whereupon they goe but slowly."

Some antiquaries are inclined to believe that Kinblethmont was the scene of the battle of Drumderg-Blathmag, which the Annals of Ulster (Johnstone's Extracts, p. 61), state to have been fought A.D. 728-29. Numerous traces of ancient burial, and other old remains, have been found in the neighbourhood.

The Knights' Templars, as in most parishes of Scotland, had an interest in that of Inverkeilor, and the farm of Templeton and St German's Well of Kinblethmont, point to the place over which the Templars held superiority. Mr Miller, in his excellent work—Arbroath and its Abbey, p. 136 —conjectures, with much probability, that in this locality was situated the chapel of S. LAURANCE of Kinblethmont, to which, and to the monastery of Arbroath, Richard of Melville, then (1189-99) lord of the district, gifted (Reg. Vet. de Aberb., p. 99) ten acres in the plain or meadow of Kinblethmont, half an acre in the village, with the teinds of the mill of the same, also pasture for the chaplain's horse, cattle, and sheep.

The chapel of the Blessed Virgin Mary "de Quhitfeild" (Reg. Nig. de Aberb., 165), stood at the hamlet or village of Chapleton of Boysack. It is surrounded by venerable trees; and at the old kirk-yard is the family burial place of the LINDSAY-CARNEGYS of Kinblethmont.

But the ruin of Redcastle, picturesquely situated near Lunan Bay, is probably the more generally interesting object of antiquity in the parish. It was engraved by Grose (1790), and is a fine subject for the pencil from many points of view. The lands and manor of Redcastle were given by William the Lion to Walter of Berkeley (the reputed founder of the Barclays in Scotland), from which race, by a female, the property passed to an ancestor of King John Baliol. As before shown, Redcastle subsequently came to the Stewarts of Lorne, from whom the Argyll family inherit the territory and title of that name.

During the time of the Stewarts, Redcastle underwent a siege by a son of Lord Gray (Mem. Angus and Mearns); but, being unable to take the Tower, he set the adjoining buildings on fire, and nearly suffocated the inmates.

The lands and barony of Redcastle were acquired by Sir John Carnegie about 1621; and, owing to "the loyaltie" of the family, their circumstances became so crippled, that shortly before the death of the fourth Earl of Northesk, Redcastle, along with the baronies of Lunan, North Tarrie, and a portion of Ethie, were sold by public roup. Redcastle—which is held of the Crown " for payment of ane Ridrose at the feast of John the Baptist, in name of blench-farm, if asked allenarly"—was bought at 22 years' purchase, 8th Dec. 1724, by the Countess of Panmure, through whom it came to the Earl of Dalhousie.

Ethie is the oldest inhabited mansion-house in the parish. It stands within a mile of the Redhead, surrounded by good old trees; and, although tradition ascribes the building to David, Abbot of Arbroath, afterwards Cardinal Beaton, Guynd states that it was " laitly reedified by John [first] Earl of Ethie."

The only villages in the parish are those of Ethiehaven, Leysmill, and Chance Inn. The first is occupied by a fishing population; and at the second, where there is a railway station, a considerable trade is carried on in pavement quarrying. The stone, known by the name of *Arbroath Pavement*, is cut and dressed by machinery—an ingenious process, which, although now pretty generally adopted in granite polishing and similar works, was the invention of the late JAMES HUNTER, manager of Leysmill quarries, who died in May 1857.

At Chapelton of Boysack, to the east of Leysmill, there has long been a school in connection with the Established Church. It was taught for some years by JAMES THOMSON, an industrious writer upon antiquities, who died at Dundee in 1864, aged 72. While at Chapelton, he published a volume of Poems (72 pp., 1818), illustrative of local traditions, &c.; and in 1847, long after he left the district, appeared his History of Dundee, which is a work of much greater value than is generally admitted. Another teacher of this place, Andrew Thomson, published (1841), a metrical version of Scottish Geography.

The village of Chance Inn—about half-way between Montrose and Arbroath—is peopled by tradesmen and merchants common to such places. Near it are the Parish and Free Churches of Inverkeilor, also the Parochial and Female Schools.

Mortlach.

(S. MOLOCH, BISHOP.)

IT is believed that a church was founded at *Morthelauch* (? *Mohr-tullach*, great hills), by MOLOCH, a supposed disciple of S. Columba, early in the 7th century. He was a Scotsman (Butler's Lives), and a zealous assistant of S. Boniface. His relics were long kept in great veneration at the kirk of Mortlach. Another writer adds that the church " has a bell called *Ronnach*, said to have been brought from Rome."

The present church, which is prettily situated in the valley of the Dullan, has been frequently repaired; and Tradition affirms (forgetting that kirks as well as castles in Scotland were constructed of but frail materials in Canmore's time) that a portion of the present kirk of Mortlach is that to which King Malcolm, on obtaining his famous victory over the Danes, added, in fulfilment of a vow, three lengths of his spear!

As it now exists, the church of Mortlach consists of a nave and north aisle. A man's face, in the north-west wall, rudely carved in stone, is said to represent BEYN, the first dignitary of the See of Mortlach. He died in 1041, and was " buried at the postern door of this cathedral," as were his two successors, Bishops DONERCIUS and CORMAUCH, who died respectively in 1098 and 1122.

The Bishopric of Mortlach was erected by Malcolm II. in 1010; and Mortlach was the seat of the Bishop, until about 1125, when, during the time of Nectan, the fourth Bishop, the See was transferred to Aberdeen, at which period it owned five churches and their territories.

In 1157, Bishop Edward held all the property of Mortlach, including " the town and *Monastery* of the same"—an expression which shows that there had been a school or seminary at Mortlach for training missionaries for the Early Christian church.

The church of Mortlach, which is rated at £20 in the Old Taxation, was a parsonage of the Cathedral of Aberdeen. In 1574, it was served, along with four other adjoining churches, by Mr George Leslie, as minister, who had a stipend of £166 Scots, with the kirk lands, out of which he paid "the reidare of Murthlak'" a sum of £20 a year. The church is in the gift of the Crown.

The east end is probably the most ancient part of the present church; and I am inclined to think that the "oldest bits" about it are the tombstones, or coffin slabs, now part of the paving of the kirk.

From the present position of the slabs, the inscriptions cannot be properly deciphered; but, the late Rev. Mr Cowie of Cairnie, when schoolmaster of Mortlach, copied these inscriptions while the kirk was undergoing repair about 1811, and engrossed them into the kirk-session books. It is from these (transcribed by the kind permission of the Rev. Mr Cruickshank), compared as far as possible with the originals, that the following copies are printed. One slab "in the passage" presents a plain calvary raised upon steps, with a shield on each side of the shaft. One of the shields exhibits the Innes coat, the inscription being round the margin of the stone:—

Hic . iacet . . . . . [? cons]tabularius . de . balbenie . qbi . obiit . die . mensis . . . . anno . dni . mccccxx . . n . spousa . . . .

nna . innes . eius . qve . obiit . . . . die . mensis . decembris . anno . dni . mccccxix.

[Here lies . . . . constable of Balvenie, who died on the . . . . day of . . . . . in the year 1420. Here also lies his spouse . . . . NNA INNES, who died Dec. 1429.]

—The constable appears to have been contemporary with James Douglas of Balvenie, who (Rymer's *Fœdera*) was sent to London, on 19th Aug. 1423, as a commissioner for the relief of James I.

From a slab ("under window at east end of church"), upon which a cross of the wheel pattern is incised, and a sword under the left arm:—

Hic . iacet . honorabilis . vir . Johannes . Gordon . de . Brodland . qbi . obiit . apud . Bochrom . anno . Dni . mdxxxiij.

[Here lies an honourable man JOHN GORDON of Brodland, who died at Bochrom, A.D. 1533.]

"Under Pittyvaich seat":—

. . . . re resurrectionis hic in pace requiescunt cineres a . . . .

Mr Cowie gives the name of "GORDON" from a slab under the stair; also the following from another slab "in the churchyard":—

Hic iacet honorabilis vir Duncanus Gordon cum Marjoria . . . . sponsa qui obiit . . . .

The next object in point of antiquity and interest to those slabs, within the church, is a stone effigy in armour. It is built into the north wall, in an *upright* posture. This had at first formed part of a recess tomb, like those at Fordyce; and being placed near to the old Kininvie sepulture, the figure in all probability represents ALEXANDER LESLIE (a descendant of the fourth baron of Balquhain), who acquired Kininvie from the Earl of Athol in 1521. Four years later Leslie built the house of Kininvie, part of which building still stands, and dying about 1549, he was interred within the kirk of Mortlach, where the family long continued to bury. Their tomb is now outside the church.

The first baron of Kininvie left several sons. Walter, the eldest, who succeeded to Kininvie, died in 1562, and the third son, George, received the lands of Drummuir from his father. It was a grandson of George of Drummuir who became Earl of Leven; and the eldest daughter of the fifth Leslie of Kininvie was mother of Archbishop Sharp. The following (from a tablet at Mortlach), erected by the Archbishop's uncle, is in memory of his (the sixth laird's) wife :—

Here lyeth the pious, vertoous gentlewoman, HELEN GRANT, goodwife of Kininvie, daughter to Belenton, who lived with her husband John Leslie of Kininvie, 60 years, and departed the 11 of May 1712, the 82 year of her age.

The seventh laird, who was provost of Banff, sold Kininvie and Tulloch, in 1703, to his third brother James, who built the middle part of the house of Kininvie in 1725, and died in 1732. He was twice married, and the following inscription relates to his first wife :—

Here lyeth HELEN CARMICHAELL, daughter to —— Carmichaell of Clapertounehall in the countie of Midle Lothian, and spous to James Leslie of Tullich, who departed this life the 15 day of May 1717. I.L : H.C. Memor lethi fugit hora.

Another slab bears the name of a brother-in-law of the eighth laird :—

Here lyeth the pious and vorthie gentleman, JOHN GRANT of Navie, who was maried to Helen Leslie, daughter to John Leslie of Kininvie, who departed the last of August -7—. J.G : H.L.

—The eighth laird of Kininvie and Tullich entailed the estates in 1730, and dying two years afterwards he was succeeded by his only child James as ninth laird. The ninth laird married a daughter of Stewart of Lesmurdie, by whom he had three sons and three daughters. The first and third sons both succeeded. The first, who sold Buchromb in 1795, had an only daughter, and the second died unmarried in 1839, in which year the estates came to the son of their eldest sister Jean, by Robert Young, factor and commissioner to Sir A. Grant of Monymusk. This son, who was a solicitor in Banff, and took a leading part in the affairs of the county, married a daughter of James Donaldson of Kinairdy in Marnoch (*v.* p. 235); and a marble tablet at Mortlach bears this record of their deaths :—

Sacred to the memory of ARCHD. YOUNG-LESLIE of Kininvie, who departed this life 31 Oct. 1841, aged 74. And of his spouse, JANE DONALDSON, who died on 30 Nov. of the same year, aged 63. This tablet is erected by their children.

The above were the parents of the present laird, of whose lady and a daughter there is the following record :—

Sacred to the memory of BARBARA-KING STEWART, the beloved wife of George A. Y. Leslie of Kininvie, and daughter of Gen. William Stewart of Elgin, C.B., who died 12th Aug. 1853, in her 36th year; and MARY-JANE, their infant daughter.

—Mr Geo. A. Y.-Leslie had three sons and three daughters. The eldest son, Archibald, an officer in the 23d R. Welsh Fusiliers, lately constructed a Family Tree, from which, and notes kindly furnished by my friend Robert Young, Esq. of Elgin (author of excellent histories of Burghead, the Parish of New Spynie, &c.), this notice of the Kininvie family is mainly compiled.

From a mural monument (Joannis Faid, me fecit), within, and near S.W. corner of the kirk :—

Hoc conduntur tumulo reliquiæ ALEXANDRI DUFF de Keithmore et HELENÆ GRANT, uxoris suæ charissimæ, qui quadraginta annos et ultra felici et fœcundo connubio juncti, vixerunt. Uterq, quidem ingenue natus, ille ex nobilissimia Fifæ Thanis per vetustam familiam de Craighead, paulo abhinc superstitem proximo & legitime oriundus; illa ex splendida & potenti Grantæorum familia eodem quoq, modo originem trahens. Ortu non obscuri, suis tamen virtutibus illustriores, opibus affluxerunt, & liberis ingenue educatis floruere; pie, juste & sobrie vixerunt, et sic in Domino mortem obiere, illa Anno Domini 1694, ætatis suæ sexagesimo.

[In this tomb are laid the remains of ALEX. DUFF of Keithmore, and HELEN GRANT, his dearly beloved wife, who lived in a happy and fruitful union for more than 40 years. Both were well born, he being very nearly and lawfully descended from the most noble Thanes of Fife, through the old family of Craighead, not long extinct, and she deriving her origin, in like manner, from the renowned and powerful family of the Grants. Of distinguished birth, yet more illustrious for their virtues, they abounded in wealth, were happy in a flourishing family of liberally educated children, lived piously, justly, and soberly, and so died in the Lord, she A.D. 1694, in the 60th year of her age.]

—Alex. Duff of Keithmore (according to Mr Baird's interesting " Genealogical Memoirs of the Duffs,")* was an officer under Montrose, went abroad in 1646, and on his return home was imprisoned for some time by the Covenanters. He " was a little man," and becoming corpulent, was called by his friends *Croilic Duff*.

"Tho' abundantly active and diligent, a great share of his Success in acquiring money is ascribed to his Wife. . . . . She was a sturdy, big-boned woman, and at last became so fat and bulky, that it is said it required an eln of plaiding to make her a pair of hose, and that one time when she threw herself hastily into her Chair without taking notice that the House cat was lying squat upon the Seat, she prest puss so effectually to Death with the weight of her body, that it never waged a foot more. . . . . During the Usurpation of Oliver Cromwell, she had concealed a great leather bag full of ducatons in the Ceiling of the Hall at Keithmore, and the rats had just finish't gnawing a Chasin in the bottom of the bag, when a large company was at dinner, a shower of Dollars fell on the floor."

Besides an ample dowry which Keithmore got by his wife, he succeeded, at the death of her brother, " to 100,000 merks, including the Wadset of Allachy itself." Keithmore, the date of whose death has not been recorded upon the monument at Mortlach, died in 1700, aged 76; and, exclusive of large purchases of land made by his eldest son, he is said to have left " 24,000 merks of Land rent."

Keithmore and his lady were both buried within the kirk of Mortlach, in front of their monument. Below it, in two separate recesses within the thickness of the wall—almost lost to view by the adjoining pews—are freestone busts of Mr Duff and his lady. Keithmore left a family of three sons and four daughters. The daughters were all married. The sons were respectively designed of Braco, Dipple, and Craigston; and the eldest son of Dipple, after representing the county of Banff in Parliament for several years, was created a Peer, first by the title of Baron Braco, then by that of Earl of Fife. From him the present Earl of Fife, and Viscount Macduff, is the fifth Peer in succession.

Although the averment in the Mortlach inscription of the descent of Alex. Duff of Keithmore from Macduff, Thane of Fife, is not borne out by charter evidence, record proves that the surname of Duff has been one of respectability and consequence in Banffshire from at least the time of king David II.

The property of Keithmore was a wadset which Duff received from the Marquis of Huntly about 1640-6. It is situated in Auchendown, and the house commands a good view of the ruins of the castle of that name, and of the valley of the Fiddich, &c. It belongs to the Duke of Richmond, as successor to the Dukes of Gordon; and is occupied by an enterprising tenant, who has much pleasure in pointing out the slabs (one dated 1680), with Alexander Duff's initials, arms and family motto—VIRTUTE ET OPERA—as well as the " Strype of water," by the side of which Keithmore's wife, fearing the approach of king William's Dragoons, had a bag of gold and silver coins secreted by " her Grand Child, old Lesmurdy, a boy then 17 or 18 years of age."

Another tablet (marble) near the Duff monument bears:—

M.O.V.S.: Mr. HUGONIS INNES, filij honorabilis viri Joannis Innes de Leichnet, qui, cum annos triginta quatuor sacra in hoc templo peregisset, obijt anno Christi MDCCXXXII, natus annos LXVIII. Posuit hoc monumentum pia ac dilectissima conjux Eliz. Abernethie, filia domini de Mayen.

[Sacred to the memory of Mr HUGH INNES, son of an honourable man, John Innes of Leichnet, who was minister of this church for 34 years, and died in 1732, aged 68 years. His pious

---

* The " Genealogical Memoirs of the Duffs"—a most delightful piece of Scotch Family History, written by Wm. Baird of Auchmeddan, Esq., about 1763-75—were lately printed for private circulation by Major Gordon-Duff of Drummuir.

and dearly beloved wife, Elizabeth Abernethie, daughter of the laird of Mayen, erected this monument.]

—"This gentleman (Old Stat. Acct., xvii. p. 432), was possessed of a considerable share of bodily strength and personal courage; and, in those days, if various anecdotes which are told of him be true, it seems he had occasion for the exercise of these qualities in the discharge of his clerical functions."

The Inneses of Lichnett were descended from James, second son of Sir Robert Innes of that ilk, and his wife Grisal Stewart. One of them, John, was a Colonel under the Marquis of Argyll, to whom, on 1st March 1649 (Acct. of the Family of Innes, 140), he was "the first divulger" of the desertions from the army in consequence of its unwillingness to march to the North.

The minister's wife, whose progenitors were long designed of Mayen in Rothiemay, is said to have been descended of Abernethy of that ilk in Perthshire, and latterly of Saltoun. It was not until 1706, during the time of Mr Innes, that the General Assembly sanctioned the disjunction of Mortlach from the Presbytery of Fordyce and its annexation to that of Strathbogie, although the arrangement had been followed from the time of the Revolution. Mrs Innes is buried at Banff; and Mr I.'s successor, Mr SIME, who died in 1763 of putrid fever, was one of thirteen victims to that malady, whose bodies lay unburied at Mortlach at one and the same time.

Four other marble tablets within the church are respectively inscribed as follows :—

Sacred to the memory of Major LUDOVICK STEWART, Pittyvaich, and formerly of H.M. 24th Regt. of Foot, who died on the 25th of Dec. 1848, aged 66 years. Also of his wife MARGARET FRASER, who died on the 17th of Oct. 1859, aged 62 years. Their children GORDON-ELLIOT, Lieut., 22d Regt. Bombay N.I., died 12th Jan. 1840, aged 24 years. [2 drs. named.]

Sacred to the memory of Mrs ANN STEWART late of Pittyvaich, whose remains are deposited in this churchyard. She died 5th Feb. 1823, aged 81 years.

—The word "of" is misapplied in the above, the Stewarts having been merely *tenants* of Pittyvaich. The property belongs to Lord Fife.

Sacred to the memory of the Rev. MORRIS FORSYTH, minister of the Gospel at Mortlach, who departed this life 19th Feb. 1838, in the 68th year of his age, and 33d of his ministry.

From a neat tablet built into the east wall of the kirk :—

To the memory of Major JOHN CAMERON, C.B., E.I.C. Native Infantry, on the establishment of St George, who after serving his country in India for 32 years, both in a civil and military capacity, and particularly in most of the principal events during that period, died on the 15th of June 1838, while officiating as Resident at the Court of Hyderabad, aged 47 years. This tablet has been erected to his memory, and placed in the church of his native parish, by a few of his friends in India, as a mark of esteem and affection for his public and private character.

Possibly the oldest tombstone in the churchyard, is one with a bold carving of the Farquharson arms near the middle. An inscription in old English characters, closely run on, and oddly arranged toward the end, is cut in relief round the margin of the slab. The true reading seems doubtful; but the following is probably not far from being the correct one :—

✠ hic facet honerabulis bir robertus farquharson de lauchtitvany quī obiit mar de quinto mēri anno dn̄i mº qūº xlo sexto cum sua propiqirt'.

[Here rests with his kindred an honorable man, ROBERT FARQUHARSON of Lauchtitvany, who died at noon on the [5th, or 15th] of March [1417, or 1517.]

—It is said that Cuming of Kellas, when refused burial in his ancestral tomb at Altyre, avenged the insult by changing his name to FARQUHAR—thus breaking off allegiance to his parent clan, which, in those days "when might was right," was no ordinary loss to a chief. From him many of the Farquharsons are descended, possibly also the old laird of Lauchtitvany. Provost Cuming of Elgin, who died laird of Auchry, in 1689, was at one time designed of Lochterlandich (v. p.

175.) It is certain that before the 15th century, the Cumings owned Lochterlandich, and other property on the North side of Glenrinnes as well as in Glenlivat, facts which possibly go to prove that the tombstone in question relates to some of the Cumings who took the name of *Farquharson*. (*v*. Miss Cuming-Bruce's History of the Family of Cuming.)

A flat slab, which " lay in the passage towards west end of church" in 1811 (now in the churchyard near to the south wall), presents a shield in the centre with the Moir and Reid arms impaled. The following inscription is round the sides of the stone :—

HEIR . LYES . ANE . HONEST . MAN . CALLED IOHNE . MOIR . HVSBAND . TO . ELSPET . REID WHO . WAS . KILLED . . . . EFENCE . OF HIS . OVIN . HOVS . AT . THE . VALK . MILN . OF BOLVENIE . THE . 13 . DAY . OF . OCTOBR . 1660. MEMENTO . MORI.

—According to tradition, Moir, who was reputed rich, was attacked by "the Cateran band," and killed by a gun-shot, while barricading the door of his house. The house—or more probably one that had been raised upon or near its site long after the affair happened—was till lately, and probably still is, pointed out by the peasantry as that in which Moir was shot. Whether "Iohne" had been an ancestor of Dr ALEX. MOIR, a native and once schoolmaster of Mortlach, who so generously left the interest of £600 for educational purposes to the parish is uncertain, though by no means improbable. The next inscription is from a slab, with mortuary emblems :—

Hir lys the corps of the deceased IANAT CATTACH, vho departed this life Ivly 3, 1751, spovs to Iohn MacKendie in Belmorn, hir age is 72.

Upon a broken table-shaped stone :—

Here lies the body of ALEXANDER CANTLIE, late in Newton of Clunymore, who died 16th June 1807, aged — years. Done by the care of his brother, Francis Cantlie, masson.

JOHN SPENCE, Balandy, d. 1777, a. 82 :—

My God who gave me strength to walk
The world to and fro,
And by his mighty handy work,
I'm here interr'd below.
So in the silent grave I ly
Along with many more,
Untill the day that I appear,
My Saviour Christ before.

Rudely cut upon a flat, undressed granite boulder

Heir lyes the desesd body of IAMES MCLANICHAL, who departed this lif in Achmor Nomr. 7, 1726. I M. I M. Heir lye the deseed I M vho deportet Febery 2, 1733, his age 49.

Here lyes the dust of ALEX. FARQUHAR who lived in Priestswell, and died May 22, 1733, aged 76 years. And of BARBARA GORDON, his spouse, who died Nov. 1736, aged 70 . . . . .

Priestswell is in the vicinity of the church.

This stone is erected by Alex. Anderson, officer of excise, in memory of his spouse HELEN GORDON, who died 3d March 1810, aged 23, daughter of John Gordon in Tomnavoullan, who left 3 children, John, Alex., and Margaret. In memory of JOHN GORDON, in Tomnavoullan, who died 6th June 1831, aged 92 years. I.H.S ✠ His spouse MARGARET GORDON, died 13th July 1844, in the 78th year of her age, and left no family alive, but an only son William.

—" William," the reputed Crœsus of Glenlivat, still lives at Tomnavoulan. Although past fourscore, he is an able and willing dispenser of " Highland hospitality."

Here lies the body of WILLIAM KELMAN, farmer in Lessmurdie, who died Aprile 26, 1793, aged 80 ; and HELEN MCBARNAT, his spouse, who died 1st Dec. 1785, aged 75.

In memory of Mr ALEXANDER THOMSON, who taught the school of Mortlach 23 years, and died March the 21st, 1804, in the 57th year of his age. This stone is placed here by his friends and pupils, as a mark of respect for his character as a worthy member of society, and an unwearied teacher of youth.

Within an enclosure :—

The Rev. ALEXANDER GRANT, late minister of Glenrinnes, was interred here, Aug. 1, 1806, and his Mother in 1777. This stone was repaired in 1807 by George Grant in Drumfurrich. Here lies also the remains of the said GEORGE GRANT, brother of the Rev. Alex. Grant, who departed this life at Elgin, 23 April 1816, aged 85, in memory whereof this inscription has been added by desire of his son, Alex. Grant, late of the Island of Jamaica, on visiting his native county from London in Aug. 1829. JANET DONALDSON, relict of Geo. Grant, Drumfurrich, died 1834, aged 78. By her son, Alex. Grant, Aberlour, 1844.

—The above-named Alex. Grant, of the Island of Jamaica, bought the estate of Aberlour, in Strathspey, from J. Gordon, Esq. A sister of Mr Grant's married Dr McPherson, farmer, Garbity; and their daughter, Miss McPherson-Grant, is now proprietrix of Aberlour, a most lovely place, to which she succeeded by her uncle's will.

From a table stone :—

In memory of ROBERT LORIMER, senior, who departed this life at Glenbeg in a good old age, about the year 1702. His sons WILLIAM, JAMES, and THOMAS, all died unmarried. His fourth son, ROBERT, junior, lived in Myreside, and died there. This monument was erected by his grandson, Dr John Lorimer of London, in the year 1795.

—Dr Lorimer left £200 for the maintenance of a bursar at the school of Mortlach, and a like sum to enable him, if so inclined, to prosecute his studies at Marischal College, Aberdeen. Upon a table-shaped stone, enclosed by a railing :—

This stone was placed here by John McInnes, Dandalieth, in memory of his parents, JOHN MCINNES, Braehead, who died 21st Nov. 1816, aged 84; MARGARET LUKE, his spouse who died 4th Feb. 1813, aged 74 . . . . . . JOHN MCINNES died at Dandalieth, 19th May 1850, aged 74, and is here interred.

A monument of Peterhead granite bears :—

This stone is erected by James Sturm of London, in memory of his parents ALEXANDER STURM, merchant, Dufftown, who died 7th April 1848, aged 65 ; and MARGARET MURRAY, his wife, who died 6th May 1847, aged 75.

—The erector of this monument, who died at Hampstead, May 7, 1869, aged 57, was sometime a clothier in Aberdeen. He afterwards became a furniture dealer in London, and left upwards of £25,000. Besides handsome legacies to relatives and friends, he left £500 to each of eight charitable institutions in London. He also left a legacy of £500 to the National Life-Boat Institution, directing that a boat, named *James Sturm*, should be employed on the coast of his native county. He bequeathed £2000 to found two scholarships for five years each in the University of Aberdeen, for natives of Mortlach, of the age of fifteen years, who have been taught in the school of that parish ; also £500 for the education of females of Mortlach in the principles of the Established Church of Scotland; and a farther sum of £500, a portion of which and interest, to be expended for the relief of infirm poor persons of the village of Dufftown.

Here lys in hope of a blessed resurrection BARBARA BARRON, spouse to John Barron, oyster in Meuelock, who departed this life the 12th of January 1779, her age forty one. Also there son GEORGE, who departed the 13th of Oct. 1769, in the fifth month of his age.

—The above John Barron gifted a pewter basin to the kirk, which is thus inscribed :—" Given by John Barron, Elder, to the kirk of Mortlach. Mr John Tough, minister, 1768." Some profane wag has scratched a verse of doggrel rhyme upon the basin, the first couplet of which runs thus :—

" This bason was presented by me, JOHN BARRON,
Who ever took the Scripture for my warran'."

Helen Clark, mentioned in the next inscription, was a sister (*v.* Fordyce) of the late Sir James Clark, M.D. :—

✠ In pious memory of JOHN GORDON, who succeeded to the farm of Tullochalum 1771, and died there 1820, aged 82. MARY DAWSON, his spouse, died 1824, aged 72. And of their children, WILLIAM, who died in Jamaica, 1802 ; ANNE, died at Tullochalum, 1811 ; THOMAS, Capt. 92d Regt., " Gordon Highlanders," died in Jamaica, 1819 ; JAMES, died at Aberdeen, 1824 ; Rev. JOHN, died at Edinburgh, 1832 ; GEORGE, SS.C., Edinburgh, died at Paisley, 1838. Also of HELEN CLARK, the beloved wife of Alex. Gordon, who died at Tullochalum, 1822, aged 28 years. R. I. P.

From a stone in the east wall of churchyard :—

Erected in memory of WILLIAM MCCONNOCHIE, late farmer in Boghead of Auchendown, who died 13 Dec. 1824, aged 81. Done by his son John :—

Omnes eôdem cogimur : omnium
Versatur urnâ, seriùs, ociùs
Sors exitura, et nos in æternum
Exilium impositura cymbæ.

—The above, from Horace's Ode to Dellius, is thus translated by Dr Francis :—

["We all must tread the paths of Fate;
And ever shakes the mortal urn,
Whose lot embarks us, soon or late,
On Charon's boat, ah! never to return."]

A table-shaped stone (enclosed) bears :—

This stone was placed here by the Parishioners of Mortlach, as a mark of respect to the memory of the Rev. GEORGE GRANT, who discharged with fidelity the duties of a minister of this parish for the space of eleven years, and died 10th Oct. 1804, in the 44th year of his age. Also interred here the remains of HARRIET-ANN STUART or GRANT, thereafter IRVINE, widow of the said Rev. George Grant, who died at Aberdeen, 5th Sept. 1847, in the 69th year of her age.

Erected by a few friends in memory of JOHN UTLEY WIGNALL, Inland Revenue officer, who died at Dufftown, 17th Jan. 1866, aged 27 years.

———

A sculptured stone, round which S. MOLOCH'S fair was held in old times, stands in the haugh of the Dullan, near the kirk. Both sides of the stone are ornamented with objects common to the same sort of antiquities. Near to this stone, about 1810, a gold bracelet of curious workmanship was found, which was given to Alexander Duke of Gordon. The stone has been engraved in the Sculptured Stones of Scotland (vol. i., pl. xiv.); and, according to Tradition, the monument was "set up" by King Malcolm when he overcame the Danes. An entrenchment on Conval Hill is called a Danish encampment; and it is said that, as at Gamrie, the skulls of three Danes were long preserved at the kirk of Mortlach. It is certain that, until repairs were made upon the church in 1827, three skulls were kept in the wall of the old part of it.

S. WALOCH is said to have had a mission at Balvenie (Bp. Forbes' Kalendar of Scottish Saints) long before the time of S. Moloch ; and a well at Balvenie was noted in old times for its virtues in curing various diseases.

It is further averred that Bishop Beyn lived at Balvenie, and conferred the name (Bal-Beyn, i.e., Beyn's town), upon the locality. More probably, its origin is to be found in the Gaelic compound, Bal-bhana, "the town of green fields," which aptly describes the verdant aspect of the place and its many pretty surroundings.

The Cumins are said to have been early proprietors of the lordship of Balvenie, which, being afterwards held by the great family of Douglas, was forfeited by Sir John Douglas, lord of Balvenie, in 1455. About 1460, Sir John Stewart Earl of Athol, uterine brother of James II., had a gift of Balvenie from the Crown, on the occasion of his marriage with Lady Margaret Douglas, "the fair maid of Galloway." She left two daughters; and the Earl having married as his second wife, a daughter of the Earl of Orkney, she bore him a son, from whom were descended the Stewarts, afterwards designed of Balvenie. The Stewarts sold Balvenie about 1606, from which date until 1687, when the property was acquired by Alexander Duff of Braco, ancestor of the Earl of Fife, it had several owners, including the Inneses.

The castle, which is guarded on the north by a great ditch, with built sides, is popularly said to have been at first erected by the Danes, and "has a large parlour in it, yet called The Danes' Hall." The western portion appears to be the oldest; and the S.E. part bears unmistakable evidence of the Stewarts. The National Arms occupy a niche over the entrance door—upon which hangs a strong gate or yett of curiously wrought iron— and the Athol legend is boldly carved upon the front wall :—

☞ FVRTH . FORTVIN . AND . FIL . THI. FATRIS.

A shield (within the castle court) is charged with the Athol and Gordon arms impaled. These possibly refer to the fourth Earl of Athol, who died in 1579, and to his lady, a daughter of the house of Huntly. Upon another slab is a much defaced coat, over which is the motto—"SPES. MEA. XVS," (Christ my hope.)

The castle, which is surrounded by some grand old trees, has a commanding position near the junction of the Dullan and the Fiddich, between the railway station and village of Dufftown. In its palmy days the house of Balvenie had consisted of a large square, occupying about a Scotch acre in extent, with a strong lofty tower at the gateway, and turrets at each of the four angles of the building.

The castle was unroofed about a hundred and sixty years ago, since which time it has gradually become so much dilapidated that restoration would be almost impracticable. Had this been gone about at the time the first Earl of Fife built a costly, but now neglected mansion, a little farther down the glen, Balvenie might have been at this day one of the noblest seats, as it is one of the most interesting ruins in the North. Billings gives two capital engravings of it in his Baronial and Ecclesiastical Antiquities of Scotland; and there is a good view (1787) in Cordiner's Remarkable Ruins.

Of a very different type from the ruins of Balvenie are those of the castle of Auchendown. These stand upon a high conical and grassy mound, the base of which is washed by the Fiddich, without a tree or bush to protect them from the storm. From the peculiar position and form, as well as the extent of the ruins, they present a singularly weird appearance, particularly when viewed from the ford at Glenfiddich—superior, in some respects, even to Melrose Abbey, when seen by pale moonlight. Indeed, so much was the Queen struck with the grandeur of the scene that during her short stay with the Duke of Richmond at Glenfiddich, she sketched the castle from several points of view.

The property of Auchendown belonged to Ogilvy of Deskford, before it came to the Gordons, which was about the year 1535. In 1592, the castle was burned by the Macintoshes out of revenge for the murder of their chief, whose head is said to have been treacherously cut off by the hand of Sir Adam Gordon's lady, and fixed upon the gate of Auchendown Castle. These circumstances gave rise to the ballad of the "Burning of Auchendown." The castle was never rebuilt; and not a trace remains of the Gordons, either in armorials or initials, if any ever existed, about the noble ruins of their old stronghold of Auchendown.

The writer of the old Statistical Account of the Parish of Mortlach says that the heroine of the song of "Tibby Fowler" lived in Auchendown; and, speaking from the report of some old people who had seen her, the reverend writer adds, that she "was a plain looking lass, with a swinging tocher."

The *Village of Dufftown* (from which the Castle of Auchendown is about three miles distant), was founded in 1817, by Lord Fife. It contains a considerable population, with a neat Roman Catholic Chapel, a Free Church, branch banks, and a number of good houses. In consequence of the salubrity of the climate, Dufftown and its neighbourhood are much frequented by strangers during the summer months, to whom Balvenie, Auchendown, and the varied and romantic scenery of the Dullan and the Fiddich are objects of much interest, and particularly the locality of the Giant's Chair, upon the former river.

The GLENRINNES portion of the parish, which lies between Dufftown and Glenlivat, was a mission station until within the last few years. It is now a *quoad sacra* parish, with the necessary accompaniments of a church, school, manse, and burial-ground.

Finhaven, now Oathlaw.

(? THE NINE MAIDENS.)

SIR ALEXANDER LINDSAY of Glenesk, father of the first Earl of Crawford (*v.* Edzell), rebuilt the kirk of Finhaven about 1380, and bestowed it upon the cathedral of Brechin, in the choir of which the prebendary had a stall.

The old place of worship stood near the Castle of Finhaven. Some of the Earls of Crawford, and the later lairds of Finhaven, and their families were buried at the church ; but, so far as known, no tombstone at Finhaven bears the name of any of the old owners of the property.

Only two monumental fragments remain. One, though small, is a good example of the coffin slab ; the other is a flat stone, with the figure of a priest rudely incised. The words below are round the margin of the latter ; and the surname, which is partly obliterated, had probably been *Bruce*. This is inferred from the Bruce arms being upon a shield at the feet of the figure :—

✠ hic . iacet . honorabilis . vir . dns . recherd . br . . . vicarius . De . finhebgn . qui . obiit . 2º . die.

HENRY QUBIT, or WHITE, prebendary of Finhaven, was an original member of the College of Justice, and died about 1541. He was possibly connected with Brechin, since he left the rents of a toft and tenement of land adjoining that city to the chaplain of the altar of S. Catherine at Brechin (Reg. Ep. Brechin.)

---o---

OATHLAW.

Although *Oathlaw* has been the name of the parish from about the beginning of the 17th century, and the church situated in that locality, the whole district was previously known as FINHAVEN, or FINAVEN. Oathlaw is supposed to have been merely the site of a chapel, dedicated to S. MARY, and dependent upon Finaven. So far as I know, Tradition and *Mary's Well* are the only authorities for these ideas.

The parish was disjoined from the Presbytery of Brechin, and annexed to that of Forfar, in 1731. The present church was built in 1815. The old bell, which is at the parish school of Careston, is inscribed :—

SOLI . DEO . GLORIA . 1618 . I . M.

The kirk of Oathlaw is rather a neat building, surrounded by some fine old trees. Within it is a tablet with this inscription :—

In memory of MARY ELIZABETH HILLOCKS, the beloved wife of Captain James Webster, who departed this life in the faith of our Lord Jesus Christ, January 2, 1834 ; and of their only children, DAVID, died January 10, 1834, aged 2 years and 9 days ; MARY, died Augt. 3, 1834, aged 3 years 7 months 19 days. This tablet is (with permission of the Heritors), erected by a sorrowing husband and father.

—A headstone, within an enclosure at the east end of the kirk, refers to the parents of the above-named lady, whose husband was a seaman, and a son of Provost Webster of Forfar :—

1831. Erected by David Hillocks at Mill of Finhaven, in memory of his beloved wife, ISABELLA BROWN, who lived respected and loved, and died in the faith of her Lord and Saviour Jesus Christ, on the 11th February 1831, aged 97 years. DAVID HILLOCKS died 6th June 1839, aged 86. Also much and justly regretted.

—Mr Hillocks was long local factor on Finhaven, Careston, and Hallyburton ; and his wife was a daughter of a factor at Aboyne. Mr H.'s brother, sometime farmer of East Newton, afterwards a grain merchant in Montrose, died about 1859, aged 96. Their father was farmer of Peebles, near Arbroath.

An Iona cross (ornamented with the family arms and motto), within a railing, in S. E. corner of burial-ground, bears upon its base :—

In memory of DAVID GREENHILL-GARDYNE of Finaven, who died 19th Oct. 1867, in his 72d year.

—Mr Greenhill-Gardyne, who succeeded his cousin, Mr Carnegy-Gardyne in the lands of Finhaven, &c., was a son of Mr Greenhill of Fearn, and his wife Clementina Gardyne of Middleton (*v.* INVERKEILOR.) Like his cousin, he assumed the additional name of *Gardyne*. He erected the present mansion-house at Finhaven, where he died as above. Mr G. was a District Judge in the H.E.I.C.'s Civil Service. Besides Finhaven, he owned Craignathro, near Forfar, also Glenforsa, in Argyll, which last he bought from Lord Strathallan. His son and successor, Lieut.-Colonel G.-Gardyne (by his wife, a daughter of Dr Wallace, Arbroath), was an officer in the Coldstream Guards. He married the Hon. Amelia-Ann Drummond, daughter of Viscount Strathallan, by whom he has issue.

Round the sides of a flat stone (in the centre of which are also traces of a Latin inscription), are these words :—

. . . . . . ELMVS . FODE . QVI . OBIIT . OCTOB . . . . . . ETIAM . ALEX . FODE . EIVS . FILIVS . QVI . OBIIT . 25 . MAII . 1618.

—" Fode" looks like a corruption of the old Forfarshire name of *Fothie* or *Fithie*, which sometimes takes the form of *Fudie*.

Heir lyis IOHN MARNO, svmtym indvelar in Ovthlaw, who depairted in November 1675, his age was 76 yeirs . . . . .

—" Marno," now *Marnie*, is probably assumed from Marnoch, or S. MARNAN.

Heir lyis ROBERT MOOR, svmtym indvellar in Bogardo, hvsband to Evphan Ese ; he depairted this lyf the 1 of Agvst 1694, of age 76 yeirs. Also his children lye heir IOHN, KATHREN, and IANET MOOR, &c.

—" Ese" or Essie is still a surname in Angus, and of local origin. From another stone :—

☞ Heir lyes THOMAS HOOD, hammerman, svmtym indveller in Wilds Hillock, who departed this present life the 18 day of Ianvarie 1699 years, and of his age the 87 year ; also IANET SVTAR his wife, and his children :—

Death is the horison wher ovr sone doth set,
Which will throvgh Christ be a resvrection grate.
The glass is rvne.

From a head-stone :—

WM. CUTHBERT, wright, Carsburn, d. 1768, a. 72 ; a son JOHN d. in infancy :—

Heir lys the Father and the Son,
Together in the dust ;
Consider this, all that pass by, —
That follow fast you must.

Upon the east side of a head-stone is the following inscription. The couplet is altered from Ben Jonson's epitaph on the Countess of Pembroke :—

Monumentum. Here lyes MAY PROPHET, spouse to Mr Thos. Raiker, minister at Oathlow, born Novr. 5, 1715, maried Feby. 4, 1742, departed this life July 20, 1798, in the lively hope of a resurrection to Immortal life, aged 83.

Before mankind a better wife shall see,
Time, O Death, shall strike a dart at thee.

[On west side of same stone :]—

THOMAS RAIKER was born on the 11th of June 1711, ordined Minr. of this parish on 24th Decr. 1740, and died 30th June 1803. He was at the sametime a regular and zealous servant of his Divine Master and attentive to his own concerns. Let those who were edified or benifited by the labours of his long life, cherish and imitate what was praiseworthy in his character.

Rests before this stone, the mortal clay
Of THOMAS RAIKER, till that awful day,
When Christ will send his angel thro' the skies,
And to the dead proclaim—ye sleepers Rise.
Then may the Saviour to this Servant say—
Enjoy a Crown thro' an eternal day.

—Mr R.'s father was an officer of excise at Anstruther Wester, and his wife was the daughter of a merchant in Kirriemuir. He left £20 to the poor of the parish ; was never three Sundays out of his own pulpit, and preached on the last Sabbath, except one, previous to his death. (Scott's Fasti.) Mr Raiker's epitaph is locally attributed to the late Rev. Mr Buist of Tannadice, who, in speaking of Mr R. being "attentive to his own concerns," possibly had the fact in view that during his 65 years' incumbency Mr Raiker saved some £5000 off a stipend of about £70 a-year. From a head-stone near to Mr Raiker's :—

Sacred to the memory of the Rev. ANDREW CROMAR, who, after being minister of Oathlaw for the short space of four years and six months, died on the 10th day of November 1835, in the fortieth year of his age. "He cometh forth as a flower and is cut down." "What I say unto you I say unto all, Watch."

[On the west side of same stone :]—

GEORGE PHILIP CROMAR, wine-merchant, Arbroath, son of the Rev. Andrew Cromar, died 12th

Dec. 1862, aged 31 years; and is here interred. JANE CROMAR, daughter of the Revd. Andrew Cromar, and wife of David Ritchie, Rio de Janeiro, died 1st April 1863, aged 32 years; and is interred at Petropolis, Brazil.

—The Rev. Mr Cromar, who belonged to Lumphanan, was sometime tutor in the family of the Hon. Gen. Ramsay of Kelly. It was through the General's influence that he got the kirk of Oathlaw.

Mr Cromar was succeeded by the Rev. Harry Stuart, a native of Birse, who was appointed to the living through Lord Hill, Commander-in-Chief of the Forces, in recognition of his services as a chaplain in the army, and for the valuable evidence which he gave in 1835, before the Commission which was appointed to inquire into Military Punishments, and the Discipline of the Army in general. Mr Stuart published, in 1853, an appeal in favour of Agricultural Labourers in Scotland, which, whether for straightforward heartiness in the cause, or graphic delineation of peasant life and character, is one of the best works that have appeared upon the subject.

The parish school and school-house are at the Kirkton of Oathlaw. A tablet with the following inscription, the admonitory part of which is from Juvenal (Sat. 14), is upon the school-house:—

Auspiciis Nobilissimi CAROLI, Comitis de ABOYNE, Bar. de Finhaven, Patroni, cum cæteris Prop. et Poss. fundi parœchiæ de Oathlaw. Virginibus puerisque.
Nil dictu fœdum aut visu' hæc limina tangat
Intra quæ puer est
Maxima debetur pueris reverentia.
A. S. 1784.

[Under the auspices of the Most Noble CHARLES, Earl of ABOYNE, Baron of Finhaven, Patron, and of the other Landed Proprietors in the parish of Oathlaw. For boys and girls.
Let nothing unbecoming to be spoken, or seen touch the threshold, within which a child is. The greatest reverence is due to children.]

Antiquarian and historical notices of Finhaven having been already given by the writer in the "Land of the Lindsays," readers are referred to that book—more especially to Lord Lindsay's delightful work of the "Lives of the Lindsays." It need only be stated that the hill of Finhaven is remarkable as the site of an extensive vitrified fort; and that, in General Roy's time, and for many years afterwards, there were traces of a Roman camp at Battledykes.

A stately portion of the ruins of the Castle of Finhaven occupies a rising ground near the junction of the Lemno with the South Esk. This is probably a portion of the house to which Earl Beardie fled after the battle of Brechin; and in which he exclaimed that he "wud be content to hang seven years in hell by the breers (eyelashes) o' the e'e," rather than have lost the victory which had fallen to his antagonist, the Earl of Huntly.

A stone bridge crosses the Lemno on the great North Road; and that over the South Esk is dated 1796.

The Kirk-session records of Finhaven and Oathlaw shew that "the Ladie of Finhaven dyed on Sabbath morning the 20th Aug. 1738, and was buried on Friday thereafter in the Isle." This relates to the first wife of James Carnegy of Finhaven, who, in a drunken brawl in 1728, accidentally killed the Earl of Strathmore upon the streets of Forfar (v. Land of the Lindsays.) The following extracts are curious:—

1734, March 15, "Agnes Clerk, spouse to John Fairweather in this town of Oathlaw dyed and was buried tomorrow."

1735, Nov. 3, "The church officer's sick child buried here"!

On 4th July 1736, charity was "given to two strangers that were dumb, being taken by the Turks at sea, and their tongues cut out."

The annexed wood cut is a representation of the tombstone of Richard Bruce, vicar of Finhaven, referred to at p. 335:—

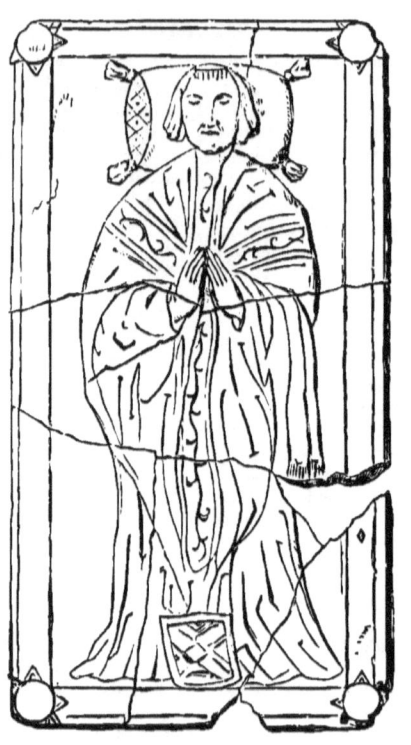

SUPPLEMENT.

Alford—(page 120.)

A costly granite monument, on the north side of the burial ground of Alford, bears :—

To the memory of the Revd. JAMES FARQUHARSON, LL.D., F.R.S., for 31 years the faithful and beloved pastor of this parish, who died much lamented Decr. 3d 1843, aged 62. This monument was erected out of grateful and affectionate remembrance by his parishioners.

—Dr Farquharson, who was the son of an excise officer at Coull, was 12 years schoolmaster at Alford before he succeeded to the church. He was a successful student of meteorology, and wrote upon the Aurora Borealis, the Currency, the Native Forests of Aberdeenshire, &c. His wife was a sister of the under-mentioned Mr Farquharson Taylor, to whose memory a handsome granite monument, with draped urn, is thus inscribed :—

In memory of FARQUHARSON TAYLOR, Esqre., J.P., farmer, Wellhouse, who died 13th July 1857, aged 58. Erected by the parishioners of Alford in testimony of their respect for his sterling integrity as Factor for many years, on the estates of Haughton, Breda, and Carnaveron ; and in affectionate remembrance of his high character and worth as a Neighbour and a Friend.

—Mr Taylor's grand-father, who was farmer of the Kirktown of Alford, died in 1800, aged 70. His own father died in 1837, aged 81.

In memory of WILLIAM WATT, sometime Reporter to the Aberdeen "Free Press," who died 27th March 1834, aged 30 years.

The next inscription records the fact of a man becoming a father in his 82d year :—

Erected by Wm. Lawson in Mill of Commerce, parish of Midmar, in memory of his parents WILLIAM LAWSON, who died 29th Novr. 1782, aged 84 years. Also of his spouse JEAN FORBES, who died 29th July 1816, aged 78 years. Also of EFFIE, their daughter, who died 27th Octr. 1793, aged 13 years. Also of WILLIAM, son of the above Wm. Lawson, who died in infancy.

From a granite obelisk :—

In memory of GEORGE THOMSON, Guard S. N. E. Ry., injured while on duty on 22nd, and died on 23rd August 1862, aged 27 years. This stone is erected by his fellow-servants and friends, by whom he is deeply regretted.

Auchterless—(208.)

The following inscription relates to ancestors of Edward Ellice, Esq., who has represented the St Andrews District of Burghs, since 1837 :—

Here lyes ADAM BARCLAY, sometime in Knockleith, and CHRISTIAN CHALMERS, his spouse. He died 12th of August, 1695, and She the 18th of April, 1696. Also, ISOBEL BARCLAY, their daughter, & GEORGE ELLICE, her husband. She died 28th of December, 1727, and He the 23d of June, 1736,

Also WILLIAM ELLICE, their son, who lived at Mill of Knockleith, and MARY SIMPSON, his wife. He died 19th August, 1756, aged 37, and She the 15th of February, 1786, aged 76 years.

—Adam Barclay was possibly tenant of the farm of Netherthird of Knockleith, for, according to the List of Pollable Persons for Aberdeenshire, 1696, Netherthird was tenanted by, apparently, his widow, "Christan Chalmers," when she and her family, "Hary, Elisabeth, and Isobell Barklays," were charged 36s of poll duty. As Christian Chalmers died on 18th April, the tax must have been fixed before that date in 1696.

———o———

Benvie—(192.)

Mr Henry Fithie, who was admitted minister of Benvie before 4th April, 1627, and whose name is upon the old kirk bell of that parish, was translated to Mains about 1633. He was deposed in 1649, along with seventeen other ministers in the Synod of Angus (Scotts' Fasti), for loyalty to King Charles.

Mr Fithie, who possibly officiated at times after his deposition, continued in favour with the Earl of Panmure; and the following interesting letter appears to refer to some official engagement which he had made with his Lordship, through his factor, Mr Pilmure. It is addressed "For the verie noble lord the earle of panmure":—

My Lord—As I promised to Mr Johne pilmure at the recent of yo.. Lops. letter from him so I intendit to hane been with your l... on Sundays night ; but that day an issue of bloud brak vpon .. wherby I was altogither vnable to ride or go anie wher. yet I hoped that it might hane closed on munday and that i might h... mend all that short iourny after the close therof ; but I must take pn .. once vnder this arestment, and craue your lop humble pardon that I can not be assistent this day as your lop desyred, I abyd your Lop
humble Seruant t . . . .
my pour   M. HENRIE FITHIE.
Claypotts ye 6 of June 1653.

Mr Fithie probably retired to the Castle of Claypots after his deposition. He died sometime before 1st May, 1655, as of that date "Mr James Fithie, only lawful son of the deceased Mr Henrie Feithie, late minister at Mains," had a gift from Patrick, Earl of Panmure, of the chaplaincy of St Salvador, "foundit for ye Lady Marie Church of Dundee." Mr James Fithie was appointed minister of Mains in 1663 ; and, as his second wife was named Martha Johnstone, she may have been related to Mrs Edward of Murroes (*infra*, p. 123).

As elsewhere stated (Mem. Angus and Mearns, p. 43), *Fithie* is an old Forfarshire name, and was originally assumed from lands in the parish of Farnell. Henry of Fythie was one of the Commissioners appointed by Robert the Bruce to inquire and report what rights and privileges the town of Arbroath had from his predecessors. Fithies were designed of Boysack at one time, and a Henry Fithie was provost of Arbroath (Nisbet, i. 353).

A handsome communion bread plate, which belongs to the kirk-session of Dundee, presents a shield, charged with a crane, pierced by a sword in base (for Fithie), and three stars in chief, probably showing descent from a second son. The donor of this plate, who was a merchant in Dundee, and sometime proprietor of Benvie and Balruthrie (Mem. Angus and Mearns, 305), married Margaret Strathwhan, or Strachan. The following inscription is round the shield :—

IOHANNES FITHEVS, IN AMORIS TESSERAM, ECCLESIÆ TAODVNENSI AD SACRAM CŒNAM CELEBRANDAM VAS HOC ARGENTEVM DONO DEDIT.   1665.

[John Fithie presented this silver vessel, as a token of his attachment, to the Church of Dundee, to be employed in the celebration of the Holy Supper. 1665.]

But it ought to be added that, apart from its intrinsic value and antiquity, this plate is an object of much local interest, in so far as it bears, in conjunction with the mark of the Assay Office of Edinburgh, the arms of the town of Dundee. I am indebted for this interesting fact to the Rev. Mr R. R. Lingard-Guthrie of Taybank, who,

I believe, has the merit of discovering the Dundee mark or stamp, which he has found not only upon the Fithie plate, but also upon later pieces of silver work at Taybank, &c.

The Dundee arms or mark shows that the pieces of plate upon which it appears were made by local craftsmen. Mr James Rettie, jeweller, Aberdeen, who is well versed in these matters, informs me that when plate was sent from the provinces to the Assay Office at Edinburgh, the arms or mark of the town in which the maker resided was added to the regular Hall Mark. He also refers to Chaffers' work on " Hall Marks," from which it appears that the plate originally made at St Andrews bore the St Andrew Cross, and that of the city of Perth the spread eagle. Plate made at Aberdeen bore the three castles, and that of Dundee had the pot and lily.

Although I have seen no record of the silversmiths of Dundee, I have no doubt but much that is interesting could be gleaned from their Minute Books. The trade was practised there at an early date, as is proved by a tombstone near the north-west corner of the *Howff*, which bears to have been erected to the memory of a " goldsmith" who died in 1603, at about the age of 70. This stone is much defaced, but as . . . . AY— the last two letters of the surname—and the Ramsay eagle can be traced upon it, the name of the craftsman is placed beyond doubt.

Having been contemporary with, this Dundee goldsmith may also have been related to, the celebrated *Davy Ramsay*, clockmaker to King James, and a reputed descendant of the Ramsays of Auchterhouse. It may be repeated (*v.* Mem. of Angus and Mearns), that Lord Dalhousie is in possession of a curious watch, inscribed " David Ramsay, Scotus, me fecit," and which is said to have belonged to Mary Queen of Scots.

It may also be added that, in a deed signed and sealed in the church-yard of St Clement, Dundee, 11th May 1427, it is stated that Thomas Maule of Panmure used a newly made seal by Donald the goldsmith (Reg. de Panmure). Donald had probably been a local artificer.

Bervie—(26.)

There was probably an earlier bridge across the Bervie than that of 1695 ; at least the following charter notice shows that it was proposed to erect one towards the close of the 15th century :—

" Ch. to Alexander Straitoun of Knox for supplie to him to help to big a brig on the water of Jnuerbervy of the kings fishings of the said water and cheifely the fishing betuixt the Sea marck in the shirrifsdome of Kincardine qlk was never given before to any excepting all former donationes given to any other gentlemen with pouer to him to putt Cruives and coupis on the said watter and to make a Clouss in the brig for his mair Commodious fishing bleuche for a reid roiss at St John Baptists day at the toun of Jnuerbervy 28 May 1474 Edinr " (M.S. Notes of Scotch charters at Panmure.)

---o---

Carmyllie—(246.)

The parish of Carmyllie was formed out of several adjoining parishes ; and, as before stated (p. 246), a chapel was erected there in the early part of the 16th century, of which Malcolm Strubble was chaplain. By the deed of erection the chaplain and his successors were bound to keep a school at the chapel of Carmyllie for the instruction of youth (Reg. de Panmure).

" The presentation of ye chapell of Carmyllie, givein to Mr David Lyndsay be y° lerd of Carmyllie, wt consent of his curators," supplies the names of two of the old ministers of the district. The deed (here printed from the original at Panmure, by the kind permission of Lord Dalhousie), is dated the same year (1609) as Parliament ratified " the Erectioun of the kirk of Carmylie in ane parochkirk, conforme to the actis of the kirk maid thairanent" (Acta Parl., iv. 442.)

As Dr Scott (Fasti) states that Mr George Ouchterlony was admitted minister of Carmyllie before 28th Dec. 1611, Mr Lyndsay had not been long there. A person of the same name and surname was admitted to Kinnettles (Fasti), before Sept. 1610. The following is a copy of Mr Lyndsay's presentation to Carmyllie:—

Be It kend till all men be yir prnt. letters, me James Strachauchn of carmylie, wndoubted patron of ye chapellanrie of Carmylie, with consent of my curators wndersubscryvand for yair Interest, wnderstandent the qualification, literatur, and gwid vnderstanding of Mr Daniel Lyndesay, sone lawfull to James Lyndesay, burges of Dunde, and of his earnest desyr and Intention to Preache the Word, Therffoir I hayff nomted. and presentit, and be yir prntis Nōatts and presenttis the sd Mr Dauid In and to the chapellanre of carmylie, lyand within the diocie of brechin and shreffdom of forfar, haill frwits, duttics, profeitts, and casualitie ptning yrto, Dwering all the dayes off his lyftym, now waccand In my handis and at my Disposition & presentation be ye deceas off Mr Thomas Strachachyn, last chapellain yroff, humble requyring Andrew, bishop of brechin, to admit and resaue him yrto, and authorise him with his testimoniall of admission yrwpon In dew and competent form as affeirs. Lykwayes humble requyring ye lordis off counsell & sessioun to grant & direct letters at the Instance of ye sd Mr Dauid, for ansuering & obeying him of ye frwits, rentis, profeits, & emolemtts of ye sd chappellanre off ye crope & yeir of god jᵐ sex hundreth and nyn yrs. Instant, & forder dueriug his lyftym. In witness qroff to this my presentatione, subscryvet be me & my curators, my seill Is affixt att brechin ye first day of Maij jᵐ sex hundreth and nyn yrs befoir yir vitnes the sd John Nory.

   James Strauchine.
  Alexr. Strachauchin,
   of brigtoun, curator.
  Georg Strathen,[?] curator.
  Al. Strathauchin, fear of brigton,
    curator.

Coldstone—(284.)

An "Iona Cross," within a railing near the gate of the church-yard, is thus inscribed:—

"I will lay me down and take my rest."

Sacred to the memory of JOHN FARQUHARSON of Corrachree, Lieut.-Colonel H.E.I.C.S. Died 19th July 1871.

—Colonel Farquharson married a sister of Mr Farquharson of Whitehouse in Tough, but left no issue. The Colonel was a grandson of the last Farquharson of Tullochcoy, and representative of the Invercy branch (*supra*, pp. 215.) His mother, Isabella McHardy, who belonged to Cabrach, had a nephew, some time sheriff-substitute of Lanarkshire, and his eldest daughter is now the wife of Mr Merry, M.P. for the Falkirk Burghs.

Upon a granite obelisk:—

In memory of FRANCIS BEATTIE, A.M., for 49 years schoolmaster of this parish. Born 1st Jany. 1785, died 24th Septr. 1855. Erected by his grateful and attached pupils who mourn in him a zealous teacher, a wise counsellor, and a constant friend.

From a granite head-stone:—

To the memory of the Rev. JAMES WATTIE, M.A., parish schoolmaster of Crimond from 1813 to 1856, also tenant of the farm of Bellastraid in this parish —to which he latterly retired—where he had been born, and where he died 31st July 1872, aged 83 years.

—In early life Mr Wattie became a tutor in the Island of Eig, where he acquired some knowledge of the Gaelic language, and a taste for traditional lore. He afterwards cultivated the latter gift with considerable success; and it is to be regretted that he did not commit his knowledge on these matters to writing.

His own sayings and doings would form a chapter rich in the curiosities of human character. He was tall and rather spare in person. When he went abroad in his own neighbourhood, he generally carried a staff nearly as long as himself, and wore a heavy cloak which, even in the warmest days of summer, covered no end of flannels and greatcoats. Although learned, well read, and of a sociable disposition, he is said to have been more frequently seen than welcomed by his friends.

Mr Wattie was exceedingly vain of the attentions of the great, and seldom lost an opportunity of thrusting himself into their presence. It is told that soon after he became a preacher, he was introduced to Lord Aberdeen, afterwards Premier, and that his Lordship signified his intention to procure a church for him. Mr Wattie allowed few chances to pass without reminding his Lordship of his promise by letter; but as writing proved ineffectual, he determined to make personal application. In course of time an opportunity occurred, and upon Lord Aberdeen remarking that the church sought after was scarcely suited for Mr Wattie, the latter, in his own blunt way, is said to have inquired, "Then, my Lord, what sort of a church do you think would suit me?"— to which it is said the Earl laconically replied— "The L—d only knows!"

It is pleasing, however, to have to add that though he did not recognise his gifts as a preacher, his Lordship perceived his skill as a farmer, and when Mr Wattie came to reside as his tenant at Bellastraid, he gave him every encouragement, and left nothing undone to make his latter years comfortable.

——o——

Cowie—(55.)

Upon a table-shaped stone :—

To the memory of RAYMOND STEWART, a Black Man, a native of Granada, who lived for thirty years in the service of the late Mr Farquharson of Breda, in this country, and was much respected. He died at Elsick the 3d January 1834, leaving money which he had saved for charitable purposes.

From two flat slabs :—

1772.—JOHN THOM, tenant in Elrick, died 27 March 1763, aged 72. ANN BURNET, his wife, died April 24, 1779, aged 76. [Nine children recorded dead.]

To the memory of JAMES THOM, once tenant in Elrick, who died 6th January 1839, aged 83 years. Also of his wife MARGARET WILLIAMSON, who died 4th January 1859, aged 82 years; and JAMES THOM of the fourth generation of the name of Thom in Elrick, son of James Thom, farmer, Elrick, who died 27th February 1841, aged 28 years.

——o——

Cupar-Angus—(73.)

A U.P. Church was established at Cupar-Angus in 1743, and a Relief Church in 1787. The undermentioned Messrs Small, Allan, and Muirhead, were respectively, the 2d, 4th, and 5th pastors of the former, and Mr Dunn was the 4th pastor of the latter body (Dr Mackelvie's Annals).

[1.]

1773 : Hic jacent cineres Domini THOMÆ SMALL, veri Christiani, & fidelis pastoris, ut speramus, in Ecclesia Associata, Cupar Angus, qui in opere Evangelii assidue laboravit, donec Deo placuit in gaudium Domini sui eum vocare. Obiit quinto die Maii, anno millesimo septingentesimo septuagesimo secundo, ætatis suæ vigesimo nono et . . . . .

[Here lie the ashes of Mr THOMAS SMALL, a true Christian and faithful minister, as we trust, in the Associate Church, Cupar-Angus, who laboured diligently in the work of the Gospel until it pleased God to call him to the joy of his Lord. He died 2d May 1772, in the 29th year of his age, and . . . .]

[2.]

To the memory of the Rev. ALEXANDER ALLAN, minister of the First Un. Assoc. Congregation, Cupar Angus, who died on the 30th January 1824, in the 72d year of his age, and 43d of his ministry. This stone is erected by the gratitude of his flock.

Qualiscunque fuerit pietate, ingenii dotibus, studiis, officiisque, cordibus viventium vigeat, lapis sepulchralis taceat.

[Of his piety, his intellectual endowments, and his zeal in the discharge of his duties, let a vivid recollection dwell in the hearts of the living; but let the tomb-stone be silent.]

—Mr Allan was author of a work on the Power of the Civil Magistrate in matters of Religion.

[3.]

To the memory of the Revd. CHARLES MUIRHEAD, pastor of the United Associate Congregation, Cupar Angus, who died 2d Aug. 1830, in the 31st year of his age, and 5th of his ministry. This stone is erected by the gratitude of his flock.

The course of his ministry was brief, but the extent of his great literary acquirements, the maturity of his judgment as a theologian, the enlightened fidelity of his official labours, the sanctified sweetness of his disposition, and the heavenly serenity of his dying hour, will be long remembered by the surviving few who had the happiness of knowing his worth.

[4.]

Here are interred the remains of the Revd. WILLIAM DUNN, A.M., late minister of the Relief Congregation, Coupar Angus. He died the 17th of May 1829, in the 56 year of his age, and 21st of his ministry. This stone is inscribed by the Members of the Relief Congregation in remembrance of his unwearied exertions while their pastor. Separated by 15,000 miles from the dust below, whither she had followed their surviving children, lie the remains of MARTHA CROSBIE, the beloved wife of the above, who died at Melbourne, Australia, on the 5th December 1852, aged 63. Her end was peace.

— Mr Dunn wrote the Life of St Columba, and several other works.

From a headstone :—

WILLIAM SMALL, spovse to Marjory Elye, in Kethick, departed this life Agvst 27 day 1712, and of age 48.

> Devot and pious vinto God
> He vas vpright to man.
> . . . .

A head-stone, which presents a shield charged with the odd figures of two spirit measures, a drinking quaich, &c., bears this inscription :—

1766: This is erected by Robert Fisher & Jean Small his spouse, in Kethuick, in memory of their son PETER FISHER, who died 17th July 1765, aged nine weeks—

> Parents freet not at God's comand,
> When he your children doth demand.

———o———

Dun—(222-5.)

A handsome cross of polished granite has been raised alongside the monument to Lady Hallyburton, mentioned on p. 222. It is to the memory of her only son, and is thus inscribed :—

Sacred to the memory of WILLIAM-HENRY KENNEDY-ERSKINE of Dun, the son of the Hon. John Kennedy-Erskine and Augusta Fitz Clarence, his wife. Born 1st July 1828, died 15th Septr. 1870.

I will trust.—Isaiah 12.2.

This monument is erected by his Widow, Catherine Kennedy-Erskine, in loving remembrance of him who made the happiness of her life.

—Mr Kennedy-Erskine left a son and two daughters. He was of an affable, kindly disposition, and much beloved by his tenantry. A marble slab, erected to his memory by the parishioners of Dun, is placed over the entrance to the parish church.

A much defaced tombstone in the church-yard bears the following simple record of one who, like Marjory Scott of Dunkeld, had seen and survived some of the more eventful and stirring scenes in the history of our country :—

Here lys . . . . s YOUNG, husband to Margaret Smith. He died ye 27 Febr. anno 1699, of age 90 yeirs.

The next three inscriptions are from old headstones built into the kirk-yard dyke:—

[1.]

☞ Here lyes an honest virgin, MARGRET SIMSON, who died ye 16 of March anno 1699, of age 21 year.

[2.]

W. F. : I. M. : I. F. : Here lyes WILLIAM FINDLOW, who dyed May 29, 1702, being of age 72. Here lyes JEAN MILNE, spouse to William Findlow.

[3.]

Over a rudely incised carving of the Strachan arms—a hart (?) tripping—is the following :—

1696 : Here lyes ROBERT STRACHAN, younger, who died ye 10 of October anno 1696, of age 8 years.

The next inscriptions are from two of the oldest of several tombstones which relate to ancestors of a family named Thomson, who were sometime farmers at Leuchland, Arrot, and Findowrie, &c., in the parish of Brechin; and one of whom was long town-clerk of Montrose :—

Here lyeth the body of IAMES THOMSON, late tenent in Mains of Dun, who died Feby. 8th 1719, aged 36. As also IS. THOMSON, his spouse, who died Iuly 12, 1742, aged 58.
Tho' Boreas' blasts, and Neptune's waves, &c.

—This stone, which bears to have been erected in 1757, presents the coulter and sock of a plough, and the initials " Ia. Thⁿ., Is. Th., Ro. Th., Is. Th." The verse (*sup.* p. 276), of which the first line is given, possibly shows that James Thomson was at one time a sailor. The other stone, initialed " Ia. Th , Ma. Low, Io. Th., An : St :" bears :—

Mors neminem fugit. 1751.
Here lyeth the body of IAMES THOMSON, late tenent in Balwylo, who died Nour. 2nd 1735, aged 53. Also MART., his daughter, died Sepr. 11th, 1721, aged 2.

Thus speak ye dead to those that passing by,
Behold death's triumphs with a careless eye—
By death we're landed on ye silent shore,
Where billows never break, nor tempests roar ;
Secure from care, from endless trouble free'd,
We rest in hope of glory to succeed.
When high in air ye mighty trump shall sound,
& call ye dead from all ye world around ;
When fresh in youth ye just in Christ shall rise,
And never fading glories bless their eyes ;
Thrice happy they in him who've put their trust,
They fear not ye decay of Time, nor terrors of the dust.

The following inscriptions, abridged from three adjoining tombstones, relate to a family, some of whose members were among the most enterprising agriculturists and stock-rearers in Angus :—

HELEN MITCHELL, wife of David Scott in Balwyllo, died 26th April 1824, aged 59 years. DAVID SCOTT, late of Newton, died the 20th January 1846, aged 90 years.

DAVID SCOTT, younger of Newton, died 12th February 1845, aged 53 years ; and his third son

JONATHAN D. G. SCOTT, 28th Regt. B. N. Infantry, died 16th Jany. 1839, aged 27 years.
ROBERT SCOTT, farmer, Balwyllo, died 5th July 1843, aged 48 years.

—The deaths of four sons and three of Mr Scott's daughters are recorded upon the same monument, the last-mentioned of whom, DAVID, surgeon-major, Bengal Medical Service, died at Umballa, 16th Sep. 1867, aged 42.

From a head-stone :—

1872 : Erected by a few friends to the memory of WILLIAM MACKIE, Schoolmaster of this parish for 41 years. Born at Brechin, 2nd Nov. 1799, died at Dun, 1st June 1863. The just shall be held in everlasting remembrance.

———o———

Dunottar—(51.)

The next two inscriptions are from marble slabs built into the wall of the Mariscbal aisle :—

Sacred to the memory of ROSE CHRISTIAN, wife of Peter Christian, writer in Stonehaven, and youngest daughter of James Young, late sheriff-substitute of this county, who closed a virtuous and amiable life, 21st April 1833, aged 57 years.

To the memory of JEAN COWAN, second wife of HUGH FULLERTON, sheriff-substitute of Kincardineshire, who died 1st June 1833, aged 42. Erected by her husband as a tribute of affection. He died 20th January 1846, aged 66, and is here interred. Their only son ALEXANDER, died at Tuticor, in East Indies, 4th May 1855, aged 26.

From an adjoining table stone :—

Mr GEORGE MILNE, writer in Stonehaven, died 7 Aug. 1798, aged 54 years. His widow MARY MILNE, daughter of James Young, some time sheriff-substitute of this county, died the 5th of December 1843, at the age of 76 years, and is here interred.

Abridged from a table-shaped stone :—

JAMES FARQUHARSON, Esq., late of Coldrach, in Braemar, died in Stonehaven, 19th November 1794, aged 74 years. Two daughters, CATHERINE, died 3d Oct. 1828, aged 77 ; JEAN, 18th Feb. 1833, aged 83. His youngest son, MURRAY FARQUHARSON,

Capt. in the 1st West India Regt., sometime Lieut.-Col. of the 2d Regt. of Aberdeenshire Local Militia, died at Elsick, 2d Nov. 1837, aged 76.

JAMES BURLEY, Cowieswell, d. 9 Jan. 1783, a. 50;
MGT. MONCUR, his sp., d. 7 Nov. 1796, a. 63 :—

Our life is but a winter day,
Some only breakfast and away ;
Whilst others do to denner stay.
Large is his debt who lingers out the day,
Those who go soonest have the least to pay.

—The above is an inferior copy of a well-known epitaph upon an innkeeper, said to be at Barnwell, co. Cambridge, which reads :—

"Man's life is like a winter's day—
Some only breakfast, and away ;
Others to dinner stay, and are full fed,
The oldest man but sups, and goes to bed.
Long is his life who lingers out the day—
He who goes soonest has the least to pay."

The next inscription is from a table-stone :—

In memory of ANN GORDON-ROSE, daughter to Charles and Jane Gordon-Rose of Blelack, who died the 10th of July 1797, in the 5th year of her age.

(*Mem.* p. 52.) The castle of Dunottar, &c., were sold by Sir Patrick Keith-Murray, Bart., in July 1873, to Major Innes, of Cowie and Raemoir, for about £80,000.

———o———

Durris—(105.)

The following newspaper cutting, from a report of a meeting of the Royal Geographical Society, held in London on 12th Jan. 1874, (Sir Henry Rawlinson in the chair), refers to a proposed act of munificent liberality on the part of Mr Young of Durris and Kelly, which is but rarely to be met with :—

"I have sincere pleasure (said the chairman) in announcing to you what, I think, will make all geographicalists thrill with pleasure, and it is, that Mr Young, a very liberal friend of Dr Livingstone, who instituted the expedition, and has already paid £2000 from his own pocket towards the expenses of that expedition, has announced to us officially that he is quite prepared to take upon himself all the subsequent expenses of that expedition. We have accepted this handsome offer, and of course we shall reduce the expenditure within the narrowest possible limits ; but at the same time, it is very gratifying to find that there is that public spirit, that appreciation of Dr Livingstone, and that interest in geography which prompts a gentleman like Mr Young to come forward and place funds at the disposal of the society. On reporting his offer to the council to-day, I was authorised to transmit a unanimous vote of thanks on the part of the council to Mr Young, and I think it would be gratifying to them if the present meeting would supplement that vote by permitting me to present the thanks of the whole of the Fellows of the Royal Geographical Society. I believe I may take it for granted that I have your authority for doing so."

Unfortunately for the cause of Science, Mr Young had no opportunity of fulfilling his generous intentions, for soon after these were announced, a telegram brought to England the melancholy intelligence of the death of the great traveller.

The following (received at the London Office of the *New York Herald*, 29th March 1874,) gives an interesting account of Dr Livingstone's last days :—

"The Malwa arrived off Suez at eleven on Saturday night, having Mr Arthur Laing, and Mr Jacob Wainwright aboard, with the body of Dr Livingstone. He had been ill with chronic dysentery for several months past. Although well supplied with stores and medicines, he seems to have had a presentiment that the attack would prove fatal. He rode a donkey, but subsequently was carried, and thus arrived at Muilala, beyond Lake Bemba, in Bisa country, when he said, ' Build me a hut to die in.' The hut was built by his followers, who first made him a bed. He suffered very greatly, groaning day and night. On the third day he said, 'I am very cold ; put more grass over the hut.' His followers did not speak or go near him. Kitumbo, Chief of Bisa, sent flour and beans and behaved well to the party. On the fourth day Livingstone became insensible, and died about midnight. Majuahua, his servant, was present. His last entry in his diary was in April 27th. He spoke much and sadly of home and family. When first seized he told his followers he intended to exchange everything for ivory to give to them, and to push on to Ujiji and Zanzibar and try to reach England. On the day of his death his followers consulted what to do, and the Nassick boys determined to preserve the remains. They were afraid to inform the chief of Livingstone's death, and the Secretary removed the body to another hut, around which he built a high fence to ensure privacy. Here they opened the body and removed the internals, which were placed in a tin box, and buried inside the fence under a large tree. Jacob Wainwright cut an inscription on the tree as follows:—'Dr Livingstone, May 4, 1873,' and superscribed the name of the head man Susa. The body was then preserved in salt and dried in the sun for twelve days. Kotumbo was then informed of the death, and he beat drums and fired guns as a token of respect, and allowed the followers to remove the body, which was placed in a coffin formed of bark. The Nassick boys then journeyed to Unyanyembe about six months, sending an advance party with information addressed to Livingstone's son, which met Cameron. The latter sent back bales of cloth and powder. The body arrived at Unyanyembe two days after advance party, and rested there a fortnight. Cameron, Murphy, and Dillon were together there. The latter was very ill, blind, and his mind was affected. He committed suicide at Kusakera, and was buried there.

"Here Livingstone's remains were put in another bark case, smaller, done up in a bale, to deceive the natives who objected to the passage of the corpse, which was thus carried to Zanzibar. Livingstone's clothing, papers, and instruments accompanying the body. When ill, Livingstone prayed much. At Muilala he said, 'I am going home.'

"Webb, the American Consul at Zanzibar, is on his way home, and has letters handed to him by Murphy from Livingstone for Stanley, which he will deliver personally only. Chumah remains at Zanzibar.

"After Stanley's departure, the Doctor left Unyanyembe, rounded the south end of Tanganyika, and travelled south of Lake Bangneales, crossed it south to north, and then along the east side, returning north through marshes to Muilala. All papers sealed and addressed to Secretary of State, in charge of Arthur Laing, a British merchant from Zanzibar. Murphy and Cameron remained behind."

The remains of the great explorer were interred within Westminster Abbey, on Saturday, 18th April 1874, in presence of his own family, his faithful follower, Jacob Wainwright, and a large assemblage of mourners, many of whom were of the highest intellectual and social standing in Europe. The coffin-plate bore this inscription:—

"DAVID LIVINGSTONE,
Born at Blantyre, Lanarkshire, Scotland,
19th March 1813;
Died at Ilala, Central Africa, 4th May 1873."

In *Punch* of 18th April 1874 appeared the following befitting tribute and epitaph to the memory of Dr Livingstone:—

Droop half-mast colours, bow bareheaded crowds,
 As this plain coffin o'er the side is slung,
To pass by woods of masts and ratlined shrouds,
 As erst by Afric's trunks Liana hung.

'Tis the last of many thousand trod
 With failing strength, but never-failing will,
By the worn frame now at its rest with God,
 That never rested from its fight with ill.

Or if the ache of travel and of toil
 Would sometimes wring a short, sharp cry of pain
From agony of fever, blain, and boil,
 'Twas but to crush it down, and on again !

He knew not that the trumpet he had blown
 Out of the darkness of that dismal land,
Had reached and roused an army of its own,
 To strike the chains from the slave's fettered hand.

Now we believe he knows—sees all is well—
 How God had stayed his will and shaped his way,
To bring the light to those that darkling dwell,
 With gains that life's devotion well repay.

Open the Abbey doors and bear him in,
 To sleep with king and statesman, chief and sage,
The missionary come of weaver kin,
 But great by work that brooks no lower wage.

He needs no epitaph to guard a name
 Which men shall prize while worthy work is known;
He lived and died for good—be that his fame—
 Let marble crumble, this is LIVING-STONE!

———o———

Ellon—(61.)

The church bell of Ellon bears to have been cast by "BAIRD & ELLIS, ABDN. 1828."

In consequence of recent alterations upon the church and church-yard of Ellon, several old tombstones have been discovered. The first-quoted inscription is from a flat slab. It presents some mortuary emblems, and the letters are cut in raised Roman capitals. Although the inscription may be of little value to the general reader, the monument is of some local interest, in so far as it bears the name and craftsman's mark of— "THOMAS TAIT, SCULPSIT, V." This was the reputed great-grandfather of the Archbishop of Canterbury (*supra*, p. 97.) The inscription runs thus :—

Hoc sub cippo requiescit corpus PATRICI CATTANACH, quondam in Mickle Miln de Essilmont, qui, 18vo mensis Iulii die anno Domini 1717—atque ætatis suæ 56to, diem obiit supremum. Hic etiam requiescunt quatuor illius liberi, duo ALEXANDRI, IACOBUS, atque filia ISABELL. Hic quoque iacet filia, nomine MARIA, quæ vigesimum agens annum 6to Iannarii die, 1727, vita excessit.

[Beneath this stone rests the body of PATRICK CATTANACH, sometime in Mickle Miln of Essilmont, who died 18th July 1717, in his 56th year. Here also rest four of his children, two ALEXANDERS, JAMES, and a daughter ISABELL. Here also lies a daughter, named MARY, who departed this life 6th January 1727, in her 20th year.]

The following is a line-for-line copy of the inscription previously given on p. 60 :—

SALVS . PER . CHRISTVM . VIVE . VIVAS.
[Forbes and Ramsay arms impaled.]
I F W   I R
1637
Built by I : F : of W :
Son to W : F : of Tolqu :
& I. R : Dautr to Balmain
in 1637   Rebuilt by
T : F : of W : & M : M :
in 1755.

—William Forbes of Tolquhon acquired the lands of Waterton from Alex. Bannerman of Elsick, about 1633. The original builders of the aisle were I. (? T.) Forbes and his wife Jean Ramsay ; and the rebuilders were Thomas, their great-grandson, and his wife Margaret, eldest daughter of Montgomerie of Aslons. It was the last-named laird who sold the lands of Waterton to the Earl of Aberdeen, about 1770 ; but dying before the purchase was completed, the transaction was carried through by his grandson, John Forbes, in 1775 (*Watertoune Papers*.)

Several tombstones belong to a family named LIGERTWOOD, some of whom were advocates, merchants, masons, &c., in Aberdeen. Mr John Ligertwood, the present sheriff-clerk of Aberdeenshire, is come of this family ; another, who died in 1834, aged 77, was proprietor of Logierieve, Uduy. The following inscription, abridged on p. 60, is here given in full :—

Here lyes in hopes of a blessed resurrection, JAMES LIGERTWOOD, born in Cairnhill, June 11th, 1681, and died there January 5th, 1745 ; as also two of his children, JAMES & MARJORY LIGERTWOODS. Likewise MARJORY LIGERTWOOD, his spouse, who died the 15th of Janr. 1772, aged 80 years. Also MARGARET GORDON, spouse to Thomas Ligertwood, who died 19th Janr. 1782, aged 56 years. And THOMAS LIGERTWOOD, late farmer in Cairnhill, who died Octr. 1782, aged 64 years.

The next two inscriptions are from table-stones:—

JANET THOMSON, wf. of Alex. Clark, wright, Old Aberdeen, d. 1809, a. 74 :—
"She was a dutiful wife, an affectionate mother, and a patron of Industry and Temperance."

This stone was erected in memory of JOHN BEAN, sometime chymist in London, son of . . . Bean, late in Ardgrain, who . . . . 1781, aged 84 years . . . . .

From a slab, upon which a bell, a book, cross bones, and a skull are represented :—

Remember Lord how short a time
I shall on earth remain ;
o wherefore is it so that thou
hast made all men in vain.

Here lies in hope of a blessed resurrection The Corps of GEORGE BOWMAN, sometime in Laverocklairs, who departed this life, 26th of August 1743, aged 54 years. Also CHRISTIAN GARIOCH, his spouse, who died the 29 of Janr. 17–4 aged . .

From a granite slab on east of churchyard :—

In memory of GEORGE CHALMERS, LL.D., who died at Hornbillocks, in this parish, in March 1787, aged 77 years. Erected by John Chalmers, Rose Street, Aberdeen, 1838.

ARCHD. AINSLIE, officer of Excise, a. 42, and a dr. 3 years, d. 1817 :—

        A funeral thought
Hark, from the tombs a doeful sound
  My ears attend the cry
Ye living men, come view the ground
  Where you must shortly lie.
Great ones, this clay must be your bed
  In spite of all your towers,
The tall, the wise, the reverend head
  Must lie as low as ours.

MARGT. CHALMERS, wf. of David Wood, shipmr., Abdn., d. 1817, a. 28 :—

All you that stop to read this stone,
Consider how soon she was gone ;
Swift was the flight, and short the road,
She clos'd her eyes, and saw her God.
A loving wife, a tender mother dear,
A true and faithful friend lies here ;
Ready to forgive, & fearful to offend,
Beloved in life, lamented in her end.
Grieve not for me, my child & husband dear,
For we shall meet when Christ the Lord appears;
As I am now, so must you be,
Therefore prepare to follow me.

ROBT. SCROGIE, wright, Ellon, d. 1833, a. 89, his wf. ISABEL KELMAN, d. 1832, a. 86 :—

Tis safer, Lord, to hope in thee
And have my God my friend,
Than trust in men of high degree,
And on their truth depend.

S. MARY'S EPISCOPAL CHURCH,

Erected in 1870-1, chiefly through the exertions of Mr M'Leod, the present incumbent, stands a little to the north-east of the old place of worship. It was erected after designs by Mr Street, R.A., and is surrounded by a burial-ground.

The new church is a handsome building in the Early English style, with narthex, nave, and chancel. A belfry and vestry are upon the north side of the church, and an organ recess is at the south-east corner of the nave. The nave itself has a semi-circular timber roof. An aumbry is upon the north side of the altar, and a piscina and sedilia on the south. The chancel-screen and pulpit are of carved free-stone ; the lectern, stalls, and altar rails are of English oak ; and a handsome baptismal font, of red granite, stands in the porch.

Six of the fourteen windows in the church are already filled with stained glass, as described below. Two of these, which are in the chancel, and respectively represent the Crucifixion and Resurrection of Our Saviour, are inscribed as follows :—

✠ Grateful to a Heavenly Father, Richard Boyle places this memorial of his love for his child, ELEANOR BOYLE, who died at Ellon Castle, August 11, 1871, aged 25.

—This young lady was the daughter of the Hon. and Rev. R.-Cavendish Boyle (fourth son of the eighth Earl of Cork and Orrery), rector of Marston-Bigott, Somersetshire, and his wife, Eleanor-Vere, youngest daughter of the late Mr Gordon of Ellon. The next refers to a brother of Mrs Boyle :—

✠ To the Glory of God, and in affectionate remembrance of BERTIE E. M. GORDON, William, Charles, and Everetta Gordon have placed this window.

—Mr Gordon was second son of the late laird of Ellon, and Colonel of the 91st Argyllshire Highlanders. He was a man of great courage and presence of mind, and it was owing mainly to his judicious and gallant conduct that the lives of his men were saved when on board the "Abercromby Robertson," at the time she was wrecked in Table Bay. He died at Ellon Castle, and his remains were buried at the east end of the church of S. Mary, where, in addition to the above tribute to his memory, his widow has erected a cross of polished grey granite, raised upon two steps. Upon the steps of the cross at the head of the grave, and upon a plain slab at the foot, are these inscriptions :—

"Until the day break."
BERTIE E. M. GORDON.
Born December 17th, 1813 ; died July 27th, 1870.

In the grave, with bitter weeping,
Loving hands have laid him down ;
There he resteth, calmly sleeping,
Till an angel raise the stone.

—Colonel Gordon's father, who died at Ellon Castle in 1873, in his 90th year, was buried beside his wife in the old church-yard of Mary Culter. He was a highly respected landlord—a fine example of the "old country gentleman"—and took a great interest in the church of St Mary of Ellon. A brass, on the north side of the altar, is thus inscribed :—

In loving and reverent memory of ALEXANDER GORDON of Ellon, whose fatherly care and beneficence are here recorded by his youngest son, in humble gratitude to Almighty God.

Mrs Gordon, who died in 1848, was a daughter of Richard Cumberland, by a daughter of the third Earl of Buckinghamshire. The offertory plate of St Mary's, which has the Sacred monogram, ihs, in the centre, surrounded by symbolical representations of the Four Evangelists, bears the following inscription :—

✠ Deo et ecclesiae de Ellon in mem : ALBINIÆ ELIZABETHÆ GORDON. Ejus animæ propitietur Deus.

[To God and the church of Ellon, in memory of ALBINIA ELIZABETH GORDON. May God be merciful to her soul.]

✠ Domini est terra et plenitudo ejus. Alleluia. [The earth is the Lord's and the fulness thereof.]

On the south side of the nave of the church are the memorial window and monument to Mr Gordon of Eslemont, noticed at p. 61. An adjoining window of two lights, in which Christ is represented Blessing Little Children, is to the memory of ANNE, ETHEL, and MARGARET, daughters of Mr and Mrs Wolrige-Gordon, now of Eslemont. Mrs W.-Gordon, who became heiress of Eslemont, was a niece of Mr Gordon. Since his death, a new mansion-house has been erected at Eslemont, and the ruins of the old moated castle of the Cheynes, which possibly indicate a work of about the close of the 16th century, are still preserved among some old trees, near the gate of the new mansion.

Another window of two lights, upon the south side of the church, representing the Sermon on the Mount (supra, p. 60), is thus inscribed along the base :—

He taught them as one having authority.
In memory of JOHN TURNER, Esq. (of Turnerhall), born 22nd July 1796, died 2nd August, 1834 ; and of ELIZABETH-HELEN URQUHART, his wife, born 20th June 1800, died 5th January 1837.

In memory of ANNA-MARGARET, wife of the Revd. George Kemp, Rector of St Alphage, London, and eldest daughter of John and Elizth.-Helen Turner, born June 10, 1831, died Decr. 1861.

The only other window which has yet been filled is upon the north side of the nave. It represents the Marriage Feast of Cana of Galilee ; and, as indicated by two adjoining brasses, it is to the memory of Messrs THOMSON and MILNE. They were both farmers, the former at Pitmedden, and the latter at Waterton.

———o———

Farnell—(92.)

A headstone (erected to JOHN DEAR, weaver, Bonnington, who died in 1726, aged 65), upon which the lay of a handloom, and a weaver's shuttle, &c , are neatly carved, bears :—

My days are swifter than a weauers shuttle. Job the 7 & 6.
I have cut off like a weauer my life. Isaiah 38 & 12.
   The Weauers Art it is renowned so
   That rich nor poor without it cannot go.

CHARLES FERRIER, tenant, Fithie, d. in Ap. and his wife ISOBEL LEITH in May 1729 :—

Here rest in hope of a most glorious life,
A frugall husband, and a faithfull wife,
Whose hearts were so unite with Divine love,
That death could not those sacred bonds remove.
But rich perfumes broke up, or blown by wind,
Do leave a lasting fragrant smell behind,
So these blest souls now purg'd of earthly dross,
Who on eternal love themselves repose,
Have left on earth an obelisk of fame,
A dear remembrance of their precious name.

JOHN FERRIER, wright, Montrose, died 15th Dec. 1860, aged 86 years.

JOHN SMITH, Greenlaw, d. 1723, a. 45, &c. :—
>Under this monument of stone,
>Lyes both the father and the son :
>Our nature's frail, we are made of dust,
>And to the earth return we must :
>One part of man in ground doth ly,
>The other mounts abone the skye
>The immortal soul to God resigned.
>A happy union the rest to be,
>Even to all eternitie.
>Remember man thou'rt made of nought ;
>Thou sold thyself, Christ hath the bought,
>And ransom'd the from death, the grave,
>Which to obtain his life he gave.

ELISABETH TAYLOR, wf. of John Crichton, tenant in Woodwrae, d. 1747, a. 61 :—
>My bones in grave lyes here below,
>A resting place hath found, yet know,
>God hath a time when he'll me raise,
>Eternaly to sing his prais.
>Espous'd I was to a Husband dear,
>Liv'd with him five and twenty year ;
>Now children four I left him have,
>I rest in hope God will them save.

DAVID COWLLIE, shoem., Karkrie, d. 1734, a. 40 :—
>When death doth come in his full rage,
>He spares not young nor old ;
>But cutts men down of any age—
>He'll not be brib'd by Gold.
>Take warning then ye that may see,
>And read this passing by ;
>And learn so to live as ye
>May not be fear'd to dy.

—Some of the above inscriptions were possibly the composition of Mr JOHN SIM, the parochial schoolmaster of the period, who, in 1730, entered upon a lease of 19 years of the half of the Croftheads of Farnell, valued at 40 merks, and which he held as part payment of his salary.

Two of the teachers of Farnell, JAMES BOWICK and the Rev. EDWARD MASSON, were distinguished in their day. The former, who was a native of Arbroath, wrote a Life of Erskine of Dun, &c. ; and the latter, who was born at Laurencekirk, published *Philhellenia*, or translations from the Greek. In the Introduction to this *brochure* the author states, in apology for the part he took in the Greek war, that he was then (1824), "young, and the spirit of the Covenant and the Grampians came o'er me. Besides, a solemn sense of duty made me accept the special invitation of the Greek Government, and of the great Scottish naval hero (Lord Dundonald, then High Admiral of Greece), to become secretary to the Greek Fleet, and take a personal share in the struggle of civilization against barbarism—of the Cross against the Crescent." Mr Masson, who was latterly professor of Greek in the Assembly College, Belfast, died at Athens, 7th July 1873, in his 73d year.

There are three headstones to a family named RUXTON, who were tenants of Mains and Mill of Farnell for three (misprinted "four") generations, *supra*, p. 324, in which page also is the more obvious misprint of "1841" for 1741.

An adjoining table-shaped stone bears a renewed inscription, to the memory of DAVID DUQUHARF, East Fithie, (husband to Isobel Marnoch), who died in 1713, aged 55 :—

>Death is the passage through which we go,
>It's just to all, spares neither rich nor low ;
>If all the virtues could have made it stand,
>Then here lies he who never one could brand
>With any vice or yet perjury :
>But its ordained that all men once must die.
>As he lived Godly so he died in peace ;
>His fame survives an honour to his race.

The following inscription was composed, and carved upon the stone, by a late beadle and gravedigger at Farnell, who was a tailor by trade :—

M A	1840	W
A L	ERECTED BY	W
J E 1817	JOHN WALKER	17 W
B E 1823	IN MEMARY OF	24 W
G O 1840	OUR PARANTS	E G 26 W
JOHN	WALKER DEYED 21	FEB 1823
MARGET	PETER DEYED 1	AUG 1820
BOTH	INTERED HER 5 OF	THEIR
	CHILDREN.	

———o———

Fettercairn—(254.)

A slab, which was recently discovered in the church-yard of Fettercairn, ornamented with representations of a wright's mallet, chisel, compasses and square, &c., and initialed, I. R., C. M., D. R. ....., bears this inscription round the margin:—

☞ HIC . IACET . PIVS . ET . HONESTVS . IACOBVS ROCHVS . QVI . COMMVTAVIT . LVCEM* . IN . ANNO DOMINI . 1642 . HIS . AG . 43 . Y. [* *sic.*

[Here lies a pious and honest man, JAMES ROCH, who exchanged life for death, in 1642, aged 43 years.]

The writer of the following letter, dated 21st May 1523 (?), was probably a brother of the laird of Claypots, near Dundee, from which place it is dated, and addressed to his "cuyne" (cousin), the laird of Carmyllie. It is here printed from the original at Panmure :—

Honobl SSr and Cuñe, ples zou well, I ame adveset yt ze ar to be fra zor place ye maist pt of yis soñer quharfor praie zou yt ye will caus deliver to my bruder ye berar my blak govne ye vestiment wt ye ptnitis and ye siluer chalice for I seir yt ye thric pt of ye fruitis of ye bñficis sal be taken yis zeir as it wes ye last zeir under Gods kepe ys At Claipotts ye xxj day of May '23 zowr Cuyne
                                                        M JA STRACHAUCHIN
                                                        psone of fothercarne
To ane honobl man thes com
Thomas Strachauchin of Carmily.

—I have learned nothing of the history of Mr Strachauchin or Strachan, except that on 27th February 1556, when an application was made to the sheriff of Forfarshire to appoint tutors to "Johne Thornetoune of yt Ilk," "Master James Strathauchin, persone of Fetterkerne," was nominated as one of the nearest of kin to Thornetoune on "the moder syde," along with "Johne Strathauchin of Claypottis, and Johne Nevay, younger, apparand of yat Ilk."—(Deed at Panmure.) Other ministers of Fettercairn bore the surname of Strachan, one of whom became Bishop of Brechin, and married Anna, sister to Barclay of Ury.

Fetteresso—(75.)

The first four inscriptions are from tombstones within the old kirk of Fetteresso, the first of which bears a carving of the Fullarton arms, prettily executed in raised Roman capitals :—

[1.]

Memoriæ et pietati ...... patris svi amantissimi, M. IOHANNIS FVLLARTONI, genere, meritis, fortvna, privatim pvblico' clari, monvmentvm hoc P. F. Ob. 10 die Ivlii A.D. 162-, ætatis svæ 79.

[This monument, sacred to the memory and piety of his most loving father, Mr JOHN FULLARTON, a man of distinguished birth, merits, and good fortune in his public and private life, who died on 10th July, 162-, aged 79 years, was erected by his son.]

[2.]

M. S. GEORGII LOGI, Clerici Vicecom : de Kincardine, prope sepulti, filij, mariti, parentis, heri optimi, amici vero strenui & sinceri, in negotijs periti simul & integri, multisq, demum virtutibus ornati, prematura, heu ! nimis morte abrepti, 35to nempe ætatis anno. Tabellam hanc exarandam moerens curavit amicus. Obijt 2lo Apr. 1752.

[Sacred to the memory of GEORGE LOGIE, sheriff-clerk of Kincardine, who lies buried near. He was an excellent son, husband, father, and master, a warm and true friend, an able and upright man of business ; and, finally, was adorned with many virtues. He was cut off by a death, alas ! too premature, in the 35th year of his age. A sorrowing friend caused this tablet to be erected. He died 21st April 1752.]

[3.]

In memory of Mrs ELIZABETH LOGIE, widow of Mr William Garden, late at Braco Park, parish of Pitsligo, who departed this life at Woodcot, the 20th of May 1819, aged 66 years. This stone is placed by her son and daughters in grateful remembrance of an excellent and affectionate Mother.

[4.]

Sacred to the memory of WILLIAM YOUNG, many years sheriff-clerk of Kincardineshire, who departed this life at Mill of Forest, in this parish, on the XIX day of March MDCCXC, in the LXXIII year of her age ; and of his spouse, ELIZABETH FORBES, who died at

the same place on the IX day of Aug. MDCCCIV, in the LXXXI year of her age. Also of their eldest son WILLIAM YOUNG, who departed this life at the same place, on the X day of June MDCCCXV, in the LIII year of his age, all of whose mortal remains lie buried under this stone, which was erected by Jane Keith, Hellen, and James Young, children of the before-named William Young and Elizabeth Forbes, as a memorial of their dutiful and tender affection for the best of parents and of brothers, the remembrance of whose virtues and worth will live in their hearts till they follow them to the grave—
The sweet remembrance of the just,
Shall flourish when they sleep in dust.
Here also are interred the remains of ELIZABETH FARQUHARSON, mother of the above-mentioned Elizabeth Forbes, by her husband John Forbes of Kincardine; she died at Mill of Forest MDCCXXX.

A flat stone, near the east end of the church (*outside*), bears this record of other and earlier members of the family above-mentioned :—

Memoriæ ROBERTI YOUNG in Mergie, qui fato concessit 19 die Septembris, A.D. 1714, ætatis suæ 50 . . . et MARGARETÆ FORBES, ejus sponsæ, quæ vitam deposuit 8 die Februarij, A.D. 1734, ætatis suæ 66, Johannes Young, Clericus Vicecomitatus de Kincardin, eorum filius natu maximus, hunc cippum ponendum curavit. Nati illorum sex fuere, viz. predictus Johannes, Jacobus, et DAVID, qui spiritum tradidit 5to Aprilis 1724, ætatis suæ 16; GULIELMUS, qui peradolescens naturæ cessit, et Abredoniæ sepultus fuit; ISABELLA, quæ mortua est 16 Novembris 1727, ætatis suæ 32; . . . . et MARGARETA, quæ in pueritia obijt. Reddenda est terra terræ, sic jubet necessitas.

[To the memory of ROBERT YOUNG in Mergie, who died 19th Sept. 1714, aged 50, and of MARGARET FORBES, his spouse, who departed this life 8th Feb. 1734, aged 66. John Young, sheriff-clerk of Kincardine, their eldest son, caused this stone to be erected. They had six children, viz., the aforesaid John, James, and DAVID, who died 5th April 1724, aged 16; WILLIAM, who died very young, and was buried at Aberdeen; ISABELLA, who died 16 Nov. 1727, aged 32; . . . . and MARGARET, who died in childhood. Dust must return to dust, so necessity requires.]

The next two inscriptions relate respectively to the great-grand, and grand-parents, of (*v.* p. 75) the Rev. John Longmuir, LL.D., Aberdeen :—

J. L. 1790. C. B.

In memory of JAMES LONGMUIR, who lived once in Hill of Monduff, and died 4th March 1782, aged 80 years. CHRISTIAN BEATTIE died March 3d, 1799, aged 99. CHRISTIAN LONGMUIR, their daughter, died Jany. 8th, 1801, aged 55.

To the memory of JOHN LONGMUIR, once tenant in Midtoun of Cowie, who died 28th April 1795, aged 61 years. Also ELIZABETH COLLIE, his spouse, who died 13th June 1823, aged 91 years. And of their children, ANDREW, once shipmaster in Aberdeen, who died at Leith, 7th October 1802, aged 41 years. ALEXANDER, REBECCA, and WILLIAM, died in infancy.

Come see the house, &c. [*v.* p. 173.]

It is said that the house of Fetteresso, now the property of Mr Duff (*supra*, p. 76), was built by the Keiths about the time of the Reformation, and that it continued ever after to be their chief seat. The letter given below, being dated from Fetteresso, probably goes to disprove the statement by Douglas (Peerage, ii. 194), of Earl Marischal's having been kept prisoner in the Tower of London from 1651 until the Restoration. It also shows that certain of the Earl's friends had become security for his " good behaviour" to the powers that were; and the letter, which is here printed for the first time, is addressed " For the Right Honble my Lord Panmure" :—

Fetteresso, the 25 September '57.

MY LORD,—I hau sent Arthur Straton to conclud wt Captan Hutton wher he shall waitt on your L. Morphe and My nephvo Pitsligo to Engadge for my good behavour It is my Lord I Confes a favor of sl an hye natur thatt your L. is pleased to becom my surte as I shall never be able sufficentlie to acknoeledge the sam but on thinge I promise your L. thatt I will break my necke and fortun befor I break this bonds or bring your Lo. and my frends in the Least hazard. besyd, I hau aqyaintd Arthur Straton to draw up ane band Conforme to thatt with your L. aid the rest shall Subsryue wherin I will obleidge my selfe to keip your L. and all the rest barmles. he will also aquant your L. wt his Jurny to Edr.; and I shall desyr your L. will give him your advyse and drectines for in any thinge that shall concerne me I do Confed in non mor then your L. who hes gue me Large and ample praffes of your kyndnes to me for the wche I subrye my selfe quhill I am, My Lord,

    Your L. most faithfull and humbl. Servand,
          MARISCHALL.

—William, 7th Earl Marischal, the writer of this letter, was a strong supporter of the Stuarts, in consequence of which he was excepted from Cromwell's Act of Grace and Pardon. His mother became the third wife of the first Earl of Panmure; and when her daughter, by Earl Marischal, was married to Lord Hopetoun, on 29th October 1657, "the mariage feast stood at Boshen, in Angus, the Earle of Panmore, his house" (Lamont's Diary.) The house of Boshen or Balishan, which was built by Earl Patrick's father five years after his marriage with Margaret, daughter of Erskine of Dun (Reg. de Pan.), appears to have stood near the site occupied by the present House of Panmure.

It was on 20th March of the same year as the above letter was written (which shews, by the way, that Earl Marischal had not improved his spelling while in prison), that General Monck issued an order by which the grass of Fetteresso was prohibited from being appropriated to any other purpose than the service of the army. This was done by the lieges being briefly warned that "the grasse within the parke of ffetteresso, belonging to the Lady Marshall, is ordered for the supplying of severall Troopes with grasses this sumer."

The *traditionary* account of Barclay of Ury's attack upon a servant of the Earl of Panmure is told, *supra*, p. 82. The *true* version (taken from a copy of the indictment, which I have lately seen), is as follows:—

Edward Shaw (brewer), and another of Lord Panmure's servants (R. Rannie, postilion), while riding on horseback on the high road from Kirkcaldy to Kennoway, on 11th Aug. 1701, met a man, who turned out to be Mr Barclay of Ury *(the son of the gentleman to whom the assault is locally attributed),* "travelling Southward on Foot in the Figure and Dress of a Runner or Horse-hirer, without any Upper-coat, in a Waistcoat without Sleeves, his Garters tied below his Knee, with a large Pole or Kent over his Shoulder, followed by another Man upon Horseback, carrying a Cloakebag." Supposing the pedestrian "to be of equal Rank and Station with themselves," one or other of them addressed him "in an easy, familiar Way," by saying, "Fellow Traveller, How do you do? or how far do you go? or Words to that Purpose: Whereupon, conceiving, as it would seem, that he was thereby affronted to be addressed in this familiar Stile, (he) did return the Compliment with very abusive Language, and without any further Cause of Provocation, having clubbed the Great Kent or Pole" .... aimed a Stroke at Rannie, which he escaped, by his horse jumping to aside. Having recovered his stick, Barclay aimed a stroke at Shaw with it which knocked him from his horse, by which he had "one of his Legs quite broke, and fractured a little above the Ancle."

The indictment concludes for the payment to the said Edward Shaw of the sum of £500 sterling, "in Name of Assythment and Damages." The "List of Assize for the Trial"—forty-five in number—includes the names of twenty landed gentry of the south of Scotland, and twenty-five Edinburgh merchants. One of the twelve witnesses was "James Reid, Servant to Thomas Fotheringham of Pourie, Esquire."

—o—

Fearn—(268.)

From a flat fragment near the middle of the kirk-yard:—

.... HIN ET INCOLA DE FERNE ET DAVID WATSON EIUS FILIUS QUI OBIIT 2DO NOVRIS 16..

The following inscription relates to the father of Isabella Black, who died in 1717 (misprinted 1723 on p. 268):—

Margret Bell erected this in memorie of hir husband IOHN BLACK, somtime in Windsore, who died the 5 of December anno 1709, of age 52 years.

. . . .

The following is a more perfect copy of an inscription and epitaph, given on same page:—

Hier lyeth IOHN REID, who was smith here the space of .. years. He died in the month of March 1702, his age 70 years .... HOOD, his spouse dyed on the ninth of November hir age 64 years & their children :—
Full seventy years he livd upon this earth,
He livd to dye—the end of life is death—
Here he was smith six lustres and three more,
The third three wanted; it had but two before.

. . . .

JOHN HOOD, blacksmith, on children (1714) :—
These corps interred below,
Lyes hide from eyes,
Whose souls advanced with Christ
Above the skyes.
Above all treads the Smith hath this renown—
The hammar and the royal crown.

—The hammer and crown are carved upon the stone.

JOHN DUKE and JANET PICKEMAN, Tannadice, on twin children, &c. (1687—1713) :—
I hope in heaven thire blessed souls do sing—
O grave where is thy victory,
O death where is thy sting?
While we have time to cry for grace we ought,
Seeing all flesh unto the dust are brought;
The life of man is like ane dial shade,
Or like the grass that suddenly doth fade.

An adjoining tomb-stone, erected by Isabel Thom, shows that her husband, DAVID LEIGHTON, tenant of Shanford, died in 1794, aged 92. Some of his relations are said to be interred in " Neither kirk-yard of Sinciras."

Some notice is taken in p. 269 of John Macintosh, who took an active part at the "battle of Sauchs." He was farmer of Leadenheudrie (misprinted "Leadeudrie"), which belonged to the Earl of Southesk; and tradition says that he received many favours from the Earl for his services at "the battle." But it would appear that Macintosh's gratitude to his Lordship lasted only so long as he was able to benefit him, as is proved by the following extract from a letter, dated 18th Sept., 1725, addressed by Mr Ochterlony, factor, Brechin Castle, to Mr David Maule, W.S., Edinburgh :—

... "The tack goven by Provost Gordon being expired, the possession called the Waterhead, is sett to on George M'Kenzie, a son of Dalmor's, who wretts att Edinburgh. This was done by Mr Cameron, upon the sollicitation of on McIntosh, a very undutifull Tennant of my Ld. Southesks, and an awowed enemy to all the suffering Gentlemen in this countrey."

Sculptured records of the parents of James and Dr H. W. Tytler were lately found near the manse. These consist of two slabs, which had possibly been built into the old manse. They bear respectively these initials and dates:—

"17   M. G. T : I. R.   47"
"M. G. T : 17—: I. R."

—Mr Geo. Tytler died in 1785, aged 79, and his wife, Janet Robertson, died in 17—, aged —.

The only monument to a clergyman at Fearn is that which relates to the late Rev. DAVID HARRIS, who died in 1867, in the 93d year of his age and the 65th of his ministry. Mr Harris died "Father of the Church of Scotland." His wife, GRACE DOW, who predeceased him in 1845, aged 62, had a taste for Scotch Ballad poetry and music, of which she left a large collection.

Their eldest son, GEORGE, who was appointed assistant and successor to his father, became sad and disheartened, and died in 1860, aged 42 years. Having studied medicine, he was of great service to the poor of his own parish and neighbourhood, with all of whom he was a favourite. He was naturally of a warm-hearted, loveable disposition, a good scholar, and geologist. He also possessed a great fund of humour and anecdote, and had a keen sense of the ludicrous. On being called upon to attend the funeral of an old man, soon after he became assistant to the late Mr Wilson at Gamrie, and being anxious to notice the leading characteristics of the deceased in his prayer, he asked information from some of the assembled company, but without success. At last—just after he had resumed his position, and was about to begin prayer—a man stepped across the barn, in which the party were met, and tapping Mr Harris upon the shoulder, whispered into his ear—" I can tell you, sir, what Sann'ers (Alexander) cou'd doe (do)—he cou'd dance upon a peat wi' ae fit! (one foot.)

Local rhymes, consisting of an enumeration of names of places, are common not only in Scotland, but in many other countries. Although they have often little meaning, they sometimes indicate that all the places named are to be seen from any one of them. This is not far from being the case with regard to the following, which refer to places in the parishes of Fearn, Tannadice, &c. :—

"Deuchar sits on Deuchar hill,
Lookin' down on Birnie Mill ;
The Whirrock, an' the Whoggle ;
The Burnroot, au' Ogle ;
Quieehstrath, an' Turnafachie ;
Waterhaughs, an' Drumlicharrie."

The following are a few more examples of the enumeration of names of places near one another, and in the same district:—

"There's Blackha', Buckit hill ;
Lochtie an' the Lint mill ;
Cowford, the Waulk mill ;
The Millton an' Balmadity ;
The Bogie an' Ba'quharn ;
The Farmerton o' Fearn."

—o—

Fordoun—(62.)

When St Palladius' chapel was being repaired in 1872, the workmen came upon a coffin-slab which had been long used as the inner lintel of the north door of the chapel. It is about 4 feet 10 inches in length, by about 20 inches in breadth, and presents some incised carvings.

In the centre is a sort of shaft with a bulging base of about 9 inches in breadth, and a circular top of about a foot in diameter, with a six-leaved ornament, resembling an old-fashioned shield or targe. A sword, with antique pommel and guard, is upon the left side of the shaft, and upon the right are the more interesting and rare figures of a bow and arrow.

As the style of this slab corresponds with those that were common in Scotland during the 14th and 15th centuries, it had probably covered the grave of a Wishart or a Strachan ; for these two families were then the most important land-holders in the eastern parts of Fordoun (Proceedings of So. Antiq. of Scot., vol. x).

An old tomb of the Irvines of Monboddo—a property which came to them through the Strachans—occupies the north-west corner of the chapel. It bears a Latin inscription (*supra*, p. 63), of which the following is probably a better translation than that previously given :—

[In the hope of a blessed resurrection here as in a perfumed chamber sweetly sleepeth in the Lord, Capt. ROBERT IRVIN, Laird of Monboddo, who piously departed this life, 6th July 1652, in his 80th year.

In this tomb lies IRVIN, a man happy in his wife and family, a lover of virtue and honour, and the scion of an ancient house. The rest is known to the Muse and the Seine, famed for its vine-nourishing waters.]

Three marble tablets have been recently erected near the Irvine tomb, and are respectively inscribed as follows :—

[1.]

The Burying place of the Family of Monboddo. JAMES BURNETT of Lawgaven married the daughter and heiress of Col: IRVINE of Monq. and thus came into the property. They are buried here. He was succeeded by his son, JAMES BURNETT, who married a daughter of Sir T. Burnett of Leys, and died   , and they are buried here. He was succeeded by his son, JAMES BURNETT, who married a daughter of Sir Wm. Forbes of Craigievar, and died   , and they are buried here. He was succeeded by his son, JAMES BURNETT, afterwards Lord Monboddo, who married Miss FARQUHARSON, a relation of the Keith Marishall family, and died in 1799, and both are buried in Edinburgh. He was succeeded by his daughter, HELEN, who married KIRKPATRICK WILLIAMSON, Esq., and died in

1833, and is buried here. She was succeeded by her son, JAMES B. BURNETT, who died in 1864, and is buried here, as are his two younger sisters, GRACE and MARGARET, and his younger son ARTHUR.

[2.]

In memory of Mrs H. W. BURNETT of Monboddo, who died 17th Feb. 1833.

—This has special reference to the heiress of Monboddo, mentioned in inscription [1.] She had three sons and four daughters by Mr Williamson. The eldest son succeeded to Monboddo, and the two younger were John, a surgeon, who died in India, and Arthur, who was sometime sheriff-substitute of Peeblesshire. Mrs Burnett appears to have inherited from her father a love for the study of the classical languages, for down to the time of her death, she continued to use a Greek New Testament in church.

Her younger sister, ELIZA—"whose amiable disposition and surpassing beauty" were the admiration of all who knew her—has been celebrated by Burns both in his Address to Edinburgh and in an Elegy upon her death. She died of consumption, 17th June 1790. Her portrait, painted by Raeburn, is at Monboddo.

The following relates to a great-grand-son of Lord Monboddo's, who was sometime in India :—

[3.]

✠ Sacred to the memory of ARTHUR-COFFIN BURNETT, Born 1840, died 1871. [John iii. 16.]

The next inscription is from one of three tombstones, erected to families named respectively Gordon and Kerr, at the east end of St Palladius' Chapel :—

Sacred to the memory of GEORGE GORDON, merchant in Auchenblae, who died on the 12th day of October 1830, aged 75 years ; and of ISOBEL KERR, his spouse, who died on the 9th day of November 1830, aged 70 years. Erected by their grateful and affectionate family, of whom ALEXANDER, born 2d July 1781, died 27th November 1858 ; MARGARET, born 29th August 1792, died 11th Feby. 1860 ; ELIZABETH, born 13th Dec. 1785, died 15th June 1866.

—George Gordon, originally a stone mason, was sometime postmaster, and the last baron bailie of Auchinblae. His son, William, who became a partner in the firm of Aberdein & Gordon, mill-spinners, Montrose, was the father of Mr Alex. Gordon of Ashludie (*supra*, p. 112.)

On north side of aisle :—

1814 : In memory of ALEXANDER MILNE, A.M., who having been 46 years schoolmaster of Fordon, died 16th December 1812, aged 72 years. Also of ELIZABETH MILNE, his spouse, who died 7th Jany. 1825, aged 75 years. And of their children, CATHERINE, died aged 21 years ; JOHN died aged 3 years.

Within an enclosure on north side of church :—

GEORGE MACKENZIE, Capt. 55th Regt. of Foot, died Sept. 24th 1791, aged 21. JAMES MACKENZIE of Drumtochty, died May 22nd 1799, aged 24. ANN MACPHERSON, relict of John Mackenzie of Strickathrow, died Nov. 12, 1810, aged 75.

—The above-named John Mackenzie, who died in Dec. 1775, made money as a surgeon in India, and bought Stracathro from his brother Colin, "of the Island of Jamaica," sometime before 1767. Mrs Mackenzie sold Drumtochty to the late Mr G. H. Drummond, banker in London, by whom the present fine mansion-house was erected. The property was again sold to the late Mr Jas. Gammell, banker in Greenock, ancestor of the present laird (*supra*, p. 64.).

Drumtochty belonged in old times to a branch of the Raits, afterwards of Halgreen, for about the year 1440, John Rait of Futhes (Fiddes) had a charter of the lands of Drumtokie, in Kincardineshire, and of the half lands of Campsie, in Angus, on his own resignation. Soon after that date, the said John Rait gave a charter of the west half of Drumtochty to his son Henry, and another of the east half to Thomas of Gillmouk. It also appears that Alexander Calder, son to Hew and Janet Ogilvie, his spouse, had a charter of Drumtochty, on the resignation of his father and of Elizabeth Rait, his spouse (*MS. Notes of Scotch Charters at Panmure*.)

Three spring wells, called respectively the Nine Maidens', Bright's (? S. Bridget), and Marot's (? S. Margaret), are upon the lands of Friars Glen or Glensaugh, the barony and superiority of which were given by Lord Oliphant, 26th Oct., 1473, to Mr Thomas Guthrie (*Ibid.*)

Auchinblae, which is the chief village in the parish of Fordoun, appears to have been in existence early in the sixteenth century, for in 1506, George, Abbot of Arbroath, as superior of the district, gave a lease to John Strachan and his spouse, Mariote Martin, of "moderne ... villam nostram de Auchiublay" for the annual payment of £3 6s 8d Scots, with a "rynmart weddyr," &c. In 1510 the same parties had a renewal of their lease of Auchinblae, to which was added "le Awrne Aylhows," within the barony of Newlands. It also appears that in 1525, John Strachan and his spouse, Egidia Gardin, and her son James Gardin, had a lease of the same and some other adjoining lands from Abbot David, afterwards the celebrated Cardinal Beaton (Reg. Nig. Aberb.) These, as before said, were the same Strachans who held Monboddo, the heiress of which carried the lands to the Irvines.

But the village of Auchinblae, as well as the lands of Glenfarquhar, now belong to Lord Kintore, who succeeded to them as heir to the Lords Falconer of Halkerton and Glenfarquhar. Their first property in Fordoun was that of Phesdo, which was acquired towards the close of the 16th century, by the second son of Sir David Falconer of Halkerton (Laird of the Lindsays.) Sir David was uncle to Patrick Falconer of Newton, whose initials and those of his wife—P. F: G. B.—are upon a stone at Newton, dated 1629. His wife had probably been a Barclay.

Sir David Falconer of Newton, second son of Sir David of Glenfarquhar, died Lord President of the Court of Session, and was buried in the Greyfriars' Church-yard of Edinburgh. His tomb bore the following inscription, which, along with the translation, is copied from Monteith's Theater of Mortality (1704, p. 44.) :—

"M. P. Q. S. Tenet hoc sepulchrum cineres, D. DAVIDIS FALCONARI, a Newtoun, e familia Halcartoniana oriundi ; supremi senatus præsidis integerrimi ; Carolo 2do & Jacobo 7mo., consiliarii fidelissimi ; in summum illud fastigium, summa in Reges fidelitate, & insigni in negotiis vigilantia,

universo patriæ voto, bono publico admoti : qui, dum nimia hac vigilantia, patriæ plus quam sibi viveret, obiit, 15 Decembris, 1685, ætatis 46.

"This sepulchre contains the ashes (or remains) of Sir DAVID FALCONAR of Newtoun, descended of the family of Halkertoun, most upright President of the Session, and most faithful counsellor to King Charles the 2d, and King James the 7th. Advanced to that high pinacle of honour by the unanimous desire of the countrey, and for the publick utility ; by reason of his greatest loyalty to his prince, and for his great and notable vigilance and dispatch of busiuess ; by which nimious vigilance, while he lived more to his countrey than to himself. He died as above."

It was about 1620 that Sir David Falconer acquired Glenfarquhar. He was the brother of Sir Alexander, who was created Lord Halkerton in 1647. His Lordship was deprived of his office as a Lord of Session after the murder of Charles I., but was reinstated on the Restoration of Charles II. He died in 1671 ; and the following Sonnet, addressed to him by Drummond of Hawthornden (Archæologia Scotica, iv., 102), shows that the poet feared that his own loyalty to the Stuarts might also bring him into trouble, a misfortune which was possibly averted by his death, which took place during the following year :—

"I FEARE to me such fortune be assign'd
As was to thee, who did so well deserve,
Brave HALKERTONE ! even suffred here to sterue
Amidst base-minded freinds, nor true, nor kind.
Why were the Fates and Furies thus combined
Such worths for such disasters to rescrue ?
Yet all those euills neuer made thee swerue
From what became a well resolued mind ;
For swelling greatnesse neuer made thee smyle,
Despising greatnesse in extreames of waut ;
O happy thrice whom no distresse could dant !
Yet thou exclaimed, O Time ! O Age ! O Isle !
Where flatterers, fooles, baudes, fidlers, are rewarded,
Whilst Vertue sterues vupitied, vnregarded !"

Two inscribed stones are built into the farm steading at Mains of Glenfarquhar. One bears 1671, and the other is initialed and dated thus :—

S. A. F.   1674   D. H. G.

—Both stones refer to the time of Sir Alex. Falconer, who was created a Baronet in 1670-1, and whose son became the fourth Lord Falconer of Halkerton. Lady Falconer had probably been a Graham.

It is interesting to notice that the oldest spellings of the names of Fordoun and Dunnottar are exactly the same (except that the syllables are reversed), the former being *Fother-dun*, and the latter *Dun-fother*. Both may have had a common origin (*supra*, p. 52.)

―――o―――

Gartly—(43.)

When a new stock was lately given to the kirk-bell of Gartly, the schoolmaster kindly copied the inscription, which the height of the bell from the ground prevented being given in our first notice of the parish. As was then anticipated, the inscription runs thus :—

IOHN . MOWAT . ABD : ME . FE : 1738.
IN . USUM . ECCLESIE . DE . GERTLY.
SABATA . PANGO . FUNERA . PLANGO.

It was also found that the inscription upon one of the stones of the belfry (which was conjectured to bear the name of the Rev. Mr Rethe or Reid), bore :—" YIS . IS . BETHEL."

―――o―――

Inveravon—(145.)

The old place of worship at the Haugh of Kilmaichlie (p. 146), was dedicated to S. MACHALUS (Bp. Forbes' Kal. of Scottish Saints.)

The first par. of same page (col. 2) should read :—
There was a Roman Catholic Seminary at Scalan, in Glenlivet, for a number of years; but it was removed in 1799 to Aquhorties (*supra*, p. 189). About thirty years afterwards it was taken to Blairs, in Mary Culter.

In the inscription from the *table*-shaped monument (not " headstone ") to " Captain ALLAN GRANT," the surname ought to be spelled *Grantt* throughout.

The following (*supra*, p. 150), is from another table-shaped tombstone at Inveravon :—

In memory of MARGARET STEWART, who died 25th March 1841, aged 88 years. She was many years a faithful servant in the family of the Rev. George Forbes, minister of Lochell, by whose son, Sir Charles Forbes, Bart., this stone is placed over her remains, in testimony of his grateful recollection of MAGGIE STEWART's kindness to him when a boy. 1842.

―――o―――

Inverurie—(180.)

S. POL'NAR'S CHAPEL is believed to have been a subsidiary place of worship to the church of Inverurie. It occupied one of those rath or fort-looking knolls which are so common in the locality, and stood about three miles to the north-east of the town of Inverurie, upon the north bank of the Don. The place was sometimes called *Rathael* or *Rathuilt*. The former name probably signifies " the rath or fort of the cliff," the latter " the rath of the barn."

The burial-ground is enclosed by a stone wall, and planted with trees and bushes. The kirk was situated near the middle of the enclosure; but only the ivy-clad ruins now remain. The chapel appears to have been about 36 feet in length, by about 18 feet in width. The only inscribed stones now visible are four slabs in the east end of the church, upon which are these initials and dates :—

W F
I G   A. F. 1662   E. F. 1662   P. F. 1666.
59

In the View of the Diocese of Aberdeen, it is stated that the lands of Badifurrow were " lately possessed by the Fergusons (now of Pitfour), and at present [c. 1732] by Forbes of Badifurrow." The above initials and dates probably belong to the Fergusons; for in 1696, the Poll Book shews that Lucress Burnett, relict of the deceased William Ferguson of Badifurrow, was then tenant, and that her children Patrick, Walter, and Mary, were living with her. The heritor of Badifurrow is stated to be "out of the kingdom."

As a part of the possessions of the Abbey of Lindores, the lands and fishings of Badifurrow were given to Patrick Leslie by James VI., c. 1600, when he was created Lord Lindores (Antiq. Abdn. and Bff.) Dr William Leslie, Bishop of Raphoe, is said to have been of the Leslies of Badifurrow. He is described as very learned and courageous, and as "the oldest Bishop in the worlde in his time."

The property of Badifurrow, now Manar, belongs to Mr Gordon, whose grand-father was originally a watchmaker. After having been some time in the E.I.C.'s Service, he joined a brother at Madras, who carried on the business of a jeweller. On returning home he bought Badifurrow, and gave it the name of Manar, after the Gulf of Manaar, near which, it is said, he acquired much of his wealth.

The chapel of S. Pol'nar is still used as a burial place, and therein lie the remains of Mr Gordon, who bought Badifurrow, and those of his son and successor, &c. The last-named, who married a daughter of Henry Lumsden of Auchindoir, died 17th June 1874, aged 61, and was succeeded by his son Henry.

The great-grand-father of the present laird of Manar, came from Cabrach, and was tenant of Old Merdrum, in Rhynie. One of his brothers, who was farmer of Drumferg, was grand-father of General John Gordon, who died at Culdrain in 1861 (*supra*, p. 258.)

The Pol'nar Burn runs past the east end of the burial ground, and falls into the Don, near the Chapel Pool, which is a favourite resort for anglers.

———o———

Keith—(165.)

The monument to the Gordons and Stuarts of Birkenburn, from which the inscription at p. 165 was copied, has been replaced by a granite monument, with this inscription:—

In memory of the GORDONS and STUARTS of Birkenburn. Also of ALEXANDER KYNOCH, merchant in Keith, who died 15 Oct. 1867, aged 52.

—Mr Kynoch married Magdalen Stephen, daughter of a West India planter. She was granddaughter of the first, and niece of the last Stuart of Birkenburn. Mr Kynoch's father came to Keith from Aberdeen, and to his original trade of a coppersmith joined that of a provision merchant. A grand-son of the last-mentioned, through a relative named Shand, succeeded to the property of Hillside of Portlethen, &c., and takes the name of Kynoch-Shand. Upon a plain headstone :—

To the memory of the Rev. JAMES BUNYAN, minister of the first United Ass. Cong. in Keith, who died 1st June 1828, in the 71st year of his age, and 41st of his ministry. He was an able and faithful preacher of the Gospel; and having, through life, been zealous in his duty, bearing afflictions with patience, he resigned his spirit into the hand of his Redeemer with confidence. Erected as a memorial of affection by his widow Anna Clark.

The burial ground of Keith has been recently enlarged, and laid out with much taste.

[*Errata.*—In the inscription from the tombstone of James Thurburn (p. 167), the year "1798" is a misprint for 1793 (see also pp. 103-2).
In the next page the surname of "Jamieson" is misprinted for JAMIESON ; and (col. 2, line 12,) *Keith* should be substituted for "Fife-Keith."]

———o———

Kirkmichael—(69.)

[1.]

Here lies JAMES GRANT of Ruthven, Bailiff of Strathaven and Glenlivet, who, in the 73d year of his age, departed this life, Dec. 9, an. 1743.
This was a man remarkable
at home, abroad, still hospitable;
a good companion, trusty friend,
and still obliging to mankind.
Pallida mors, &c. *(supra*, p. 91.)

[2.]

Here lys the body of ISOBEL M'LACHLAN, spovs to James Grant, who departed this life . . . . . . year of his age, Oct. 20, 1722.

Laurencekirk—(292.)

The following inscription (from a head-stone on the south side of the kirk), is carved in beautifully interlaced Roman capitals :—

☞ Here . . . . James, David, Margrat, Mare Stvart, lavfvl children . . David Stvart and Jean Wallace his spovs, vho departed this lyf in the yearis of God, 1671, 72, 7-, and 77.

No sooner cam they from the voumbs dark cave
Bvt back again they most . . to the grave
For non of them bvt on did years atine
In vhom God's spirit vorking might be seen
Vherby he did apear to take delyght
In them that he an . . . . . . ke to perfyt
Vhich Christ himself provideth in his book
Concerning babs in the 18 of Lvk.

. . . .

A flat slab, near the stone from which the above is copied, bears :—

. . . . s . David . W . y .
. . . . Mains of Lavr . . .
. . . . life November
the . . day . . . .
D . W : M . N

—These few words are all that now remains of an inscription which referred to David Wysse or Wise, son of Alex. Wyse, Mains of Thornton. He was twice married, first to (" M. N.") Margaret, daughter of Alex. Nairn, (?) Pitreddie (Marriage Contract dated at Montrose, 9th Nov. 1681), and next to Margaret Burnett. In his last will and testament (a copy of which is engrossed in the kirk-session books of Laurencekirk), David Wysse is described as " sometime in Mains of Lawristown, now residenter in Montrose;" and by this deed he left his second wife, in full of all demands upon his estate, an annuity of 200 merks, his whole household furniture, and his cow.

Mr Wysse had a son and two daughters alive at the time he made his will, for he therein leaves "Alexander Wysse of Lunan, my son, and Margaret Strachan his spouse, the sum of 6000 merks Scots money to be life-rented by them or either of them, during their lifetimes, and to the said Alexander Wysse hail children equally amongst them in fee, excepting David Wysse, his eldest son, who is to have no share thereof with the oyr children." He also left the liferent of 1000 merks to each of his two daughters, Elizabeth and Margaret, and their husbands. The former was married to Arthur Shepherd, sheriff-depute of Kincardineshire, and the latter to James Allardice, in Powburn. The last-named, and Alex. Jamieson, writer, Montrose, were sole executors under the said will, which was dated at Montrose, 20th March, 1732, and witnessed by Mr Hendry Ogilvy, minister of Lunan, Peter Japp, wheelwright, William Rob, smith, and Alex. Beattie, "servitor" to Alex. Jamieson, all in Montrose.

In addition to the above-mentioned legacies, David Wysse left 250 merks to each of the Kirk-sessions of Lunan, Montrose, Ecclesgreig, and Laurencekirk, payable within six months after his death. He died before 7th July, 1732, and appears to have been survived by his second wife, Margaret Burnett.

The above-named Alexander Wysse, who married Margaret Strachan, bought the estate of Lunan, 30th October, 1723, from John Ogilvy of Balbegno. It was about thirty-six years in the family of Wyse, David, the son of Alexander Wyse, having sold the same to William Imrie, in 1759, and retiring to Dundee, he died there in ——. His eldest son, Thomas, of Clermont, in Jamaica, returned home, and bought the property of Hillbank, in Dundee, where he died in 1816. He married a daughter of Wm. Chalmers of Glencricht, town-clerk of Dundee, by whom he had four sons and two daughters. Their eldest surviving son, Dr Thomas-Alexander Wise, representative of the Wysses or Wises, of Lunan, claims through his great-grandmother, the above-named Margaret Strachan, to be the representative and heir-of-line of the old family of Strachan of Thornton, in the Mearns, who were created baronets in 1625.

The English portion of the next inscription is carved in raised Roman capitals, and the Latin, previously given from an older tomb-stone at Dun (*supra*, p. 223), is incised :—

☞ Here lyes vnder the hope of a gloriovs resvrrection, ALEXANDER COVIE, hvsband to Margaret Beatie, sometime in Mil of Halcartovn vho departed this life the 3 of March 1709, and of his age 79 years.

Disce mori, qvievnq, legis mea scripta, viator :
Omnes æqva manent fvnera : Disce mori :
Disce mori : Frater discat cvm præsvle, clervs
Cvm ivniore senex, cvm sapiente rvdis.
A. C : M. B : I. C : A. C.

From a slab fixed to the east wall of the kirk :—

☞ Here lyes in hope of a glorious resurrection, ROBERT MORTIMER, messenger, husband to Susanna Smith, who departed this life the 6th day of December 1734, aged 46 years. Two of his children are also buried here, viz. JAMES & WILLIAM.

Sic transit gloria mundi.
R. M : S. S : J. M : W. M : R. W.

The following additional notes regarding the lands of the Castle, or Castleriggs of Kinghorn, in Fife, now the property of Mr Shank (*supra*, p. 292), cannot fail to be interesting.* It is stated by Douglas (Peerage, ii. 562-3), that the lands of the Castle of Kinghorn and others were given to Alexander, second Lord Glamis, and his wife Agnes, in 1463. This statement is corroborated by the following extract, copied from an old MS. vol. of Notes of Scotch Charters at Panmure :—

"Ch, of con. of a Charter granted be the kings mother Marie, to Alexr. Lord Glamues & Agnes his spouse, of the Lands of the Castell of Kingorne with mylne, & myluclands of Kingorne, be his oun resig., with the lands of Balbardy in fyffe, also resigned be him. warde of rege. Edur. 19 October 1463, and confirmed Edur. 18 October 1463."

* The paragraph (pp. 291-2) immediately succeeding the inscription from the tombstone of the Rev. Mr Shank, at Laurencekirk, ought to read thus :—
—Mr Shank, who was a grandson of the minister of Drumoak, Aberdeenshire, was presented to the church of St Cyrus in 1759 (Scott's Fasti). It was about 1781, when he succeeded to the fortune of his namesake, Alexander Shank of Castlerig, in Fife (only son of the Rev. Martin Shank, of Banchory-Ternan), that he resigned the charge of St Cyrus. By his wife, &c.

Although the above grant does not appear to have included the Castle of Kinghorn—for it was held "cum monte" by Kirkcaldy of Grange in 1564—it is evident that it comprehended that piece of property which has been long known as "the Castle rigges" of Kinghorne. In proof of this it need only be stated that these lands, which consist of about 13 acres imperial, and yield an annual rental of £45 sterling, were long held by the Glamis family. As shewn by the rental of the Earl of Kinghorn's " ffewdewties and Teynddewties" for 1660, the "castle rigges" were then occupied by three different tenants, and at the following rents :—

Cristiane Reidie payes valued teynd bolls for 8 aiker of the Castlerigges............ 4 b
Johne Smetowne payes for 4 aiker of the Castlerigges valued teynd bolls............ 2 b
Alisone Wallace payes for 4 aiker of the Castlerigges valued teynd bolls............ 2 b

There are thirty separate entries in the paper from which the above is copied. The only other surnames in it are those of Orrock, Blak, Syme, and Gordon.

The name of *Castleriggs* does not appear in the MS. from which the next excerpts are made. It is a dateless Valuation Roll of Fifeshire, but apparently the same as that to which the date of 1695 is given in Sibbald's "History of Fife." It is here printed because it contains the name of Hendrie Shauks, a reputed ancestor of the present laird of Castleriggs :—

"The trew Rentall of such heretors Estate in the Shire of ffife as the samen was taken up by the Commissioners of Valuation, w* the valued rent on the margin :"—

£24. William Birrell } both held "aikers" under the
       William Smyten } Earl of Strathmore, to whom, over their rents, each paid "twa bolls of bear."
£48. *Hendrie Shauks*. The rent of his aikers is ane chalder of bear, and over that rent to the Earle of Strathmore, four bolls of bear.
£12. James Douny. The rent of his aikers is fourteen bolls of bear, and over that to the Earle of Leven of few, twelve bolls twa firlots of bear.

The extract given below is from the Session Registers of Kinghorn. It relates to the baptism of the future minister of Banchory-Ternan (*supra*, p. 4), who (Scott's Fasti) was previously incumbent of Auchtertool, in Fife, Although I have seen no proof of the fact, I am inclined to believe that Margaret Dauney, who was the wife of the Rev. Mr Shanks of Banchory, had been in some way related to "James Douny," mentioned in the above Rentall—probably a daughter:—

Julii 1670. henrie shanks Bailye & Agnes balfour, their childe born the 28 of Junie, named Martine, was baptized the 10 of Julie : W. Johne bruce, baylie, patrick Wallace, Williame Smeaton, Mr William Bett.

It may be added that the surname of Shanks appears twice in the baptismal register of Kinghorn during the 16th century—in 1577 and 1578 respectively. In each instance "Martine Shankis" is a witness to a baptism. This was probably the father of "Hen. Schankis," who was made an elder of Kinghorn in 1608, and who, in 1624, was allowed "to set up ane foir-face to the boukar of his dask to saue his wyfe and wynis fra being tred upo' be these y^t gois in to the yll." In Mr Hepburn's interesting little book of extracts from the Kirk-session Registers of Kinghorn, it is also stated that "the house of Henry Shanks, the kirk-treasurer of those days, may still be seen above the railway viaduct."

This old house presents two nicely carved, but slightly defaced, coats of arms, in pale, with crest, over the principal door. Upon the left of the shield are much the same coat and crest as now borne by Shank of The Villa, and the Balfour coat has a crescent in base, which probably shews descent from a second son. The initials and date of "16 : H. S : B. B : 38," are upon the door lintel below the arms, but the arms and initials appear to be in a later style of carving than the date, and correspond more with the time of Henry Shanks and Agnes Balfour.

Although I have seen no grave-stone at Kinghorn bearing the name of Shank, there is one at Ceres to the "memory of JOHN SHANKS, fewer of Thirdpart, Town House Customs, and Miln of Ceres," who died in 1755, aged 70. If not a brother, John Shanks may have been otherwise related to the minister of Banchory.

It may be added, in connection with the town of Kinghorn and the name of Shanks, that possibly the oldest and finest carved grave-stone there bears an inscription to Robert Glen of Euchky, town-treasurer of Edinburgh. During his period of office (1564-5), and when the "Heding Aix" or *Maiden* was being made, he paid certain sums of money to Patrick and Adam Shang (? Shank), carpenters in Edinburgh, who appear to have been the principal makers of that celebrated instrument of punishment (Proceedings of So. of Antiq., vii. 548.)

Reference has been made on p. 293, to the interesting collection of portraits of original feuars of Laurencekirk, and others, which is preserved in the Gardenstone Arms Hotel of that place. Believing that a list of these may be appreciated, I subjoin the names of the persons represented, copied from the backs of the drawings, with additional notes within brackets, viz. :—

David Beattie, factor.
[Father of James Beattie, Prof. of Nat. History, Mar. Coll., Aberdeen, and uncle of the author of "The Minstrel."]
John Scott, parochial schoolmaster.
[Long Baron Bailie of Laurencekirk. One of his daughters became the wife of Mr P. Mason, corn merchant, Montrose.]
Bailie Garden.
[Mr Garden, who was an Aberdeen advocate, and Baron Bailie of Peterhead, became factor for Lord Arbuthnott. He married a daughter of the Rev. Mr Moir of Ellon, and having removed from Mains of Fordoun, he died at Birness, in Logie-Buchan. He was connected in some way with the Gardenstone family, and a portrait of Lord Gardenstone, which belonged to him, was given to the town of Laurencekirk by his youngest daughter. Mr Garden was maternal grandfather of Mr John Garland, Cairnton.]
Mr Badenoch, Johnstone.
[Paternal uncle of Mr J. Badenoch-Nicolson of Arthurhouse and Glenbervie.]
Alex. Smart, Powburn.
[Grandfather of the late Mr Alex. Smart, writer, Stonehaven.]
Mr Dewar, Aberdeen.
John Rae, manufacturer.
[Grandfather of Mr Rae, farmer, Haddo.
John Dallas.
Mrs Cruickshank, aged 78 [innkeeper].
Wm. Cream, innkeeper.
[Father-in-law of Dr Fettes, Baron Bailie of Laurencekirk].
John Silver, baker.
Peter Ramsay, mason.
James Laurence, blacksmith.
[Formerly at Charter Stanes, afterwards at

Laurencekirk. It was after him that Charter's Square, in the village, was named. Among the many old stories that are told of "Charters," it is said that the Rev. Dr Cook and he having quarrelled on some occasion, and the Doctor having asked him, in a lofty tone—"Do you know who I am, sir?" "Charters" rejoined—"Brawly that!—you are my servant ae day i' the week, an' the ither sax if I want you!"]
William Rue, tailor.
John Charles, tailor.
John Rae, gamekeeper.
James Hay, forester.
James Murray, forester.
Robert Trail, hedger.
Lord Colville, Ochiltree.
[Said to have been a local character.]
Mr Brich, artist, 1790.

—o—

Lintrathen—(280.)

[1.]

Here lyes JANET CANDOW, spous of John Deuchers, Hamerman in Burnside of Kinclune, Departed this life September 26, 1721; and of her Children JOHN and ROBERT, who died in their infance.

Under this ston intombled lyes,
    Ane woman of honest fame;
And of hir uirtues while she liud,
    Hir name doth still remain.
And to hir husband and parents dear,
    Ane help and comfort uas;
But nou the Lord hath crouned hir,
    With joy and heauenly bliss.

[2.]

Heir lyes DAVID STIL spovs to Ianet Wright. He lived in Fornitie and departed this lif the 5 day of December 1705, his age was 58 yeares.

Operations for the supply of water to Dundee (*supra*, p. 281), having been commenced at Lintrathen, the fragment of a sculptured cross was found at a short distance from the church. This interesting relic, which is either part of an arm or the top of a freestone cross, is ornamented with the interlaced work so common to this class of objects. It had probably stood upon the toft referred to in the curious charter of 27th June 1447, by which the bell of S. Meddan of Lintrathen was resigned to Sir John Ogilvy (*supra*, p. 280.) There is little doubt that it is a portion of the Cross of ST MEDDAN, before which devotees and pilgrims had often knelt, and round which fairs or markets had also been held.

—o—

Logie-Dundee—(196.)

When the burial-ground of Logie-Dundee was levelled, and otherwise put into a good state of repair, soon after it was closed against interments by order of the Privy Council, two or three additional tombstones were found. One, initialed and dated D. K : E. C. 1722, presents a bold carving of a blacksmith's crown and hammer. Four other stones bear the following curious inscriptions:—

[1.]

Here lys Georg Roger and Mary Roger thy both did on the 14 day of December 1723 the lad was 8 years the las 4 years . . . . . and Margrat Roger died the 7 of Ivn 1725.

[2.]

. . . . In 1744 James Allan uas infeft in the burial ston at the death of Alixander roger in 1744 & is also interrd under same stone Lelyabeth roger & her children & barbara henderson & her children & Jannet Farguson.

[3.]

1791   JOHN   X   ROBERT
died X decr X th20 X
Agd X 53 X yer

[4.]

Erected by John Watson and his Spous Beatty Whitson Pleasantes in meamery of there Daughter ELISBATH, who died Febr 19th 1808, aged three years.

[*Errata.*—p. 197 (col. 1, line 5) *for* posture *read* position ; (l. 17) *read* genuine worth, integrity, &c.]

—o—

Longside—(100.)

The following inscription is from the oldest of several tombstones which relate to a family named Scott. One female descendant became the wife of the late Mr Russell of Kininmonth, brother to the laird of Aden, and another married the Rev. Dr Christie, late of Kildrummy, Aberdeenshire, now of Kilrenny, in Fife:—

A. S : M. A : W. S : I. S : M. G.

Here lye, in hopes of a blessed resurrection, ALEXR. SCOTT, some time in Nether Aden, who departed this life on the 8 day of Feb. 1699; & MARGARET ARBUTHNOT, his wife, who died the 13th Septr. 1756, aged 94. Also IEAN STRACHAN, lawful spouse to William Scott in Nether Adan, who departed this life on the 28th day of March 1716; and MARY GORDON, his second wife, who died the XII of May MDCCLXIV, in the 67 year of her age. There are likewise interred here the remains of the said WILLIAM SCOTT. He was born at Dumstone, the XIX of June MDCLXXXIII, and died at Peterhead, the XXV of June MDCCLXV.

From a flat slab (s. p. 96):—

Here lyss IAMES DUNCAN, who departed this life, the 3 of May 1703, lawfull son to Alexr Duncan in Enervedie.

From a table-shaped stone near west door of church:—

In memoriam GULIELMI BROWN, A.M., scholae Longsidensis praefecti per annos quater fere septenos evigilantissimi, qui Nonis Martii, Æ. C. 1761, aetatis vero quinquagesimo octavo labente anno, diem obiit supremum, Maria Vallas, ejus vidua moerens moestaque, hunc posuit lapidem. Hic quoque conduntur reliquiae ejusdem MARIE WALLACE, quae quarto Cal. Feb., Æ. C. 1796, aetatis vero sexagesimo sexto, diem obiit.

[To the memory of WILLIAM BROWN, A.M., for about 28 years a most energetic master of the school of Longside, who died 7th March 1761, in the 58th year of his age, Mary Wallace, his sorrowing widow, erected this stone. Here also are laid the remains of the said MARY WALLACE, who died 29th Jan. 1796, in the 66th year of her age.]

From a table stone:—

To the memory of JOHN NICHOLSON, in Nether Innervedie, a loving husband, a kind father, and industrious farmer; an agreeable neighbour, and a sincere Christian, who died in 1798, aged 84. And of JEAN MATTHEU, his wife, who died in 1796, aged 74. Their four sons dedicate this small monument of filial duty to the best of parents.

And may their children learn from them,
In virtues paths to tread—
Like them respected when alive;
Like them esteemed when dead.
R. I. P.

—The first of the above-mentioned four sons succeeded his father in Nether Innervedie; the second became farmer of Smallburn, and was grandfather of Mr Nicolson, Dean of the Diocese of Brechin; the third, farmer of Braeside, married a daughter of the author of Tullochgorm; and the fourth went abroad. The family are said to have come from Skye to Glenlivat during the Civil Wars, and to have changed their name from *Macdonald*.

The next two inscriptions are from head stones:—

GEO. WALKER, Fortry, d. 1827, a. 94:—

"His grave is here pointed out as the resting place of a man who practised the truth "AS IT IS IN JESUS," in all its simplicity."

Erected by Andrew Webster, farmer in Ardlaw, in memory of his wife, ISABELLA PORTER, who died the 11th of Septr. 1870, aged 72 years. Also of her Aunt, ISABELLA PORTER, who died the 30th of Septr. 1868, in the 101st year of her age.

Athough unrecorded by any tombstone, I am told that the remains of LIZZIE WILKIN are interred at Longside. She died at the reputed age of 103. Her father was carpenter to Earl Marischal at Inverugie, and it is said that she remembered of him making "drumsticks" for the rebel army of 1714-15.

A slab, which exhibits a nicely carved, but much defaced coat of arms, with the motto "Spero," a crest, helmet, and mantlings, &c., is built into the east dyke of the kirk-yard. The shield is charged with the Forbes and Barclay arms impaled, the former having a crescent, and the latter a boar's head for difference. The crest is also composed of a crescent; and, as the "difference" corresponds with that used by Forbes of Savock, as described by Nisbet, who also states that this branch of the Forbeses was come of a second son of the laird of Tolquhon, it is probable that the slab had marked the burial place of Forbes of Savoch and his wife, the latter of whom may have been a Barclay of Towie.

The church-yard of Longside has been recently enlarged and otherwise improved. An interesting example of a "lich-gate," which forms the west entrance to the old portion of the kirk-yard, is built of stone. Although an inferior specimen to that at Blackford, in Perthshire, it is quite entire.

It need scarcely be said that those erections were used for sheltering coffins while graves were being made, and the burial service read. They were named from the Saxon word *lich* or *lire*, which signifies "a corpse or dead body." The well-known ceremony of "the lyke wake" or corpse watching, has its name from the same word, which also appears in "lyke-stanes."

Although "lich-stanes" are still found in some out-of-the-way places in Scotland, they are by no means common. I know of examples near Newburgh, in Fife, and there are others in Buchan. The latter are upon the old Mormond Hill road, between Strichen and Rathen, and bodies were rested upon these stones when they were being conveyed for burial from the one place to the other. I have also met with the name of "Lich-ar-ford," which doubtless has a similar meaning, and points out the ford or the crossing of a burn or river by which dead bodies were conveyed to their last resting place.

---o---

Lunan—(241.)

The inscription given below, to the memory of Walter Mill, the well-known Scottish martyr, was composed and set up at Lunan by the late Rev. Mr Gowans. It has long ago disappeared; but, being correct in reference to facts, it is probably to be regretted that it was not adopted in preference to the one now within the church :—

"M.S. Reverendi GUALTERI MILL, hujus Ecclesiæ olim pastoris eximii, qui veritatis studiosus Jesu Christi a Pontificiis ejusdem insectatoribus—jam major octogenario in foro Andreapolitano igne crematus est tertio Kalendas Maii MDLVIII. Hoc pos : R. J. G., I. W. 1818."

[Sacred to the memory of the Reverend WALTER MILL, formerly an excellent minister of this Church, who, being zealous for the truth as it is in Jesus Christ, was, when upwards of eighty years of age, burned (to death) by the Popish persecutors of the same, in the market place of St Andrews, on the 29th of April, 1558. This monument was erected by R. J. G. [Rev. John Gowans, and] I. W. [Isabella Webster, his wife], in 1818.]

—The most graphic, as well as the most trustworthy account of the apprehension and burning of Mill is probably to be found in Pitscottie's "History of Scotland," pp. 519-23 (*supra* p. 241).

In addition to notes of writs regarding the proprietary history of Lunan, which Major Blair-Imrie has so obligingly communicated (see *supra*, p. 243), he also gives the following interesting account of his own ancestors :—

"William Imray, or Imrie, who bought Lunan from David Wise, 27th Nov. 1759, was the son of a farmer in Aberdeenshire. He assisted his father upon the farm for some time, and while quite a youth, left home without communicating his design to any one, and walked along the coast road until he reached Redcastle. Having mounted the hill on which that old ruin stands, he lay down, fell asleep, and dreamt he was Laird of Lunan. He went to England, sailed several times to India, married a woman with money, and became the owner of a hotel in Fountain Court, Strand, London. This tavern, which at that time was the favourite resort of the Forfarshire lairds when they went to London, ultimately degenerated into the well-known 'Judge and Jury' Tavern, over which for so many years presided that celebrated character, the Lord Chief Baron Nicholson, of facetious memory, whose dry judicial humour was more remarkable than the purity of his language.

"The incident at Redcastle left a deep impression on William Imrie's mind, and having become rich in London, he returned to Scotland, and there realised the dream of his youth.

"William Imrie's children all died in infancy, and his wife only survived her removal to the old mansion house of Lunan for the short space of six weeks. He had a sister married to —— Simpson, and their child, Agnes, became the wife of Alexander Taylor (whose mother was Jane Silver of Netherley), at Cushnie, in Fordoun. He left Lunan to his niece's husband in life rent, and to their second son, William, in fee, and died in 1790.

"When Alexander Taylor (great-grandfather of the present Mr Blair-Imrie) succeeded in 1790, he assumed the name and arms of Imrie. He died on the 21st September, 1813, and was succeeded by his second son, William Taylor-Imrie, who died unmarried in 1849, leaving his property to his nephew, Lieut.-Colonel and Brigadier James Blair.

"In acknowledgment of the public services which Brigadier James Blair had rendered for 36 years in India, it is said that the Home Government directed that his papers should be forwarded, with a view of conferring upon him the honour of knighthood. By some inadvertence the papers were mislaid, and before the error was corrected death had transplanted him to that land of peace, where worldly honours could avail him nothing. Shortly after his death, his brother officers erected an obelisk to his memory at Lunan." (See *supra*, p. 242.)

---?---

Maryton—(235-8.)

When the church-yard of Maryton was improved in 1872, some interesting old tombstones were brought to light, which had been hidden from view for a great number of years. Amongst these was a mutilated slab of red sandstone, upon which was cut, in low relief, the effigy of a baron dressed in the costume of the sixteenth century. A shield, charged with the arms of the family of Wood (an oak tree growing out of a mount), between those of Tulloch of Bonnington (two cross-crosslets), adorns the lower portion of the slab. The initials V. V. are below the shield, and the following traces of an inscription are upon the sides of the stone:—

. . . ulcimus . wod . olim . domin . . . .

—As the carving of this fragment seems to belong to the first half of the 16th century, it was probably the tombstone of WILLIAM WOOD, who is described in 1520 as the son and heir of Dorothea Tulloch of Bonnington and her husband, Walter Wood. He married *Margaret* Ogilvy (misnamed "Elizabeth" in Douglas' Peerage), eldest daughter of the second Lord Ogilvy of Airlie. William had a brother, John, who was alive in 1493, but the latter appears to have died, and possibly without issue, before 1520.

It appears that in 1528-9, William Wood had a feu of Newbigging and Kirkton Mill in Inverkeillor, with the astricted multure, and "ryng boyer," &c. (Reg. Nig. Aberb.) On 3d March, 1530, he acquired a charter, on the resignation of James Durham of Ardcastie, "of the 6 part of the lands of Fullartoun, a third part of the lands of Ennenie, a 6 part of ane 18 part of Kinnaird, and a 6 part of ane 18 part of little Carcarrie." Two years later he acquired charters of the same lands, Fullarton excepted, upon the resignation of Wm. Earl of Montrose (*MS. Mem. at Panmure.*)

William Wood, who was alive in August, 1532, had a son, James, who married Elizabeth, daughter of Lord Ruthven, and from them was descended John Wood of Bonnington, who, as before shown (*sup.*, p. 237), was created a baronet.

Besides the lands of Bonnington and others adjoining, the Woods also owned those of Letham and Idvies; but, about 1682, their affairs became much embarrassed, and their estates were adjudged to be sold in the time of Sir John Wood. He was succeeded in the title, and possibly in any part of the family inheritance that remained, by his eldest son, James, who was alive in 1728.

The surname of Wood, or *De Bosco* (as it was anciently written), is one of the oldest in Scotland; but the clan being numerous, it is difficult to say to which branch the first Wood of Bonnington had belonged. He may have been related to Andrew Wood, *Hostiarius*, who is a witness to the resignation by Walter Tulloch of certain lands in the Mearns, 1488 (Montrose Dukedom Case, 99*b.*)

It is certain that, on 5th July, 1493, the king confirmed a charter by Dorothy Tulloch, with consent of her husband, William Wood, of the lands of Bonytoun and Balnamoo, which were hers hereditarily, to John Wood, their son, reserving their life rent. But as Dorothy was a co-heiress, this must refer only to one half of the property, since, on 23d Nov., 1498, Jonet Tulloch, "one of the Ladies of Bonytoun," resigned the lands of Balnamone and Bonytoun, with her part of the mill thereof, to Thomas Lord Innermeath, who, in June, 1508, conveyed back these lands to David Garden, son and heir apparent of David Garden of Cononsyth, and his wife Janet Tulloch (*Miscell. Aldbar*, MS.)

It was on 18th March, 1377, that Walter Tulloch—possibly the same individual as was Deputy Chamberlain of Scotland for parts north of the Forth—received charters of Bonnington, on the resignation of John de Capella (Reg. Mag. Sigill., 130; Chamb. Rolls, ii. *passim*.)

Slabs, all less or more injured, and bearing the inscriptions given below, were found at the time the church-yard was improved. Besides its quaint orthography, the first quoted inscription contains a denunciation in regard to the stone upon which it is carved, that will remind the reader of a similar threat in Shakespear's epitaph regarding his own bones:—

[1.]

 . . . ANd OF Ye AIGES OF . . .
[A shield, charged with a blacksmith's crown and hammer, and initialed, W. S., is here carved.]
☞ WO . bE . TO
HIM . yAT . PV
TIS . yIS . TOO
ANy   .   WdER
WS   .   WHA
dESECIT . IN . A
NOA . MVCLX
XXIV . yN . yAR

[2.]

Heir lyis VILLAME LIETCH and DAVID LIETH tvoe briether sovn tyme in Old Montrois, vho departet the nynthe of March the year of God 1666 yires of aige 63 yires, and the other departit the tvantie thrie of Decembre the yeir of God 1642 yires of aige 6—

W. L : D. L.   1673.

The mortuary emblems of a bell and a sand-glass are carved upon the last-noticed slab. Upon the next are a blacksmith's crown and hammer, also a shield charged with a bird of some sort (probably a pelican, for *Paterson*), initialed A. P : R. :

[3.]

Blessed ar the ded vhich die in the Lord yea saith the spirit that they may rest from their labovr and their vorks do folov them.

Heir lyes IAMES DALL hvsband to AGNIS PEATERSON his spovsse. Thois tvo personos desesed September 22 and Febrvar the 10 the yer of god 58 and 55 and of age 45 and 63. and ISOBELL REAT spovse to Thomas Dall vho deceased in September the 10 the yeir of god 42 and of age 44 Memento mori 1643.

[4.]

. . . .

Heir lyes an faithfull brother, WALTER GREIG, hovsband to Margret Black, who died the first of Ivly, the year of God, 1643, of age 48 years.

☞ Here lyes MARGRET BLACK, spous to Walter Greig, elder, who died ye 15 of April anno . . . . of age 78.   W. G ; M. B ; W. G. I. H.

The next two inscriptions possibly relate to cadets of the Melvills of Baldovie, a property to the eastward of the kirk of Maryton. It will be remembered (*v*. Melvill's Diary) that the celebrated Reformers, Andrew and James Melvill, were sons of Melvill of Baldovie:—

[5.]

. . . .
A. M.   B. R.   1667.

Here lyes ALEXANDER . . . . . L hovsband to Bessie Ramsay sometyme in Cotovn of Old Montrose vho departed this lyfe in the Lord the . . of May the year of God 1667.

[6.]

Death is the end of all tribvlation,

And therfor to vyse men a swet consolation :

Here lyes WILLIAM MELLVIL, hvsband to Barbra Mikeson who died in the Lord the 5 of Avgvst the year of God 1677, of age 55 years.

W M
W M   B M
YOVNGER   E W
IEAN ANNA
MELLVILL

[7.]

Heir lyes IOHN GRIEG and IANET . . . . . .
his spovs vho deceased both in on ag 72
the yeir of . . . March 1670 6
I. G.   M. W.   C. E. C.
MEMENTO MORI.   1673.

[8.]

Heir layes ELIZABETH LONKINE, lafvl spovse to Valter Dall in Ananise, & mother ... to Iohn Gray in Cottovne, a w ... ovs, religiovs . ife, vho departed this life to a better, of her age 65 November .. 70 . . . .
.. ovng man vho died of age 21 Septemb . . 4, 1670.

I G . E L   I G
   1673   I D

—The word ANANISE is carved in such a curiously interlaced form in the above inscription, that it looks more like "NANSE." The name is variously spelled Inaney, Enene, Eunenie, &c. The place itself, now familiarly known as *Ananias*, is of some historical note, in so far as the lands were given by William the Lion to Crane, the heriditary gate-keeper of the King's castle of Montrose (Mem. Angus and Mearns, p. 46; *supra*, p. 237.)

[9.]

Let us be attentive to the call of the Almighty.
A G A K. W G M D

WILLIAM GREIG with his spouse MAGDALENE DUN, who died in the year of our Lord 1702, and in ye 67 of her age. He dyed in the year 17 .. , aged 84 years. And ANDREW GREIG, their son, farmer in Marytown for the space of 28 years, departed this life, August 8th, in the year 1718, aged 64 years. His son WALTER GREIG succeeded him, and died 24th August 1761, aged 63 years. ELISABETH BEATTIE, his spouse, died Decr. 1786, aged 84 years.

Although their bodies Mulder here to dust,
To wait the Resurrection of the Just;
Their souls in trouble rest in peace,
Ordain'd of God for all the chosen race.

Their children were Elisabeth, Ann, Jane, Andrew, Christian, Margaret, Marjory, Kathrine, Walter, and Robert Greigs.

[10.]

Heir . lies . CHRISTAN . RANY . davghter . to Iames . Ra . . . . . the . Cott . . . . f . Dysart . . . departed . t . . . life . the . 12 . of . May . 1705 her . age . 18 . yeares.

Monifieth—(106.)

From a flat slab, with carvings of a mariner's compass, anchor, &c :—

Here lyes JOHN KNIGHT, shipmaster in North Ferric, who departed this lyf the 8th of November 1721, and of his age 82, as well as his spouse ISOBEL HILL, who departed this life the 4 of Nevember 1713, and her age 68—

Tho' Boreas blasts on Neptune's waves
  Hath Tossed us to and fro,
Yet by the order of God's decree
  We harbour here below.
Where now wee lye at anchor sure
  With many of our fleet,
Expecting on day to set sail
  Our Admiral Christ to meet.

THOS. ARCKLAY and JANET CWPER in Hillock— 3 children d. 1732-41 :—

Lo children three, by God's decree,
  Dissolving here do ly,
Their tender years with floods of tears,
  Lament ought you and I.
Let's cry, alas, all flesh is grass,
  Here fades all worldly pleasure ;
Let's dart our eyes beyond the skies
  & seek for heavenly treasure.
As heaven decreed, we've all agreed
  That soul from body sever,
Eerth to the clod, the soul to God
  Shal live and reing for ever.
Ye parents kind, who stay behind,
  Pale Death hath made you sorry ;
Yet comfort take, we shall awake
  & meet in endless glory.

Within an enclosure :—

Sacred to the memory of DAVID HUNTER, fourth son of General Hunter of Burnside. Born 20th April 1801 ; died 16th Aug. 1834. This last tribute of affection is erected by his deeply afflicted widow, Sarah Kerr Hunter.

'Repose, then, Precious clay !
Thou art in safer custody than mine.
The purchase of atoning Blood ! What though
The sods of earth now cover thee, and rage

The elements around thee? Angels watch
The sleeping dust; nay, more, Omnipotence
Is th' invisible Guardian of thy tomb.'

A costly freestone monument, with columns, and three inscription tablets of polished Peterhead granite, is built into the north dyke of the churchyard. It was "Erected by Thomas Kerr of Grange of Monifieth, A.D. 1867." The panels are respectively inscribed:—

[1.]
In memory of THOMAS KERR of Grange of Monifieth, born 30th December 1737, died 22d December 1811; also of CATHARINE KERR, his spouse, born 1st January 1730, died 1st January 1808; and of ELIZABETH KERR, their daughter, born 8th June 1768, died — May 1839.

[2.]
In memory of DAVID KERR of Grange of Monifieth, born 12th October 1766, died 5th October 1843; and of ANN ANDERSON, his spouse, born 16th March 1769, died 18th June 1840.

[3.]
In memory of the following children of David Kerr and Ann Anderson, viz. DAVID, their younger son, born 23d May 1803, died 11th June 1832; and MARGARET KERR, born 5th July 1800, died 31st May 1865.

—Thomas Kerr was some time farmer at Pitskellic. He bought the property of South Grange of Monifieth in 1795; and his son David, who died in 1843, bought that of Newbigging, in Monikie, in 1821. Thomas, erector of the monument, and grandson of Thomas Kerr of Grange of Monifieth, possesses both estates, also North Grange.

Within an enclosure are two inscribed table-shaped monuments. One records the death of CHARLES KERR, tenant in Fore Boath, who died in 1795, aged 48. The other bears:—

1848: Inscribed by Thomas Kerr of North Grange, in memory of his father ROBERT KERR, who died the 8th of July 1813, in the 79th year of his age. MARGARET KID, his mother, who died the 16th of July 1813, in the 80th year of her age. [Also 2 brothers and 3 sisters named.] THOMAS KERR of North Grange died at Denlind, the 3d of April 1864, in the 90th year of his age.

A plain head-stone thus records the death of a patriarch, who was born in Fettercairn:—

1843: Erected by David Rennie, farmer, Mill Omachie, in memory of his wife ANN KID, who died 9th April 1818, aged 57 years. The above DAVID RENNIE, died 3d March 1857, aged 102 years. Also, his son THOMAS, who died 12th Dec. 1860, aged 66 years.

Abridged from a marble slab:—

In memory of JOHN ARKLAY, late of Hillock, who died 12 June 1828, aged 87. MATILDA CRAMMOND, his relict, died 8 Dec. 1830, aged 72. Their son ROBERT ARKLAY of Ethiebeaton, died 2 June 1837, aged 58; JOHN, son of Robert, was drowned whilst bathing at Monifieth in the river Tay, 18 Aug. 1837, aged 11. ELIZABETH SIM, spouse of Robert Arklay, died 26 Aug. 1859, aged 75. ROBERT ARKLAY died 1859, aged 70. AGNES, their youngest daughter, died 1862, aged 31.

The next two inscriptions are also abridged. The former is from a monument on the south side of the kirk, and the latter, "erected by the members of his congregation," is from one in the south-east corner of the burial-ground:—

The Revd. JOHN BISSET, minister of this parish, died 5th March 1839, aged 61 years 11 months. ISABELLA DICK, his spouse for nearly 16 years, died 1825, aged 47.

The Revd. PETER MYLES, minister of this parish for 14 months, died 24th Feb. 1855, aged 28.

A neat Free Church was erected a little to the north-west of the Parish Church of Monifieth in 1872. In the following year the interior of the Parish Church was improved at an expense of nearly £1000 sterling.

Mem.—In noticing the Chapel of Ease at Broughty Ferry (*supra,* p. 115), there are two misprints, viz. "1826" for 1827, and "1SJS" for 1863.

Monquhitter—(175-8.)

[1.]

To the memory of ISOBEL RETTIE, sometime in Balhangie, his respected mother; and of JEAN OREM, daughter to the Reverend Mr Orem, his beloved wife, this monument of filial piety and connubial love is gratefully dedicated by John Russell of Balmade. The one died Nov. 12th 1770, aged 69; the other died July 27th 1771, aged 38.

[2.]

WM. ALLARDYCE, Corbshill, d. 1782, a. 43 :—
A gen'rous heart he had,
Could melt at woe;
The poor man's friend he was,
To none a foe.

[3.]

Under this stone is deposed the body of ISABELLA IRVINE, who died the 17 of Oct. 1787, in infancy. This stone is erected by George Irvine, Esquar of Bayndlie. [The Lord gave, &c.]

—"Bayndlie," or Boyndlie, in the parish of Tyrie, now belongs to a branch of the Forbeses.

The next inscription probably relates to a descendant of Guthrie of King Edward. The first of this family succeeded to the baronetcy of Guthrie of Colliston, in Angus. They were come of a younger son of Guthrie of that Ilk :—

[4.]

Died at Cuminestoun, Octr. 1797, in his 70 year, WALTER GUTHRIE, manufacturer. Piety, virtue, and faith diffused in his heart contentment and peace. As a husband, a father, and Christian monitor, he was revered by his family. His industry, integrity, and medical skill, were grateful to society. His life was the life of the righteous, and his death illustrated their comforts.

Religion cheers the vale of tears,
Excites our hopes, & lulls our fears;
It guides the good through evry scene—
They live esteem'd, and die serene.

[5.]

In memory of ALEXANDER GRIEVE, late merchant in Cuminestown, who died 20th April 1806, aged 73 years; and also of his spouse, MARGARET CLARK, who died 26th November 1807, aged 58 years. He bequeathed two hundred pounds to the Kirksession of Monquhitter, the interest of the same to be paid yearly to poor industrious families in the parish, not on the poor's Roll. Blessed are the dead who die in the Lord.

[6.]

Sacred to the memory of JOHN CHALMERS, surgeon, Fyvie, who died 14th June, 1833, aged 34 years. For the unwearied attention with which he discharged his professional duties, and his kind consideration of the condition of the poor, his memory will be long cherished, and his loss regretted in the neighbourhood, which was the field of his useful labours.

Although modern, the next inscription is sufficiently quaint :—

[7.]

Erected by Sophia Stewart, in memory of her beloved husband, ALEXANDER CRAN, feuar in Cuminestown, who died 16th June 1833, aged 60 years, by mutual concent of Andrew Lorimer, his Successor.

---o---

Nevay—(68.)

"S. NEVETH, Martyr, was one of the sons of Brychan. He is said in the Welsh Genealogy of the Saints to have been a bishop in the north, where he was slain by the Saxons and the Picts. The ecclesiastical district of Nevyth (Nevay) now united to Essie, near Meigle, lies within the old Pictish territory. Perhaps S. Neveth was buried at Nevay." (Bishop Forbes' Kalendars of Scottish Saints.)

As the ivy-clad ruins of the church of Nevay, or Kirkinch, are among the most picturesque in the county of Forfar, some of the 17th century monuments are also fine examples of their kind, in the art of carving. Were the grave-yard trenched over and put in proper order, some equally, if not more, ancient and interesting stones, would probably be found in the course of operations.

The church of *Essy* (p. 67), which had S.

BRANDON for its patron (Kalendars of Scottish Saints), was dedicated, in 1246, by David, Bishop of St Andrews (Robertson's Concilia.)

The shield upon the mutilated Tyrie stone, within the ruins at Novay, is flanked by the initials I. T. The Tyrie coat (? a cheveron bet. 2 crescents), is defaced, but the impalement of a lion rampant (? for Crichton) still remains. The inscription (*supra*, p. 69), reads thus :—

. . . . . . YRIES . IN . NEV . . . . . .
. . . . . . E . FOLLOVIS . . . . . .

The rest of the inscriptions are from monuments in different parts of the Church-yard :—

[1.]

Heir lyis THOMAS TYRIE, sumtym indvellar in Novay, sone to vmvmhyl David Tyrie, and husband to Iauet Veilaut, vho departed the 10 of October 1651, his age vas 3- yeirs :—
Heaven keips his savel, heir the bodie lyis ;
On earth he vas both vertvvs cynd and vyse.

MEMENTO MORI.

[2.]

Heir lyis ane honest man IOHN RIVIN [? Rynd] in Navey . . . . rted Ia . . . . and his spovs ELSPET . . . . March . . . .
Yov vho is in pomp, I Death arcast yov, stay ;
I lay al pomp and honovr in the clay.
J. R., E. W., M. i. 1645.

[3.]

The hour is run :
Heir lyis ane . . nest man IOHN WARDROPER . . Templetvn . . . . . arted November . . . . . .

[4.]

AD. IW : ID. ID. HB.

Heir lyas JAMES DOOG, lavfvll son to Androv Doog and Iean Wardroper, indvellers in Gateside of Ballgrvgo, who dayed in 1715, of his age 29 :—
His nattralle temper uns so good,
His vertve in his blossovme ;
And to his parants vas so kind ;
It was ther griefe to loss him.
A holy, harmless life hee lead,
From wice hie was estranged ;
Bvt nov the Lord hath crovned him
To joy, from girefe is ended.

[5.]

☞ Heir lyes IOHN . . . . . . DVGATS, children of Gilbert Dvgat and Elizabeth Scot in Templetovne, their ages are 20 days . . . . yeares . . . . as was . . . . . 10 of November 1667, departed . . . Febr. 1678. . . . .

Beneath this stone lyes . . . . . . sone . . . . .

The following traces of an inscription are from a flat slab at the west end of the ruins. It bears a shield, charged in pale, a cheveron, between three roundels, possibly for Myreton of Cambo, and a St Andrew's cross, probably for Maxwell :—

[6.]

☞ Heir lyis . . . . . . gentlewoman . . . MARGRET M . . . . tvn of age 55 . . ars . . . .

There are several tombstones to a family named Barron (*v.* p. 69, in which the date of "1853" is misprinted for "1753.") The oldest stone bears a pretty long Latin inscription, of which the following is a portion :—

[7.]

H. S. S : ANDREAS BARON, mercator, qui obiit 4° Id' Octobris A. Æ. C. 1714 ; et conjuge MARGARETA FAIRWEATHER, quæ ob. die Paschali 1692, &c.

—The latest of the Barron stones is in memory of ANDREW BARRON, who died in 1851, aged 82, and his wife MARGARET SMITH, who died in 1826, aged 55. It was erected by their daughter, Margaret, wife of Charles Clark of Princeland, Coupar-Angus.

[8.]

HEIR LYIS ALEXANDER NEAVE
X IEAN STORACH.

[9.]

Heir lyes IEAN PULLAR, spouse to Iohn Anderson, who lived in Navy. She died Apryle 7, 1755, her age . . . .

—A table stone at the west end of the ruins is erected by Elizabeth Murray in memory of her husband, ROBERT ANDERSON, tenant, North Nevay, who died in 1801, aged 38, leaving four children—Margaret, Andrew, Janet, and Robert.

Newtyle—(138-41.)

When the church of Newtyle was taken down in 1870, to make room for the present building, bits of old carved stones were found in and about the walls, and also some grave-stones in the burial ground. Probably the most interesting of these relics was the top stone of an awmbry, about 2 feet 4 inches in height by about 1 foot 9 inches in breadth. It bore ornamental carvings, and these words upon a scroll or ribbon :—

```
      IACOB'. HOC   ╷  FIER . FEC . .
      ΛVSƎꓯΛT        †       SIꓹVƆIΛ
```

[James Lyndesay, vicar, caused this to be erected.]

—On 13th March, 1519, Mr Andrew Dure was presented to the vicarage of Newtyle, on the death of Mr Wm. (? James) Lyndsay (Reg. Nig. Aberb.)

Two of the fragments possibly relate to the Oliphants, who were early proprietors in the district (*supra*, p. 141.) One bit bears the Oliphant and (?) Crichton arms, with the initials, I. O : —. C. ; and upon the other bit are these words :—

```
. . . . . . OLYPHAN . AND . H . . . .
AGE . YE . . . . 1603.
```

Upon a third fragment :—

```
         VIR . FGREGI' . PRÆDICA
         IO . SEPTIMO . QUIEDU
         . . . . . . . NO
```

The lintel of the old kirk door was also discovered among the debris. It bore the following text, in interlaced capitals, which has been attempted to be imitated over the principal entrance to the new church :—

```
         . . . . . .
         GATE . OF . YE . LORD
         INTO . VHICH . YE
         RYCHTEOVS . SAL . ENTER.
```

A coffin-slab, with bevelled sides presents the following, as here arranged :—

```
1603 . AND . OF . HIS . AGE . 75 . HEIR . 'W
HEIR . LYIS . IOHN . MICHEL . VITTA
LER . IN . BALMAV . AND . HVSBAND . TO . ISBO
BEL . DOG . I . FER . GOD . . . . . . . . . . . . . . . . . . . .
WHA . DEPARTIT. YE. 17. DAY . OF. NOVEMBER. ANNO
```

The next inscription and epitaph are from a stone, which has the initials, R. M : I. S., upon the left, and those of the seven children referred to below upon the right side of a shield. The shield bears an *owsen-bow* or ox-collar, &c. :—

Erected by George & Alexander Masons in memory of there father ROBERT MASON, late tennant in Pitnepie, who died Aprile 20th 1748, aged 84 years ; & IEAN IACKSON, his first spouse, who died Aprile 20th 1708, aged 40 years, by whom he had 5 children. His second spouse, Isobel Spankie, survives him, by whom he had 2 children.

Struck by the fiery dart of Death,
Here ROBERT MASON Lies,
Awaiting the Eternal Call
Of Christ beyond the Skies.
He while on Earth mankind did aid,
& genarously befriend,
For which we hope, Almighty God
has bless'd his latter end.
He by god's blessing often did,
Lame people Safe restore,
To wonted Strength, although their bones,
were bruised very sore.
MEMENTO MORI.

The first portion of the following inscription is in raised interlaced Roman capitals, chiefly round the verge of the stone, the rest is in incised capitals, and disposed as indicated below :—

Heir . lyis . INON . MITCHELL . indweller . in Craighead . hvsband . to . GRISSELL . GREIN . who deceased . the . 20 . d . of . May . 1678 . and . of . his age . 78 . and . she . departed . the . 2 . d . of March . 1675 . and . of . hir . age . 82.
and . vise
Heir . is . intombd . on . kinde . svllan
tymes . thrice
Who . lived . one . and . nynes . thrie
as . he . did . finde
Of . years . the . [climac]terick . great
cord . wutvind
When . d[oaths dar]to . his . siluer
I.   M.   G.   G.

Another tombstone, upon which there is a shield near the top, charged with the initials, A. W : K. G., the date of 1730, and an old fashioned plough, coulter, and sock, bears this epitaph :—

Here lyes interred belou this stone,
The dust and ashes of ANDREW WHITTON,
And of his age ninety even,
But now I hope he lives iu heaven.
He was a freind to rieth and poor,
His living was in Auochteryre;
Ane honest wpright husband man,
But nou hes lying in the ground here.
Also interred belou this ston,
A child of nonage, whos nanio was IOHN;
His children seven remaining be,
And of his oyes thirty-three.

—The stone which bears the above inscription presents some mortuary emblems, also the initials of the seven children above referred to. It stands within an enclosure on the west side of the burial-ground, where there is a monument of Peterhead granite thus inscribed:—

Erected to the memory of ANDREW WHITTON, Esqr. of Couston, who died 14th May 1861, aged 68 years. Also of his mother, CHRISTIAN ROBERTSON, who died 12th March 1835, aged 74 years; and of his father, ROBERT WHITTON, who died 26th October 1840, aged 82 years.

—The first-named in the above inscription was succeeded in Couston and Scotston by his son, now local factor for Lord Wharncliffe.

From a head-stone:—

Sacred to the memory of ANNE DALRYMPLE, school-mistress, Newbigging House, who died the 21st Febr. 1839, aged 63 years. Erected by a few of her Pupils, as a token of their respect for her memory.

The church bell of Newtyle is dated 1736.

The patronage of the kirk was acquired by Sir George Mackenzie of Rosehaugh, King's Advocate, from George, Earl of Panmure.

The top of the old awmbry, and four of the fragments above noticed, as well as the stone with the curious inscription to Gilbert Mille (*supra*, p. 140), have either been buried or destroyed since I took note of them in 1870. The marble tablet to Mr Alison, who was long factor for the Belmont estates (*supra*, p. 139), lies broken and uncared for within the burial-ground.

Oathlaw—(335.)

From a lately recovered tombstone:—

1732: Here lyes ELIZABETH VOLUM, dau.. ter to Iohn Volum & Iannet Cato in Main Shott of Finevan, & HELEN VOLUM, their daughter, who died the 10 of Iune 1731, aged 19 years.

—The above were probably descendants of a family named Volume, who were once proprietors of Woodwrae (*v*. Land of the Lindsays.) They appear to have fallen into a state of indigence, for in 1636 and 1638, the Brechin Session records show that "Alexr. Wellom, sometyme of Woodurae," received charity from that body.

Robert Volum, in Kirriemuir, who was served heir to his uncle, Thomas Dunlop, dyer and burgess, Arbroath, 8th Sept. 1668 (Retours), was probably of the same stock.

The name of Volum is now better known in Buchan than it is in Angus. Catto, which is quite a Buchan name, may have been assumed from the district of Cairn Catta, near Peterhead.

---o---

Pert—(213.)

The first two inscriptions are copied from flat slabs in the kirk-yard of Pert, and both bear mortuary ornaments, &c.

[1.]

Hir lys ain fames yovth son to IOHN SMITH, somtym goodman in Galro, vho departed this lyf Febrvar the 20 day and of ag 27, 1666

Com al and se as yov go by
En houred corps hir lov do ly
As ye ar nov so one vas ay
As ay am so sal ye be
Remember man that thov most dei

[2.]

Here lys IOHN IAMIE, vho departed this lyfe in the year 1708, and of his age 86 Ian. 2 day. And MARGRAT . . . . spovso vho departed this lyfe in the year 1702, and of her age 84.

Here lys DAVID IAMIE and IOHN IAMIE, and IEAN PITCARNES and MARGRAT GLEAG ther spovses.

. . . .

The following is a complete copy of the inscription, given in an abridged form on p. 211:—

Sacred to the memory of MARY ALLARDICE, daughter of James Allardice, Esquire of that Ilk, in the Mearns, and second wife of James Macdonald, Esquire, long sheriff-substitute of that county, and only son of Thomas Macdonald, advocate, Aberdeen. She died at Inglismaldie, 4th January 1801, in the 75th year of her age. Also to the memory of the said JAMES MACDONALD, Esquire, who died 23d of August 1809, in the 83d year of his age. They lived together upwards of 42 years in greatest happiness, and in the practice of every Christian virtue, beloved and revered by their family, and by all who know them. This stone is erected by their only daughter MARY, only surviving child of six children, and wife of Charles Ogilvy, Esquire of Tannadice. Also, here lies the body of MARGARET OGILVY, daughter of the above Charles Ogilvy and Mary Macdonald, who died 25th Oct. 1805, aged 3 weeks.

—The remains of Mr Ogilvy of Tannadice and his wife also lie at Pert. Having made money as a medical officer in the H.E.I. Co.'s Service, Dr Ogilvy bought the lands of Tannadice towards the close of the last century, and built a mansion-house there. He was succeeded by his son, an officer in the army, and upon his death in 1845-6, the property came to his elder sister, Mrs Balfour-Ogilvy (see *supra*, p. 48). His younger sister married Mr Ogilvy of Inshewan. Dr Ogilvy's father was laird of Murthil, and long a medical practitioner in Forfar. His daughter, Jane, was the second wife of Walter Ogilvy, seventh Earl of Airlie, and grandmother of the present Earl.

There are two head-stones at Pert erected by Mrs Ogilvy (daughter of Mr James Macdonald, Inglismaldie), to the memory of two domestic servants. One stone bears that JAMES BROMLEY, who had been 30 years in her father's service, died Sept. 1809, aged 73, and the other shows that ELIZABETH OGILVY, died in March 1804, aged 63, after a service of 50 years in the same family.

Two monuments upon the west side of the burial-ground relate to a family named DURIE, who have been long farmers in the district. The older of these stones was erected by Thomas Durie in Capo, and his wife Margaret Middleton, in memory of their daughter ISOBEL, who died in 1791, aged 14. The other bears the name of their son, CHARLES DURIE, farmer of Dalladies and Capo, who died in 1862, aged 72, also the names of two of his daughters and three of his sons.

Mr Durie, who was long an auctioneer and land valuator, was as remarkable for honesty and integrity of character as for his great good humour. His eldest son, CHARLES, who succeeded his father in the farms of Dalladies and Capo, died in 1870, aged 39. He was Secretary to the Fettercairn Farmers' Club, and was esteemed alike for his kind heartedness and general intelligence. His younger brother, ALEXANDER, died in 1872, also aged 39. He was sometime Dean of Guild of Brechin, and carried on the business of a brewer at the North Port of that city, where his maternal ancestors had conducted the same trade for nearly 200 years.

I have now ascertained that the relationship between the Rev. Mr Lunan, Rosehill, and his namesake at Daviot (as stated on p. 213), is uncertain. But it appears from documentary evidence that Mr Alex. Lunan, Episcopal minister at Rosehill, was a grandson of the Rev. Mr Alex. Lunan of Kintore, who married Jean, daughter of Sir Wm. Forbes of Monymusk. William (son of Mr Lunan and his wife Jean Forbes), married Barbara, daughter of Alex. Gordon of Merdrum, in Rhynie, 24th Dec., 1663. They had a son and a daughter. The son, also William, married Isobella, a daughter of Thain of Blackhall, in the Garioch, 4th Oct., 1691. By her he had a large family, of whom the minister of Rosehill (born in 1703), was the seventh, and his sister Ann (born in 1710), was the tenth. She married N. Cruickshank of Aberdeen. For this information, I have to thank Mr Cadenhead, advocate and procurator-fiscal of Aberdeen, who is himself a descendant of Mr Lunan of Kintore. Mr Cadenhead has made up a most interesting account of the Family of Lunan from a pretty early date.

St Cyrus—(36-9.)

The following is a more complete and accurate copy of the inscription upon the old Straton tomb than that on p. 36 :—

☞ HIC . SEPVLTVS . CI . . . .
. . . . THVRVS . STRATON . . .
MARGRET.E . LEONIS . QV.E . OBIIT . . . . . .
. . . 1646 . ÆTATIS . SV.E . 58.

[1.]

Here lyes interred the body of JAMES ABERCROMBIE, sometime Gardener in Morphie, who died the 12th July 1789.

Likewise the body of MARY VICAR, his spouse, who died the 20th January 1776.

   Crux Christi nostra Corona.
   O death, thy power.

[2.]

This stone was raised by William Gibson in Mains of Morphie, in memory of ANN ALLARDICE, his spouse, who departed this life 13th March 1767 years, in the 24th year of her age.

[3.]

This stone was erected by William Gibson, physician in Montrose, and Jean Barclay, his spouse, in memory of two beloved children whose remains are interred here. GEORGE, died 14th September 1818, aged 8 months ; DAVID STEWART, the 30th October 1818, aged 5 years.

—The erector of this head-stone was a half brother of the late Dr Gibson of Auchenrioch.

[4.]

Erected by Thomas Christie, Tenant in Mains of Woodston, in memory of his son WILLIAM CHRISTIE, who died the 5th Nov. MDCCXCV., in the 8 year of his age.

Much sprightliness this Christian youth adorned
Thro' his short life, as made him justly mourned.
 'Tis God that lifts our comforts high,
  And sinks them in the grave ;
 He takes, and when he takes away,
  He takes but what he gave.
Let patience teach us all our woes to bear,
And may eternal things engage our care.

[5.]

In Memoriam :—ELIZABETH ANDERSON, a native of this parish, widow of Robert Wills, cabinetmaker, Montrose, died 12 November 1851, aged 84 years. Sed [quod decet mulieres pietatem in Deum spondentes] operibus bonis. 1 Tim. ii. 10. The said ROBERT WILLS, died 25 Septr. 1818, aged 65 years.

—The above inscription is from an obelisk which stands upon the south side of a head-stone to the memory of JOHN WILL, weaver, Brownhill, and his spouse IEAN FERN, who both died in 1751.

Ellon—(61, 347.)

[1.]

Under this tomb-stone are not hidden Gold and Silver Treasures of any Kind, but the body of JOHN CRUICKSHANK, the younger son of Patrick Cruickshank and Christian Walls : They resided long at Fordmouth of Arnage, in this Parish. John Cruickshank died on the 11th day of March 1830, aged 80 years. This stone was erected by GEORGE WYNES, late in Stewart Field, who died the 14th March 1817, aged 56 years.

[2.]

Sacred to the memory of FORBES FROST, bookseller in Aberdeen, who died 28th June, 1845, aged 57 years. He was the son of WILLIAM FROST, gardener at Dudwick, and of MARY LEASK, his Spouse, who along with their two daughters, MARY and HELEN FROST, are interred here.

[3.]

GEO. ROBERTSON, sailor, died 1816, a. 27 :—

 Nine years I sail^d the Rageing main,
  Till death, the terror of all men,
 Hath taken me on my Native Shore
  To meet with Christ, to part no more.
 No more he'll Plow the Briny deep,
  In Search of Gold or Earthly store,
 But underneath this Turf he'll sleep,
  Till time shall end, and be no more.

APPENDIX

OF

ILLUSTRATIVE PAPERS AND NOTES.

Awmbry at Airlie Church.

APPENDIX

OF

Illustrative Papers and Notes.

I.—(pages 1-3.)

The Parish School, and the Reids of Banchory-Ternan, 1631-1753.

The following extracts from a Deed of Mortification, regarding the Old Schools of Banchory-Ternan (for the use of which I am indebted to Mr Steuart, inspector of poor), are not only illustrative of the history of the Parochial Schools of Scotland generally, but are fitting additions to the notices already given of the family of Reid, who were so long ministers of the parish of Banchory :—

It is recorded that, by will, dated 1st February 1639, Dr Alexander Reid left the liferent of (1), £100 towards the increase of the minister's stipend at Banchory-Ternan; (2), £100 to the poor "born or bred," or, who have lived the greater part of their lives "in the paroch," the same to be "distributed amongst them at the feast of the Nativity and Resurrection of Our Saviour; and (3), £100 to the school of Banchory for "one who shall there teach arithmetic, and write a fair hand."

. . . .

The same deed also shows that Dr Alexander Reid, who was physician to Charles I. (*supra*, p. 3), and "son lawfull to umqhle James Reid, sometime minister of the said Kirk of Banchorie," mortified 4000 merks Scots, for behoof of the two teachers, and for upholding the "edifice of the said schoole, and hospitall under the same." For the same purposes 1000 merks were given by Mr Alexander Burnett, agent and indweller in Edinburgh. Two-thirds of the annual rent of these 5000 merks were given to the master, and one-third to the under-master; but upon condition that the former should pay at the rate of 8 pounds, and the latter 4 pounds yearly towards the repair of the "edifice," if, at the sight of the Laird of Leys, the parish minister, and elders, it "shall be found damnified."

Dr A. Reid also left his "Books of Humanity, as Poets, Oratours, and Prophane Historiographers to the Grammar School of Banchorie-Ternan." But of these, as of the "Liberarie," which was subsequently given by Sir Thomas Burnett, neither a catalogue nor a volume is now known to exist.

In addition to these gifts to his native parish, Dr Alex. Reid left £400 sterling (which was owing to him by "the Right Honorable the Earl of Annandale and his sureties") to be invested by the Magistrates and Town Council of Aberdeen, the interest of one-half of which was to be divided "amongst the Regents of the Old and New Town College," and the other half was for the benefit of the schoolmasters of the Old and New Towns of Aberdeen.

Besides his original gift of 4000 merks towards the endowment of the school for males, Dr Alexander Reid also mortified the sum of 1800 merks for the "sustension" of the mistress of the "womans schoole." This was supplemented by his brother Mr Robert Reid, parish minister, to the extent of 200 merks; and Sir Thomas Burnett of Leys also contributed to the same object, by giving "ane house for a schoole for the education and virtuous upbringing of young women and maids of the said town of Banchorie, and dedicated the same to the said use in all time coming."

It appears by deed of mortification, dated 29th Oct. 1651, that Sir Thomas Burnett of Leys built "ane schoole [at Banchory-Ternan] having ane chamber for the maister and under Doctor of the said schoole, and ane room or ane other chamber for ane Liberarie, and such books as upon inventure, and ane perfect Catalogue are delivered in custody to the Maister of the said Schoole . . . . that the said schoole having been all ance burned by negligence, I having re-edified the same, having four hospitall vaults or chambers under the said schoole for four old poor and four to attend them, the young being mulls, to be taught be the maister and under Doctor of the said schoole, gratis, paying nothing for their instruction."

The school and schoolhouse at Banchory-Ternan, which had "an chamber for the master," was erected in 1650, upon the north banks of the Dee, to the south of the present railway station. The former part was used as a school until 1799, when the great flood of that year undermined it, and the latter was occupied by the teacher until 1829, when both his house and garden were destroyed in the same way. In 1799 the school was removed to an old house upon the north side of the turnpike road, where it remained until 1824, when a new school was erected. A school-house was built in 1829-30; but in 1854, when the Deeside Railway was being constructed, the school-house had to be removed, and the present school-buildings were then erected near the parish church.

It ought to be mentioned that another member of the Banchory Reids attained eminence as a surgeon in the Royal Navy. This was Dr George Read, whose monument is still at Banchory (*supra*, p. 3), and for the erection of which he thus provides in his will, dated 23d August 1753 :—" As I intend, if it may please Almighty God, to be buried amongst my ancestors at Banchory-Ternan, I leave the sum of £100 stg. [to the poor of the parish], and £10 for a gravestone."

II.—(106-116.)

Rentals of West Ferry and Monifieth, before 1654.

The following is copied from a dateless MS. at Panmure, which is docquetted " rentalls of monifeith," by Earl Patrick, who died in 1654 :—

Rentall of the west ferrie yearly q^{ll} it was in my Lord balmerino possesione & the which rentall is now agmeuted by the Laird of Powrie.

Item payed be David Rodger elder to my Lord balmerino for ane aiker of land with the teind yrof and ane house	020 : 00 . 0
Item payed be Johne Ramsay & Isobell Knight his spouse for ane aiker of land wt the teind yrof and ane house	020 : 00 . 0
Item be them ane singell toft	005 : 08 . 0
Item be Issobell Artchor for ane aiker of land with the teind yrof and ane hous	020 : 0 . 0
Item be Issobell Hay for ane aiker of land with the teind yrof and ane hous	020 : 00 . 0
Item be Henrie Knight for ane aiker of land with the teind yrof and ane house	020 : 00 . 0
Item be Issobell Charters widdow for ane aiker of land with the teind yrof and ane hous	020 : 00 . 0
Item be Grissell Smyth & her spouse for ane aiker of land with the teind yrof and ane house	020 : 00 . 0
Item be them ane singell toft	005 : 08 . 0
Item be Issobell Charters and some tyme be Johne Howathsone ane aiker with teind and ane house	020 : 00 . 0
Item be Thomas beatoun for ane singell toft	005 : 08 . 0
Item be David Rodger younger any double toft	010 : 16 . 0
Item be Thomas Andersone ane single toft	005 : 08 . 0
Item be Hindla Johnstoun ane singell toft	005 : 08 . 0
Item be William Knight ane double toft	010 : 16 . 0
Item be Hendrie Knight James Abbut George Sandersone and Thomas beatoun for the salmond fishing of the west crook belonging to the fferrie	040 : 00 . 0

Item be tennents in the west fferrie forsaids are obleidged to furnish to my Lords house all sorts of whyt fish in the sumer seasone at ten shilling for the hundreth and thretteiu shilling four penyes in winter and febry. haddoks at on lib. 6s 8d pr. hunder

148 : 12 : 0

Item payd for the maines of Balumbie ten chalder victuall viz. Item of bear Item of wheitt Item of meall Item of money rent thrie hundreth merks	200 : 00 . 0

Rentall of my Lord Balmerinos Lands in Anguse.
Silver dewties lib
Payed be the bonnet makers for the
walke milne . . . . . 022 : 00 : 0
Payed be John Airth for the Lavorik
Land . . . . 010 : 00 : 0
Payed be Margaret whyt for her house 001 : 06 : 8
Payed be David for his hous 006 : 00 : 0
Payed be Henrie Scott younger . 001 : 00 : 0
Payed be Pa: Jack for ane hous and a
yaird . . . . 001 : 10 : 0
Payed be James gaivane for his house
& chope . . . . . . 002 : 00 : 0
Payed be James Lovell for his hous &
chope . . . . 003 : 00 : 0
More payed be James gaivane for ane
house formerly possest be Margaret
Smairt . . . . 001 : 00 : 0
Payed be Mitchell guild . . . 003 : 00 : 0
Payed be Cristane Jack for the maill
of ane house . . . . . 001 : 00 : 0
Payed be Alexr Carmichell for his hous 007 : 06 : 8
Payed be Henry Whytlaw for ane
house . . . . 005 : 13 : 4
Payed be Pa: Key . . . 001 : 00 : 0
Payed be Alexr milne for ane house . 001 : 10 : 8
                          113 : 16 : 8

Payed be the laird of grange for his
fishings of gall and buddon fourtie
sevin pound . . . . . . 047 : 00 : 0

Besides the "Rentall of the West ferrie," and the "silver dewties" given above, the same paper contains a list of payments to Lord Balmerino in bear, meal, capons, hens, chickens, and geese. These were paid by five different tenants,—(1) Alex. Kid, for third part of Barnhill and Balmossie Mill; (2) Thomas Miller, for part of Barnhill; (3) David Patillock, who also paid 12 bolls wheat, for Balmossie; (4) John Bull, for Burnside; and (5) "the Bonnet Makers, for the Walke Milne."

III.—(121-2.)

Fothringham of Powrie.

Archibald Fothringham, son to the laird of Powrie, entered the service of the Chevalier, and became a Lieutenant in the Earl of Panmure's regiment. He was taken prisoner at Sheriffmuir, and carried thence to Stirling Castle, along with other rebel officers, on 14th Nov. 1715.

Fothringham appears to have been afterwards sent to Edinburgh, whence he made his escape, as thus graphically narrated by the Countess of Panmure, in a letter to her husband, dated 3d June 1716 :—" Last week Poorie made his escape from his Lodgings in ye Canongate, having gott liberty to come out of my Lord Winton's house to take a course of Physick, so he had onlie sentrys on him; and Borrowfield and Glenlyon has made their escape from Stirling."

It is probable that Thomas Fothringham, who petitioned the King to grant him a pardon for the unpremeditated murder at Florence, in Aug. 1737, of Dennis Wright or M'Intyro, was a member of the Powrie family. The cause of quarrel is not stated; but according to the copy of the Petition, now before us, it appears that both were "heated with drink" at the time, and that the affair began by "throwing of Bottles & Glasses; and afterwards (as the petition continues) your Petitioner having unluckily got into his hand a Hanger that was lying in the Room, I gave the said Dennis a wound in the Belly." Wright, who died within two days after the accident, emitted a declaration, dated 20th August, which contains this frank and highly honourable statement:—"I forgive him with all my heart, and I do by this my Declaration, put a stop, as far as in me lyes, to all prosecutions that may arise on account of this accident." (*Papers at Panmure.*)

IV.—(125.)

The Guthries of Westhall, c. 1682, *et sub.*

In Macfarlane's MSS. (vol. iii. pp. 275-9), in the Advocate's Library, Edinburgh, the words "Westhall, with a dovecot," are deleted in Ochterlony's Account of the Shire of Forfar, and "Mr John Guthrie of Westhall," substituted. Mr Guthrie had probably succeeded Mr Archibald Pearson in these lands (*supra*, p. 160.)

Mr John Guthrie had two daughters, Isobell and Margaret. The former was married first to Bishop Norie of Brechin (Marr. Contract in the possession of the Rev. Mr R. R. Lingard-Guthrie of Taybank, dated — April 1708), and next to David Gardyne of Lawton, who "fought under Prince Charles at Culloden" (*supra*, p. 323.) Her sister and co-heiress (misnamed *Ann* in Nisbet's Heraldry) became the second wife of Sir David Ogilvy of Barras, to whom she bore a family of sons and daughters. One of the daughters, Susanna, married Mr James Ogilvy, minister of Essie, who was also designed of Westhall. Mr Ogilvy, who died in 1802, was long survived by his widow; and their son, William Ogilvy, was also designed of Westhall.

Mr James Ogilvy of Westhall, and minister of Essie, was a son of Mr George Ogilvy, minister of Kirriemuir (Scott's Fasti), by his wife, —— Trail.

V.—(127, 294.)

Rev. Mr Rose, Episcopal Minister of Lochlee, 1723-58.

The interesting paper, printed below, regarding the Rev. Mr Rose, is from a copy by the Rev. Mr Moir, now of St John's Episcopal Church, Jedburgh, formerly Dean of the Diocese of Brechin. Mr Moir found the original among the papers of his maternal grandfather, the late Rev. Mr Jolly, and gave it to Mr Rose's great-grandson, Lord Strathnairn. I am obliged to the courtesy of the Right Rev. the Bishop of Brechin for the use of Mr Moir's copy of the paper:—

"A brief account how I have been supported in the Exercise of my Priestly Office since its commencement Barnabas-Day one Thousand, seven hundred & twenty-three—

I passed my Tryals in the Old Town of Aberdeen; Before The Right Revd. Bishop James Gadderar, The Very Revd. Dr George Garden, Doctor James Garden, Doctor George Middleton, The Revd. Mr William Murray, all living in the Old and New Town of Aberdeen, June ninth & tenth 1723, Upon St Barnabas-Day said year. Present, the above-mentioned Clergie and several Laity. I was ordained a Deacon by the Right Reverend Dr James Gadderar, Bishop of Aberdeen, in the House of Dr George Garden in New Aberdeen. I was consecrated a Priest in the same year upon St Bartholomew-Day by the above-mentioned Bishop in the House of the Rev. Mr William Murray in the Old Town of Aberdeen. In the said year Bp. Gadderar in his visitation course of his Diocese, during which time (ten weeks) I officiate for him in the Honble. the Viscount of Arbuthnott's Family, settled me optionally in Skeen Elder and Younger, their Familys for which cure I was to have had twenty lib: St. yearly. At which juncture of time I had an unanimous call given by Lochlee and Lethnott Parishes, which I preferred to the above-mentioned settlement. Lochlee Parishioners bound themselves to pay to me yearly fourteen lib: Ster. which they paid punctually for several years. Lethnott promised five lib: ten sh: St. yearly, qch they never pd me. The Collections of both Houses were applied by proper Managers and me to pay all publique things and satisfy the demands of the Poor—the Superplus was given to me.

"Since my entry to my present charge to 1745, I was privately supported by the Interest & Addresses of Lord Panmure & his Family, but nothing from their own Pocket. Some years before 1745 to 1747, I was grately supported by the Right Honble. Lady Sinclair, & from 1747, my wife & I have an annuity during Life five lib: St. From 1750, to his death, Sir Alexander Ramsay was my great Benefactor; & from 1747, I was much obliged by the good offices of John Erskine of Dun, Esq., and James Carnegy Arbuthnott of Balnamoon, Esq. for several years. And for the space of Thirty years, George Skene of that Ilk was my true Friend. My present Sallary, arisable from the good will of the after-mentioned Familys and places:— From Balnamoon Family, four Bolls of Meall, one Boll of Oats, & one of Bear. From Keithock a Boll of Malt. From Lady Smidyhill, half a guinea. From Lady Findowry two Bolls of Meall, besides altar collections. From Lady Ballbegno, & Miss Ogilvie three bolls of meall besides altar collections. From Lochlee House at Milltown yearly nine Pound St. From all the Retainers to Woodside from Caraldstone, Brechin, Lethnott & Navar Parishes Three Pound sterling. From Woodside Collections, altar & daily, deducing publick charges, seven lib: st. From Lochlee Collections deducing publick charges three lib. sterling. By prudent management & tinceous Application these Funds and my share of the Charity Fund may be continued with my Successor in office. The truth of their Presents is attested at Milltown in Glenesk, January the eleventh One Thousand seven hundred and fifty-eight by the Subscription of

(Signed)   "DAVID ROSE,
    Priest of the Scots Church."

VI.—(135.)

The Montgomeries in Knapp of Marykirk, c. 1630-7.

The following extract, from a dateless "Rentall of the Lordschip of Brechin," but of about the beginning of the 17th century, throws some additional light upon "the Montgomeries, in Knap" of Marykirk:—

"The Corns and Landis of haltoun occupat be Robert Montgumrie, payes yearly off Bear, ix chr. v bs.; Meall, xviij chr. x bs.; Linning clayth, viij. don. elnis; Caponis, xij; Swyne, j. It is to be rememberit the Landis off haltoun of auld, befor ye sett of ye last nynetene yeir tak, payed Tua dosone elnis Linning claythe."

The story of the wealth of the Montgomeries was probably mythical, for it appears that "Ion and George Montgowmries" were £226 8s 3d in arrears of rent for crop 1636-7. *(Original Rentals at Panmure.)*

VII.—(159.)

Funeral Expenses of Miss Arbuthnott of Findowrie, 1704.

The many curious items which are charged in the following account, in connection with the funeral of Miss Arbuthnott of Findowrie, in 1704, will form an interesting accompaniment to the inscription from her tombstone, printed on p. 159. The "accompt" is copied from the original among the Findowrie papers, kindly lent through the late Mr P. Chalmers of Aldbar, by the late Mr J. Carnegy-Arbuthnott of Balnamoon:—

Accompt of Elizabeth Arbuthnott's funeralls and others Disbursed by the Laird of Ballmadies—

	lib.	s.	d.
To 2 pounds cut Tabacco 2lb 5s, 2 Dozen pipes for late wake 4s	02	09	00
To expence for bringing home her grave cloaths	00	14	08
To 18 gallons of ale	14	08	00
To 6 pecks flower	04	00	00
To candle	01	14	08
To ½ peck Oates 5s, grass 2s, stable fee 2s, corks for the barrels 2s, 2 penny Loaves			
& 2 pints ale 6s, to the man for Scobing the barrels 1s, to Custome 4s, in all	01	02	00
To Expence for the horse that went with Doctor Arbuthnett, being a night In Town	00	08	00
To hens Chickens and geese	04	12	10
To expence in bringing them home	00	05	02
To Eggs	00	04	08
To Double tree and nails, and expence in bringing them home	02	07	10
To Expence in bringing home necessaries for ffindaurie and his sert	00	04	02
To 5 Serts for carrying the buriall Letters	03	00	00
To the serts expence for going to Dundee to bring home five hunder merks for defraying the funerall expence	00	07	00
To carrier, and expence for bringing home canarie	00	13	06
To expence to the sert who went through the countrey seeking doves	00	04	00
To 9 Duckes at 4s per peire	01	16	00
To a hen and eggs	00	06	00
To a Sert for going to Kerrimuir for more fowls, & for a mure fowl	00	07	00
To two Sheep	06	13	04
To Elizabeth Arbuthnett's grave Cloaths, as per acct and receipt	27	13	06
To 2 bolls Meal	12	00	00
To flower bread	00	16	06
To expences for horse & serts for bringing home the plumb Cakes, and silver worke from Montrose	00	12	00
To an pair mourning Shoes	02	06	00
To an ell black ribbans	00	16	00
To James Guthrie for Capers, Cordendron orange pill, & Cinnamon, as per accompt	06	08	00
To sweat meats, as per accompt	07	11	10
To almonds 12s, an side of beef 9 lib, mourning greath 6 lib, in all	15	12	00
To an pair buckles 7s, 6 pound candle 1 lib 6s, 8 dales 4 lib 16s	06	09	00
To express for Evlick	00	16	00
To custome for the carts 12s, To corn and expence for men and horses 10s, 2 bungs 10s, in all	01	12	00
To 2 pecks flower	01	08	00
To spice	00	03	04
To 2 pints ale drunken by the carter	00	04	00
To misscompted by the Bearer in paying the above accompts	00	05	10
To an Lamb	01	14	00
To Ardovie's man for bringing doves	00	04	00
To Edzells servt. that kill'd the deer, and			

for ale to them	01 06 08
To expence to the sert who went with Letters to the Mearns, ffingzean, and Edzell	00 15 04
To Andrew Ogilvie for his service	01 00 00
To eggs	00 02 06
To 12 gallons of ale and an half at the Late wake and buriall, from ffrancis Scott	08 06 08
To choppin aqua vitæ	00 13 04
To an boll Oates for gentlemens horses at the buriall	06 06 08
To James Arbuthnett for the coffin, per discharge	66 13 04
To the Master household 5 Dollars, To the Cook 4 Dollars, The Carter 1½ Dollar, in all	30 09 00
To money distributed among the poor	10 00 00
To bailif Ogilvie and Mr Dempster, for brandie, plumb cakes, bisket, &c., per two accompts	49 11 06
To expence to the sert that returned the Silver worke	00 06 06
To 2 skins for breeches to ffindowrie's sert	01 04 00
To 1 pair mourning gloves 12s, To James Mitchell for making three suite of Cloathes, &c., 8 lib 2s, in all	08 14 00
To Andrew Ogilvie	00 10 00
To Drink money to sert 14s, to a . . . . . : in all	07 00 00
To the mortcloath, and making the grave	03 08 00
To Alexander Gibson for serving the Cook three days	00 09 00
Summa Totalis	328 00 04

Carved Stones at Balmadies.

In addition to our remarks upon the parish of Rescobie (*supra*, pp. 155-61), the subjoined notices of some carved stones at Balmadies may be interesting.

Two of the fragments are preserved in the farmsteading. One consists of an old corbel, and the other presents the date of 1603. In the north pillar of the west gate of the mansion-house, there is also a stone with ornamental work upon it, and these traces of a legend :—

. . . . . DER . . . IRTVS . SIDIMET.

A cluster of slabs, of various dates, is built into the south-east gable of the stables of the mansion-house. Two of these had been skew-put stones, and both bear shields. One is initialed I. O., the other A. B., and they are respectively charged with the coats of Ochterlony and Beaton of Balfour. These appear to be the oldest carvings about the place. Probably both belong to the last half of the 16th century, and may refer to the time when the property was held by the old race of Ochterlonys, to whom it belonged from about 1480 (*Mem. kindly communicated by the late Mr Pierson of Guynd.*)

It was in 1624 (*supra*, p. 159) that Alex. Pierson and his wife Isobel Beatoun acquired Auchtermergities or Balmadies; and it seems probable that, although of a prior date, the uppermost of the shields above referred to, which is initialed A.P. I.B., dated 1613, and charged with the Pierson and Beaton arms, may have been brought from some other of the Pierson properties, and placed at Balmadies by them.

Mr and Mrs Pierson (the latter of whom died before 1641) had a son and successor, also called James, and it was probably he who had the following admirable inscription carved in stone, which has luckily been preserved to us, and which, no doubt, had graced either the front of the house, or the chimney-piece of the hall of the family mansion. It is in raised Roman captals, and runs thus :—

O . DOMVS . HOSTEM . ARCE . HOSPITIB
PATEAS . ET . AMICIS ⋅⋅⋅(((⋅)))⋅⋅⋅—⋅⋅⋅(((⋅))) ⋅⋅
SIC . NVNQVAM . DISPAR . TE
TENEAT   DOMVS   1657.

[My foes keep out, O house, to friends and strangers open be;
And may such ever be the mind of him that holdeth thee.]

A lintel, below the inscribed tablet, presents these initials :—

        M   D
  ⊙ A P ⊙ M M ⊙

The above refers to Mr Alexander Pierson and his wife, Dame Margaret Murray, whose gravestones are at Chapel-yard. They died respectively in 1700, and 1694 (*supra*, p. 159.)

Their son, James Pierson, who married a daughter of Lindsay of Evelick, and died in 1745 (*supra*, pp. 159-60), executed, in 1739, a disposition of his whole estate (Balmadies, Lochlands, Barngreen, Berryfold, and Smiddycroft) in favor of his second son, Robert, advocate, with certain reservations in favor of his eldest son, John, and his youngest son, Thomas (*MS. Mem.*) John died unmarried in 1763; and Robert Pierson, advocate, who then came into absolute possession of the property, married Anne, daughter of Fraser of Kirkton and Hospitalfield. He was grandfather of the late Mr Jas. A. Pierson, who succeeded to Guynd on the death of his maternal uncle (*supra*, p. 247.)

[Since the preceding sheet was printed off, I have seen a deed which shows that Piersons were designed of Balmadies in 1614.]

The present mansion-house of Balmadies was built about 1820, when the property belonged to the late Mr Henry Stephens, the well-known author of "The Book of the Farm."

An old door-lintel, built over the back entrance to the manse of Rescobie, is thus inscribed:—

M . IO . SPALDINVS.

B . A . 1602.

—The above has reference to Mr John Spalding, minister of Rescobie, and his wife Barbara Auchenleck. One of Mr Spalding's sons became his colleague, and predeceased his father (Scott's Fasti.) Mr Lindsay (*supra*, p. 156) probably succeeded Mr Spalding.

VIII.—(164.)

The Lands of Balfour, in Kingoldrum, 1539.

"The first ffew chartour of Balfour, grantit be David Beton, Cardinal and Abbot of Aberbrothick," was made in favour of James Ogilvie of Cookstone, Marjorie Durie his spouse, and their heirs and assignes, whom failing to the nearest lawful heirs and assignes of the said James Ogilvie whatsomever.

The deed (of which the following is an abridged translation) conveys to Ogilvie and his heirs "all and sundrie the lands of Balfour, Kyrkton, Ascrawys Ower and Neyther, the mill of Kingoldrum, with the astricted multures, lie multer sheif, ring bear, of all the baronie of Kingoldrum, viz. the lands and towns of Easterpersy, Mydpersy alias Balgruy, Westerpersy, Ascrewys Ower & Nethyr, Kirktone, Balfour, Balduwy, Kinclune, Meklecany, Litlecany, Aucheroch, with their tofts, crofts, outsetts, pertinents, and cottages." These lands are described as lying within the barony of Kingoldrum, regality of Aberbrothock, and sheriffdom of Forfar, and were to be held in feufarm of the said David and his successors in the Abbacy of Arbroath, for an annual payment of £42 6s in money, with certain cane payments, or an augmentation of the rental to the extent of £44 payable at Whitsunday and Martinmas, together with three suits yearly to three chief courts of the regality of Aberbrothock. Ogilvie's heirs were bound to double the feu-duty the first year of entry, but neither he nor they had power to dispone any portion of the property "without ye sd David and his successors speciall licence had and obtanit yreto."

The original charter of Balfour, which is dated at the Monastery of Arbroath, 20th February 1539, is a deed of more than ordinary interest. It contains (as printed below) the signature of Cardinal Beaton, also those of twenty-four members of the Convent of Arbroath. Although differently spelled, the names marked thus †, occur in the Colliston charter of 1544 (Reg. Nig. de Aberb., Appendix; *v.* also pp. 316, 410, 439.):—

† DAUID CARDLIS STI ANDRE.

Come'datar' de ab'broahok.

Johes b'ad sup'spor manu ppio

Johne Wardlau ad id	† David scot
† Dauid craylle ad id	† Johanes Logy
† Dauid teynder	dauid Kay
Nycholas purwys	† Johannes peirson
aly'r gyb	† Valter' Baldeuy
† Johannes Renie	Patri' Mray
Thoma' stott	† Wilelm' craund
† Thoma' ruydfurd	Alanus mrttyun
Johis gyll	Thomas saidlare
Robert' Dauidson	Robt' d'uard
† Andreas barde	Thomas Nych
	† Willmis wedd'burn

The charter of Balfour, and several later deeds, also an Inventory of titles down to 1612, are at Panmure.

It would appear from these, that James Ogilvy of Cookstone, whose original feu-charter was confirmed both by the King and the Pope, died before 18th November 1588, as of that date, John, Commendator of Aberbrothoc, granted a precept for infefting "James Ogilvie of Balfour as heir to wmqll Mr James Ogilvie of Balfour, of all and sundrie ye sds lands," &c.

It is also proved that during the lifetime of his father, and on 1st October 1558, Mr James Ogilvie and Margaret Steuart his spouse, had seisin of "the fourt part of ye said lands of Kinclwne, with ye teind sheiwes yrof includit, whilk wer never in use to be seperat from ye stock, with all and sundrie yr pertinents, annexis, connexis, dependentijs," &c. These were to be held of the Abbey for certain yearly payments in money and kind, and for giving suit to the three head courts, or to such other courts of the regality, as the fenar shall be cited to attend, "to be holden at Cairdenkouneth [Cairneonan] as use is, or any place in yr tolbuith w'in ye burgh of Aberbrothock yearly."

The fourth part of the lands of Kinclune, which was disponed by Ogilvy in the year 1618, appears to have been the first portion of the property which was sold by the Ogilvies, who long continued to hold the estate. In a memorandum of 9th November 1698, it is said that "yis put ballfour his Grandfather . . . is yett living." Balfour came to the Fothringhams through a female descendant of the Ogilvys, towards the middle of last century. It was sold by the Fothringhams about 18—, since which time it has frequently changed hands.

IX.—(177.)
Conn of Auchry, 1644.

The following inscription referred to *(supra* p. 177), is copied from *Archæologia Scotica* (iv. 376), where it is stated that the monument is surmounted by a bust of George Conæus, and a shield charged with his family arms. It appears from the inscription that the Conns of Auchry were a branch of the Celtic sept of Macdonald :—

"D.O.M. GEORGIO CONÆO, Scoto Aberdonensi, Patricij Domini de Achry ex antiqua Magdonaldi familia et Isabella Chyn ex baronibus de Esselmont filio, qui inter conterraneos eloquentia et doctrina Duaci et Romæ haustis, librisque editis immortalitati se commendavit ; prudentia vero et agendi dexteritate summorum principum, ac præsertim Cardinalis Barberini, in cuius aula diu vixit, cuiusque legationes Gallicanam Hispanicamque secutus est, benevolentiam promeruit ; quem Urbanus VIII. Pontifex, ingeniorum maximus existimator, quanti fecerit, et ad Magnæ Britanniæ Reginam Henrichettam in Catholicorum solamen allegatione, et ingenti in ipsius morte, quae ne in editiori loco positus clarius elucesceret retuerat, moerore testatus est. Obiit die x Januarii an. M.DCXL. in aedibus Vicecancellarii, qui amico funus amplissimum in hac basilica faciendum curavit, et Monumentum posuit.

φῶς ἐν τῇ σκοτίᾳ φαίνει, καὶ ἡ σκοτία αὐτὸ οὐ κατέλαβεν."

[Sacred to the memory of GEORGE CONÆUS, a native of Aberdeen in Scotland, son of Patrick, Laird of Achry (a scion of the ancient family of Macdonald), and Isabella Chyn, of the baronial house of Esselmont, who immortalised himself among his countrymen by his eloquence and learning acquired at Douay and Rome, and also by his published works ; who, by his prudence and skill in the conduct of affairs, won the goodwill of powerful princes, and, in particular, that of Cardinal Barberini, at whose court he long lived, and to whose embassies to France and Spain he was attached ; and his high esteem for whom Pope Urban VIII., an admirable judge of ability, testified both by sending him on a mission for the comfort of the Catholics to Henrietta, Queen of Great Britain, and by his profound grief at his death, which had prevented him from shining with greater lustre in a more elevated position. He died 10th January, 1640, in the house of the Vice-Chancellor, who caused a most sumptuous funeral to be given to his friend, in this church, and erected this Monument to his memory. The light shineth in darkness, and darkness comprehended it not.]

—Maidment, in his Catalogue of Scottish Writers, gives a list of five different works by Conn, among which is a Life of Mary Queen of Scots, published at Rome in 1625.

X.—(185.)
The first Earl of Strathmore.

Reference has been made to the part which the third Earl of Kinghorne, afterwards the first Earl of Strathmore, took in the Civil Wars, also some extracts are given on page 185, from his memorandum book, when he visited Paris in 1683. His Lordship was a grandson of the first Earl of Panmure, and being left a minor, his uncle, the second Earl of Panmure, was appointed one of his guardians and trustees. The young Earl was educated at St Andrews, and, through the courtesy of the late Earl of Dalhousie, who kindly allowed the following interesting "Inventor" to be published, a glimpse is got into the Scotch College life of the nobility of the period, in so far at least as relates to the sort of articles with which their chambers were furnished :

APPENDIX. 387

An Inventor of furnishing in My Lord Kingorn his chamber in the Colladag of St Androus 22 of November 1655, wher of som cam from Glames the Last of October 1654. To witt

Item three imbroudred panels
Item tuo imbroudred broun velvet coortaines
Item an peice of rid velvet imbroudred with my Lord Kingorn his armes and name plaised above the chimney
Item ane turkie carpet
Item tuo velvet cusshens
Item tuo turkie worke cushens which cam wnlynd and wnstuffed
Item four pair of sprainged bed plaids
Item five peaces of arras hangings
  Thes things foullouing wer sent from Glames for furnishing My Lord Kingorn his chamber in the colladge at St Androus the Last of October 1655, to witt
Item three feather beads
Item three boulsters
Item four pair of sprainged bedpleds
Item sex paire of course bedplyds
Item a peice of strypt hangings
Item tuo ..... cussens
Item five codds
Item three soued coverings
  All thes Inventored and taken in costodie at St Androus 22 of November 1655 by me Robert Maule   ROBERT MAULE.

Received the 23 of Januar 1656. Six pair of Sheets. Thrie cloathed chaires. Thrie lathered chaires. Two chamber pots. Thrie vhyte Iron Candle Sticks. Six codvarees vith a 7 torn & rent Item 6 febr. 3 codvarces old and two dornck servits as they ar.

I Robert Maul testifyes yt I receaved al these things by my subscription at St Andrews the 4 of March 1656   R. MAULE.

In addition to the above interesting "Inventor," the following "particulars of furnishings bought for the carll of Kingorno" for the winter of 1655, as well as for his "servant," caunot fail to form an acceptable addition to the information we already possess of the Domestic Life of the 17th century:—

  Ane note of some necessare things for my Lord Kingorn for winter cloathes
Item five elle and a haffe of Londone cloath at sex quarters broad to be a cloacke a suite and a close-bodied coate for my Lord Kingorne
Item ane hat and hat band for my Lord Kingorne
Item for ane elle of stenting

Item three elles of small tuedling to lynne the breeches and doublet
Item ane elle and ane haffe of playding to be under lyning to the breeches
Item a paire of grait pockats and ane paire of lesser
Item three elles of stringing to the knees of the breeches
Item a dozene of glaspes and eyes
Item a coller and tua bellie peeces
Item four elles of wattings
Item halfe ane elle of lupping
Item five dozen of small buttens to the doublet and breeches
Item sex dozen of grater buttens to the coate
Item twa dozen and ane halfe of grait buttens to the cloacke
Item ane dozen and ane halfe of smaller buttens to the cloack necke
Item a long tailled butten for the cloack necke
Item ane ounce of silke wherof ten drope of round silke for the butten holes and sex drope of small silke for shewing the seemes
Item for halfe ane elle of sairg or a quarter and a halfe of taffatie to face the cloack and suite
Item tua paire of gray stockings
Item tua paire of gloves
Item tua paire of shooes
Item   elles of rebans to trime the suite and hat, and for the shooes.

  A note of necessaries for Robert Maule servant to my Lord Kingorne
Item three elle and three quarters of Yorkshyre cloath to be a suite and a closse bodied coat of darke couler suting with the cloathe he gat the last yere
Item ane elle of stenting
Item three ells and halffe of tuedling for lyning to the doublet and breeches
Item ane paire of grait pockats and ane paire of lesser
Item three elles of stringing to the knees of the breeches
Item ane dozen of glaspes and eyes
Item halfe ane elle and halfe ane quarter of loupping
Item a coller and tua bellie peices
Item three elle and a halfo of wattings
Item five dozen of buttens to the sute
Item sex dozen of graiter to the coate
Item tuelve drape of silke where of eight drape of round silke to the buttens holes
Item ane hatt and hat band
Item a paire of gray stockings
Item a paire of gloves
Item a paire of shooes

Item halfe a dozen of bands and cuffes
Item halfe a dozen of handcurchars
Item shirts foure
Item   elles of ribans to trime the sute

As the above "Inventor" shows the equipment of the Earl of Kinghorn (afterwards Strathmore) when a student at St Andrews in 1635, and his personal outfit for the winter of the same year, the following letter, from the Findowrie papers, exhibits the Earl in the character of a true soldier and a gentleman. I am indebted to the late Mr James Carnegy-Arbuthnott of Balnamoon, through the late Mr Patrick Chalmers of Aldbar, for the use of the letter. It is addressed, "(for The laird of ffindourie, Yōr.," and is as follows :—

At the Incampment of the Angus regiment
18th June 1685 in Strathblain

Sir

As I have alwayes made it my bussenes to adjust the severall Comands of my Militia regiment with persones fitt for it, It hes bein lykwayis my endevour so to suport the credit of the Service, that few comes into any Comand therein but such as (modestly speaking) are als good as those who were befor; I have at present a cleir vaikancie by A Shamfull desertion (which I scorn to persew); this is known to the Lords of the Secret Comittee at Edr. als weall as to the genell persoues in the field. Yow ar the persone who is my choyse, And I assure yow its most acceptable to the whole Gentlemen my Companions in the Comand of the regt. Your translane is easie from A ruyter of horse to the Comand of that Companie which was Cookstouns, formall Goodnights. . . . . . So I intreat Yow come downe imediatlie now before wee march, which is impatiantlie expected by

Your werie reall freind & Sert,
STRATHMORE.

XI.—(225.)
The Erskines of Dun.

I found the original of the letter printed below, among the Panmure Papers. It was used as a cover to a MS. in the handwriting of the gentleman to whom it was addressed, and docquetted thus :— "1633—a note of things bought for my self withe prycis."

Besides being curious in itself, the letter is interesting, in so far as it bears to have been written by the survivor of the "two zonng boyis, to whom poison was administered by their paternal uncle and aunts at Montrose, in 1610 (*supra*, p. 225.)

The writer of the letter succeeded his uncle's son as laird of Dun in 1621. On 23d December 1631, he had a charter of the barony of Dun, &c., in favour of himself and his eldest lawful son, John Erskine, by his wife, Margaret Lindsay, daughter of the first Lord Spynie. He is described as *Sir Alexander Erskine of Dun*, in a charter of the lands of Newbigging, 26th July 1637 (Wodrow's Collection (Mait. Club), vol. i. 414.) Sir Alexander may have been knighted through the influence of his "Louing Wukill, the Laird of Panmure, one of the Kingis Majesties bced chamber," to whom the letter, which is a beautiful specimen of caligraphy, is addressed:—

Right Honbl and Louing Wukill,

I hope my lest letteris be come to zour handis, long befor this tyme. I knowe it wer onnecessarie to me to renoue my request to zou in that bussines for I assure my sclff ze will be carefull of zat in regard it may tend so far to my waill. Sr the Laird of bonitoune hes spoking to me of ane purpose wich he tellis me he proponnit to zou him selff at zour lest being in Scotland. I find him werie willing and desyrous to bestoue his eldest sone wpon zour dauchter. Sr he hes desyrat me to wrett to zou to lett zou knowe that he will be willing to remitt the haill conditions to zour selff, what ze will be plesit to give wt zour dauchter, or what coniunct fie sall be giwine to zour dauchter, and at zour sight to give his sone ane fie of his Estait. Sr I will assure zou on thing ther is not ane better disposit zouth in this kingdome nor zoung bonitoune is, give ze mynd to bestone zour dauchter in this kingdome it is not ane offer to be neglectit, housoeuer Sr, ze are oblist to the laird of bonitouns respect to zou and zour hous, ther is to my knowlege the occasions of good fortunes offerit to him, but he hes ane grytter mynd to dell wt zou then wt anie qhuatsumeuer, and will not enter in termes wt anie till he haue ane answer from zou, wretting to me. Sr giff ze mynd to dell, it will be fittest that the matter continen till zour awne cumming to Scotland. Sr according as ze in joyne me be zour letter I sall most carefullie and secretly obey zour desyr. I heir the Kingis maiestie is to be in Scotland this zeir, Sr iff ze think it fitting that I prouyd my selff to repaire to Edinborie at that tyme to attend his maiestie's seruice, and to haue the honor to kisse his M/ handis, I will dou it? wtherwayes not. I knowe ther is sundrie places of seruice wich belongis Scottismane to dou to his Majestie during the tyme of his stay heir, iff ther be anie of them ze think fitting for me, or may be ane occasione of his maiestie's fauor and cuntinance heirefter, I knoue it wald cost zou but ane word, Mr George flegger cane informe zou of the haill places that will be weakand, or is to be giwine to anie. Therfor Sr, I will most humblie intreat zou to mak chose of soume place, for I hope, god willing, to discharge my self of anie thing In that kynd as weill as wtheris. Sr I hope ze will excuse my rudnes, and homlie wretting to zou, for iff I reposit not more in zou nor into anie wther, and haid grytter confidence of zour fauor to me, I wald be loth to troubill zou. I assure my selff ze will not tak exceptions that I troubill zou wt requestis in this kynd, for ze knaue, Sr, I haue not entrese to anie hes suche pouer. So wissing zou all happines, I rest and sall euer remane,

                    Zour Louing Nepheu to serve zou,
                                    A. Erskine off Dun.
Dune the 8
of februarij.

The laird of Dun's pleading with his uncle, in behalf of "zoung bonitoune," appears to have been unsuccessful. His uncle's two daughters both married Earls. The oldest became the wife of the second Earl of Northesk, to whom she bore the third Earl, and other children. The second daughter married first the Earl of Kinghorn, and secondly the Earl of Linlithgow. By these two marriages she was the mother of three Earls, vizt. :—The Earl of Kinghorn (whose outfit as a student at the College of St Andrews, in 1655, is printed on pp. 386-7), the Earl of Linlithgow, and his brother, the Earl of Calendar.

Sir Alexander Erskine of Dun died in 1655, and having been predeceased by his eldest son, Sir John Erskine, he was succeeded by his younger son David, by a second marriage. David Erskine of Dun married a daughter of Lumsden of Innergelly, in Fife, and was father of Lord Dun (great-grandfather of the Marchioness of Ailsa, *supra*, p. 221), of Alexander, merchant in Montrose, ancestor of the Erskines of Balhall, and other children (Wodrow's Collections.)

XII.—(296.)

"*Testificatione anent the waisting of the parioche of Navar*," 1645-6.

The "Testificatione," printed below, has reference to the ravages which were committed in Navar by the soldiers of the Marquis of Montrose in 1645, at which time they also burned the kirk of Lochlee, and harried adjoining districts (*v.* Land of the Lindsays). The minister, who was son-in-law to Guthrie of Pitforthie, was previously Preceptor of the *Maison Dieu* of Brechin. He was translated from Navar to the church of Brechin about 1650.

We wndersubscryevand, Testifies to the honoll estaites of parliament, thair comitties and vtheris haveand thair power, That the parochine of Navar, belonging to the laird of Paunmuire, Lyand wtin the shrefdome of fforfar, Is totallie waisted by the creweltie of the malitious enemie of this kirke and kingdome, qrby, to our certaine knowledge, he hes bein frustrat of his rent thir tua yeires bygane, In regaird the saidis landis ar in a great pairt unprofitable and lying waist, And suche as ar labored ar wnable to pay any dewtie, The tenents not being able to labor aboue to serve thair owen necessaties. And sicke lyke, the minister of the said parioche Is constrained, becaus of the freqnent Incursions of the broken and barbarous heighelanders, To retire himself wt his whole famelie to the toun of Brechine, They haveing befoir his removeall, plunderit his hous, taken away and destroyed his haill cornes, and victuall, and buikes. This we testifie to be of veratie be thir pntis, subscryvit wt our handis as followes, at Brechine, the Tenth day of Januar 1646.

Mr L. Skinner,	G. Symmer of Balzordie
minister at Navar	J. Guthrie of patforthie
	Jhn Symer elder of brathie
	Johne Symmer feir of Brathinche
	Dauid Levingstoun of dilapie
	George Straton off athdouie

In Memoriam:

The subjoined Inscription from "Maule's Cairn" in Glenesk is here printed as a slight but grateful tribute to the memory of the late EARL OF DALHOUSIE, who died at Brechin Castle on 6th July, 1874.

MAULE'S CAIRN.

ERECTED A.D. 1866,

BY

FOX EARL OF DALHOUSIE, K.T., G.C.B.,

IN MEMORY OF

The Right Hon. MONTAGU, Baroness Panmure;
The Hon. Col. LAUDERDALE MAULE, M.P.;
The Hon. WILLIAM MAULE-MAULE;
The Lady PATRICIA YOUNG;
The Lady RAMSAY;
The Lady MARY HAMILTON;
The Lady GEORGINA DOWBIGGIN;

AND ALSO OF

Lady RAMSAY MACDONALD;
The Lady CHRISTIAN MAULE,
and HIMSELF,

When it shall please God to call them hence.

GENERAL INDEX.

A BROTHER LIES 173
A deep and rapid 280
A godly man 205
A humorous 233
A pearl precious 296
A watchman 153
Abbé of Brechin 130
Abel, Geo. 258
Aberchirder. (v. MARNOCH)
Abercrombie, Jas. 376
ABERDOUR (Deer) 55-9
ABERLEMNO 7-10
Abernethy of Rothiemay 29
Abernethy-Gordon, Benj. 307
Addison,G. 192,Janet,Jean,223-4
Adam and Eve 253
Adam, Wm. 182, 312
Adams, Dr Francis (poet) 6 ; 189
Adamson, Janet 9
Ætatem ornavit 257
After the cares 317
Ah ! early lost ! 202
Ailsa, Marquis of 221 ; 389
Ainslie, Arch. 347
AIRLIE 162-3
Aitken, Jean 120
"Ajax's Speech" 19
"Albert Cairn" 216
ALDBAR 10-11
Alexander, John 265, Mary 97, Robert 34
ALFORD 116-121, 339
Alison, James 138
All men live 112
All shall die 39
All time relations 280
All who pass by 210
All ye in life's gay morn 47
All you that stop 349
Allan, Alex. 343, Barbara, Geo. 286, Jas. 287, Joseph 228, Wm. 248
Allardyce castle 27
—— of A. 211, Dunottar 222
—— Ann 379, Mary 211, 375, Wm. 8, 371
Altho' by nature 29

Altho' this tomb 285
Among the earth 205
Among the rest 203
An honest man 47
Ananias lands 237, 369
Annabella, Queen 72
Annand of Auchterellon 59
—— Wm. 12
And he come who is 77
And is she gone 97
And must this body die? 197
Anderson of Candacraig 152
—— Arch. 216, Alex. 41, 112, 313, Geo. 9, 14, 187, John 14, Thos. 58
Ane epitaph 34
"Angel's Whisper" 112
Angus, Descrip. of. (v. Edward)
Aodh or Eth, King 179
Arbroath Couvent 385
Arbuthnott of Findowrie, Miss 159, (funeral expenses) 383
—— Abbot 100, Jas. 97, Dr John 174, 236, Robert 24
Andes, Malcolm (hist.) 209
Arklay, John 370, Thos. 369
Arkley of Dunniuald 124
Arnhall Chapelton 252
Arnott, Jas. 64
Arsludie or Ashludie 112
As a mark of respect 101
As our shorter day 260
As pensively you pass 102
Auchendoun castle 334
Auchleck, H. 30, John 54
AUCHTERLESS 206-9, 339
Auchterlony. (v. Ochterlony)
Austin, Wm. 251

BACKBOTH CHAPEL 35, 249
Baden, Alex. 140
Badenach-Nicolson 91 ; 363
Badenoch of Whiteriggs 64
Badenoch, Wm. 117
Bain, Geo. 187
Baird of Auchmedden 56, 329, Ury 80

Balbirnie, Helen 183, Jas. 248
Balbithan 307
Baldarroch witch 7
Balfour 164, feu-charter of (1539) 385
—— Janet 309
Balgavies 9
Balinhard. (v. Carnegie)
Balishan of Panmure 354
Ballantyne, John 75
Ballindalloch 147, 210
Ballumbie 121
Balmadies 384
Balmoral 216-17
Balneillie 224
Balvenie castle 327, 333
BANCHORY-TERNAN 1-7 ; schools 379
Bannatyne, G. (poet) 141
Bannerman of Elsick 55, 287
Barron, John 332
Barclay of Caldham, Johnston, 134, Mathers 41, Towie 45, 86, Ury 80-4, 211, 354
—— Adam 339, Dr Geo. 208, John 253, (poet) 312, Robt. 243
Baron, And. 372
Baromdon, John 15
Bass of Inch 22, Inverurie 180
Baxter of Kincaldrum 197
Be mindful 154
Before mankind 336
Below this monument 184
Below this stone 163
Below this tomb 280
Beneath this stone 166
Beattie, Alex. 292, Elizabeth 320, Francis 342, George (poet) 39, Dr Jas. (poet) 65, 292, 293, Jas. 21
Beaton of Melgund 10
—— charter by Cardinal 385
Bell, Euph. 9, Rev. Dr Pat. 249, Thos. (comedian) 73
Bells, old church 1, 163, 268, 279, 308, 326, 335

GENERAL INDEX.

Bell founders—
Barclay, R. 221, D. 308, Burgerhuys, John 89, 190, Michael 192, 235, 280, Dickson & Co. 250, Easton, John 308, Ehem, And. 155, Gely, Albert 20, Jansen, Peter 207, Kilgour, F. 175, Maxwell, Robt. 8, Mears, Thos. 23, 63, Mowat, John 27, 43, 104, 117, 165, 226, 359, Orminston, Wm. 246, Ouderogge, C. 296, Ser, Jacob 108, Stens, Peter 1, 169
BELLIE 11-16
Bellie, Jas. 309, Pat. 289
Bennet, John 197
BENVIE 192-3, 340
Bequest, curious 40
Bereans 137, 253
Bergstrome, P. O. 124
BERVIE 23-7, 341
Besler (Batchelor) Jas. 202
Boyn, Bp. 326, 333
Bidie, Wm. 188
Binny of Fearn 105, 268
Bisset of Lessendrum 257-8, Lovat 276
—— John 309, 370
Bishops, R. Cath. 278
Black, Anna 73, Jas. 44, 295, 311, John, Isabella 355
Blackhall lands 30
Blair, John 182, Wm. 139
Blair-Imrie of Lunan 241-2, 366
Blelack Howff 281
Blest is the man 268
BOG WELL 51
Bonesetter 38, 373
Both in one grave 204
Bowick, Jas. (poet) 351
Bowman, Jas. 60, 112, Geo. 348
BOYNDIE 199-201
Boyne castle 200
Breadalbane, Marquis of 243
BRAEMAR 217-20
Brewster, Wm. 61
Brich (artist) 364
Bride, a lost 44
Bridges—
Alford 121, Auchmull 311, Banchory on Dee 7, Bervie 26, (charter regarding, 1474) 342, Brawny 131, Buxburn 285, Carron 53, Cluny 220, Courtford 48, 270, Craigellachie 301, Crathes 106, Cruden 317, Don 180, Dreip 31, Dun 225, Dye 31, Ellon 62, Feugh 7, 31, Fochabers 16, Gannochy 253, 295, 311, Glenoffock 131, Invercauld 220, Isla 103, 168, Keith 168, Kincardine o' Neil 240, Lady Bridge 31, Leuchars 19, Mark 131, Marnoch 234, Marykirk 138, Newe 155, Noran 48, Northwater (Lower) 43, (Upper) 213, Park 106, Pitmuies 35, Pooldhulie 155, Pouskeenie 131, Pow 95, Shiach 106, Stonyford 297, Tarf, Turret 131, Vinny 35, Wellford 48, 270, Westwater 297, 311
Bridgeton (St Cyrus) 40
Brodie of Idvies 35
Brokie, Alex. 52
Brougham, Lord 119
BROUGHTY FERRY 115-6, 370, old rentals 280
Brown, David 41, Jas. 57, Jas., John 205, 286, Matthew 240, Wm. 365
Bruce-Gardyne. (v. Gardyne)
Bruce of Innerquhomery 95-6
—— Barbara 119, Jas. 58, 182, 310, Richard (vicar) 335-8
Bryce, Pat. 247
Buchan of Auchmacoy 197-8
—— Mrs (imposter) 201, Wm. 179
Buchanan, John 212
Buckie, town of 276-7
Bucklitsch, J. H. J. 302
Budworth, John 183
Buick, John 204, Wm. 203
Buist, John, and family 47
Bunyan, Jas. 360
Burgon, R. Cowan 25
Burley, Jas. 346
Burn, Jas. 224
Burnes of Montrose 135
Burns, Wm. 225
Burnett of Leys 1, 2, Monboddo 63, 356-7, Sauchen 4
—— Alex. 259, Bishop 2, 303, Jas. 228, Robt. 286, Wm. 41
By honest industry 236
Byers of Tonley 61
Byres, Jas. 199
Byron, Lord 220

CAIDYOW, Walter 17
Caird, David 248
Cairn Greg 115
Cairn-o'-Mounth 31, 256
Cameron, Major 330
Campbell of Blackhall 30
—— Agnes 41, Archibald 101, David 37, John 73
Candieglerach, 1
Candow, Janet 364
Cant, And. 31
Cantlie, Alex. 331
Cardean, David 162
CARESTON, 259-60

CARMYLLIE 246-9, 341
Carnegie, lands of 247, 249
—— Earls of Northesk 343-4, 321, 326; Earls of Southesk 93-4, 238, 249, 253, 269; of Balmachie 295, Craigo 90, 209-10, 323, Finhaven 337, Glen 182, Redhall 325
—— Chas. 94, Robt. 312
Carny, Alex. 245-6, Jas. 228
Carracci (artist) 277
Carment, Jas. 276
Cattach, Janet 331
Cattanach, Geo. 266, John 164, Margt. 187, Pat. 348
CATERLINE 173-4
Cathrow, Alex. 182
Causey Mounth 84
Chalmers of Aldbar 8, 10, Christian 339, Elspet 77, Geo. (hist.) 16, LL.D. 348, 258, Hugh 233, Jas. 88, 184, John 44, 371, Mary 298, Wm. 208, 227
"Chappell of Grace" 27
CHAPELYARD (Rescobie) 159-61
CHAPEL-HOUSE (Abdnsh.) 264
Charles X. of France 168
Charmers 103
Cheyne of Esselmont 59, 178
Child, wife 196
Christie, Geo. 234, Jean, Duchess 12, John 248, Wm. 252, 376
Christian, Rose 345
Clark or Clerk, Jas. 259, Geo. 57, John 360, Wm. 24
"Clavies" 149
Clayhills of Invergowrie 193
Cloch-na-ben 31
CLOVA (Abdnsh.) 260-1
Cluny-Crichton castle 6
Cook, Dr Geo. 291
Cookney church 76
Cob, David 191, 224
Cook, Jas. 303
Cocks or Cox (Lochee) 195
Cockfighting 46
COLDSTONE 283-5, 342
College furnishings (1655) 387
Collie, Wm. 5
Colman (poet) 293
Come see the house 173
Come all and see 374
Come shed a tear 314
Con of Auchry 177-8, 386
Conjugium Christi 222, 320
Conveth 288-93
Corrimulzie 220
Corgarff castle 155
Cormauch, Bp. 327
Cornhill of Park 28-9

GENERAL INDEX.

Cooper, Geo. 310, Wm. 124
Cossins of that ilk 185
Coulie, David 351, Susan, Wm. 223
Courteney, Randell 138
Coutts of Hallgreen, banker, &c. 26 (*errata*)
Cowan, Jean 345
COWIE 53–5, 343
Cowie, Alex. 362
Coxton tower 272
Crabb, David 302
Craigievar 189
Cran, Alex. 371
Cranstoun, Margt. 153
Crathes castle 2
CRATHIE 214–17
Crawford, Earls of. (*v.* Lindsay)
Cromar District 281–5, 342
Cromar, Alex. 224, Aud. &c. 336–7
Crooks, Thos. 224
Croll, Alex. 252, Robt. 25
Crombie of Phesdo 63–4, 134
Crosbie, Martha 344
CRUDEN 312–18
Cruden, Geo. 198, Wm. (poet) 210
Cruckshank, Eliz. 275, Jas. 208, John 376, Pat. 313, Wm. 79, 183
CUIKSTOUN 92–3
Cullen, Three Kings of 270
Culqubanny 155
Culter house, lands 17
Cuminestown 177
Cumin or Cuming of Auchry 175, 330, Culter 4, 17, Inverallochy 17
Cuming, Alex. 298
CUPAR-ANGUS 72–4, 343
"Curracher" (boatman) 147
CUSHNIE 187–90
Cushnie, Pat. 51.

DAKERS, DAVID 46
Dall, Agnes 34, Jas. 368, Janet, Thos. 158
Dalgarno, Margt. 57
Dalgety, Alex., And. 9, John 138
Dalhousie, Earl of. (*v.* Maule)
Dalrymple, Ann 374, Mary 28
Daun, Geo. 21
Dauney, F. 4
Davidson of Pettens 285, Tillychetly, &c. 4, 118
—— Adam 68, And. 205, Geo. 285, Jas. 228, Wm. 179
Dawson, Alex. 51, Robt. 318
Deeply the widow 63
Dear, John 350
Dear as thou wert 160
Dear pilgrims 183

Death is the end 41
Death is the horizon 336
Death is the passage 351
Dempster of Auchterless 209, Careston 209, 260, Dunnichen 108–9, 139 (letters by 108, 139)
—— Thos. (historian) 209
Dennies, David 236
Dennis, Lady Eliz. 17
Desswood 240
Deset nor proud 63
Deuchar of Deuchar 269
—— David 351
Deus dedit 35
De Witt (artist) 185
Dick, Dr. Thos. 116
Dickson of Clocksbriggs 157
Dingwall of Brucklay 58
—— Geo. 208
Disce mori 223, 362
Disruption of 1843 234
Doig of Cookston 90, Reswallie 158
—— Dr. David 90, Jas. 372, Isobel 373
"Dominie Deposed" 19
Don, John 140, Thos. 309
Donald Bain 161, Geo. 5
"Donald Dig" 214
Donaldson of Kinairdy 235, 328
—— Jas. 309
Doth infants pain 236
Douglas of Bridgeford 173, Tilwhilly 2
—— Bishop 3, Robt. 61
"Doupin' Stane" 19
DOWNAN (Bauffsh.) 146
Downie Park 48
—— John 207
Downys, Donald 154
Drowstie 129
Drum Stone 228
Drumin 147
DRUMBLADE 277–9
Drummond, Jas. 194, Bp. 312
Drumnagair 27
Drumrossie 20, 22
Dubois (artist) 168
"Dubrach Grant" 219
Duff of Braco 101, Culter 17, Fetteresso 76, Hatton 207, Keithmore 17, 328–9, Genealogy of 56, 217, 220, 259
—— John 202, Wm. 104
Dufftown 334
Dugat, Gilbert 372
Duirs, Dr. Wm. 288
Duke, John 355
DUN 220–6, 344, 388
Dunn, Wm. 344
Dunbar, Alex. 266, Michael 265, Nath. 154

Duncan, Agnes 191, Jas. 365, Janet 309, John 316, Jonathan 297, 310, Major 164, 168, Thos. 96
Dundarg castle 59
Dundee plate-mark 340
—— Viscounts (*v.* Graham, Scrimgeour)
Dunlop, Ludovic 226
DUNOTTAR 48–53, 343
Dunnideer 22
Durham of Pitkerro 109–10
DURRIS 104–6, 346
Duray of that ilk 309
Durie, Chas. 375, Jas. 236, Joshua 319, Margt. 312
Duthie, Robt. 33, (poet) 79
DUTHIL 142–3
Dykar, Wm. 18
DYSART. (*v.* MARYTON)

EACH revolving year 73
Earth, take thy earth 248
Easie, Euphan 336
Eaglesgreig. (*v.* ST. CYRUS.)
Ecclesmonchty 114
ECHT 65–6
Edward, Rob. (of Murroes), and family 122–3
Edwards, Anne 54, John 234
EDZELL 307–11, iv., xxviii.
Eglisjohn 220
Ellice, Geo. 339, Wm. 340
ELLON 59–62, 347, 376
ELCHIES 297–9
Elphinstone, Lords 261–2
Elphinston of Bellabeg 65
—— Marjory 178
ELSICK, chapel, lands 55
Enslie, John 306
Enercrity, David 89
Entombed here lies 128
ENZIE 277–9, 15, 27
Ere yet his lips 66
Errata, vii.
Errol, Earls of. (*v.* Hay)
Erskine of Dun 210–13, 220–2 225, 334, (letter by, 1633) 388, Linlathen 111
—— John 222–3, Kath. 77
ESSIE 67–8, 371
Esplin, Thos. 262
ETHIE 318, house of 326
Expect, but fear not death 119

FAITH, JAS. 176
Faith makes us sons 210
Falconer of Glenfarquhar 62, 132, 302, 358
—— Bp. 211, Wm. 145
Farewell, vain world 205
FARNELL 89–95, 350

3 E

GENERAL INDEX.

Farquhar of Hallgreen 27, Newhall 78, Pitscandly 155-6
—— Alex. 331, Jas. 5, Margt. 134
Farquharson of Allargue 153, 283, Auchriachan 70, Baldovie 163, Balnour 25, Balnabodach 215, Breda 120, 153, Coldrach 345, Corrachree 229, 342, Haughton 117, Invercauld 214, 217-18, Lochterlandich 330, Monaltrie 214, Tullochcony 215, Wardes 20, Whitehouse 284-5
—— Dr. Jas. 339, Kath. 77
Farskin, kirk of 273
FASQUE 254-5
FEARN (Angus) 268-70, 354
Fenton, Jas. 280
Ferguson of Badifurrow 359
Fergusson, And. 236, David 91, Jas. (astronomer) 102, 166
Ferrier, Chas., John 350
FETTERCAIRN 250-6, 352
FETTERESSO 75-85, 352
Fettes or Fetus, Geo. 25
Fielding, Serj. Alex. 79
Fife, Earls. (v. Duff)
Fife-Keith 168
FINHAVEN 334-5
Finlay-More 218
Findlay, Wm. 344
Finlayson, Alex. 68
Fisher, Peter 344
Fitchet, John 310
Fithie, H. 192, (letter by) 340, John 193, 340, Wm. 336
Fix'd is the term 79
Fleemin, Jamie 100
Foote, Robert 253
FOCHABERS 11, 15 (v. Bellie)
Foggieloan 234-5
Forrest, Janet 60, Jas. 236
Forbes of Ardmurdo 305, Auchernach, Dunottar 150-1, Auchmedden 58, Badifurrow 359, Balfluig, 117, 283, Brux 262, Craigievar 186-9, Deskrie 154, Invererman 151-2, Kincardine 353, Newe 149-50, Savoch 365, Thornton 134, Waterton 60, 348
—— Alex., David 291, Elizab. 174, 227, 352, Geo. 44, 284, John 236, Kath. 227, Margt. 57, 284, Robt. 178, 283, (poet) 19, Wm. (poet) 19
FORDOUN 62-5, 356
—— John of 65
Forsyth-Grant of Ecclesgreig 42
Forsyth, M. 326
Fothringham of Powrie 121-2, 381
Foudlen, Glens of 22
Four hundred years 218

FOYERS 67
Frail man 212
Fraser of Durris 104, Findrack 238-9, Foyers 67, Philorth 59
—— Jean 240
Frendraught Aisle 43
Friend, would'st thou 153
Frioekheim 35
From dust I came 204
From what befalls us 128
Frost, Forbes 376
Full seventy years 268
Fullarton, Kath. 223, Hugh 345, John 352
Funeral letter (1672) 10
Fyfe, John 296, Kath. 202, Margt. 296

GALLOWAY, ALEX. 304-5
Gammell of Drumtochty 64
GAMRIE 85-9, 244
Garden of Midstrath 127-8, Troup 87, 176
—— Geo. 54, Jean 275, Margt. 195, Peter 209, Bailie 363
Gardenstone, Lord 87, 290-3, 363
Gardiner, Geo. 58
Gardyne of Gardyne 32-3, 322-4
Garioch of Kinstair 120, Mergie 79, 301-303
GARTLY 43-5, 359
—— Wm. 22
Garvock, John 176
Gavin of Langton 243
Gavin, Capt. Wm. 79
Geddes, Dr. Alex. (poet) 277, Agnes 271, Janet 168, Geo., Thos., John 14
Geekie, Janet 193
Gellie, John 306
Gibb, D. 26, Jas., etc. 252, Walter 202, Wm. 68
Gibson, Jas. 91, John 248, Wm. 124, 128, 376
Giffard of Strachan 31
Gillan, Margt. 300
Gill, And. 271, Geo. 200
Gillatly, D. 19
Gillies, John, and family 259
Giles, John 166
Gladstone of Fasque 30, 254-5, 311
GLAMIS 180-6, 386-8
Glashan, James 166
Glass, David 63
Glassel 5
Gleig, family of 135
Glen, Alex. 258, Janet 236
Glen Dye 31
Glenkindie 155, 230
Glenlivat, 146-7

Glenmark 131
GLENMORISTON 66-7
Glenny, Jas., etc. 304
Glenrinnes 334
Gold, Alex., Isob. 312
Goldsmiths (Dundee) 341
Good, sober, pious 184
Goodall, Walter (historian) 29
Gordon, Duke of 12, 13, 15 (v. Huntly), Lord Adam 311, Lord George 12
—— of Aberdour 56-7, Ardmealie 232, Auchendoir 286, Auchleuchries 313, Auchentoul 235, Avochie 232, Birkenburn 165, 360, Bleluck 281-2, 346, Brodland 327, Buckie 275, Cairnfield 275, Dalpersie 265, Ellon 62, 349, Eslemont 61, 350, Farskan 274, Glastirim 274, 278, Glenbucket 69, Lesmore 262, Letterfourie 277, Manar 360, Park 28
—— (Croughley) 70, (Miumore) 146
—— Adam 13, Alex. 76, 176, Anna 104, Donald 282, Duncan 327, Elizab. 258, Elspet 13, George 44, 357, (poet) 169, Hugh 177, Jas. 155, John, &c. 331-2, Mary 271, 306, Mr. 117, Robt. 176, 258
Gorme, Janet 211
Gowans, Ellen 242, 366
Graham of Montrose 12, 148, 169, Fintray 201-3, Morphie 37-8, Largie 172
Grainger, Jas., of Kinneff 171
GRANGE 100-4
Grantully. (v. GARTLY)
Grant of Grant 142, Aberlour 332, Ballindalloch 143-4, Burnhall 66, Cloghill 145, Elchies 298-9, Glenlochy 70, Glenmoriston 66-7, Hilton 174, Kilgraston 70, Kincardine O'Neil 240, Tullochgorm 142
—— Allan 145, 359, Alex. 331, Chas. 145, Sir Francis (artist) 70, F. W. 300, Geo. 332, Jas. 145, 360, Joseph (poet) 30, John 142, 144, Peter 219, Wm. 142, 144
Grassick, Geo. 154
Gray of Carse 156
—— Alex. 29, Agnes 191, Jean 299, Margt. 223, Robt. 233
Great is the wonders 140
Green, Grisal 373
Greenhill-Gardyne. (v. Gardyne)
Greenhill of Fearn 323, Finhaven 335

GENERAL INDEX.

Greenlaw, Gilbert, Bp. 305
Gregory's Walls 22
Gregory of Kinairdy 32, 235
—— Helen, Wm. 51, Jas. 5
Greig, Alex. 236, Walter 368, Wm. 77
Grieve, Alex. 371, Nath. 60
Grig, King 52
Grim, Wm. 161
Gudefellow, Jock 296
Guthrie of Colliston 371, Gagie 126, King Edward, Westhall 318, Pitforthie 108, 389
—— Helen 184, Walter 371
Gycht, Bog of 12, 15.

HALL, JOHN 204
Hallgreen castle 26
Halliday, And. 104
Hallyburton, Lady 222, 344
Halkett, John 72
Harris, David, Geo. 355
Harper, John 265
Hart, Edward 129
Hastings of Dun 224
Hatton castle 141
Haures, Christian 208
Having now found 24
Hawker, P. J. 307
Hay of Errol 72, 313. Rannes 273-4, 322, Tullybole 15, Ury 75
—— Adam 175, Peter 141
Headhouse or Hoodhouse 120
Heav'nward directed 145
Heaven keeps the soul 372
He as a rock 252
He who was sober 248
He'll order death 137
Henderson, Cath. 227, Wm. 184
Hendrie, John 141
Hepburn of Rickarton 76
—— Geo. 55
Herald, Wm. 46
Herd, David (poet) 136
Herdman, Thos. 51, Wm. 184
Her stately person 69
Here are repos'd 69
Here doth ly 278
Here gentle reader 249
Here in this bleak 287
Here is intombed 373
Here James lyes 93
Here lies a child 34
Here lies a sweet 183
Here lies consigned 96
Here lies the man 9, 233
Here ly the dust 141
Here lyes a harmless 112
Here lyes a youth 34
Here lyes ane bereaved 24
Here lys an honest 9

Here lys below this stane 119
Here lys beneath 192
Here lys interred 230, 374
Here lys the father 336
Here one doth lye 278
Here rest in hope 350
Here rests together 212
Here rests the bones 34
Here with the aged 21
"Hie, bonnie lassie" 171
"Highland shearars" 148
Hill, Jas. 112, Alex., John, Thos. 193, Robt. 130
Hillocks, David, &c. 335
His natural temper 372
His was the soul 47
Hood, Thos. 336
Hodge, John 41
Hodgston, Jas. 212
Hogg, Jas. 227
Houyman (minrs. Kinneff) 171
Horne, Jas. 125, 184
Horsley, Dean 196
Hospitals, ancient 31
How useful they 203
Howe, Alex., Jas., Ann 286
Howie, Alex. 104
Howison, Janet 194
Huddleston, Robt. 242
Huie, Ann S. 246
Hunter, David 266, 369, Jas. 204, 326, John 61
Huntly castle 15
Huntly, Earls, Marquis of. (v. Gordon)
Hutton, And. 310
Hutcheon, John 78

IDVIES of that ilk 35
If at this humble urn 30
If honour writ 29
I lived almost 205
I am now inter'd 182
I rest in hope 33, 202
I when the trumpet 236
Imlach, Alex. 124
Inrie of Lunan 241, 366
Innes of Artanes 178, Cowie 53, Coxton 271-2, Durris 105, Edingight 101, 103, Leuchars 53, 270, Lichnett 329, Muiryfold 101, 232, Tippertie 199
—— Alex. 274, Anna 327, Prof. Cosmo xxii., 53, 105, 270, John, Jean 53, Hugh 329
Inchmarlo 4
In hopes in peace 9
In one coffin 299
In one house 21
In the cold bed 112
In the grave 349
In this lone spot 247

Incney 367, 369
Ingenious youth 212
Inglis, David 129
Inglismaldie 137-8
INSCH 20-3
INVERAVON 143-9, 359
Inverbervy. (v. BERVIE)
INVERGOWRIE 193-6
Invermark 130-1
Invernochty 154
INVERKEILOR 318-26
INVERURIE 178-80, 359
Ireland, W. F. 227
Ironside, Geo. 54
Irvine of Boyndlie 371, Cults 17, Drum 10, 229, Kelly 10, Monboddo 62, 356
Its pride and its pomp 125

JACK, JAS. 191, Robt. 195
Jackson, Wm. 141
Jaffray, Alex. 287
Jamie, John 374
Jameson, Alex., Jas. 360, 168
Jarron of Balbinnie 8
Jobsons (Newtyle) 140, 202
John-ton of Caskieben 303
—— Alex. 119, 176, Aud. &c. 317
Jolly, Peter 128-9, 382
Jopps (Insch) 20
Junor, Sandy 254
Justice and truth 116

KEITH 164-9, 360
Keith-Marischal, Earls of 49, (letter by) 353-4, Field-Marshal 49
—— of Caldhame 138, Ludquharn 96, Troup 86
—— Alex. (hist.) 314-15, 39, Elizab. 50, Geo. 53, 302, John 302
KEITH-HALL 301-4
Kellie, Jas. 187
Kelman, Wm. 331
Kennedy of Kermucks 62
Kennedy-Erskine of Dun 225, 344, 389
Kethenys, Ingram of xvi.
Kerr, Alex. 101, Thos. 370
Kidd, And., Wm. 99. David 182, 248
Kid, Tho. 58
Kilbattoch. (v. TOWIE)
KILDRUMMY 260-7
Kilgour, Robt. 314, Wm. 54
Kinairdy house 32, 235
KINCARDINE O'NEIL 238-40
Kincardine castle 62
Kindrocht. (v. BRAEMAR)
King, Arthur 306

GENERAL INDEX.

Kingennie 112
Kinghorn castle 362
Kinghorn, Earls of. (v. Lyon)
KINGOLDRUM 163-4, 385
Kingoldy 174
Kingswells 287
KINKELL (Aberdeenshire) 304
Kinloch, John, etc. 253-4
KINMUCK (A'c d'enshire) 304
KINNAIRD (Angus) 92-5
KINNEFF 169-74, 23, 119
Kintore, Earls of. (v. Falconer)
KIRKDEN 32-5. (v. Idvies)
Kirkland, Alex. 212
KIRKMICHAEL (Banffshire) 69-71, 360
Kirkside 36, 42, 376
Knight, Isobel 13, John 369
KNOCKANDO 299-301
Know, mortal 158
Knox, John 23, Robert 28
Kyle, Bishop 168, 277
Kynoch, Alex. 360

LAING, ALEX. (poet) 284, Jas. (hist.) 209
Laird of Strathmartin 204
L'Amy of Dunkenny 68, 181
Landon, L. E. (poetess) 167
Langlands, Janet 182
LAURENCEKIRK 288-94, 361
Lauriston 37
Laws, bill of 115
Lawrance, Wm. 236, Jas. 363
Lawson, David Wm. 289, 339
Lay, Wm. 63
Leadenhendrie 355
Lean not on earth 248
Lees, Sir Edward S. 111
Leighton, David 355
Leitch, Alex. 236, Isobel 248, David and John 295, 368
Leith-Hay. (v. Hay)
Leith-Lumsden. (v. Lumsden)
Leith-Ross of Arnage 59
Leith, Sir Alex. 229-30, Alex. 266
Leith of Whiteriggs 64-5
Leithel, Alex. 191
LEOCHEL 186-7
Lessel, Robt. 170
Leslie of Kininvie 327-8, Coburty 55
—— Alex. Jas. 65, 3
LETHNOT 294-5
Let marble monuments 248
Let none suppose 34
Levs, Loch of 6
LHANBRYDE 271-2
"Lich-gate" 366
LIFF 190-2
Life's everlasting gates 112

Legertwood, Jas., John 60, 348
Like to the seed 158
Lindsays of Edzell, Glenesk 130, 308-9, Balgavies 9, Blainiefedden 157, Evelick 69-70, 159, Fearn 260. Spynie 319, 325
—— Ann 69, David 235, Isobel 224, Jas. (vicar) 373, Robt. 230, (Whisteberry) 172-3
Lintown, Wm. 51
LINTRATHEN 279-81, 364
Livingstone, Dr. 346-7
Lo, here lies one 183
LOCHLEE 127-31, 382, 390
Lochngar 220
LOGIE-BUCHAN 197-9
LOGIE-DUNDEE 196-7, 364
LOGIE-MAR 281-3
LOGIE-MONTROSE 209-10
Logie, Geo., Eliz. 352
Logy, Margt. (Queen) 48
Longmore, Adam 166
Longmuir, Alex. 104, Jas., John, 353
LONGSIDE 95-100, 364
Lorimer, Robt. 111, 332
Love conygal 63
Lovell of Ballumbie 124, 194
Low, George (naturalist) 310, Margt. 136, 252, Robt. 228
Low, children three 369
Low here 39
Lumgair, Ogilvy of 50
Lumsden of Cushnie 188-9, 263, Auchendoir, Clova 263-5, Blairmonmonth 79, Corrachree 188, 229
—— John 153, Robt. (poet) 188, 229
LUNAN 241-3, 366
Lunan, Alex. 129, 212, 375 (errata)
Lundin, Walter of 193, Wm. 179
Lyall of Gallery 91, 212, Kinnordy 92, (Careary) 91-2
Lyell of Gardyne 32-3
—— David 260
Lyon of Glamis 48, 181, 185, 362, 386-8
—— Alex. 230, Jas. 181, Janet 268, Margt. 34, Peter 316
Ly still, sweet maid 173

MACDUFF 244-6
Macfarlane, Thos. 272
Machar, Isobel 280
Mackenzie of Drumtochty, Strathro 357
—— Daniel 194, Geo. 227
Mackie, David 77, Isobel 275
Mackay or M'Kay 28, John 165

M clenan, Mr. 215
Macpherson-Grant of Ballindalloch 143-4, 209
Mactier of Durris 105
Macvicar, Archd. 72
M'Combie of Easter Skene 227
M'Connach, Hugh 120, 281
M'Connochie, Wm. 333
M'Donald, Alex. 219, 145, Donald 129, Jas. 145, Pat. 67, Wm. 99
M'Gregor, Joseph 179, Robt. 71
M'Hardy, John 154, 284
M'Innes, John 283, 332
M'Intosh, L. 219, John 269, 355
M'Kondachy, John 167
M'Lachlan, Isobel 360
M'Laggan, John 282
M'Lanichal, Jas. 331
M'Lean, Archd. 303, Jas. 167, 272
M'Leod, Finlay, Peter, 67
M'Pherson, Geo. 258
M'Queen, Donald 286
M'Sween, Donald 53
M'William, Jas. 265
M'Willie, Wm. 144
MAINS 201-3
Mair, Wm. 5
Maitland, Adam 21, 207
Malcolm, Wm. 189 (errata)
Man's life on earth 112
Mann, Wm. 176
Marriage pledges 148
Mar, Earldom of 267
Mar's Stone 22
Marischal, Earls of. (v. Keith)
Mark, Geo. 19
Marno, John 336
MARNOCH 231-5
Marshall, Jas. 203, Wm. (composer) 13
Martin, Wm. 18, D. 30
Martyr's mont. (Dunottar) 50
MARYKIRK 133-8, 383
MARYTON, 235-8, 367
Masson, Prof. Edward 351
Mason, Robt. 373
Mathison, Geo. 279
Mathers, Kane of 41
Mathew, Alex. 202, Grissel 162, 195
Maundach, Jan (poet) 143
Maule of Panmure 130-1, 193, 219, Melgund 10
"Maule's Cairn" 390
Maxwell, David 206
Mearns, Men of the 52
Mearns, Alex. 21
Meff, Wm. 18
Meiklejohn, Lieut. 152
Mellis, Geo. 228

Meldrum of Crombie 231-2
Melgund castle 10
Melville, Alex. 368, Geo. 286,
  Margt. 135, Wm. 368
Memess, Robt. 51
Menzies, John 13
Mercer, Benj. 265
Michie, Capt. 152, John 154
Middleton, Earl of 138, 238, 256
Mildness of temper 160
Mill, Jas.; John Stuart 213-14
Mill (Boyndie) 199-200, Walter
  (martyr) 241, 366
Miller of Ballumbie 124
Milligan, Wm. 35
Milne of Kinstair 167
Miln, And. 77, Alex. 16, 64, 357,
  Cath. 248, Chas. 236, David 9,
  Elizabeth 13, Geo. 345, Jas.
  61, John 129, Marjory 228,
  Wm. 265, 289
Milner, Peter 186
Miltonhaven 41-2
Mylne of Mylnefield, 194-5
Mitchell, Adam 21, And. 7, Alex.
  44, Geo. 140, 260, Gilbert 140,
  Jas. 8, John 191, 373, Thos. 7
Mitchell, Major 152-3 (errata)
Moatach Well 22
Moir, And. 60, Jas. 35, 306, John
  331
Mollison, Wm. 303
Monboddo, Lord 63, 356. (v.
  Burnett)
Monck, Gen., 'protextion' by 182
Moncur of Knap 24
—— John 58, Kath. 191, Wm. 79
MONIFIETH 106-15, 369, old
  rentals 380-1
Montealts of Fearn 269
Montgomerys in Knap 135, 383
Monkeigie. (v. KEITH-HALL)
MONQUHITTER 173-8, 371
Montrose, Marquis of. (v. Graham)
Moor, Robt. 336
Moram, David, Janet 110, 113
Mores, Elspet 293
Morrice, David 251, Wm. 240
Morison, Jas., letter to laird of
  Troup, 87, John 28
Morphie, Stone of 37
Mortimer, Robt. 362, Edward 167
MORTLACH 326-34
Moug, John 140
Mowat, John 77
Muchals castle 84
Mudie of Arbikie 35, 241, 320-22
Muirhead, Chas. 314
Mullo, David 195
Munro, John 300
Murray of Melgund 10
—— Jas. 224

MURROES 121-6, 381
Murdoch, John 166
Muschet of Cargill 72
My bones in grave 351
My friends in Christ 210
My God who gave 331
My parents here 252
My voyage is made 88
Myles, Peter 370

NAPOLEON I. 168, III. 158
NAVAR 296-7, 389
Neave, Alex. 372
Neish of Laws 115, Tannadice 48
NEVAY 68-9, 371
NEWDOSK 311-12
NEWHILLS 285-7
Newton, Lord 322
NEWTYLE 138-41, 373
Nichol, Dr. J. P. 226
Nicol of Ballogie 78
Nicolson of Glenbervie 91. (v.
  Badenach)
—— Bp. 278, John 365
Nine years I sailed 376
Nipt by the wind 21
Niven of Peebles 264
Niven-Lumsden, Sir H. 264
No beauty 325
No lingering sickness 105
No sooner cam they 361
Northesk, Earls of. (v. Carnegie)
Now, cruel death 248
Now she is whom 116
Now slain by death 306

OATHLAW 335-8, 374
Ochterlony of Guynd 7, 161, 247,
  Balmadies 161, 384, Flemington 7, Kelly 247
Ogilvy, Glen of 182, 185
Ogilvy, Earls of Airlie 281
—— of Balfour 385, Barras 169-
  70, Culpbin 199, Dunlugas
  207, Inverquharity 203-4,
  Lumgair 50, Milton 169, Tannadice 211, 373
—— Alex., Jas. 280, Henry 242
Ogston of that ilk 3, 256
—— Barbara 176, Jean 57
"Old Mortality" 50
Oliphant, Lords 141, 169, 373
Orr of Bridgeton 40-1
—— Jas. 236
ORDIQUHILL 27-29
Ord, Helen 275
Of Barclay's single life 109
Of manners mild 227
Oft shall sorrow 69
O dear child 73
O dear John Dalgety 183

O death, fierce is, &c. 92
O death, O grave 268
O man, live thou 155
O mortal man 195
O my soul 112
O painted piece 179
Oh, that it were 137
O that men 141
Once lovely youth 208
On earth I waulked 111
Our life is short 77
Our life is but 345

PAIN was my portion 79
Panmure, Earls of. (v. Maule)
Panter, Patrick 85
Panton, Geo. 176
Par meus eloquio 252
Paterson, John 270, 223, Margt.
  223-4, Rebecca 207, Wm. 198
Paul, Geo. 325, Pat. 272, Wm. 202
Peebles, Chas. 203
Peace to his body 99
Peace to thy soul 11
Peat, Alex. 252
Pedey, Alex. 241
PERT 210-14, 374
PETER CULTER 16-20
Petrie, Jas. 236-7
Philip, J. (artist) 120, Pat. 182
Pickieman, trade of a 9
Picts' houses 94, 125, 154, 161,
  267, 284
Pierson of Balmadies, Guynd 159-
  61, 247, 384
"Pin the widdie" 252
Pitfodels, Reids of 3
Pittarrow, Wisharts of 64, 356
Pitempan 206
Playfair, Principal 181, 183
Popular Rhymes 53, 285, 317-18,
  356
Porter, Isabella 365
Porteous of Lauriston 40
Poussin, N. (artist) 290
Pratt, Dr. 100, 317
Presentation to a church (1609)
  342
Preshome 277
Prince Albert 216, 256
Proctor, John 230, 299, Pat.,
  Wm. 184
Prophet, May 336
"Puri nativi" 36, 48
Pyot, Jas. 158

QUAKERS 80, 82, 287, 304
Queen's "Leaves" 220, 256
Queen's Well, The 131

RADULPH (sacerdotis) 20
Raiker, Thos. 336

GENERAL INDEX.

Rait of Hallgreen 26-7, Anniston 323, Bryanton 320-1, Drumnagair 27, Drumtochty 357
—— Henry 93, Wm. 25, John 320
Ramsay of Balmain 2, 231, Banchory-Lodge 2, 30
—— Dean 2, Geo. 207, Jas. 140, Wm. 57, 140-1
Rare William 183
Rattray, Lt.-Col. 48
RATHVEN 273-9
Reader, repent 164
Reader, suppose 99
Reaping machine 249
Reddenda ex terra terra 51
Redcastle, Redhead 244, 325
Reid of Glassel 5, Newmill 263, Pitfodels 3
—— ministers of Banchory-Ternan 3, 379
—— Alex. 5, 379, Geo. 130, 303, John 268, 276, 335, Thos. (poet) 3, Dr. Thos. 32, Wm. 130
Reidie, Lord 69
Remember all 38, 162
Remember man 38, 89, 129, 268, 348
Rennie, David 370
Repose, then, precious clay 360
RESCOBIE 155-61, 384
Rests before this stone 336
Rettie, Isobel 371
Revd. and grave 265
Reynold, Alex. 57
Rhynd of Carse 157
—— Jas. 247-8, John 372
Rickard, Geo., &c. 269
Rickarton church 75
Riddoch, Margt. 246
Ritchie, Jerom 266, John 189, 260
Robb, Alex. 191, John 313
Roberts, Elizabeth 208
Robertson, Geo. 376, Dr. Joseph 186-7, Dr. Robt. 72, John 189, 211, Wm. 249
Roch, Jas. 252
Roger, Geo. 364, John 240, Wm. 157
Rolok, R. and V. 162
Roman, John (archdeacon) 7
Ross of Arnage. (r. Leith-Ross)
—— Alex. (poet) 127, 240, 281, 289, Jas. 13
Rose or Ross, Alex. 208
—— David (Lochlee) 129, 294, 382, Kath. 165
Rosehill chapel 137
Rose-Innes of Netherdale 232-3
Rostinoth 7, 193

Rothiemay 29
Rothiemurchus 142-3
Row, John 294
Roxburghe, Duke of 272
Roy, Peter 219
Ruddiman, Thos. 11, 201, 289
Ruddoch, Isabel 16
Russel, David 272
Ruthven, Earl of Forth 110
Ruxton, David 324, 315

SADLER, JOHN 272
ST. ANDREW'S (Elginsh.) 270-1
ST. CYRUS 36-43, 376
ST. NINIAN'S (Banffsh.) 277-9
ST. POLNAR (Abdnsh.) 359
Saints—
 Aidan 159
 Andrew 11. 43, 116, 155, 197, 217, 254, 270
 Anthony 293
 Apollinaris 178, 359
 Arnold 169
 Boniface 193
 Brandon 199, 371
 Bridget 48, 71, 226, 260, 271
 Catherine 65, 256
 Columba 66
 Congal 104
 Cowan or Congan 176
 Donan 206
 Drostan 20, 55, 127, 311
 Ennan 48
 Freland 65, 238
 Fergus 180
 Finnan 45
 Gregory (mispd. Mary) 277
 Grig or Cyricus, 36
 Hilary 257
 Huchomy 234
 John 65, 85, 137, 162, 155, 169, 234
 Kieran or Caran 85
 Laurence 37, 288, 307, 325
 Macconoc 318
 Macalen 297
 Macarius 267
 Machalus 359
 Madoe 159
 Maelrubha 32, 164
 Mark 250, 256
 Marnan 186, 231
 Martin 169, 204, 209, 253
 Mary 23, 27, 53, 59, 68, 190, 208, 220, 235, 246, 273, 285-6, 294, 325, 334
 Meddan 162, 279, 364
 Menimis 234
 Michael 69, 304
 Moloch 261, 326
 Murdoch 114, 318
 Muren 114

 Nathlan 53
 Neveth 371
 Nine Maidens 185, 206, 241, 334
 Ninian 49, 89, 201, 268, 277
 Niniar or Manir 214
 Olaus 312
 Orland 184
 Our Lady 106, 114, 231
 Palladius 62
 Paul 168, 277
 Peter 16, 142, 143, 168, 193, 273, 277
 Philip 174
 Ronan 267
 Ruffus or Maelrubha 32
 Rule or Regulas 36, 106
 Rumon 82
 Serf or Servanus 301
 Thomas 168
 Ternan 1, 45
 Triduana 155-61
 Walock 281, 285, 333
Sandeman, G., C. 47
Sanders, Wm. 12
Sangster, Jas. 44
Sauchieburn, 137
Sauchs battle 269
Savoch chapel 62
Scalan 359
Scologs of Ellon 61
Scottish Regalia 169-70
Scott, Alex. 190, 252, Robt. 161, 345, David 345, Wm. 238, 365
Scougal, Henry 209
"Scourger" 147
Scrimgeour of Dudhope 192, of Tealing 122
Scrofula 163
Scrogie, Robt. 349
Sculptured Stones—
 Aldbar 10
 Coldstone 284
 Corrachree 188
 Edzell 307, iv.
 Farnell 89
 Fordoun 65
 Glamis 184-5
 Inach 22
 Invergowrie 193
 Keilor 141
 Kingoldrum 163
 Knockando 301
 Lintrathen 364
 Marykirk 137
 Monifieth 106, 115
 Mortlach 333
 Pitmuies 35
 Pitscandly 161
 Strathmartin 205-6
 Tannadice 47
Seaton, Mary 53
Seton of Cariston 260

GENERAL INDEX.

Shand, Jas., Sir C. F. 135, Helen 14, John 311
Shank of Castlerig 4, 291-2, 362-3 (v. *errata*)
—— Janet 21
Shanwel, John (abbot) 74
Sharp, Geo. 161
Shaw, Edw. 354, Wm. 6
She honoured as she bore 68
Shepherd, John 283
Sheriffs, Dr. E. B. 254, Wm., &c. 266
Shiels, Anna 179
Shilgreen, Isabel 89
"Shirra Muir" ballad 215
Sibbald bequest 126
Silent grave 207
Silver of Netherley 78
Simpson of Concraig 18
—— Margt. 223, 344; Jas., John 233
Siste, Viator! 113
SKENE 226-9
Skene of Skene 226, 229
—— Geo. 306
Skinner, Rev. John, &c. 90-9, Laurance 389
Slidders, John 141
Small, Geo. Jas., Dr. (hist.) 246, J. G. (poet) 25, Olifer 163, Rob. 141, Thos. 343, Wm. 344
Smith, Alex. 44, Colvin (artist) 105, 219, Geo. 165 6, Janet 184, Jas. 246, 253, John 54, 351, Peter 8, 316, Thos. 316, Wm. 66, 306
Smith-Skene, Capt. 196
Sod Kirk 76, 264
Souter, Jas. 25
Southesk, Earls of. (v. Carnegie)
SOUTHESK HOWFF 93-4
Spanzie, Jas. 193
Spark, Robt. 290
Spink, And. 110
Spital (The) 31
Spence, John 9
Sprot, And. 300
Stay, passenger 242
Stay, reader, stay 60
Stephens of Balmadies 385
Sterling, Gilb. 316
Steven or Stevenson, And. (poet) 85, Kath. 223
Stil, David 364
Stiven, Chas. 292
Stewarts of Innermeath, Lorne, Redcastle 244, 322, Carnaveron 119, 174, Tannochy 275
—— Charles 173, James 73, (Deskrie) 146, (Minmore) 146, (Pittyvaich) 145, 330, Raymond 343

Stirling-Graham, Miss 201
Stirling, Jas. (artist) 19, 120
Stocket forest 287
Stonehaven, Newtown of 85
STONEYWOOD CHAPEL 286
Stop, passenger 128, 137, 306
STRACHAN 29-32
Strachan of Carmyllie 342, Claypots 352, Glenkindie 230-1, Monboddo 358, Thornton 132-4, 165
—— Jas. (letter by (?), 1523) 352, John 238, Bishop 249, Robt. 344, Wm. 173
STRATHDON 149-55
STRATHMARTIN 294-6
Strathmore, Earls of (v. Lyon)
Strathnairn, Lord 129, 294, 382
"Stragler woman" 148
Straton of Kirkside 36, 42, 376, Lauriston 37
—— Alex. 51, Geo. 389
Struck by the fiery dart 373
Stuart-Forbes of Fettercairn (v. Forbes)
Stuart of Birkenburn 165, 360, Bogs 279, Edinglassie 153, Ordens 199
—— John, LL.D. 166, 220, Geo. 224, Harry 266, 337, Thos. 316, Margt. 359, 361
Sturm, Alex. 332
Sturrock, Stroak 114, 158, 372
Superstitions, various 43, 103, 106, 126, 148, 225, 249, 256, 282
Sure death may kill 162
Symers, Alex. 295, Geo., John 389

TAILLIOUR, MAGNUS 51
Tait (Archbishop), Geo. Wm. 96-7, Thos. 61, 79, 306
TANNADICE 45-8
Tawse, And. 284
Taylor of Kirktonhill 134
—— Dr. Alex. 189, Farq. 339, Joseph 117, John 233, Thomas 182, Walter 89
Taylor-Imrie of Lunan 241, 366
Tealing xvi.
Tenant, Thos. 176,
Thain, John, David 204, Jean 189, Margt. 193, Wm. 233
That James had failings 79
The grave, great teacher 128
The loving wife 268
"The men of Ross" 142-3
The penetrating art of man 34
The saints are pilgrims 39
The smiles of fortune 44
The tender grass 93
The tyrant death 252
The weaver's art 350

Theirs none in question 63
They were a couple 116
Think ye 46
Thir lines engraven 46
This charming child 203
This couple lived 124
This dormitory 57
This dust which here 63
This honest man 141
This life they steer'd 116
This little band 176
This man and his wife 68
This stone doth hold 259
This stone in memory 159
This stone is set 182
This woman 223-4
This worthy pair 162
Tho' Boreas blasts 369
Tho' .Eleos blasts 276
Tho' this fine art 9
Tho' 84 be long 99
Tho' young in years 30
Thom, Barb., 140, John, James 343
Thomson, Alex. 119, 281, Geo. 75, 339, Jas. (hist.) 326, 345, Robt. 54, Thos. 202.
Thornton of that ilk 251, 352
—— Alex. 183
Thurburn of Murtle 18, 360, 164, 167 (v. *errata*)
Thy life, dear man 276
Thy name aye 205
Tillychetly 4
Tilwhilly castle 3
'Tis here the fool 92
'Tis safer, Lord 349
To honour the dead 202
Tocher, Alex. 246
Tomintoul 71
Torn, John 242
TOWIE 229-31
Trail, Jas. 41
Trew, H. L. 6
Trouble sore 71
Troup, John 54
Trustach forest 6
Tulloch of Bonnington 237, 367
—— Alex. 300
Turnbul, Margt. 245
Turner of Turnerhall 60, 350
Tyrie of Drumkilbo 23, 69, 372, Dunnideer 23, 228, Lunan 243
—— Eliz. 2, 228, Thos. 372
Tytler, Jas. and Henry W. (poets) 269, 355

UNCONSTANT EARTH 158
Under this monument 91, 351
Under this stone 202, 223-4, 251, 364
Unknown to pomp 14

GENERAL INDEX.

Unmark'd by trophies 282
Urquhart John 110, 113-14
URY HOWFF 80-4

VAIN MORTALS 105
Vain tears give o'er 293
Vallentine, John 251
Vallognes of Panmure 193
Vayne castle 269
Virtuous and learned 8
Volum of Woodwrae 374

WADDLE, WM. 192
Wallace, John, Thos. 158-9, Jean 187, Mary 365, Margt. 300
Wallace's castle 88
Wallack, Robt. 211
Walker, Alex. 309, David 38, Geo. 224, 365, Jas. 50, John 306, 351
Walram of Normanville 29
Walton, Eliz. 272
Warden, Isobel 298
Warburton 37, 41
Wardroper, John 372
Watt of Logie 190 (v. *errata*)
—— John 200, Wm. 178, 339
Wattie, Jas. 342
Watson, Alex. 9, Bishop 289, Chas. 219, David 354, Hugh 140, Jas. 164, 233, 269, John 364, Wm. 300
Wauchop of Culter 17
We are but earth 68
We do not 93
We of this child 162
Webster of Balruddery 191, Meathie 111
—— James 38, Janet 91, John 247
West Ferry, old rentals of 380-1
Whamond, Jas. 46
What havock 164
What's mortal here 127
When death's darts 248
When death doth come 351
When first I drew 39
When low in dust 88
When minstrels 184
When mortal man 314
When silver hands 223
When this man liv'd 159
While here on earth 205
While manly beauty 18
While nature shrinks 162
White, Alex., David 139, 253
Whitton, And. 374
Whoe'er thou art 223
Whose turn is next? 212
Whyte, Abbot John 57
Wighton, David 68, Jas. 191
Wignall, J. Utley 333
Will, curious 40

Wilkie, Jas. (poet) 231, Margt. 183
Wilkin, Lizzie 365
Wills, Robt. 376
Wilson, Alex. 228, Jas. 90 1, 246, Geo., Pat. 102, 176, Wm. 246
Winchester, Col. R. 239, Jesper, &c. 270
Wink, John 300
Wise of Lunan 244, 361
Wishart, Geo. 64, Jean 119
With husbands two 192
With temper meek 154
Within this grave 223
Within this isle 117
Within this narrow house 18
Wo be to him 368
Wood of Bonnington 237, 367, 388, Balbegno 250
—— Jas. 260
Wright, And. 162, Dennis 381, Isabel 163
Wyllie, Jas., Thos. 310

YE GENTLEMEN 103
Ye readers all 58
Yet where, O where 29
You, who is in pomp 372
Young of Aldbar 11, Durris 105, 346, Stank 172, 344, 352-3
Youngson, And. 58
Youth fades 246

PRINTED AT 'MONTROSE STANDARD' OFFICE.

www.ingramcontent.com/pod-product-compliance
Lightning Source LLC
Chambersburg PA
CBHW032141010526
44111CB00035B/764